Re-Inventing Radio
Aspects of Radio as Art

Printed with support of the Austrian Federal Ministry of Science and Research.

Re-Inventing Radio
Aspects of Radio as Art

Edited by   Heidi Grundmann, Elisabeth Zimmermann
Reinhard Braun, Dieter Daniels, Andreas Hirsch, Anne Thurmann-Jajes

A publication by Verein werks in cooperation with the
Ludwig Boltzmann Institute Media.Art.Research. (Linz), MiDiHy Productions (Graz),
and the Research Centre for Artists' Publications at the
Weserburg–Museum of Modern Art (Bremen).

Revolver, Frankfurt am Main

Contents

Preface

The Editors
R. Braun, D. Daniels, H. Grundmann, A. Hirsch,
A. Thurmann-Jajes, E. Zimmermann

«*In order to translate the understanding of radiophonic space or, rather, spaces into present-day artistic practice it is important to remember that during the early twentieth century it was common to think of wirelessness in terms of* communication *because it existed prior to the redundancies of contemporary mass media,*» Douglas Kahn wrote in 1994.[1] More than a decade later, the rise of W-LAN, satellite communications, GPS, and other wireless technologies—and especially the ubiquitous cell phone—have made it possible to talk about a return of wirelessness or, in the context of art, about a «return of wireless imagination.» This (deliberate) reference to the Italian Futurist Marinetti—and, by implication, to the beginnings of the relationship between avant-garde art and radio as a technology of communication and war—formed part of the title for an international conference dedicated to «100 Years of Radio» (in memory of Fessenden's «first broadcast» at Christmas 1906). The conference—a collaboration between the Ludwig Boltzmann Institute Media.Art.Research., Linz, Austria, and *Kunstradio*—became a key point of departure for the realization of this book, in which media theory, art history, and the practice of international artists interlink. Some authors in this volume have been part of earlier international events and conferences, periodically organized by *Kunstradio* in the nineteen-eighties and nineties, on aspects of the theory and practice of radio art. A communicative relationship between media and art theory and artistic practice is also a feature of this publication.

A unified history of radio art is still missing and may be impossible to write. One, if not the dominating, strand of the many potential histories of radio art deals with the work of artists in and for large broadcasting institutions. Klaus Schöning, founder and longtime producer of the Studio Akustische Kunst at WDR (West German Radio), Cologne, coined the term *Ars Acustica* for this mostly commissioned type of art. In 1989, *Ars Acustica* was adopted as the name of a newly founded group of producers of radio art in the member organizations of the European Broadcasting Union (EBU), with its associated members in Australia, the United States, Israel, and Canada. The *Sound Workshop* of the then Yugoslav National Radio in Belgrade was a founding group member, and at the beginning of the nineteen-nineties producers representing experimental departments of Eastern European radio corporations joined the group.

But since the end of the nineties, several well-known and particularly prolific *Ars Acustica* program slots in public radio have been closed down or altered beyond recognition. They are among the victims of the fundamental reorganizations with which many broadcasting corporations react to the onslaught of the forces of liberalization and commercialization, digitalization, convergence, and remediatization. Today a majority of the remaining *Ars Acustica* programs are based in music departments, and such programs increasingly define their content as sound art (a term which is not synonymous with the, by Schöning's definition, radiogenic *Ars Acustica*).

The publication *Re-Inventing Radio* deals neither with the complex issues of sound art in radio, nor with the problems of a radio art predominantly bound to the highly controlled and curated space of public radio corporations in crisis—nor can, unfortunately, the recent development of a well-functioning network of

1   Douglas Kahn, «Radio Space,» in *Radio Rethink: Art, Sound and Transmission*, ed. Daina Augaitis and Dan Lander, exh. cat. Walter Phillips Gallery (Banff: Banff Centre Press, 1994), p. 111.

2   Erkki Huhtamo, «From Cybernation to Interaction: A Contribution to an Archaeology of Interactivity,» http://classes.design.ucla.edu/Fall06/10/CybernationToInteraction.pdf (accessed February 8, 2008).

3   See http://www.mediafiles.at, an online information system for Austrian media art.

4   Carl Loeffler and Roy Ascott, «Chronology and Working Survey of Select Telecommunications Activity,» *Leonardo* 24, no. 2, *Connectivity: Art and Interactive Telecommunications* (1991), pp. 236–40.

small radio initiatives in Europe be discussed here. However, *Re-Inventing Radio* does approach the rich history of radio art in independent and free radio, for example in a contribution by Anna Friz, who is familiar with such contexts from her own practice as a radio artist and, at one point, also as a station manager.

«**One of the common features** of many technocultural discourses is their lack of historical consiousness. History evanesces as technology marches on. This is not caused by some ‹postmodern› logic; rather, it is a reflection of the dominance of the ‹engineer approach› to culture.»[2] Huhtamo's words have inspired the work of the association MiDiHy and its Graz-based archive mediafiles.at.[3] MiDiHy, one of the partners in the production of this book, is represented by coeditor and author Reinhard Braun: «Positions of the nineteen-sixties and seventies seem to be of special importance, as they continue to form the basis of up-to-date discourses on media and art, allowing for a reconstruction of intermedial forms of art. If so far the emphasis of mediafiles.at has been placed on Austrian projects from the realms of video, TV, and telecommunications, the book *Re-Inventing Radio* not only represents a necessary international evaluation of the relationship between art and radio, it also closes an important gap in the understanding of the changing concepts of media in general.»

Re-Inventing Radio explores a radio art whose roots outside an institutionalized *Ars Acustica* were somewhat obscured in the nineteen-sixties and seventies by the modernist division of communications art into separate and separately discussed media-specific entities—such as TV art, satellite art, or telecommunications art and radio art, and so forth—as opposed to an elaboration on their shared concerns with access to communications technologies and their appropriation and deconstruction in art projects.

In 1991, Carl Loeffler and Roy Ascott compiled a «Chronology and Working Survey of Select Telecommunications Activity,»[4] starting with examples from 1977. Their short introduction illustrates that the experiments of telecommunications art referenced in our book were able to overcome the art-theoretical separation of artists' media-specific use of different technologies by incorporating them as networked elements of temporary fields of action, exchange, and communication at a distance. Loeffler and Ascott write: «Telecommunications is hereby defined as electronic transmission of information through computer networks, radio, slow-scan video, telephone, television and satellites. The projects listed here ... were interactive, establishing two-way communications.» This corresponds with some attempts in the nineties to define the increasingly networked practice of radio art as part of telecommunications art, rather than as *Ars Acustica* or sound art.

The history of radio art, which the material contained in *Re-Inventing Radio* partly illustrates with examples from different periods, has its roots in conceptual art, mail art, Fluxus, intermedia, performance art, and telecommunications art. There are also connections to the Experiments in Art & Technology (E.A.T.), and not only in their model of close collaboration between technicians/engineers and artists of different disciplines, a model which has also played an important role in several phases of radio art. Billy Klüver, for instance, relates that the legendary *9 Evenings* performances, which took place in 1966, were to a high degree radio-based and radio-controlled, enabling artists/performers and engineers to interact and communicate from different corners of the huge New York Armory Hall venue: «The wireless is like the crown of the whole thing. There's nothing like it that exists on the market. Actually what we're doing is putting radio in the theatre. We asked the FCC [Federal Communications Commission] for 15 frequencies for continuous performance between the 13th and the 23rd of October [1966]. This is really much more fantastic than anything else that has been done.»[5] Seen from a present-day perspective, it is relatively easy to see how Bill Bartlett—important initiator of a series of telecommunications projects in the nineteen-seventies and eighties—would, as he mentioned in an informal conversation in 1978, have been influenced by E.A.T.

The majority of the contributions to *Re-Inventing Radio* were written in 2007. But it also includes reprints of select earlier texts, interview excerpts, and project descriptions. The mixture of old and new contributions, theoretical essays, artists' texts, portraits, and project descriptions, in addition to the numerous illustrations, has made a straightforward, linear approach to sequencing

---

5 Billy Klüver, «Theatre and Engineering: An Experiment. 2. Notes by an Engineer» *Artforum* 5, no. 6 (February 1967), quoted after Meredith Morse, «e-Collaborations in Sixties America: *9 Evenings*, the Dancer's Body, and Electronic Technologies,» *Scan Journal of Media Arts Culture*, http://scan.net.au/scan/journal/display.php?journal_id=92 (accessed February 8, 2008).

6 There are perhaps more references to activities in Canada and by Canadian artists than one would have expected in this volume. This is due to the nationwide system of community and campus radio and the longstanding tradition of artist-run galleries and production centres, which have provided the necessary infrastructure for a high level of activity in radio and communications art.

the material difficult. So, although the book is loosely structured into three main sections, there has been no attempt to organize it into clear, visible chapters, as each section contains texts which could easily find a place in one of the others. In other words, *Re-Inventing Radio* is not a linearly structured book but more of a mosaic inviting associative approaches.

Examples of artist-run festivals, spaces and organizations, and innovative projects and exhibitions initiated and curated by artists are a recurring motif in *Re-Inventing Radio*.[6] We were ourselves surprised to find that in many cases the same projects are referenced by different authors in their contributions. We have decided not to interfere with these overlapping references, trusting that different views of these iconic events or projects might lead to reflection on the processes of emerging histories and perhaps encourage more detailed research and evaluation.

Such research is to be facilitated in the future through the new archiving activities of two partner institutions supporting this volume's publication and of the editors representing them:

The Ludwig Boltzmann Institute Media.Art.Research. in Linz, Austria under its director Dieter Daniels pursues, among many other areas, an archivization and restoration project for early Austrian artists' net projects and intends to include the *Kunstradio On Line* archive, which contains material on over thirty years of radio art. A new strong impulse for the archiving of radio art originates from the Research Centre for Artists' Publications at the Weserburg–Museum of Modern Art in Bremen, Germany (director Anne Thurmann-Jajes). The collection of the Research Centre comprises several archives with approximately 80,000 international publications and has thus become the largest and most outstanding collection of published artworks since 1950 in Europe. Every year four to six related exhibitions, publications, and events provide a comprehensive overview on specific artists or topics.

Re-Inventing Radio serves as catalogue book to a first exhibition of radio art at the Weserburg–Museum of Modern Art, in which the Research Centre for Artists' Publications features the newest field of its collecting and research efforts: an archive-in-progress of radio art, comprising at the time of its founding material from the archives of radio corporations such as the *Ars Acustica* archive (West German Radio [WDR], Cologne), the *Kunstradio* archive (Austrian National Radio [ORF], Vienna), the *Ars Sonora* archive (Spanish National Radio [RNE],

Madrid), and the *Pro Musica Nova* archive of Radio Bremen. Independent radio archives—insofar as they exist at all—will be added to the digitalized research databank catering to researchers and, in a less complex form, to the general public. The exhibition under its title Art on Air: Radio-Art in Flux (April to August 2008) focuses on radio art from German-speaking countries and its international connections and influences. The exhibition is accompanied by a conference and an Internet platform dedicated to the complex issues of archiving a volatile art such as radio art.

It may perhaps seem that the current interest in archivization and documentation of radio by artists suggests a period of summarization, signaling that radio as a medium is somehow at an end. Nothing could be farther from the truth, for the prediction of radio's imminent demise has been recurring regularly at least since the advent of television in the nineteen-fifties. Recent developments in podcasting, streaming media, and the Internet—together with the obvious crisis of major public broadcasting organizations—have once again raised the specter of a senile and dying media centenarian. But by a strange trick of metamorphosis, radio seems once again to be eluding its nemesis. For radio, after all, was never really about «broadcasting» but rather about space and communication. The new wireless media, which appear to be instrumental in its death, are in fact an extension of radio. And the new frequencies becoming available through the digitalization of television are being recycled mainly as wireless (radio) communication frequencies.

As this book attempts to illustrate, artists have long been aware of the excitement of radio beyond its identity as a mass medium. The notion of extended or expanded radio has inspired artists to integrate radio into exhibitions, public space, global communications projects, performances, and installations. A close look at radio work by artists, especially since the beginning of the digital revolution in the nineteen-seventies, is crucial for understanding the shape of the networked future increasingly dominating our culture.

Acknowledgments

The Editors

First and foremost we would like to thank the authors for writing and contributing their texts to this volume, having trusted that somehow, against all financial odds, the book would indeed be published. They have also provided us with valuable images from their personal archives. Without their ideas, thoughts, projects, and generous cooperation this publication would not have been possible.

Many of the authors have at some point or other worked with *Kunstradio*—a weekly program on the cultural channel of Austrian National Radio (ORF) and a platform for international radio art for over twenty years. The archives of *Kunstradio* were a valuable source for many but by no means all of the projects featured in this volume.

The lion's share of organizational efforts for this publication have rested with the small non-profit association werks, Vienna.

Special thanks go to Dawn Michelle d'Atri, the editing office of this complex publication. She made the most of it, especially of the many texts translated from German into English.

We also would like to thank the Ars Electronica Festival as well as the many different public funding agencies who have, in the end, facilitated this publication, putting faith in our concept.

The Last Radio Broadcast

Friedrich Kittler

Nobody listens to radio. What loudspeakers or headsets provide for their users is always just radio programming, never radio itself. Only in emergencies, when broadcasts are interrupted, announcer voices are stifled, or stations drift away from their proper frequencies are there any moments at all for hearing what radio listening could be.

«ANNOUNCER: I'm speaking from the---roof of Broadcast Building, I'm speaking from the roof of the Broadcast Building, New York City. The---bells you hear---are---ringing to---warn the people to evacuate the city as the Martians approach. Estimated in last two hours---three million people have moved out along the roads---to the north---Hutchinson River Parkway still kept open for motor traffic. Avoid bridges to Long Island, hopelessly jammed. All communication with New Jersey shore closed---ten minutes ago.---No more defences.---Our army's wiped out---artillery---air force---everything wiped out. This may be the---last broadcast.---We'll stay here to the end.---People are holding service below us---in the cathedral.---Now I look down the harbor. All---all manner of boats, overloaded with fleeing population, pulling out from docks. Streets are all jammed.---Noise in crowds like New Year's Eve in city. Wait a minute the---enemy now in sight above the Palisades. Five---five great machines. First one is---crossing the river. I can see it from here, wading---wading the Hudson like a man wading through a brook.---A bulletin's handed me---Martian cylinders are---falling all over the country. One outside in Buffalo, one in Chicago---St. Louis---seem to be timed and spaced.---Now the first machine reaches the shore. He---stands watching, looking over the city. His steel, cowlish head is even with the skyscrapers. He waits for the others.--- They rise like a line of new towers on the city's west side---now they are lifting their metal hands.---This is the end now.---Smoke comes out--- black smoke---drifting over the city.---People in the streets see it now.--- They're running towards the East River, thousands of them---dropping in like rats.---Now the smoke's spreading faster. It's---reached---Times Square.---

This essay is reprinted in revised translation from: Friedrich Kittler, «The Last Radio Broadcast,» in *ON THE AIR: Kunst im öffentlichen Datenraum*, ed. Heidi Grundmann (Transit: Innsbruck, 1994), pp. 71–80.

People are trying to run away from it, but it's no use. They're falling like flies. --- Now the smoke's crossing Sixth Avenue --- Fifth Avenue --- one thousand yards away... it's fifty feet...

OPERATOR FOUR: 2X2L calling CQ...2X2L calling CQ...2X2L calling CQ New York. Isn't there anyone on the air? Isn't there anyone on the air? Isn't there anyone...2X2L...»[1]

The War of the Worlds, as Orson Welles called the most influential radio drama of all times just before the outbreak of the Second World War, is a pure and simple media war: an empire goes under because the rocket machines of a foreign and extraterrestrial empire successively take out its infantry, artillery, and air force; an empire goes under because its public broadcasting stations, having been universally relegated to signal corps command in the emergency situation, cease functioning; an empire goes under because not even the non-public radio message «to everyone,» being in effect of the same source as wireless telephony, elicits any responses. And in the precise second that the radio command center 2X2L likewise suspends its radio messages, all that remains to be heard «on the air,» which is only a metaphor for the ether, are the the rocket machines of the Martians, whose roar then blends into the static. And for a single moment, before the Columbia Broadcasting System regains control of the ether with its signature tune and station identification, everyone is listening to the radio.

As is well known, this resulted in the biggest radio listener panic in U.S. broadcasting history on October 30th—or Halloween Eve—of 1938. As if the «last radio broadcast,» which, incidentally, was ostensibly only broadcast from the «Broadcast Building» rather than from the CBS Building on censorship grounds, had truly and honestly issued orders, the empirical radio consumers precisely followed the example set by the imaginary populations of New Jersey and New York in the radio drama. Approximately one million people are reported to have reacted as hysterically on that Halloween Eve as the three million described by the fictional reporter. And this in turn was initially followed by, as is widely known, sociological research projects that ultimately led to data on empirical radio listener behavior, but additionally, as is less widely known, to plans by the U.S. Naval Command for carrying out the evacuation of the population in the war with Japan, already foreseeable in 1938, exactly according to the scheme proposed by the fictional War of the Worlds.

For the Second World War—in contrast to the First World War where signal corps and inter-brigade communications only appeared with difficulty on the field and in radio drama fiction—was a high frequency war from the outset. The path taken by Orson Welles from the old theater stage to the Mercury Theatre On The Air already anticipated the radio games and multiplex broadcasts of 1942 to 1945. Like Hermes or a messenger from the gods hailing a coming high frequency war, theater ceased representing the victory message of recently concluded wars as it had since the Persians of Aischylos's time. It was not simply by chance that Orson Welles, following Pearl Harbor, helped support the American war effort radiophonically: as announcer for the GI Journal of the American Forces Radio Service, as dramatist of a patriotic Air Force piece sponsored by Lockheed, and finally also as orator for Roosevelt's final presidential campaign in 1944.

But *The War of the Worlds* was already a warm-up for and introduction to high frequency wars. If the Mercury Theatre on the Air serves as a metaphor for the ether, and the ether in its nonexistence is only a metaphor for a vacuum, which as such carries all radio waves, then early warning radio dramas (*Frühwarnhörspiele*) of an impending world war bring the high frequencies, meaning the inaudible itself, to the necessarily low frequencies of hearing. For once, since CBS had placed itself under U.S. Army Signal Corps command (according to an announcement by its technical assistant director), an entertainment program cut in all those signals against whose reception all civilian radio sets had been systematically sealed since their introduction in the nineteen-twenties. The two forms of panic—in fiction as well as in reality—therefore resulted not just from the fact that the radio drama, only one month after the Munich Agreement (appeasement of Hitler by Chamberlain), employed the brand new radio form of live broadcast,[2] but also from its simulation of an entire military command network: spanning the National Guard to infantry battalions and field artillery regiments to bomber fleets. For this reason alone, forty minutes long not a single woman is to be heard. And when, finally, a Secretary of the Interior, whose voice—despite all CBS censoring—is an equally quiet and clear imitation of the Fireside Chat radio voice of President Roosevelt himself, calls out for the grace of God in defense of his country and of the supremacy of mankind, the military radio complex receives the political stamp of approval.

For the American nation—in the words of its fictional Secretary of the Interior—being expected to be «united, courageous, and consecrated to the preservation of human supremacy on this earth» already represents that catastrophe subsequently caused by the landing of the Martian rockets. In his introductory statement as «director of the Mercury Theatre and star of these broadcasts,» Orson Welles describes the opening situation as follows:

«We know now that in the early years of the twentieth century this world was being watched closely by intelligences greater than man's and yet as mortal as his own. We know now that as human beings busied themselves about their various concerns they were scrutinized and studied, perhaps almost as narrowly as a man with a microscope might scrutinize the transient creatures that swarm and multiply in a drop of water. With infinite complacence people went to and fro over the earth about their little affairs, serene in the assurance of their dominion over this small spinning fragment of solar driftwood which by chance or design man has inherited out of the dark mystery of Time and Space. Yet across an immense ethereal gulf, minds that are to our minds as ours are to the beasts in the jungle, intellects vast, cool, and unsympathetic, regarded this earth with envious eyes and slowly and surely drew their plans against us.

«In the thirty-ninth year of the twentieth century came the great disillusionment. It was near the end of October. Business was better. The war scare was over. More men were back at work. Sales were picking up. On this particular evening, October 30th, the Crossley service estimated that thirty-two million people were listening in on radios» (11).

Every word of this description of the opening situation is saturated with misrepresentation as can only be afforded by large empires in their blindness to foreign policy: the misrepresentation of the U.S. for the world. After the New Deal overcame the economic Great Depression and the Munich Agreement alleviated the previous war psychosis, the unity of the U.S. did in fact find its expression radiophonically. For the listener ratings agency Crossley, which incidentally had regularly supplied Orson Welles's radio drama series and had predicted *The War of the Worlds*'s success chances at a measly 3.6 %,[3] had of course not surveyed thirty-two million listeners worldwide, but only nationwide.

However, a system of comprehensive radio coverage, as «CBS and its affiliated stations» claimed to represent, was already in and of itself open to interception. No «abyss of ether,» which doesn't exist anyway, protected the supremacy of mankind from planetary doppelgängers. As a radiophonic union, the U.S. and, a fortiori, the Earth—having become high frequency transmitters—constituted targets of attack for an enemy, who had only just become conceivable as an entirely different planet through this unity. While in 1938 high-frequency-sensitive radar astronomy didn't yet exist—as Jodrell Bank was to develop it after the end of the World War based on plundered Giant Würzburgs (*Würzburgriesen*)—all optical telescope observatories from Princeton to Chicago to Toronto already had their instruments trained on a Mars whose equally cold and mortal intelligent beings were, conversely, themselves keenly eyeing the earth from their rockets.

At first these rocket launchings only attracted astronomical ridicule, as had Schiaparelli's theory of intelligent Martian channels at the turn of the century. But as soon as the reputed «volcanic eruptions» being observed revealed their periodicity, the appearance of a natural catastrophe—in spite of all later information theory—fell apart: the chance planetary event turned into a planetary enemy who, just like the Germans in Peenemünde (German WW II rocket launching base) hardly six years later, were to fire one rocket after the other off into space. (Also much as the V-2 launches on the Peenemünde testing pad were to be observed by camera-equipped Royal Air Force Spitfires.)

The sleepy farmer and radio interview partner in whose fields the first «rocket machine» (22) goes down is only familiar with rockets from an Independence Day and a National Anthem that both reminisce about solid-fuel signal rockets from the American Civil War. In 1938, air strikes without a previous declaration of war—as started in Pearl Harbor and, with modern liquid rockets (these V-2 descendants), having become a constant threat—still had to be explained to the population at large. Not by chance alone did this farmer, an allegory for all radio drama listeners in the radio drama itself, sleep through the Martian rocket landing on the radio, of all places. Therefore a fictitious Professor Farrell, as if the military testing grounds at Peenemünde had already been observed by espionage, may and must call the fuel of the liquid rockets by its proper name on the basis of spectrographic analysis: hydrogen.

However once on earth, after their landings in New Jersey and other states, the Martian rockets display an unusual ability to mutate. The planetary enemy, as soon as he has left his metaphorical ether, metamorphoses from star wars weaponry into blitzkrieg weaponry. As «fighting machines» (22) at «express-train speed» (23), the former Martian rockets operate in the metropolitan area between Princeton and New York precisely as were otherwise only the tank generals Guderian and Rommel in their operation «*Sichelschnitt*» (Sickle Cut) prone.

For the blitzkrieg as a combined system coordinating between the independent tank divisions and tactical bomber squadrons was, particularly in the France campaign of 1940, the exact tactical opposite of all the mass destruction techniques originating in the First World War. «The *Schwerpunkt*—place of main effort—was not the place where major resistance was encountered. On the contrary, the advanced elements by-passed and avoided opposition, wriggling and infiltrating wherever possible, fighting only where there was no alternative. The momentum of the attack was vital to success, and so no element would move off the roads to go cross-country without very good reason, for this would slow the advance.»[4]

The strategic emphases of «*Operation Sichelschnitt*»—and Deighton's excellent analysis forgets to note this—consequently lay in the enemy communications systems, by which armies are principally trailed, and which, in the case of the French and British army, this sickle cut proceeded to systematically eradicate. The enemy position accounts (available to the broadcasting public for once) have just the same to report from the War of the Worlds: «The monster is now in control of the middle section of New Jersey and has effectively cut the state through its center. Communication lines are down from Pennsylvania to the Atlantic Ocean. Railroad tracks are torn and service from New York to Philadelphia discontinued.» (22).

«Langham Field, Virginia: Scouting planes report three Martian machines visible above treetops, moving north towards Somerville with population fleeing ahead of them. The heat ray is not in use, although advancing at express-train speed, invaders pick their way carefully. They seem to be making a conscious effort to avoid destruction of cities and countryside. However, they stop to uproot power lines, bridges, and railroad tracks. Their apparent objective is to crush resistance, paralyze communication, and disorganize human society» (22f.).

With so much strategic vision on the part of enemies, who can hardly camouflage their operative similarity to Guderian's radio-equipped armed tank divisions,[5] the assault on American media systems as such can only lead to the destruction of the radio medium itself. The historical fact of a high frequency system with thirty-two million low frequency ears provides the necessary prerogative for its own annihilation. That a New York reporter declares his microphone transmission to be the «last radio broadcast» just before he and the microphone crash on the floor, thus heralding through the continued presence of a contentless transmission channel (in defiance of Freud and McLuhan) the final disengagement of mankind from technology: all this is not coincidental, but rather—as previously the periodicity of the Martian explosions—symptomatic of strategic calculation. Enemies plan while natural events occur at the roll of the dice. In vertiginous paradoxy, likely only comparable to the state-supporting victims of «*Operation Sichelschnitt*,» the radio drama proclaims to its listeners in the state of New Jersey:

«We are informed that the central portion of New Jersey is blacked out from radio communication due to the effect of the heat ray upon power lines and electrical equipment» (22).

The paradox becomes even more dizzying when the heat wave from enemy rocket machines, hence the general destruction of high frequency systems, happens to coincide with the silliest and therefore most entreating wish admitted to by Orson Welles from behind his Halloween mask:

«This is Orson Welles, ladies and gentlemen, out of character to assure you that War of the Worlds has no further significance than as the holiday offering it was intended to be. The Mercury Theatre's own radio version of dressing up in a sheet and jumping out of a bush and saying Boo! Starting now, we couldn't soap all your windows and steal all your garden gates, by tomorrow night…so we did the next best thing. We annihilated the world before your very ears, and utterly destroyed the CBS. You will be relieved, I hope, to learn that we didn't mean it, and that both institutions are still open for business. So good-bye everybody, and remember, please, for the next day or so, the terrible lesson you learned tonight. That grinning, glowing, globular invader of your living room is an inhabitant of the pumpkin patch, and if your doorbell rings and nobody's there, that was no Martian…it's Halloween» (31f.).

Upon which CBS, as if to demonstrate again its continued and uncontested existence, starts up with the bass drums and trumpets it has usurped from Tschaikowski's First Piano Concerto as its signature tune and announces the end of the radio drama: «Tonight the Columbia Broadcasting System and its affiliated stations coast-to-coast has brought you *The War of the Worlds* by H.G.

Wells—the seventeenth in its weekly series of dramatic broadcasts featuring Orson Welles and the Mercury Theatre On The Air» (32).

However, not all well wishing will lead to relief and consolation. CBS has, in the meantime, been swallowed up not by Japan's bomber fleets but by its media companies. And the fictitious Ramón Raquello—lurking in the background of *The War of the Worlds* as the mask of the radio drama's band leader Bernard Herrmann, only to have his radio hits interrupted more and more frequently by emergency reports—has meanwhile, at least in fiction, much as the radio drama itself due to the Second World War, forfeited any claim once laid to any index of fictionality. In Pynchon's *Vineland*, the husband of the heroine's mother is thus described:

«He was back east playing congas with Ramón Raquello the night they interrupted ‹La Cumparsita› with the news from Mars.»[6]

1   *The War of the Worlds / Der Krieg der Welten: Vier Hörspiele*, ed. Werner Faulstich (Tübingen, 1981), pp. 27f. The other page references in the text also refer to this edition.

2   See John Houseman, «Mémoires de la radio: Extrait de Run-Through,» in *La guerre des mondes d'Orson Welles* (Paris, 1989), p. 93. (With thanks to Heidi Grundmann / Vienna.)

3   Ibid., p. 88.

4   Len Deighton, *Blitzkrieg: From the Rise of Hitler to the Fall of Dunkirk* (London, 2007), p. 157.

5   On the secret order of October 9, 1939 regarding not wearing out tank divisions with the destruction of cities, see ibid., p. 159.

6   Thomas Pynchon, *Vineland* (New York, 1997), p. 78.

Orson Welles, *The War of the Worlds*, radio broadcast rehearsal, New York City, NY, U.S., October 10, 1938.

Orson Welles, *The War of the Worlds*, radio broadcast, CBS's Mercury Theatre On The Air, New York City, NY, U.S., 1938.

Inventing and Re-Inventing Radio

Dieter Daniels

The advent of technical media can never be pinpointed to a specific date or a single individual. Photography, film, and television illustrate this by example, as does radio. The initial conceptualization of these media often astoundingly emerges in parallel, in several different places at the same time, with several stages of development usually necessary before a functioning medium can be established. For this reason, the concept of an «invention» must be supplemented with the aspects of its «relatedness» and «utilization.» «Relatedness» stands here for various genealogical branches as well as for the possible connections between completely separate origins by means of «marriage,» out of which emerge new branches of «relatedness.» «Utilization» in turn denotes the usage to which a medium is subjected by its users, a circumstance that cannot be controlled by the inventor or the producer and is, at times, diametrically opposed to its original intention.

The year 2006 presented several good reasons to celebrate a century of radio. For instance, on Christmas Eve 1906, Reginald Fessenden made the first public broadcast of speech and music. Coincidentally, further technical foundations for radio were laid the very same year, including the invention of the electron tube and the detector. Although it would take another fifteen years for radio to achieve its breakthrough as mass medium, 1906 nevertheless represents a crucial formative moment for radio. The fact that this 2006 anniversary was marked by only marginal public acknowledgement signifies how little historical awareness exists—in comparison, for example, to the worldwide celebrations of 100 years of film in 1995—and how weak the theoretical underpinnings of radio still are.[1]

A second reason for now devoting more attention to the dawn of radio history is the current synthesis of Internet audio streaming, W-LAN, podcast, and mobile telephony to create a common hybrid medium with broadcast radio. This trend heralds a dissolution and diversification of the classic mainstream medium of broadcast radio. The transition from wireless telegraphy to broadcast radio, having begun in 1906, is now undergoing a revision one hundred years later, with the original potential of networked communication for integrating users returning to everyday life. Radio art has anticipated this trend in many ways during the past thirty years, developing exemplary scenarios for a non-hierarchical, decentralized, and participative form of radio. Radio art can thus be regarded as the springboard for a re-invention of radio, having recalled to consciousness the aspects of media «relatedness» and their alternative «utilization,» which had been marginalized by radio as mainstream medium.

The Fourfold Invention of Radio

Four stages can be discerned in the «invention» of radio, spanning over a period of four decades:

circa 1880: utopia and practice of telephone distribution
1895: wireless technology
1906: broadcast of voice and music
1920: amateur radio boom in the U.S.

1   The disregard for this date was one theme of the symposium The Return of Wireless Imagination – 100 Years of Radio, January 17 to 19, 2007, RadioKulturhaus Wien, hosted by *Kunstradio* and the Ludwig Boltzmann Institute Media.Art.Research. This event likewise occasioned the compilation of the essays by Wolfgang Hagen, Wolfgang Ernst, Daniel Gethmann, and Inke Arns for this volume.

2   Norbert Wiener, *Invention: The Care and Feeding of Ideas* (Cambridge, MA and London, 1993), pp. 7–9.

3   In this respect, see the essays by Wolfgang Ernst and by Wolfgang Hagen in this volume, which examine the technical history of radio from an epistemological and media-archaeological viewpoint, as well as the essay by Daniel Gethmann, which explores the political, economic, and social development of radio.

Only after this long course of development does one-to-many broadcasting become the «killer application» of wireless, which has ever since dominated the wave spectrum and further technological progress. The complexity and colorful history of such «inventions» is retraced by Norbert Wiener in his book *Invention: The Care and Feeding of Ideas.* Wiener's four stages of invention do not completely coincide with the stages of radio development proposed here, but there are certain analogies:[2]

- Change in the intellectual climate (effectiveness of the individual is enormous)
- Existence of proper materials or techniques (not a part of the original idea but necessary for its execution)
- Social climate and particular date (often same invention made independently in many places)
- Economic climate (depending on individual and class as entrepreneurs)

A significant breadth of time and space may lie between these stages, as demonstrated by the centuries-long process of «technology transfer» from China to Europe, in which paper and gunpowder later proved fundamental to the development of printing and firearms.

Consequently, caution is called for when pinpointing the birth dates of media! By means of the right facts, an inverted order could easily be constructed: in 1883, Paul Nipkow «invented» an «electric telescope»—but only on paper, for he received a patent but lacked the means for constructing his design. This, however, did not prevent German television stations from celebrating 100 years of television in 1983. The year 1895 is recognized as the year film was born. Applying the assumption that the development of radio began in 1906, the following odd sequence of media would ensue: in 1883 television, then in 1895 film, and finally in 1906 radio. In actuality, television as mass medium only became conceivable through the synthesis of film and radio, and its institutional and technical history as wireless image broadcasting began in the late nineteen-twenties.

Hence, instead of a techno-historical representation, the proposed approach here can be more aptly characterized as «media anthropology.»[3] It is only from this perspective that those social, cultural, and economic factors—decisive for the above-named «relatedness» and «utilization,» rather than «invention,» aspects of media—become manifest. To provide an example: in 1876 and 1887 respectively, two completely independent discoveries or inventions were made, which ended up converging in today's employment of radio as mass medium. In 1876, the electric telephone was invented by Bell and the mechanical phonograph by Edison and, in 1887, the experimental measurement and transmission of electromagnetic impulses by Hertz and the gramophone record by Berliner. Radio's commercial success as mass medium of the hit parade can only be understood through the convergence of these four factors, which led to the «marriage» of Hertz's laboratory experiments with the mass production of records as sound carriers, thus having given rise, starting in the nineteen-twenties, to a new chain of «relatedness.» As early as the eighteen-seventies, utopias likewise emerged—parallel to the technical foundations—for radio and television as future mass media. These planted the seeds in public consciousness, creating what Wiener refers to as the first stage necessary for an invention: the right «intellectual climate.» Accordingly, the four stages in the development of radio and their interconnections will be examined in the following.

1880s
The Utopia and the Practice of Telephone Distribution

A tele-distribution anticipating the one-to-many principle of broadcasting would already have been possible in principle with the telephone. As a matter of fact, when Graham Bell introduced his telephone, the American press feared that news distributed via the faster medium could pose some serious competition. Soon thereafter, practical attempts were made at using the new medium for entertainment. At the Exposition International d'Électricité (World Exhibition of Electricity) in 1881, for example, people stood in line to hear music from the Paris Opéra transmitted for the first time in stereo. Even before the invention of the telephone, a caricature in *Punch* in 1849 foresaw the possible consequences of music transmission via telegraph line, of which there were rumors coming from America: «The grand point of the invention seems to be, that, if songs can be car-

4 *Punch* 17, no. 440 (1849), p. 225.
5 Albert Robida, *Le XXème siècle* (Paris, 1883).

ried along the lines, our popular vocalists may treble or quintuple their present salaries, by singing in four or five places at once.»[4] What Wiener posits as the last stage of invention, the right «economic climate,» was thus already imaginable over 150 years ago.

Caricaturist Albert Robida sketched in 1883 in *Le XXème siècle* a vision of electrical sound and image transmission via *téléphonoscope* as part of a complete media system. This had far-reaching social, cultural, and economic implications, just as this vision would become a reality in the face of radio and television in the twentieth century.[5] Robida's most significant thesis lay in the predicted synthesis of telephone, phonograph, and *téléphonoscope*, forming the foundation for a new industry using the distribution capacity of these media to propagate a whole range of new multimedia offers. The tele-theater company he imagined as being founded in 1945 has 600,000 subscribers worldwide, whose subscription fees pay the respective theater, which can then reach an audience of up to 50,000 for each performance. A big music factory in downtown Paris electrically supplies all subscribers with the performances they have booked. The occupation of musician, limited to a few factory employees, is therefore virtually disappearing, as is likewise the piano from the home.

Live stereo transmission from the Paris Opera to the World Exhibition of Electricity, Paris, France, 1881.

Comparable technical utopias can be found in another futuristic novel on the twentieth century, Edward Bellamy's *Looking Backward 2000–1887*, where they are, however, tied to socio-utopian ideas.[6] Here, technical progress and human insight into the evils of capitalism have given rise to a new form of society based wholly on the principles of cooperation and equality. Cash has been replaced by credit cards with equal rationing thereof. The production of goods is centralized; people order items based on samples, and merchandise is delivered via a pneumatic tube system directly to the customer's home. Making music in the home has also become superfluous since four programs are available around the clock, transmitted live from concert halls via telephone to every home, with perfect acoustics. Interestingly, Robida's humoristic-capitalist and Bellamy's moralistic-socialist visions of the future both draw on the same imagined media distribution technique.

Returning now from the realm of science fiction back to reality: starting in 1893 until the Second World War, Budapest boasted a program for news and music called «Telefon Hírmondó.» This operation set a new record as regards the media-technical acceleration of information distribution, offering brief and precise news updates twenty-eight times a day.[7] The most ambitious and disastrous attempt to use the telephone network for the distribution of electrically generated music was the Telharmonium, invented and built by Thadeus Cahill in 1900. It inspired Ferruccio Busoni's radical musical theory and anticipated the synthesizer by decades, but it never managed to supply the necessary number of lines with simultaneous audio signals, despite it having been redesigned in 1906 and 1911, causing the loss of significant amounts of venture capital.[8]

Despite all of these utopias, caricatures, and practical attempts, the expansion of industrial production and distribution methods—aimed at encompassing a nonmaterial commodity like the electrical delivery of culture and information—nevertheless did not make substantial inroads during the nineteenth century. The resulting question of «why» is one of the unsolved riddles of media history.

---

6   Edward Bellamy, *Looking Backward 2000–1887* (Boston, 1888).

7   See Miklós Peternák, «Der Beginn der zentralen Programmsendung – Budapest 1893,» *Lab* (Kunsthochschule für Medien Köln) (1997), pp. 373ff.

8   See Wolfgang Hagen on the Telharmonium in Dieter Daniels and Barbara Schmidt, eds., *Artists as Inventors – Inventors as Artists* (Ostfildern, 2008).

1895
Wireless Technology

Wireless technology was not initially recognized as a completely new medium, but as a further development of cable telegraphy for areas that are hard to reach by cable. In 1895 and 1896, wireless telegraphy, like all important media previously, was being developed by many inventors simultaneously, of whom we can only name a few here: Guglielmo Marconi, who received the Nobel Prize for this innovation; Alexander Popov, honored annually in Russia with Radio Day on May 7; Oliver Lodge, who is cited in the Encyclopaedia Britannica; Nathan B. Stubblefield, who despite initial success as an inventor would end up starving to death, identified on his gravestone in Kentucky as the «Father of Radio»; Professor Adolf Slaby, who personally apprised Kaiser Wilhelm and his wife of the latest developments at Hubertusstock Palace near Potsdam; and finally, Nikola Tesla, who today enjoys great popularity in media art as well as amongst devotees of esotericism.

Apart from a simultaneity of ideas that never ceases to amaze, the unpredictable «marriage» of media can once again be demonstrated here: likewise in 1895, that banner year for radio, the Lumière brothers in Lyon as well as the

News transmission at the dining table per *téléphonoscope* from Albert Robida, *Le XXème siècle*, Paris, France, 1883.

Skladanowsky brothers in Berlin, along with additional inventors in Washington, New York, and London, all projected films before the public for the first time. From a present-day perspective, the convergence of the two media radio and film led to television. But at the time of its emergence, radio initially remained strictly bound to the paradigm of cable telegraphy and had no connection whatsoever with the simultaneous practice and utopia of tele-distribution.

On the contrary: for Marconi and all the other inventors, the radial broadcast capacity of wireless posed a problem, with interferences from numerous stations not only disrupting military use and jeopardizing the secrecy of classified communications but also making civilian use difficult. Marconi reports: «This defect preoccupied me to such an extent that my main research efforts were directed for many years at eliminating it.»[9] The idea of broadcasting to random recipients was not even mentioned as a possibility at the international conferences on wireless telegraphy in 1903 and 1906.

Of all the wireless inventors in the years surrounding 1895, only Nikola Tesla recognized the potential for radial and global broadcasting. He justified the construction of his Wardenclyffe Tower for international broadcasting (which was never completed and presumably would never have functioned) by citing the «moral effect» to be expected from a global communication envisaged to change the course of history. This socio-utopian dimension links him to Bellamy's belief in a happy future through technology. In 1904, Tesla noted:

World Telegraphy ... will prove very efficient in enlightening the masses, particularly in still uncivilized countries and less accessible regions, and ... it will add materially to general safety, comfort, and convenience, and maintenance of peaceful relations. It involves a number of plants, all of which are capable of transmitting individualized signals to the uttermost confines of the earth. Each of them will be preferably located near some important center of

9   Marconi 1937, quoted in Friedrich Kittler, *Grammophon, Film, Typewriter* (Berlin, 1986), p. 363. The fact that a conference celebrating 100 years of radio already took place in 1995, based on Marconi's invention of wireless telegraphy in 1895, can be primarily attributed to the fact that the English word «radio» fails to differentiate between point-to-point and one-to-many communication. See the International Conference on 100 Years of Radio, IEE CP 411, ISBN 0 85296 649 0 (1995).

10 Tesla in an article in *Electrical World Engineer*, March 5, 1904, quoted in Margaret Cheney, *Tesla: Man out of Time* (Englewood Cliffs, NJ, 1981), p. 178.

11 Lee de Forest, *Father of Radio: The Autobiography of Lee de Forest* (Chicago, 1950), pp. 86 and 449.

civilization, and the news it receives through any channel will be flashed to all points of the globe. A cheap and simple device, which might be carried in one's pocket, may be set up anywhere on sea or land, and it will record the world's news or such special messages as may be intended for it. Thus the entire earth will be converted into a huge brain, capable of response in every one of its traits.[10]

1906
Broadcast of Voice and Music
Reginald Fessenden and Lee de Forest

Tesla served as the great paragon for Reginald Fessenden and Lee de Forest, the pioneers of broadcasting. Like Tesla, both were minister's sons who from the onset approached their radio activities with a parareligious touch—the reason Fessenden decided to hold his first test broadcast on Christmas Eve in 1906. In the case of Lee de Forest, reading Nikola Tesla's texts on high-voltage electro-technology aroused the desire «to myself enter into that tenuous realm that is the connecting link between God and mind and lower matter.» He later reflected on his contribution to radio, stating that he was «proud to have had a prominent part in this new evangel.»[11]

Let us try to imagine the fascination «wireless» must have held for people one hundred years ago. The discovery of wireless telegraphy in 1895 opened up what is termed the «ether,» an as yet unknown and still mysterious sphere, charged with just as many hopes and enigmas as cyberspace would be at the end of the following century. Human and technical communication signals mixed in with the hissing and crackling of cosmic radiation—the code of the Morse Alphabet freed itself from the wire and swung its way onto the yet poorly understood waves of the electromagnetic spectrum. At first, it was considered improbable that modulated tones, meaning human voices or music, could be transmitted by such waves.

This assumption only changed on that momentous Christmas Eve in 1906, which Reginald Aubrey Fessenden spent not at home but rather, with his family, in front of the microphone at his sparely furnished wireless laboratory in Brant Rock, Massachusetts. He played the song «O Holy Night» by Gounod on his violin, sang a few stanzas, and read aloud some verses from the Gospel according to Luke. Listening in were professional radio operators on ships at sea as well as amateurs who found wireless telegraphy a fascinating hobby. For many of them, it must have been surprising to suddenly have heard, instead of the monotonous peeping of Morse Code, musical harmonies and human voices emanating from their headphones. Some marine radio operators couldn't believe their ears and «called in their officers to listen alongside them; soon the radio cabins were full of people.»[12] Fessenden had alerted listeners to the date and frequency for his experiment per advance telegraph in order to ensure that an audience would witness the success of his test.[13] After all, the experiment was also designed to act as an advertisement for his development of the «wireless telephone,» without him even having yet contemplated a mass medium.

The first inventor to have used the term «broadcasting» for a transmission of music and speech to all those with a receiving device was Lee de Forest.[14] He made a further important discovery applicable to radio in 1906: the first electronic amplifier tube, or triode. He dubbed it «Audion,» alluding to the new acoustic world of sound that it could facilitate through transmission. Replacing the extremely expensive, large, turbine-like high-frequency transmitter used by Fessenden—which generated alternating current frequencies through a high number of revolutions—a small vacuum tube entered the picture, affordable even for amateurs producing an audio signal strong enough for broadcasting.[15] This invention ushered in the transition from electromechanical to electronic broadcasting and receiving, making radio's route to mass medium possible in the first place. The types of inventor embodied by Fessenden and de Forest are just as distinct as their technologies: Fessenden and his team worked with scientific ad-

12 Erik Barnouw, *A Tower in Babel*, vol. 1, *A History of Broadcasting in the United States* (New York, 1966), p. 20. See also Daniel Gethmann's essay in this volume.

13 Christopher H. Sterling and John M. Kittross, *Stay Tuned: A Concise History of American Broadcasting* (Belmont, CA, 1978), pp. 28–29 and 40. Fessenden maintained that he had already made a test broadcast on December 11, 1906 for invited specialists and the press; see Reginald Aubrey Fessenden, *The Deluged Civilization of the Caucasus Isthmus* (Boston, 1923), p. 117. He broadcast again on New Year's Eve, comparable to his Christmas broadcast; Barnouw 1966 (see note 12), p. 20.

14 Significantly, this first use of the term takes place in 1907 in a love letter from the aspiring poetry writer de Forest. The term originally stems from agriculture, indicating the scattering of seeds by hand. See Dieter Daniels, *Kunst als Sendung: Von der Telegrafie zum Internet* (Munich, 2002), p. 97.

15 The radio tube is another parallel invention, developed simultaneously by Lee de Forest and Robert von Lieben in 1906 (see the essay by Wolfgang Ernst in this volume). The Audion tube was, starting in 1907, initially used for amplification only on the receiving side; only later did de Forest discover that it can also amplify the broadcasting signal. Likewise in 1906, the simplest and least expensive form of receiver was discovered, the crystal detector that would find widespread use well into the nineteen-twenties.

vising and industrial capital, whereas de Forest began as an amateur and, despite his intermittent successes, remained a solitary figure. Lee de Forest is the last hero in a long line of inventors-as-tinkerers, who, like Edison and Marconi, produced results through mere trial and error, without a scientific background and above all without mathematically calculating the physical processes involved.

———

1920–22
From Radio Amateur to Radio Boom

———

Even after the experiments conducted by Fessenden and de Forest, the transmission of sound remained the exception, while Morse Code continued to prevail as the lingua franca of the frequencies. This also applied to the networked community of amateur radio enthusiasts spread out across the entire North American continent, as described by Francis A. Collins in his book for young readers, *Wireless Man,* of 1912: «An audience of a hundred thousand boys all over the United States may be addressed almost every evening by wireless telegraph. Beyond doubt this is the largest audience in the world. No football or baseball crowd, no convention or conference, compares with it in size ... The skylines of every city

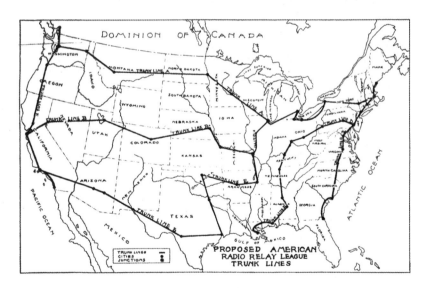

Proposal for the network of the amateur association American Radio Relay League (ARRL) by Hiriam Percy Maxim from *QST*, February 1916.

in the country are festooned with the delicate antennae of the wireless operators. They will be found skillfully adjusted to thousands of barns or haystacks
in the most remote parts of the country.»[16] Until the Radio Act passed in 1912,
no rules or regulations restricted amateur use of the ether. In North America of
that era, the frequencies of the electromagnetic spectrum might even be called a
natural resource. Many amateurs were only acquainted over the air, making for a
true grassroots community beyond industrial or state control. Just before World
War I, the amateur association American Radio Relay League—anticipating that
telephone and telegraph lines might be damaged by hostilities—proposed a nationwide amateur network, which in some aspects prefigured the distributed relay
network of the Internet. But instead, all amateur wireless stations were ordered to
close down for security reasons and did not go back on-air until 1919.

Wireless telegraphy has opened up a new communications space that is in
principle accessible to everyone. The «tech talk» of the amateurs often makes
the social and aesthetic dimensions of the medium appear less significant.[17] The
medium itself is their primary theme: just as the e-mails exchanged by hackers
usually center around computers, radio amateurs generally communicate over
the airwaves about radio technology. McLuhan's dictum «the medium is the message» can be taken quite literally here.[18] But the point is in fact less the actual

16 Francis A. Collins, *The Wireless Man, His
    Work and Adventures on Land and Sea* (New
    York, 1912), p. 26. According to estimates
    made by the *New York Times*, several hundred
    thousand amateurs were already active
    by 1912. See Susan J. Douglas, *Inventing
    American Broadcasting 1899–1922* (Baltimore
    and London, 1987), pp. 199–200.

17 See *QST*, the magazine for amateur radio
    enthusiasts that has been published regularly
    from 1915 to the present.

18 Later on, this even becomes part of the state
    regulations imposed on amateur wireless to
    prevent them from interfering with broadcast
    radio. This had lead to frustration on the part
    of artists trying to collaborate with radio ama-
    teurs for the project *Kunstfunk* in Vienna in
    1984: «In a sense, Kunst-Funk was a senti-
    mental attempt to experience what radio might
    have been like if it had not become a central-
    ised mass medium. But the strict licensing
    regulations and restrictions on content (e.g.,
    no meaningful information aside from name,

address, call-letters, and discussion of
equipment—and radio amateurs are regularly
monitored, and prosecutions for infringements
can result in confiscation of equipment or
worse) have resulted in a ghetto mentality
by radio amateurs, which makes them extremely
suspicious of outsiders and frightened of
coming into conflict with the authorities by
trying anything new—such as working with
artists.» See http://alien.mur.at/rax/
KUNSTFUNK/index.html (accessed October 22,
2007).

19 See Dieter Daniels, «The Miracle of Simultaneity:
    Anticipations of Globalisation at the Beginning
    of the 20th Century,» in *Ohne Schnur: Art and
    Wireless Communication*, ed. Katja Kwastek,
    exh. cat. Kunstverein Cuxhaven (Frankfurt am
    Main, 2004), pp. 36–61.

20 In Europe, starting in 1919 several broadcasting
    pioneers likewise begin making regular music
    broadcasts, however these did not culminate
    in as widespread of a movement as in the U.S.
    due to the fact that in Europe the state
    maintains control over all broadcasting and
    reception activities.

content of the communication than the way the communication process itself is used and structured—a process whose networked, international, and simultaneous presence implies eminently aesthetic experiences. While American amateur radio fans were perfecting their technique, simultaneity was being propagated in the poetry and paintings of the European avant-garde. Guillaume Apollinaire, Robert Delaunay, and F. T. Marinetti, in particular, related the idea of simultaneity directly to wireless technology, without however putting this idea into media practice.[19] Not until the radio art of the last thirty years, for example the projects *Chipradio* (1992) and *Realtime* (1993), has a comparably explicit aesthetic self-reflection of the changing medium occurred within the medium itself. In the heroic age of media and modernism, this connection between American amateur practice and European aesthetic reflection has failed to materialize.

The American radio amateurs would end up playing the decisive role in the breakthrough of broadcasting as a mass medium. Following the caesura of World War I, during which all private radio was prohibited for reasons of national security, the so-called «radio boom» emerged in 1920 in the U.S. and Canada, as pioneers began to step up broadcasting of music and speech.[20] In addition to the networked community of amateurs sending and receiving Morse Code, a «normal

"Wait until the dumb-bells get poisoned with these litle dit-dit's"

Cartoon from the magazine for radio amateurs *QST*, May 1922.

audience» also began to take an interest in sound broadcasting. A then-contemporary cartoon illustrates how the amateur apparatus operated by a male radio fanatic was all at once transformed to a new center of attraction for the entire family, all wanting to listen to the music emanating from the device. The amateur movement thus gave birth to the first radio listeners in a genuine sense. This transition from medium of communication amongst initiates to medium of reception for anyone forms the true moment comprising the «invention» of radio as mass medium.

Only after some delay did the industry also recognize this chance to revive demand for radio technology, which had been flagging since the end of the war. This is the reason for the second date that is often cited as the first radio broadcast: a live report of the counting of votes in the American presidential election of November 2, 1920, broadcasted by the station KDKA, operated by the Westinghouse Electric Company engineer Frank Conrad, who had spun his hobby as a radio amateur into his profession. But neither does this famous political live broadcast, heard by several thousand listeners in 1920, mark a concrete beginning of the mass medium of radio—because where did these listeners actually come from? The history of the broadcasters therefore does not answer the question of the actual driving force behind the radio boom. There is no «first radio broadcaster,» and radio does not have an «inventor.» The idea behind it was not born of a single mind, nor of several minds in parallel, as with so many other media inventions; instead, it has grown as a phenomenon out of a social process that is based in heart not on a new technology but rather on a new utilization. The audience was already there before broadcasters even got started. Or, to put it more dramatically: *radio was invented by the listeners*.[21]

For the first time in media history, the users were the force dictating the launch of a mass medium. The do-it-yourself community of wireless amateurs created the basis for the «early adopters» among radio hobbyists, who, however, were no longer interested in Morse communication but rather only in receiving sound broadcasts. In this way, the avant-garde, so proud of its autonomy, ulti-

21 For a more detailed description, see Daniels 2002 (see note 14), pp. 131ff.
22 On the commercialization of radio, see Dieter Daniels, «A Hundred Years of Radio's Potential,» in *Relating Radio. Communities. Aesthetics. Access, Beiträge zur Zukunft des Radios*, ed. Golo Foellmer and Sven Thiermann (Leipzig, 2006), pp. 34–49.

23 See Patrice Flichy, *The Internet Imaginaire* (Cambridge, MA and London, 2007).

mately paved the way for its own marginalization. Starting in 1922, the electronics industry began to manufacture ready-to-use radio receivers for the consumer and was soon unable to meet rapidly escalating demand. Six hundred new stations went on the air that year, and the radio boom grew into a mass movement, from which there was no turning back. The sound of the new medium gave the «Roaring Twenties» its name. This spelled the end of the once open, communicative, and networked structure of the medium, with the new «killer application» of broadcast radio forming a centralized transmission medium, whose further «formatting» would soon be geared toward commercial criteria.[22]

Broadcasting would go on to become the most powerful instrument for mass distribution in the history of mankind, yet this did not come about based on an industrial or state mandate but rather through its own bottom-up momentum stemming from the amateur movement. This is a process that could only have taken place in the U.S., where a large quantum of legal freedom provides the requisite leeway, while in European countries, radio was not to prevail until two or three years later, introduced top-down as a state-controlled instrument. This difference between the U.S. and Europe was repeated in the nineteen-nineties with the breakthrough of the Internet as a mass medium, likewise emerging from a grassroots community.[23] In both cases, the varying legal regulations are merely an expression of the fundamentally different role media technology plays for society: in the U.S., the terrain of the ether and also of cyberspace have been conquered and marketed based on individual initiative, in keeping with the tradition of the «go west» mentality, while in Europe the state has always taken it upon itself to intervene as a regulating and cultivating force.

Re-Inventing Radio

The birth of radio was based on a new way of implementing existing technologies, shaped decisively by the users and not by industry or individual inventors. This is what makes media archeology and radio theory so pertinent and necessary for the present return of the wireless and the new role of the user in the Internet. The current signs of dissolution of the centralized mass media radio and television make the initial ideas hatched one hundred years ago, at the beginning of the era of broadcasting, seem quite up-to-the-minute again: «Broadcast Yourself» is the motto chosen by youtube.com, words that could also have formed the central message of radio pioneers like Fessenden, de Forest, and the radio amateurs. Today, this promise made by YouTube pulls millions of short videos onto the most successful video distribution platform on the Internet, worth the immense sum of 1.65 billion dollars to the operators of Google. Many of these videos were shot with mobile phones, and they can be called up and viewed wirelessly as well. This convergence of the media television, radio, Internet, and mobile telephony is no longer a coincidence of technological history but alternately a hotly contested development goal in the industry, with the ultimate aim of fusing marketing strategies for the requisite technologies and products. But even for this new developmental push, the impetus came not from the industry but from the users. Podcasting, the precursor to platforms like YouTube, experienced a boom in 2004 comparable to that of radio in the nineteen-twenties, arising primarily from linking blogs with other forums for user-generated content.[24] Along with Tom Sherman, Andrew Garton, and Matt Smith, in this volume artists from different generations comment on this situation of yet another «paradigm shift.»

With the breakneck speed of digital media developments, it's easy to forget that many of the concepts that are today changing and reformatting the principle of broadcasting under the catchword Web 2.0 have already been around for decades, in a similar form, in the realm of media art. This includes early pre-Internet telecommunications art (see, for example, Daniel Gilfillan on Robert Adrian or Candice Hopkins on Hank Bull in this volume) and, since the mid-nineties, models for the connection of radio, Internet, telephone, and ISDN lines, such as *State of Transition* (1994), *Horizontal Radio* (1995), and *Other Voices* (1999). In these projects, Daniel Gilfillan discovers not only a serious consideration of migration issues but also strategies of «subverting broadcasting practices of standardized content and transmission procedures» and a demonstration «that alternatives to a globalized telecommunications structure and homogenous cultural

24 On the emergence of podcasting, the daily newspaper *USA TODAY* writes: «Big tech and media companies could not have foreseen this potentially disruptive hitch to their grand strategies... Like the blogging phenomenon, podcasts have come out of nowhere to attract an enthusiastic grassroots following.» Byron Acohido, «Radio to the MP3 Degree: Podcasting,» *USA TODAY*, Feb. 9, 2005, http://www.usatoday.com/tech/news/2005-02-09-podcasting-usat-money-cover_x.htm.

25 See Daniel Gilfillan, «Broadcast Space as Artistic Space,» in this volume.

26 See August Black, «An Anatomy of Radio,» in this volume.

27 Bertolt Brecht, *Werke XXI, Schriften 1* (Frankfurt am Main, 1992), pp. 217 and 553. The speech «Der Rundfunk als Kommunikationsapparat» («Radio as Communication Apparatus») was held in 1930, not in 1932, and has only been accessible again since 1966. See Klaus-Dieter Krabiel, *Brechts Lehrstücke* (Stuttgart, 1993), p. 108.

content are possible.»[25] Even more radically, the concept of centralized broad-casting is put into question by examples of artist-developed and artist-run open platforms for user content like ORANG–Open Radio Network Group, until 2002, or the Cultural Broadcasting Archive of the Federation of Austrian Free Radios and r a d i o q u a l i a ' s *Frequency Clock*, as discussed by August Black.[26] Looking back, we can today regard these media art practices as an anticipation of the current sea change in the media hierarchy of broadcasting.

From this present-day perspective—against the backdrop of the develop-mental history of radio as sketched above—the development of radio art can be considered on the whole an ongoing re-invention of the medium and of its lost aesthetic and communicative potential. This history of re-invention was already initiated in 1927 with Bertolt Brecht's criticism of radio as an «antediluvian invention.» The demand he voiced in 1930 that «radio must be transformed from a distribution apparatus into a communication apparatus» has, since its reitera-tion by Hans Magnus Enzensberger in the nineteen-seventies, become a standard postulate in all left-wing media criticism.[27] Ten years after the American radio boom, Brecht actually should have been calling for a return of radio to its com-municatively networked origins—but he fails to make this connection. Brecht's

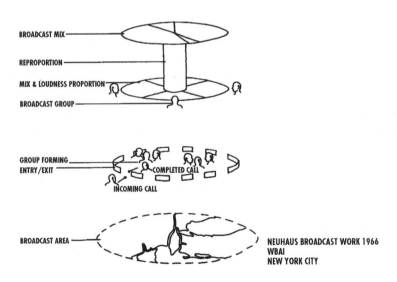

Max Neuhaus, *Public Supply I*, network diagram, 1966.

settling of accounts with radio rests upon his experience with «Lindberg's flight,» a failed attempt at a participatory radio play just one year before. Brecht thus also stands for the conflict between institutionalized broadcasters and artistic interventions running through the entire continued history of radio art.

That radio art, just like other forms of art, transpires in the mind of the beholder—and not in the hopeless attempt to change the broadcast institutions—can be concluded from John Cage's approach. After having created a few radio pieces under contract, Cage subjected the medium to a radical re-invention in 1952, at the high point of the Top 40 format, using it no longer as programming source but rather as randomly generated raw material. In *Imaginary Landscape No. 4*, for twelve radios and twenty-four performers, he turns reception into composition by means of a live remix of stations. «It is thus possible to make a musical composition the continuity of which is free of individual taste and memory (psychology) and also of the literature and ‹traditions› of the art. The sounds enter the time-space centered within themselves ...» is how Cage describes his goals.[28] Questions of authorship and public, as they come to fore in the networked radio art of the nineties, are already in evidence here. At the same time, this re-empowerment of the listener/receiver is a reaction against the slackening of format radio into mere background noise: «You can leave the room, and when you come back, you've missed nothing,» writes *Time* magazine in 1958, sounding almost like a paraphrase of Cage's programmatic redefinition of radio reception as creative process.[29]

Max Neuhaus's series of broadcast works, starting in 1966, marks the beginning of the artistic re-invention of radio as a temporary appropriation and *mis*-use of the technical broadcasting system infrastructure. For *Public Supply* (1966) and *Radio Net* (1977), Neuhaus first found access to a regional broadcasting studio (WBAI New York), and later to the network of National Public Radio, for experimenting with a fundamental redefinition of their basic media-technological structures. By re-staging the «relatedness» between radio and telephone, lost in

28 John Cage 1952, quoted in John Cage, *Silence* (Cambridge, MA, 1967), p. 59.

29 See on format radio Wolfgang Hagen, *Das Radio: Zu Geschichte und Theorie des Hörfunks – Deutschland / USA* (Munich, 2005), p. 326.

30 Max Neuhaus, «The Broadcast Works and Audium,» in *Zeitgleich* (Vienna, 1994).

31 The internationality and permanence which Neuhaus intended for *Audium* was an inspiration to internationally networked projects such as *Immersive Sound* (1998) and *Sound Drifting* (1999), both of which streamed nonstop from different locations over longer—potentially infinite—periods with a generative «soundpool»/«sound drifter» taking over in absence of people.

the mists of media history, Neuhaus opened up the broadcasting communications space to the audience. The dedicated lines over which stations exchange programming, generally not heard on-air, were turned into circulating, listener-based audio loops in *Radio Net*, creating a collective compositional instrument spanning a width of 2,400 km and a length of 4,800 km. Neuhaus additionally constructed new control devices and interfaces, enabling live mixing of the simultaneous audio sources. His goal, though, was not to achieve artistic control over these broadcasts as author/composer, but rather to install a self-executing system, unfolding—through the aesthetic participation/interaction of the user/listener—a social dimension. Radio no longer functions here as distribution medium, but instead as an autopoetic feedback system and as a «virtual place» for open communication «programmed by the people who use it,» as Neuhaus writes of his more recent autonomous telephone-radio installation, the yet unrealized *Audium*.[30] Here, Neuhaus explicitly refers to the anthropological component of his broadcast work by which he aims to emphasize the emotional and cross-cultural aspects of the human voice based on intonation and inflection.[31] This can be regarded as the practical counterpart to the earlier postulated necessity for a media-anthropological theory of radio.

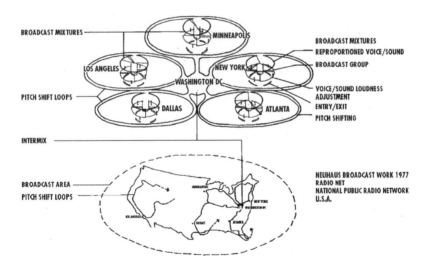

Max Neuhaus, *Radio Net*, network diagram, 1977.

A further chapter in this synthesis of technical and conceptual re-invention of radio can be ascertained in the amalgamation of broadcast medium, Internet, data lines, and telephone for the projects initiated and organized by *Kunstradio* since the nineteen-nineties, especially in the *Horizontal Radio* project of 1995 as well as in others mentioned above.[32] This ongoing artistic and programmatic practice was labeled «Re-Inventing Radio» for a meeting of radio artists and radio activists at the Garage Festival in Stralsund (2004) as well as a subsequent conference and the *Long Night of Radio Art* at Ars Electronica the same year. Finally, the potentially ever-progressing *Re-Inventing Radio* project gave rise to the initiative for this book. The concept of re-invention is explored by several of the authors in this volume. «To rethink, reconceptualize, and revive the radio medium as an active, thinking, and engaged medium» is how Daniel Gilfillan sums up the objectives of these projects.[33] According to Anna Friz, this context also allows for «revisiting and reimagining trailing edge or ‹residual› technologies such as terrestrial radio.»[34] And Tetsuo Kogawa goes even further by deconstructing the «casting» in both broad- and narrowcasting by reminding us that radio is «not only a media form but also a phenomenon of radiation» and resonance.[35]

These experimental models of radio art in the nineteen-nineties are acting in a «time window,» where the liberating potential of the new technologies is emphasized, similar to the nineteen-sixties concepts of self-empowerment by media. Some artists see it as their task to keep this «time window» open as long as possible.[36] But is not the final affirmation for any avant-garde its going down in history while its models and proposals concurrently dissolve into the sphere of daily cultural practice? Today, the new paradigms of radio are comprised by the hybridization of the former mass medium with Internet and mobile phone technologies—as well as by the new role of the users and their active selection (exchanging, tagging), modification (remixing, sampling), and production (pod-

---

32 We will forgo a more detailed analysis here since several authors in this volume expound on *Horizontal Radio*. See, for example, Gilfillan, Dalò, and Arns in this volume.

33 Daniel Gilfillan, «Broadcast Space as Artistic Space,» in this volume.

34 Anna Friz, «Becoming Radio,» in this volume.

35 Tetsuo Kogawa, «Radio in the Chiasme,» in this volume.

36 See Robert Adrian, quoted in Kwastek 2004 (see note 19), p. 33.

37 The current interest shown by media artists in media archeology is therefore, as in Inke Arns's view, not nostalgic but rather a retrospection on the never-realized utopias of the media and, in this sense, a corrective for contemporary and future developments. See Inke Arns, «The Realization of Radio's Unrealized Potential,» in this volume.

casting, blogging) of content. The current hype of Web 2.0 is a testing ground for methods of commercial exploitation of this potential, where, if successful, the models developed by media amateurs and artists would ultimately be used to contravene their own goals, similar to the media transformation prompted by the radio boom of 1922. Are the radio and media artists hence the legitimate successors to the amateurs, who one hundred years ago reveled in the fascination of the ether, experimenting with a new application for radio, thereby unwittingly triggering the emergence of electronic mass media? Taking this perspective, some of the following contributions on the invention and re-invention of radio can be correspondingly read as part of a cyclical movement of twentieth-century media history, today echoing certain motifs from its early days.[37]

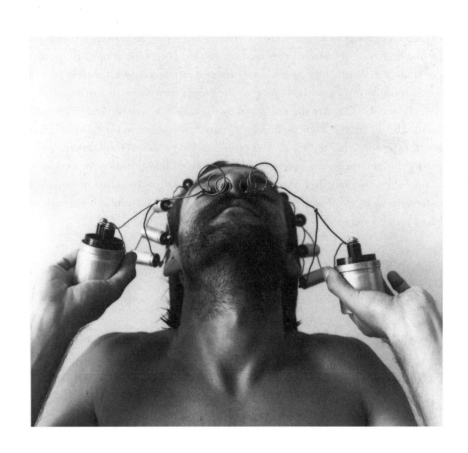

Tom Sherman,
*Negative Ion Breathing
Apparatus*, 1974.

Blanking

Tom Sherman

There is a new psychological phenomenon emerging in this era of hypertele-media, information abundance, and information overload. People of all ages and walks of life are blanking; that is, they are shutting down or experiencing momentary ruptures of consciousness or, in very severe cases, blanking sometimes lasting for days. Blanking is not attention deficit disorder (ADD) or daydreaming (dd), but a sudden breakdown of consciousness brought about by sensory and cognitive overextension induced by hyperconnectivity.

These days, we rarely choose to focus on one coherent stream of information. Rather we simultaneously gather data from multiple sources. Instead of simply listening to the radio or watching TV, we listen to the radio *and* watch TV and read a newspaper, magazine, or book, while we have something to eat, while we have a conversation on the phone, while we stroke our dog's tummy with our bare foot. This is how we function in leisure time: we choose to compose our immediate information environment from multiple sources, mixing our multilayered reality on the spot.

We've become good at packing more and more sources of data and information into shorter and shorter days. In school or the workplace we have learned to concentrate on specific, required tasks in chaotic environments characterized by high levels of noise. We are always in training, learning to swim in more and more confusing, turbulent currents of data. Successive generations have become better at coping with louder, busier, more crowded, more discordant surroundings. When we come home to a dark, quiet apartment, we need to flip switch after switch, turning on our info-appliances until we achieve our preferred quota of information. We panic without this pressure, a media presence that is akin to atmospheric pressure. We sleep as an escape from exhaustion, but with our televisions and radios and computers left on.

Many of us have multimedia workstations to turn up the volume day and night. Many work at home, with our workstations transformed into playstations and vice versa by simply pointing these machines in different directions.

This essay is reprinted from: Tom Sherman, *Before and After the I-Bomb: An Artist in the Information Environment*, ed. Peggy Gale (Banff: Banff Centre Press, 2002).

Perhaps more accurately, the difference between work and play is determined internally, psychologically, as we adopt these different attitudes. We mix our multichannel, multidimensional realities internally, in a private place, wet and cool and blue with bioelectrical equilibrium.

Hyperconnectivity is the buzz. When we're flying high, we tie into anything and everything, and we enjoy building bridges between audio and video and data, and touching and looking and tasting and being here and there, while wanting to be somewhere else, alone together in sweet intensity. We're strong and immense and spread out in tandem with the forces of the universe.

But then we blank, and it's frightening to go down, to crash without sound or punctuation. To terminate into emptiness. First, it's scary, and then it's disappointing, an experience racked with futility. [A loved one strokes our hair in the distance.] Our fingertips are frozen in the curl of our empty hands. Emerging from blanking you realize that overload has been achieved. You've gone further than ever before. You have pushed yourself into the organic reset mode. You'll have to stay quiet or disconnected for a while, but step-by-step, you'll begin to reload again. Then you'll progress as if dancing through a series of inevitable contacts; tying yourself into this and that until you feel whole again; up and running, functioning, expanding, turning up the volume, finding the rhythms, opening your eyes, wider, stepping out farther, reaching across, bridging impossible distances and differences, until again you blank.

«Blanking» was originally written for the online project *SUBVERTICAL ORG*, October 1996. *SUBVERTICAL ORG* was the title of a web work Sherman made as part of a show called *Temple of the Third Millennium*, Urban Exile, Sydney, Australia, January 1996. Urban Exile's web archives have unfortunately vanished.

«Blanking» is included on Tom Sherman and Bernhard Loibner, *PERSONAL HUMAN*, compact disc, ORF *Kunstradio*, Vienna and Ars Electronica, Linz, © 1997. See also http://www.kunstradio.at.

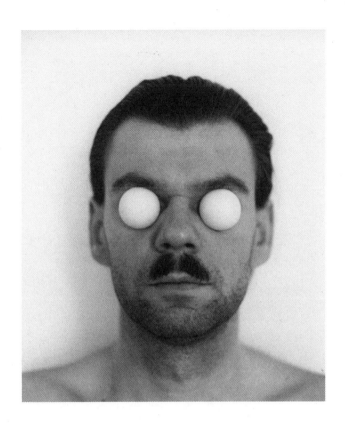

Tom Sherman,
Ganzfeld #2,
The ordinary ping-pong
ball, cut in half, pro-
vides an even field of
white light. That's the
definition of a ganzfeld,
«an even field of white
light,» 1975.

Alternating Currents and Ether

Two Paradigms of Radio Development
U.S. vs. Europe

Wolfgang Hagen

It is a strange circumstance that a symposium on 100 years of radio in 2007 in Vienna causes us to remember a long-past and distant event in American history. Ultimately, we will have to clarify what this event has to do with the history of European radio.[1]

1

Our starting point: two broadcasts, if they actually existed and if the term «broadcast» makes sense at all in this context—if, then, on Christmas Eve and New Year's Eve of 1906 in Brant Rock. From the east coast of Massachusetts, 150 miles south of Boston, Reginald A. Fessenden, the lone engineer, eccentric, outstanding theorist, and equally ingenious experimenter, transmitted peaceful violin music and recorded singing to a few ships at sea. He had pre-announced the transmission by telegraph. This he told us himself a few decades later. A few earwitness reports, arising after another few decades, would nail the forgotten event down more firmly.

What did Fessenden do? He transmitted clearly audible modulation with the aid of an alternating current transmitter with amplitude modulation. It probably sounded like a better telephone line. Today, we would say: Fessenden used the first longwave transmitter to transmit speech and sound on a frequency of about one hundred kilohertz. Because it was a special transmitter that he was working with, we also know: if anyone could do it, then only Fessenden.

His longwave transmitter, then, was simply a steam-driven machine generating alternating current—a current generator. The frequency of its alternating current was very high, that is, the machine rotated very quickly and was, at the same time, extremely stable in terms of torque. The microphone that Fessenden used modulated the strength and voltage of this alternating current. If Fessenden's lips had touched this device, he would have been dead on the spot. Fessenden used an electromagnetic sine wave modulated by speech and sound. He knew what he was doing. Epistemologically, he was pursuing a radio mechanism based fundamentally on the wave paradigm.

Here we must clearly distinguish the technological from the epistemological aspect. Fessenden's current generator, built by Ernst Alexanderson, a pupil of Charles Steinmetz, was mechanically still extremely unstable. It could not take more than a few hours of running at one hundred thousand rotations per minute. And its power was weak. Broadcasting power? Maybe twenty-five watts or a few more.

So if it was the beginning, at Brant Rock in 1906, then technologically it was a very precarious one. Altogether it was a very civilian, partly amateurish, thoroughly experimental event with a low range. The first test run of a little local radio, as it were.

The very non-amateurish epistemology behind this experimentation was alternating current. Fessenden knew precisely what he was doing, even if his means were humble. Epistemology means «knowledge of knowledge.» The chain of knowledge that knows something about the knowledge of alternating current goes back seamlessly from Fessenden to Alexanderson, who built the machine for him, to Charles Steinmetz, who supplied the theory and the necessary characteristics of the machine, to Nikola Tesla, the great propagandist and spiritualist of alternating current in the U.S. of the eighteen-eighties and nineties. «In almost every step of progress in electrical engineering, as well as radio, we can trace the spark of thought back to Nikola Tesla,»[2] Alexanderson later said, thus clearly defining the context of Fessenden's experiment.

1   Wolfgang Hagen, lecture, ORF Broadcasting House, Vienna, January 19, 2007; see his essay in this volume.

2   Quoted in Margaret Cheney and Robert Uth, *Tesla: Master of Lightning* (New York: Barnes & Noble, 1999), p. 157.

Thomas Edison,
Electrocuting an Elephant,
film, 1903.

Participant sitting in
Nikola Tesla's laboratory,
publicity photograph,
Colorado Springs, CO, U.S.,
circa 1900.

Nikola Tesla invented the induction motor and the induction generator. He built the first practicable alternating current transformers. His patents, marketed by Westinghouse, allowed the electrification of the U.S. by safely transporting electricity over distances of hundreds and thousands of kilometers. For instance from the Niagara Falls to New York. Tesla was the winner of the «Battle of Currents» in the U.S. in the eighteen-eighties and nineties, beating Thomas Alva Edison, who strictly refused any dealings with alternating current, operating with his direct current generators only in wealthy districts, as direct current can only be transported without loss for a few hundred meters.

And indeed, a fierce social dispute concerning access to electricity took place in the U.S.—and notably not in Europe—shortly before the 1900 turn of the century, a dispute fought with images conveying the essence of electricity that are nothing short of supernatural. Tesla put on a real show, launching loud bangs and eerie sparks into the universe, while Edison demonized alternating current as a deadly evil, electrocuting an elephant in public on an alternating current platform. For only his direct current devices, only direct current was «good» electricity. The battle for electrification was inflated with illusory images—and with deceptive arguments and notions. For concepts such as essence, substance, and form, that may have held good for the mechanical world of the Modern Age, cannot be applied to electricity.

His whole life long, Tesla hence believed in telepathic phenomena—and not only upon the death of his mother. He made all of his inventions by means of imaginary inspirations.

On one occasion, ever present in my recollection, we were enjoying ourselves in the City Park, I was reciting poetry, of which I was passionately fond ... «*Sie rückt und weicht, der Tag ist überlebt, Da eilt sie hin und fordert neues Leben, Oh, dass kein Flügel mich vom Boden hebt Ihr nach und immer nach zu streben! Ach, zu des Geistes Flügeln wird so leicht kein körperlicher Flügel sich gesellen!*»[3] As I spoke the last words, plunged

3 The sun retreats—the day, outlived, is o'er
It hastens hence and lo! a new world is alive!
Oh, that from earth no wing can lift me up to
soar And after, ever after it to strive!

. . . .
Alas! To wings that lift the spirit light
No earthly wing will ever be a fellow.
(Goethe, *Faust I*, Faust monologue «Outside
the gate of the town»)

4 Nikola Tesla, *Lectures, Patents, Articles*, sine
loco, sine anno, p. 198.

in thought and marveling at the power of the poet, the idea came like a lightning flash. In an instant I saw it all, and I drew with a stick on the sand the diagrams which were illustrated in my fundamental patents of May, 1888.[4]

The outcome (supposedly): the most important of the numerous induction motor patents held by Tesla, with which he secured his lifelong wealth, sporting new suits, spats, and shoes everyday and enjoying lifelong residence in the best hotels. The history of radio in the U.S. is epistemologically founded upon the alternating current wave from the context of Nikola Tesla. It is multiply overloaded with the specter and madness of a psychotic inventor, who delivered largely practicable, detailed blueprints for his dynamos, circuits, and motors, the origins of which, however, are shrouded in the dark mystery of visions, delusions, and telepathic phenomena. What Tesla describes in these crazed visions is the un-place of electricity. It simply cannot be described with the means of modern science.

The following words stem from Heinrich Hertz himself: «We form for ourselves images or symbols of external objects; and the form which we give them is such that the necessary consequents of the images in thought are always the

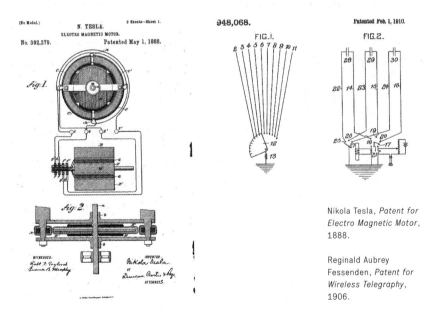

Nikola Tesla, *Patent for Electro Magnetic Motor*, 1888.

Reginald Aubrey Fessenden, *Patent for Wireless Telegraphy*, 1906.

images of the necessary consequents in nature of the things pictured. In order that this requirement may be satisfied, there must be a certain conformity between nature and our thought.»[5] Electricity can only be «represented» in the four Maxwellian equations. They describe with mathematical precision the interrelationship between electric and magnetic vectors in four-dimensional space.

In all other respects, electricity eludes any ontological definition. At best, we can find correspondences between images and follow-up images of images. The fact that classical metaphysics is overtaxed in terms of model theory when facing the problem of electricity is what resounds in Tesla's delusions but also paves the way for building innovative electricity machines.

2

The fact that radio history is not just radio history—and American radio history is certainly not European—is illustrated by the example of Hans Bredow. Not that he failed to notice Fessenden. All of these very young radio pioneers around the globe were watching each other very closely. In his memoirs *Im Banne der Ätherwellen* from the nineteen-fifties, Bredow could not help but declare Fessenden as the first person to make radio with high-frequency generators because he was able to modulate undamped vibrations. The go-getting young gentlemen from Telefunken were only too familiar with Fessenden's American patents. Bredow hastens to add that a certain Professor Goldschmidt in 1911 and Count Arco from Telefunken in 1912 had done it better and more effectively. The old father of German radio from 1923, slave-driven and deprived of power by the Nazis, but as loyal to the Emperor as ever, wrote this as late as 1954. Right down to his choice of words, he repeats in detail what he had already written as editor in his Telefunken newspaper back in 1910.[6]

The young Telefunken boss Bredow, the later-to-be radio founder of the Weimar Republic, was forced to deal with Fessenden for the simple reason that his was an inexpensive and simple system, weak in range but of high electroacoustic quality. Telefunken was forced to copy Fessenden's patents because the company

5 Heinrich Hertz, *Die Prinzipien der Mechanik in neuem Zusammenhange dargestellt: Drei Beiträge* (1894; repr., Thun et al.: Deutsch, 1996), p. 67.

6 Hans Bredow, *Im Banne der Ätherwellen*, vol. 1, *Daseinskampf des Deutschen Funks* (Stuttgart: Mundus Verlag, 1954), pp. 267–68.

7 *Telefunken-Zeitung* 1, no. 6 (1911), p. 81.

8 Bredow 1954 (see note 6), p. 200.

had been wanting to get in on the exploding colonial world markets of electric wireless telegraphy since the first decade of the twentieth century. Fessenden, the technologically so dangerous rival, had to remain a footnote. As of 1911, every two months the *Telefunken-Zeitung*, with director Bredow as editor in chief, would above all praise the company's own sales in Asia, Africa, Latin America, China, and the South Pacific.

German colonialism was, even then, for Bredow simply a question of dominating the ether. At the last international radio conference before World War I, in London in June 1913, Telefunken handed out a paper in which it read: «Of the approximately 3000 radio stations in operation [around the world], some 45% use the German system, while all the other systems, Marconi, de Forest, Fessenden, … Rochefort, Poulsen, etc. divide up into the remaining 55%.»[7] And he adds in his memoirs of 1954: «One could thus have claimed, without any arrogance, that German radio had taken the lead before World War I and won an international standing.»[8]

As early as 1906, radio had become a colonial instrument of power both in Imperial Germany and Victorian England. If the discourse of «postcolonial studies» were more conclusive in terms of media analysis, we could leave it at this

Telefunken Wireless Transmission Station, 1906.

diagnosis. The European dispositives of early radio development were aggressively militaristic and colonialistic, while the American ones proved amateurish and overloaded with the paradigm of alternating current as energy and salvation for humankind/civilization/nation. Bredow, Marconi, Telefunken, and all the other European «electricians» were not concerned with transmitting music and speech but rather with imperialist control of the command codes of power, military logistics, and trade information, that is, technologically speaking: with telegraphy. When, likewise in 1906, one somewhat eccentric but ingenious engineer at Telefunken by the name of Wilhelm Max Schloehmilch began to experiment with and talk about wireless telephony—even demonstrating transmission of Caruso records to the Emperor—he was sharply reprimanded by Telefunken boss Arco to refrain from this fooling around. His equipment ended up in a museum just three years later, where it can still be viewed today.

Ever since Marconi had demonstrated it to European engineers in 1897, although he himself did not understand enough of it technically, all wireless systems in Europe were geared to achieving extreme ranges. Again, postcolonial discourses would find much food for thought in the Telefunken newspaper as of 1910. Every issue outdid the previous one in the ecstatic hysteria of ranges. To transmit from Nauen to German South West Africa, that is victory. Technologically, this was only possible with gigantic spark transmitters, exploding out into East Havelland with sparks as thick as a man's arm and deafening bangs at the transmitter site. It would not have been possible to secure the majority of radio on merchant ships with high-frequency alternators à la Alexanderson or Fessenden. That would not have made the radio operators trained by Telefunken proud. And Bredow was sitting in the middle.

But in questions of media, to take a postcolonial perspective is to take the easy way out. It both overrates and underestimates colonialism prior to 1914. The European radio dispositive is the spark, but not (only) because its oscillation generates electromagnetic waves that reach as far as the South Pacific.

Rather, the radio spark is connected with a complex epistemology that, if at all, has a structural relationship to colonialism. The radio spark, you see, is based upon ether. To the extent that nothing more omnipotent than ether existed

9   Adolf Slaby, *Entdeckungsfahrten in den elektrischen Ozean: Gemeinverständliche Vorträge*, 5th ed. (Berlin: Simion, 1911), p.118.

in pre-1900 physics that can be caused to tremble by electric sparks, we may concede that ether was congruent with colonialism.

«If we cause any kind of electric vibration, it creates a wave motion in the sea of ether surrounding us,»[9] writes Adolf Slaby in his *Voyages of Discovery into the Electric Ocean* of 1911. Ether and the spark that causes it to move is the paradigm of European radio epistemology. It is not necessary to cite Heinrich Hertz in order to illustrate the epistemological dimension of ether in modern-day physics. Hertz was certain that the sparks in his laboratory in Karlsruhe at Christmastime in 1887 caused a displacement motion in the ether. As early as the start of the nineteenth century, Fresnel and Young had indisputably demonstrated the wave structure of light, thus proving that light must swim in the ether in some way. In 1883, the «Michelson-Morley experiment» had been expected to prove ethereal drift of the earth through ether, but failed. Yet at first this «dead end» did not cause any European scientists to doubt the existence of ether. William Thomson, alias Lord Kelvin, the leading mind in Europe, had, after all, already determined the specific weight of ether, and his widely accepted atomic model consisted in eddy structures of ether as the state of matter. By means of his experiment, Hertz had thus simply confirmed this epistemic figure of ether once again, thus underscoring the irrefutability of its existence once more.

The physical properties of ether must have seemed almost crazy. It had to be a totally transparent substance, finer than any structure as yet known, all-pervading and invisible. At the same time, however, it had to transport transverse oscillations—oscillations that are transverse to the direction of their propagation. For it was shown that light is such a transverse oscillation. However, such oscillations are transported only in the very hardest of bodies, for instance in diamond or special steel alloys. Invisible and yet as hard as diamond? Reading the contemporary descriptions of ether from the nineteenth century, here again the depth of contradiction of a crazed discourse is no far stretch (from today's point of view). For the classical Newtonian mechanics of celestial bodies, this substance was obsolete. Planetary orbits need no ethereal substance to be explained. But the deeper the Modern Age penetrated electricity, leading to Hertz's proof of electromagnetic radio waves in 1887, the more this went to confirm a figure of madness that the concretion of ether was increasingly growing to be after 1890.

Electricity and the media it engendered have one thing in common: both generate illusory images that are the effect of going beyond understanding. After all, you do not have to understand electricity to use it. Tesla may have had delusions, but in the end his motors were effective enough to allow Fessenden to transmit radio. Hertz had to consider the existence of ether proven by his experiments, but his sparking dipoles were effective enough to bring Telefunken imperial business until as late as 1914.

Media need not be understood to be used. This is both their degree of freedom and their bane. But even one hundred years after Brant Rock, nothing has changed.

Lecture presented at the conference 100 Years of Radio – The Return of Wireless Imagination, ORF Broadcasting House, Vienna, a collaboration between *Kunstradio* and the Ludwig Boltzmann Institute Media.Art.Research. The conference was part of Vienna *Art's Birthday* Celebrations, January 17–19, 2007.

Transmission Culture

Brandon LaBelle

There will come a time when in our individualistic
harmonious state all work will consist of
thinking and crystallizing thought into sound or
directionable spheres which will set in motion
machinery or controlled fourth dimensional
design.[1]
— *Buckminster Fuller*

The radio transmission conducted atop the Eiffel Tower in July 1913 not only made possible the standardization of time for the Western nations, it also radically transformed, and set the stage for, an architectural object: the Tower as a symbolic expression of modern engineering now turned into an electrified point from which electro-communications is thrown.[2] The vertical tower, in reaching for the heavens, now in turn radiates horizontally, reaching out in all directions to make connection, to signal and transform the landscape from a visible field to an invisible network. The standardization of time not only sets the clock according to a rhythm of production and consumption but also extends poignantly the relation of such rhythm to the dynamism of communications.

Turning the Eiffel Tower into a transmission tower inaugurates a new form of architecture, one imbued with a sense of complexity, for transmission must be understood to both fuel the potentiality of global communications while infusing this with a degree of monstrous imagination. Already, the Eiffel Tower in its moment of construction in the eighteen-eighties signaled the total upheaval of the urban skyline by its radical implementation of cast-iron framing developed for bridge and factory design. As Sigfried Giedion observes, «Viewed from the standpoint of construction, the whole tower is an adaptation of the lofty supports of iron bridges, increased to cosmic dimensions.»[3] Such cosmic dimensions take on greater promise with the capping of the Tower with transmitting antennas.

The construction of steel frame towers for radio transmission took greater hold in the nineteen-twenties, with the construction of the Berlin Radio Tower in 1926. Standing 150 meters, the Berlin Tower consists of four corner support structures that sweep upward, gentling tapering to the top. As Moholy-Nagy's montaged photograph of the Tower suggests, the jointed tapestry of metal framework is embraced as an expression of man's technological rationality. Such rationality in turn equates with a spiritual mythos according to Kandinsky, interweaving geometry and abstraction with the poetics of the soul.[4] Science and technology were integrated into an overarching project of the imagination, turning the extravagances of artistic expression into forms of idiosyncratic engineering: from the synaesthetic to the occult to the pataphysical, modernism is replete with instances of applying rational thought to the fringes of cultural production, incorporating the technological as both social and utopian project as well as harbinger of a new sensorial organization, which, in the hands of artists and dictators alike, turns transmission into the cornerstone of the new Nation. While modernism's techno-spiritualism spawned fantasies of universal languages, a metaphysics transcending the globe in the potential of connection, it in turn found balance with the practicalities and entertainment possibilities of reaching the masses, as witnessed with the broadcast of the first regular television programming in the world beginning in 1935 from the Berlin Tower.[5] Notions of synaesthetic plenitude, and the inner resonance of spiritual bodies, which for other modernists, such as Velimir Khlebnikov, find further potential in the promise of mass transmissions, are counterbalanced by an appeal to the quotidian,

1   Buckminster Fuller, *Your Private Sky: R. Buckminster Fuller* (Baden: Lars Müller Publishers, 1999), p.106.

2   The event was decided upon at the International Conference on Time held in 1912, establishing the need to «rationalize public time.» The Eiffel Tower had been used for radio transmission beginning in 1903. See Stephen Kern, *The Cultures of Time and Space, 1880–1918* (1983; repr., Cambridge, MA: Harvard University Press, 2003).

3   Sigfried Giedion, *Space, Time, and Architecture* (Cambridge, MA: Harvard University Press, 1997), p.281.

4   In Kandinsky's publications, *Concerning the Spiritual in Art* and *Point and Line to Plane*, the artist theorizes the relation of sensation and abstraction to questions of inner experience, devising synaesthetic correspondences, for instance, yellow corresponds to the sound of middle C on the piano.

5   The Eiffel Tower also served as an experimental TV transmitter in 1935, broadcasting on shortwave, marking the beginning of European television broadcasting.

6   The Tower is soon to be made obsolete with the development of the new Tokyo Tower to be completed in 2011, which will stand as the tallest structure in the world measuring 610 meters high.

in which news reports, radio dramas, and commercials address the average citizen. The potentiality of transmission is thus placed on an uneven ground where state control, information and entertainment, and the fantasies that govern both avant-garde utopias as well as the imagination of television producers converse. In Japan, such conversations find articulation with the construction of the Tokyo Television Tower in 1958. As a symbol of the new Japan arising out of its long defeat following World War II, the Tower meant to express the country's ascendancy as a global power and openly drew upon the Eiffel Tower as a model for its design. Measuring thirteen meters taller than the Eiffel Tower, the Tokyo Tower is constructed from an iron frame reaching 333 meters high and has served as an important transmitting relay.[6] The symbolic importance of the Tower can be further understood in relation to the tensions embedded within transmission: while seeking to signify the nation's future promise, the Tower was regularly featured as the site for fantasies of destruction in Japanese films, with the likes of Godzilla smashing it to pieces in the various films made throughout the sixties.

Transmission towers thus become galvanizing rods around which intersecting perspectives converge, bringing together the belief in the power of transmission to spawn new forms and structures of being—democratic, spiritual, fantastic—

TV Tower,
Tokyo, Japan, 2006.

while offering new forms of capital gain to the forces of commercialism and military might.[7] As architectural forms, they are suggestive of new possibilities for inhabitation and urban connection based on the atmospheric and the connective, and at the same time, they come to burden the spaces of living with the weight of their messages. To transmit thus is an ideological wager upon which gain and loss are measured according to technology and its ultimate use and application. It is around transmission towers that I want to locate a cultural momentum toward the medial that drives architectural, electronic, and urban avant-garde projects throughout the modern period. Such projects may be understood from this vantage point to collapse back onto the otherwise banal transmitting tower, haunting or supplementing the infrastructures of communications from within.

Towers
Electrical Imagination

«The interpenetration of continuously changing viewpoints creates, in the eyes of the moving spectator, a glimpse into four-dimensional experience.»[8] Giedion's whimsical descriptions of the Eiffel Tower resound equally with the advent of radio communications, which were to amplify the «interpenetration of viewpoints» and realize a bolder glimpse onto four dimensions through live media. While these steel frame constructions exemplify the very move of transmission itself by architecturally appearing as light, structural, and without interior—the steel frames are pure form, seemingly immaterial and lightweight, reaching from the earth out into the sky—the use of concrete in the fabrication of transmission towers signifies a centralized core.[9] Concrete transmitting towers, initially appearing throughout Europe beginning in 1953 (with the Southern German Radio [SDR] Stuttgart Television Tower), allow not only for aesthetic benefits but for struc-

7   One might add the promise in acting as a tourist attraction, which both the Eiffel Tower and the Tokyo Tower have served radically, with each receiving well over a million visitors each year.

8   Giedion 1997 (see note 3), p. 284.

9   Steel frame towers appear more widely along highways, as local broadcasting stations, and as the carrier of electrical and telephone cabling, cutting through the landscape, as connecting and relaying towers, appearing less now as architectural and governmental symbols than concrete towers.

10   By the nineteen-eighties, there were roughly 180 transmission towers spanning the West German countryside. See Erwin Heinle and Fritz Leonhardt, *Towers: A Historical Survey* (London: Butterworth Architecture, 1989), p. 227.

11   Jonathan Sterne, *The Audible Past* (Durham: Duke University Press, 2002), pp. 153–54.

tural ones, for concrete is ultimately more resistant to wind change, reducing the level of transmission interference by minimizing the vacillation of its antennas at such heights. In addition, concrete profoundly reduces the amount of vibration through muffling, to which steel frames are particularly susceptible.[10]

The vertical apparatus of the transmission antennas finds earlier expression in telephone and telegraphic poles that draped across the United States beginning in the mid-nineteenth century. With the advent of electric telegraphy in 1837, and Morse Code (invented by Samuel Morse) in the same year, the ability to transmit messages began to fragment the landscape both by its infrastructural forms as well as the corresponding medium of electrical current. The first electrical telegraph line was developed in 1844 using thirty-foot wooden poles, following railroad lines and roads that would come to dominate the American landscape by the turn of the twentieth century. The design and appearance of these forms came to embody the invisible, magical, and ghoulish medium of electricity and its ability to carry information, to connect by traveling great distances according to a speed beyond human capability. «Sound telegraphy does not reproduce sound so much as link it, enmesh it in a relation of correspondences, and organize it according to the logic of an indexical code—a particular kind of signification.»[11]

Eiffel Tower,
Paris, France, 2007.

Marking the development of sound telegraphy—the deciphering of Morse Code not by its visual marks as in early telegraphy, but by the sound of the mechanism driven by electrical current from the sender—Sterne emphasizes how sound was to become a new kind of syntax, a form of communicative code by which listening would act as a new sensory technique. Such technique, and its related mechanism of the telegraphic machine, has its counterpart in the transmitting towers and electrical cabling physically linking sender and receiver in an elaborate network that would become an expansive infrastructure for nation building. Thus, sound's signification in turn is further iterated not solely in the mechanics of the telegraphic machine, the point of reception, but in the expansive infrastructure of transmitting and relaying poles and towers that would come to speckle the landscape and dominate the skyline. The tower made manifest the currents racing across distance, making tangible, alongside the clatter of the machine, the transmutation of code. With the advent of radio after 1899, both the infrastructure of the new nation, and its auditory habits and cultures, would intensify as wireless tower transmission, would lead to constructions with higher and higher antennas in order to reach more distant points. Property value, information access, visual beauty, and national borders would all come to synthesize into a complex knot of social, economic, and political intensity, leading to legislation on all these issues, as well as the very construction of the towers.

The transmitting tower formally echoes an entire mythology surrounding obelisks, monoliths, pyramids, ziggurats, steeples, minarets, and defense towers that historically come to embody forms of power and magic. As a formal language, the tower expresses an ongoing relation of earth and heaven, operating to channel correspondence and communication, between man and god, between church and society, and between enemies, demarcating time and space while monumentalizing historical events. It in turn comes to symbolize, as we have seen with the Eiffel and Tokyo Towers, the nation as an identifiable force, enigmatic by being both physically exact as well as by projecting a sense of omniscience: the tower both draws in and projects out the spirit of a nation. In its most audacious, the transmission tower continues this legacy by literalizing this connective image, linking the force of physical engineering with communicational media. One might look

12 Originally standing in its place was the Royal
    Palace, which was initially damaged during the
    war and demolished in 1952.

toward the Berlin TV Tower located in Alexanderplatz to recognize this interplay. Constructed between 1965 and 1969 after extensive debate throughout the fifties, the TV Tower aimed to facilitate two functions, namely, to provide necessary transmission capabilities to East Berlin as well as to act as a symbol for the communist GDR.[12] While the GDR struggled to locate the necessary funds throughout the fifties for such projects, in 1964 Walter Ulbricht, the party leader, was persuaded to combine the two projects, inspired by the city proposal by Hermann Henselmann from 1957 which located the TV Tower in the heart of the city (a rare gesture in European cities). When finally opened in 1969, the Berlin TV Tower succeeded in providing television programming to East Berlin, combating the heavily watched West German television stations as well as boldly marking the city as a living monument to the communist state.

The transmission tower in turn is generative of methods of sabotage, espionage, spying, and other fringe techniques that supplant or supplement the nation with medial transgression, turning the national symbol into an ideological and military weapon. For transmission towers are also receiving towers, enabling nations to monitor each other's broadcasts and communications, forcing the very codes of which Sterne speaks to implement more and more covert script, forcing

TV Tower,
Berlin, Germany, 2008.

the ear into new positions of listening. Electrifying visions of other worlds, turning up the volume on the interchange between earth and the sky, charging the medium of air with a radical ambiguity, the transmission tower may in turn bring us back to Kandinsky's inner, spiritual resonance. Fuelling the imagination with new horizons of possibility and communication, the transmission tower sets the scene for alien communications, utopian fantasy, an interlinking of minds, and a general unease and paranoia as to what may come speeding through the radio, the phone lines, the television, to locate itself within the home. Thus, transmission towers vacillate within the imagination by lending support to the very fantasy of communicational technology: to extend the limits of the body, whether individual or political, social or aesthetic.

Fitted with disk platforms, directional and mirror antennas, and aerials for wireless and television transmission, transmission towers come to symbolize a kind of oscillation between the power of state control and the potentiality of personalized expression, which may be said to reside at the very heart of radio and other broadcast media. «Transmission towers are tangible manifestations of our immersion in this cosmos of communication.»[13] As Bertomen suggests, our «immersion» takes the condition of a cosmic experience, accentuating the field of radio—radio not strictly as content, but as the very medium of radio waves or electromagnetism—as intrinsically other, and beyond total comprehension. For Bertomen, such cosmic depiction subsequently undoes the ability to fully apprehend from a single perspective a field of knowledge, replacing the authoritarian panopticon with a vision of fragmented and multiple points in a leveled field of exchange. As she continues: «In the dispersed electromagnetic medium, this singular glance of authority has been fragmented, democratized by the multitudes that now participate in its formation. The radio network might be considered the physical heir to the workings of the moral consciousness.»[14]

Radio thus comes to embody the very possibility of sharing beyond the particularities of nation states, governmental offices, and it does so partially by formalizing such networks through the spindly appearance of the transmission tower. For «[t]ransmission towers and the network of communications they support are paradigmatic of a distinctively new conception of the world, one that also

13 Michele Bertomen, *Transmission Towers: On the Long Island Expressway – A Study of the Language of Form* (New York: Princeton Architetural Press, 1991), p. 9.

14 Ibid., p. 52.
15 Ibid., p. 60.
16 Ibid., p. 61.

demands new strategies for perception.»[15] While Bertomen locates this radical alteration away from a single perspective or apex of knowledge, governed by an architecture of tangibility and visibility, in turn such perspective falls short in recognizing to what degree such a communications network—of towers and their ultimate transmission—is fully regulated by an infrastructure of control and policy: what information can be transmitted and who has access become questions that undermine the belief that «modern transmission towers suggest an antithesis to the understanding of knowledge as an immediately comprehensible overview in favor of one in which all points in the system provide equal and compatible points of access and comprehension.»[16] This is nowhere more poignantly glimpsed than in the mounting of personal transmission devices for the broadcast of illegal signals. To erect one's own transmitter not only necessarily infringes upon the landscape of existing towers, it in turn trespasses on the territorial field of frequency and related law. Transmission towers in themselves, as a language of form, may indeed point toward an upheaval in the paradigmatic base for the apprehension and understanding of knowledge, but it equally does so by implementing new forms of control. As Deleuze has so eloquently sought to highlight, the technological future of democratized media (which identifies also

Ironton Radio Tower, transmission tower for an AM/FM radio station, Ironton, OH, U.S., 2006.

a kind of secret passage from a «society of enclosure» to a «society of control») only brings forth more strict and stealth mechanisms for maintaining and policing what may pass through such media.[17] According to Deleuze, it would be the very appearance of freedom suggested by transmission towers, and their related network of connective and decentralized power, that would warrant a more thorough identification and understanding of the underlining structures or «codes» controlling this appearance.

The Atmospheres of Urbanism
Situationism and the Promise of Ambience

In following the development of transmission and related infrastructures of towers and networks, I've been interested to identify a cultural perspective surrounding notions of freedom and progress, communications and policy, generated by the aerial imagination. It is my view that such imagination is both sparked by as well as initiating of technological fantasies and products, fusing cultural visions to scientific research while fuelling such research with degrees of potentiality. How might transmission towers, as quotidian objects, reveal a kind of material history of transmission culture?

The development of urbanism following the Second World War not only led to programmatic shifts in understandings of architecture, exemplified in the CIAM group initially established in 1928; it in turn fused architecture with a larger set of coordinates, ultimately leading to embattled arguments as to the social and connective effects of space itself. While architects such as Le Corbusier sought to find suitable form for the new city by dealing up cubic volumes, a combination of vertical towers with open green spaces, the potentiality opened up by the advent of new electromagnetic communications and technologies of transmission radically broke apart the conventional understanding of space as based on cubic volume. The formal and material play of Le Corbusier, while aiming for the transformation of European cities, nonetheless remained extremely conservative alongside subsequent architectural manifestos and movements following the war. Exemplified in groups such as the Situationist International, Team 10, and the later Metabolists, questions of urbanism, architecture, and space be-

17 Gilles Deleuze, «Postscript on the Societies of
    Control,» *October* 59 (Winter 1992), pp. 3–7.

come infused with the further implementation of electrical circuits, networked technologies, communicational structures, and the potentiality of the immaterial and the unfixed so characteristic of radio broadcast. While Le Corbusier and the related CIAM group focused largely on built forms, traditionally gravitating around the image and notion of the home, the situationists and related Team 10 members found more inspiration from questions of social space and its related languages and systems. To move to such questioning entailed a more thorough glimpse onto the structures and infrastructures of city life, from transportation networks to mobile supports. A number of elements align themselves within this perspective, notably the automobile, which was to become an object of continual inspiration (and disgust), leading to projects such as David Greene's *Living Pod* (1965) and Ron Herron's related *Walking City* (1964), which overlays vehicular design with urban planning: the city as a continual shifting of bodies and buildings, fused in a mobile system. In addition, we might add the increasingly present image of the transmission tower and its related antennas, relay stations, and networks of cabling, circuitry, and transformers that increasingly intersect with buildings and their related landscapes throughout the modern period. For these came to truly embody and make tangible the new frontier of urban experience: in contrast to architecture as an object located in a fixed landscape, functioning as part of a larger governmental and bureaucratic office of planning, the functional, de-aestheticized, proto-proletariat objects of the steel frame tower harnessed all the romantic fantasies of libidinal desire, the flows and slippages of unconscious projection, and the continual upheaval of city life, exemplified in the situationist's theory of psychogeography. Psychogeography was to come to express an interpenetrating of subjective rhythms and fevers with an objective study of the urban landscape; it recognized the two as interlocked phenomena, whereby the self's interior presence was both determined by and determining of the external space of existence. The city itself was to be seen as a living form truly embodying this dynamic. By nature, the city is a controlled and structured territory, objectified by the material aspects of its continual construction and decay, while at the very same time receiving and conducting a heightened sense of embodied flow, rhythm, and social interaction, fuelling the imagination with mobility, energy, and the sensuality of a continually modulating and fleeting exchange in and amongst others. As a practice, psychogeography took the form of drifts through the city (*dérive*) as a means of unraveling the script of bourgeois life and infusing time with degrees of play and ambiguity. «Drift therefore became a transgression of the alienated world,»[18] allowing the appropriation of existing systems and official structures for the pleasures of the experiential.

By and large the city represented and offered itself as a magnetized, energetic field by which new behaviors and new architectures would meet. What this new architecture would be found its operative language through the notion of «the atmospheric.» That psychogeographic drifts and encounters sought out particular regions of a city, highlighting the ruinous, the local, the informal, against the terrain of the bureaucratic, it did so according to an inexact science, following intuitive sensations and modes of feeling that often relied upon a sense of the atmospheric or the ambient (as well as the drunken): the atmospheric is more an overall condition determined not solely by architecture or specific materiality, but by the organization and modality by which space is *occurring*. As Gernot Böhme suggests, «Atmospheres stand between subjects and objects ... their great value lies exactly in this in-betweeness.»[19] The atmospheric thus interrupts as well as complements and completes architecture, and importantly urban experience, by *filling* in: where architecture and urbanism fall short, atmospheres lend dynamic support.

All such instances, of atmospheres and psychogeographies, find ultimate expression in architectural and urban proposals, such as Constant's well-known *New Babylon* project begun in 1958, which was an elaborate city plan consisting of sectors determined by mood and ambience. Yet the *New Babylon* finds early iteration in Constant's drawings and diagrams related to playground designs he was developing (alongside Aldo van Eyck) in the Netherlands in the mid-fifties, which consist of labyrinths and ladders, all networked together to form a maze of intersecting lines, arcs, and trajectories. These weave together to suggest a spatial structure that is more half-object than architectural form, for none of it adds up to a completed depiction, rather they seem to define a set of parameters by which individual movement and activity may take place. That is, they are

18 Simon Sadler, *The Situationist City* (Cambridge, MA: MIT Press, 1998), p. 94.

19 Gernot Böhme, «Acoustic Atmospheres,» *Soundscape Journal* 1, no. 1 (Spring 2000), p. 15.

20 See Yona Friedman, *Towards a Scientific Architecture* (Cambridge, MA: MIT Press, 1975).

21 Mark Wigley, *Constant's New Babylon: The Hyper-Architecture of Desire* (Rotterdam: Witte de With and 010 Publishers, 1999), p. 18.

22 Libero Andreotti, «Architecture and Play,» in *Guy Debord and the Situationist International*, ed. Tim McDonough (Cambridge, MA: MIT Press, 2004), p. 226.

inherently «in-between» form and function. The playground is conducive in this regard, not only for being organized around play, but also by operating more as skeletal architecture recalling the steel frames of transmission towers. Thus, for Constant and his visions for a new urbanism (termed «unitary urbanism»), the city was but a network sewn together by a series of girders, ladders, and potential movements, that itself came to articulate, through a formal language, the reality of broadcast media and its related architecture. The city was but a medium for the networking of desire and its related play, and the means to amplify such elements was to make the city, as Yona Friedman terms, an «extensive infrastructure» open to adjustment and readjustment.[20]

Echoed in turn in the psychogeographic maps produced by Constant and others, notably Guy Debord and Asger Jorn, the cutting up and montaging of the geographic resulted in nodes and connective lines, splotches of ambiguous terrain alongside tense vectors, where «parts of the city that lack atmospheric intensity are simply removed» and «zones of intense ambience float free on the blank page, linked only by unidirectional red arrows that define flows of attraction.»[21] As Wigley's description of Debord and Jorn's *Naked City* (1957) publication outlines, the psychogeographic map was a redrawing of the city of Paris according to a circulation of ambient presence. Such an image is suggestive of transmitted and radial media, which was to be put to use in a proposed situationist exhibition for the Stedelijk Museum in Amsterdam for the fall of 1959, during which time participants were to roam the city over the course of three days communicating through radio transmission.[22] The Museum was to act as a kind of hub around which vectors and drifts would be inserted into the city by the force of attraction and repulsion, a kind of primary magnetism by which urban space and embodied experience would converse, and the street would come alive as avenues of communication, embodied and transmitted.

Constant's development of *The Ambient City* finds early influence during his meetings with the sculptors Steven Gilbert (an earlier member of the Cobra group, along with Constant) and Nicolas Schöffer between 1953 and 1956, whose ideas on the future city are radically suggestive of what would later become the *New Babylon* project. Schöffer's early sculptural works consisted of steel frames and supports enlivened by the incorporation of kinetic movement, sound, and light projections, expressing his theories of «spatiodynamism» that began to surface in 1948. The use of steel frames for Schöffer provide an optimal structure by being «transparent» and «airy, penetrable from all sides.»[23] Transparent and airy, they in turn function to support the application and amplification of temporal media, such as light and sound, or what he calls «radiation.» Without limit, the work's radiation thus becomes the real effect.

These sculptural works he presented to Constant, whom he invited (along with Gilbert) to collaborate on a large-scale project, which turned into a manifesto titled «Neo-Vision» in an attempt to establish a concentrated forum on the intersection of art and architecture informed by new thoughts on communications and related technologies. Following these discussions and meetings, a collaborative team was formed for the making of a large-scale sculpture to be exhibited as part of the International Building and Public Works Exhibition in Paris in 1956. Consisting of Schöffer, the architect Claude Parent (who was to later collaborate with Paul Virilio in the Architecture Principe group), composer Pierre Henry (whom Schöffer would continue to work with throughout his career), engineer Jacques Bureau, and with art critic Guy Habasque,[24] the *Spatiodynamic Tower* project echoed Schöffer's earlier sculptures, particularly his *Spatiodynamic City*—a construction depicting a networked city consisting of long, translucent volumes accommodating a variety of functions, transportation arteries with helicopters roaming the skies and cars traveling underneath, all stitched together by an elaborate system of communications and structural supports allowing the city to grow, and even become mobile. The new *Tower* work appeared as a series of steel frames suggestive of ladders, playground objects, and transmission towers suspended with light beams, sound systems, mirrors, and motorized sections, all of which were to suggest potential forms to a new vision of urbanism. As Guy Habasque wrote, «The possibility of animating space in an entirely new way is indeed coupled with the introduction of a temporal element which had never been taken into account in the conception of a work of art.»[25]

23   Nicolas Schöffer, «Definition of Spatiody-
     namism» in *Nicolas Schöffer* (Neuchatel:
     Editions du Griffon, 1963), p. 20.
24   The project was aided with the involvement of
     the Phillips Company, who built the electronic
     brain, which would power the work.
25   Guy Habasque, «From Space to Time,» in
     Schöffer 1963 (see note 23), p. 12. It is worth
     noting that Schöffer also envisioned practical
     uses for the *Tower*, significantly radio trans-
     mission and radar. Later, Schöffer would
     ultimately build the first cybernetic sculpture,
     CYSP 1 (1956), which, in addition to being

     animated through the movements of mirror
     plates and sound, would come to move in space
     according to input from the environment. This
     was premiered at the Sarah Bernhardt Theater
     in Paris along with dancers and later, on top of
     Le Corbusier's Unite d'Habitation in Marseilles,
     as part of the avant-garde art festival, 1956.
26   See Henri Lefebvre, *The Production of Space*
     (Oxford: Blackwell, 2000).
27   Steen Eiler Rasmussen, *Experiencing Architec-
     ture* (Cambridge, MA: MIT Press, 1980), p. 33.

Schöffer's work was to become an integral part of what would become Cybernetic Art, by providing an early model of not only how technology might be utilized in sculptural form, but how sculptural form might become suggestive of a future built upon an integration of man and technology: the plastic arts were to become spatialized and dynamic according to the promise and urgency of atmospheres and networks, systems and their organization—communicational bonds that must be understood to remodel how cities are imagined and built. In this regard, Schöffer's work runs parallel to the ongoing critique of modern architecture, and can be further summarized in the work of Henri Lefebvre.[26] According to Lefebvre, urban planning had succumbed to a belief in opticality by relying upon the «visible» and «readable.» As a consequence, visions of the urban future were complicit with a mode of production that overwhelmed and overshadowed what Lefebvre termed the «tactile» and the experiential—opticality leads to an understanding of space as inherently «abstract,» thereby alienating everyday life from the very spaces of its occurrence. As Steen Eiler Rasmussen in turn proclaims, «It is not enough to see architecture; you must experience it. You must dwell in its rooms, feel how they close about you, observe how you are naturally led from one to the other. You must be aware of the textural effects ...»[27] The tac-

Nicolas Schöffer,
Chronos 8, Kalocsa,
Hungary, 1982.

tile is sympathetic to what the situationists termed «the atmospheric,» for both seek to undo the reign of opticality in city planning, inserting in contrast a belief that individual experience within space occurs through a dynamic and sensual relation to materiality that goes well beyond the apprehension of sight and the production of space as spectacle. The embrace of moods, atmospheres, and ambiences leads to the use and implementation of electronic media, transmission, and live circuits, turning space into a temporal medium sensitive and sympathetic to the fevers of real presence. To refuse the abstraction of city space, and the subsequent notion of the «spectacle,» the street was to become a live wire for the passing and exchange of ongoing play and imagination. «The only authentic communication is the one presenting itself from the outset as a form of common action, of everyday life collectively reinvented, in an immediacy dispensing with all representation ...»[28] In this regard, Schöffer's *Tour Spatiodynamique Cybernétique*, exhibited in 1961 in Liège, may similarly express such themes by building a transmission tower not only for broadcast but for the self-generative organization of a feedback system: transmission towers, in representing mass media, were stitched into the new cybernetic city, where mass media was an interactive tool for the promotion of new sensations and exchanges. Consisting of a fifty-two-meter, orthogonal steel tower fitted with thirty-three rotating axes, driven by motors to put into motion sixty-four mirror plates as well as polished steel blades that reflect and refract light into a medley of projections and reflections, the Liège *Tower* became a living system. In addition, the *Tower* was fitted with microphones and other sensing devices, which responded to the environment, feeding the electrical brain of the *Tower* with information that in turn structures and influences its movements. Such cybernetic workings suggest methods for the production of atmospheres and situations that Constant's *New Babylon* proposes in model form. Feedback systems, informational links, and communicational networks thus have at their core a belief in the restructuring of urban life in the support of temporal sharing and ultimate modulation.

28 Vincent Kauffman, «Angels of Purity,» in
    McDonough 2004 (see note 22), p. 293.
29 Ibid., p. 306.

Airy City

«In a sense, the boundless games of the situationists are meant to be played out not in urban space but in the sky...»[29] The construction of atmospheres, the networking of planes and sectors, the circulation of flows of desire and communications find a formal language reminiscent of transmission towers, circuit boards, and playgrounds: the steel-framed structures which were to increasingly dot the landscape, beginning with the inauguration of the Eiffel Tower as a transmitting tower in the beginning of the twentieth century, extended upward from the earth to pierce the skies, constituting a kind of material vocabulary for the imagining and modeling of future cities based on atmospheres. For as *New Babylon* and other works, by Schöffer and Yona Friedman, appear more as structural supports than completed volumes, they are a series of beams and girders, frames and ladders, by which to support the movements and circulation of bodies and interactions. In this regard, transmission towers provide a key image for reimagining the production of space that need not result in static form. For they are objects whose form can only be understood in considering what they generate more than what they statically represent. In addition, they seem to suggest a radical form of integration between man and machine, desire and architecture, finding parallel in the development of cybernetics beginning in the late nineteen-forties with the publication of Norbert Wiener's seminal *Cybernetics, or control and communication in the animal and the machine* in 1948. Cybernetics was to wield an important influence upon following generations working not only with computer science, mathematics, biology, and zoology, but with art and its involvement with electronic systems, networking, and transmission, taking off throughout the sixties with the works of the art-technology groups such as E.A.T. and Pulsa. Prior to the actual utilization of electronics and circuitry, we can glimpse sorts of proto-constructions in marginal architectural projects and proposals, as with the situationists, where the fusion of bodies and architecture would take on bolder systematic visions, linking individual behavior not solely to an architectural object, but to an urban plan that held in its wake the relation of man and machine. That Le Corbusier would analogize the home as a «machine for living» underscores a greater inertia within modernism, marking technology as a new frontier, not only of tools but modes of behavior—situationist attacks against the Corbusian vision highlight a subtle yet poignant difference. For the situationists, machines for living were not only about rational planning and systematic design, but also about breakdown, noise, dreamy effect, and drunkenness … Thus, notions of transmission (desire and code), the built (network and architecture), and their synthesis would appear on both sides of an ideological fence that sought to define in what way the modern environment was to appear and in itself behave.

«Sociological and cultural theorists so well hide the question of power that experts can write thousands of pages about communication or the means of mass communication in modern society without ever observing that this communication is unidirectional, that the consumers of communication have nothing to respond to.»[30] The situationists' critique of urban space goes hand in hand with a critique of mass media, and more generally, mass culture, echoed in understandings of Schöffer's work: «The sensations produced by Schöffer's sculptures belong to a real therapy for the ‹mal du siècle› and, in addition, they accord with other processes, psychophysiological ones, which also exert an influence on exchanges and blockages of circuits of information.»[31]

The city as mass space runs parallel to mass media, as both aim to conduct the means by which individuals may participate in the formation of both the structures and infrastructures, by which experience and interaction may take place. It produces junctions of exchange, the meeting place of disparate forces that come to further the ongoing unfolding of stimulation and play that for the situationists were at the core of modern life. Constant's *New Babylon* is thus both a model of a future city, which will «make possible the creation of an infinite variety of environments»[32] through technologies of atmospheres, as well as a circuit board for the construction of a new form of mass media, whereby people will have something to respond to, for «communication is only ever found in action undertaken in common.»[33]

Prior to situationist experiments, the city and electronics find articulation in the work of Buckminster Fuller, whose architectural and engineering visions sought to integrate theories of mathematics and communications with questions of manufacturing and design. Against the prevailing questions of architectural design, Fuller's eccentric projects progressively sought to include a sense of communications and time, aiming to model new architecture in support of modern-

30 Note from the editor, originally in *Internationale situationiste* 7 (1962), trans. Tom McDonough, in McDonough 2004 (see note 22), p. 129.

31 Doctor Jacques Ménétrier in Schöffer 1963 (see note 23), p. 91.

32 Constant, «A Different City for a Different Life,» in McDonough 2004 (see note 22), p. 101.

33 See note 30, p. 130.

Mountain Blästerfjället,
Jämtland, Sweden,
February 2007.

lived experience. Curiously, his early work, in particular his *4-D Tower* from the late nineteen-twenties, functions as both an apartment block, designed to support free movement and the management of affordable housing, as well as structures of communications technology. Fitted with radio transmitters, the *4-D Tower* could function as a communicative device, stitching the inhabitants together into a network of related towers, fusing life with being in extensive contact. «In our individual homes no matter where we may be we can speak into our combination radio-telephonic-recording-dictator recording our commands graphically (word or picture) to our machines which will involve only real thinking and study of statistics by the directors of industries machines.»[34] Living was thus infused with the potentiality of technological connection. Such communicational ease seems to parallel Fuller's engineering visions, moving his architectural projects into forms of pure suspension: the construction of buildings based on central axes from which floors would be suspended down in lightweight materials, opening up buildings by eliminating the bulkiness of side supports. Apartment blocks seem to hover in the sky, flowing down in modular patterns which in turn support a great deal of flexibility. «A room should not be fixed, sound not create a static mood, but should lend itself to change so that its occupants may play upon it as they would upon a piano.»[35] Such open-ended and individualized architectural visions point toward an overarching cultural question, which would continue to find argument throughout modernism: the built environment, in being a technology, necessarily comes to define (to support as well as limit) the glimpsed potentialities of freedom.

Pirate Radio
Pirate Territories

At the same time Constant's *New Babylon* was surfacing in 1958, offshore radio broadcasting was initiated off the coast of Denmark. Converting an ex-German fishing vessel, Radio Mercur started broadcasting in the summer of '58, anchored off the coast between Sweden and Denmark. Following the steady development of radio broadcasting throughout Europe and the United States since the early to mid-nineteen-twenties, with the British Broadcasting Corporation

34 Fuller 1999 (see note 1), p. 106.
35 Ibid., p. 111.
36 Matthew Fuller, *Media Ecologies* (Cambridge, MA: MIT press, 2005), p. 39.

being established in 1927, offshore radio transmitting is part of a general culture of pirate radio broadcasting that aims to usurp the larger media structures. The early Baltic offshore radio ships, from Radio Mercur to Radio Nord and Radio Syd, ran between 1958 and 1962, when joint legislation was implemented among the Scandinavian countries officially outlawing offshore radio transmission. While pirate stations developed in tandem with state control of radio, and with the emerging network of commercial stations appearing in the United States at this time, offshore transmissions offer a compelling version by also occupying and setting into relief the very question of spatial and national borders: offshore broadcasts both insert additional content to the media structures while disrupting the management of national borders. Appropriating and converting ships into transmitting vessels, dodging the authorities on the seas, and sending out signals toward coastlines, offshore transmissions function as physical and medial additions to given nations: they literally append to the edge of countries as part of their own extensive communications infrastructures, to mirror back through broadcast, dropping back in to the territorial specifics extra messages.

The offshore transmitter is a radio on the waves, spread out over this nebulous and vague territory of the water, to interrupt the signal space of national broadcasting with, what Matthew Fuller terms, the «medial organ» which inaugurates new forms of connection and thus knowledge by always already promising another consciousness.[36] Pirate radio is both a broadcast aimed at other cultural materials while also structuring such materials according to another medium, that of piracy itself: to be pirate is to thwart the media structures at large, aiming directly for the public listener set within their own place inside the medial environment. Pirate listeners are kinds of marooned islanders awash in the greater medial environment seeking out signals from isolated ships. Such recognition ultimately led Ronan O'Rahilly to launch the infamous Radio Caroline in 1964. As a record producer and manager, Ronan had sought to promote the recording of the artist Georgie Fame, but was continually turned down by the major radio stations, whose airtime was sponsored by the major record and publishing companies. To combat such restrictions, Ronan had the artist independently recorded and a record released and was further inspired by the existing offshore stations, such as Radio Mercur, to develop alternatives to mainstream broadcasting.

Anchored in the Thames Estuary, Radio Caroline was fitted with a 168-foot-tall mast topped by an antenna aimed to withstand the harsh environment of the sea, a 10 kilowatt transmitter, plus generators, record players, tape machines, and a mixer, all of which were housed in a studio built into the ship. Run by a crew of ten Dutch sailors, the ship maintained a continual circulation in and around the Thames Estuary, with the crew working for six weeks straight, and with DJs being transported to and from the ship by the use of a small shipping vessel, which also brought mail and supplies. After one week of broadcasting, the ship received 20,000 letters of fan mail, along with complaints from the Belgian government that it was interfering with maritime broadcasting.[37] Thus, Radio Caroline was a kind of floating medial vessel, an organ not only interrupting the circulation of transmitted signals but also transfiguring the very means by which signals were sent and broadcasting sustained.

Offshore pirate radio stations may curiously fulfill Buckminster Fuller's vision of a communicational architecture, echoing his own interest and involvement with ship building, and the management of naval ships. As a naval officer in Upstate New York in the nineteen-tens, Fuller understood the efficiency and discipline needed to maintain the movements of life on board. The ship could serve as a model for how to construct cities, based on the efficiency of design and engineering, with the sense of essential needs of humanity. The ship, too, was understood as a moving vessel participating in a larger network of command and exchange, a transmitting and communicational vessel charting its course in relation to the movements and intensities of a larger chain of command and control. The ship was an autonomous vehicle but one which could serve as a model for humanity. To support individual taste, Fuller's 4-D architecture, as a piano to be played by occupants and driven by individual direction through his «radio-telephonic-recording-dictator,» mirrors Radio Caroline's, and others', desire to create alternatives to mainstream broadcasting. The tension of media structures thus drives locational and vehicular expressions, placing ideological viewpoint onto geographic coordinates whose control is a constant battle. Airwaves are thus inexplicably about terrestrial culture.

The immediate success of Radio Caroline in 1964 (which continued well into 1967 when the British government passed the Marine Offences Act, erupting into often-fierce battles between offshore stations and the police, and even amongst competing pirate vessels) can be understood in relation to the cultural revolution

37 See Ralph C. Humphries, *Radio Caroline:
    the pirate years* (Mon., UK: The Oakwood
    Press, 2003), p. 21.

emerging within music in the mid-sixties, to which it ultimately catered. Playing records by The Rolling Stones, The Animals, The Hollies, and The Beatles, striking up a steady base of listeners dissatisfied with the likes of the BBC, whose monopoly only assured diluted and generalized programming, Radio Caroline essentially galvanized the cultural momentum at this time, doing so by partially appearing as alternative, illegal, and pirated. The promise of transmission from an offshore perspective is also the promise of hearing something one cannot find elsewhere, and thereby participating, or incorporating one's identity, into aerial transgressions. Such instances of pirate radio broadcasting contributes to a perspective on the radiophonic imagination, by not only supplying alternative content but by defining radio's borders according to an ambiguous terrain. For offshore radio floats freely in the waters, situating the alternative as not only being in the ether, occupying bandwidth space, but by steering clear of terrestrial borders.

The poetics of transmission towers, in piercing the sky with a potentiality of electrical extension, finds its complement in the lateral expansion that bursts the seams of national borders and their related broadcasts: the tower sends the imagination up into the sky while offshore transmissions bring us back to earth, and to the tensions of being on the outside. Thus, radio may be understood to negotiate the unsettled spectrum of the imagination and its realities, granting fuel to those who seek the outside, through a kind of contagious fugitivity, while building infrastructures for internal communications.

Becoming Radio

Anna Friz

Radio is not a static medium, and so continues to have the potential for unexpected mutations. Artists are striving to reimagine radio through radio/art practices that challenge current conventions in terms of form and content. Experimental radio has never been easy listening, and so has flourished in micro-political forms: from licensed independent campus/community stations, to temporary, clandestine, low-watt broadcasts, to online collaborative networks. My own work as a radio artist has developed within such independent or appropriative contexts as Canadian campus/community radio, artist-run media culture, and pirate interventions, with a focus on the critical (re)use of terrestrial radio technology. Though independent radio is largely volunteer-based, the relative or complete lack of overhead institutional structure has also fostered a unique and eclectic radio art practice that is able to move radio into unexpected territories.

I am motivated by the belief that radio remains relevant because of its accessibility and its persistent, if commonplace, «magic.» The steady decline of radio into generic corporate formats does not satisfy the desire for meaningful contact, nor do state or corporate interests thwart ongoing work by independent engineers and artists. There has been a remarkable resurgence of interest in radio among artists and community activists, particularly in the past few years. Revisiting and reimagining trailing edge or «residual» technologies such as terrestrial radio calls into question currently accepted paradigms of communication, while providing a frame for the hybrid radio networks and various wireless initiatives spearheaded by independent artistic communities. The radio art projects and interventions described in this essay are created under the rubric of «minor media» and aim to reconsider the materiality of radio, both technically and ontologically; proposing an embodied radio practice, or «becoming-radio.»

Minor Media

In the early nineteen-nineties, Gregory Whitehead wrote that «a revitalized practice of radio art languishes in cultural limbo because today's wireless imagination applies itself exclusively—fervently!—to questions of intensified commodity circulation and precision weapons systems» (Whitehead 1992, 254). This was not a new criticism of radio as generic and controlled by state and market interests: Canadian radio artist and theorist Dan Lander noted that the development of radio art and an art of radio were hampered from the early days of radio history by institutions of command and control, such that artists have historically had little free access to the airwaves. As a result, «most practitioners have grown to accept a level of control and censorship that is not normally tolerated with forms of artistic and cultural expression such as painting and literature» (Lander 1994, 14). Jacki Apple wrote that even in previously supportive institutional settings in the U.S., «art and the artist have already been virtually banished from the airwaves» and predicted that «[i]n the 21st century radio as we have known it may disappear altogether ... or, as an obsolete technology relegated to the subculture fringes, it may exist only in pirate form, a weapon of the world's underclasses; a tool for artists, revolutionaries, shamans, and other questioning voices in our brave new tech world» (Apple, see website). Together these three comments summarized the state of the mainstream North American radio situation in the early nineties: restricted public access to radio in the name of protecting the public; radio programming driven by convention, not experimentation; and, in the language of recent technological developments, radio as the aging horse who should be put out to pasture. To this Whitehead adds that the public is also unable to imagine radio as anything more than a tool for command and control.

Over a decade later, twenty-first-century radio artists are still struggling with these same issues of state and corporate control, generic and syndicated media formats, public radio sectors that are steadily eliminating the few programs with an interest in experimental work, and the public expectation that radio will consist of music, news, weather, and advertisements. However, radio would seem to be in no danger of disappearing just yet as Jacki Apple's prediction of activists and artists appropriating radio technology has come true: a growing number of people have been busy soldering their transmitters and raising antennas to make community radio and radio art. In Canada and increasingly in the U.S., there is a flourishing (though minor) independent radio sector where many artists gain experience and find latitude to experiment. When theorizing independent radio art activities in the current radio spectrum, rather than speak of center and margin, it may be more useful to think in terms of mainstream versus minor networks; where the two are not necessarily in opposition, but where the minor may operate both within the mainstream and autonomously from it.

Already in the early nineties Félix Guattari noted that mass communications were moving toward more conformist, centralized systems as well as toward miniaturized systems easily appropriated by marginalized groups (Guattari 1996, 73). Oft-quoted by radio activists, Guattari's involvement with the free radio movement in Italy in the early eighties led him to theorize minor media as an important part of becoming post-mass-medial: that is, bringing about an end to state and corporate media hegemony, as «mass media have to be re-appropriated by a multiplicity of subject-groups who are able to administer them on a path of singularization» (Guattari in Broeckmann 1999, 79). «Becoming minor,» in a community radio sense, is a strategy of modifying or mutating major technology (technology in the dual sense of culture and hardware) into readily accessible machines, often combining analog and digital devices. This conception of technological appropriation and use is better «adapted to group subjects and not to subjugated groups» (Guattari 1996, 74). Most importantly, micro-radio narrowcasters are not engaged in radio solely to critique mainstream commercial or state-run radio and society, but also to enable the expression and interests of alternative or marginal communities, and to be heard by others in those communities. For instance, the explosion of unlicensed broadcasting in the United States in the mid-nineties, enabled by increased public access to terrestrial radio and digital (online) technology, was an expression of distinctive political, linguistic, and/or ethnic cultural communities as much as a response to the hegemony of corporate interests in the U.S. radio landscape. When minor media begin to proliferate, they de-totalize the major and act as a destabilizing agent in the face of mainstream corporate control (Broeckmann 1999, 78).

Guattari expressed concern that minor media remain vulnerable to state and/ or corporate co-optation (1996, 106): «Is it possible to envision a proliferation of ‹minority becomings› capable of diversifying the factors of subjective autonomy and economic self-management within the social field?» The emphasis here must be on «becoming»; that minor media, if they are ever to challenge corporate behemoths such as Clear Channel Communications or Disney, will do so through dynamic heterogeneity and experimentation. «The individuals must, at the same time, become solidary and ever more different» (Guattari in Broeckmann 1999, 82). Here Guattari champions new forms of subjectivity, both oppositional and creative of new lines of flight. All these minor efforts may be seen as «molecular revolutions» and «soft subversions» that Guattari hoped would pervade individual and collective practices to decenter the mainstream institutions of command and control (Guattari 1996, 111). Community radio must do more than represent community; it must enact and embody community.

Molecular revolutions tend not to effect dramatic change, but despite the continued centralization and conglomeration of corporate control in global communications, today there is a substantial momentum to create and expand autonomous community radio in countries around the world, and to maintain global networks of these local efforts. In this way the micro-political has become translocal.

Canadian radio broadcasters enjoy a measure of freedom unheard of in many countries in the form of campus/community radio.[1] In Canada, the radio dial is allotted to three sectors: national public radio (the English-language Canadian Broadcasting Corporation or CBC and French-language Radio-Canada), private (commercial) radio, and community and campus-based community (c/c) radio. This third radio sector distinguishes itself from the public and private (for-profit) radio sectors by being single-station operations run almost or entirely by volunteers, maintaining non-profit status, supporting multiple modes of address and

[1] The first campus station was established at Queens University in Kingston, Ontario in 1922; subsequent independent radio stations were not licensed until the mid-sixties. Community radio had its beginnings in northern trapline radio among remote First Nations communities.

[2] Canadian campus-based community radio stations are based on a college or university campus, though members of the station need not be students. These stations draw a significant portion of their funding from student fee levies and maintain a variable amount of student involvement on the board of directors or other management committees. Most c/c radio stations are also funded through listener donation.

style on-air, broadcasting in multiple languages, reflecting the different needs of urban or rural broadcast, and often broadcasting on low-power or even micro-power transmitters.[2] Though bound by their mandate and license, c/c and community radio stations vary greatly from station to station, and region to region. These stations share a mandate to supply programming that is absent from the mainstream, so in addition to supporting Canadian music and culture (including a daily average of 35 % Canadian content in music programming), no more than 4 % musical «hits» may be played in the music programming, and stations are licensed only with the submission of a «promise of performance» that details a significant commitment to promote cultural, gender, and ethnic diversity reflective of the community in which the station intends to broadcast.

The spirit of community radio is one of open access. A prospective volunteer does not need any previous training in radio to become involved at the station. Station outreach is targeted toward community and social groups that are woefully underrepresented by mainstream media, so alternative political and cultural views as well as modes of address are sought out and featured. As a result, community radio provides fertile ground for experimental music and radio art, limited only by the programmer's imagination and the station's budget. Community

The Shoebomber and others, live radio mixing at CKUT FM, Montreal, Canada, 2006.

radio has notably also been a starting point for women into electronic music and sound production, an area of new media that is otherwise typically dominated by male producers and artists.[3]

Campus/community radio provokes the audience into listening for the unexpected while encouraging them to come to the station and become programmers, thus beginning a kind of circle of transception between the listening community and the radio station. Radio art in this context is not necessarily the purview of «experts» or «professionals» but instead enacted by a community of listeners and creators in shared radio space—where space is something actively produced rather than a vacancy waiting to be filled. The ramshackle character of such stations (with their small budgets, inherited equipment, used furniture, and anti-consumer political ethos) encourages a do-it-yourself ethic and aesthetic that is also common in radio artwork produced on unlicensed airwaves.

One manifestation of transceptive radio art on c/c radio has been *24 Hours of Radio Art* at CiTR 101.9 FM radio station at the University of British Columbia in Vancouver, Canada. Initiated by Peter Courtemanche in 1992, from 1994 to 1996 *24 Hours of Radio Art* happened on «Private Radio»—a homemade transmitter (built by Robert Kozinuk based on Tetsuo Kogawa's 2-watt transmitter plans and broadcasting at FM 89.3) located at the Western Front artist-run centre in Vancouver. In 1999, as program director of CiTR, I curated *24 Hours of Radio Art* for *Art's Birthday* on January 17th at the station, with our first online stream provided by First Floor Eastside and the Western Front. While some members of the station had already been producing live-mixed shows with collage, DJing, and original composition, *24 Hours of Radio Art* provided an opportunity for other programmers to step outside their regular show format and try something unusual. The event also brought in sound artists who were listeners but had never considered volunteering for the station before. This combination produced the most varied, eclectic, hilarious, and sometimes downright unlistenable day of broadcasting: from the regular host of the francophone show, who created a layered mix of three Celine Dion records played backwards at different speeds, to a show constructed entirely from tape loops, to Hank Bull and Patrick Ready reviving the *HP Radio*

3   Dr. Andra McCartney of Concordia University, Montreal, who has been conducting a five-year ethnographic study of women sound producers (*In and Out of the Sound Studio*), found that as many as 45 % of the women she interviewed had previous experience as programmers on c/c radio. See http://s171907168.onlinehome.us/civicspace/?q=en/taxonomy/term/15 (accessed November 13, 2007).

Show and roasting wieners on a wire stuck into an electrical outlet in the studio, to political soundscapes, to a microphone placed in the station's lounge to broadcast us as we all sat back and had lunch. Listeners phoned in, and their voices were added to the on-air mix.

The model of *24 Hours of Radio Art* has since spread to other stations, particularly during *Art's Birthday* celebrations. CKLN 88.1 FM Toronto celebrated *Art's Birthday* in 2007 with a twenty-four-hour event, but rather than preempting the regular programming for that period, organizer Darren Copeland encouraged as many scheduled programs as possible to adapt their usual show format to the theme, thus pushing programmers and listeners to challenge their expectations of radio on both sides of the dial. CKUT 90.3 FM in Montreal has also participated in various international radio and network art events such as *Radiotopia* (2002), *Extended Radio* (2005), and *Art's Birthday* (2007), preempting regular programming to make way for a more loose, improvised madness in the studio. In each case, the station is able to create an opportunity to introduce artists to the station as well as for current programmers to experiment with radio art. At CiTR, listeners and volunteers dropped by the station to witness the chaos in person and became audibly implicated in the mix. These events also serve as deviations from

Christine Duncan
performing as part
of the Radio Theatre
group, *Deep Wireless*,
Toronto, Canada, 2006.

the program schedule that, even at independent radio stations, tends to follow the standard format of shows beginning on the hour, with talk, music, news, and station identification. *24 Hours of Radio Art* transformed the radio station and its community into a more spontaneous instrument. Other notable collaborations between c/c radio stations and artist-run centres include *send + receive festival* and CKUW in Winnipeg, Manitoba (1999–2007); *This City Is A Radio* co-produced by CFCR and *paved* Art and New Media in Saskatoon, Saskatchewan (2006); and *Deep Wireless Festival of Radio Art* and CKLN in Toronto (2003–2007).

Special events such as *24 Hours of Radio Art* also program the strange, beautiful, noisy, and sometimes very abstract radio-making in the middle of the day, rather than confining uneasy programming to evening or late-night radio. They provide opportunities for radio volunteers and artists to meet, observe one another, jam, discuss interests and gear, and begin to build a community of experimentation at the station. Speaking for myself, first as a listener and (starting in 1993) as a volunteer, it was through campus/community radio that I became exposed to collaged and bricolaged audio works, field recording and soundscape composition, sound poetry, absurdist radio plays, critical remixing of media debris, and improvised radio-making. C/c radio provided the training on recording and editing equipment, the studios with which to make my own original works, and the confidence to experiment live on the air.

Micro and Mobile

Campus/community radio had challenged me to create original work and to rethink what was possible on the radio, so I next turned to the idea of dissolving the formal studio to take up a more itinerant radio practice. In this sense, I, like other radio-makers and media artists, became interested in extending radio beyond the format of broadcasting from a fixed frequency or location to become more mobile and unstable. Despite the restrictions of FM radio (a one-way broadcast medium), I wondered if Brecht's dream of transception might not still be possible in a social rather than strictly technical reconfiguration of radio. What potential might there be in bringing listeners and broadcasters face-to-face, in making the transmission process transparent? By pulling radio out of the formal studio, how could radiophonic space be (re)created, current conventions challenged or highlighted, and characters or imagined spaces (part radio, part acoustic) brought to life?

In May 1998, I undertook a project through the Western Front with performance artist Sharon Feder entitled *B.E.A.R.*, which was a staged occupation of the empty bear enclosure in the now-vacant Vancouver Zoo. *B.E.A.R.* was an exploration of political protest as spectacle, of increasing public alienation through commercial mediation, and of the role of media in establishing and forming public political identities. First we staged a «take-over» of the CiTR FM airwaves on two nights leading up to our occupation, where we broadcast political soundscapes and spoken word collages. We taped these sessions and then rebroadcast them, layered with our live commentary, on a 2-watt FM transmitter from the bear enclosure for the duration of our eight-hour performance. The zoo site was an elaborate concrete and stone area with a deep, dry moat that had been designed to house polar and brown bears. We rappelled into this pit, dressed in paramilitary gear with our equipment in backpacks, and once inside quickly set up the transmitter on the highest ground available. The signal was audible throughout Stanley Park where the zoo was located, and we later heard that some spectators had been drawn to the site because they stumbled across the radio broadcast on their car radios. For people who simply wandered by and paused to see what we were doing, we had installed solar-powered radios along the fence at the edge of the bear pit that broadcast our mix. During the first four hours, we were dressed in paramilitary clothing with face masks, and did not speak. The radio became our ersatz voice, while we, through movement and gesture, embodied the stoic politics implied by the collaged political, musical, and media debris that comprised our broadcast. After four hours, we removed our masks, stripped away the military clothing to reveal red long underwear underneath. In our more vulnerable «rebel» personas, we began to talk back to the crowd acoustically and on the microphone to the radio. Our radiophonic interventions on licensed (CiTR) and pirate airwaves constituted a real and symbolic occupation of media space, extending our bodies beyond the confines of the bear enclosure, adding an—at times aggressive, at times absurd—audibility to our performance, and serving as an unruly interruption of the regular program. As Montreal media artist Katarina Soukup notes, «[l]ow power and pirate radio are ways of subverting the mediated national corpus by secreting unregulated signals into the sanctioned mediasphere. Hence in relation to state and corporate interests in radio, low power broadcasting can be seen as a kind of grotesque radio» (Soukup, see website).

For *B.E.A.R.*, we had borrowed a transmitter from Peter Courtemanche, but I was so inspired by the potential in mobile micro radio that I wanted to build my own. I participated in a transmitter-building workshop with Rob Kozinuk, who taught how to make a 2-watt FM transmitter adapted from Japanese media artist Tetsuo Kogawa's design.[4] What I especially appreciate about employing low-watt transmission is that it is extremely localized media (with a broadcast radius ranging from some meters to several kilometers under ideal circumstances), and it is highly portable (from palm-size at less than 1-watt to a larger 40-watt transmitter the size of a shoebox that runs off a wet-cell battery or a motorcycle battery). Broadcasting less than 5 watts of FM does not require a license in Canada, and pirate broadcasts that exceed 5 watts are prosecuted only if a station were widely advertised as pirate or if complaints were made about station interference. The liberal climate of Canadian radio removes some of the political radicalism of running an unlicensed transmitter (especially considering that campus/community radio already provides an effective platform for alternative views and music), but for me working outside of a licensed station means I am able to focus my attention and transmitter on more ontological and formal questions about radio and the nature of transmission itself. From 2000 onwards, I have used small transmitters ranging from 50 milliwatts to 12 watts FM to create performances, installations, and interventions. As a mobile broadcaster, I have intermittently broadcast pirate community radio from my house (*Radio Free Parkdale*), haunted the neighborhood from the roof of a local hotel (*Radio Spidola* broadcast from the Drake Hotel in Toronto, 2005), set up a transmitter and microphone on a Montreal street corner to broadcast political protest soundscapes and solicit testimonies from passersby following the 2001 Free Trade Area of the Americas protests in Québec City (*NRRF Radio*, 2001), and secretly broadcast from atop an abandoned grain silo in the port of Montreal (*The Clandestine Transmissions of Pirate Jenny*, 2002–2003).

Other Canadian media artists have embraced the mobility of micro radio, such as Katarina Soukup's radio-in-motion projects *Radio Bicyclette* and *Radio Bicyclette 2: Urban Legends* (1998–99). For *Radio Bicyclette*, Soukup was in-

4   For Kogawa's updated design, see http://
anarchy.translocal.jp/radio/micro/howtotx.html
(accessed October 2007).

spired by stories of pirate radio broadcasts in response to the Soviet crackdown in Prague in the spring of 1968—particularly of people riding through the streets with radios blasting the pirate stations on their bicycles as political mayhem exploded in the city. She traveled to Prague to record oral histories and mixed these with archived broadcasts from 1968. These compositions were then broadcast from a 1-watt FM transmitter installed on the back of her bicycle, while the audience/participants rode with her and tuned in to radios receivers mounted on their bicycles. The use of mobile transmission allowed Soukup to reproduce the political materiality of a historical radio moment in contemporary urban settings some forty years later. Interested participants were given an active role to play in the piece (as cyclists with radios, they were also broadcasting to the street acoustically). Finally, the format also implicated passersby as inadvertent participants who witnessed the cyclists and radios. Thus radio is cast as a medium for public engagement, where participatory public space is actively produced on the ground and on the correspondingly localized airwaves. With *Radio Bicyclette 2*, Soukup employed the same technical system but broadcast compositions of city soundscapes and urban tales, with the intent to «invigorate the art of listening in and to the metropolis» (Soukup, see website).

Katarina Soukup,
Radio Bicyclette, Next
AttrAction Ap/Art,
event, Galerie Articule,
Montreal, Canada,
May 1999.

Sharon Feder and
Anna Friz, *B.E.A.R.*,
Vancouver, Canada,
1998.

In the U.S., the unlicensed low-power FM (LPFM) boom of the nineteen-nineties was a direct response to increased media conglomeration, lack of community access to local radio (particularly in some towns where there was no longer even a local commercial radio station), and commercialization and homogenization of content through syndication. Unlike Canadian c/c radio, U.S. college stations might sound exactly like commercial radio, so the need for genuine alternative radio was dire. At the height of the LPFM activity, there were over 2,000 pirate stations operating.[5] free103point9.org is a transmission arts center based in Upstate New York and Brooklyn that was founded as a micro-casting collective in 1997, some of whose original members had previously been radio pirates in Florida. free103point9's hybrid mobile approach to radio (using low-watt transmitters and online streaming) provides access to the airwaves for community groups and local musicians, and «most significantly to a group of under-served artists shaping conceptual works specifically for radio transmission.»[6] The free103point9 mission statement goes on to advocate for the liveness and presence that may be enacted by radio: «Transmission practices harness, occupy and/or respond to the airwaves that surround us. There is an inherent ‹liveness› to this work. In a performance-based setting, audience members are newly engaged, becoming participants rather than passive viewers and listeners. Installation or sculptural transmission works are often dependent on the present, reacting to whatever occupies the surrounding frequencies in a single instance, or changing that information by adding new signals to the spectral environment.»

Two signature events in free103point9's repertoire are *Tune(In)))* and *Tune (Outside)))*. In each case, four or more low-watt transmitters are set up to broadcast on different frequencies, each with a roster of artists creating live sound, while listening participants are given radios with headsets so they can scroll through the dial to find to the various frequencies. This event has been hosted inside galleries and venues internationally, as well as out on free103point9's Wave Farm property in Upstate New York. With everyone listening to radio on headphones, the acoustic space is fairly quiet, but often participants will share ear buds (effectively mixing two stations, one in each ear), and their movements on the dial will take them past conventional stations and interfrequency static. In this way, radio manifests as a public intervention (everyone is in a space listen-

5 In 2000, the Federal Communications Commission (the U.S. federal radio licensing body) established LPFM licenses as a new class given out to small civil society groups for FM stations of under 100 watts. As of June 28, 2006, LPFM licenses were extended into major urban areas, though there are rarely any new frequencies made available for such licenses.

6 free103point9 mission statement, http://www .free103point9.org (accessed October 2007).

ing to radio together) into private space (intimate listening on headphones), and the radio spectrum is highlighted as an environment in itself. In particular, it is a pleasure to «tune outside» to radio art in a relaxed rural setting, reminding participants of the ubiquity of radio waves and the need for re-occupation of those waves, even outside major cities. There is a layering of presence—acoustic and radiophonic—that allows for interesting juxtapositions and expression.

My recent radio performance works also highlight the shared experience of listening to radio(s) and seek to conjure imagined radio spaces as a kind of group dream. I use up to four low-watt transmitters that broadcast on four separate frequencies, which are received by between twelve and sixty-five radios suspended from the ceiling of the performance space. The four-frequency pattern of reception in the radio array creates an immersive radiophonic environment with dynamic panning effects. *You are far from us* (2006–2007) is a solo performance for four transmitters and sixty-five radios with no other sound system in use. Here I consider the interplay of public and private spaces through which the radio passes, and in this I seek a poetics of radio, made of intimate sounds revealed, performed by a chorus of receivers. Though the format uses conventional one-to-many radio broadcasting, and though this is a solo rather than clearly interactive

Campfire Sounds,
free103point9
Wave Farm, Acra,
NY, U.S., July 2006.

Anna Friz and
Annabelle Chvostek,
*The Automated Prayer
Machine*, performance,
Hamburg, Germany,
2004.

performance, my intent is to gesture toward what else radio might become—a medium for conscience and consciousness as well as dreams. These are the inaudible and imagined transmissions in times of crisis. The main sounds in the piece are sounds from the body (normally unheard in official radio voices and studios) seeping through the veneer of mediation with a focus on breath: deep restful rhythm broken by restless or nervous breathing, a series of suspensions and release, and fragments of tense witness reports from radio news. I recorded human breathing over baby monitors, walkie-talkies, and other cheap analog electronics, so that they were compressed and degraded to be rendered affectively fragile and monstrous.

These examples of mobile, micro-radio broadcasting demonstrate the layering of sonic spaces, imagined and remembered, acoustic and radiophonic, invoked by all participants in the circuit. Space is activated, and radio may become embodied in the context of minor media. Gregory Whitehead has noted that «radio happens in sound, but sound is not really what matters about radio» (1992, 254). Extended radio is not solely a story about black boxes and wireless reach, novel programming or unusual listening environments. While cultivating an experimental radio practice, it is nonetheless easy to refer to and therefore think about radio always through its technological manifestations—the microphones, transmitters, and receivers powered by human subjects that herald the deceptively one-way format of radio as we know it. But radio is about traces and reverberations; resonance of the living mortal desires to communicate. That we are so often thwarted in our dreams of union realized through profound communication makes this the most mortal dream of all. Whitehead posits «dreamland/ghostland as the natural habitat of the wireless imagination» but goes on to state that «mostly, this involves staging an intricate game of position, a game that unfolds among far-flung bodies, for the most part unknown to each other» (254). Mobile and micro-radio art bring these formerly far-flung bodies into contact and context and allow for something else to happen. Through such palpable, embodied radio presence, I have been inching closer to the understanding that transmission is us, that the dream and reality of transception is us; and that even across distance and time, radio is us.

7   I refer to the common notion that the radio voice is disembodied: «*I hear voices, but there's no*BODY *there!* As early as 1930, Rudolph Arnheim wrote that the effect of radio was basically at the level of the body...Faced with no-body, the ensuing listener response is anxiety» (Corbett 1993, 76).

Becoming Radio

If we see the wireless as implicated in the production of a post-human subject, we must rethink radio, seeing it no longer as a quaint, nearly obsolete technology but instead as the leading edge of later developments in cybernetics. Alternatively, if we hold on to our awareness of the nineteenth-century roots of wireless technology, we will find ourselves rethinking our understanding of the term «posthuman.» We may understand the posthuman not as *a new type of being*, part human and part informational circuit, but as a *new perspective* on the complex and enmeshed relations that human beings have always had to the technologies we develop (Squier 2003, 276).

I want to understand radiophonic subjectivity as imminent, partial, resonant, and embodied through an aggregate of body and electronics. Recording and broadcasting technologies allow voices to be heard far from their point of origin, yet they are not divorced from the bodies that uttered and sustain them.[7] All discussions of dead or disembodied voices to the contrary, radio is not psychosis. We are not confronted with the voices of the dead, but the traces of the living, whether or not they still live. Before recording and broadcasting technologies enabled the voice to be heard over distance and time, the sound of the voice assured the immediate presence of the speaking subject: the subject was immanent in the voice. With the advent of radio, the speaker is heard, though no longer present «in the flesh»; their body is deferred and yet their physicality resonates in the timbre, tone, and intonation of the voice—a physicality that includes technological resonance as well (choice of microphone, levels, added filters, EQ, or other effects, the signal transduced to radio waves and back into audible sound through the receiver, to the ears of the listener). With minor media such as community and micro radio, the circuit of transmitting bodies is smaller and more apparent—the broadcast takes place in a localized site such that transmission and reception are intimately interwoven in situ, while the less conventional format of c/c radio allows for more of the «secretions» of this aggregate radio body to emerge: the lip-smacking, sniffing, coughing, breathing, pauses, and filler words; the uneven mic technique, the limits of cheap equipment, and the sound of the environmental context—be that a living room, the street corner, or a forest. Extended or hybrid radio practices add digital networks to terrestrial radio, bridging localities to invoke the translocal. But the materiality of radio need not disappear in these circuits—we are extending ears and voices through radio, and thereby extending subjectivity and presence through resonance with radio technologies.

Félix Guattari and Gilles Deleuze note that a history of minorities is always defined in relation to the majority, and this discussion of radio art has been no exception. However, what I have sought to highlight through this limited account is the dual movement of radio as minor media: on the one hand to trouble or withdraw from the mainstream, on the other enacting the becoming of minor agency. For Deleuze and Guattari, «becoming is a process of desire» (Deleuze and Guattari 1987, 274) and of «modes of expansion, propagation, occupation, contagion, peopling» (239). Thus I propose becoming-radio as antidote to the major communications paradigms of dialogue versus broadcast that position sender and receiver as polar points, as beginning and end. Becoming-radio understands radiophony as transceptive; where a line of becoming «has neither beginning nor end, departure nor arrival, origin nor destination» (293), so that becoming is truly always in motion, in the middle. Becoming-radio is the in-between in a circuit of transmission that includes listeners, soundmakers, eavesdroppers, boxes, antennas, keyboards, desires, dreams, and nightmares; where no position is fixed. Thus transception does not flow from a device that both sends and receives; rather the transceptive potential of becoming-radio flows from the becomings-minor of embodied radio community and practice.

Works Cited

Apple, Jacki. *New American Radio and Radio Art*. New American Radio website. http://www.some where.org/NAR/writings/apple.htm (accessed October 2007).

Broeckmann, Andreas. 1999. «Minor Media: Heterogenic Machines.» In *Acoustic Space: Net Audio Issue* 2.1, pp. 78–82.

Corbett, John. 1993. «Radio Dada Manifesto.» In *Radiotext(e)*. Edited by Neil Strauss. New York: Columbia University, pp. 71–84.

Deleuze, Gilles, and Félix Guattari. 1987. *A Thousand Plateaus: Capitalism and Schizophrenia*. Translated by Brian Massumi. Minneapolis and London: University of Minnesota Press.

Guattari, Félix. 1996. *Soft Subversions*. New York: Semiotext(e).

Lander, Dan. 1994. «Radiocasting: Musing on Radio and Art.» In *Radio Rethink: Art, Sound, and Transmission*. Edited by Dana Augaitis and Dan Lander. Banff, Alberta: Walter Phillips Gallery, pp. 11–31.

Soukup, Katarina. *Promiscuous Technologies and the Radiophonic Grotesque: Spilling out of the Electronic Corset*. Simultaneita: New Media Arts Magazine. http://www.simultaneita.net/promiscu oustechn.html (accessed February 21, 2007).

Squier, Susan M. 2003. «Wireless Possibilities, Posthuman Possibilities: Brain Radio, Community Radio, Radio Lazarus.» In *Communities of the Air: Radio Century, Radio Culture*. Edited by Susan Merrill Squier. Durham and London: Duke University Press, pp. 275–304.

Whitehead, Gregory. 1992. «Out of the Dark: Notes on the Nobodies of Radio Art.» In *Wireless Imagination: Sound, Radio, and the Avant-Garde*. Edited by Douglas Kahn and Gregory Whitehead. Cambridge, MA: MIT Press, pp. 253–64.

Ordinarily Nowhere

GX Jupitter-Larsen

A graffitist who tags the airwaves with noise; his seemingly nonrepresentational sounds seeping off the speakers: this is my radio art. I am that graffitist. For years, I seldom documented my radio shows because I was perfectly happy with the idea that the residues of my broadcasts were still zapping through outer space. At the time, I saw no need to provide evidence of something that was still whole and still very much active.

In fact, the only reason I ever started to record any of my radio shows was so that I could reuse key elements in subsequent broadcasts. It was all due to my enthusiasm for variations on a theme.

Excerpts from a radio broadcast would also then be incorporated into successive live performance art as pre-recorded audio. Recorded performances were, in addition, incorporated into subsequent radio shows. Audio from radio would be used as video or film soundtrack; just as the audio taken from raw video could be used as the substance of radio broadcasts. Needless to say, occasionally a live performance, not originally meant for radio, would still end up being broadcast live over the airwaves.

The idea being that each new broadcast would be built upon the ruins of its predecessor. During my most active years on the air I was actually homeless, traveling constantly all over the world. I didn't have a routine or regular show of my own. I therefore started treating every moment of airtime that I could get as a cross section of a larger accumulative effect. I might not have had my own show, but I still managed to have my own series. It didn't matter how or why I was on the air. Be it public, pirate, or state radio; local or international; be it for an hour or a minute; as host, co-host, or guest; every radio appearance I did was manipulated as another episode of my ongoing run of radiant racket.

It might have been a series in my mind, but I never mentioned this to my listeners. I wanted to keep them guessing. I wanted them to figure it out for themselves. I wanted every broadcast I did to just fade behind the circumstances of them never really knowing what they were listening to; or even if they had been listening to anything at all in the first place.

After a few years of this radiophonic polywave, the contextual translation of mediums would become so multilayered; any original format-complexion was long disfigured beyond all recognition. It was a kind of entropy, and such consideration as this could only lead me to do one thing: the live broadcasts of amplified erosion. Slowly pushing live microphones into power grinders proved very useful. Sandpaper combined with contact-mics became my most relied upon method. Drilling also became a recurring motif, as altering wood into sawdust made for adventurous after-hours radio.

Noise can tell all kinds of different stories. During his life, mathematician Ross Rhesymolwaith lived on the windy coast of Wales near Portmeirion. He would always leave all the windows of his cottage open so he could feel the wind against his face while he did his calculations. To celebrate this image, an amplified calculator was balanced on top of a small fan. The blades of the fan slapped against the face of the calculator. An intense reverberation was the sum effect.

It wasn't a linear progression, but from 1983 to 2006, my radio shows became increasingly dense with sound. Despite the many different subjects of many of my broadcasts, and the many different circumstances under which my radio art occurred, each broadcast was just that much noisier than the one before. After twenty-three years of ever-intensifying radio, I found the noise had become so compact that I had to start chipping away at the sound in order to obtain yet another kind of hole.

There are many ways to build a hole. Amplified handheld hole-punches make a nice «clici-clic» sound. Digging in the ground with live microphones are also far more than adequate. Once in 1991, at the Museum Moderner Kunst in Vienna, I dug small radios out of a garbage bin using an amplified shovel. This performance was later aired in its entirety on the ORF program *Kunstradio*.

Now, there's no way I can bring up Vienna or radio art without mentioning Heidi Grundmann. I had been active in radio for some years before I first met this cultural analyst extraordinaire in 1987, however it was because of Heidi's constant counsel that I continued in radio as consistently as I did. As often as possible, she included me in the several international symposia and exhibitions related to telematic art that she had organized and curated. She never wasted a chance to take me aside to remind me of the importance of radio as an essential element in my body of work or life experience. I would have kept on doing radio, but since I'm so easily distracted by random circumstance, I have no doubt that I would not have been as methodical, if it had not been for her considerate friendship and support.

Although the radio I did in the Pacific Northwest (*Newsounds Gallery*) and Central Europe (*Kunstradio*) are my best known, some of my most memorable were aired on KFJC out of Los Altos Hills in the San Francisco Bay Area. During much of the nineteen-nineties, I was a regular guest on two different late-night

GX Jupitter-Larsen,
Building Empty Holes,
radio performance,
Geometry of Silence,
Vienna, Austria, 1991.

programs. My visits would normally consist of a one-, two-, or even three-hour-long mix of live radio static and feedback.

The climax of this distortion came in 1996 when I did a collaboration with Mayuko Hino. A powerful emotional outburst is always the overwhelming effect given by any performance of this Japanese former porn star, and our radio partnership was no different. She did her thing with a theremin while I rubbed a mic against some sandpaper. It went on for twenty minutes, and it was really, really loud. Really good harsh noise has always made me feel all warm and fuzzy inside.

Since 1999, KXLU in Los Angeles has been one of my best venues. Damion Romero's weekly program, *Psychotechnics*, has been a highly acclaimed showcase for contemporary noisicians since 1990. Being able to occasionally co-host Damion's program has given me ample opportunities to translate my different performance-art pieces into effective live radio. A prime example of this was in May of 1999. Earlier that same year I had designed a noise belt. Now, just by looking at this thing, you would never know it was a sound-generating device. It looks pretty much like most championship belts of Pro Wrestling, but inside the belt is something else: a lot of wiring. Damion plugged my Untitled Title Belt directly into the station's control broad. The belt was left to feedback on itself and over the airwaves for the better part of an hour. No effects or processing were utilized. They were beautiful tones, metallic in nature.

The Untitled Title Belt has been used in radio, performance art, and yes, even in the theatrical stage of actual Pro Wrestling. Briefly, while I was a performer with the Oaktown Wrestling Alliance in 2003, I was able to bring my belt into the squared circle. I never got to turn it on, but it was part of my attire. For me, this completely legitimatized the device as true Wrestling regalia.

The greatest possibility in radio as a medium is that of the accidental listener. An accidental listener is someone who, while looking around the dial for something else to listen to, ends up hearing you instead, and sticks around long enough to decide yea or nay. It happens a lot in any kind of true broadcasting. The potential audience is open-ended and limited only by geographical vicinity. The accidental listener is important because such audience members encourage debate. I know this personally, from the kinds of immediate phone calls I would get during many of my broadcasts.

I think debate is very important in any art. If I didn't know how people misunderstood my work, I'd have less of an idea of what I was actually about as a person. By comparing others' misunderstandings with my original intent, I gain a deeper appreciation of the workings of my own mind. This helps maintain my peace of mind.

Narrowcasting, by its very definition, is preaching to the converted. The real limit to any kind of narrowcasting is the lack of true accidental listeners. Take podcasting: the only people who will ever hear a particular show are those who were specifically searching it out in the first place, or, at least, something else just like it. There's simply far less chance-operations involved in the audience composition of narrowcasting; and therefore, there's far less debate with narrowcasting.

The only real type of broadcasting possible on any computer network is that of the computer virus. No other file format can be as successfully disseminated to a wide and random populace. Viruses don't have to be malevolence. I myself have worked with hackers in the past, looking into the possibilities of benevolence viruses that would go around a network, secretly fixing bugs in other people's computers. Therefore I would suggest using something like a worm to transmit

Both radio and entropy are recurring themes in
GX Jupitter-Larsen's visual work.

something like a podcast. Instead of having a person go around looking for a podcast, the podcast could actively go around looking for accidental listeners. A worm is a type of computer virus that self-propagates across a network, exploiting security or policy flaws in a widely used service. Such a virus could act as a carrier, with a podcast being the payload. The targets being those unsuspecting individuals who would just suddenly find an unfamiliar podcast sitting on their desktop. I'm sure such a broadcast as this would certainly spark a debate.

Not speaking of The Totimorphous, are you super, or superceded?

Will future futurists relay on yesteryear's futurism and continue the tradition of techno-fetishism, or will the superfuturists of tomorrowland surpass the superceded futurists of the past with a clean and decisive break from history? If so, what motif will this new superfuturism take on? If our new future will no longer be measured by technological development, what will it be measured by?

I'm not talking about a non-technological causality here, just one in which people have a relationship with technology that is different from the one they have currently; a kind of relationship that does not appropriate the assembly line as a calendar.

«The future will be measured in orgasms,» said noise poet blackhumour. He went on to contend that it was the past that needs to be predicted, and not the future.

Is the future such an old-fashioned idea? The future, I think, should be our means of getting past ourselves. It should be about seeing beyond our own constraints.

What I think should happen is some kind of non-temporal-based futurism. Any superfuturist actually living in the future would be forced to look inward for what lies ahead, and not outward at some calendar for some poetic date that's been imagined. After all, anti-time is when time isn't.

Airtime

Sergio Messina

When it comes to radio, I've been a very lucky man. I've often found myself in the right place at the right time, in the right company. Of course then you help luck along, but timing in these matters is essential—and that's mostly chance. Since the age of nine I was the kid with the tape recorder—it was, along with a portable turntable, my most precious possession, and I spent my afternoons recording from the radio. Italian sixties public broadcasting was very formal, and even when the shows for young people had cool music, it was presented the old way. The late sixties and early seventies were very restless, and the distance between young people and the state radio and TV (the only ones available at the time) became immense. This is why, when pirate broadcasting began in 1975, the success was huge—and by the end of the year there were already 150 *Radio Libere*—free radios, as they came to be called. I was fifteen when, in June 1975, I walked into the one-room studio of Radio Roma 103 (one of the seven or eight stations of the city) and declared: «I have a 90-LP record collection: can I work here?» I have to thank forever Enzo Buscemi, owner, manager, and star of the station, for his reply: «You have the 3 to 5 p.m. slot, every day (including Sundays).» In the subsequent three years, I failed one at school, but I learned a job I still do. It was an amazing time, when anything on the radio was possible. The most radical differences were about music (now you could play, and hear, just about anything), language that became much closer to how young people spoke, and the relationship with the listeners that was really different: they could call and ask for songs or to be put on the air (something unheard of in the media at the time, but very frequent today). I remember whole shows spent chatting with listeners on the air and playing wild new music with an eye on the door, in fear of a Postal Police bust.

By 1980, the Italian broadcasting scenario had changed for good; there were several thousands of FM radios: commercial stations, who mocked American radio and played chart music, and local radios (still numerous today), who retained some of the original free radio spirit (local ads, music dedications, open phone, etc.) but mostly played Italian melodic stuff. Then there were a few more political stations that featured information, had little or no advertising, and played the coolest music available. It was at that time (early eighties), and through Radio Città Futura (a left-wing station in Rome), that I started DJing live. We had a very popular daily music show, and we simply moved it to a club; the success was quite large, and I supported myself DJing for a few years. But I was growing restless, and while I loved to play dance music in clubs, I felt that perhaps on the radio I could experiment, I could dare more. I started to mix sound effects to music, to create sonic ambients where the radio show would take place, to create pre-recorded clips where music wasn't the main ingredient, to «open the window» to the sounds of the world (a few times literally speaking with my head outside, to catch the traffic).

In 1984 I came across another very important person in my life (and quite relevant to this story), Pinotto Fava. He was the curator of *AudioBox*, the radio art program of Rai, the Italian public broadcasting company. *AudioBox* broadcasted stuff that made my «extravagant radio» sound tame: it was learning time again for me. I've collaborated on and off with *AudioBox* for over seven years, producing other people's works and doing my own things. Through *AudioBox* I met three generations of artists, performers, and radio people, and I've had the chance to hear unbelievable stuff. Pinotto Fava (who comes from theater and has a very special sensibility for narrative radio and a healthy skepticism about the word «art») had an intensely «public service» mentality—very rare in experimental/art radio. But this attitude (and his nose for talent) created variety, provoked healthy generation clashes, and made *AudioBox* very adventurous for listeners.

At one point, in 1988, I had the honor of hosting the first *AudioBox* live broad-casts (one-hour shows, four per week, for six months). My format was simple: I'd spend countless hours listening to the immense *AudioBox* archive, sampling fragments (sometimes several minutes long) and mixing them live, with scattered comments—but full credit for each sample. Plus occasional live performances and bits of other media (cinema, TV, etc.). The result was a vortex of radio, some-times quite solid, often light and diverse. I still meet people that remember these shows, and I know some artists (very few) hated me: I destroyed the integrity of their pieces.

In 1990 I was called again by Pinotto Fava, this time to work on a new, impos-sible project. Besides being a radio program, since the early eighties *AudioBox* had also been an international conference on radio and art. It was held at various universities in the south of Italy. But this time Pinotto had something slightly different in mind: he planned to take over Matera (an amazing, timeless city in the heart of southern Italy) and turn it into an immense sound installation. We held over forty different performances, some technically quite challenging, in a town whose historic center (the Sassi) is mostly reachable on foot (or by donkey) but not by car. The program covered a very wide spectrum, from improvised

Sergio Messina,
Marinetric, performance,
Geometry of Silence,
Vienna, Austria, 1991.

music to performance theater, with a common matrix: Matera, its churches (over 120, carved in the stone mountain), courtyards, and public spaces. I've heard important radio art experts say that we had produced the most perfect amalgam of landscape and sound art so far. I'm not sure, but I guess we came pretty close. Rai didn't feel the same way, and the *AudioBox* festival has never happened again. The end of the festival somehow marked the beginning of the decline for *AudioBox*. Year after year the budget cuts, shorter airtime, the move to another channel, the standardization of Rai's broadcast standards, and finally Pinotto Fava's pensioning (without a replacement) created the conditions for the end of *AudioBox* in 1998—after nineteen groundbreaking years.

Meanwhile, in the fall of 1989, I had made *RadioGladio*. This is an odd story: an Italian judge had discovered *Gladio* (or «Operation Stay Behind»), a secret organization created in Italy in the late forties by the American intelligence, to prevent a communist revolution and make sure the left stayed at the opposition. They had money, weapons, explosives (as well as close contact with some dangerous right-wing extremists), all apparently financed by the U.S. I asked an American friend if they knew anything about this, having also paid for it, and he said it wasn't in their news. So I made a little reggae beat and, in DJ style, I told the *Gladio* story: *RadioGladio*. I handmade 300 cassettes and sent them to random Americans, from radio stations to magazines, political organizations—I even sent one to Howard Stern (little did I know). The cover said «*RadioGladio*, a radio message from Italy to USA» and «No Copyright.» It also said «duplication is encouraged,» and it spread very fast: people made copies (it was only four minutes long) and sent them to American friends. Since there were no names on it, people started calling me *RadioGladio* (and some still do). Thanks to a common friend, Frank Zappa also received a copy, and praised it in an interview. Unfortunately, *RadioGladio* got me banned from Rai: «It's too easy to write a political manifesto and sing it,» was one remark I received. But lots of people picked it up; I have to thank Andy Caploe for helping me spread it in the U.S., and Heidi Grundmann for having me play it live on stage at the Funkhaus in Vienna.

I met Heidi in 1991 at the Matera festival and gave her a music/radio cassette demo of what I was doing at the time. She invited me to play in Vienna in 1991, and it was the first of many visits to Austria, and of many great sonic (and human) adventures with *Kunstradio*. I have done some solo work for *Kunstradio* over the past fifteen years (including a Marinetti tribute in 1991, and an operetta in 1999), but the best part for me is having been on some of the teams Heidi Grundmann put together over the years, culminating with the amazing «Kunstradio All Stars» for *Recycling the Future*, in 1997. It was a difficult number: take many different electronic solo performers, from different backgrounds and generations, and have them do collective work, and radio improvisations. The results were extraordinary and, as I have written before, show a possible path that—still to this day—is seldom beaten but full of potential. *Kunstradio* has been a very crucial crossroad for many people besides me: imagine clever acoustic and radio curatorship, combined with a sharp political perception of art. Mix it with a tireless curiosity about the future and top it with Austrian technical excellence (showcased in endless Kura productions): that's hard to beat.

Meanwhile, in Italy I made over 150 concerts between 1992 and 1996 (besides making two albums, producing a few with other bands, and scoring a hit single). These shows were basically live radio on stage, where I was the speaker but also made the music. And the more it went on, the less music I had: it was going toward a digital version of Lenny Bruce, with lots of talk and samples of voices, odd music, television, and so on. All very radiophonic, but quite untouchable by most Italian stations. So I figured I'd have my own private radio.

Sergio Messina,
Klangpark,
Ars Electronica,
Linz, Austria, 2000.

I had found out about web streaming in 1995, thanks to *Horizontal Radio* (and *Kunstradio*). Then I played with it again in 1997 during *Recycling the Future*, and this time I was sold. Not only that summer did I put a whole album in MP3 online (one of the first legally on the web, and still there), but I started developing an idea that combined a certain *AudioBox* spirit with webcasting. In 1999, *Radio Lilliput* was born. It had two simple missions: to provide free counseling for Italian musicians on copyright, contracts, publishing, management, and so forth, and to offer public access web airtime to anyone. All you had to do was choose a free slot, and you'd get a login and password: that slot was yours every week, forever. Slowly, quite an interesting community of webcasters developed around this (now defunct) website, that had also become a music/tech webzine. The success of *Radio Lilliput* was also its poison: for broadcasting, we «borrowed» bandwidth from a large commercial webfarm, thanks to their simpatico webmaster. One evening in 2000 we simply used it all, blacking out the whole server for a night. We got kicked out; but by that time, there were commercial services that offered the same type of access, so *Radio Lilliput* was no longer necessary.

Much of my work today is still closely related to radio. I run a Sound Design course in Milano; we teach students how to use sounds, music, and technology to make soundtracks for many occasions, from fashion shows to installations, from music selection to video soundtrack mixing, commercial or otherwise (the techniques are the same). While teaching, I realize I have an edge over pure musicians, an additional perspective: tempo for me can be both musical time, the metronome, and radio time, the clock. It's known that radio can twist your perception of time, making the clock seem wrong (both ways: ten minutes can become one, but also thirty). This is also true for music, but it's very difficult for music authors to become their own audience, while for me is natural: when you do live radio you have to do it all the time, as listeners take no prisoners. Also, I haven't stopped to put music in acoustic locations. I use soundscapes to place my tracks somewhere: in a park, in a large cave, or on the beach. And finally, last year I went back on stage after a long time. I picked it up from where I left: talk and digital. I'm touring with *Realcore*, a one-hour, stand-up anthropology show, an infotainment talk (with one hundred slides) on the digital porno revolution and its peculiarities. People say that two of the effective elements of this performance are the rhythm of the presentation and my voice. I'm glad to hear that, and I have to thank radio for both. So, I might have made some of it, but—as you can see—when it comes to radio, I've been quite a lucky man.

Landscape Soundings

A Project by Bill Fontana

In May 1990, *Kunstradio* (Austrian National Radio's radio art program) and the Wiener Festwochen (Vienna's annual international festival) collaborated to assist in the realization of *Landscape Soundings/Klanglandschaften*, a live sound and radio sculpture by Bill Fontana. For two weeks, sixteen microphones that had been most carefully positioned by the artist captured the sound events taking place in the Stopfenreuther Au, a protected part of the Danube marshes near Hainburg on the Slovakian border.

By means of a collage of various old and new transmission technologies, these sound events were delivered live to an improvised studio at the Museum of Art History in Vienna and distributed to seventy speakers, again carefully placed and arranged, along the façades and in the cupolas of both the Museum of Art History and the Museum of Natural History, and in the formal garden

Bill Fontana,
Landscape Soundings,
Danube marshes,
Austria, 1990.

between them with its monument to the Empress Maria Theresia. A stereo mix of the live signals was transmitted simultaneously and continuously to the ORF Broadcasting House in Vienna, where program producers were free to use the sounds at all times. Within a few days, and with increasing frequency, the live sounds could be heard on all of the radio channels of the Austrian National Radio. The success was so overwhelming that, following a suggestion by Ernst Grissemann, the radio broadcasting director at the time, the last five minutes of the sculpture were eventually broadcast live on all ORF radio channels simultaneously: for five minutes the space of Austrian radio (at the time a monopoly) became the site of a live sound sculpture blotting out any other radio content.

During the fourteen days of its realization, *Landscape Soundings* developed into a project which paradigmatically touches upon some of the most important aspects of telematic radio art: the phenomenon of simultaneity as well as the dissolution of the traditional concept of the finished work of art; the co-authorship between artists and non-artists as well as the new definition of the role of the artist who—when preparing his or her work within the public, that is, the institutionalized domain—becomes an initiator, (project) manager, and facilitator, responsible for motivating other people involved to find, if necessary, highly unorthodox solutions. *Landscape Soundings* not only highlighted the poetics of a fragile and endangered natural environment by and through the live transmissions but, by eavesdropping on nature, also addressed the surveillance character of new recording and transmission technologies which are infiltrating every aspect of the social space.

An introduction to *Landscape Soundings/Klanglandschaften* can be accessed on http://kunstradio.at/FONTANA/LS/index.html. The documentation was designed by Robert Adrian in 1999. Two CDs were produced by Bill Fontana in connection with the project: *Landscape Soundings* (1990) and *Virtual Nature* (1994).

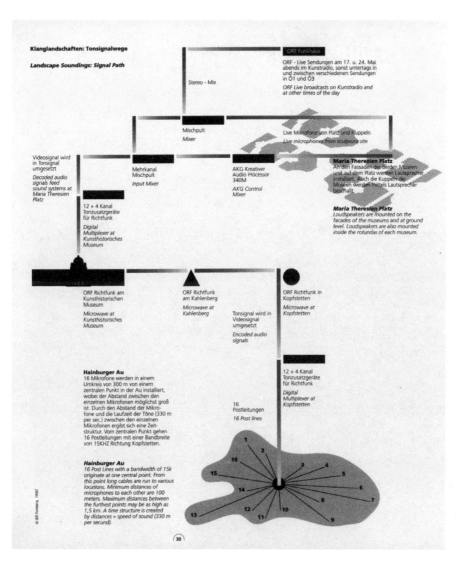

Klanglandschaften: Tonsignalwege

Landscape Soundings: Signal Path

Stereo - Mix

ORF Funkhaus

ORF - Live Sendungen am 17. u. 24. Mai
abends im Kunstradio, sonst untertags in
und zwischen verschiedenen Sendungen
in Ö1 und Ö3

*ORF Live broadcasts on Kunstradio and
at other times of the day*

Mischpult
Mixer

Live Mikrofone von Platz und Kuppeln
Live microphones from sculpture site

Videosignal wird
in Tonsignal
umgesetzt

*Decoded audio
signals feed
sound systems at
Maria Theresien
Platz*

Mehrkanal
Mischpult

Input Mixer

AKG Kreativer
Audio Processor
340M

*AKG Control
Mixer*

Maria Theresien Platz
An den Fassaden der beiden Museen
und auf dem Platz werden Lautsprecher
installiert. Auch die Kuppeln der
Museen werden mittels Lautsprecher
beschallt.

Maria Theresien Platz
*Loudspeakers are mounted on the
facades of the museums and at ground
level. Loudspeakers are also mounted
inside the rotundas of each museum.*

12 + 4 Kanal
Tonzusatzgeräte
für Richtfunk

*Digital
Multiplexer at
Kunsthistorisches
Museum*

ORF Richtfunk am
Kunsthistorischen
Museum

*Microwave at
Kunsthistorisches
Museum*

ORF Richtfunk
am Kahlenberg

*Microwave at
Kahlenberg*

Tonsignal wird in
Videosignal
umgesetzt

*Encoded audio
signals*

ORF Richtfunk in
Kopfstetten

*Microwave at
Kopfstetten*

Hainburger Au
16 Mikrofone werden in einem
Umkreis von 300 m von einem
zentralen Punkt in der Au installiert,
wobei der Abstand zwischen den
einzelnen Mikrofonen möglichst groß
ist. Durch den Abstand der Mikrofone und die Laufzeit der Töne (330 m
per sec.) zwischen den einzelnen
Mikrofonen ergibt sich eine Zeit-
struktur. Vom zentralen Punkt gehen
16 Postleitungen mit einer Bandbreite
von 15KHZ Richtung Kopfstetten.

Hainburger Au
*16 Post Lines with a bandwidth of 15k
originate at one central point. From
this point long cables are run to various
locations. Minimum distances of
microphones to each other are 100
meters. Maximum distances between
the furthest points may be as high as
1,5 km. A time structure is created
by distances ÷ speed of sound (330 m
per secund).*

12 + 4 Kanal
Tonzusatzgeräte
für Richtfunk

*Digital
Multiplexer at
Kopfstetten*

16
Postleitungen

16 Post lines

© Bill Fontana, 1990

30

Bill Fontana,
Landscape Soundings,
diagram, 1990.

Radio Art as Interference

José Iges

Through their conscious action in the context of the radio medium, artists quite often try to «interfere» in the standardized and therefore nearly always too pre- dictable broadcast schedule by endowing the content of their projects with a greater capacity to alienate. We use that term in the sense of *ostranenie* (defamil- iarization) as enunciated by Russian Formalist Viktor Shklovsky: «If we reflect on the general laws of perception, we notice that as actions become habitual they al- so take on a mechanical character.» In this context, the concept, which Shklovsky referred to as *ostranenie* and which originally came from literary theory, is ca- pable—if used as a method—of restoring the intensity, originality, and capacity of transmitting information to an element that, according to Italian theorist Gillo Dorfles, «would otherwise remain automated, devoid of interest, unless it is ex- tracted, alienated from its habitual associative context by means of an artifice.»

Quite a considerable number of radio works have been proposed from that point of view. In short—and by way of paraphrase of what artist Marcel Duchamp enunciated about the intentions behind his Readymades—it is a communicative strategy that forces the listeners to question their conventional approach to the decoding of messages supplied by the medium, which predisposes them toward creating «new thoughts» for those messages in their minds. For instance, it became impossible to continue to listen in the usual way to the news coming from the Gulf War in 1991 after having heard the BBC's «fake news report,» which British artist Rod Summers had created under the title *Sad News*. In it, one could hear the mechanically rendered statement, «I'm sad, very sad,» whenever the announcer introduced the comment from a politician.

Thus, we refer to works which have been intended by the artists as *interferences* by the artists in and/or with the radio medium as a source and/or target, although, given the customary nature of radio programming content, one could be tempted to state that, in the current state of radio broadcasting, *the whole of radio art constitutes an interference in that medium*. We are fully aware of the fact that in radio, and in telecommunications in general, interference is understood as any process that alters, modifies, or destroys a signal during its transfer between sender and receiver. If in wave mechanics such a phenomenon takes place through the superimposition of one or more waves, we will try to ascertain in the following that in a broader sense the efficiency of the communicative strategy of interference occurs through the friction between notions, uses, or assumptions.

Historical Examples

All too often, we artists have resorted to the conventions peculiar to the genres of radio news services—mainly bulletins, reports, interviews, and documentaries—for our acts of interference.

The first example brings us to 1924, the year in which French engineer Maurice Vinot, under the pseudonym Gabriel Germinet, carried out rehearsals for the final broadcast of a radio drama titled *Maremoto* (Seaquake), jointly designed with Pierre Cusy. With this piece, its authors had won one of the two prizes given in a contest, launched by the newspaper *L'Impartial français* on May 3, 1924, under the title *Radiophonie*. The work was to be broadcast by Radio-Paris on June 23 of the same year. Two days before, there had been a rehearsal of *Maremoto*, but someone had left the broadcast antenna plugged in. Thus haphazardly, the listeners who tuned their receivers to Radio-Paris's wavelength (1780 m) on that June 21 at 6:15 p.m. thought they were picking up what clearly seemed to be a

---

1   See Friedrich Kittler's essay, «The Last Radio Broadcast,» in this volume, originally published in both German and English as Friedrich Kittler, «The Last Radio Broadcast,» in *ON THE AIR: Kunst im öffentlichen Datenraum*, ed. Heidi Grundmann (Innsbruck: Transit, 1994), pp. 71–80.

shipwreck: noise of strong winds, falling objects, heavy seas, distant Morse tele-graph signals, and, all of a sudden, a woman's voice repeating, «Hello, hello ... this is steamer Ville de Saint-Martin, in danger at 23° 15' 25" latitude North and 14° 35' 40" latitude East ... a serious leak has sprung ... request for immediate help ...»

As radio author and critic Roger Richard points out, the excitement caused was such that the Department of the Navy indicated to Radio-Paris, through the Department of Telecommunications (P.T.T.), that «in order to ensure safety at sea, as well as to guarantee public order and the smooth running of everyday life, it would be in the public interest to ban the radio script titled *Seaquake*.» This proves the effectiveness of the realization and the magnitude of the illusion, although it should also be noted that, in those days, radio was taking its first steps as a medium, and its users were accustomed to the primitive, horizontal communication between amateur radio operators, a field where it was common to encounter distress signals coming from vessels in danger.

The most famous outcome of this kind of practice to date was the CBS broad-cast of Orson Welles's adaptation of *The War of the Worlds* by H. G. Wells in 1938.[1] Two superimposed strategies lent verisimilitude to that work. The first consisted in the use of radio news genres, so obviously different from radio dra-ma, within a broadcast that, according to the schedule, was a radio drama. Some of the settings in the play were borrowed from such genres as the report, the news bulletin, or the interview. Others came from the practices of entertainment radio in those days: broadcasting of dance music from a dance hall, airing of records. The second strategy consisted in the rendering of the above-mentioned with painstaking realism, or rather «radiophonic realism,» since the simulated reality was the «norm» within the medium for those genres. In sum, the singular-ity of Welles's work relied on «radio-within-radio,» or better, on the specific ap-proach to producing radio in the forms accepted in certain genres of radio news. That is to say, a seemingly veritable entertainment program was created and later interfered with fake news flashes: this double simulation was central to granting credibility to the message.

Mirages
Disorientations

The strategy of interference produces in the listener a feeling of disorientation equivalent to finding oneself in a no-man's-land or a landscape covered in fog. Contours aren't safe, references have worn away, and the rules to be followed in order to move around that territory aren't clear. Along with the general situation that results from the works currently being analyzed, there are other specific instances that generate a certain kind of acoustic «mirage» in the audience, a point referred to in the following.

We will begin by placing ourselves in 1990, when *Kunstradio* and the Vienna Festival produced *Landscape Soundings* by American artist Bill Fontana.[2] The act of bringing to the center of Vienna nature sounds that could be considered to be «archaeological» in that location in 1990 was the aim of Fontana, whose installations are characterized by transmitting sound environments from one location to another. Along with that «mirage,» another one took place: for a few minutes, the live mixes created by Fontana unexpectedly entered through some «windows» opened in the program schedules of ORF's Ö1 and Ö3 stations. The impact that such organized nature sounds would have as it interfered in the usual daily programming of any FM station—devoted to broadcasting general news and cultural information, literature, classical, and/or up-to-date music, pop music, as well as sports—can easily be imagined.

Another such case, featuring a remarkable palette of nuances, was *Trafic*, a broadcast belonging to the project *Droit de cité*, produced by Mario Gauthier and Claire Bourque for the CBC in Montreal, June 15–21, 1992, as part of the *7th Electroacoustic Spring*, in a section entitled *Radio Sound Ecology*. With a duration ranging between ten and thirty minutes, the various authors—among them Gauthier, author of the proposal himself—interrupted the music programs being broadcast with their «sound portraits» of various aspects and places in the city of Montreal. In all cases, the sounds were brought live into the studio and, once there, were mixed and partially transformed according to the criteria of the

2   See Bill Fontana's project description, «Landscape Soundings,» in this volume.

3   The *Ars Acustica* group consists of the radio art producers within the public broadcasting organizations of the EBU, the European Broadcasting Union.

various authors. In *Trafic*, which was aired on the morning of June 15, 1992, starting at 7:30 a.m. and lasting seventeen minutes, interference took place in a program that usually broadcast classical music: the announcer was presenting a Beethoven quintet and, in an extremely long cross-fade, the live sounds of the city traffic began to come in over the music, until they disappeared. Thus, the rumble of road traffic became for a few minutes the musical protagonist, although almost as an acoustic mirage, since the process ended up being reversed and normal broadcasting resumed.

Since its inception, the *Ars Acustica* group[3] proposed its first public appearances outside radio itself, following the example of *Acustica International* (WDR, Cologne) or *Rassegna AudioBox* (Rai, Matera, 1988 and 1990) and, subsequently, of symposia such as Geometry of Silence (Geometrie des Schweigens, ORF, Vienna, 1991). Thus in 1992, organized by the BBC, papers and productions by most active radio stations in the group were presented at a forum held in London under the title *Radio Beyond* between May 28 and 29 of the same year. During the first day, radio art producers presented their lectures or performances, depending on the case, while on the second day short radio pieces, dedicated to «the sound of the continent,» could be heard through the public address system of Liverpool Street Station. The juxtaposition of those artistically organized sounds and the customary train service announcements occurred as interferences in the aforementioned channel—the public address system—and, in a certainly remarkable, almost metaphorical manner, the alienation caused in the chance listener ran parallel to the one experienced by audiences when exposed to radio art genres. In both public spaces—the station concourse or the radio—art acted by turning a topical communications space into an heterotopy, in a space for «otherness,» for the unusual and the diverse, in the sense defined by French philosopher Michel Foucault. Let's recall another two such experiences occurring in the nineties: one of them took place at the L'Arte dell'Ascolto Festival, where its director, Roberto Paci Dalò, brought the sound of radio art to the beach in Rimini through its public address system. Something very similar was implemented by the author of these lines at the 1998 edition of ARCO (Contemporary Arts) Fair in Madrid, by using the public address system of the trade fair—halls, transit areas, car park—for a whole week.

Ars Sonora Productions

The next examples are two works by Spanish authors produced in 1993 in Ars Sonora (RNE Radio Clásica): *Clases de música en la granja* by Catalonian composer Llorenç Balsach and *Zambra 44.1* by Madrilenian Adolfo Núñez.

With *Clases de música en la granja*, its author creates a parody on two levels: on the one hand, it adopts the formal attitude of the typical radio show featuring an interviewer and a guest—the latter being the imaginary Doctor Liebermann. This is a characteristic format in what is known as «generalist» radio, that is to say, the type of radio usually made in mediumwave. On the other hand, as we shall see, the strictly musical contents broadcast are part of a musical tradition ranging from Rossini's *Cat Duet* and Mozart's *Musical Joke* to part of Balsach's own instrumental music. The work, mixed at the RNE studios, Madrid—though the author had previously created the musical fragments using a sampler and a computer at his own studio—begins with precisely the *Cat Duet* by Gioacchino Rossini. The presenter points out to us that, in fact, two real cats are interpreting the score. And stemming from that assertion begins the interview with Doctor Liebermann, who proceeds to unfold, before an astonished audience, the sonic results of her research on drugs aimed at enabling farm animals to sing. The interview format is absolutely customary—Questions and Answers, with a tone of fake openness so peculiar to that kind of announcer—and dealt with by the interviewee with great soberness. The examples featured become increasingly unbelievable and hilarious, since they develop from the musical ambiguity of the grunts of some pigs, the bleating of sheep, or the neighing of donkeys or horses to the creation of a true orchestra with all the animals, which Balsach himself would assumedly accompany on the piano. In reality, it is all sheer emulation, from the interview to the music fragments, which are created by means of a music notation program where the notes are substituted by samplings of animal sounds, thus enabling their feigned «musicality» as interpreters.

In *Zambra 44.1*, composer Adolfo Núñez draws up right from the beginning three types of radio programs, without intending to pass them off as authentic. The intention is to look for a certain structural and linguistic legitimatization for his proposal by being ironic about certain ways of making radio from within the very medium. The piece begins with a news report where the introductory music has been substituted by a burst of dynamic clapping and flamenco guitar strumming. Over these sounds, the announcer says: «The truest information in Onda Veró.» Thus, right from the outset it is obvious that there is no intention to mislead the audience by simulating an authentic news report in order to slip other content into it, but rather to take on—for that section of the work—the form of a news report. Apart from this, all the major sections typical of current affairs broadcasts—including sports and crime news—are featured, being broken up by means of little jingles allusive to the various themes.

The two remaining sections—which are fully composed, meaning that all the things we hear have been either literarily written or electroacoustically realized by the composer in the studio—include a fake program by an equally fictitious pop radio station and a contemporary music concert broadcast by a radio station like RNE's Radio Clásica. Throughout the piece, the texts, read by two announcers (a man and a woman), use terms from *caló* (the dialect of gypsies in Spain) or flamenco *coplas* (Spanish folk songs of Andalusian origin) and are pervaded by humor. The work unfolds progressively, like an increasingly faster zapping, in which we find, however, that from one station to the next those texts remain as invariances, reaching from comments of a newscaster to those of a commentator on the latest pop hit to those of an electroacoustic music concert announcer.

Concha Jerez and
José Iges, *Argot*,
performance installa-
tion view, Geometry
of Silence, Vienna,
Austria, 1991.

The Notion of Interference in the Radio Works of
Concha Jerez and José Iges

The concept of interference runs as a leading thread through the sound and visual installations that Concha Jerez and the writer of these lines have authored since the late nineteen-eighties. A notion that, conceptually articulated through the reflection of a given space and the dialogue with its features, has reached formulations and results that are also found in several of our radio works.

The first piece we will tackle is *Argot*, created in November 1991 at the Geometry of Silence symposium curated by Heidi Grundmann. The piece was realized at Vienna's Museum Moderner Kunst (at its former headquarters) as an installation piece as well as a radio performance for *Kunstradio*. It could be considered an interaction between two powerful media contexts, the radio and the museum. While the female performer progressively activated different sounds throughout the various rooms of the museum, the basic text of the work unfolded, in turn being broadcast to twenty-six radio receivers located at the central space of the above-mentioned building. The process of adding both sound sources resulted in the creation of the piece as an interaction between the spaces of the museum and that of radio, since the basic text—in four different languages—was gradually subjected to transformations with the passing of time, while the remaining sounds—vowels and consonants—were used for an acoustic «sounding» of different rooms of the building, both processes being superimposed in the radio mix. The text itself entailed a self-referential connection with the piece and related it to the museum space and thus resulted in a reflection—play of mirrors—by the authors on the role of art and artist in modern society.

In October 1993, the live broadcasting of *Bazaar of Broken Utopias*—like the previous work, a co-production of *Kunstradio* (ORF) and *Ars Sonora* (RNE)—took place at the ORF studios in Innsbruck within yet another radio art conference.[4] It featured the live appearance of the authors and of special effects technician Bernardo Mingo. In this case, the work interfered with itself and was thus being morphologically organized: sounds from various electronic toys ironically underlined, or caused to disappear, the reading of a text—just passed—by the European Conference on Security and Cooperation, while sounds taken from shortwave stations as well as a montage of interviews on utopia as an abstract notion and personal aspiration also interfered and intervened.

4   See Grundmann 1994 (see note 1).

The case of *Limites du décor* is different, for it initially was a performance—*Límites del decorado*—in 1999, that as a result of an invitation by René Farabet, who produced it for Radio France's *Atelier de Création Radiophonique*, became a radio piece the following year. In it, the interfering element came from the cross play of its content: a cynical text, whose roots lay in pataphysics, vaguely vindicating child labor and some genocidal acts, was linked to the threatening sound of an air raid and the sudden apparition of a shapeless mass of national anthems and sounds of electronic toys. By way of counterpoint, brief fragments of our radio piece *The Whistling of Iron Horse Crossing the Threshold of Heaven*, which had actually been created in Paris in 1994 in relation to the migration phenomenon toward Europe, were included.

The last example dates from October 2003. Its title was *Noticias en Tierra de Nadie/News on a No-man's Land*, and it took place in fifteen interference mini-spaces, as we called them, ranging between two and three minutes in length and that, always featuring different news items and for a span of three weeks, were daily broadcast at the same time in *Radio Círculo* (belonging to the Círculo de Bellas Artes de Madrid), in particular after their morning cultural news service. The actual news items were almost entirely fictitious and dealt with burning

Concha Jerez and José Iges, *Bazaar of Broken Utopias*, live radio performance, video still, *On the Air*, Innsbruck, Austria, 1993.

issues related to politics, economics, and modern society, both national and international. Some of those news items—the most unbelievable ones—were, by the way, real and thus contributed to spreading a certain shadow of doubt over the remaining ones, since listeners could from then on enter a critical—reflexive, alienated—frame of mind in relation to every piece of news they subsequently read or listened to. Between each of the two news items, a short musical section in which fragments of various national anthems were mixed—partially modified by electronic means but, in any case, recognizable—could be heard.

Thus, there was an aestheticization of the genre as in the already mentioned piece by Núñez. However, the basic intention was different, since it attempted, on the one hand, to critically emphasize those current issues *forgotten* by the news media and, on the other, to point out the difficulty in telling the real from the fake in what the media daily furnish. Furthermore, a frequent difficulty of establishing that distinction exists, even for newscasters themselves, who, being increasingly overloaded by the flux of information circulating online, have begun to claim for themselves a filter status, that of validators of the information being provided. It is the old argument between horizontal communication and vertical broadcasting, experienced in the early days of radio and now reemerging on the Internet. At the end of the day, they are different approaches to politics: approaches of which art is not unaware. And neither is radio art, as we have attempted to illustrate in this essay.

Concha Jerez and
José Iges, *Food for
the Moon*, inter-
media intervention,
Zeitgleich, Hall in
Tirol, Austria, 1994.

Art without Time and Space?

Radio in the Visual Arts of the Twentieth and Twenty-First Centuries

Katja Kwastek

In the Futurist Manifesto of 1933, Filippo Tommaso Marinetti and Pino Masnata propagate «*La Radia*» as «*A new art,*» as «*A pure organism of radio sensations,*» as «*The reception amplification and transfiguration of vibrations emitted by living beings living or dead spirits...*» and finally as «*An art without time and space without yesterday and tomorrow.*»[1]

The fact that invisible electromagnetic waves in space can contain and transmit information—worldwide and simultaneously—had inspired in artists such enthusiasm that they anticipated a sweeping renewal of the arts.

Even though the new media technologies in use today in the mass-media information and entertainment industries seem to have effectuated much more far-reaching changes in society than in the visual arts (although the possibility that Marinetti and Masnata would have viewed the present-day media industry as precisely this new art shouldn't be ruled out), their significance for the development of the art from the twentieth and twenty-first centuries should not be underestimated.[2]

The nineteen-sixties marked a moment in art history when impulses stemming from the Futurists and Dadaists, from Marcel Duchamp and the Surrealists, began to ripen into a completely new concept of art: on the one hand, as part of the development that art theorist Lucy Lippard terms the «*dematerialization of Art*»[3] and, on the other, through the increasing incorporation of everyday and found objects, of materials from nature, industry, and media, into artistic work. Lippard describes the dematerialization more precisely as an expansion of the conceptualization of art to include «*art as idea*» and «*art as action,*» that is, encompassing purely conceptual approaches as well as performative projects (and thus incorporating temporal components). With the integration of everyday objects in their artworks, proponents of pop art and the Nouveaux Réalistes, in particular, proclaimed presentation to be an artistic strategy of equal value to representation. Both tendencies, in terms of intention initially appearing almost diametrically opposed, played a decisive role in the genesis of so-called media art.

And although one might have expected the realization of the new radio art propagated in the above-quoted Futurist Manifesto to take the form of dematerialization as described by Lippard, it has been the detour through object art which has enabled the immaterial radio waves to first gain entry into the visual arts.

Yet as will become apparent in the course of the following remarks, the boundaries between performative and object-focused arts are becoming—with

1   Quoted from Douglas Kahn and Gregory Whitehead, eds., *Wireless Imagination: Sound, Radio, and the Avant-Garde* (Cambridge, MA, 1992), p. 267.

2   Up until the mid-twentieth century, social forms of communication made their way into the visual arts only as motifs (ranging from Johannes Vermeer's *Woman Reading a Letter* to the depictions of Morse Code and telegraph lines by the Futurists), with a few significant exceptions in the early twentieth century, such as the design of transmitting and receiving stations in Russian Constructivism, for example the *Radio Orator*, designed by Gustav Klucis for broadcasting radio messages to large crowds, or Vladimir Tatlin's design for a «Monument to the Third International.» See Dieter Daniels, «The Miracle of Simultaneity: Anticipations of Globalisation at the Beginning of the 20th century,» in *Ohne Schnur: Art and Wireless Communication*, ed. Katja Kwastek, exh. cat. Cuxhavener Kunstverein (Frankfurt am Main, 2004), pp. 37–61.

3   Lucy Lippard, «The Dematerialization of Art,» in *Changing: Essays in Art Criticism* (New York, 1971), pp. 255–76.

4   Interview with Tom Wesselmann from 1964, quoted from the exhibition catalogue *Pop Art*, ed. Marco Livingstone (Munich, 1992), p. 58.

5   See Thomas Buchsteiner, ed., *Tom Wesselmann 1959–1993* (Ostfildern, 1994), p. 21; on the integration of radios, see also ibid., p. 15.

6   *Broadcast*, 1959, Slg. Powers, Carbondale, Colorado, in *Robert Rauschenberg: Retrospektive*, ed. Walter Hopps and Susan Davidson, exh. cat. Museum Ludwig Köln (Ostfildern, 1998), p. 290, fig. p. 291. Many thanks to Heidi Grundmann for alerting me to Rauschenberg's radio works.

7   Robert Rauschenberg, *Oracle*, 1962–65, Musée National d'Art Moderne, Centre Pompidou, Paris, in ibid., fig. pp. 296–97; description pp. 312–13. In the meantime, technology has been updated for electronic scanning and infrared transmission.

8   Billy Klüver on *Oracle*. See http://www.artmuseum.net/w2vr/archives/Kluver/04_Oracle.html (accessed February 8, 2008).

the increasing mobility of devices—more and more blurred, with public space now taking on greater consequence as a material stage for wirelessly communicated sounds.

«Confront Art and Life Directly»
Radio in the Object Art of the Sixties and Seventies

While Richard Hamilton's 1956 collage *Just what is it that makes today's homes so different, so appealing?*, celebrated as an incunabulum of pop art, still represented the new entertainment media of television and cassette player in picture form, Tom Wesselmann and Robert Rauschenberg would soon incorporate the actual devices into their collage compositions.

Starting in the early nineteen-sixties, Wesselmann integrated not only radios but also television sets into his pictures. He was interested in *«the dimension ... it gave a picture, something that moves and emits noises.»*[4] Being able to receive actual radio and television programs was important to him, as he wanted, according to Marco Livingstone, *«to confront art and life directly.»*[5]

As early as 1956, Robert Rauschenberg had hidden a working radio behind the canvas of one of his paintings, which visitors could operate using controls at the front of the picture,[6] and from 1962 to 1965, in collaboration with sound engineer Bill Klüver, he created an installation titled *Oracle*, comprised of five mobile sculptures made of scrap metal (car door, window frame, stovepipe, etc.), with radio programs emanating from their interiors. The frequency scanners in these radios were, aided by motors, in constant operation, generating ongoing channel changes. In this work, Rauschenberg was searching for ways to integrate sound into his sculptures that could be influenced by the viewers:[7] the viewers could regulate the apparatus volume and the frequency search speed at a special console, connected to the objects via radio control. Additionally, the viewers were invited to shift the various objects in space. Bill Klüver describes the effect of this work as follows: *«The impression was that of walking down the Lower East Side on a summer evening and hearing the radios from open windows of the apartment buildings.»*[8]

Wesselmann and Rauschenberg reflect in these works on radio's status as mass medium, on its potential, in terms of both aesthetics and content, as an inexhaustible sound producer, a supplier of entertainment and information. At the same time, they effectively draft manifestos for the new conceptualization of art: for they are not simply integrating everyday objects in their works but rather functioning technical devices. Hence, they ignore the traditional boundary between visual and acoustic art, and moreover, with the live broadcast, they incorporate into their works a component over which they themselves have absolutely no influence.[9] Apart from the radio apparatus itself, this component does not age along with the works themselves. The insertion of various everyday objects or newspaper clippings in the scope of object art have still allowed for a deliberate selection of the latter, based on formal and conceptual criteria. Here, however, the acoustic material used in the work is continually updated, meaning the gestalt of the artwork changes perpetually with the alternating radio programs.

The fact that here a live medium is being tied to an art form of an object-based nature is not to be underestimated as regards its significance for art theory. This phenomenon can be examined more closely by contrasting the works above with a piece by Edward Kienholz. In his series of «*Volksempfängers*» (Nazi-era radio receivers), Kienholz addresses the sociopolitical function of radio. In the nineteen-seventies, he had purchased a few of these mass-produced, nineteen-thirties radio devices at the Berlin flea market and incorporated them into various installations. While he first considered having Hitler's voice sounding from the radio, he soon changed his mind and instead integrated passages from Wagner's *The Ring of the Nibelung*, one of the reasons being that, as a foreigner, he didn't want to presume he could select the adequate National Socialist speeches.[10] Alternatively, he chose Wagner as something «*weighty*,» corresponding to his idea of the cultural situation of the time.[11] The installations in question thus deal with the role of radio in the Third Reich's propaganda machine, yet expressly as an American's analysis of his own conception of German history.

Unlike the works of Wesselmann and Rauschenberg, these radios do not pick up live broadcasts—device and sound are instead witnesses to, or merely symbols of, history. Most of Kienholz's installations using radios make obvious show

---

9   The substantial influence of the works of John Cage is evident here. Cage had already composed his *Imaginary Landscape No. 4* for twelve radios and twelve performers in 1951. Rauschenberg and Cage were close friends.

10 A statement made by Kienholz in a discussion on January 30, 1970, quoted from Roland H. Wiegenstein, «Ed Kienholz, die ‹Volksempfängers› und der ‹Ring des Nibelungen,›» in

Edward Kienholz: Volksempfängers, ed. Jörn Merkert, exh. cat. Nationalgalerie Berlin (Berlin, 1977), pp. 12–19, here p. 13.

11 According to Jörn Merkert, Kienholz was not aware of Hitler's enthusiasm for Wagner. See «Jörn Merkert: Ed Kienholz und die Sprache der Dinge,» in Merkert 1977 (see note 10), pp. 20–53, here p. 34.

12 See Wiegenstein in Merkert 1977 (see note 10), p. 16.

of their antennas and stage diverse communication situations. The fact that the broadcast sound is produced by a tape is disguised, creating the impression that even on the electromagnetic frequencies the artist has succeeded in turning back time.

In *Die Bank (The Bench*, 1976), seven older radios (six of them *Volksempfängers*) are lined up on a bench, while an eighth, a contemporary one, stands on its own pedestal. The seven radios play Wagner and the eighth modern music. Kienholz himself views the installation as a portrait of a man traced from the National Socialist seizure of power to the present. The man's changing political and social attitudes are mirrored in the various devices and how he treats them (manipulation, wear and tear, rubbing out the swastika emblem, etc.).[12]

Three aspects fundamental to the integration of radio technology in the visual arts could be elucidated through an analysis of the above-described works from the nineteen-sixties:

They pertain to function and instrumentalization, the mythification and identification potential of the medium of radio. They incorporate immaterial elements in their works which cannot be influenced by the artist and which are subject to constant change. And they develop various strategies for dramatizing time in visual art, including juxtaposing the work's time of origin, its thematic time, and its reception time.

As far as the concrete form taken by the works is concerned, they adhere to the object in two ways: firstly as regards the radio as apparatus in its function as information source and symbol carrier (only Rauschenberg hides the device in sculptures, which in turn evoke their own worlds of symbolism), and secondly by holding fast to the artwork as a material object to be installed in an exhibition space. The (current or historical) media environment—or, in the case of Wesselmann, «life»—is integrated into the artwork in the guise of the apparatus.

In the following, whether, and to what extent, present-day media artworks have advanced from object to «art without time and space» will be explored along with the relationship these projects have to developments in radio technology and culture.

From Object to Space
«Hertzian Space» in the Media Art of the Nineties

The 1992 piece *Radio-Aktiv*[13] by Christian Terstegge visualizes the dense network of frequencies with the help of a series of household sponges, in which radio receivers and speakers are embedded—viewers see only the dipole antennas hanging down below the sponges. A random generator constantly changes the broadcast frequency of each individual radio, enabling the installation to make the variety of voices and melodies potentially present in the space audible, overlaid by noise on the unoccupied frequencies. Like Kienholz, Terstegge underlines the visibility of the antennas in the installation. But while in Kienholz's works the antennas merely refer to the potential for reception or contribute to its pretense, Terstegge's piece is a live artwork that takes on distinctive qualities with every visit, in every new exhibition: not only are the character of the radio programs and the content of the broadcasts subject to constant change, but the number of received stations differs greatly depending on the exhibition location.[14] In technical terms, the work thus displays analogies to Rauschenberg's *Oracle*, with both utilizing the station search function in a sculptural installation with numerous radio receivers. But while Rauschenberg turned the cacophony of the stations into a modern oracle, staged the scrap metal sculptures as «gifts of the street,»[15] and gave high priority to the influence exercised on the work by the viewer, Terstegge is concerned with the emerging, almost abstract soundscape. The household sponges serve as a mere metaphor for sending and receiving, no longer first and foremost objects but rather media, mediators, underlining the transient and ephemeral nature of the sounds flowing through them. This impression is enhanced further by their serial arrangement. The objective is to make the ubiquitous multiplicity of information perceptible as such and to demonstrate its spatial dimensions. The radio device is no longer a window to the world or a mouthpiece of the world in private space, for here the electromagnetic waves themselves as the bearers of the frequencies, along with a not clearly delimited data space, are the protagonists of the work.

13   1992, collection of the artist, see Kwastek 2004 (see note 2), pp. 149–53.

14   Simon Penny had already developed an—unfortunately no longer existant—installation in 1988, in which reeds were hung to form a kind of mobile, set into motion by the radio waves surrounding them, seemingly picking up information from them. Here, the receiver is likewise metaphorically transformed. See http://ace.uci.edu/penny/works/loyoyo.html (accessed October 16, 2007).

15   Robert Rauschenberg, interview by Billy Kluever, March 31, 1991, quoted in Hopps 1998 (see note 6), p. 313.

16   Roy Ascott, «Gesamtdatenwerk,» *Kunstforum International* 103 (1989), pp. 100–106.

Focusing on the data space as subject reflects a nineteen-nineties trend reacting to two developments in media technology: firstly, the increasing significance of digital data and its networking, which Roy Ascott for instance describes as a *Gesamtdatenwerk* (comprehensive data work),[16] and secondly, the rise of mobile technology, namely the application of wireless transmission technology not only for the distribution of information but also for communication, via telephone and later portable computer. The immaterial data space has thus experienced a quantitative and qualitative expansion and, above all, a new meaning in human consciousness.

The logical consequence follows that artists no longer limit themselves to reflecting on radio in their works but also accommodate the entire breadth of the electromagnetic spectrum, while increasingly incorporating mobile devices into their work.

In order to make visible the entire bandwidth of what is also known as «Hertzian space,» British architect and artist Usman Haque, for example, visualized the frequencies through light. In his project *Sky Ear* (2003–2006), he lets a «cloud» of helium-filled balloons float up into the sky, whose integrated LEDs react to the changing electromagnetic currents in the atmosphere. He makes the influence people wield on the Hertzian space surrounding them particularly apparent by

Robert Rauschenberg, *Oracle*, interactive sculpture (1962–65), installation view, Leo Castelli Gallery, New York City, NY, U.S., 1965.

having visitors call the cloud using mobile phones, thereby exerting a visible impact on the electromagnetic spectrum. The result is an ever-changing, crackling, multicolored glowing light display, as beautiful as it is unsettling.

The fascination and unease that results from comprehending the existence of the information inscribed in the electromagnetic waves also provides the springboard for Marko Peljhan's projects, which are described in more detail in this volume by Inke Arns and which represent a direct political aspiration. Through radio performances and his own mobile laboratories, Peljhan taps into all accessible radio frequencies, intercepts local and global transmissions, and analyzes them in his artistic research projects and performances.

In comparison to the projects of the nineteen-sixties, a shift in interest can thus be discerned from the device as theme to a preoccupation with the frequencies such devices allow us to pick up, and then further to a general exploration of the electromagnetic spectrum. Hertzian space is not explored as a neutral data carrier, however, but rather in its relationship to real space, in the varying shapes it takes in different places: Christian Terstegge is interested in the distinctive appearance of his installation depending on its exhibition venue; Usman Haque leaves the exhibition space behind and lets his *Sky Ear* rise up into the sky over public spaces on different continents; and Marko Peljhan constructs a mobile laboratory in order to research the spectrum of frequencies in a wide variety of localities and the information encoded therein.

British artists Anthony Dunne and Fiona Raby, in turn, put the receiver itself in constant motion, detecting the wirelessly present information in public space. In the project *tuneable cities*, they employ what was long the most widespread mobile receiving device: the car radio. They start from the observation that the driver in a vehicle traverses regions without receiving any information about them: car radios are generally programmed to always return to the frequency of the station first entered, that is, the radio program at the point of departure. But if the radio were instead to switch over to local stations, the changing radio programs would afford the driver impressions of the regions and cities of travel.

Elaborating on this idea, the artist duo built a broadband scanner into a car (which in addition to radio can also pick up other frequencies) and drove through the streets, not only aiming to receive local radio stations but also to discover how

17 Anthony Dunne, *Hertzian Tales: Electronic Products, Aesthetic Experience and Critical Design* (Cambridge, MA, 2005), pp. 137–42.

18 Ibid., pp. 1 and 21.

much information residents radiate into their surroundings by means of electro-magnetic waves, emanating from installed bugs, mobile phones, baby monitors, and so forth. In fact, the car trip demonstrated that more than half of the houses were broadcasting *domestic soundscapes*.» The artists also equipped birds with radio transmitters and wired radios to receive atmospheric radio sounds. Finally, they constructed car radios configured for the selection of the «new stations» (birds, atmosphere, baby monitor) in place of the buttons for normal channels.[17]

The projects of Dunne and Raby provide us with an occasion for an excursus on the persistent meaning, but the altered role, of objects in media art. The object as found device, in which form it played the leading role in radio-related works in the nineteen-sixties and seventies, can no longer be found in more recent works. But the object is still prevalent in a new guise, for instance as interface design or taking the form of critical pseudo-devices such as those created by Dunne and Raby, who describe their works as «Design Noir» or «post-optimal objects.» According to Anthony Dunne, the classic task of the designer of electronic objects is to create semiotic interfaces for incomprehensible technologies, transparent interfaces[18] making device operation easy and understandable. Dunne quotes Virilio, who has described interactive user friendliness as a metaphor for human

Christian Terstegge, *Radio-Aktiv*, installation view, *Ohne Schnur*, Cux-haven, Germany, 2004.

enslavement to supposedly intelligent machines, since people unconditionally accept the necessity of such machines and their functionality.[19] Dunne thus regards post-optimal objects to be those that make the distance between human and machine visible again, emphasizing moments of irreconcilability.[20] In addition to the aforementioned modified car radio, Fiona Raby also constructed, for example, the *Faraday Chair*, which protects the sitter from electromagnetic radiation. The two artists additionally developed a series of so-called placebo objects, which are purported to react to electromagnetic radiation, or shield the user from it, but in actuality investigate people's anxieties and their limited grasp of technology.[21]

From Distribution to Communication Medium?
Interactive Radio Art

Dunne and Raby center their considerations on the human as producer and consumer of electromagnetic waves as well as on the relationship of real space to the data traffic.

As was already the case with Wesselmann and Rauschenberg, the electromagnetic waves are Readymades, though not static objects selected once but rather constantly changing. Nevertheless, they remain found elements of our everyday culture. The artists make the information already existing in space visible or audible, while exerting no influence over the information type and content. This at first corresponds with the idea of the radio as broadcasting medium, receivable but not participatory, followed later by the concept of abstract data space, which can be visualized or intercepted but not actively changed. Attempts to involve the receiver in the process of data traffic have been repeatedly undertaken— whether by manipulating the station scan speed as in the case of Rauschenberg or by exploring the possibilities of the telephone call in Haque's electromagnetic

19 Ibid.

20 «By poeticizing the distance between people and electronic objects, sensitive scepticism might be encouraged, rather than unthinking assimilation of the values and conceptual models embedded in electronic objects»; ibid., p. 22.

21 See Kwastek 2004 (see note 2), pp. 193–99 and Anthony Dunne and Fiona Raby, *Design Noir: The Secret Life of Electronic Objects* (London, 2001), pp. 75–157.

22 Reference is due here, however, to Max Neuhaus, who in 1966, in his work *Public Supply*, had already connected radio and telephone technology in order to broadcast sounds generated through the telephone receivers directly over the radio. This work had no visible components, however, and found its way out of the broadcasting studio via the traditional broadcasting channel.

cloud—but a true reciprocity of information exchange has not been achieved. This is a characteristic of radio, already criticized by Bertolt Brecht, that has—in the medium of radio—never been successfully changed: the demand for a communication medium has not been met by radio. Other media, such as the telephone and meanwhile the Internet, fulfill this function notably better. While as early as the nineteen-sixties forms of communications art were created that explored possibilities for reciprocal interaction, for exchange, and for common action, they used not so much radio technology[22] as mail and telephone, later also fax and satellite, and then finally the Internet.

Using hybrid forms and exploiting the increasing mobility of end devices, artists have nevertheless found ways of carrying out a public dramatization of communication even using radio technology, while still preserving the radio-specific characteristics. The *Radio Ballet*, a performance having been put on by the Hamburg artists' group LIGNA in various German cities since 2003, astounded the unsuspecting observer, when suddenly several hundred passersby standing on the platforms of the Hamburg or Leipzig main railway stations synchronously raised their hands, all sat down on the ground, or stretched out their arms, as if controlled by magic hand. These purportedly innocent bystanders were actually

LIGNA, *Radio Ballet*, Leipzig, Germany, 2006.

all equipped with mobile radio receivers with headphones and had been instructed beforehand via Internet to show up at the train stations at a specified time,
with the receivers set to a specific frequency, in order to carry out the gestures
conveyed over radio. This performance is related to the idea of the flash mob,
particularly prevalent in the summer of 2003, consisting of lightning-fast mass
assemblies collectively carrying out brief actions (coordinated ahead of time via
Internet or mobile phone).[23] Equipping the participants in the LIGNA radio ballet with radio receivers allowed for a more extensive repertoire, however, and a
more precise temporal coordination of the various actions. The actions and gestures called for by LIGNA were all activities prohibited at German train stations,
such as begging or settling down with the ostensible intention of staying there.
LIGNA's intent was to show how the common action of a group (organized through
a combination of various media technologies) could undermine such rules of
conduct, while at the same time pointing out the kind of behavioral discipline
imposed on us in supposedly public space.[24] The radio ballet can be understood
as mobilization of the masses, as constituting a protest against prescribed rules
by means of spontaneous solidarity, but also as a measure for surveillance or
heteronomy. The «listeners» play the decisive, active role in this project but are,
on the other hand, merely the extended arms of the radio instructions they implement in public space.

In another performance project organized relatively spontaneously by a group
of artists during the 2004 ISEA (Inter Society for the Electronic Arts) Festival in
Helsinki, the distribution of roles is not defined quite as clearly. Here, the relations between listeners and participants, public and private sphere, are reflected
upon on various levels. The project took the form of a city tour, the theme being
the so-called *Grillis*, traditional snack bars of long-standing tradition in the city.
Originally, mobile sausage sellers hawked their wares from converted bicycles,
but nowadays the *Grillis* are usually permanent stalls, some nearly one hundred
years old. What was unusual about the tour was less the theme than the means
chosen to communicate it. Various group participants carried portable radios and
the guide herself spoke into a mobile phone connected to a local radio station,

23 See Howard Rheingold, *Smart Mobs: The Next
Social Revolution* (Cambridge, MA, 2002),
in which the smart mob is distinguished from
the flash mob by the claim that the assemblies
organized as smart mobs pursue a political
or social aim, that is, do not merely serve
entertainment ends.

24 See «Radio Ballett: Übung in unnötigem
Aufenthalt erfolgreich,» http://www
.ok-centrum.at/ausstellungen/open_house/
ligna.html (accessed October 16, 2007).

as did other assistants interviewing passersby. The project was broadcast live on the radio, hence enabling participants to either follow it directly or via their accompanying radios. The listeners ascertained in the process that sound emanated from the radio with a slight delay. Live voice and supposed live broadcast redoubled the tour in a disruptive manner. Most notably, however, this performance engendered a subtle encounter with media-age communication forms: although the group participants were together physically in one place, communication took place by means of radio, so that the activity could potentially be followed by any resident of Helsinki regardless of location in the city. The group itself was, just like the radios the people had with them, extremely mobile in contrast to the *Grilli* stalls, having converted from mobile sales vehicles to permanent stalls. At the same time, the accompanying radios made the outing more open than traditional guided tours, since the devices, like a loudspeaker, amplified the voice of the guide and alerted passersby to the situation. The action thus consisted of a subtle mix of face-to-face communication and its mediation through the media, of private tour and public broadcast.

While the issues of media criticism and the temporal structure of the medium addressed here stem from a long tradition, as illustrated above, the relationship between material components and immaterial information is today being reconceived in such a way that neither the object nor the data space, as material or immaterial components, constitute the focus, but rather the recipient, who is localized in real space, forming the interface with the data space.

Another important innovation lies in the fact that both latter projects do not solely implement radio technology but also combine it with other media. The combination of Internet and radio, or radio and mobile phone, is an indication of a general media amalgamation, making it increasingly difficult to render answerable the question as to the specificity of the medium of radio in comparison to other media. The «institution of radio» is reacting to these developments with podcasts and net radio, programs which can be called up as needed at any time, and also saved and thereby heard anywhere the user happens to be. This personalization of media results in the connection between data space and real space increasingly being created by the individual recipient, who calls up or broadcasts information anywhere, at any time, using the accompanying mobile devices. The technologies employed for this purpose are manifold and prove difficult to differentiate distinctly.

Radio Art
From Apparatus/Object to a Mode of Spatial and Aesthetic Experience

The fascination with Hertzian space superimposing real space is tendentially strengthened rather than weakened by the fact that the former is extremely heterogeneous and has long since been detached from the radio as apparatus or institution. This becomes apparent in the last project under consideration here: American artist Teri Rueb's *Drift* (2004), a site-specific installation designed for the Cuxhaven *Wattenmeer* (tidal flats) on the German North Sea coast. At an issue station, the visitors are each given a small backpack with headphones and then instructed to make their way through the tidal flats. During the hike through this unique topography, there are long phases where no sound at all emanates from the headphones, forming a contrast to the natural sounds of the landscape: sea birds, wind, water, ship motors, and sounds of their own movements across the sandy, soggy ground.

Suddenly, however, the visitors hear footsteps and realize these are not their own. After a while, a voice begins to tell of hikes, landscapes, pathways. Occasionally the visitors hear an entire train of thought, but at other times the text suddenly breaks off, lost along with the sound of the footsteps. Some time later, they hear a further text, also accompanied by walking sounds, dealing with questions of roaming, searching, or being lost. These are fragments of literary texts, for example by James Joyce, Thomas Mann, or Dante.

Listeners who turn around, heading back in hopes of hearing a text again, will be disappointed. Finding the text again may well prove impossible, and the listeners wonder if this is due to their own lack of orientation skills, or to the technology used, or whether it is perhaps a conceptual component of the work. Searching and roaming are consequently not only themes of the texts but are likewise inherent in the experiential mode of the work itself.

The reason why the sound fragments are so transient can be discovered in the accompanying graphic projection in the exhibition section: the texts roam—analogous to the North Sea tides—across the landscape. The visitor hence happens completely at random upon the texts, only to be heard in a completely different

25 For more on Teri Rueb, *Drift*, see Kwastek 2004 (see note 2), pp. 211–19.

place a few hours later. The ephemeralness of the data space corresponds with the character of the landscape in which the data is audible: it, too, being subject to constant change, flooded by the sea in a regular rhythm, emerging again—depending on weather conditions, wind and currents—in new form. Hardly any points of orientation are offered by this vast expanse inviting the walker to roam aimlessly. Sounds and landscape thus enter into a symbiosis, the audio space indissolubly interwoven with the material space.[25]

The aesthetic experience of this installation consists in roaming through wavering clouds of sound, seemingly wandering through a mysterious data space. Yet technically, one carries the data space along in the backpack—all sounds are saved on the small computer inside. The only direct connection with Hertzian space exists through an integrated GPS device which constantly plots the listener's current position. The computer subsequently plays the sound data according to this position and to the time determined by the tidal situation.

This work thus technically has little to do with radio technology as a constant stream of information transmitted over electromagnetic frequencies, picked up by receivers and made audible. But the visitors' aesthetic experience is nevertheless like wandering through clouds of sound or text that they themselves

Teri Rueb, *Drift*,
locative art project,
Ohne Schnur, Cuxhaven,
Germany, 2004.

render audible. This experience unfolds the work's intention of making tangible the wandering data streams and relating them to the constant changes in nature as well as to our own real and emotional movements.

Surely it is not «art without space and time,» as invoked by the Futurists, that is presented to us here. Nonetheless, Rueb raises the question of whether the ideas of a continuous space and a linear time are still the constants governing our society—a society in which an entirely man-made information space seems to be crowding the material world into the background.

The aesthetic the artist devotes to this purpose is an aesthetic anchored in the tradition of radio art. The immateriality of the information, its accessibility and temporality, and its strange, varying localization between real space and Hertzian space, between present and past, are elements that have motivated the incorporation of radio into artistic projects from the very beginning.

The days of scanning for a station, of the apparatus-bound capacity, of radio as dominant information channel are now definitely of the past. Innumerable radio programs offer—via traditional stations, Internet connections, or mobile phone—individually consumable information and entertainment, as do many other media. Yet the fascination of Hertzian space—information floating invisibly through space—is today more pertinent than ever. Facilitating the experience of this fascination, shaping it or illuminating it critically, is one of the important themes of contemporary media art. As to whether this is accomplished with traditional radio technology or by means of other devices, which after all create a related aesthetic experience, seems to be of secondary importance.

Audiomobile

A Project by Matt Smith and Sandra Wintner

AUDIOMOBILE[1] is a project for mapping cities with sound. *AUDIOMOBILE* invites small audiences to explore «sonic maps» by riding in a multi-passenger vehicle which is equipped with surround sound and GPS (Global Positioning System) technology. The sonic maps consist of audio samples created by local sound artists and are superimposed onto selected landmarks in the city, according to locations chosen by them.

The individual audio elements are triggered by matching the output coordinates of the onboard GPS with the geographical location of the vehicle in the city as it glides through various urban scenarios. As a result, an array of audio samples, sound clips collaged with looping ambiences and complete narratives, generate an ever-changing audio «cityscape» projected into the vehicle in sur-

Artist Run Limousine (ARL), *Audiomobile*, view from inside the car during a ride, Quebec City, Canada, 2005.

Artist Run Limousine (ARL), *Audiomobile*, interior and two guests of the Artist Run Limousine, Vancouver, Canada, 2003.

round sound. The position of the vehicle determines not only which sounds are being played but also from which direction (loudspeaker) they originate.

AUDIOMOBILE has been performed with the Artist Run Limousine[2] in Vancouver (2003), Saskatoon (2004), and Winnipeg (2004). In Linz (2004), Quebec City (2005), and Vienna (2005) it took place in luxury minivans with onboard navigation systems. In each of these cities, between five and ten local sound artists contributed an average of 150 individual sound files and corresponding locations.

The versions created by the local artists in the individual cities were completely distinct from each other, not only due to the individual samples, played through AUDIOMOBILE, but also because both traffic patterns and geographical features of each city are instrumental to the project—it is a sound sculpture that comes into existence by driving around within the sonic map created by the local artists. Every time AUDIOMOBILE goes on one of its tours, a new version of that city's performance is created. Participants directly influence the AUDIOMOBILE «score» by choosing routes and directing the driver into areas of their choice. The intimacy of the passenger compartment also promotes dialogue between individual passengers, which adds a further layer of communication to each tour. AUDIOMOBILE encourages exchange between people and the environment and attempts to replace anonymity and detachment with familiarity and identification.

A strong inspiration for AUDIOMOBILE was the idea of creating an «alternative soundtrack» for a city, by people who inhabit it for people who inhabit it, rather than developing a guided tour concept, which has since been realized commercially by numerous companies and cities. The inspiration was certainly a cinematic one, in which the view out of the vehicle onto the passing city becomes the context for the unfolding soundscape. AUDIOMOBILE allows for artistic expression that directly associates place with sound and uses movement (travel over time through space) as a temporal and sequential base. As such, AUDIOMOBILE is a truly nonlinear media experience, with every performance being original and unique.

---

1 The AUDIOMOBILE project has involved, along with Matt Smith and Sandra Wintner, many other artists at each location. For more information, see http://www.firstfloor.org/ARL/Audiomobile/.

2 The Artist Run Limousine (ARL) was a mobile artist run space in the shape of a white Cadillac Fleetwood stretch limousine run by Matt Smith, Sandra Wintner, and others. In October 2004, the original Artist Run Limousine unglamorously broke down in Golden, BC and has since been abandoned. See http://www.firstfloor.org/ARL/.

Radio as Exhibition Space

Doreen Mende

> Listening to music is listening to noise, realizing
> that its appropriation and control is a reflection
> of power, that is essentially political.[1]
> — *Jacques Attali*

More and more often, established art institutions are hosting shows on the theme of sound.[2] To date, radio art has received little attention in this context. But in recent years, interest in this field has been increasingly reflected in small-scale conferences and exhibition projects, and in the founding of numerous free radio stations.[3] Could radio technology provide a presentation space that reexamines exhibition strategy? Using the example of the *EAR APPEAL* show,[4] I will discuss the relationship between the presentation of art in a physical exhibition space and the specific qualities of radio-based exhibitions, as well as an «Audio Culture»[5] in contemporary art practice that argues in social terms.

If one goes back in time a little, then—in art from the nineteen-fifties through the seventies—Audio Culture plays a decisive role in artistic practice on a par with other media. It is no coincidence that Henry Flynt—philosopher, anti-art activist, and coiner of the term concept art—begins his «Essay: Concept Art»[6] with the words: «‹Concept art› is first of all an art of which the material is ‹concepts,› as the material of for ex. music is sound.» The dematerialization of the art object, in whose terms Lucy Lippard described art between 1966 and 1972,[7] corresponds to the spirit of Audio Culture. The development of art in this period features a coming together of heterogeneous positions that are united by their interest in the division between art and life. To name just a few examples: as a key figure in Fluxus and concept art, John Cage used sound and silence in his compositions based on the principle of chance; every detail of the surroundings became material for a composition whose objective was nothingness. In the fifties, Ray Johnson developed «correspondence art»—later mail art—as an artistic praxis that produces process, activity, and networking. From the early seventies, the dematerialization and placelessness of art became more differentiated thanks to the simplification of electronic recording technology. Christine Kozlov, another pioneer of concept art in the U.S., chose the tape recorder as a test setup in her piece *Information: No Theory* (1970) as a way of questioning the credibility of information in the dawning age of mass media.[8] At the beginning of the seventies, William Furlong and Barry Barker founded the magazine *Audio Arts*,[9] a programmatic format for sound recording as artistic practice and for the creation of a public outside of institutions. All of these are practices that push up against the boundaries of the institutional exhibition space.

Nonetheless, the white exhibition space became the matrix for artistic debate. The visible architecture became the frame of reference for the negotiation of territorial, contextual, and metaphorical boundaries between inside and outside. From the ideology of the White Cube, artists derived material for their examinations of the art institution in postwar modernity. Debate focused, however,

1　In Jacques Attali, *Bruits: essai sur l'economie politique de la musique* (Paris: Presses Universitaires de France, 1977). English version: Jacques Attali, *Noise: The Political Economy of Music* (Minneapolis: University of Minnesota Press, 1985).

2　Sonic Boom (Hayward Gallery, London, 2000), Sonic Process (Centre Pompidou, Paris, 2002–2003), Anti Reflex (Kunsthalle Schirn, Frankfurt, 2005), and in particular the mediaspecific Sonambiente shows in Berlin (1996 and 2006).

3　Resonance FM (London), reboot.fm (Berlin, 2004), *Radio_Copernicus* (Warsaw and Berlin, 2005), Garage Festival (Berlin, 2004), Bienal Internacional de Radio (Mexico City), Radio Gallery (London, 2006).

4　From October 19 through November 18, 2006 at Kunsthalle Exnergasse in Vienna. Artists: Rashad Becker, Justin Bennett, Benjamin Bergmann, Elisabeth Grübl, Arthur Köpcke, Genesis P-Orridge, Ultra-red, Ruszka Roskalnikowa, Paula Roush, Mika Taanila,

Annette Weisser. Curator: Doreen Mende. *EAR APPEAL ON AIR* broadcast on *Kunstradio* on October 29 and November 5 and 12, 2006.

5　*Audio Culture: Readings in Modern Music*, edited by Christoph Cox and Daniel Warner, was published in 2004. In the following, «Audio Culture» will be used to refer to artistic work with sound.

6　In 1961, Flynt spoke of conceptual art for the first time; the essay was published in 1963 in *An Anthology* by La Monte Young.

7　*Six Years: The Dematerialization of the Art Object from 1966–72*, edited by Lucy Lippard, published 1973, reprinted 1997, contains a bibliography listing interviews, documents, artworks, and symposium papers that make up a chronological index.

8　Susanne Neuburger, «…with their own intrinsic logic,» *springerin*, Theory Now issue (February 2006).

9　For more information on Bill Furlong and the *Audio Arts* project and archives, see Bill Furlong at http://kunstradio.at/BREGENZ/KIDS/index.html.

not on its visibility, but on a conceptual questioning of space-defining reality. Art became a seeing machine, an instrument for the analysis of that which takes place both outside and inside the institution.

After World War II, the technical perfection of radio technology increased and its popularity grew. This period was characterized by the arrival of a mass-media toolkit: the transmission of information in the form of electromagnetic signals from broadcaster to receiver allowed private homes to connect with the outside world at the push of a button: private space became the venue for public presentations. But the content changed, too. The range of themes grew to include audience participation and a focus on individual concerns: the public domain became private. Radio was just the beginning of this transfer.

The aim of the *EAR APPEAL* show was to bring an invisible element of reality into the exhibition space and to discuss links between audio and society without falling into the trap of a media-specific exhibition. Instead, the focus was on the possibility of portraying our society in audio, and on sound as a potential instrument for the control of individual actions. What interests me in particular about Audio Culture—following concept art—is its potential for analysis and place-lessness combined with its rendering visible of social issues by using sound as

Mika Taanila, *Thank You For the Music*, film still, *EAR APPEAL*, Kunsthalle Exnergasse, Vienna, Austria, 2006.

analytical and conceptual material. So when an exhibition focuses on the links between Audio Culture and society, then the presentation space must be conceived of and examined in terms beyond its physical architecture. Nonetheless, a museum-like exhibition architecture was necessary at the Kunsthalle as a counterpoint to the immaterial space of radio, in order to—drawing on the experience of nineteen-nineties artistic praxis—deal with institutional manifestations. A space-filling display system using grey partitions structured the exhibition according to a topological principle.

In addition to their pieces for the show at the Kunsthalle, several of the *EAR APPEAL* artists—Justin Bennett, Rashad Becker, Paula Roush/msdm, Ultra-red, and Annette Weisser—were asked to devise works for radio to be broadcast by *Kunstradio* on Austrian public radio's cultural channel Österreich 1 (Ö1), while the show was running, and to remain available online as downloadable MP3s. *EAR APPEAL ON AIR* was explicitly part of the overall exhibition concept in that the series of radio programs was designed not as an accompanying program but as an extension of the exhibition space. The radio pieces all featured one of two aspects: working with found urban sounds or reflecting on the technology of the radio as a way of achieving an impact at the point of delivery in the external world. This created a concrete interrelation between inside and out that was put into practice and continued within the space of radio. What makes the presentation of Audio Culture on the radio significant? Assuming that the presentation of art consists of a complex mesh of spatial, technological, institutional, and situational conditions, the specific character of presenting Audio Culture on the radio lies above all in its placelessness, situation-specificity, and everydayness. A radio set can be installed in various places and remain switched on around the clock: a radio set can host an instant, immaterial, and transportable exhibition, just as hats, publications, and boxes[10] have become exhibition venues. The inside and outside of the radio space are manifested in the radio receiver's on/off switch. But making an exhibition also means creating a space characterized by selection

10 Robert Filliou, *Galerie Légitime* (1962); Seth Siegelaub and John Wendler, eds., *The Xerox Book* (New York, 1968); see also, Ina Conzen, ed., *Art Games: Die Schachteln der Fluxus-künstler* (Stuttgart: Staatsgalerie Stuttgart, 1997).

11 Jacques Rancière, *Le Partage du sensible. Esthétique et politique* (Paris: La Fabrique, 2000); translated into English as Jacques Rancière, *The Politics of Aesthetics: The Distribution of the Sensible:* (New York: Continuum International, 2004).

12 From *érgon* (Greek) «work» and *onomatopoiein* (Greek) «create a name.»

and presence. If, depending on broadcasting times, radio can be listened to on the street, in the car, at work, at home, or while jogging, then more than anything else, art becomes totally mixed up with the casual nature of everyday life. But this blending of art and everyday life is distinct from that activated by conceptual Fluxus artists like George Brecht and John Cage. Does art have a chance in the everyday white noise of radio if the listener does not have to give up his or her passive, receptive role? How can a «distribution of the sensible»[11] be both called into question and reconfigured?

In the context of *EAR APPEAL*, the brilliant *reading/work piece No. 1* by Fluxus artist Arthur Köpcke represented an important historical reference. Made as early as 1963, his instruction piece *music while you work*, part of his chef-d'oeuvre *manuscript* (1963–65), takes social norms to absurd lengths: *piece No. 1 music while you work* parodies BBC radio's Light Programme which, from the war years until well into the nineteen-sixties, was designed to increase the productivity of factory workers by means of animating, functional music: «Artistic value must NOT be considered. The aim is to produce something which is monotonous and repetitive» (BBC). In a version documented on video, Köpcke begins by sweeping a room to music coming from the radio: the text instruction requires that he interrupt his work whenever the music stops—so that neither the music nor the work can ever be brought to an end.

For his new sound installation *Ergonomatopoese*,[12] Berlin artist Rashad Becker interviewed around forty working individuals to obtain an acoustic portrayal of what is understood by «work» based on the activities that typify professions ranging from trader through artist. After an introductory exchange, Becker asked the interviewees to reproduce the sounds of their work using their own sound-producing organs. Although it comes as no surprise, it is significant that the phonetic vocabulary is far less developed than the ability to portray working conditions using optically coded words. Woven together collage-style, the recordings of the onomatopoeias produced a space within the exhibition in which to think about the concept of work, which is as diverse as the sounds that buzz, rustle, and whistle around the space, triggered by the visitor's movements. Another striking thing is that the more neoliberal the structures of the work in question are, the harder it is to capture the notion of work, something which cannot be attributed solely to the phonetic inexperience of the participants. For his *Kunstradio* piece entitled *Radio kenn' ich nur vom Hörensagen—Ohranwendung in der Wertegemeinschaft*

(I only know radio from hearsay—the use of ears in a community of shared values), Becker edited the interviews and onomatopoeias into an experimental radio play consisting of sounds and distorted but recognizable language. Instead of commenting on the knocking, snapping, and hissing noises, the fragments of the original spoken passages all revolve around the transition from language to sound: «Do I make a sound like ...,» «For a sound like ...,» «Would I dress up for a sound like ...,» «With a sound like ...,» and so on. The radio piece cannot be separated from the work at the Kunsthalle. Whereas the latter achieves a sense of three-dimensionality using hypersonic directional loudspeakers—creating an auditory experience entirely different to that of listening to the radio, which the artist puts in context in a text in the accompanying booklet—the radio piece includes the level of everydayness that can only exist outside and in the immediate physical vicinity of the listener.

Both Paula Roush/msdm (mobile strategies of display & mediation) and the Ultra-red group (for *EAR APPEAL*, Dont Rhine and Manuela Bojadžijev) used the Kunsthalle as a meeting place and discussion venue. Generally speaking, radio took on the role of postproduction as well as that of publication and distribution.

After periods in London and Leipzig, London artist Paula Roush localized her *Protest Academy* in the show in Vienna as a vital structure for cooperation, exchange, education, and information-gathering about audio tactics that articulate social or political resistance. When does sound become information and protest? As the setting for a workshop and as an installation in the exhibition, visitors had access to the protest archive begun in London in 2005 containing newspaper articles, CDs with songs of protest and peace, an opera libretto, theoretical texts by Toni Negri and Gilles Deleuze, and a variety of projects and documentation by artists including Oliver Ressler, Temporary Services, and Melanie Jackson. For her performances and collaborations, Paula Roush used the archive, with entries divided up into the four categories «What are we doing? What's happening to us? What needs to be done? I prefer not to.» At the same time as being a collection of materials, the archive also acts as working material. On the radio, a record

13 From the Spanish: gathering, meeting. In the context of the anti-globalization movement, especially in Latin America, this form of political meeting has evolved where relevant social themes are discussed publicly on the basis of networking.

produced by Paula Roush and the artist Isa Suarez was played which brings together the contents of the archive in edited form. Like the archive, the four tracks on the record are ordered using the four categories, allowing the sound material to be presented in different contexts, such as live jam sessions or performances. Protest slogans can still be heard among the sound collages, but this reworking questions the degree to which information must be comprehensible if a praxis of resistance is to become effective protest.

As well as being the focus of research by Ultra-red into migration and its impact on social structures, *Surveying the Future* is also the title of the radio piece by the group for *EAR APPEAL ON AIR.* The radio piece is an edited version of an «*Encuentro*»:[13] on October 21, 2006, Ultra-red theorists, activists, and artists organized a public gathering to discuss «What is the Sound of the War on the Poor in Vienna.» With Tania Martini, Roland Atzmüller, Jakob Weingartner, and Fahim Amir, Ultra-red explored various locations in Vienna like the Lugner City shopping mall, the Gürtel, or the Brunnenmarkt, which were presented at the *Encuentro* in the form of talks and audio recordings. The way the question was framed actively encouraged a differentiation of concepts and attributions. What is sound? What is war? Who are the poor?

Paula Roush,
Protest Academy,
installation and
intervention, *EAR
APPEAL*, Kunsthalle
Exnergasse and
Kunstradio On Air,
Vienna, Austria, 2006.

Both the audio recordings and what was said during the discussion were used by Ultra-red as analytical material to explore links between social structures and planned urban development. In a method of «militant investigation» devised and used for political analysis above all by the Marxist labor movement in Italy (Operaismo), the activation of debate and network-building are central elements in the artistic audio praxis of Ultra-red. The aspect of informal education, influenced by the theories and praxis of the Brazilian pedagogue Paulo Freire (1921–1997), as laid out in his main work *Pedagogy of the Oppressed* (1968), also plays a key role. The piece by Ultra-red for *Kunstradio* uses radio technology as an instrument for the creation of a public. In addition, the radio also provides a place for the activation of communal learning that is negotiated on a collective level and which articulates critical awareness. The radio transports the public brainstorming session at the Kunsthalle back to the locations in question.

The transfer of content from the exhibition to the scene of the action—to concrete places in Vienna and, in conceptual terms, out of the institution—marks an important aspect of the overall exhibition concept, implemented directly via presentation on the radio. The British artist Justin Bennett, based in The Hague, has been working since 2003 on his piece entitled *Sundial*: in major cities like Barcelona (2003), The Hague, Rome, Guangzhou, Paris (2005), and Vienna (*EAR APPEAL*, 2006), over a twenty-four-hour period the same number of individual sound recordings were made, forming an edited acoustic panorama of the cities in question. But it is not so much about merely documenting a specific urban soundscape or making an interpretative study of the diverse connections between people in the city and their surroundings. Instead, in edited form, Bennett indexes the specific characteristics of the sonic environment of Kunsthalle Exnergasse as a kind of cartographic inventory, but without prescribing a definitive legibility. Transferred to the radio, the subjective city map becomes a piece of musique concrète.

EAR APPEAL commissioned a new piece by Annette Weisser on the theme of radio as a place of cultural production and cultural coding: in one of the old broadcasting studios at Austrian State Radio, she cooperated with *Kunstradio* to produce the audio and video work *Kanon* based on the old children's

---

14 «C-A-F-F-E-E, trink nicht so viel Kaffee. Nicht für Kinder ist der Türkentrank, schwächt die Nerven macht dich blass und krank. Sei du kein Muselmann, der das nicht lassen kann» (C-A-F-F-E-E, don't drink so much coffee. This Turkish drink is not for kids, it weakens your nerves, makes you pale and ill. Don't you be like a Moslem who can't do without it). Set to music by Carl Gottlieb Hering (1766–1853).

song «C-A-F-F-E-E.» Instead of the original lyrics,[14] Weisser sang and whistled, in a five-voice canon with herself: We Know What We Are By What We Are Not—a line taken from a magazine article about the «clash of cultures.» Various film sequences show the artist recording her voice parts, scan murals featuring idyllic Austrian nature scenes, or wander around the space, lingering on the décor and the control room window. The recording studio, originally built as a broadcasting studio in the nineteen-thirties, becomes a matrix for the construction of cultural identity and refers to the place where it is produced and duplicated. The daily broadcast of the radio piece made affirmative use of the way radio functions, at the same time as reflecting on it via the audiovisual feedback to the presentation at the Kunsthalle. In the exhibition space, then, we experience something like a double making-of: specifically, the making of the piece itself and, generally, the development of radio technology as a mass medium for the shaping of political opinion. Using the melody of a well-known children's song, Weisser plays with the programmed recognition effect with which we are familiar from ubiquitous radio. But the cultural canonization is undermined by the rhythmic new lyrics, thus activating more attentive listening, something that comes as more of a surprise when listening to the radio than it does in an art space.

Annette Weisser, *Kanon*, video/DVD/*Kunstradio* broadcast, installation view, *EAR APPEAL*, Kunsthalle Exnergasse, Vienna, Austria, 2006.

Radio is almost unparalleled among media in its ability to provide independent distribution strategies, distance from art institutions, and the positioning of art in the listener's everyday surroundings. Admittedly, in terms of exhibiting art, Audio Culture only indirectly leaves behind a visual work capable of being documented. We are dealing either with a process of transformation from sound to language, to image, or with the playing back of a sound recording which in a conventional exhibition space can only be presented in limited or altered form on account of the acoustic conditions, but which as a readymade (field recording) automatically triggers attentiveness. Contemporary exhibition practice in art features codes that cause us to perceive selectively and specifically. Radio lacks this very concrete and often-criticized frame of reference. In its historical evolution into a mass medium, radio technology is so strongly linked with everyday reality outside the exhibition space that the moment when the radio listener is called on to listen is far less precise that it is in the art space, when reading a publication, or on receipt of a Mail Art postcard. On the other hand, by removing sound from its original context as an objet trouvé and doubly recontextualizing it—that is, as material in an artwork and as radio art in an unspecified everyday situation—every sound played on the radio is institutionalized. In this light, radio as an exhibition space appears as impermeable as the physical space of the art institution. Is art really transported outside? Audio Culture in general and radio art in particular call for exhibition formats that manifest content, produce context, and bear in mind the institutional space of the radio.

Willem de Ridder, *European Mail-Order Warehouse*, 1965, installation for a photograph by
Wim van der Linde: boxes with objects by George Brecht, Robert Watts, Henry Flynt,
Alison Knowles, La Monte Young, and many others are piled up on a couch in Willem de Ridder's
house in Amsterdam. Among them sits Dorothea Mejer, de Ridder's girlfriend at the time. The
boxes as well as the print publications were designed by George Maciunas, who had appointed
Willem de Ridder as chairman of Fluxus activities in Northern Europe. Under its director
Willem de Ridder in Amsterdam, the conceptual shop *European Mail-Order Warehouse* offered
and sold the same boxes as the New York FLUXSHOP Loft by Maciunas. Neither shop existed as
physical sales room, rather both of them used postal distribution structures as instruments
of display. The illustration shows a reconstruction of the *European Mail-Order Warehouse*
within one big box by Jon Hendricks for the Fluxus exhibition of the Gilbert and Lila Silverman
Collection, 1984. Willem de Ridder lives near Amsterdam. His website (www.ridderradio.com)
obeys Fluxus principles even today: every week de Ridder replies live to questions formulated
by listeners on the spur of the moment and/or based on their everyday experience.
(Description by Doreen Mende.)

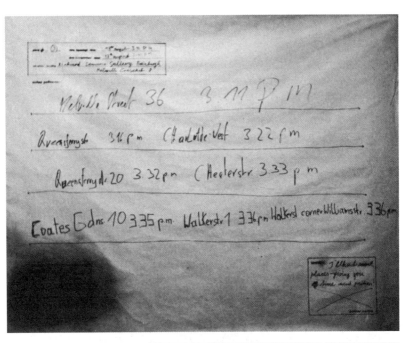

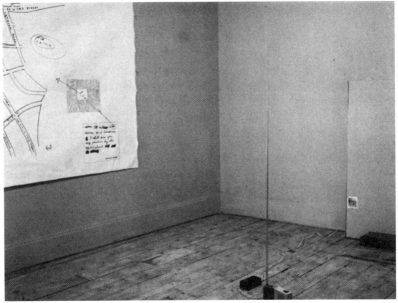

Inside – Outside

A Project by Gottfried Bechtold

Edinburgh Festival 1973

Every day during the opening hours of The Austrian Exhibition at the Demarco Gallery in Edinburgh, Gottfried Bechtold went on walks in the gallery's surroundings—equipped with a mobile handheld transmitter. Again and again the artist communicated his exact location to a small portable VHF receiver placed on the floor in the center of the installation space. Installation visitors found canvases pinned to the walls as well as pens and pencils readily available to them for marking and listing the locations indicated in the artist's transmissions. Thus, drawings in progress by the visitors/radio listeners emerged and became vital parts of the installation. A further, slightly different version of *Inside–Outside* took place at the Institute of Contemporary Arts (ICA) in London.

Gottfried Bechtold in action for *Project for Bregenz*, Bregenz, Austria, 1973.

A year earlier, in 1972, Bechtold had realized *100 Days in Kassel* at documenta V. For this project, the artist transmitted his location in the city several times a day to the Fridericianum, the main documenta venue. There, the artist's messages were broadcast over the public address system and protocolled in type script.

As a direct precursor to the Edinburgh/London project *Inside–Outside*, Bechtold realized *Project for Bregenz*, in his Austrian home town, in 1973.

Inside–Outside was part of the Austrian Exhibition at the Demarco Gallery, Edinburgh Festival, 1973. The exhibition presented a survey of Austrian art of the nineteen-sixties and early seventies curated by Richard Demarco.

Communication Breakdown

Caoimhín Mac Giolla Léith

In view of the relatively arcane, obscure, or private nature of some of Garrett Phelan's more recent artworks, it is useful to recall that his earliest artistic enterprises were highly collaborative, accessible to a wide public, and generally facilitatory in intent. In 1993, Phelan, along with Mark McLoughlin, set up *Random Access Soundworks* in Bow Lane Recording Studios as a workshop for artists working in the visual domain who were interested in using sound as a creative medium. Each artist selected was provided with professional pre-production advice, a high-spec recording studio, and a qualified sound engineer for forty-eight hours, all paid for by funds procured from the Irish Arts Council. The work produced was then published and distributed free of charge to a selection of key venues, publications, and individuals involved in sound art internationally. Three compilation CDs were produced between 1993 and 1998. During this same period, Phelan and McLoughlin also set up *A.A.R.T.–Radio (Audio Artists Radio Transmissions)*, a temporary, licensed radio station designed to provide an alternative arts programming format to that of the national networks by airing the work of some two hundred artists, many of whom were renowned internationally for their pioneering use of sound within an expanded notion of the visual arts. Run on a modest budget with technical assistance from veterans of pirate radio, yet

This essay is reprinted from: Caoimhín Mac Giolla Léith, «Communication Breakdown,» in *MADE*, ed. Garrett Phelan (Dublin, 2004).

fully ratified by the relevant authorities, *A.A.R.T.* broadcast over a ten-day period in autumn 1994 from the Irish Museum of Modern Art, Dublin as part of From Beyond the Pale, an exhibition offering an alternative, anti-canonical reading of the history of twentieth-century art. Five years later, *A.A.R.T.* reconfigured itself as a four-day-long, live-broadcast, collective «research and development project» emanating from Arthouse in downtown Dublin and avowedly bent on the acoustic exploration of «the physics of radio.» Issues of authority, ratification, and access were at the heart of Phelan and McLoughlin's work throughout this period.

1993–98 were fruitful years on a number of fronts for Phelan/McLoughlin, who described themselves at the time as «a curatorial production team working in and promoting peripheral art forms.» Many of the concerns initially addressed in their collaborative works have remained crucial to Phelan's subsequent work as a solo artist. In addition to those already cited, these include the related questions of communication and codedness, iconicity and obscurity, public art and private language. The first artwork produced by the partnership, with the invited collaboration of fashion photographer Brendan Bourke, was *HERO* (1994). This was a large-scale, photo-text work depicting a rifle-toting figure in generic paramilitary garb mounted on a horse in a field, accompanied by the legend TO RIDE/ TO SHOOT/ TO TELL/ THE TRUTH. By invoking the motto of the Pony Express, the work equates violence with truth-telling and conflates the American myth of the conquest of the West with the iconography of Irish militant politics. The romance of a high moral code is blended with the low farce of heroic self-delusion to produce the slightly ridiculous image of a paramilitary cowboy. *HERO* may be seen against the contemporary background of a simultaneous legislative push in the U.S. to restrict the carrying of arms and attempts in Ireland to relax the broadcasting ban on representatives of paramilitary interests. Brendan Bourke also collaborated with Phelan/McLoughlin a year later to produce a video work, *Yellow: Minimum Analysis, Maximum Action* (1995). A cigar-smoking crooner in a tuxedo strolls onto a soundstage with a bright yellow backdrop. He seats himself on a high stool as the music swells, and there he awaits his cue. This he repeatedly fluffs only to leave the stage at the end of the song without ever singing a note. This «yellow-pack» comedy of errors, a display of ludicrous indecisiveness entailing the endless deferment of dubious pleasures, was designed to be screened in the specific context of a supermarket. A third work, *Kippure* (1995), was produced in response to the publication of a Government Green Paper on

Broadcasting and was installed in a group show in a commercial art gallery. It comprised a panoramic photograph of the eponymous radio transmission mast in the Dublin mountains accompanied by a 1-watt radio transmission of pre-recorded ambient noise from the windblown summit of Kippure. This transmission could be picked up on a radio Walkman within the confines of the gallery and its immediate vicinity, incidentally emphasizing the porousness of the gallery space. In their different ways, the vacuous political icon, the bungled commercial schmaltz, and the «empty» radio transmission featured in these three works all signal a fundamental breakdown in communication.

Convolutions of communication also featured in the installations *Time is, Time was, Time is past* (1996) and *What God Hath Wrought* (1997), both of which invoked the spirit of Samuel Morse, a man who forsook his early endeavors in the visual arts for the invention of pioneering technologies of communication. *Time is, Time was, Time is past* was a complex, two-part artwork involving the transmission in Morse Code of the work's title by the 2nd Field Signal Corps of the Irish Army and its subsequent representation, in both documented and recorded format, within the context of an elaborate installation at Le Confort Moderne, Poitiers, France and subsequently at the Irish Museum of Modern Art (which is

Phelan/McLoughlin,
KIPPURE, installation,
1995.

housed in a former military hospital), involving photography, light, sound, and radio transmission. The backdrop of the installation was a stylized «drawing in light» of a nineteenth-century signal tower, one of a series of towers dotted along the Irish coast, which were used by the British to protect Ireland from French Naval Forces during the Napoleonic Wars. The work's title is a quotation from Erasmus Darwin, friend and colleague of the Irish telegraphy inventor Richard Lowell Edgeworth. The title of *What God Hath Wrought*, on the other hand, echoes the first message ever sent in Morse Code.

The visual component in this work took the form of a wall text in vinyl in which the title of the piece was «spelt out» in the dots and dashes conventionally used for the written rendition of Morse Code. By enlisting the aid of the Irish Army, Phelan registered the apparent necessity of covert communication for the purpose of maintaining public order, or in the interests of national defense. Yet the most commonly known message to be regularly transmitted in Morse, SOS, is an urgent communication of individual or collective distress. This play between notions of obscurity and concealment, on the one hand, and of communicative efficiency and immediacy, on the other, may be read reflexively as a comment on the relationship between contemporary art and its various audiences, a reading the artist himself endorses. Phelan distinguishes at least three levels of audience with whom an artwork might be expected to communicate in different ways: what he refers to as the work's «principal audience,» that is, the artist(s) who produces it; «a secondary audience which is informed to some degree of the work's existence and content,» which is to say an «art audience»; and a third «accidental audience,» who might encounter the work unexpectedly. Needless to say, the degree of control it is possible to exert over the potential meaning of a given artwork vis-à-vis these three audiences varies considerably.

The question of the mediation of meaning in contemporary art was explicitly addressed in one of Phelan and McLoughlin's final works as a team. For... *one truth teaches another...* (1997), they employed the artist Maurice O'Connell as a «spokesperson» and contracted him to broadcast a series of nineteen daily «discourses on contemporary art,» each addressing a topic suggested by the commissioning artists and lasting one hour. This oblique contemporary echo of Joshua Reynolds's *Discourses on Art* took place within the context of a group show at the Royal Hibernian Academy's Gallagher Gallery, whose historical indebtedness to the model of Reynolds's Royal Academy is considerable. By delegating the

Phelan/McLoughlin, *Time is, Time was, Time is past*, detail, Le Confort de Moderne, Poitiers, France, 1995.

Phelan/McLoughlin, *Time is, Time was, Time is past*, original installation, Le Confort de Moderne, Poitiers, France, 1995.

responsibility for communicating with their audience to a third party, Phelan and McLoughlin might initially appear to be relinquishing some control over the production of meaning and willingly diminishing their authority as artists/producers. This, however, was decidedly not the case. On the contrary; the inordinate constraints under which the ordinarily freethinking (and, indeed, freewheeling) O'Connell was required to operate were designed, as Phelan puts it, «to get him to deliver what we wanted him to,» rather than allow him the freedom to be presented as their intermediary, and the myriad conditions under which he was bound hinted at the dogmatic nature of traditional academic thinking while at the same time functioning as a wry reminder of our natural human resistance to situations in which we cannot be sure that we say what we mean or mean what we say.

Black Brain Radio

A Voice That Dims the Bliss of Union

Sarah Pierce

> Radio is provided with its cloak of invisibility,
> like any other medium. It comes to us ostensibly
> with person-to-person directness that is private
> and intimate, while in more urgent fact, it is
> really a subliminal echo chamber of magical
> power to touch remote and forgotten chords.[1]
> — *Marshall McLuhan*

Picture in your mind's eye, a reserve of land that extends out from the edge of a metropolis towards the sea. Along the southeast stretch, running adjacent to the mouth of a wide river, the land curves in the direction of a broad strand. Before the strand is a low, man-made hill, the landfill of a retired dump, covered in wild flowers. Beyond it industrial docklands stretch out in the distance where skeletal cranes hover over low-lying cement beds. In this *terrain vague*, urban space disperses into what we name the outskirts, the periphery, the fringes. The places farthest from the city center where boroughs meet unclothed and unprotected. Pasolini's Roma. Stripped bare. This is where the city is its most essential—water, gas, waste, concrete. Architecture, always the more obvious, celebrated intervention is neither revered nor lasting here. Structures divested of glory, organs exposed, limbs raw. Cables, towers, drains. Our will to reconstruct our surroundings infiltrates the land, the air, the sea. Unseen energies concentrate and expand, channeling our existence. Through invisible wavelengths, we tune in.[2]

In a history of radio, the story goes that the world's first radio broadcast took place in 1916 upon the Irish Easter Rising when rebels used wireless telegraphy to transmit a mass message, informing anyone who might be listening, in Morse Code, that an Irish republic had been claimed in Dublin.[3] Forty-eight years later, in 1964, Marshall McLuhan wrote, «Radio is not only a mighty awakener of archaic memories, forces and animosities, but a decentralizing pluralistic force...»[4] Radio, like all media, has the power to form opinion, but it does so along local lines, tapping communal principles as opposed to universal ones. It is the nature of radio to dissent, to deviate, to interrupt and disrupt, especially in times of violent implosion. Unlike television, the mighty pacifier, radio incites both fascism and revolt. It has global appeal, yet no globalizing tendencies—in India, in Asia, in Africa, in Europe, in South America it works to nativize, to recuperate. Radio speaks the tribal drum. The more we identify with its cadence, the more localized we become. Radio unites us in blindness; where voices go unheard, it amplifies. The symbolic and real effects of radio on the twentieth century, and its ties in the twenty-first to the most intimate, private, and small communities, lead us to the world of *Black Brain Radio*.

The role of radio in Garrett Phelan's work traces back to 1994. In collaboration with artist Mark McLoughlin, Phelan established *A.A.R.T.*,[5] located temporarily in the Irish Museum of Modern Art in Dublin. The station broadcast for a ten-day period, reconfiguring again in 1999 over a four-day live transmission from Arthouse in Dublin's city center. Set up as an alternative arts program relative to national Irish radio, *A.A.R.T.* introduced the work of some two hundred artists to the Irish airwaves, including many well-known international artists using sound in an expanded media.[6] The meaning of these broadcasts was invariably

1 Marshall McLuhan, «Radio: The Tribal Drum,» in *Understanding Media: The Extensions of Man*, 6th ed. (New York: Signet, 1964), p. 263.

2 As a point of passing interest, this description wittingly echoes Phelan's portrayal of the Irishtown Nature Reserve in *The Electro Skylark*, a site of daily walks where he has done recordings, and where he did much of his thinking about *Black Brain Radio*.

3 Peter Mulryan, *Radio Radio* (Dublin: Borderline, 1988), p. 2. See also McLuhan 1964 (see note 1), p. 266.

4 Marshall McLuhan 1964 (see note 1), p. 267.

5 Audio Artists Radio Transmissions

6 For more on the early use of sound and radio in Phelan's work, see Caoimhín Mac Giolla Léith, «Communication Breakdown,» in this volume, first published in *MADE*, ed. Garrett Phelan (Dublin: Garrett Phelan, 2004). See also Annie Fletcher, «Knowledge and Life,» same volume.

7 *Black Brain Radio*, Temple Bar Gallery & Studios and in partnership with the Irish Museum of Modern Art (IMMA). The transmission was broadcast around the clock over a thirty-day period from January 19 to February 17, 2006 to listeners within the greater County Dublin area on 89.9 FM.

impacted by the «medium» content of the project, which was bound up in the modality of radio. Exercising official (licensed) and high-tech means of production, *A.A.R.T.* arose out of a do-it-yourself mutiny against the powers-that-be who monopolize art's *dissemination*, especially in relation to types of expression that are not easily absorbed into an official canon. The context for these early broadcasts was an exhibition that attempted to highlight alternative or peripheral practices. One must question whether this type of strategic sanctioning by museum curators opens up the canon to its fallacies and fallibility, or reestablishes its precepts by ghettoizing what remains «outside.» A truly cynical position claims that these temporary infusions actually change the way we experience art.

In a significant return to radio in 2006, Phelan presented a month-long artwork entitled *Black Brain Radio* on 89.9 FM in Dublin.[7] The pre-recorded broadcasts, read aloud by the artist, are the result of compiled media sources—shortwave and longwave radio, cable link, newspaper articles, webcasts, and so on—translated into two-minute audio segments. Phelan spent approximately two months collating and editing the information, ending up with thirty days of material; roughly three hours of content per day in ninety, two-minute segments that repeat several times over a twenty-four-hour broadcast. Using an MP3 player

Garrett Phelan,
NOW:HERE, installation
drawing, Pallas Heights,
Dublin, Ireland, 2003.

Garrett Phelan,
RACER UNTITLED,
Firstsite, Colchester,
U.K., 2006.

to randomly shuffle the segments, the artist recited each three-hour broadcast back into a recorder, in effect reducing the various formats into one streamlined verbal message. Phelan's working methodology, at once automated and manic (described by Phelan as «days of nothingness»[8]) calls to mind an endless ingestion of information that simultaneously repeats and expels. As a result, the form of public address initiated by *Black Brain Radio* moves beyond the familiar pace of talk radio into a kind of disengaged semiconscious state of autism. Big Bang-quicksand-Uganda-Jesus Christ-warfare. The two-minute segments shift without warning, with no perceptible tonal segue between subject matter, so that any interpretation of content requires listeners to follow unusual, disjunctive, obsessive patterns of thought that are not fully established or developed.

The manner of output in *Black Brain Radio* triggers associations to other projects by Phelan, both collaborative and solo, where the seat of technology is communication.[9] Or is it the other way around? From *Kippure* (1995), *Time is, Time was, Time is past* (Phelan/McLouglin 1996), and *Scum of the Earth* (2002) to recent works that comprise *Formation of Opinion* (2003–ongoing), we come to understand communication *as* technology, as an amalgamation of hidden, coded, obscure, specialized languages that inscribe all forms of transmission. As such,

8   Phelan during a private interview with the author on January 8, 2007 at Trinity College, Dublin. Listening to *Black Brain Radio*, we can detect background noises—typing, a telephone ringing, occasional behind-the-scenes conversation—which dramatize the artist's tendency to «multitask» in order to cope with the tedium of recording the daily broadcasts. See also David Bell's introductory remarks in *The Cybercultures Reader*: «My experience of machines is always mediated by cultural factors; I'm never just sat at my computer, typing, without simultaneously logging on to all the ideas and images that clutter the mediascape and my own mindscape.» See David Bell, «Introduction I, Cybercultures Reader: a user's guide,» in *The Cybercultures Reader*, ed. David Bell and Barbara M. Kennedy (London: Routledge, 2000), p. 8.

9   It is important to note that *Black Brain Radio* contains several outputs besides radio broadcasts, including gallery installations, daily drawings, and a weblog. Phelan anticipated that many people listening to *Black Brain Radio* would tune in by accident.

10 Phelan's preoccupation with electromagnetics is analogous to McLuhan's: «If the human ear can be compared to a radio receiver that is able to decode electromagnetic waves and recode them as sound, the human voice may be compared to the radio transmitter in being able to translate sound into electromagnetic waves.» See McLuhan 1964 (see note 1), p. 83.

11 Phelan charts out *Formation of Opinion* in four chapters: 1) Reception of Information (the works *NOW:HERE, LUNGLOVE, GOD ONLY KNOWS, BLACK BRAIN RADIO*), 2) Cognition, 3) Action, and 4) Success and Failure.

12 *A Regurgitated Conversational Monologue of Little Political Consequence*, in *Enthusiasm!*, curated by Sarah Pierce and Grant Watson in association with Resonance 104.4 FM, London, Frieze Art Fair, October 12–15, 2006.

«discovery» in Phelan's work more often yields a «failure to assimilate» than any type of interactive, friendly, sociable encounter, and we frequently find ourselves utterly alone amidst the communal systems at play. In large-scale installations such as *NOW:HERE* (2003), *LUNGLOVE* (2004), and *GOD ONLY KNOWS* (2005), the immediacy of text and drawing as «technologies» correlates to the complex acoustic and visual material of works that precede *Formation of Opinion*, such as *RACER* (1997–2003). Seeing and hearing in *RACER* are closely connected— eye and ear are hyperaesthetic, hypersensitive, and charged.[10] This synthesis of sound and vision as magnetic, powerful forces foreshadows *Formation of Opinion*'s first phase, aptly referred to as «reception of information.»[11] Despite what is at times a visual surplus, it is interesting that in much of Phelan's work we enter a darkness, an infused privacy where we strain to see or where vision is conditional. Invisible elements beacon, like a compass that allows us to focus, to hone in. Likewise, images of blindness and speechlessness signify subjective shifts between impairment and agency, surrender and resurrection in works such as *Scum of the Earth* and, more recently, in a ten-minute radio performance, where the artist himself is blindfolded as he simultaneously listens to and recites a pre-recorded script.[12]

Garrett Phelan,
Black Brain Radio,
detail of marketing,
installation at IMMA,
Dublin, Ireland, 2006.

In her work on subjectivity and virtual reality, Margaret Morse writes, «Subjectivity can never be real or full, as it is always based on *simulation*.»[13] The spatial and temporal divisions between you and me, here and now, are fictive gaps that we use to smooth out the contradictions «between the world and language.» Our tacit agreement with one another is to enact a process of simulation, or what Algirdas Julien Greimas calls the «enunciative fallacy»—a fictitious reality based on proximity, contiguity, and simultaneity. Through language we approximate the world. What surfaces again and again in Phelan's work is a tendency for language to disrupt, for memory to dislocate, and for technology to destabilize our sense of reality as we receive, anticipate, and recover information. Speech in *Black Brain Radio* is an act of simulation, a way to re-present already selective «realities.» Phelan reads each text, committing it to his voice, thereby acting as an intermediary for the multiple subjectivities of *Black Brain Radio*. The very seamlessness of this narrative actually produces ruptures or gaps in the text, moments of suspension that, again, rely on a certain blindness, or *blindsidedness*. We are «in the dark,» without reference points or footnotes, without points of origin or coordinates in which to orient ourselves. We receive blindly. Dissociated information accumulates, leading us nowhere.

In a remarkable encounter entitled, *The Instant of My Death/Demeure: Fiction and Testimony*, Maurice Blanchot and Jacques Derrida each deliver texts that, coupled together, profoundly explore the philosophical and political implications of narrating personal experience. The first essay, by Blanchot, is a short piece in which he recounts a moment when a young man who has been brought before a firing squad during World War II suddenly finds himself released, just at the moment of his death. The incident, written in third person, is suggestively autobiographical—owing to the title and several remarks in the text, and also to a letter Blanchot once wrote about a similar incident in his own life. Insofar as

---

13 Margaret Morse, *Virtualities* (Bloomington: Indiana University Press, 1998), p.11.

14 Jacques Derrida, *Demeure: Fiction and Testimony*, trans. Elizabeth Rottenberg (Stanford: Stanford University Press, 2000), p.43. N.B.: Parts of this essay alter and adapt an earlier text by Pierce on Phelan's work, entitled «Species of fiction: *Field craft* and *The Electro Skylark*,» in *Mother's Annual* (Dublin: Mother's Tankstation, 2006). The author originally applied this analysis to *Field craft* and *The Electro Skylark*; both deal directly with observation through first-person narration.

15 See Jean-Luc Nancy, *Being Singular Plural* (Stanford: Stanford University Press, 2000), p.1. In every singular expression or interpretation, Nancy hears a multiplying of voices. The voice is shared. Every voice is in itself opened, plural, exposing itself to the outside world. It addresses itself to another, an outside. «We do not have meaning anymore because we ourselves are meaning—entirely, without reserve, infinitely, with no meaning other than ‹us.›»

The Instant of My Death raises questions about what such an experience might mean, near death becomes, in the instant that the man is released, a symptom of a life he *no longer possesses*. The second text is an extended critical essay by Derrida, whereby he asks, through exegesis of Blanchot's text, what it means to write about an experience that one cannot claim as one's own. Testimony, always public, has as its condition an event that cannot be rendered communicable. To retell is to lose the singularity of «what happened to me, to me, to me alone.»[14] While *Black Brain Radio* does not rely exclusively on testimony, it is distinctly presented in first person, in one voice, Phelan's. Yet, we know his voice is not his alone; that in essence the voice of *Black Brain Radio* is plural.

When testimony is shared, when a secret is no longer one's own, when the «personal» transitions into the public, into community, into the world, we arrive at the fundamental problem of *the political*. To whom, to what, does my life belong? If we consider *Black Brain Radio* within terms of literature, as a narrative that both claims and subsequently displaces Phelan's ownership or authority over the text, we can begin to understand its political relevance as a process of transposing singular beings into plural meanings.[15] To rephrase Margaret Morse's description of subjectivity: *community* can never be real or full, as it is always

Garrett Phelan,
Black Brain Radio,
detail of the marketing
installation, Temple Bar
Gallery, Dublin, Ireland,
2006.

based on simulation; community is an enunciative fallacy based on proximity, contiguity, and simultaneity. Here, *Black Brain Radio* enters a discussion of globalization. From our cars, our homes, our places of work, we receive a stream of migrating references, a temporal interplay more akin to a map of «incidents» than a map of geographies. If globalization is the reality of being interconnected, and captures the speed at which these connections occur, then *Black Brain Radio* offers an opposing logic. It is the reality where we emerge not as a globalized network, but as *code inconnu*. The more we connect, the more miscommunication and omission become fundamental, even essential, to our experience. Paolo Pasolini often used the word «sacred» to describe the images that he excluded from the frame. What we see is merely one part of reality—the truly essential remains unseen. Just as Pasolini adapts the filmic frame, Phelan exploits our frame of reference, and what we hear is not the whole story. *Black Brain Radio* reverses globalism's pretext of cause-and-effect and in doing so conceals one secret to reveal another.

In order to appreciate *Black Brain Radio* in relation to its primary medium, it is necessary to understand that it radically relinquishes radio to multiple outputs, leaving us *denativized*. A kind of apositivistic epistemology is at play, where information disorganizes us; fills «us» with uncertainty. McLuhan's tribal drum gives rise to sporadic messages rife for misinterpretation. *Black Brain Radio* is site-specific, yet specifically un-sited. We connect through an ungroundedness, which carves out commonalities that are difficult to manage under any guise of the «global.» There is no mythical *communality* to our togetherness. We are the depth of our misery, the mendacity of our conceits, our fickle bonds, our exceptional divergences, our boredom, our violence, our mistakes.

A black brain. Dense yet penetrable. Masking the very subjects it represents. Its content is absence. A nervous void where each synapse has the potential to paralyze or liberate. The incongruities of those moments when we reveal ourselves to the world are precisely when we exceed a singular existence. Every experience from birth to death is recorded somewhere in the brain. An electrical circuit, amidst countless billions, there, simply waiting to be remembered. *Black Brain Radio* is our experience. *Black Brain Radio* is us.

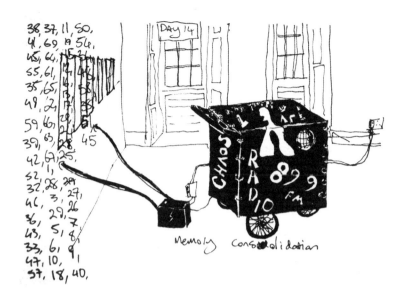

38, 37, 11, 50,
4, 69, 9, 54,
45, 64, 15
55, 61, 4,
35, 65, 4,
49, 2,
59, 6,
39, 65, 28 45
42, 67, 25,
1,
52, 28, 29
32, 28, 27,
46, 3, 26
36, 29, 7
43, 5, 8,
33, 61, 9
47, 10, 9
57, 18, 40,

Memory Consolidation

43, 50, 41, 66,
53, 20, 26, 62,
23, 30, 36, 72,
53, 10, 16, 3,
57, 40, 52, 7,
27, 45, 32, 4,
37, 55, 42, 5,
17, 25, 63, 6,
44, 35, 73, 8,
54, 15, 67, 9,
24, 59, 64, 46,
34, 29, 68, 47,
14, 39, 60, 48,
28, 19, 70,
38, 51, 69,
14, 21, 61,
18, 31, 71,

DAY 29

CHANGE

IS OUR ONLY
COMMONALITY

Garrett Phelan, *Black Brain Radio Archive*, pen on
paper, 2006. From archive of drawings, made on
consecutive days during the entire project duration
and displayed along the walls of Temple Bar Gallery
as an exhibition in progress.

Media Space

Networked Structures in Early Radio Communication

Daniel Gethmann

In light of the first optical telegraphic connection, established by Claude Chappe in 1794 between Paris and Lille via twenty-three signal stations, a new paradigm has emerged in the discourse on the networked structure of communications. For a conception was formed in regard to this network, which by the mid-nineteenth century had branched outward in a star shape, where crosslines between the connections joining different localities would be spanned, in order to enable several transmission paths between transmitter and receiver without having to remain solely dependent on overcoming the shortest connection.[1] The transition from optical to electrical telegraphy has expanded this network structure on such a scale that the worldwide system of cable connections gives even the category of space a whole new cognitive dimension: beyond their communicative mission to redefine the national terrain in the aftermath of the French Revolution, the telegraphic communications networks, soon realized on an even grander scale, gave rise to today's concept of so-called globalized spaces. The fact that their conception of dynamic dispositives is induced in the media itself demonstrates to what extent the potential of media technologies reaches beyond the mere reproduction of social structures.[2]

As early as 1858, U.S. President James Buchanan dispatched a greeting to Queen Victoria in England via the first, short-lived transatlantic cable, characterizing this suboceanic cable as the decisive factor in this new means of communication, as a technological instrument that would achieve no less than «to diffuse religion, liberty, and law throughout the world.»[3] In the second half of the nineteenth century, this discourse would be used to legitimate rapid European colonial expansion, both fostered by and dependent upon the extension of the worldwide telegraph network. As a «Tool of Empire,»[4] the telegraph connections at the time of Guglielmo Marconi's initial experiments—that is, the year radio was invented—were already so extensive that one could send a message around the globe and back, as William Henry Preece, chief engineer of the British General Post Office (GPO), the most important global telegraph network at the time, asserted in 1895: the message is carried on its way exclusively over cable networks, meaning human messengers are no longer necessary to span gaps between unconnected telegraph lines, and it takes approximately fifty-six hours for the message to circle the earth, at a cost of about eighteen dollars per word.[5] Rudyard Kipling describes this submarine telegraph network in 1896 in his poem *The Deep-Sea Cables*, in which he puts into words the notion of the new concept of space induced by this technology:

1   Patrice Flichy argues that the network concept used to describe communication, derived from the organic discourse on the circulation of blood, appears almost concurrently in administrative discourses carried out in municipal organizations, the common thread being a perception of the city as organism. The idea of a networked communications structure is based on the emerging telegraph networks and describes a structure in which previously unconnected lines are subject to a common arrangement, so that «the fastest possible transmission did not necessarily coincide with the shortest transmission route.» See Patrice Flichy, *Tele. Geschichte der modernen Kommunikation* (Frankfurt and New York, 1994), p. 57. On the routing of telegraph lines, see Rolf Oberliesen, *Information, Daten und Signale: Geschichte technischer Informationsverarbeitung* (Reinbek, 1982), pp. 59–62.

2   See the detailed explanation provided in Harold Adams Innis, *Empire and Communications* (Oxford, 1950).

3   «May the Atlantic telegraph, under the blessing of heaven, prove to be a bond of perpetual peace and friendship between the kindred nations, and an instrument destined by Divine Providence to diffuse religion, liberty, and law throughout the world.» Greeting telegram from President James Buchanan to Queen Victoria in 1858, quoted in Paul M. Kennedy, «Imperial Cable Communications and Strategy, 1870–1914,» *English Historical Review* 86 (1971), pp. 728–52, here p. 730. When the first commercial radio-telephone connection bridged the Atlantic nearly seventy years later, the publisher of the *New York Times*, Adolph S. Ochs, posed on January 7, 1927 to the publisher of the London *Times*, Geoffrey Dawson, the question—pertaining to the new media space of electromagnetic waves—as to who in the face of this communications technology could still possess the temerity to claim that prayers were not heard up in heaven?

4   See Daniel R. Headrick, *The Tools of Empire: Technology and European Imperialism in the Nineteenth Century* (New York and Oxford, 1981).

5   See Henry Muir, «The Telegraph Systems of the World: Their rapid growth, their wide extent, their close cooperation,» *McClure's Magazine* 5, no. 2 (July 1895), pp. 99–112, here p. 101.

... There is no sound, no echo of sound, in the deserts of the deep,
Or the great gray level plains of ooze where the shell-blurred cables creep.
Here in the womb of the world—here on the tie-ribs of earth
Words, and the words of men, flicker and flutter and beat—
... And a new Word runs between: whispering, «Let us be one!»[6]

By the turn of the century, the appeal «Let us be one!» had long since been achieved by the cable connections, so that even the draft of a new French telegraph law on January 30, 1900 describes its political effects as prompted by the motive of creating a legal framework for cable communication with the country's own colonies, surmising that England, and thus the British Empire, probably owed its global influence more to telegraphy than to its famous navy.[7]

The structures of this—by the end of the nineteenth century—virtually closed, globe-spanning network, comprised of economic interests and telegraph cables with their local stations, were to take on a new dynamic at the beginning of the twentieth century through the invention of radio. Radio had the effect of delimiting the local spatial structures, with the communication route nodes—forming a telegraphic paradigm, spanning from the ancient Greek fire telegraph to the transatlantic cables, bound to geographically concrete localities (and relays)—consequently bringing points at all locations into communication with each other.[8] Michel Foucault describes this change as follows: «We are in the epoch of simultaneity: we are in the epoch of juxtaposition, the epoch of the near and far, of the side-by-side, of the dispersed. We are at a moment, I believe, when our experience of the world is less that of a long life developing through time than that of a network that connects points and intersects with its own skein.»[9]

The understanding of the world as a «network that connects points and intersects with its own skein» demonstrates to what a large extent our idea of the world depends on our communications conditions. The concept of this novel network structure thus implies a break between the concrete locale of the telegraph and the points in communications space. What were the forces within the network structure that negated the notion of the world as an organism full of cable connections as nerve strands—the center of which surely lay at the end of the All Red Line in London—in favor of a dynamic matrix where points can communicatively connect without locality and presumably without extension? Even before Marconi's experiments, physicist Oliver Heaviside provided in 1891 an answer to this question in the introduction to his multivolume *Electromagnetic Theory*, citing

«James Clark Maxwell's field theory,» which in his view was at heart a «theory of dielectric displacement.»[10] The very word «displacement» used to describe this theory articulates its revolutionary impact on our concepts of space, which would henceforth be subsumed instead under Maxwell's «radiational theory.»[11] The theory focuses on the electromagnetic field, confirmed by the experiments of Heinrich Hertz (1886–88) showing that electromagnetic waves by their very nature overcome the category of a locality within the network of communication, as Heaviside laconically remarked: «Still, however, the theory wanted experimental proof. Three years ago electromagnetic waves were nowhere. Shortly after, they were everywhere.»[12]

For both of these contrary characteristics of electromagnetic waves—being nowhere and being everywhere—a concrete locality no longer plays a role. Instead, transmitters in a radial network replace the former cable communications relays, giving rise to a multidimensional media space, the properties of which, in Heaviside's notion, are ensured by a self-inherent medium «continuously filling all space,»[13] constituting the precondition for the fact that transmission of electromagnetic waves between any two points in communications space is possible at all. The locality and thus the matter itself represent, in this concept, more

6 Rudyard Kipling, «The Deep-Sea Cables,» in *Complete Verse* (1896; repr., New York, 1989), p. 173.

7 See Daniel R. Headrick, *The Invisible Weapon: Telecommunications and International Politics 1851–1945* (New York and Oxford, 1991), pp. 102–105; Kennedy 1971 (see note 3), p. 748.

8 The dispositive of point-to-point telecommunication comprises—as communications configuration in the transition from telegraph networks to wireless radio stations in the early twentieth century—all conceivable forms of the expanding radio communications. These were defined in the United States Radio Act of August 13, 1912, which was designed to create a legal basis for controlling the expanding realm of radio: «That the expression ‹radio communication› as used in this act means any system of electrical communication by telegraphy or telephony without the aid of any wire connecting the points from and at which the radiograms, signals, or other communications are sent or received.» United States Radio Act, 1912, reproduced in Captain Linwood S. Howeth, *History of Communications Electronics in the United States Navy* (Washington, 1963), pp. 570–74.

9 Michel Foucault, «Von anderen Räumen,» in Michel Foucault, *Schriften*, vol. 4 (1967; repr., Frankfurt am Main, 2005), pp. 931–42, here p. 931. This translation from French to English by Jay Miskowiec, see http://foucault.info/documents/heteroTopia/foucault.heteroTopia.en.html (accessed October 2007).

10 Oliver Heaviside, *Electromagnetic Theory*, vol. 1 (London, 1891/1893; repr., New York, 1971), p. 5.

11 Oliver Heaviside, «Theory of Electric Telegraphy,» in *Encyclopaedia Britannica*, 10th ed., vol. 33, s.v. «Telegraphy» (London, 1902), pp. 213–18, here p. 213.

12 Heaviside 1891/1893 (see note 10), p. 5.

13 «Perhaps the simplest view to take of the medium which plays such a necessary part, as the recipient of energy, in this theory, is to regard it as continuously filling all space, and possessing the mobility of a fluid rather than the rigidity of a solid. If whatever possess the property of inertia be matter, then the medium is a form of matter. But away from ordinary matter it is, for obvious reasons, best to call it as usual by a separate name, the ether.» Oliver Heaviside, «On the Forces, Stresses,

Network of optical
telegraph lines in
France, 1846.

than a random, entity-like arrangement in an enveloping, experimental media space «which immediately surrounds it,»[14] whose property of omnipresent diffusion is defined a priori before all further space-shaping factors. No longer tied to a specific location, the reality which we term «field» can epistemologically «no longer be thought of as a complex of physical things, rather it is the expression for an embodiment of physical relations.»[15] These relations call into question the notion of the world as one single, large organism, reconceiving it in the context of relational network connections within the field. The mechanics of the body thus lose significance inasmuch as the question of transmission potential within the comprehensive and dense media space pushes the optimally arranged, site-bound structures into the background. At the same time, the widely expanding transmission space enables the transition from a station-bound communication form to a multidimensional, dynamic addressability of wireless systems. In this sense, wireless telegraphy and telephony initially add to the closed networks, with cable connections between two localities, the structural innovation of spanning from transmitting and reception stations an open network to ships at sea, in effect releasing the control over maritime traffic from domination by local harbors.[16] Wireless, point-to-point communication accordingly enables an ad-

and Fluxes of Energy in the Electromagnetic Field,» in *Electrical Papers*, vol. 2 (London and New York, 1891/1892), pp. 521–74, here p. 524.

14 Ibid., p. 524.

15 Ernst Cassirer, *Philosophie der symbolischen Formen*, vol. 3, *Phänomenologie der Erkenntnis*, 2nd ed. (1954; repr., Darmstadt, 1990), pp. 544–45.

16 «The sea may be viewed as the actual field in which wireless telegraphy acts, on the one hand because sea water forms a better transmission medium for electrical waves than the earth, and on the other because on the seas there is the possibility and the need for traffic between floating stations.» Domenico Mazzotto, *Drahtlose Telegraphie und Telephonie* (Munich and Berlin, 1906), p. 358.

17 «Hence the waves accommodate themselves to the surface of the sea, in the same way as waves follow wires. The irregularities make confusion, no doubt, but the main waves are pulled round by the curvature of the earth, and do not jump off.» Heaviside 1902 (see note 11), p. 215.

18 Ibid.

19 This hypothesis, which couldn't be proven scientifically until twenty years later, was formulated in 1902 both by Heaviside and by Arthur Edwin Kennelly, a Harvard professor and former colleague of R. A. Fessenden. See Arthur E. Kennelly, «On the Elevation of the Electrically Conducting Strata of the Earth's Atmosphere,» *Electrical World and Engineer* 39 (March 15, 1902), p. 473. The description «Heaviside layer» was suggested by W. H. Eccles in 1912 in the context of his physical calculations of the spread of waves. See W. H. Eccles, «On the Diurnal Variations of the Electric Waves Occurring in Nature, and on the Propagation of Electric Waves Round the Bend of the Earth,» *Proceedings of the Royal Society*, A, vol. 87 (1912), pp. 79–99, here p. 94.

20 The conceptual prerequisite for the notion of an all-encompassing media space of transmission consisted in experimentally demonstrating its ability to extend across the curved surface of the earth. In the theory positing the spread of electromagnetic waves via a «sufficiently conducting layer in the upper air,» the media space is conceived of as its own, terrestrially boundless, but by no means infinite, space. Its definition is thus based on

Survey map of inter-
national telegraph
connections, Berlin,
1886.

Daniel Gethmann
Media Space

dressability at a «dispersed» locality (Foucault) at sea, where communication transactions in spatially dynamic networks constitute a new topography of passage comprised of moving points.

From the analogy that the electromagnetic waves «accommodate themselves to the surface of the sea,»[17] Heaviside as a logical consequence posits his 1902 spatial-theoretical theory of a multidimensional, enveloping media space, while formulating what is probably his most famous hypothesis: «There may possibly be a sufficiently conducting layer in the upper air. If so, the waves will, so to speak, catch on to it more or less. Then the guidance will be by the sea on one side and the upper layer on the other.»[18] Only the reflection of the electromagnetic waves in the ionosphere, later referred to as the «Heaviside layer,»[19] facilitates their nature of being everywhere, precisely through the restriction of their dispersion. The media space widely spanning the earth hence becomes concrete only when its unlimited expansion is no longer conceived as infinite.[20] For its conductive enclosure by the sea's surface on one side and the ionosphere on the other is what forms the conceptual premise for the concept of a Heaviside space: the multidimensional and enveloping media space enabling the transmission of electromagnetic waves, unfolding at the beginning of the twentieth century.

a differentiation made by Bernhard Riemann in his 1854 habilitation lecture with regard to the constructions of space «when these empirical determinations are extended beyond the limits of observation.» It seemed to him vital in this respect to «distinguish between unboundedness and infinite extent, the former belonging to the extent-relations, the latter to the measure-relations.» Bernhard Riemann, *Über die Hypothesen, welche der Geometrie zugrunde liegen* (Göttingen 1854/1867; repr., Darmstadt, 1959), p. 21.

21 Oliver Heaviside already raised the question in an unpublished letter to the editor of *Electrician* in spring 1902, «if the recent success of Mr. Marconi in telegraphing from Cornwall to Newfoundland might not be due to the presence of a permanently conducting upper layer in the atmosphere.» Quoted in W. H. Eccles, «Wireless Communication and Terrestrial Magnetism,» *Nature* 119, no. 2987 (January 29, 1927), p. 157.

22 Hans Bredow, Christmas address to the American people, recorded in Berlin, Vox Studios, December 9, 1924 (archived at the *Deutsches Rundfunkarchiv* [DRA], Frankfurt am Main), quoted in Peter Dahl, *Radio:*

Sozialgeschichte des Rundfunks für Sender und Empfänger (Reinbek, 1983), p. 103.

23 Using an electrolytic detector and a telephone receiver, Fessenden succeeded on December 23, 1900 in wirelessly transmitting spoken language over a distance of one mile with a spark gap transmitter and two fifteen-meter-high antenna masts. He spoke the first test words on behalf of the Weather Bureau in Rock Point, Maryland, after having an apparatus constructor named Brashear build an «interrupter» designed by S.M. Kintner, which was capable of interrupting the electric circuit 10,000 times per second. The device was produced «by scribing fine grooves longitudinally on a phonograph cylinder» (Hugh J. Aitken, *The Continuous Wave: Technology and American Radio, 1900–1932* [Princeton, 1985], p. 61) and achieved more or less the expected frequency. In addition, Fessenden also integrated a carbon microphone into the spark transmitter: «Transmission over a distance of one mile was attained but the character of the speech was not good and it was accompanied by an extremely loud and disagreeable noise, due to the irregularity of the spark.» Reginald Aubrey Fessenden, «Wireless Telephony,» *Transactions of the*

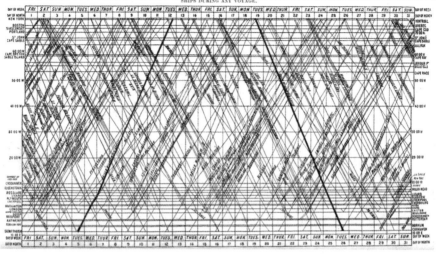

Marconi Telegraph
Communication Chart,
October 1909.

Initial evidence for this novel concept of space was previously provided, on December 12, 1901, by the experimental and media-technological breakthrough that occurred when Guglielmo Marconi, stationed in St. John's in Newfoundland, received a radio signal from Poldhu in Cornwall, having managed to cross the Atlantic despite the curvature of the earth.[21] But only after radio as medium of space had unfurled its electromagnetic law of everywhere, thus promising to make communication in future completely independent of spatial distance, could the virtual radio space develop within the Heaviside space of electromagnetic waves, a space whose characteristic feature the German radio pioneer Hans Bredow described in his 1924 Christmas radio broadcast, addressed to the American people, as follows:

> Man's ancient battle against the limitations of space and time has entered a new stage, ... now that it has become possible with the help of radio to spread news in a fraction of a second over the entire earth. This development has led to us viewing the world today as a common conference room, no matter whether we are neighbors or antipodes.[22]

American Institute of Electrical Engineers 27, part 1 (January 1 – June 30, 1908), pp. 553–629, here, p. 570. See also Reginald Aubrey Fessenden, «Wireless Telephony,» *The Electrical Review* 60 (February 15, 1907), p. 252.

24 Oliver Heaviside twice refused offers of employment in Fessenden's company (between October 1904 and January 1905) as advisor on the more complex mathematical issues. Fessenden needed assistance due to the fact that while setting up his transatlantic radio stations in Brant Rock, Massachusetts and Machrihanish, Scotland—for the purpose of sending wireless communications, including as voice connection over the ocean—he faced analytic mathematical problems in his attempts to improve signal transmission and reduce atmospheric interference, problems he was long unable to solve. See Paul J. Nahin, *Oliver Heaviside: Sage in Solitude. The Life, Work, and Times of an Electrical Genius of the Victorian Age* (New York, 1988), pp. 280–81.

25 Reginald A. Fessenden, «Wireless Telegraphy,» *The Electrical Review* 58, no. 1485 (May 11, 1906), pp. 744–46; and no. 1486 (May 18, 1906), pp. 788–89, here p. 789. Italics in original.

26 In preparing for his Christmas broadcast in 1906, Fessenden in fact realized, after the sudden loss of his Scottish radio station, how insignificant the planned range was for a public presentation of his new high-frequency alternator. Instead, he regarded public experimental presentation itself as being the decisive factor that would help his media technology to catch on, as had already been demonstrated by Guglielmo Marconi in the case of wireless telegraphy. Therefore, the purpose of Fessenden's first radio broadcast should not be confused with its content, because the primary focus was a large-scale demonstration of a successful technical experiment as opposed to a mere «transmission of ordinary speech, and also transmission of phonographic talking and music by wireless telephone between Brant Rock and Plymouth.» In addition to alerting the marine radio operators to the broadcast via telegraph, a personal invitation from the *American Telephone Journal* was also sent out by mail on December 11, 1906 to select professional colleagues, including Elihu Thomson and former co-workers such as Arthur Edwin Kennelly, in which recipients were informed not only of the above-quoted content but also of the purpose of the presentation:

The metaphor of the common conference room (*Sprechsaal*) is derived from the distancelessness of the world made possible by radio, having been first made audible in the innovative leap represented by Reginald Aubrey Fessenden's famous Christmas radio broadcast in December 1906, featuring violin music and poetry recitation. Fessenden was no longer interested only in transmitting the voice—this he had already achieved on December 23, 1900[23]—but now also in experimenting with transmitting the voice in Heaviside space.[24] Offering commercial radio service across the Atlantic—initially only for wireless telegraphy—seemed to him a very profitable proposition compared to the costs of the suboceanic cable. Fessenden derived from this the following economic consequence, formulated in 1906 in his business model for the National Electric Signaling Company (NESCO): «[it is] only in working across seas that wireless telegraphy can hope for an *immediate* return without the expenditure of several millions of capital ... It was for this reason that it was decided to commence commercial work in competition with cable companies rather than with landlines.»[25] In order to make this free competition possible in the first place, he set up a radio station in Machrihanish, Scotland in 1905 identical to the one in Brant Rock. On January 10, 1906, the two stations started communicating via a wireless telegraphic transmission and reception system founded on a synchronous rotary spark gap transmitter invented by Fessenden in 1905, leading in the course of the year to regular nighttime operations. A storm destroyed the Machrihanish radio station on December 5, 1906, however, so it could not be involved as planned in the experimental setup for the Christmas broadcast using the high-frequency alternator installed in the summer of 1906 in Brant Rock.[26] But expanding the experiments on voice transmission to the Heaviside space only became an option at all after Fessenden had intercepted a confidential report concerning the first transatlantic voice reception via radio. This happened due to events on a November night in 1906, one month prior to the storm, when a technician by the name of Stein in Brant Rock was exchanging information on how to operate the high-frequency transmitter with a colleague at the station in nearby Plymouth, a distance of 18 km. A technician named Armour at the radio station in Machrihanish, Scotland suddenly picked up «five or six sentences totaling between fifty and one hundred words»[27] of their conversation and recorded the words in the station's reception book. Since he didn't want to reveal what had happened via radio, he sent Fessenden a written report, the details of which were confirmed by Stein. Because the high frequency used for telegraphic radio communication over the Atlantic coincided with that used for the radio telephone connection between Brant Rock and Plymouth, the technician in Scotland had, according to Fessenden's records, «overheard Mr. Stein at the Brant Rock station giving instructions by wireless telephone to his assistant at the Plymouth wireless telephone station ... After ascertaining these facts, I decided to give a demonstration of transatlantic wireless telephony at the earliest possible moment.»[28] Yet Fessenden didn't make public mention of this first transatlantic radio reception until twelve years later, since he had first wanted to wait for the results of further tests: «A program of transatlantic telephonic tests was drawn up, and arrangements were made to carry out a series of telephonic tests between Brant Rock and Machrihanish.»[29] This project was interrupted by the destruction of the Scottish station, however, and with it the option of verifying his findings in a public experimental presentation. Fessenden decided to initially remain silent about the discovery of this extraordinary transmission range, while nevertheless recognizing the new market opportunities it harbored for the radio technology he had developed: «I believe, however, that there is a field for wireless telephony for long distance lines.»[30]

«A limited number of invitations have been issued to witness the operation of the National Electric Signaling Co.'s wireless telephone system between Brant Rock and Plymouth, Mass., over a distance of between ten and eleven miles.» Quoted in Fessenden 1908 (see note 23), p. 580.

27 Reginald Aubrey Fessenden, «The First Transatlantic Telephonic Transmission,» *Scientific American* 119, no. 10 (September 7, 1918), p. 189; see also Aitken 1985 (see note 23), pp. 73–74; John S. Belrose, «Reginald Aubrey Fessenden and the Birth of Wireless Telephony,» *IEEE Antennas and Propagation Magazine* 44, no. 2 (2002), pp. 38–47, here p. 44.

28 Fessenden 1918 (see note 27), p. 189.

29 Ibid.

30 Fessenden 1908 (see note 23), p. 606; on October 21, 1915, AT&T engineer B.B. Webb finally spoke into the microphone of the U.S. Navy transmitter in Arlington, Virginia— amplified by 300 Audion tubes connected in parallel—and was understood in Paris, with the Eiffel Tower functioning as antenna. «In these earlier tests, however, speech was received in Paris only at occasional moments when transmission conditions were exceptionally favorable.» H.D. Arnold and Lloyd Espenschied, «Transatlantic Radio Telephony,» *The Bell System Technical Journal* 2, no. 4 (October 1923), pp. 116–44, here p. 117.

31 See Dominik Schrage, «‹Anonymus Publikum›: Massenkonstruktion und die Politiken des Radios,» in *Politiken der Medien*, ed. Daniel Gethmann and Markus Stauff (Zurich and Berlin, 2005), pp. 173–94.

32 See Daniel Gethmann, «Technologie der Vereinzelung: Das Sprechen am Mikrophon im frühen Rundfunk,» in Gethmann and Stauff (see note 31), pp. 305–18.

33 «The inclination to search for, find, and celebrate forerunners is the most pronounced symptom of an inability to apply epistemological criticism. Before allowing two paths to merge seamlessly, one should at least first make sure they are really one and the same path.» Georges Canguilhem, «Der Gegenstand der Wissenschaftsgeschichte,» in *Wissenschaftsgeschichte und Epistemologie* (Frankfurt am Main, 1979), p. 34.

34 For a more detailed handling of this approach, see Daniel Gethmann, *Die Übertragung der Stimme: Vor- und Frühgeschichte des Sprechens im Radio* (Zurich and Berlin, 2006).

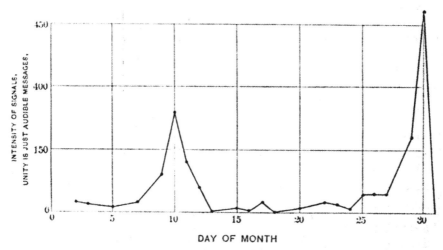

DAY OF MONTH

FIG. 47.—Curve showing variation of intensity of transatlantic
messages for the month of January, 1906

Diagram depicting
the message signal
strength between
the Fessenden trans-
mitters in Brant Rock,
MA and in Machri-
hanish, Scotland at
night, January 1906.

In contrast to wireless telephony from point to point, the famous Christmas 1906 broadcast was addressed to all radio stations within range; its effect was to release radio from its primarily military use by for the first time programmatically bringing together the technical experiments employing a high-frequency alternator for voice and music transmission with the social experiment of a public radio for everyone. The «hundred-year radio history» can thus be considered the connection of a technical and a social experimental situation, from which the third, the artistic, cannot be separated. In fact, the combination of the technical with the social experiment of radio is the essential factor for creating public radio, which originated with Fessenden's broadcast. This is why, despite the previous technical history, we speak today of 100 years of radio. At the beginning of this social experiment, however, neither the contents of broadcasts, nor the impact of radio on the structure and form of new of listener groups,[31] or even the development of specific radiophonic forms of communication[32] are of primary importance. Instead, the effects of the radio-spatial distancelessness contributed to a social reconception of the space globalized by wireless networks. These effects emerge from the point-to-point communications situation, revealing an analytical gaze upon being disengaged from the question of its alleged «forerunnership»

35 The prerequisite for the emergence of the virtual radio space within the Heaviside space lies not so much in the first voice communication experiments but rather above all in the replacement of the extremely expensive high-frequency alternator with the inexpensive and readily available tube technology based on the triode invented by Lee de Forest in 1906. Integrating this triode into the transmitting and receiving apparatus formed the springboard for the development of the local and popular radio broadcasting culture.

36 See reports on the tests in the *American Telephone Journal* issues of January 26 and February 2, 1907; Fessenden 1908 (see note 23), p. 580.

37 At the end of its first expansion phase (1899–1930), UFCO owned 1,409,148 hectares of arable land in Central America, only five percent of which (76,553 ha) were devoted to growing bananas. See Charles Morrow Wilson, *Empire in Green and Gold: The Story of the American Banana Trade* (New York, 1947), pp. 153–67; Stacy May and Galo Plaza, *The United Fruit in Latin America* (New York, 1958), pp. 5–6; Constance Orozco, *The United Fruit Company in Central America: A Bargaining*

Power Analysis, Texas papers on Latin America, nos. 91–07 (Austin, TX, 1991).

38 «Urgent communications from company offices in the United States were first telegraphed to Galveston, Texas; then they were dispatched by cable (usually out of order) via Mexico to San Juan del Sur, Nicaragua; here the messages were transferred to land lines owned and operated by the Nicaraguan government; after much delay, land lines owned and operated by the government of Costa Rica picked up the communications. The latter systems were frequently out of order and, when strife or ill will prevailed between Nicaragua and Costa Rica or the staffs of their respective national telegraph systems, the messages never crossed the boundary at all. But when and if the messages reached Costa Rica's capital, they were dispatched by United Fruit land lines to the Limón headquarters, and then by Carib Cayucos down the reef-strewn coast to Almirante Bay and Bocas.» See Wilson 1947 (see note 37), p. 154.

39 Lee de Forest had previously used the transmitters to issue reports on the «America's Cup» regatta. See ibid., p. 155.

for the formation of a virtual radio space by means of broadcasting,[33] but instead giving rise to an independent radio dispositive, asynchronously associated with public radio. Rather than interconnecting the various development phases in radio history with an epistemological focus on analyzing only their respective contributions to the establishment of public radio, we will instead examine in the following the question of the different media and communicative dispositives within a discontinuous history of radio as medium,[34] the differentiated investigation of which can also lend new contours to an analysis of its respective specific power effects.

After 1906, when radio in its second phase began to be increasingly identified as an apparatus for «wireless telephony,» imprinting itself on the virtual radio space within the Heaviside space,[35] an overlap was also witnessed between the communicative configuration of point-to-point communication and of the one-to-many principle. Marine radio as an early, non-military use of radio formed the experimental field for various forms of public communication. With his talent for publicity, Fessenden invited not only his professional colleagues and the local trade press to witness the reception of his first broadcast[36] but also alerted—via wireless telegraphy from Brant Rock, Massachusetts, three days before Christmas Eve 1906—all military and marine radio stations within range to his upcoming program. For this reason, in addition to the U.S. Navy radio operators and the invited journalists, there was also a third listener group witnessing the broadcast, the employers of whom seized upon Fessenden's program as an impetus to radically rethink their use of radio: the marine radio operators employed by the banana importer United Fruit Company (UFCO).

Founded in 1899 in Boston as a fusion of several smaller companies, UFCO quickly assumed market leadership in banana trade and developed into one of the first multinationals, acquiring extensive property in Central America and the Caribbean and moreover establishing an international communications structure.[37] The inadequate telegraphic cable connections in the region, along with complex production and transport logistics, made pioneering work in wireless communication necessary,[38] prompting the company to install two respective de Forest radio transmitters in Puerto Limón, Costa Rica and in Bocas del Toro, Panama as early as 1904, thereby erecting Central America's first radio stations.[39] In 1907, UFCO switched its shipboard equipment to radio devices designed by R. A. Fessenden, who had received numerous confirmations of reception from marine radio operators following his first radio broadcast, reportedly received after his second broadcast at New Year's, even from UFCO ships in the Caribbean.[40] Thus, a direct radio connection, using Fessenden's apparatus, spanning such a distance now for the first time seemed to be within the realm of possibility, and in «July 1907 the range was considerably extended and speech was successfully transmitted between Brant Rock and Jamaica, Long Island, a distance of nearly 200 miles.»[41] With the UFCO's ships in turn having good reception, these first broadcasting experiments consequently ended up (rather paradoxically) convincing the company to invest in point-to-point communications technology. The much greater range afforded by Fessenden's transmission and reception technology for wireless telegraphy can be deemed decisive here:

Experiments were then made between Brant Rock and the West Indies, a distance of 1700 miles, during the spring and summer of 1907. It was found that ... while there was great absorption for frequencies of 200,000 there was comparatively little absorption for frequencies in the neighborhood of 80,000 and messages were successfully transmitted in daylight with this latter frequency. No messages were received in daylight with

40 See Helen M. Fessenden, *Fessenden: Builder of Tomorrows* (New York, 1940), p. 153.
41 Peter Lertes, *Die drahtlose Telegraphie und Telephonie*, vol. 4, *Naturwissenschaftliche Reihe* (Dresden and Leipzig, 1922), p. 4. «In July 1907 the range was considerably extended and speech was successfully transmitted between Brant Rock and Jamaica, Long Island, a distance of nearly 200 miles, in daylight and mostly over land, the mast at Jamaica being approximately 180 ft. high.» Fessenden 1908 (see note 23), p. 581.
42 Fessenden 1908 (see note 23), p. 612. Fessenden believed that the target ranges for these reception experiments, conducted in the spring of 1907, could also be achieved in regular operations. He based this assumption on having received at Brant Rock, Massachusetts so-called echo signals from the Machrihanish, Scotland transmitter on various nights during 1906—signals that each echoed after circa every two tenths of a second. Fessenden attributed the delay to the fact that the signals arriving later must have come from the other side of the globe: «on certain nights there appeared to be indications at the

Boston station of a double set of impulses being received, one about a fifth of a second later than the other. It is too early yet to make any definite statement in regard to this matter, but there is some reason for thinking that the second set of signals arrived at the station after going the longer way round.» Fessenden 1906 (see note 25), p. 745; see also Belrose 2002 (see note 27), p. 45.
43 Fessenden 1908 (see note 23), p. 606.
44 Lee de Forest, *Father of Radio: The Autobiography of Lee de Forest* (Chicago, 1950), p. 4.
45 See Susan J. Douglas, *Inventing American Broadcasting 1899–1922* (Baltimore and London, 1987), p. 95.
46 Cleland Davis, quoted in Chen-Pang Yeang, «Scientific Fact or Engineering Specification? The U.S. Navy's Experiments on Wireless Telegraphy circa 1910,» *Technology and Culture* 45, no. 1 (January 2004), pp. 1–29, here p. 1. See also Aitken 1985 (see note 23), p. 87; on the conception of a «British Imperial Chain» in collaboration with Marconi, see Peter J. Hugill, *Global Communications since 1844: Geopolitics and Technology* (Baltimore and London, 1999), pp. 97–107.

the higher frequency, though messages transmitted from the same station and with the same power and frequency were officially reported as having been received at Alexandria, Egypt, a distance of approximately 4000 miles.[42]

This enormous range, projected by Fessenden likewise for «wireless telephony for long distance lines»[43] at the meeting of the American Institute of Electrical Engineers on June 29, 1908 in Atlantic City, persuaded UFCO to award Fessenden a large contract and in parallel to set up their own «Invisible Empire of the Air,»[44] even before Lee de Forest's invention of the Audion tube. The structure of this system essentially had less the character of a technical than of a social experiment with radio, with the effect of establishing a new socioeconomic order in globalized space predicated upon the new media technologies decisive for the emergence of this concept of space in the first place. The radio strategy pursued by Mack Musgrave, the first director of the United Fruit Telegraph Service, thus illustrated the effects of the radio-spatial distancelessness facilitating an unprecedented economic and political expansion of the company. The way in which this developmental step still realizes its wireless network structure within the hierarchical spatial matrix of cable telegraphy, based on a central station connected point-to-point with the other stations, while judging Fessenden's broadcasting as a mere public relations measure for his transmission technology, evidences the extent to which the emergence of new political and economic structures are related to early radio networks.

UFCO, for instance, had by 1908 set up a radio station network reaching from Bluefields and Rama, in Nicaragua, via Guatemala to Cape San Antonio in Cuba, which was meant to establish contact to a larger station in New Orleans, Louisiana via a Caribbean relay station installed by UFCO in 1907 on the small Swan Island, located circa 1,500 km to the south of New Orleans.[45] At the same time, the company's fleet of twenty-five ships was also outfitted with the new system, which under good weather conditions allowed even the Caribbean radio stations to hear broadcasts from Fessenden's station in Brant Rock. The plan was to communicate in Central America via Morse Code for the time being, but soon there was the additional option of voice communications, for which Fessenden once again received a large-scale commission. This kind of network structure for radio communication in the Caribbean and Central America had previously been set up only by military operations on behalf of the state, with the aim of circumventing or even improving on the existing communications technology of closed telegraph networks. Along these lines, the director of the radio division of the U.S. Navy Bureau of Equipment, Cleland Davis—upon awarding to R. A. Fessenden, in 1909 in Arlington, Virginia, the U.S. Navy contract for building the strongest radio transmitter to date—characterized radio technology as an opportunity for countering the telegraphic cable connections of the British Empire with an «imperial chain,»[46] a chain of wireless stations akin to those already set up by UFCO.[47] James Schwoch argues in this context that it was only in the interplay of state and private enterprise that radio became a key technology in the political and economic expansion of America during the first decades of the twentieth century.[48] In the process, it formed the communicative foundation for the emergence of new multinational power structures, which in the case of UFCO unfurled an economic scale and political power attributable previously only to sovereign states.[49]

On the way there, the company expanded its business model in 1913 under the direction of George S. Davis, the new manager of UFCO's radio division, and founded the subsidiary Tropical Radio Telegraph Company, the leading

47 After having compared the costs of cable telegraphy with those of wireless telegraphy, the same conclusion was reached in Germany in 1907: «To connect islands and for regions subject to severe storms, wireless telegraphy will probably be the only acceptable alternative in the future.» Gustav Partheil, *Die drahtlose Telegraphie und Telephonie nach Geschichte, Wesen und Bedeutung für Militär und Marine, Verkehr und Schule gemeinverständlich dargestellt* (Berlin, 1907), p. 86.

48 See James Schwoch, *The American Radio Industry and Its Latin American Activities, 1900–1939* (Urbana and Chicago, 1990).

49 «The banana empire is not primarily an aggregation of mutually interacting governmental and industrial agencies, but the expansion of an economic unit to such size and power that in itself it assumes many of the prerogatives and functions usually assumed by political states. The United Fruit Company, rather than rely upon the State Department to pull diplomatic wires, trains its own political representatives to deal with Caribbean

governments. The corporation, which not only monopolizes the banana trade in the most important producing regions but also owns or controls railroads, docks, steamships, radio, housing facilities, leading wholesale and retail stores and other enterprises, and which also controls the livelihood of many business men, farmers, laborers, and professional men, can speak with such force that politicians accede to its will.» Charles David Kepner, Jr. and Jay Henry Soothill, *The Banana Empire: A Case Study of Economic Imperialism* (1935; repr., New York, 1967), p. 341.

50 See Albert W. Buel, «The Development of the Standard Design for Self-Supporting Radio Towers for the United Fruit and Tropical Radio Telegraph Companies,» *Proceedings of the Institute of Radio Engineers* 12, no. 1 (February 1924), pp. 29–64. The founding of the subsidiary Tropical Radio was made possible by the 1912 purchase by George S. Davis of the Wireless Speciality Apparatus Company, founded by one of the developers of the crystal detector, J.G. Pickard, ensuring UFCO important patent rights for the development of its own tropicalized radio devices.

manufacturer of transmission and reception technology at that time.[50] By 1921, the company had invested nearly four million dollars in radio technology and thus in the control of its holdings in Central America and the Caribbean[51]— with additional, even larger stations in Santa Marta (Colombia), Cape Gracias á Dios (Honduras), Costa Rica, Panama, Cuba, Guatemala, Jamaica, and Nicaragua—as well as in communications, with its so-called «Great White Fleet» of passenger ships. Following the end of the First World War, Tropical Radio, thanks to these investments and a wealth of experience in the employment of the technology in tropical climate conditions, from which its own technical developments benefited, was in a position to take a place at the table as equal partner when it came to negotiating the allocation of American radio rights and to forming a «Radio Trust.» The UFCO with its Tropical Radio Company was thus one of the founding members of the Radio Corporation of America (RCA), in which it held a 4.1 percent stake, supplementing its means of controlling its possessions with the addition of state-run news channels.[52] «From a money-losing subsidiary of the banana business the company by 1920 had launched itself on a program that would make it the dominant international communications company in the region by the end of the decade.»[53] Its economic strategy was successful, for Tropical Radio managed not only to operate radio stations in remote coastal regions of Central America but also, through aggressive diplomacy, to build transregional stations near the respective capitals of every country in the region that were licensed for public international news broadcasting. By the year 1928, Tropical Radio was accordingly conducting international radio communications in all Central American countries as point-to-point communication, so that the UFCO's expansive initial phase of founding and development culminated in due course with a strong position on the world market as well as a monopoly in banana exports from Costa Rica, Guatemala, and Panama. This hegemony was founded in substantial investments in the transport infrastructure (shipping and railway lines) and control over international communications networks throughout Central America.

The experiment in social reconception within the context of postcolonial economies, made possible by such predominance, ultimately led, in the discourse on a networked structure of communication, to the realization that it was by no means sufficient to merely decouple transmission from the surmounting of the shortest distance in order to realize the technical utopia of one big global community in the everywhere of radio-spatial availability. Martin Heidegger noted in 1950: «The hasty elimination of all distances alone does not bring closeness; because closeness does not consist in a low degree of distance.»[54]

Acknowledgements
Thanks to Dawn Michelle d'Atri for her indispensable aid in refining the English version of this essay.

51 See Christopher H. Sterling and John M. Kittross, *Stay Tuned: A Concise History of American Broadcasting* (Belmont, 1978), p. 35.

52 See Erik Barnouw, *A Tower in Babel*, vol. 1, *A History of Broadcasting in the United States* (New York, 1966), pp. 72–74; Aitken 1985 (see note 23), pp. 446–47.

53 David McCreery, «Wireless Empire: The United States and Radio Communications in Central America and the Caribbean, 1904–1926,» *Southeast Latin Americanist* 37.1, Montgomery, Alabama (Summer 1993), pp. 23–41, here p. 33.

54 Martin Heidegger, «Das Ding,» in *Vorträge und Aufsätze* (1950; repr., Pfullingen, 1954), pp. 157–75, here p. 157.

Networked Radio Space and Broadcast Simultaneity

An Interview with Robert Adrian

Daniel Gilfillan

From our positioning in the early years of the twenty-first century, it is easy to fall into that pervasive trap of explaining the complexities of the world around us using solely the vocabularies, metaphors, and discourses prevalent with the rise of the eternally new information economy. Yet falling into this trap fueled by advertising hype, new business models, and the promise of global economies elides an entire history of thought and engagement with the role and function of art in exploring the finely tuned connections between knowledge, information, and communication. In a very real sense, the bits of information we work with on a daily basis are shaped by the discourses at play in each of the artistic fields or scholarly disciplines we find ourselves representing, by the media in which the information travels (book, newspaper, radio, television, film, stage production, painting, sculpture, body movement, Internet), and by the structures of knowledge in which the information is conceptualized. The medium of radio and the techniques of broadcasting are not often associated with network connectivity, levels of interactivity, or the mutual experience of simultaneity. These same elements also do not traditionally surface in conversations about the plastic and visual arts. For that matter, the art world and the radio world are rarely brought together in the minds of the mainstream, who tend to relegate the place of art to galleries and museums and the place of radio either to much contemporary, template-style programming or to the nostalgia of the radio-centered family living room. Among the interstices that have arisen in the overlapping and intersecting of these two worlds is an idea of an electronically produced space that assumes its fluid, amorphous shape through bringing together the fleeting temporality of radio broadcast and the virtual presence of network connectivity and, in doing so, allows for a temporary space for artists to collaborate regardless of physical, political, social, or economic limitation. This networked radio space is one type of electronic space that has been exposed within existing international telecommunications infrastructures by media and telecommunications artists as a viable space for simultaneous and synchronous artistic experimentation and collaboration.

One such artist is Robert Adrian, whose work has ranged from early outdoor landscape sketches and paintings, polymer clay miniatures, a series of experimental paintings that explore the concepts of surface and space, a move to paper-based collages arranged in arrays as wall installations, and then later a transition to large sculptural installations involving not-yet-readymades, such as model airplanes. Not to be missed or ignored in this trajectory of artistic work is Adrian's experimentation with and long-held commitment to the devices and spaces of telecommunications as areas for artistic practice to reside and take shape. This particular work with telecommunications art has left no communications device unexplored for its artistic applications (teletype, telefacsimile, slow-scan and closed-circuit television, computer, radio, etc.), and this exploration highlights Adrian as a perceptive and innovative user and critic of these devices in creating a space for artistic experimentation. He comments on this work with telecommunications space in his 1989 essay «Electronic Space,» where he details its elusive composition as belonging to both the temporal specificity of performance art and the spatiotemporal immateriality of conceptual art:

The electronic space in which telecommunications artists—along with transnational corporations, stock markets and the military—operate is a complicated concept made possible by another phenomenon of art in

---

1   Robert Adrian, «Electronic Space,» http://alien
    .mur.at/rax/TEXTS/ra-eraum-e.html (accessed
    February 26, 2007). A German version is
    available as «Electronischer Raum,»
    Kunstforum International 103 (1989), pp. 142–
    47, here p. 142.

the 1970's ... conceptual art. Conceptual art demands a conceptual space in which to exist and a culture that has grasped that elusive notion will have no trouble at all de-materialising its power structures into something as relatively concrete as the electronic space of international electronic communications networks. Our interest in this space should be no surprise: Art has always gone where the power is.[1]

In addition to the interstitial play between the durational qualities of performance and the dematerialized aspects of conceptual art, Adrian's description of this electronic space mentions another characteristic as key to its coming into existence—the breakdown of a culture's power structures, those ideologies and institutional forces of a culture that restrict, limit, or otherwise seek to control physical or intellectual movement. Aligned typically within or along various legal, economic, political, gendered, racial, and ethnic categories, these power structures are themselves often called into question through much performance and conceptual art, precisely because both resist archivization or the creation of any physical art product, which could then be subsumed within these same power structures.

Robert Adrian, *76 Airplanes: 76 paper aircraft models*, installation, Aurora Borealis, Montreal, Canada, 1985.

While the variety of media types and approaches in Robert Adrian's work may suggest a disparity of sorts, it more importantly reflects reactions to changing trends in the art world vis-à-vis the art market and addresses the need to shift artistic practices as a response or challenge to the consumerist forces of this very same art market. Key to understanding this apparent disparity rests with this question of materiality: whether or not a material object is produced that can be bought and sold within the art market. Adrian addresses this himself in an interview from 2001:

> Although I saw no conflict between operating in the immaterial world of telecommunication systems and making physical artworks, it slowly became clear that the two activities were perceived as unrelated and contradictory by both the art institutions (galleries, museums, etc.) and most of my network partners. It became a slightly schizophrenic situation in which I could not mention my activities in one area while talking with people in the other without encountering stony silence. This is probably because many of the pioneers of the kind of low-tech telecomm with which I was involved had been active in the 70's with performance, video, etc. but after 1980, when the galleries and museums suddenly re-embraced the painted object and the market boomed, the people with no product to sell were pushed to the margins.[2]

This schizophrenic, caught-at-the-crossroads mindset that Adrian references is illustrative of many, if not all, artists caught between the financial needs of daily subsistence and the theoretical/knowledge needs folded up within artistic practice. While this underscores once again the same binary between materiality and immateriality that telecommunications art engages, it also addresses the perceived disparity in Adrian's work between the presence and absence of material art objects, by clearly showing that the time-driven movements of performance art and the impermanent knowledge processes of conceptual art are part and parcel of all artworks, regardless of material specificity. In other words, the processes

2 Robert Adrian, «Interview,» in *Robert Adrian X*, exh. cat. Kunsthalle Wien (Vienna: Folio, 2001), p. 65.

3 Jackson Pollock, «Interview with William Wright,» in *Jackson Pollock: Interviews, Articles, and Reviews*, ed. Pepe Karmel (New York: Henry N. Abrams, 1999), p. 20. Interview conducted in late 1950 and broadcast on radio station WERI in Westerly, Rhode Island in 1951.

involved in bringing any artwork to fruition exist within this constantly seesawing effect that shifts preference in the art world between materiality/immateriality, appearance/disappearance, presence/absence, and visibility/invisibility. Artists thus always find themselves in a constant state of negotiation, between content and form, between subject and object, between theory and practice, and between concept and market, when the onus of such negotiation should continually fall to representatives from the art market, who need to understand trends and practices as set by the artists rather than by the loop design of the market itself.

When American modernist painter Jackson Pollock was asked to comment on his unconventional painting technique in a 1951 radio interview, he teased out some intriguing connections between artistic expression and innovations in technological progress:

> My opinion is that new needs need new techniques. And the modern artists have found new ways and new means of making their statements. It seems to me that the modern painter cannot express this age, the airplane, the atom bomb, the radio, in the old forms of the Renaissance or of any other past culture. Each age finds its own technique.[3]

Pollock locates his art directly in the midst of those information networks prevalent in nineteen-fifties America and perceives it as a node of experience which expresses visually and texturally the speed of air travel, the minute complexity of the atomic bomb, and the simultaneous ethereality and physical presence of the radio. That Pollock sees his painting technique as a reflection of the atomistic properties of energy and matter and the fleetingness of communication finds resonance in Robert Adrian's experimentation in the seventies with painting surface:

> It seemed that art—or at least painting—was fragmenting, splitting into its components all through the 70's: the act of painting was being played out as performance; video was dealing with narrative; photography with illusion; the painted object was turned into its own subject matter while subject matter dematerialised into conceptual texts or manifestos. Minimal art, conceptual art, mail art, performance art, media art, analytical art jostled and overlapped in a kaleidoscopic array of conflicting histories and possible futures. Viewing all these different fragments as the basic

elements of painting made it easy to abandon the formal preoccupation with the physical object and try to recover some of the aspects that I had been so rigorously omitting.[4]

The series of experimental paintings that Adrian produced during this time period (e.g., *Surface Tension*, *Black Silk*, and *Gray*), in which he sought «to develop a technique for making surfaces without support,»[5] that is, sans canvas backing, and, I would argue, the collection of twenty-four polymer clay miniature sculptures, *24 Jobs*, are each the result of object-producing techniques that mingle in the kaleidoscopic, fragmentary, and elusive qualities of conceptual art. Both the paintings and the miniatures reflect the tensions that the artist faces within the art world vis-à-vis the cycle of production and consumption, yet they do so along very different lines and at various points of connection to Robert Adrian's growing interest in the late seventies/early eighties with communications devices. He teases out some of these very subtle and complex connections in an interview from September 2006:

> The connection between the work that I had been doing before and the work that evolved out of experiencing communication devices—that's not too easy. Up until the end of 1977, beginning of 1978, I had been working with frontal painting for about six or seven years. I'd done a lot of what might be called *support-surface* from the French, or analytic painting—it was working with the surface. And I developed a technique where I could work basically without backing at all, but actually make the paintings face down on plastic, and then stuck the cloth on that and lifted them off, so that you experience the painting from the first layer to the last layer, not the reverse; there was no impasto covering up what was behind, you saw everything because it was transparent. You could technically or theoretically analyze the painting from front to back, the top layer was the first layer, and the last layer was the cloth.[6]

The type of analytic painting that Adrian describes here, with its focus on addressing some of the formal problems of painting as an art form, finds a solution in the technique of layered transparency, which he devises to move away from

---

4 Adrian 2001 (see note 2), p. 59.
5 Ibid., p. 57.

6 Robert Adrian, interview with the author in Vienna, September 16, 2006.

the limitations that he saw coalescing in surface-oriented painting. Rather than hiding the layers of information and communication behind top-level surfaces that comprise the paint-on-canvas approach, Adrian's technique made the process and the layers visible, transparent. There is a certain simultaneity that occurs in the application of this technique, in the sense that each individual paint layer exists simultaneously with each of the other layers. It is with this aspect of simultaneity that I want to draw some connections to Robert Adrian's collection of miniature, narrative-based sculptures known as *24 Jobs*. Made from Fimo, a brand of polymer modeling clay that hardens when baked in an oven, the collection depicts the various jobs (theater usher, houseman, art school model, painter/decorator, framer, fake painter, etc.) that the artist had to take on while also working as an artist. The array of simultaneous public, working identities foregrounded by this collection speaks to the need for the constant state of interchange running parallel to the artist's role as artist, but in some respects it is a system of interchangeability that is not always equitable, as financial concerns take precedence over the artistic.

The moments of simultaneity and the components of transparency educed by these examples of Robert Adrian's work provoke an idea of artistic space that

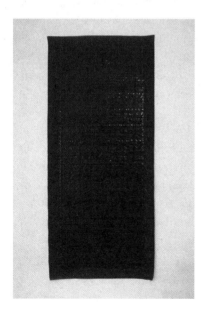

Robert Adrian,
Black Silk, acrylic
resin and cotton thread
on silk, ca. 200 × 90 cm,
1976.

moves beyond the physical space of galleries and museums—and the positioning of the observer directly in front of the artwork, or even immersion in the space of an installation—to open itself instead to the more conceptual and performative areas existing as modes of experience and modes of production in the art-making process. This re-articulation of artistic space through analytic painting to reestablish the type of knowledge and theoretical work that comprises an artwork, an art object, or an art product (depending on one's position within the art market equation) points to a central area of attraction for Adrian's interest in the networks of telecommunications space, which he contrasts with museum space: «... the fact of the matter is that museum art, gallery art, is boring and déjà vu. If it's in a museum the context will make it ‹art› but it cannot make it relevant. The exciting things, call it art if you like, are happening in the street and in the network—if they also find a place in a museum so much the better but they will serve to redefine the museum and not vice versa.»[7] Clearly, for Robert Adrian, the importance of the network and the street lies in their relevance and in their framing a sense of happening—those moments illustrating the movement and process of communication/dialogue/performance between and among artists and audiences that allow a work to happen, and thus which work within the previously mentioned parameters of durational performance and immaterial conceptuality. He also sees these virtual spaces (networks) and physical spaces (streets) as central for realigning the art market equation in favor of the artist, whose work should be guiding the evolution of the museum.

His use of communication devices and exploration of telecommunications networks range from the utilitarian (sporadic everyday communication and BBS posts linking other artists separated by physical distance) to large-scale media art happenings, like *The World in 24 Hours* from 1982, which connected the media landscapes of several cities across the globe and across several different time zones within the technical infrastructures of diverse, sometimes low-tech devices, which tangentially assisted in either rethinking or reworking the artistic parameters with which these devices had originally been conceived. *The World in 24 Hours* connected fifteen cities (Vienna, Amsterdam, Bath, Frankfurt, Pittsburgh,

7   Robert Adrian, «Electronicism,» http://alien
    .mur.at/rax/TEXTS/elecism.html (accessed
    February 26, 2007). Also available in Désirée
    Schellerer, *Translucent Writings* (Vienna:
    G. Insam, 1994).

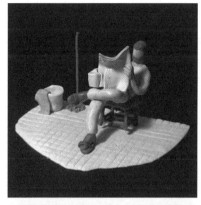 

 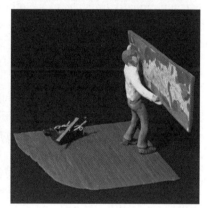

Robert Adrian, *24 Jobs*,
polymer clay miniatures,
1979.

Above left,
Baths Attendant;
above right,
Display Designer;
below left,
Painter and Decorator;
below right,
Gallery Assistant.

Wellfleet, Toronto, San Francisco, Vancouver, Sydney, Tokyo, Honolulu, Florence, Istanbul, and Athens). Like many of the telecommunications projects that Adrian either conceived or participated in, *The World in 24 Hours* incorporated an early idea of artifact transmission (still and video image, text, voice, telephone-based sound) from any of these remote locations to the central staging area in Linz, where the project segued with the 1982 Ars Electronica Festival. Transmitting via such technologies as slow-scan television, telefacsimile, computer network, and telephone-based audio, individual artists or artist groups in each of these remote locations contributed not just a stack of quantifiable material in the form of texts, video captures for SSTV transmissions, and the like, but rather instances of play-ful and thought-provoking assemblages requesting participatory and interactive engagement, ideally from any of the other participants in any of the fifteen cities. About the project and the type of participation and access it sought to promote, Adrian writes:

> If any sort of chance arises to develop new techniques by means of which private individuals can make meaningful use of these electronic media— to assert their right to genuine participation in the development of this new electronic world—then it will have to be very soon. It is probably too late even now to really change the direction of design development but we can try at least to discover ways to insert human content into the com-mercial/military world floating in this electronic space. And this is where artists are traditionally strong... in discovering new ways to use media and materials, in inventing new and contradictory meanings for existing organizations and systems, in subverting self-serving power structures in the interests of nearly everyone. Artists using electronic telecommunica-tions are trying to find human meaning in an electronic space.[8]

To say that the project anticipated the convergence of several media types (sound, text, still/moving image) in the same way we conceive of multimedia computing today would be to gloss over its true contributions in establishing an electronic

8   Robert Adrian, «The World in 24 Hours,» in *Ars Electronica: Facing the Future. A Survey of Two Decades*, ed. Timothy Druckery (Cambridge, MA: MIT Press, 1999), pp. 145–56. Also reproduced online at http://alien.mur.at/rax/24_HOURS/24-catalog-e.html. First published in German in Christine Schöpf, ed., *Ars Electronica: Festival für Kunst, Technologie und Gesellschaft* (Linz, 1982), p. 145.

9   Adrian interview (see note 6).

space for the transmission of human-based signification. In one sense, the transitory electronic space, opened up by the telephone line connections within the twenty-four-hour duration of *The World in 24 Hours*, illustrates the power of the simultaneous network in achieving moments of human connection and human collaboration even when the distances of time and space would normally pose any number of physical limitations. In another sense, the project seeks to provide an alternative model—a transparent and accessible model for creating and utilizing this type of network space for purposes other than commercial or military exclusivity—and in doing so calls these other frameworks into question.

As Robert Adrian's work with artistic appropriations of telecommunications networks grew, the number of projects he participated in or began also expanded. Vital to these was understanding the role of communication as pure content, in seeing these spaces of communication as occurring outside of meaning, and it was here that Adrian saw his work connecting to radio:

> Communications technology was to me pure content—without meaning. Meaning was unimportant—it's another spin-off—you've got the meanings elsewhere. This was communication as content, was what I called it. Just the fact of turning the machines on and being present in the [electronic] space was the work. What happened with the work was inconsequential, and basically once the machines were off it was gone anyway ... This had all kinds of other references to what art is anyway, and what art had been, and there was the problem of performance artists whose work was always appropriable, because whoever had photographs of the piece had the piece. So, if twenty-five people made photographs, there were twenty-five pieces—so there are a whole lot of references and things going on in your head about what's left over from art—in this situation what is the art, who decides, what is the role of the artist—the artist has no control—and these things referred into radio.[9]

This notion of communication as pure content goes directly to the heart of the issues surrounding artistic practice and artistic control, which Robert Adrian had wanted to address through his experiments with analytic painting and narrative-based sculpture and which other artists had sought to address through the medium of performance art. Yet, for Adrian, the fact remained that no matter how much the artist controlled the framework of production, no matter how spontaneous a performance, no matter how resistant the piece was to being captured, archivized, or hung on a museum/gallery wall, the fact remained that meaning and value were still being fixed into the work and served up as product. The creation of an electronic space via the networks of various telecommunications devices linked together, some for the first time, allowed the types of spatiotemporal happenings that characterized street-level art and performance pieces to be ported over to the more immaterial space of the network, where capturing the work of the artwork was elusive:

> ... the sad story of the graffiti artists, whose work was torn from its location in and under the street and reinvented as art in the East Village and SoHo schlock galleries, should remind us that some things are interesting, exciting and relevant exactly because they are not «validated» or «contextualized» as «art.» Artists working inside the electronic networks are unlikely to be threatened by a similar fate as there is virtually no product to display, market or appropriate.[10]

The link that Adrian sees to radio stems from this same desire for elusiveness in the creative process, for creating meaning without having an existing framework of meaning being attached to, categorized into, or otherwise captured from the moments of performance and conceptualization that occur collaboratively between artists in this network space.

It is in a set of twelve aphorisms about radio listening and radio production, created in collaboration with the Viennese *Kunstradio–Radiokunst* project, that Robert Adrian conceptualizes the connections he sees between artistic space, communications space, and radio space. These twelve points comprise Adrian's «*Kunstradio* Manifesto: Twelve Notes Toward a Definition of Radio Art,» and it is in this manifesto that an idea about radio space is adapted along the contours of simultaneity and interactivity it implicitly sets into motion. *Kunstradio* takes it for self-evident that:

10   Adrian in Schellerer 1994 (see note 7), n.p.

Wiencouver IV,
Robert Adrian and
Hank Bull preparing
to transmit *The
Haters* performance
to Vienna, Austria,
1983.

The World in 24 Hours,
Ars Electronica,
Linz, Austria, 1982.

1   Radio art is the use of radio as a medium for art.
2   Radio happens in the place it is heard and not in the production studio.
3   Sound quality is secondary to conceptual originality.
4   Radio is almost always heard combined with other sounds— domestic, traffic, tv, phone calls, playing children etc.
5   Radio art is not sound art—nor is it music. Radio art is radio.
6   Sound art and music or literature are not radio art just because they are broadcast on the radio.
7   Radio space is all the places where radio is heard.
8   Radio art is composed of sound objects experienced in radio space.
9   The radio of every listener determines the sound quality of a radio work.
10 Each listener hears their own final version of a work for radio combined with the ambient sound of their own space.
11 The radio artist knows that there is no way to control the experience of a radio work.
12 Radio art is not a combination of radio and art. Radio art is radio by artists.[11]

Each of the points in this constellation initiates encounters with and within the space opened up by the medium of the radio, yet the twelve points of the manifesto clearly situate listening and the position of the listener as the point where the experience of radio art occurs—for example with point two: «Radio happens in the place it is heard and not in the production studio»—and becomes intricately tied to the sounds and the unique spaces of each individual listener—here, point ten: «Each listener hears their own final version of a work for radio combined with the ambient sound of their own space.» Conceived in this way, radio space allows temporary spaces of performance to develop, putting both artists and listeners on equal footing in the transmission and reception of a radio art piece, and moves the value of the piece away from its technical point of transmission in the studio—away from an idea of art objects selling as art products in the art mar-

11   ORF *Kunstradio*, «Toward a Definition of Radio Art,» http://www.kunstradio.at/TEXTS/manifesto .html (accessed February 26, 2007).

Blix, *Kunstfunk*
(Art Radio), installing
the shortwave radio
antenna on the cupola
of the Secession,
Vienna, Austria, 1985.

Blix, *Kunstfunk*,
radio studio preparing
to transmit slow-scan
images, Secession,
Vienna, Austria, 1985.

ket—and toward its point of reception with the listener, in effect restructuring the commercial broadcast paradigm from one based in the marketing of information through time-specific standardized formats to one based in the interchange of knowledge without privileging these formatting concerns.

Adrian's manifesto about radio art theorizes at a much more profound level the position and role of the audience than did the very painter-centered ideas behind analytic painting, or even the ideational/notional/noumenal contours of conceptual art. Where a project like *The World in 24 Hours* (1982) or *Telephone Music* (1983) and the conferences *Interplay* (1979) and *Artists' Use of Telecommunications* (1980) served to test the waters of possibility within these networked spaces for the artists themselves, the series of radio projects that Adrian participated in acknowledged the position of the audience, in this case the listener, in the production of any piece of radio art. This expansion of the networked electronic space to incorporate outlets via radio broadcast to an audience of dispersed listeners became possible as advances in network technologies continued to grow, and as radio itself began to explore areas of convergence with computer-based and satellite networking.

Hank Bull

From the Centre to the Periphery

Candice Hopkins

> When you break a
> sentence the future leaks out.
> —*William Burroughs*

Hank Bull's Move to Vancouver

Hank Bull's move at age twenty-four from Toronto, near the middle of Canada, to Vancouver, on the West coast, would shape the future of his practice. Seduced by the early happenings at the Western Front (one of the country's oldest artist-run centres), Bull met his further collaborators, as he has said, on the coattails of mail art. At the time the medium was simultaneously «bursting at the seams collapsing under the weight of its own success.»[1] The network and its nodes, first initiated and necessitated through mail art's very structure, was shifting into something different and Bull had arrived at just the right time. In a story that has almost become iconic now, in September 1973, after learning about the Western Front through one of the artist collective General Idea's *FILE Magazines*, Bull jumped on the train from Toronto with little more than an ounce of hash, a trunk of clothes, and an accordion to his name. He wasn't sure what he would find but knew that he was looking for something different. «The Vancouver scene was mythical,» he recalls. «There was a voluminous exchange between Toronto and Vancouver, especially among the poets, but Image Bank [a collective of artists from Vancouver] and General Idea [from Toronto] were also very close, sharing a lot of ideas.»[2] At the time, General Idea was building its connections with Vancouver, and through the infamous *Hollywood Decca Dance* members of the Western Front were collaborating with the likes of Willoughby Sharp of *Avalanche Magazine* in New York and Ant Farm in California.[3] (The *Decca Dance* was organized in celebration of the 1,000,011th Birthday of Art on January 17, 1974. The event, of which Hank Bull was the musical director, took place at both the peak and the decline of mail art. A host of correspondence artists from around North America traveled to Hollywood to take part in the festivities and in the Mail Art Awards Ceremony.) In the same period, French Fluxus member, and *Art's Birthday* founder, Robert Filliou was in Upstate New York visiting with Dick Higgins, an artist and founder of the experimental Something Else Press. It was there that Filliou initiated one of his first telecommunications experiments, which consisted of him calling all of his long-distance friends in his personal network over the telephone.[4] In a gesture that would point also to the future of artists' use of communication technologies, and Bull's practice in particular, Dick Higgins had coined the term «intermedia» seven years prior. An excerpt from his *Statement on Intermedia* (1966) reads:

> For the last ten years or so, artists have changed their media to suit this situation, to the point where the media have broken down in their traditional forms, and have become merely puristic points of reference. The idea has arisen ... that these points are arbitrary and only useful as critical tools, in saying that such-and-such a work is basically musical, but also poetry. This is the intermedial approach, to emphasize the dialectic between the media. A composer is a dead man unless he composes for all the media and for his world.[5]

1   After the Western Front collaborated on the highly successful *Hollywood Decca Dance* of 1974, some participants were so overwhelmed by the mail they received that they didn't have the time to respond.

2   Robert Filliou in an exhibition catalogue compiled by Sharla Sava and Scott Watson: *Robert Filliou: From Political to Poetical Economy* (Vancouver: Morris and Helen Belkin Gallery, 1995), p. 63.

3   *The Decca Dance* was co-organized by the Western Front and Image Bank, Lowell Darling, Willoughby Sharp, Ant Farm, and General Idea.

4   These phone calls were published as an audiocassette by Voicepondence, Calgary in 1975 and can be found in the catalogue *Robert Filliou: From Political to Poetical Economy* (see note 2).

5   Dick Higgins, *Statement on Intermedia* (1966); http://www.artpool.hu/Fluxus/Higgins/intermedia2.html (accessed July 2007).

6   Keith Wallace, introduction to *Whispered Art History: Twenty Years at the Western Front*, ed. Keith Wallace (Vancouver: Arsenal Pulp Press, 1993), p. 2.

7   Hank Bull, interview with the author in Vancouver, December 2006.

Although Higgins didn't know it at the time, that same year in Vancouver the Intermedia Society had formed. True to its name, it focused on finding new relationships among previously defined mediums and media and facilitated projects ranging from jazz, to dance, sculpture, radio, sound, and performance, and points in between. Recognized as the city's first large-scale, non-institutional, artist-initiated collective, Intermedia's interdisciplinary nature eventually divided them in 1973 when their publishing section—Intermedia Press—paradoxically subsumed the organization itself.[6] During Intermedia's decline, eight people (an architect, composer, and six artists working in the intersections of video, dance, photography, performance, and literature), including two who had been actively involved throughout the span of the organization, banded together to buy a cavernous former Masonic Hall on Vancouver's low-rent East Side and named it the Western Front Lodge.

On the day of his arrival from Eastern Canada, Bull, already en-route to the Western Front, found himself sharing a bus with Front founder Eric Metcalfe (then known as Dr. Brute; Lady Brute being Metcalfe's then-wife Kate Craig), whom he knew of but had yet to meet. Metcalfe invited him to an event that night. Bull described this first introduction to the Western Front as follows:

> I was 24. At that time the gallery was one big room going back to the kitchen and it was set up with tables. It was the famous «Von Bonin» dinner. There were menus and there were people filming it ... The dinner was just about finished and people were starting to go upstairs ... I went into this big old room, and there were no lights in there or anything. It was just a sound system ... I could see some people fussing with a sound system and I thought, «That's not going to do anything.» I saw there was a grand piano and I said to myself, «Well, I might as well arrive in Vancouver,» so I sat down and I started to pound out some boogie-woogie on the piano. Suddenly a spotlight was turned on me and then out of the wings come Mr. Peanut tap dancing and Dr. Brute playing saxophone. Turned out it was being filmed for German Television, the WDR, by the famous Dr. Von Bonin ... They were making a film about art in Canada and the Western Front treated them to a special night. That's how we met.[7]

Trained as a painter, Bull was creating work at a time when the medium had reached a crux. The influence of formalism—largely inspired by the writings of art historian Clement Greenberg—was pervasive and had become the central subject of its discourse and practice. From Bull's perspective, painting had reached an end point; reduced to discourses on medium specificity, there was little left to explore. At the same time, by coincidence, Jeff Wall, a Vancouver artist now known for his staged large-format photographs (what he carefully refers to as «pictures»), also stopped painting. He had abandoned the picture frame altogether and was painting white monochromes directly onto the gallery wall.

In 1973, two months prior to Hank Bull's arrival in Vancouver, Robert Filliou had also come to the Front for the first time. His initial visit (and multiple returns to collaborate with another founder of the Western Front, Kate Craig, among many others) would influence the Front, its founders, and its programming to this day. Filliou's Fluxus sensibilities complemented the organization's already defined lean toward the merging of art and life. Enacting this philosophy consciously or not, the members of the Front lived and worked out of the space and in their first year as a collective had transformed even the most potentially mundane aspects of everyday life—cooking and eating—into grand artistic gestures, with everything from placemats to what was being served in a given night considered on their digestive, conceptual, and aesthetic grounds. (Metcalfe and Bull, although no longer associated with the programming or the board, continue to reside in the building.) Filliou would also have an impact on the Front's experimentation in new technologies namely video, radio, telecom, sound, and later, the Internet. Importantly, he would introduce the concept of the *Fête Permanente*, or as it would become known: The Eternal Network.

Between the Broadcaster and the Listener
The HP Show

Bull's first experimentation with a medium outside of painting was in performance, and through this, radio. At the beginning, Bull was interested in the effect that radio would have on the performers as a direct result of the «energy of live performance.» In 1974 at the Western Front, Bull was collaborating with a group

8   Hank Bull and Patrick Ready, «The Story of The HP Show,» in *Radio Rethink: Art, Sound and Transmission*, ed. Dan Lander (Banff: Walter Phillips Gallery, 1994), p. 47.

called the Lux Radio Players, a group of artists and people from other disciplines who got together to *perform* radio plays. The plays were conceived and performed as live events with accompanying live music and sound effects. The tapes were edited and then aired on Vancouver's newly formed Co-op radio (CFRO-FM). Two years later, Bull began his long-term collaboration with Patrick Ready for what they called *The HP Show*, which would run until 1984. Later, when their weekly time slot was moved, the name was changed to *The HP Dinner Show*, «scientifically designed to help you prepare, eat and digest your dinner,» also broadcast on Vancouver Co-operative Radio. The amount of work they created at the time was staggering. Together, with few breaks, they aired a new ninety-minute program every week for eight and a half years.

Bull and Ready's collaboration was predicated on correspondence beginning in 1967 after their initial introduction in Peterborough, Ontario. It was maintained via cassette tape, letters, and occasional visits until they both found themselves living in Vancouver ten years later.[8] (Although Bull has stated that he was taken with the idea of mail art, the only person he ever engaged with this on a sustained level was Patrick Ready.)

The Lux Radio Players, *A Bite Tonight: The World's Longest Radio Play*, Hank Bull (piano), Kate Craig and Patrick Ready (sound effects), live recording, Vancouver, Canada, 1977.

The Lux Radio Players, Glenn Lewis, and Kate Craig as the Soni Twin, a two-headed, hermaphroditic private detective, with their lines all spoken in unison, Vancouver, Canada, 1978.

Throughout the entire period I do not ever recall discussing any actual rules or systems we should use to work together, other than to casually talk about one day writing the definitive text on collaboration. The regular and constant live improvisations on air necessitated such an enveloping understanding of each others' minds, abilities, weaknesses and strengths that our everyday relationship became virtually ... a slower version of what we did on radio.[9]

A source of inspiration for Bull's thinking about radio as an artistic space was from a line by General Idea. The quote, as Bull remembers, was about «how artists, like Hermit crabs can invade the dead forms of mass media.»[10]

The title of their show, which quite deliberately oscillates between absurdity and seriousness, takes its name from the (still) ubiquitous British-born steak condiment: HP Sauce. «The acronym HP was invented when [Ready and I] were corresponding ... We needed a name. We decided to invade the mind of the HP Sauce Corporation.»[11] Their «invasion» was not limited to the company's name. Bull and Ready also channeled their energies to redesign the product's labels and place the new versions on supermarket bottles, and to performances where, carrying a large cardboard re-creation of an HP bottle complete with a periscope (the *HP Sedan Bottle*), they created films and other collaborative ventures. An

9   Ibid., p. 59.
10 Interview with Hank Bull (see note 7).
11 Bull and Ready in Lander 1994 (see note 8), p. 47.
12 Ibid., p. 49.
13 Ibid.
14 Interview with Hank Bull (see note 7).
15 Eduardo Kac, «Aspects of the Aesthetics of Telecommunications,» in *Siggraph Visual Proceedings*, ed. John Grimes and Gray Lorig (New York: ACM, 1992), pp. 47–57.
16 The description of *The HP Show* in *Whispered Art History* reads as follows: «Devoted to the idea that radio could be activated as an art medium the two hosts developed an idiosyncratic style and a quick following. A forum for new inventions [via the mechanical wizardry of Patrick Ready], telephone music and various types of listener participation, the show made heavy use of sound effects, experiments with tape recorders and scripted serials with names like *The Caveman, Tales from the Days of Sail, Captain Bonnard and Captain*

Lafarge and *Carolyne in Space*. Many of the artists who came to the Western Front would be incorporated into the show.» Quoted from Wallace 1993 (see note 6), p. 27.
17 Interview with Hank Bull (see note 7).
18 *The Radio Painting* was part of a radio art chapter of the Ars Electronica Festival in Linz, Austria in 1989. The 1989 edition of the festival was titled *In the Network of Systems*. The radio art section was curated by Heidi Grundmann (with Alfred Pittertschatscher) and was the contribution of the weekly program *Kunstradio*, on the cultural channel of the Austrian National Radio, to the festival. One focus of the radio art section was on live radio art by international artists. «Im Netz der Systeme,» *Kunstforum International* 103 (September/October 1989); http://www.aec.at (festival archive).

important inversion in some of these actions was found in the way that they were performed and filmed. One such performance, done while both Ready and Bull were walking backwards, was projected backwards. With the double reversal, the resulting projected image seems «normal,» with both performers appearing to the viewer to be walking forward. The fate of the *HP Sedan Bottle*, which was built to carry a person, was also met on film where similar strategies of reversal were employed. It was eventually blown up as a part of a «palindromic» movie.[12] Embodying the often necessarily guarded persona of those working under an assumed identity, Bull and Ready recollect that they communicated like spies at the time, in «cryptic» shorthand and tape-recorded meetings.[13]

It is the first iteration of *The HP Show* that is an important marker for the way in which Bull and Ready would make use of radio as an artistic medium. Hank credits that it was his perceived freedom in the medium—the autonomy in not having to perform in front of a live audience—that enabled them to be more creative. For them, «it was performance [art] done in the style of a radio play.»[14] Bull had a penchant for «liveness» through the performance of radio and the connection to multiple audiences it enabled. As Eduardo Kac notes, «Radio was the first true mass medium capable of remotely addressing millions at once.»[15]

The HP Show took the idea of inhabiting existing forms of mass media to its very limits. Further to this, Bull was invested in the structural qualities of radio and how these could be manipulated, challenged, and imagined anew.[16] The possibility for radio, for example, to take on what Joseph Beuys termed «social sculpture.»[17] From Bull's perspective, the difference between the ways that he was engaging in radio and the majority of avant-garde radio, for example in Germany, was that he was coming from a perspective of visual art. Perhaps the most direct enactment of this philosophy is found in a project he created for Ars Electronica in 1989 entitled *The Radio Painting*.[18] Based on a historical and conceptual understanding of painting through the discourses around the frame, Bull defined painting's «frame» as consisting of two elements: time and space. In his painting *mediated through*, radio «time» was measured by setting a metronome, and space was «framed» through direct engagement with the audience. Those listening to the broadcast were asked to phone in and identify their location, and each location would then be marked on a map, and these marks, dictated by the listeners, would complete the painting.

A radio show that further challenged the possibilities of radio, but in an entirely different form, was *The HP Underwater Special, The World's First Completely Underwater Radio Show*. A one-time experiment, it confronted the normally disembodied voice of the broadcaster, thereby bringing the very limits of physicality and breath that «voice» is dependent on to the forefront. The performance shifted the context of radio from something which takes places above ground—(radio waves rely on the atmosphere for transmission)—to under water.

> We took a white plastic bucket and keelhauled it upside down to form an airlock. Then, donning appropriate bathing costumes, we jumped over the side with the microphone covered with two condoms and came up inside the bucket. The sounds in the harbour were distant and metallic clinking, throaty motors purring, water slapping the boat's hull. Then, from inside the bucket came a suppressed scream as the microphone joined our SHOCKED heads in the airlock. We did this about eight times which exhausted about everything you could say about being inside a white plastic bucket. I was able to stay in the bucket about thirty seconds before all the air was exhausted. Hank breathed less and stayed longer. All sound for the show was guaranteed to have been recorded under, or passed through, water before it was broadcast.[19]

The HP Show, similar to General Idea's parody of the postwar U.S. glossy *LIFE* through their self-published magazine *FILE*, also played with the signifiers of consumer culture. Appropriating a brand, to paraphrase Diedrich Diederichsen, is «a small act of semiotic subversion» that involves an artist's borrowing of power from the public side of capital to momentarily use it against itself.[20] The use of techniques of masquerade, role-playing, and the «mimetic re-articulation of mass- and pop-cultural themes» was pervasive in Canadian art of the nineteen-sixties and seventies.[21] By the time Bull arrived in Vancouver in 1973, Dr. Brute (Front founder Eric Metcalfe) had just completed a massive painting, which would cover the entire façade of the Vancouver Art Gallery (the city's largest) in leopard spots, thereby camouflaging the building itself. The act of

19 Bull and Ready in Lander 1994 (see note 8), p. 58.

20 Diedrich Diederichsen, «Glad Rag,» *Artforum* (April 2002).

21 Ibid.

22 Judy Radul in Wallace 1993 (see note 6), p. 206.

painting the spots, along with the quite literal *costuming* of the building, worked to simultaneously «brand» it with Dr. Brute's most recognizable symbol of the leopard spots.

Already recognizing the potential in appropriation, a number of artists had taken on pseudonyms—a play on alterity that enabled them to simultaneously critique the relationship of the art object to commodity and skirt the system. The early members of the Western Front were known as Marcel Idea, Mr. Peanut, Dr. and Lady Brute, S.S. Tell, and Flakey Rose Hip, among other names. General Idea, in a similar vein, was comprised of A.A. Bronson, Felix Partz, and Jorge Zontal—also assumed identities. As Judy Radul remarked in writing on the history of performance at the Western Front, the boundaries between what was real and fictitious were not always clearly defined. «Although Dr. Brute occasionally appeared in performances, it is hard to say where Brute ended and Metcalfe began, typical of an art/life performance delineated not only by specific actions but by immanent possibilities for disrupting the norm.»[22] Aside from names, beginning in the nineteen-sixties, Canadian artists were also appropriating the signifiers of commodity and consumer culture itself: the business or corporation. Preceding *The HP Show* by nearly a decade in Canada was N.E. Thing Co. (founded by

Hank Bull and Patrick Ready, *HP Radio Show – Underwater Special*, ninety minutes of radio entirely recorded underwater, Vancouver, Canada, 1978.

Iain and Ingrid Baxter), Image Bank (Michael Morris and Vincent Trasov, known as Marcel Idea and Mr. Peanut respectively), and Ace Space (founded by Dana Atchely), among others. General Idea was also interrogating the association of art to money, power, and commodity through carefully orchestrated beauty pageants comprised of the most unlikely contestants, a ten-year search for a «Miss General Idea,» and their parodied publication *FILE Magazine*. Their Glamour issue articulated their position well in stating: «We wanted to be artists and we knew that if we were famous and glamorous that we could say we were artists ... We [also] knew Glamour was artificial. We knew that in order to be glamorous we had to become plagiarists, intellectual parasites.»[23]

The use of fiction and appropriation in the work of this period, as Diedrichsen has put forth, does not lead back to a kind of truth but to something else altogether. It is an action where «the *inauthentic* is precisely the goal.»[24] Understood «as a critique of ‹authenticism› or normality,» these actions both embodied and foregrounded Jean Baudrillard's future writings on the simulacra and their cult-like adoption in the New York art world in the nineteen-eighties.[25] In a move that would come at nearly the same time as the decline of appropriation/simulation art, in 1987 *FILE Magazine* would stage a farewell to the simulacra with a roundtable featuring Judith Barry and Peter Halley on the occasion of the Group Material exhibition fittingly titled Resistance (Anti-Baudrillard).[26] «As the simulacrum becomes bottomless,» Radul writes, «the use of the self as a viable or even available filter/interpreter is called into question.»[27] One wonders how this changes or is defused when the self is already layered with the constructed subjectivity of the alter ego and fictitious identities, the very taking on of these identities being both the result of and critique of commodity. It was commodity culture specific to America which Baudrillard's writings on the simulacra were inspired by in the first place.

Another figure of the post-68 generation whose ideas were relevant for radio art and Bull's practice, in particular, was Félix Guattari, who was involved in pirate radio in Italy and France and had developed a theory of «micro-politics.» Guattari figured micro-politics as an alternative strategy to the failed mode of mass revolution in France in the late sixties. One of his correspondents at the time was Japanese philosopher and artist Tetsuo Kogawa, who, out of an impulse

---

23 Ibid.
24 Ibid., emphasis added.
25 Ibid.
26 Ibid.

27 Radul in Wallace 1993 (see note 6), p. 211.
28 Bull and Ready in Lander 1994 (see note 8), p. 59.
29 Wallace 1993 (see note 6), p. 70.

to democratize mass media, sparked a «Mini FM» boom in Tokyo in the early eighties. Mini FM was a low-power FM transmitter, capable of covering a neighbourhood that could be easily made from cheap components purchased from any local electronics store. Bull first met Kogawa in Japan in 1992 and invited him to give a Mini FM workshop at the Western Front. Through the workshop, others in Canada, notably Bobbi Kozinuk, spread the technology across the country. Kogawa returned to Vancouver several times and through this the Mini FM was expanded from radio to micro television through a project at the Western Front called *Neighbourhood television* (NTV), in 1994. For *Neighbourhood television*, Kogawa developed a transmitter capable of broadcasting television images to other TV sets within a few block radius.

As *The HP Show* progressed, Hank Bull's concerns shifted to the possibilities offered though «global networking» (networking indicating a two-way, or multi-nodal, rather than one-way mode of communication). This change would thereby involve «radio as part of a larger field of communication.» With this came some of the earliest explorations by an artist of telecommunications on the I.P. Sharp Network (a form of e-mail and chat), as fax art and Slow Scan Television. «What appeals to me about radio,» Bull remarked in 1994, «is its ephemeral quality. It exists out there somewhere between the broadcaster and the listener, who is, like the Third Man, fugitive. Radio is the broadcaster's collaboration with this invisible phantom.»[28] Telecommunications would be one way of making this phantom visible.

Hank Bull is particularly gifted at connecting people and equally adept at making the space for this to happen. In 1980 to 1981, he undertook his first round-the-world trip with artist and wife Kate Craig (formerly married to Eric Metcalfe). Their intent was to «meet other artists and to explore the possibilities and problems of cross-cultural communication.»[29] Their travels took them to Europe, Southeast Asia, Japan, India, Africa, and points in between, but it was their month spent with musicians in Cameroon that Bull focused on when we first sat down in December of 2006 to talk about the formative years of his practice. In Africa, Bull quite literally took on the role of the «Third Man,»—the agent that comes between one point and another—to bring two opposite ends of the earth together.

Bull recalls that there was a feeling of urgency to their trip. For the artists it was an opportunity to think critically about globalization, and with this the rise of global capital, and its effects. Tied to this was their interest in initiating an effective and truly international network—one that did not consist of the usual suspects of Paris, New York, London, but places farther afield in India, Asia, and Africa. Their first attempt to form this network wasn't facilitated through media technologies but by real connections. It was an individual attempt (however successful) to break down cultural barriers and, with this, the imagined and mutable border between the so-called first and third worlds.[30] Having previously met Vienna-based radio producer Heidi Grundmann and artist Robert Adrian, their house would act as one of the «nodes» in Craig and Bull's global experiment. Over the course of their travels, they would periodically send packages of found ephemera—objects like candy wrappers and cigarette packages—to Vienna for safekeeping. The materials, together with photographs from the trip, would form a series of twenty collages shown in Austria and at the Canadian Cultural Centre in Paris, together with a manifesto Bull wrote entitled «Down with World Trade.»

The Form of the Network Shifts Yet Again
Experimentations in Telecommunications

Bull credits his formative ideas on communication to the influence of Bill Bartlett, telecom artist and founder of the Canadian artist-run centre Open Space. Bartlett developed an idea as Bull states, which he attributes to Brecht and his frequently quoted text about radio:[31]

> ... This vision that media, whether it is radio, telephone, and what have you, is not really communication unless it goes both ways. Radio is not a means of communication, it is a means of distributing information unless there is a way to respond to it and involve it. [At the time] Bartlett said we have technology that can make interactive communication ... the audi-

---

30 As a way to bridge the fictitious dichotomy between the first and third worlds, Bull together with Craig and others created Pidgin (hybrid) languages among other projects, which worked between different cultures.

31 Bertolt Brecht, «Der Rundfunk als Kommunikationsapparat,» *Blätter des Hessischen Landestheaters Darmstadt* 16 (July 1932).

32 It wasn't long thereafter that Bill Bartlett, disenchanted with telecommunications, its rising costs, and its inability to truly bring people together, dropped out of the scene. Interview with Hank Bull (see note 7).

33 Hank Bull, «*Wiencouver,*» in *Art + Telecommunications*, ed. Heidi Grundmann (Vancouver: Western Front and Vienna: Blix, 1984), p. 122.

ence can communicate with themselves or respond to whoever is sending out the image or the sound. It was called direct media.[32]

Perhaps Bull's single most successful attempt at bridging the gap between geographic divides, and an ongoing experimentation in direct media, is found in «*Wiencouver*,» an «imaginary city hanging invisible in the space between its two poles: Vienna and Vancouver.» In a brief history of *Wiencouver* from 1984, he writes:

> Seen from Europe, both cities are at the end of the road, one on the Pacific Rim of North America, the other just 65 km from the [former] soviet bloc. They are each on the edge of the art world's magnetic field, able to observe from a distance, and equally able to turn the other way, one toward the far east and one toward the near east. Vienna and Vancouver are wealthy, regional cities with international perspectives. This, coupled with their linguistic and historical differences, makes them ideal correspondents.[33]

Wiencouver has survived the cold-war era and continues to thrive today.

Hank Bull performing at *Audio Scene*, Lengenfeld, Austria, 1979.

The first iteration of *Wiencouver* (known as *Wiencouver I*) took place in 1979 when Bull first went to Vienna to attend *Audio Scene '79*.[34] It was there that he spoke about intermedia art and radio art and, through this, the potential to «remove the art world that normally mediates between the artist and the public.»[35] *Wiencouver II – IV* are described by Bull in 1984 as telematic exchanges between Vienna and Vancouver using mail art, Slow Scan TV, computer, telefax, and telephone music. Whenever Bull and, in turn, the Western Front would hook up via Slow Scan, the I.P. Sharp Network, and/or just the telephone with artists in Vienna, *Wiencouver* came alive.[36] It was at these times, for however brief a period, that the imaginary city of *Wiencouver* would become reality. The birth and concept of the project, through its use of the network, would conflate two very disparate places and parallels, the very ethos of telecommunications, that being the ability to connect and interact over large geographic divides. As Roy Ascott wrote in 1989, in telematic art «meaning is not created by the artist, distributed through the network and received by the observer. Meaning is the product of interaction between the observer and the system.»[37]

Notable editions of *Wiencouver* include *Wiencouver IV* (1983), an event that would go full circle to bring Robert Adrian and Bill Bartlett to Vancouver from where they and several other artists would exchange Slow Scan TV and telephone music with artists in Vienna.[38] For Bull and artists such as Bill Bartlett and Robert Adrian, it wasn't so much the content of the work unfolding at that time that mattered. What was important was «that you were connecting.» And

34 *Audio Scene '79: Sound as a Medium of Visual Arts* was an exhibition, a conference, and a series of performances by international artists, conceived of and organized by Grita Insam in Vienna and at Schloss Lengenfeld in Lower Austria. During the conference, Bull performed an iteration of what he called «*Religion Canada*,» which was a regular feature from *The HP Radio Show*. Wearing the regalia of «The Great Homunculus» (both the high priest and the God), Bull delivered the manifesto of *Religion Canada*. A critical spoof on Canada's national agencies—Immigration Canada, for example—the performance also took to task the unabashed capital interests of many large churches in North America throughout the nineteen-eighties, which turned religion into a corporate entity. With *Religion Canada* «you could send money but in return you would get absolutely nothing... we

weren't full of false promises.» Quoted from the interview with Hank Bull (see note 7). Please see http://kunstradio.at/REPLAY and editions *Audio Scene '79 «Boy Can See With His Ears»* for the text and image of the performance and his contribution to the exhibition.

35 Bull in Grundmann 1984 (see note 33).

36 Robert Adrian describes the I.P. Sharp Connection on the website http://alien.mur.at/rax/BIO/. Also see Adrian's essay «Art and Telecommunication, 1979–1986: The Pioneer Years» at http://telematic.walkerart.org/overview/overview_adrian.html (accessed July 2007).

37 From Ascott's essay, «Is There Love in the Telematic Embrace,» published online at ibid.

38 Ibid.

39 Transcribed from interview with Hank Bull (see note 7).

while the Western Front never initiated any of those major projects, they were nearly always included as a node, and they did a «pretty good job of being a node.» Before the Western Front went online and into streaming technologies in 1999, they connected via telephone to networked projects such as *Horizontal Radio* (1995) and *Natural Radia* (with Tetsuo Kogawa in Vienna, 2002). To Hank Bull, the telephone is a «truly democratic communications medium ... to the point where—and this is one of the miracles of the telephone—it is a fully multiplexed medium, which means you and I can be on the phone talking at the same time and we can hear both of our voices or, for that matter, we could even have four voices. It is not an over-to-you situation like e-mail, or a [conventional] walkie-talkie ... To paraphrase Gene Youngblood, we could call it expanded telephone» [early telecommunications technologies such as fax, ARTEX, SSTV, etc. were all telephone peripherals].[39] *Wiencouver* continues today mainly as part of the annual *Art's Birthday* celebrations on January 17th, whenever artists both in Vancouver and Vienna participate in and/or initiate this or other events.

For Bull, 1983 and 1986 held two key events. The first was *La Plissure du Texte* and following was *Planetary Network*, a part of the 42nd Venice Biennale. Conceived as an interactive multi-authored telematic publication, *La Plissure*

Bill Bartlett, 1983.

du Texte was based on the narrative form of a fairy tale. Each participating city was assigned a character following, very roughly, as organizer Roy Ascott notes, V.I. Propp's archetypes. Vancouver was the princess.[40] The title of *La Plissure du Texte* is itself a nod to Roland Barthes's *Le Plaisir du Texte* (*The Pleasure of the Text*) from 1975, an attempt to find a way outside of the realm of «both conservative society and militant leftist thinking,» which Barthes felt stifled the very ability to read and write. It was intended as a kind of textual *«jouissance,»* a means of creating a cathartic climax through the act of reading, an act that enabled a (albeit temporary) loss of self through intimate engagement with text.[41] «My belief in this new order of the text, actually a new order of discourse,» Ascott writes, «and my wish to exercise and celebrate the participatory mode of dispersed authorship which networking affords, led me to devise a project wholly concerned with the interweaving of textual inputs from a global distribution of artists. This became *La Plissure du Texte* …»[42]

Planetary Network (1986) engaged more than one hundred artists spanning three continents on the idea of «daily news.» It took place in two stages: the first—a networked *Laboratory Ubiqua*—was a two-week period of live exchanges with on-site activities and exhibitions at the Venice Biennale; the second was a two-month long virtual conference via ARTEX, sponsored by the I.P. Sharp Network.[43] Both events in 1983 and 1986 embodied the potentialities of the network and its ideals. The network component of both events were organized by Robert Adrian via ARTEX. (For *La Plissure du Texte*, the Vancouver network component took place from the Western Front, where Adrian was an artist-in-residence at the time and also organized the basic network.) The two projects were very different in structure, at least as far as the two weeks of the networked *Laboratory Ubiqua* were concerned: here Venice served as a kind of hub for the exchange using different media, among them the by then color Slow Scan TV contributions, which

40 Other characters and cities were as follows: Alma, Quebec – beast, Amsterdam – villain, Bristol – trickster, Honolulu – Wise Old Man, Paris – magician, Pittsburgh – prince, San Francisco – fool, Sydney – witch, Toronto – fairy godmother, Vancouver – princess, Vienna – sorcerer's apprentice.

41 See Wikipedia.org: http://en.wikipedia.org/wiki/The_Pleasure_of_the_Text (accessed July 2007).

42 Roy Ascott, «Art and Telematics,» in Grundmann 1984 (see note 33), pp. 34–35.

43 Participating cities were Venice, Sydney, Honolulu, Vancouver, Los Angeles, San Francisco, Chicago, Toronto, Pittsburgh, Atlanta, Boston, Bristol, Paris, and Milan.

were displayed on screens at the Biennale. The following computer conference was an online conference over ARTEX more akin to *La Plissure du Texte* but, as a three-month-long open conference, lacking the unifying structure and impetus of the «global fairy tale» that characterized *La Plissure du Texte*. The semantics at the time are also revealing: in *Planetary Network*, and earlier projects, those taking part are referred to as participants, not as artists. In both cases, importance is tied more to process than the final result. Further to this, this shift signaled the idea that many of the participants were from fields outside of art (ham radio operators, electricians, university and school children, educators, etc.), widening the scope of who took part in the events and how they were understood.

Bull, like many others who were practicing at the time, saw *Planetary Network* as the end of an era. As he recalls, the debate was whether artists should participate in this new thing called the Internet. Spurred by the Internet and alternative media art, telematic art exploded on the alternative art scene, just as mail art once did. An interesting aside to this discussion is a comment made by Canadian artist Norman White, in an interview about early telematic art. White, who through Bob Bernecky at I.P. Sharp Associates (IPSA) was the first artist to begin working on this network, reveals in the interview that he believes that the

Roberto Paci Dalò,
Hank Bull, and
Peter Courtemanche
(left to right),
Art's Birthday, Grand
Lux, The Western Front,
Vancouver, transmitting
to Tetsuo Kogawa,
Radio Kinesonus,
Tokyo, 2007.

«problem with today's technologies [the Internet included] is that they're not limiting enough. In other words, artists don't have to improvise to get around the limitations of the technologies.»[44]

With this in mind, it is fitting to close with some ideas Bull relayed at the end of our interview in December 2006:

> I see art as a path or a relationship to people and to life. It's about the way you live your life. You make your life into a work of art. It's not about making objects and selling them. It is an attitude and the objects are what are left behind from the real practice. They are not the actual art, they are the trace of the art … It's not the artist as a content provider, it's an artist as a context provider.[45]

44 Jeremy Turner, *Interview with Norman White about Early Telematic Art at Open Space in Victoria, Canada*, http://openspace.ca/web/ outerspace/NormanWhiteInterview2 (accessed July 2007).

45 Interview with Hank Bull (see note 7).

Radio Amidst Technological Ideologies

Reinhard Braun

Writing about FidoNet, Tom Jennings retrospectively notes that it was a «very strange, complicated, very large social organism, a terror-toma partially/intentionally of my creation. It still lives on, shockingly, today, and still thrives in places where people have no money and terrible telephone systems.»[1] To him, the early BBS systems were «in fact a collection of social conventions encoded in software ...»[2] But why are descriptions of network projects—structured hierarchically according to coordinators and nodes—of interest here when the title focuses primarily on a very different sphere of media, that of radio? The attempt to formulate this interest ultimately leads to debates on the ambivalent and antagonistic relationship between technology, society, and culture as a whole—the focus of the following.

In this context, Tom Jennings addresses a core conflict of this relationship, meaning to what extent can technical media be described as cultural techniques, or to what extent do they elude the control of social and cultural practices. The domain of radio as a mass medium may be considered exemplary of this latter perspective—as broadcasting that connects recipients to its «disciplinarian production of cultural knowledge,»[3] excluding them from any form of participation. While it will eventually evolve that even the sphere of radio can no longer be described in this way, it will serve for the time being as a chimera of social fantasies of order, so as to make visible the changes that the conception of media, mediatized spaces, and their entrenchment in culture and society have undergone, and have had to undergo.

A first line of approach in outlining these changes lies in the observation that the entire development of alternative communications systems would have been inconceivable without the (discursive and technological) dominance of mass media, given that they form the commercialized, institutionalized, hegemonialized, and restricted antipodes of those movements supporting free, independent network structures, that is, control of the technical means and therefore the possibility of alternative application. But even if this contrast was, and still to some extent remains, important, within this antipode we come upon a contradiction— radio in particular, both as a technology and a media space, is experiencing an unforeseen renaissance in the triumphant advance of wireless technologies of recent years and hence also in the realm of strategies for building free networks based on decentralized self-organization. It soon evolves, then, that radio (not only recently) has assumed a whole array of (likewise contradictory) forms and formats, not simply developing from a mass medium to a network but rather comprising a myriad of practices. While these practices revolve around the paradigm of broadcasting, this would also seem to assume very different functions and meanings in various contexts: from the classical distribution of programs to the simple (and inexpensive, albeit physically limited) dissemination of information, in the realm of community building, to the organization of political countermovements, and, not least, as a medium in the field of artistic practices with a broad and long tradition.

1 See http://wps.com/FidoNet/.

2 Ibid.

3 A figure of speech that I borrow from Judith Butler. See Judith Butler, «Überarbeitungen der Macht: Linda Singer und die Logik des Epidemischen,» in geld.beat.synthetik. copyshop 2. Abwerten bio/technologischer Annahmen, ed. Susanne Schultz, BüroBert, minimal club, Edition ID-Archiv (Berlin: Rotation Vertrieb, 1996), pp. 112–26, here p. 118.

4 «We define media as a historical a priori of the organization of sensory perception...In the bird's eye view and with the incredible

acceleration of the human body in space, experiences become important that revolutionize the technical organization of the collective physical constitution...Film is the development of forms of apperception preformed in modern machines; it is about deepening apperception, not about interpreting its meaning.» See Norbert Bolz, «Die Schrift des Films,» in Diskursanalysen 1: Medien, ed. F. Kittler, M. Schneider, and S. Weber (Opladen: Westdeutscher Verlag, 1987), pp. 26–34, here p. 28.

5 Vilém Flusser, Ins Universum der technischen Bilder (Göttingen: European Photography, 1990), p. 35.

In many cases, broadcasting something implies being a cultural communicator, disseminating, distributing something, enabling it to link up with other broadcasts and accordingly to a circulation of media formats. This «broadcast,» or rather that which is broadcast, not only has a vast number of manifestations and contents, it also engages with manifold communicative practices and thereby with numerous other technologically based cultural techniques. And thanks to this eminent expansion of what radio can be, it long ago became part of a tradition of artistic telecommunications projects from the nineteen-seventies and eighties, intermeshing with forms of radio art that, in turn, considered themselves constituent in this telecommunications art, constantly reflecting on the changes in radio due to new communications technologies. The broadcasting format of radio and its contents therefore exist in direct relationship to countless other media and communications formats.

For this reason, it appears necessary to expound on problems related to the discursification of media and media technologies—and particularly as regards the problematization of radio as a media technology—in an extended sphere of media practices, as the opposite poles of «radio» and «new media,» mass media and alternative media, cannot be maintained in this form, for radio has long since become immersed in the complex and diversified contemporary media landscape. And Tom Jennings's above-quoted terminology, his reference to a «very large social organism» and a «collection of social conventions encoded in software» applies without reservation to radio. The quotation also seems to spotlight a core aspect in the problematization of media technologies and social paradigms, for Jennings's diction demonstrates a concrete conception of the relationship between technology and its cultural implementation: Jennings does not abstract technology from the social contexts of its actual use, but rather he sees it tied to the specific semantics of everyday life, the «social conventions.» This emphasis on the production of a social context inverts, as it were, the narrative of media determinism. It amends the notion that describes media as a historical a priori of the organization of sensory perception and of society as a whole.[4] Vilém Flusser defined the inescapability (*Unhintergehbarkeit*) of media with the aid of the new technical image: «We live in an imagined world of technical images, and we increasingly experience, recognize, assess, and act as a function of these images.»[5] In terms of literature, Bernhard Dotzler describes the situation thus: «Since Turing, all that remains for literature is to recapitulate as far as its former control center functions are concerned.»[6] And Jens Schreiber, finally, speaks of a reality reduced to code operations, wired to provide logical functionality.[7] So technical media are thought to have put an end to the bad infinity of reality, putting social processes in a calculable—and thus controllable—framework. Within this framework, the social is divested of its sociocultural dimension: not the sometimes unsystematic, subjective narratives and drafts for action are relevant, but rather code operations and logical functionalities. Connected to many different channels and surfaces, the social individual then processes a program preset by technology. Technology becomes a culturally independent and culture-forming element in everyday patterns of action, with people handling technical apparatuses or operating in technically generated environments in a more or less capable manner. Hence Marshall McLuhan's prediction of man as machine's servomechanism would seem to have come true.[8]

According to this understanding, media would have always been implemented in society a priori (through research, industry, the market), not merely never fully under the control of this society or its cultural parameters but indeed independent of them, as permanent, autonomous machinic zones, as it were, as an unattainable framework, or «enframing» (Gestell), to borrow one of Heidegger's concepts.[9] We then, as recipients, operators, and users, can only relate to them, refer to them, in a step of translation, mediatization, (temporary) appropriation, in a mode of representation. Accordingly, artistic projects would also simply illustrate aspects of

6   Bernhard Dotzler, «Nachrichten aus der früheren Welt – und Zukunft: Zur Programmierung der Literatur mit und nach Babbage,» in Computer als Medium, ed. Norbert Bolz, Friedrich Kittler, and Christoph Tholen (Munich: Fink, 1994), pp. 39–68, here p. 57.

7   Jens Schreiber, «Stop Making Sense,» in Bolz 1994 (see note 6), pp. 91–110, here p. 101.

8   «By continuously embracing technologies, we relate ourselves to them as servomechanisms,» Marshall McLuhan, Die magischen Kanäle – Understanding Media (Dresden and Basel: Verlag der Kunst, 1994), p. 81. This rhetoric is also found in Vilém Flusser: «In this way, the original ‹man/apparatus› relationship is inverted and functions as a function of the apparatus.» See Flusser 1990 (see note 5), p. 64.

9   See Hartmut Böhme, Fetischismus und Kultur: Eine andere Theorie der Moderne (Frankfurt am Main: Rowohlt, 2006), pp. 64ff.

10 Schultz 1996 (see note 3).

11 Friedrich Kittler, Grammophon, Film, Typewriter (Berlin: Brinkmann U. Bose, 1986), preface.

12 Karl H. Hörnig, «Kulturelle Kollisionen: Die Soziologie vor neuen Aufgaben,» in Widerspenstige Kulturen: Cultural Studies als Herausforderung, ed. Rainer Winter Hörnig (Frankfurt am Main: Suhrkamp, 1999), pp. 84–115, here p. 107.

13 The most well-known are without doubt Die Welt in 24 Stunden (1982), see Dr. Horst Stadlmayr, ed., Ars Electronica im Rahmen des Internationalen Brucknerfestes Linz: Festival für Kunst, Technologie und Gesellschaft (Linz, 1982), pp. 145–56, and Horizontal Radio (1995), Linzer Veranstaltungsgesellschaft mbH; see also www.kunstradio.at/HORRAD/horrad.html.

the functionality of technology, their consequences for the «revolutionization of the collective physical condition»[10] or their virtually incredible possibilities for digitally transforming everything into anything. However, in this case, cultural and artistic practices would by no means be in a position to involve technology in a system of actions that could change technology itself and, on that basis, develop a new concept of a sociotechnical culture. If what remains of people is what media can store and communicate, as Friedrich Kittler writes, then all that remains for these people is to negotiate effects of technology and media by way of representation, without approximating their materiality, since what counts are not the messages or content but rather only their circuits.[11]

The idea that the military-industrial complex is constantly throwing new technical components at something we call the market, thereby coercing society and culture to adapt these components, to somehow implement them in everyday cultural interaction, creates a hierarchical concept of this society, with a formation of science/research/technology—not conceived as culturally determined—at the vertex of a triangle that is not even isosceles, at the base of which lies a diffuse set of social and cultural (including artistic) processes that are all somehow linked to or increasingly influenced by technology.

Only technology itself remains constant here. I would like to counter this concept with the idea that media, technology, and the societal form a common dispositive, share common terrain, that is not only interrelated in discourses but rather displays its efficacy precisely in that the various positions within the dispositive are assigned functions, each having an effect on the other positions. In this triad, no element remains stable but rather is constantly being modified by the other elements. «For the more thoroughly technical things circulate in a society, the more people (have to) involve themselves with them, the less any kind of deterministic opinion is appropriate, the less ‹technology› appears as a prefabricated substance, as a solidified ensemble of assumptions, strategies, and materials, as a lasting ‹rule›—and the more people do something with it, entrenching it in their social life by means of their practices of production and use.»[12] A project such as *Wiencouver*, which I will discuss in the following, is exemplary of many other projects[13] that by means of their usage practices involve components of media and technology in processes that reformulate technology as a prefabricated substance, consequently redefining the ideological paradigm of technology.

The «fabrication» in question is a production, a poiesis ... but a hidden one, since it is concealed in the areas defined and occupied by systems of (televisual, urban, commercial, etc.) «production» ... The counterpart to a rationalized, expansionist, but also centralized, clamorous, and spectacular production is *another* production, termed «consumption»: the latter is devious and dispersed, but it insinuates itself everywhere, silently and almost invisibly, for it does not manifest itself through its own products, but rather in its approach to using the products imposed by a dominant economic order.[14]

It should be all the more appropriate to put forward what Michel de Certeau calls for here as a form of production—of a different approach to dealing with products in the field of consumption—with regard to those practices that may be viewed as active appropriation, redefinition, adaptation, and modification of tele-media systems, thus as equally dispersed but sometimes also equally spectacular and clamorous practices of media art projects (likewise distinguishable, in most cases, for not creating their own products but rather constituting ways of handling products). «For to the same extent that we must refute the notion of ‹technology› embodying a transhistorical and transcultural nature, so too must we refute the notion that ‹society,› ‹history,› ‹culture,› and ‹nature› may be perceived detached from their mediation by technology.»[15] It is not, therefore, a matter of rescuing the subject, society, and culture from the clutches of technology—it is a matter of their mutual mediation, of comprehending «technology/science as a ‹social artefact,› i.e. as an instrument for managing unstable constructions, contingent laws, historically altered interpretations, and political definitions.»[16]

In 1979, Hank Bull was invited to Vienna to participate in the *Audio Scene '79* project which focused on sound as a medium of visual art. During his participation, he developed the idea of an imaginary city, conceived to span between Vienna (*Wien*) and Vancouver, and finally named this «city» *Wiencouver*. *Wiencouver*

14 Michel de Certeau, *Kunst des Handelns* (Berlin: Merve, 1988), p. 13; English title: *The Practice of Everyday Life*.

15 Sabeth Buchmann, «Kritik der Medientheorie,» in *Im Zentrum der Peripherie: Kunstvermittlung und Vermittlungskunst in den 90er Jahren*, ed. Marius Babias (Dresden and Basel: Verlag der Kunst, 1995), pp. 79–103, here p. 81.

16 Ibid., p. 97.

represents Hank Bull's conception of radio as a sculpture as well as an aesthetic of social action and international communication between artists. The focus, then, is on the construction of a media structure as platform for an altogether socioculturally perceived communications space—a space simultaneously defined in terms of sculpture and aesthetics, that is, initially conceptualized from the realm of art prior to an emergence as the scene of a media-based project. The sculptural dimension of this space appears as an interrelation of spaces, artistic material, activities, and collaborative situations but also of ideas and hypotheses, of temporary assumptions, texts, sounds, transmitted images, of correspondence and information. This space differs from the space drafted by developers in the early timesharing networks (accessible also to artists at the end of the nineteen-seventies) or from the radio space discussed and criticized since the nineteen-twenties in terms of its mass-media limitations. The space created in *Wiencouver* incorporates the modalities both of the employed technology and of the interpersonal collaboration. From such a perspective, the medium as artifact and form of practice only assumes its function when linked to sociocultural processes. This fosters those hybrid, amorphous, but also symmetrical media spaces of varied representations, of limited range, of variable meanings, of a liquid aesthetic;

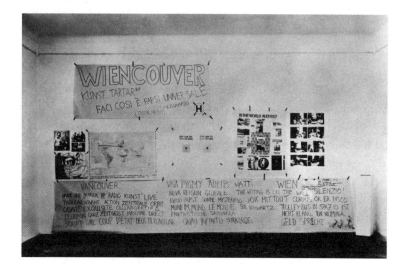

Hank Bull, *Wiencouver I*, installation, *Audio Scene '79*, Modern Art Galerie (Grita Insam), Vienna, Austria, 1979.

spaces in which ideas of cultural practices such as action, cooperation, experience, communication, distribution, and so forth, are each specifically negotiated, with the role of technology being redefined respectively; spaces in which something like shared social time is created by way of temporary and hypothetical agreements, in a word, a scope of agency involving collaborating individuals, where above all culturally relevant parameters are up for discussion and are negotiated beyond hegemonic (media) concepts; and a space in which questions regarding the function and dispositive of the applied media forms and systems are ultimately negotiated and not merely appropriated.

The expanding, elusive, and temporary gestalt of this imaginary city amidst increasingly extensive networks has survived—with interruptions—to this day. In January 2007, *Kunstradio* broadcast the *Wiencouver 1906* project, «a radiophonic meeting above the waves of the Atlantic, somewhere between Vienna and Vancouver. A transcontinental broadcast dedicated to the sounds which emanated before the emergence of wireless communication.»[17] *Wiencouver* has thus evolved since its beginnings into a complex media space, simultaneously discovered and constructed, transcending the (media) spaces of the individual projects and also incorporating a social network of individuals and institutions (since 1999 primarily *Kunstradio* in Vienna and the Western Front Society in Vancouver)—a space «that is determined by social rules and norms of partial societies, partial public spheres, and institutions … The artists occupy this space or partial aspects of this space—often only for a very short time—putting different contents and forms into this space, moving forms from one part into another, reproducing spaces in each other in real time …»[18] Hence, the city metaphor manifests itself as an attempt and also an opportunity to formulate the space of such projects as having always been «civilized,» that is, culturally influenced, as well as to understand the interactional relationships as a form of «civitas,» meaning as a politicized community of social individuals. In this sense, it cannot be said that the concept of the city constitutes an inadequate metaphor for a media phenomenon either; rather, this metaphor attempts to describe the media phenomenon as a social context.

17 See http://www.kunstradio.at/2007A/14_01_07.html.

18 Eduardo Kac, «Aspekte einer Ästhetik der Telekommunikation,» in *ZERO – The Art of Being Everywhere*, ed. Steirische Kulturinitiative (Graz: Leykam, 1993), pp. 24–92, here p. 70.

19 David Morley, «Wo das Globale auf das Lokale trifft: Zur Politik des Alltags,» in Hörnig 1999 (see note 12), pp. 442–75, here p. 467.

20 John Fiske, «Wie ein Publikum entsteht,» in Hörnig 1999 (see note 12), pp. 238–63, here p. 251.

What ensues is a new space, a media-determined scope of agency, not founded on a breach between subject/society and technology but rather construing the conflicts, the fragmentation, questions of presence and localization, questions of the construction of meanings on the basis of dividing lines running transversely to technology and culture, transecting both fields in equal measure. These divisions also pervade radio space, no longer perceived as being controlled from a center but instead merging into a space constructed in different media, a space that appears and disappears, both unifying and fragmenting experiences beyond localities. This results, in a sense, in a «diasporic ceremony»[19] of scattered but interrelated practices, contributions, translations, and transformations. John Fiske describes this way of life as the «creation of connections beyond the scope of experiential spaces»;[20] without intending to romanticize a project such as *Wiencouver*, the evolving conception of the project components over a time period of nearly three decades has repeatedly revealed this interest in (diverse geographical and cultural) experiential spaces interrelated in varied ways (by fax, Slow Scan TV, telephone, radio, etc.). Yet the technological basis of these interrelated experiential spaces must not be confused with the spaces themselves. Consequently, in these experiential spaces, technology and media no longer ap-

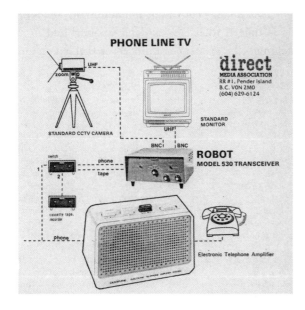

Diagram for slow-scan
TV setup, 1979.

pear as those products of a prevailing economic order but alternatively as interpreted, articulated, and transformed agents in a terrain of cultural production that regards social, technological, and scientific determinations as the «result of mutual relationalizations between elements, … that only take shape by means of these relationalization processes.»[21]

«Never is an arrangement combination technological, indeed it is always the contrary. The tools always presuppose a machine, and the machine is always social before it is technical. There is always a social machine which selects or assigns the technical elements. A tool, an instrument, remains marginal or little used for as long as the social machine or the collective arrangement-combination capable of taking it into its *phylum* does not exist.»[22] The term «phylum» is borrowed from botany and bacteriology and may be regarded as describing the principle of a division (*Stamm*) in the sense of a non-hierarchical, heterogeneous, and rhizomatic group of elements.[23] Following this conception, I understand cultural processes as heterogeneous mechanisms that rearrange and constantly redistribute the elements of these phyla, perpetually creating new associations within these elements/components, without referring to any fixed, stable starting point, an all-determining root or beginning: neither technology nor the subject can occupy this place.[24] The new connections thus do not coincide with the circuits of media applications or systems, nor do they constitute an unalterable «materiality of communication.»[25] «This is indeed what Deleuze and Guattari had in mind when coining the term ‹machinic,› the existence of processes that act on an ini-

21   Ingo Schulz-Schaeffer, *Akteur-Netzwerk-Theorie: Zur Koevolution von Gesellschaft, Natur und Technik*, http://www2.tu-berlin.de/~soziologie/Crew/schulz-schaeffer/pdf/AkteurNetzwerkTheorie.pdf, p. 207.

22   Quoted after Jean-Louis Comolli, «Machines of the Visible,» in *Electronic Culture: Technology And Visual Representation*, ed. Timothy Druckrey (New York: Aperture, 1996), pp. 108–117, here p. 109.

23   Not the tree trunk (*Baumstamm*) as the starting point of all branches but rather the bacterial strain (*Bakterienstamm*) that knows nothing but branching.

24   See Buchmann in Babias 1995 (see note 15).

25   As the title of one book puts it, see Hans Ulrich Gumbrecht and Ludwig Pfeiffer, eds., *Materialität der Kommunikation* (Frankfurt am Main: Suhrkamp, 1988).

26   Manuel De Landa, *The Machinic Phylum*, http://www.voorthuis.net/texts/Manuel_DeLanda_The_Machinic_Phylum.doc.

27   Hans Ulrich Reck, «Konnektivität und Kartographie. Über: künstlerische Praxis, Arbeit, Subjektivität, Handeln,» in *Offene Handlungsfelder*, ed. Peter Weibel (Cologne: DuMont, 1999), pp. 184–202, here p. 196. Hans Ulrich Reck also drafts art as a social agency, as a «constant opening up of scopes of agency»: «In terms of art, methods of transitoriness are of prime importance—albeit by no means exclusively—in that they are not geared to utilizing system conditions, but rather to invention and intervention, i.e. in that they draft and test their own type of action that … is neither normative nor instrumental.» Ibid., p. 194.

28   Schultz 1996 (see note 3).

tial set of merely coexisting, heterogeneous elements, and cause them to come to-gether and consolidate into a novel entity. As they say, ‹what we term machinic is precisely this synthesis of heterogeneities as such.›»[26] Within the context of such projects as *Horizontal Radio*, *Rivers and Bridges*, *Sound Drifting*, and others, this «novel entity» appears to entail a temporary coexistence of heterogeneous elements: public sphere, data networks, software, text, performative actions, ar-chives and databases, interactive production, and so on, that is, an «ensemble» of subjects and machines—related to each other in various practices—forms a phylum, an intermeshed scope of agency, with actors who project all elements of this «ensemble» onto each other, changing their (temporary) meaning «without being able to occupy or even just refer to any fixed space.»[27]

Against this backdrop of an alternate conceptualization of technocultural processes, numerous theoretical studies have opposed the aforementioned «dis-ciplinarian production of cultural reality»[28] by means of theories that, ensuing from modernism, still advocate a utopia of rationalization and control of society: according to them, modernism appears as a *scopic regime* (a concept tracing back to Christian Metz) of a panoramatic gaze that sees all, or as an electro-magnetic regime (including radio) that causes the social individuals to oscillate

Wiencouver II, flyer inviting participation in the Wiencouver Mail Art and Telecomm event, 1980.

communally and collectively, putting them on the same frequency and combining a structuring of time with a structuring of space. The ideology of the medium in the sense of modernism, which «along with its vividness, resonance, and depth also [loses] the ability to organize and lend meaning to people's lives,»[29] hence consisted/consists in the ability to control the social and the societal (the production of depth and resonance) as the ability to control space and time. The medium of modernism installs itself as a structural order of societal terrain.

Under current conditions, the participation in media (and hence in the mass medium of radio) is characterized by a comparably private and temporally displaced mode of a self-duplicating media consumption, creating participation in a space conceived as *public* under totally different conditions. This postmodern mode does not connect the addressees (consumers?) to a medium but rather already assumes general media accessibility and availability of events and processes—an accessibility, however, from which every consumer/participant group is increasingly extracting its own *version* of the published events. This puts the generalizing performance of mass media under pressure, as the general horizon of a social present—general technical control of natural and societal processes—tends to disintegrate into a myriad of divergent events and present horizons that can no longer be synchronized by these media within a coherent, tendentially controllable space, as was characteristic of the modernist function of mass media. The homogeneous—or at least homogeneously conceived—territory of mass media is disintegrating into numerous sub-territories and has, so to speak, dispersed along a host of different media channels.

Radio too is not only disintegrating into numerous disjointed and asynchronous territories—it also evolves that radio as a modernist mass medium has above all been a political project that is proving less and less suitable for controlling and synchronizing the «masses» in the course of postmodern neoliberalism. The transition to post-mass-media mechanisms of processing, control, and regulation (flat hierarchies, distributed production and mediation instances, etc.)

29 Ian Chambers, «Städte ohne Stadtplan,» in Hörnig 1999 (see note 12), pp. 514–42, here p. 527.

30 A term coined by Marshall McLuhan in 1962 in his book *The Gutenberg Galaxy*; see Martin Balts et al., eds., *Medien verstehen: Der McLuhan-Reader* (Mannheim: Bollmann, 1997), pp. 84ff.

31 David Morley (see note 19) in Hörnig 1999 (see note 12), p. 458.

must therefore be principally interpreted as a strategic reaction to the loss of the media-based coupling of society, as a political (if not to say, ideological) project aiming to not lose control completely. And once again, technologies are the linchpin in this effort to retain control and to put society as a «global village»[30] back into an order that, as the village metaphor suggests, sets a common experiential horizon, conceived not as an agglomeration, as a phylum of heterogeneous elements, but rather as an almost primal common horizon of a cultural identity owing its foundation and stabilization to technology.

Yet in the sphere of media art practices—especially in those set at the interface between communications technologies and radio, thus intermeshing, redefining, and reciprocally superimposing divergent media dispositives—it becomes increasingly clear, in my opinion, how such conceptions of the relationship between medium and reality, between medium and society, are drifting away from an essentialization of technology. They are departing from a figure such as «placelessness,» as romantic as it is ideological, having brought into play the question of the modes of power, «[creating a] strongly standardized televisual language that tends to devaluate and edge out all others.»[31] As a result, the space of radio is likewise divested of its (modern) abstractions and becomes in-

The Haters
(GX Jupitter-Larsen and Dermot Foley),
Wiencouver IV,
performance for slow-scan TV and sound transmission to Vienna,
The Western Front, Vancouver, Canada, 1983.

creasingly articulated as a specific way of creating translocal experiential spaces characterized not by conflation and standardization but by «heterogenesis»[32] and diversification. And to engender these heterogeneous and diversified spaces of experience and action, the programs are not «read» from the technical objects, media, surfaces, environments, or systems, in view of which the cultural context would be of secondary importance. Media art practices go against the figure of re-presentation, against forms of being re-presented, against the unattainability of discourses, against the unattainability of systems. They instead appear as projects, making visible processes «that define an experience in which the subject and object form and transform one via the other, and one in the function of the other.»[33]

32 Andreas Broeckmann, «Medienökologie und Ästhetik der Heterogenese,» in *Netzkritik: Materialien zur Internet-Debatte*, ed. Nettime (Berlin: Edition ID-Archiv, 1997), pp. 186–200, here p. 194.

33 Giorgio Agamben, *Profanierungen* (Frankfurt am Main: Suhrkamp, 2005), p. 60.

RadioZeit

A Project by Richard Kriesche

RadioZeit (RadioTime) was performed in October 1988 as part of the international radio art symposium With the Eyes Shut–Bilder im Kopf: Ein Symposium zur Theorie und Praxis der Radiokunst at the Styrian Autumn Festival in Graz, Austria.[1]

For his performance, Richard Kriesche invited the participants of the symposium into his—darkened—studio in Graz, which was equipped with a parabol antenna outside its window catching the signals from a weather satellite as well as with a beamer projecting live images from the satellite onto the wall opposite the audience. Also connected to the antenna was a digital sampling keyboard containing Mozart's *Kleine Nachtmusik* («A Little Night Music»). Richard Kriesche himself sat, confronting the audience, beside the projection at a table, and in the light of a small lamp he read a text called «*RadioZeit.*» To the frustra-

Richard Kriesche, *RadioZeit*, weather satellite
antenna, Graz, Austria, 1989.

tion of the audience, the voice of the reading artist was drowned in the noise of the satellite signals and the fragments of the *Kleine Nachtmusik* occasionally triggered by the data from the satellite. The performance became a perfect image for the white noise of data, the all-devouring backdrop of a digitalized society, one of the central issues in Richard Kriesche's art and theoretical thinking. For a 1989 radio version of *RadioZeit*, Kriesche used not only excerpts from the text he had read in Graz but also some freely spoken statements. On the radio, his words were intelligible. Kriesche's partners in *RadioZeit* were the musician and media artist Josef Klammer as well as a ham radio expert, along with experts from the Technical University, Graz.

In the text used in his performance and on radio, Kriesche formulated for the first time some ideas, which reappeared in a lecture appropriately named «In the Noise of the Signals» held in 1990 in Vienna at the radio art symposium Geometry of Silence, which took place simultaneously at the Museum Moderner Kunst in Vienna and at the Tiroler Landesmuseum Ferdinandeum in Innsbruck. The two museums were temporarily connected via digital telephone lines especially installed by the Austrian Post. In 1994, Kriesche's lecture «In the Noise of the Signals» was published in a slightly revised version in English in *Radio Rethink: Art, Sound and Transmission* by the Walter Philipps Gallery at The Banff Centre for the Arts.

In the above-mentioned text, Kriesche refers to radio, and specifically to car radio, in a digital (informational) age, when he writes (in 1990):

«...it was only with car radio that radio found its real definition and designation. this history of radio accompanies the section of history covering a technological society that has been set into motion. from the stationary box to transistor and ultimately car radio, from the stationary to the mobile and ultimately to the dynamic object. dynamic because the ‹apparatus radio› becomes so ‹interconnected› with the ‹machine car› that the dynamics of the machine and the statics of the apparatus raise each other to a higher level of power. as the

---

1   The symposium was organized by *Kunstradio*. Among the participants were Bruce Barber, Bruno Beusch, Vittorio Fagone, Bill Fontana, Fritz Grohs, Douglas Kahn, Georg Katzer, Friedrich Kittler, Richard Kriesche, Minus Delta T (Mike Hentz and Karal Dudesek), Radio Subcom (Oil Blo and Armin Medosch), László Révés and Gábor Bora, Klaus Schöning, János Sugár, Helen Thorington, Ed Tomney, Nicholas Zurbrugg, and Peter Weibel. For *RadioZeit*, see also http://www.kunstradio.at/1989A/19 _1_89.html.

moving car sets the radio in motion, the radio heats up the body that is now motionless—tied down with belts...car television is replaced by collages on the car window. the tv screen is replaced by the wind screen. driving along, whether along the highways or in urban rushhour traffic, corresponds increasingly to the collage technique of the dadaists. concrete dirt on the window panes, mixed up with fragments of landscape, melt together to become an inseparable unity. video clip technology with its extremely short cuts and sounds continues the trip at highest speeds in the mental space, beyond all visible speeds and laws of perception. the special significance of car radio lies in its unique fusion of the industrial and the informational communication levels...it thus becomes clear that the mobile subject, once set into motion, dissolves increasingly into a noise of the signals. in the car radio, the data of the channels blur with the sound of the motor and the temporal collages of the car windshield to become a synaesthetic perception of the world. the faster the movement, the more this background emerges. the higher the speed, the harder it gets to filter ‹stationary data› from the data background, that is to follow the program, pick out information. the multidimensional data background becomes the actual program. in it, the speed of the moving body is proportional to the noise of the signals, until at last it melts inaudibly into the background releasing only one piece of information, that of the background...in the space age this noise does not suggest distance between the scene of the action and the receiver, as it did at the beginning of the radio age, but rather a compressed speed for the subject that remains in immobility (rigor mortis!).

RADIOMAN

the electric man no longer listens to the radio—he himself is radio: set at the same time on reception and transmission. as a sign of his existence he thus leaves his marks on the data background. the drawing of marks is the basis of his existence (on video, banking card, telephone, fax, personal computer and so on). as if in recognition of the electric circuits in his own body, the ‹radioman› charges himself up with mobile electronic calculators, watches, data and dictating machines, walkmans, cellular telephones, electronic locators, laptops, notebooks. supported by batteries, he creates around himself the postmodern aura of an omnipresence. his exterior is radiant...his interior is embedded in the electronic community of the data background. he himself is a light spot (pixel) in the space of surfaces, the ‹computer planes,› of foregrounds, backgrounds and image planes. into them he plunges, to disappear and then emerge in another place as someone else. as a light spot the ‹radioman› has permanently taken on the form of the vanishing point.»

Past and Present of Radio Art

A 1995 Perspective

Heidi Grundmann

Notably often it has been pointed out that much of what artists do today was anticipated by the exponents of the avant-garde at the beginning of the twentieth century. For radio art in its current, advanced form, Dadaist sound poetry or Futurist art of noise remain important traditions. What turns out to be a veritable treasure trove for describing what artists do and think today, however, as Douglas Kahn has illustrated, are likewise the writings of those, for example among the Russian artists and authors, who took radio as a metaphor for something that, at that time, implied a (better) future: a metaphor of the new technological development, at the time still regarded as progress, that would go hand in hand with a new society and thereby with a new art.

It was in this sense that Majakowski wrote about radio—incidentally also demanding radio for poets—just as Vertov imagined his «Radio-Eye» as a «most powerful instrument in the hands of the proletariat, as an opportunity for the workers of the world to hear, see and understand one another in an organized fashion,» or that Khlebnikov envisaged radio as strengthening the muscle power of harvesters. In his story «The Moon King,» Apollinaire positions King Louis II at a piano-like instrument in a mountain, listening in on the soundscapes of distant world regions by striking different keys. And, of course, Marinetti can also

This essay was written in April and May of 1995—originally entitled «Interplay»— and presented at the Alte Schmiede, Vienna, as an introduction to the then forthcoming *Horizontal Radio* project.

always be aptly quoted in this context, with his and Masnata's manifesto «*La Radia*,» in which the two demand a «new art that begins where theater cinema and narrative end,» an «art without time or space, without yesterday or tomorrow.»[1]

Everything has turned out differently than imagined by the political and artistic avant-garde. But they were right about one thing: technology has changed society and with it, art. Along with—and as a consequence of—what we today term «new technologies,» a different art is emerging than the one having accompanied industrialization to its horrible climaxes and its demise—be it in opposition to or as part thereof.

Drama of Distances:[2] 11 sec. of a military march performed in Rome—11 sec. of a tango performed in Santos—11 sec. of religious Japanese music played in Tokyo—11 sec. of a lively country-dance performed in the village of Varese—11 sec. of a boxing match in New York—11 sec. of street noise in Milan—11 sec. of a Neapolitan romance sung at the Hotel Copacabana in Rio de Janeiro.[3]

1 See Douglas Kahn in *Wireless Imagination: Sound, Radio, and the Avant-Garde*, ed. Douglas Kahn and Gregory Whitehead (Cambridge, MA: MIT Press, 1992). This book also contains the manifesto «*La Radia*» by F. T. Marinetti and Pino Massnata in English.

2 From the *5 Sintesi dal Teatro Radiofonico* by F. T. Marinetti.

3 From «Manifesti e scritti vari: La Radia,» quoted after F. T. Marinetti, *Teoria e Invenzione Futurista*, ed. Ludiano De Maria, preface by Aldo Palazzeschi (Milan: Arnoldo Mondadori Editore, 1968). Original Italian: «*Dramma di Distanze*: 11 sec di una marcia militare a Roma—11 sec di un tango danzato a Santos—11 sec di musica giapponese religiosa suonata a Tokio—11 sec di ballo campestre vivace nella campagna die Varesa—11 sec di un incontro di pugelato a New York—11 sec di rumorismo stradale in Milano—11 sec di romanza napoletana cantata nell albergo Copacabana di Rio de Janeiro.» See also Heidi Grundmann, «Radiokunst,» in «Im Netz der Systeme,» *Kunstforum International* 103 (September/October 1989); http://www.aec.at (Ars Electronica Festival archive).

4 See Kahn 1992 (see note 1) and also Douglas Kahn, «Radio Space,» in *Radio Rethink: Art, Sound and Transmission*, ed. Daina Augaitis and Dan Lander (Banff: Banff Centre Press, 1994).

5 Wolfgang Hagen, «Über das Radio (hinaus)» (beyONd RADIO), in *TRANSIT # 2 – Materialien zu einer Kunst im elektronischen Raum* (Vienna: Triton, 1993); published in both German and English. «It is conceivable and intended in DAB that you do not choose a station but rather press a desired category button—easy listening, radio drama, news or sports, and then the receiver will search for the desired category among the 6 or 12 or 24 stations and tune it in, consider follow-ups and automatically relay important messages. In other words digital radio is an intelligent listening guidance system as well as a refined traffic guidance system. Therefore, it is being massively financed by the industry.»

Marinetti's *Drama of Distances* and his other *Sintesi* (syntheses) of radiophonic theater are scores for short radio plays (that he never realized himself). They not only anticipate various, now mature genres of radio art (the soundscape, the radio sculpture, the live event) but rather also—like the manifesto and many other avant-garde texts before—already imply «*La Radia*»: globally spanning and enveloping, as an «immensification of space. No longer visible and frameable, the stage becomes universal and cosmic,» «*La Radia*» as a «pure organism of radio sensations,» as a «synthesis of infinite simultaneous actions.»[4]

Today the globe is encircled by satellites, riddled with all manner of cables, spanned by analog and digital transmission networks, networked by computers—and Marinetti's *Drama of Distances*, the live simultaneous broadcast from many cities around the globe, manifests itself, for instance, in the now everyday football reports featuring a few minutes or seconds of running commentary from games being played simultaneously in different cities.

«Media artists»—for want of a better word—belong to the community of those who not only reflect on and analyze the vast cultural change entailed by digitization but who also see their practice and theory as a consequence of this change. Outdated conceptual instruments are no longer effective but instead serve as a kind of consensual menu bar for accessing a space of action and reflection that remains hard to describe and position. In this situation, among other things, the avant-garde «*Radia*» utopias and images become charged with a current relevance, which in turn becomes amenable to a certain historical depth as well as to a potentially disparate future.

But digital radio means: transmission is control; namely that the data package sent, which will be processed by a new generation of intelligent receivers, contains not only the audio data and values of the transmitted music and speech; but also an arbitrary number of parallel controlling signals which can allow the arbitrary separation of music from words, loud from quiet, pop from classical, radio drama from feature, news from commentary; each piece of audio information will be codifiable, and therefore the receivers of such radio transmissions are in fact small programmable computers. Whereby the end of radio is heralded, the end of the one way transmission of a source from a transmitter to a receiver.[5]

Radio is no longer primarily an auditory medium. Rather, the educational goal of a refinement of the listener's sense of hearing—as postulated for many years by radio play, feature, and music departments in public service broadcasting—is also transferred into the marketable distribution mode of audio-on-demand, including saleable off-air products such as all manner of CDs (and an aftermarket of gimmicks). The audio signals that are actually transmitted reveal themselves as camouflage for all kinds of data: for traffic control and surveillance systems, for information that can also be requested as hard copy, for advertising the sale of audio-on-demand, et cetera—as material that may be arbitrarily mixed via telephone, Internet, and/or MIDI data, and so forth.

This development, having lately attracted much attention with the buzzword «data highway,» forms the backdrop—and has done so for over fifteen years[6]—for the work of those artists who also incorporate the radio medium into their examination of the new technologies.

In fact, some media artists in Austria also focused—at a comparatively early stage (for Europe) but above all relatively continuously—on interventions into the mass media of television and radio, including in productions created by ORF (Austrian National Radio and Television) itself. These productions were not usually broadcast in the music or literature sections but alternately in youth programs, in programs exploring an extended concept of culture, and in programs on current visual arts.

In retrospect, it seems symptomatic that in 1979 a live show from the radio series *Kunst heute* (Art Today), broadcast by ORF Radio, represented one of the many networked sites of *Interplay*, the first telecommunications project to also involve European artists: in Studio AR5 at the Broadcasting House in Vienna, production headquarters of the Österreich 1 program, there was a portable terminal with a modem. The printer was rattling away, heaping up continuous thermal paper higher and higher in soft folds on the table and floor of the small studio. Gottfried Bach, head of I.P. Sharp's Vienna office, a Canadian time-sharing com-

---

6 From a 1995 perspective.

7 This name was inspired by *Kunstfunk*, a telecommunications project for slow-scan TV and amateur radio, Vienna Secession, June 13–17, 1984, http://alien.mur.at/rax/KUNSTFUNK/index.html.

8 *Kunstradio – Radiokunst*, every Thursday, 10:15 p.m. to 11:00 p.m. on Österreich 1. Of course, *Kunstradio* also pursues and produces other radio art trends in addition to those described in this essay. Occasionally, *Kunstradio* initiates and (co-)organizes symposia and events and has published a CD edition as well as a T-shirt edition designed by artists.

pany that provided free computer time for this event, was typing in messages and could hardly keep up with reading out the answers of the artists participating from Vienna, Vancouver, Sydney, Chicago, Hawaii, and so on. And no one was aware that right there, for the first time in Austria and Europe, an art project, similar to the electronic networks so successful today, was opening up into the space of the mass medium radio, and that, in an event defined by artists as an artistic project, an image was being created for what today in 1995—sixteen years later—engages the general public as the future of mass media and of the home computer.

It was above all the concept of art developed in telecommunications projects by artists from diverse backgrounds that paved the way for transforming the ORF show *Kunst heute*—renamed *Kunstradio* (Art Radio)[7] in the nineteen-eighties, while still reporting on international contemporary visual arts—into the *Kunstradio–Radiokunst* (Art Radio–Radio Art) show in 1987: transposing from a journalistic series dedicated to international contemporary visual arts—having also occasionally broadcast works created by visual artists for the radio medium—to an on-air gallery and agency for radio art.[8] *Kunstradio* in its present form also acts as an organizer of projects that are not content with remaining in the protected gallery space of the weekly program but instead aim to break out into the context of everyday radio, television, and/or other public and institutionalized spaces (museums, «urban» space, newspapers, data spaces), taking on the character of a live event in front of a physically present audience, or involving the radio audience in the program, be it by phone or via the Internet. Since April 1995, *Kunstradio* has gained, in addition to its accustomed slot on the ORF radio program Österreich 1, an additional platform for the announcement, preparation, realization, and archivization of media-specific art, and for the distribution of theory and information: *Kunstradio On Line* on the World Wide Web.

The ideas, concepts, and perceptions acquired by some of the media artists through their long-standing dealings with computer networks correspondingly manifest in their work with the radio medium, the more so because they view radio precisely as one of many media in a large, truly world-spanning media system. Radio offers the opportunity for finding expressive images for some of these ideas that are changing fundamentally—compared with traditional concepts of art, work, author, audience, originality, et cetera—as a result of current practice. Hence, the flow of the radio program, now relegated as a background medium, may be compared, for example, with the flow of data enveloping our earth, which can be entered and exited at will at varying times and in manifold places: «The Finished Work of Art is a Thing of the Past,» as Tom Sherman recently titled one of his performative texts.[9]

One way that radio artists are accounting for this is by adapting their works not to the length of a radio program but rather, for instance, to that of a carrier medium such as the cassette tape, declaring that a program can start or end at any point on the cassette. Radio artists react to the different national legal situations, but also to the digitalization transforming everything into material that can be transferred into any media and context: for example, by sending their works on cassette—with the added comment «Copying and Broadcasting Welcome» or even «No Copyright»—out into the world of cassette networks, independent, autonomous, or pirate radios and occasionally also into the world of public service media with their strict copyright regulations.

Some of the international telecommunications projects with slow-scan TV, videophone, fax, and computer networks initiated in Austria in the nineteen-eighties also involved artists, writers, and musicians from Eastern Europe, who at that time did not have access to any forms of such «new media» and therefore were compelled to develop their contributions as «telephone music.» Today (that is, 1995), these projects are regarded as precursors of the oft-invoked «interactive television»: with the aid of sound, music, speech, text, and, if possible, images, they attempted for a given period of time to lift a space—defined by the media-based interconnection of all participants (such as, for example, in Vancouver, Vienna, Warsaw, Budapest, Berlin)—out of time as a sculptural space. The variously structured events at the different locations respectively influenced the events at the other locations and were, in turn, influenced by the input of the participants/users physically present elsewhere. The prevalent present-day keyword: tele-presence. Here, it was not so much the individual contribution, occasionally stemming from non-artists, but instead the collective gestalt of such

9 The text has meanwhile been published in Tom Sherman, *Before and After the I-Bomb: An Artist in the Information Environment*, ed. Peggy Gale (Banff: Banff Centre Press, 2002).

10 Douglas Kahn has on several occasions pointed out that «since the mid-1950s, on the heels of over two decades of radio and film sound and at the front of television, highly codified sounds could be apprehended at a qualitatively accelerated pace; this pace, when compared to earlier quotational practices within music, exists now at the atomistic site of the material itself.» Quoted from «Radio Space,» lecture at the Radio Rethink symposium, Banff, Alberta, 1992.

events (some of which lasted several weeks), no longer in all ramifications re-producible or repeatable, that was considered an «artwork,» that is, a sculpture, a collective composition or narrative.

Those artists who contribute only volatile fragments to such collective works are no longer addressing recipients, who are sure of their identity and immersing themselves with admiration into a sublime work, but rather are addressing frag-mented persons, who are—even in their (much-bemoaned) passivity—plurally active and accessible at many levels, their attention drifting, briefly docking here and there, being able with increasing alacrity to develop meanings and associations from the smallest particles of sound, image, and text encoded by the mass media.[10] In genuine network projects, recipients and authors coincide. Someone, however, must also define for such projects the point of departure, the context, and a minimal conceptual formulation within which the participants/users operate. In an online opera in 1992–93, for example, FidoNet users were able to retrieve and process MIDI files from the connected ZEROnet, developed for art projects and communication between artists, and feed them back into the network in a situation defined by Seppo Gründler. A preceding project from 1987 was *RAZIONALNIK*, initiated by Seppo Gründler and Josef Klammer: a live

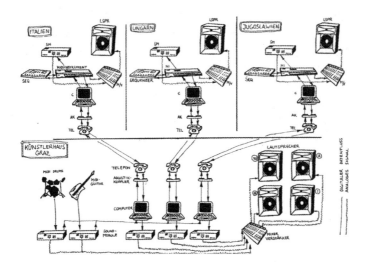

Seppo Gründler and Josef Klammer, *Razionalnik*,
diagram of the network structure, 1987.

concert held by phone simultaneously in Budapest, Ljubljana, and Graz, perhaps the first functional online MIDI concert between participants from different cities. None of the participants could perceive the overall concert as such, and the participants did not even have the usual control over events at their «own» location, as these could be influenced by the respective other locations; the «work» could only lodge itself in the memories of the participants (musicians, audience) in fragments.

Together with, for instance, *Simulplay*—a project by Australian Ross Bolleter commenced in 1989,[11] at the time of writing in 1995 having consisted of three parts in which musicians at various places in Europe and Australia improvised live, on an equal basis, via high quality telephone lines in a loose structure set by Bolleter—or the projects from the symposium The Geometry of Silence (Die Geometrie des Schweigens, 1991)—where the Museum of Modern Art in Vienna and the Tyrolean Provincial Museum Ferdinandeum in Innsbruck were connected with each other via stereo, acoustic, data, and image lines for a wide range of simultaneous events—*RAZIONALNIK* proved to be a crucial starting point for the development of a specific form of telematic simultaneous radio events, carried out and refined in various manifestations since the summer of 1992 with the participation of *Kunstradio* and, frequently, the Tyrolean media art association TRANSIT. To begin with, the *Puente Telefonico* project was held live and simultaneously in Seville at the Expo '92 outside the Austrian pavi-lion as well as in a radio studio in Vienna and on *Kunstradio*: an interactive sound sculpture consisting of twenty-seven sound rods (2.5 to 6 meters high) that did not generate sound themselves but rather, once set in motion by the audience, were transmitted to a computer during this telematic radio event. This data was then used to steer, control, and produce sounds. For *Puente Telefonico*, the interactive sound sculpture in Seville was used by musicians Seppo Gründler and

11 To begin with, *Simulplay* took place live at the Brucknerhaus Linz as well as on the (first) *Long Night of Radio Art* on Österreich 1, ORF's culture channel, as a coproduction with The Listening Room, ABC (Australian Broadcasting Corporation) and as part of a focus program of the Ars Electronica Festival 1989 dedicated to radio art and curated by *Kunstradio*. The two protagonists of *Simulplay* were Jim Denley (Linz, Austria) and Ross Bolleter (Perth, Australia). See also «Im Netz der Systeme,» *Kunstforum International* 103 (September/ October 1989); http://www.aec.at (Ars Electronica Festival archive).

12 Description of the *Puente Telefonico* project by Gerfried Stocker and Horst Hörtner, Graz, 1992.

Josef Klammer—with a phone line controlling sound events at the radio studio. in Vienna, whence Gerfried Stocker sent control signals back to the computer in Seville. In their project description for the telematic live radio event, the artists wrote:[12]

> The acoustic result of musical action, digital remote transmission and reconstruction by means of acoustic engineering is stereophonically processed and directly broadcast on the radio throughout Austria. The material passes through various forms of coding and is specifically changed by each of the transmission media. The musical material that is actually made to sound thus cannot be conclusively determined, the form of expression of the message remains negotiable and takes second place to its terminology.

This principle was further developed specifically to incorporate the medium of radio and initially realized in the *Chip Radio* project in October 1992: in the foyers of three ORF regional studios, architecturally identical in different cities, simultaneous concerts were held, influencing and changing each other through

Mia Zabelka, *Chipradio*, performance,
Regional Broadcasting House, Salzburg,
Austria, a TRANSIT project, 1992.

Chipradio, installation section in entrance hall,
Regional Broadcasting House, Innsbruck, Austria.
The violin-robot by Martin Riches was triggered
by Mia Zabelka from Salzburg, Austria, 1992.

the transmission of MIDI files via the sound, phone, data, and image lines between the regional studios. At the same time, this network concert (with a strong text component that was partly spoken live, partly played back from tape, and partly triggered as samples) emanated from one of the studios into stereophonic radio space, where it was broadcast live in the form of a collective composition on the *Kunstradio* program.[13] Another stage in the development of this concept involved *La Lunga Notte*—a telematic live radio concert between Rimini, Tel Aviv, Cologne, and Innsbruck, with varying participants around a hard core of artists and composers, broadcast by Rai (Italian National Radio), combining radio lines and phone lines to transfer data and speech[14]—and *Radio Beams*—a co-production by Dutch radio and ORF involving the media art festival in 's-Hertogenbosch and x-space in Graz. Different live mixes, controlled by the live musicians in 's-Hertogenbosch by means of light signals, were broadcast on ORF and Dutch radio respectively. The concert situation in 's-Hertogenbosch itself was in turn influenced by instruments remotely controlled from Berlin and Graz and by the light beam of a robot reacting to control signals from a head-mounted display worn and moved by Horst Hörtner in Graz, at the same time influencing the musical situation there. This situation also included the broadcast in Austria of the live transmission of the event from the Netherlands. This *Kunstradio* broadcast was, next to a videophone, the sole feedback available to the musicians in Graz.[15]

A project in 1993, finally, entitled *Realtime* again featured three simultaneous concerts at three regional ORF studios that influenced each other.[16] The telematic space of audiovisual, data, and telephone lines, having constituted the fourth site of *Realtime*, opened up into the fifth scene, the radio space of Österreich 1, and

13 *Chip Radio*, a telematic simultaneous concert, live at the ORF regional studios in Tirol, Vorarlberg, and Salzburg, and on ORF *Kunstradio*. Participants: Andres Bosshard, Seppo Gründler, Gerfried Stocker. Text: Waldemar Rogojsza. Network design: Horst Hörtner. *Chip Radio* was carried out by ORF in cooperation with the TRANSIT association and was one of ORF's contributions to the Prix Italia 1993, in the music category.

14 *La Lunga Notte* was part of the festival L'Arte dell'Ascolto in Rimini, August 1993, and was held in cooperation with the TRANSIT association, Innsbruck. See also Roberto Paci Dalò's essay «LADA – L'Arte dell'Ascolto» in this volume.

15 *Radio Beams*, a telematic live radio installation, featuring, among others, Gerfried Stocker, Horst Hörtner, Roberto Paci Dalò, Isabella Bordoni, and David Moss, October 1993.

16 *Realtime*, a telematic live simultaneous concert at ORF's regional studios in Tirol (Upper Austria) and Styria on the Österreich 1 radio program and on ORF 2 television, December 1, 1993. Participants: Isabella Bordoni, Andres Bosshard, Kurt Hentschläger, Horst Hörtner, Michael Kreihsl, Roberto Paci Dalò, Waldemar Rogojsza, Martin Schitter, Gerfried Stocker, Tamas Ungvary, Mia Zabelka, and many others. A TRANSIT project.

17 Concept for *Realtime*, 1993.

18 See Daniel Gilfillan's essay «Broadcast Space as Artistic Space» in this volume.

the sixth simultaneous venue, the television space of ORF 2.[17] Thanks to the participation of Italian writer and performance artist Isabella Bordoni, the text component of *Realtime* was substantial, just as the visual dimension of the collective event received greater attention—due to the involvement of television—than in previous events. As Gerfried Stocker noted, «The real ‹stage› of *Realtime*, however, is the ‹telematic space› of the communication and transmission media.»

Another important step in the development of telematic radio projects was taken in *State of Transition* by Andrea Sodomka, Martin Breindl, Norbert Math, Gerfried Stocker, Martin Schitter with the participation of several Dutch artists in 1994.[18] Incidentally, Andrea Sodomka, Martin Breindl, and Norbert Math, who participated in *State of Transition*, had previously focused on the open-theme structure of contemporary media and radio art, for example, in a considerably less complexly structured project (in terms of the broadcast) by playing the tracks created by numerous collaborating composers for the CD *The Future of Memory* in one of many possible sequences. The sequence of such a broadcast could be programmed differently each time by the respective program maker or, for instance, also by listeners phoning in and/or voting for which track number to play.

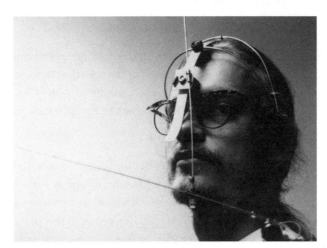

Horst Hörtner, *Realtime*,
performance with
data helmet, Innsbruck,
Austria, a TRANSIT
project, 1993.

Composer Karlheinz Essl pursued a slightly similar project by programming a digital Bösendorfer so that the listeners could phone in to influence the course of the live composition during the transmission time of the performance in the *Großer Sendesaal* (large broadcasting hall) of the Funkhaus radio building in Vienna: there were so many phone calls that the computer could not even react to all of them.

For the live *Lost Memories* project at the Kunstraum ESC in Graz and, simultaneously, on *Kunstradio*, Isabella Bordoni, Roberto Paci Dalò, and Gerfried Stocker engaged in a live performance, on-site with an audience—within an interactive installation—in which they could activate samples through their movements. Live text recitals and music blended with the samples (among other things, from historical radio plays) to form a live radio composition («*hoerspiel*»), not least thematizing and relativizing the expensive, laborious radio play studio productions of our time.

In projects of this kind, technology is not only deployed in a competent, efficient manner but also becomes the focus of reflection, its impact analyzed. This reflection deals with such issues as the time-neutral database character of digitally stored material, the changing access to technologies, the position of the human being in relation to them, and so forth. Formulation of the relevant questions has only just begun ...

> Cyberspace: Accessed through any computer linked into the system; a place, one place, limitless; entered equally from a basement in Vancouver, a boat in Port-au-Prince, a cab in New York, a garage in Texas City, an apartment in Rome, an office in Hong Kong, a bar in Kyoto, a cafe in Kinshasa, a laboratory on the Moon.[19]

In Austria today, three or four generations of artists hailing from a notably diverse range of traditions and disciplines are exploring telecommunications and radio. Above all, however, they examine the effects of digitization on our culture. All the same, it is not enough to describe their practical and, derived from this practice, theoretical work as analysis and reflection on our current media landscape and its effects. Rather, it is already one of the direct consequences of cultural change at the close of the twentieth century.

---

19   Michael Benedikt, *Cyberspace: First Steps*
     (Cambridge, MA: MIT Press, 1991).

Indeed, as far as radio art is concerned, the nature of projects of this kind is such that they can essentially only take place by involving the broadcasting media of radio and television. Yet at the same time, by uniting (collaging) with other new, in some cases interactive, communications media, they furnish images of the end of broadcasting media as we know them.

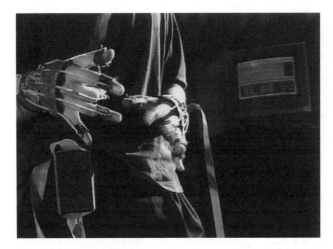

Gerfried Stocker
with data gloves, 1993.

Kunstradio On Line
start page,
January 2000.

Robert Adrian,
Kunstradio On Line,
diagram of the
original structure,
April 25, 1995.

Kunstradio On Line

Kunstradio On Line—kunstradio.at—went online in April 1995. It was founded by artists as a medium of information and documentation for the weekly Kunstradio broadcast on the cultural channel of ORF (Austrian National Radio). *Kunstradio On Line* also became a site of many live broadcasts and internationally networked projects. The original structure and design—both still the basis of today's *Kunstradio On Line*—were conceptualized and established by Robert Adrian in Netscape 1.1. *Kunstradio On Line* was hosted by THE THING Vienna from 1995 until 2000, at which time THE THING Vienna was compelled to abandon its provider functions. The website has become a unique archive of international radio art and is still produced at arm's length from the Austrian National Radio and its website http://orf.at.

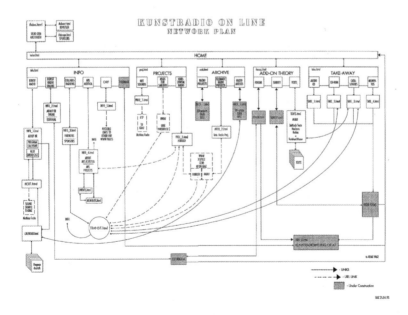

Broadcast Space as Artistic Space

Transcultural Radio, Itinerant Thought,
and the Global Sphere

Daniel Gilfillan

> The Radio of the Future—the central tree of
> our consciousness—will inaugurate new ways to
> cope with our endless undertakings and will
> unite all mankind...Let us try to imagine Radio's
> main station: in the air a spider's web of lines,
> a storm cloud of lightning bolts, some subsiding,
> some flaring up anew, crisscrossing the building
> from one end to the other.[1]
> —*Velimir Khlebnikov*

> But all that radio is, Morty, is making available
> to your ears what was already in the air and
> available to your ears but you couldn't hear
> it. In other words, all it is, is making audible
> something which you're already in. You are
> bathed in radio waves—TV, broadcasts, probably
> telepathic messages, from other minds deep in
> thought.[2]
> —*John Cage*

Velimir Khlebnikov's 1921 Futurist premonitions and John Cage's 1966 musings about the radio each sketch out the subtle hopes and connections imbued in the physical presence of the radio device. While Khlebnikov's spider webs and lightning bolts shroud his description of the future radio within an animistic realm of natural force, and Cage's explanation teases out the ethereal and immaterial qualities of radio reception, both focus on the radio's ability to connect its users (both as listeners and as practitioners) to a space of consciousness and intellect—its ability to capture and remediate those modes of thought and structures of knowledge, which often get lost behind long-held notions of radio broadcast as simply a medium for news and entertainment. Each of these artists detected a territory of unbounded space accessible through the radio as medium and the radio as device—a territory of democratic potential and collaborative reflective thought. The majority of today's mainstream and non-mainstream radio listeners would likely not think twice about the pre-recorded origin of their radio programming, in the case of the former, nor beyond the broadcasts of non-conventional music (classical, jazz, opera) or the occasional documentary-style report reminiscent of much National Public Radio broadcasting, in the case of the latter. Yet in the nineteen-eighties, the world of telecommunications art began to explore the type of broadcast- or radio-enabled space identified by both Khlebnikov and Cage. And it continues to do so to the extent that the disembodied voices and sounds of radio space have begun to inhabit the predominantly economic realm of data space normally associated with these global telecommunications and network infrastructures. That the radio and its technologies of transmission and reception have enjoyed a relatively long history as a viable medium for artistic expression remains uncontested. That the radio be positioned within a range of a/synchronous communication devices and techniques (telephone networks, web-based messaging applications, live audio streaming, etc.) as a method for connecting artists and their varying sound projects in a network of broadcast space, however, is an idea that continues to ride the waves of the cutting edge.

Three live broadcast projects, in particular, are the focus of this essay: *State of Transition* from November 1994, *Horizontal Radio* from June 1995, and *Other Voices–echoes from a warzone* from April 1999.[3] Each of these live broadcast performances engage conceptually with the varying practical (read: real) and theoretical issues of globalization in the context of the growing European Union and more specifically with a range of political, social, economic, and cultural connections between Vienna and Eastern Europe. Given Austria's geographic location in Central Europe, and with Vienna's long imperial history as center of the Austro-Hungarian empire, these broadcast projects also provide a medial and artistic layer to understanding and shaping Austria's role in contemporary critical discussions about issues of migration, national identity, and the framing of

1 Velimir Khlebnikov, «The Radio of the Future,» in *The King of Time: Selected Writings of the Russian Futurian*, ed. Charlotte Douglas (Cambridge, MA: Harvard University Press, 1985), p. 155.

2 John Cage and Morton Feldman, «Radio Happening I: July 9, 1966,» in *Radio Happenings I–V. Recorded at WBAI New York City, July 1966 – January 1967* (Cologne: Edition MusikTexte, 1993), p. 19.

3 Information about all three of these live broadcast projects can be obtained from the *Kunstradio* website, http://www.kunstradio.at. I provide more specific references to each individual project throughout the course of the essay.

ideology within post-1989 Europe. Where the 1994 collaborative project *State of Transition* explores various geographical points and economic sites where human movement occurs (airport transit halls, market squares, border crossings, cargo shipyards), in order to auscultate larger global questions of asylum for economic/political refugees, the 1999 project *Other Voices–echoes from a warzone*, arranged by artist and DJ Gordan Paunović, amplifies the cityscape of thoughts and sounds of Belgrade and its people immobilized by NATO's aerial bombing response to Serbia's leader Slobodan Milošević and the war in Kosovo. In contrast, the 1995 global radio event *Horizontal Radio* combines the technical possibilities of radio transmission and the theoretical imagination of its designers to create a networked performance environment where artists from any of the twenty-six cities involved in the twenty-four hours of broadcast could participate, collaborate, and interact on both a creative and conceptual level regardless of the varying spatio-temporal limitations that such a live global event would normally raise.

The non-hierarchical broadcast structure and the overarching theme of migration taken up by each of these projects speak to the movement of information and bodies across networks and crossings to create or establish a cultural presence, when the possibility of physical movement and physical presence is hindered by spatiotemporal distance, or by political, social, and economic regimes of power. Allowing mobility to occur through the flow of information, marketable goods and services, and signals, rather than through the movement of physical bodies across national and international boundaries, points to a set of larger research questions about the links between information as a commodity, network globalization and connectivity, and artistic access to these invariably closed systems. How does the subtraction of the physical body from within an exchange of ideas lead to changes in information reception? That is, does the removal of the physical body trigger the transformation of intellectual thought into information, and subsequently into commodity? How does information for thought become information for sale? And what role does artistic experimentation play in this intertwining of communication and economics? These are viable questions that inform and are informed by these three live performance broadcasts. Exploring thematically the varying issues surrounding migration, *State of Transition*, *Horizontal Radio*, and *Other Voices* each work by forming interconnected networks of broadcast stations, points of interactive access for its various audiences, and intermedial networks of sound-based input and output, and in the process they work by subverting broadcasting practices of standardized content and transmission procedures, effectively demonstrating that alternatives to a globalized telecommunications structure and homogeneous cultural content are possible.

Radio space, or broadcast space, draws together notions of an immaterial space known as the ether, the physics of electromagnetic frequencies, the clarity of disembodied sound, and the receptiveness of the listening subject to create a space of performance. This performance space transcends the physical limitations of the performing and listening body, blends the notional ideas behind the performance repertoire and the relational powers of the listening experience, and splices these out-of-body interactions onto equally immaterial and inaudible electromagnetic frequencies to be captured and broadcast by very real, very material, and very technical devices such as the radio receiver. When radios still had dials, what we encountered in the tuning process was an eerie sort of journey through the ether, a fantastic jaunt of disconnected voices, music, and electronic sounds until the clarity of the searched-for channel came through. This encounter with radio space highlights its immersive capacity, the ability to draw listeners in and engage them. In the introduction to his recent study, media arts professor Joe Milutis describes the ether as

> at once the attic of the universe in which antique and broken, unrecorded, or unheard transmissions can be found, and it is the misnomer for the wireless-seeming tangle of ports called the «Ethernet» that resides in the basements of institutional space and facilitates local area networks.[4]

Here Milutis establishes a delicate connection between the elusive, diaphanous qualities of this non-space and the fleeting resonance of sound, reminding us that for early radio practitioners and enthusiasts the ether served as a loose archive for both already uttered and conveyed sound and for sound yet-to-be-heard and mediated either through the parameters of broadcast or those of the listening experience—in a certain sense these are sounds in their natural state, sounds that exist within a field of electromagnetic frequencies and wavelengths. And,

4   Joe Milutis, *Ether: The Nothing that Connects Everything* (Minneapolis: University of Minnesota Press, 2006), p. ix.

5   Anthony Dunne and Fiona Raby, *Design Noir: The Secret Life of Electronic Objects* (London: August, 2001), p. 12.

6   Ibid., p. 15.

misnomer or not, Milutis links the non-space of the ether with the technocultural embrace of ethereality in the creation of cyberspace and in doing so highlights the ether as a networked space, where the crisscrossing of wires, ports, and signals, demonstrative of the global telecommunications infrastructure, have been marking out territorial claims in a type of electromagnetic frequency landgrab or foreclosure on URL «etherfront» property using tactics reminiscent of imminent domain. Industrial designers Anthony Dunne and Fiona Raby also note this territoriality in their volumes *Hertzian Tales* and *Design Noir*. They situate their research at the juncture between the immaterial world of electromagnetic frequencies and the material world of electronic objects, defining the proximal space of electromagnetic radiation that escapes from electronic objects as hertzian space. Citing hertzian space as «a medium for carrying information, an invisible alternative to wires and cables,»[5] Dunne and Raby comment on the difficulty of making this space habitable, on accounting for it in the design and architecture of new buildings and other objects, given this territoriality:

> ... like other «natural» environments, the electromagnetic spectrum is constantly under threat from commercial over-development. Unsurprisingly, industry views hertzian space solely as something to be bought and sold and commercially developed for use in broadcasting and telecommunications. The spectrum is highly regulated by the state and nearly all uses of it require a license—unauthorized use is viewed as trespassing. The high value of electromagnetic real estate has encouraged the government to explore radical plans to raise billions from the part privatization of the spectrum.[6]

Yet, even within this corporate and governmental divvying up of the electromagnetic frequency spectrum, and in the increasing move to create larger zones of immaterial wealth, where economic and knowledge transactions take place virtually, an experimental, artistic, and operative mode exists which seeks to access and transform this space of regulated telecommunications into an unrestricted space of networked performance. It is in this vein that the Austrian *Kunstradio* project, formed under the direction of Heidi Grundmann, strives to connect artists with the often inaccessible technical infrastructure of radio. In her essay «Radio as Medium and Metaphor,» Grundmann writes:

Kunstradio had to do with artists who saw themselves as the initiators of media-based processes and which logically understood its role not as the regulator of access to the radio but as an entry point to the means of production and transmission provided by public radio; as a clearing-point at which strategies were developed in partnership with the artists for avoiding bureaucratic restrictions within the institution itself.[7]

While the politics of artistic access are extremely important for an understanding of the *Kunstradio* project's raison d'être, it is in their manifesto about the nature of radio as a communications medium—and the nature of radio as an artistic medium—that this idea about radio space is adapted along the contours of simultaneity and interactivity it implicitly sets into motion.[8] The manifesto points to radio space not as a space regulated by issues of quality or tied to a fixed studio but rather as a fluid, transforming, and transitory space dependent on the networks of relationships it mediates between artists, their radio art concepts and sound objects, and their listeners. It thus theorizes at a much deeper level the position and role of the audience in the art process. The expansion of networked electronic space to incorporate outlets via radio broadcast to an audience of dispersed listeners became possible as advances in network technologies continued to grow, and as radio itself began to explore areas of convergence with computer-based and satellite networking. The stage was thus set for the types of technically and artistically experimental broadcasts that *Kunstradio* wanted to produce and support—broadcasts exploring the very nature of knowledge and

7 Heidi Grundmann, «Radio as Medium and Metaphor,» in *net_condition: art and global media*, ed. Peter Weibel and Timothy Druckery (Cambridge, MA: MIT Press, 2001), pp. 236–43, here p. 239.

8 *Kunstradio*, «Kunstradio–RadioArt Manifesto,» http://www.kunstradio.at/TEXTS/manifesto .html (accessed February 26, 2007). See my discussion of the manifesto within the context of Robert Adrian's work in the interview essay «Networked Radio Space and Broadcast Simultaneity: An Interview with Robert Adrian» appearing in this volume.

9 Gerfried Stocker, «STATE OF TRANSITION,» ed. Martin Breindl, *Kunstradio*, http://www .kunstradio.at/1994B/stateof_t.html (accessed February 26, 2007). A more complete set of materials, including concept description, website, and documentary photographs from

the performances existed on a web server hosted at the University of Graz: Gerfried Stocker, «state of transition,» http://gewi .kfunigraz.ac.at/x-space/state_of/ (site now discontinued). These materials have recently been given a renewed online presence under the direction of «alien productions,» an artist collaborative comprised of Andrea Sodomka, Martin Breindl, and Norbert Math, each of whom played central roles in the on-site performance in Graz. See http://alien.mur .at/state_of/ to access the archived version of the original website.

10 Gerfried Stocker, Joel Ryand, Andrea Sodomka, Martin Breindl, and Norbert Math, *State of Transition*, MP3 audio file, ORF *Kunstradio*, © 1994. Time settings in brackets refer to this MP3 version. At the time of this writing, neither a published version of the broadcast

information in the ever-changing landscape of telecommunications technologies, folding in ideas about artist and audience interactivity that move beyond the emptiness the term has come to represent in standard infotainment models, and splicing these together for a deeper understanding of how artists use broadcast space to field geopolitical issues surrounding migration, work with and resuscitate them notionally and conceptually, and transmit them back as broadcast for audience reception and engagement.

State of Transition
Migration, Art, and Itinerant Thought

Transition connotes movement in terms of physical location, state of mind, change in ideological structure, or emotional mien. Often it is associated with a forward progression, a move toward one thing and away from another; and hence it is always in flux and never frozen in stasis, always already retrospective, nostalgic for what was left behind, and anticipatory, expectant of what may lie ahead. The live performance and broadcast of *State of Transition* (1994) serves as an aural and peripatetic documentation of these varying moments of transition. The project is bound together with questions and problems of migration, a contemporaneous geopolitical issue facing much of Europe given the break up of the former Eastern Bloc, the increased numbers of refugees seeking political and economic asylum, and the Bosnian war taking place in the former Yugoslavia.[9] *State of Transition* takes these issues at the forefront of the European mindset and connects them to the relatively unhindered flow of information along various networks associated with the burgeoning global telecommunications infrastructure:

> Migration movements, traffic routes, immigration quotas, transit spaces, border-crossings and transitional stages of all kinds are the subject and structure of this live radio event. The businesslike euphoria that creates the illusion of the world as a global village in the cross-border flow of data contrasts with the sociopolitical reality of increasingly stringent immigration and refugee quota rules that are drawing physical borders in an increasingly clear and insurmountable manner. This must no longer be taken without contradiction [01:15–01:50].[10]

The nineteen-nineties hype surrounding the creation of a global information economy and the figurative notion of the global village separated the haves and the have-nots. While regulatory controls over trade were eased to foster the seamless flow of goods, services, and labor to support this information economy based in the virtual realms of business, there were simultaneous legal and governmental restrictions enacted to help regulate the movement of immigrants and refugees across the various borders within Europe and other parts of the world. At the center of the *State of Transition* project are the communications theories of Czech-born theorist Vilém Flusser, whose essays on migration, experience, and the telematic society form the basis of a complex process of dialogue and discourse, which Anke K. Finger distinguishes: «Th[e] distinction defines dialogue as that which produces information and discourse as that which collects information. Ideally the two coincide and interconnect, so that to live in a telematically networked society is to be both recipient and sender at once, ever processing and ever producing.»[11] In addition to the obvious connections to the concepts of radio/broadcast space and hertzian space outlined earlier by Milutis, Adrian, and Dunne and Raby, Flusser's operative notion of dialogue/discourse combines the modes of thought and engagement that comprise our processes of knowledge creation and meaning-making with the networked structures of communication that comprise our contemporary telematic society. Flusser's theories of experience embrace the ideas of transition and mobility, requiring a constantly itinerant mindset to take advantage of the high-speed data networks reshaping economic, social, political, and cultural practices and use them to create and enhance the full range of collaborative potential that non-networked modes of experience do not attain:

> Let us imagine that our central nervous system were to extend around the globe like a net. Let us further imagine that it would constitute something like a *neurosphere* situated between the biosphere and the atmosphere ... What we need to do is imagine such a neurosphere as a network of human nerves as well as material and nonmaterial cables. And we must

on CD nor a streaming-audio version have been made available for public purchase or download. Translation of related quotations by Richard Watts.

11 Anke K. Finger, introduction to *The Freedom of the Migrant: Objections to Nationalism*, by Vilém Flusser (Urbana: University of Illinois Press, 2003), pp. xii–xiii.

12 Vilém Flusser, «Ex-perience,» in Flusser 2003 (see note 11), p. 67.

further imagine human brains and artificial intelligences at the nodal intersections of such a network. Such a neurosphere spanning the globe would function to compute into experience all stimuli incessantly streaming in from all directions to transform these experiences into decisions and actions. Seen this way, the telematic society would be a mechanism for experience, a global machine for the realization of potentials [emphasis in the original].[12]

The types of neural networks that Flusser envisions splicing into the digital networks being advanced and created for the potential of a global information economy seek to unhouse the mind from the limitations of the physical body in an attempt to replicate the experience of the migrant, whose own sense of displacement and unsettledness offers a unique perspective to guide and shape our application of these network technologies. Although Flusser's ideas are couched in the optimism of the early nineties about the democratic potential of these new network technologies and do not anticipate the type of conglomeration and access issues that Dunne, Raby, and Grundmann point out, his approach intellectualizes the nature of the exile and migration experience; transforming it from the nega-

Martin Breindl, Horst Hörtner, Norbert Math,
Wolfgang Reinisch, and Andrea Sodomka,
State of Transition, performance, video stills,
Neue Galerie, Graz, Austria, 1994.

tive sociopolitical connotation of the refugee and asylum seeker looking to beleaguer the social system of the new host country to an idea of the global citizen able to navigate the spaces of experience that accompany the move from emigrant to immigrant and inhabit a space outside individual topographies.

Conceived as a «hyper-radio-environment,» the *State of Transition* performance created a networked space using what the artists describe as «key technologies of telecommunication and telepresence.»[13] The live performance occurred simultaneously in geographically distant places: the southern Austrian city of Graz and the port city of Rotterdam in The Netherlands. It also occurred along differentiated media channels by folding its performative layers through radio frequencies, across data networks, and through the physicality and provocative atmosphere of live performance. It produced synchronized live performances in both of these cities and versions of these performances specific to audience reception—radio listeners, visitors to the public performance spaces in Graz and Rotterdam, and users of the web-based interactive content tied directly to the performances. Participants in these live performances included Gerfried Stocker, Joel Ryand, and Dirk Haubrich at the V2 Center for Art and Media Technology in Rotterdam and Andrea Sodomka, Martin Breindl, Norbert Math, and Wolfgang Reinisch at the Neue Galerie in Graz. Linked telematically via an array of interactive connections that provided high-level communication between the two cities, the artist groups saw themselves more as mediators and network administrators rather than as creators. Using radio channels, visual telephone lines, data links, and the still not-yet-fully-explored artistic capacities of the Internet, the five artist-mediators worked with a range of image, text, and sound materials gathered from various outposts—the transit hall of the Vienna airport, the Hauptplatz in Graz, a highway border crossing station between Austria and Slovenia, and the EU harbor in Rotterdam. Each of these are spaces where movement, travel, and border crossings occur, and where the physical manifestations of movement can be captured acoustically through ambient, directed, and archived sound, optically through still and moving image, and textually through definitions, governmental documents, and statistics that form the hypertext backbone of the project website. In addition to these sources for the live and broadcast performances, the project drew on excerpts from short radio plays developed

13 Gerfried Stocker, «state of transition»   14 Ibid.
     (see note 9).

by disabled artists, clips from *MREZA/NETZ*—a September 1994 telephone concert that brought together musicians from each of the former Yugoslav states to interact and improvise in a musical performance format—and recordings from a collection of audio CD tracks arranged specifically for the event.

The latter two sets of sound sources help to form the remote interactive components of the performance. Here the audio clips from the *MREZA/NETZ* project were triggered to play in the performance spaces in Graz and Rotterdam via a voicebox technology as radio listeners dialed a specific telephone number in Vienna associated with the broadcast, and the audio CD tracks were merged into the piece as visitors to the website associated with the performance broadcast navigated through the online space clicking on specific keywords—these actions would select the specific clip associated with it and play it as part of the performance. Gerfried Stocker, now co-artistic director of Ars Electronica in Linz, describes this latter interactive component on the website accompanying the project:

> Each of these pages is linked with a certain track of an audio CD produced specifically for this event. So if you select a page you start the corresponding track of the CD. If you access our server, a traceroute routine will be started automatically, analyzing the route of your connection. This information will be mapped into MIDI commands controlling our sound samplers. Thus each machine involved in your link to our server will get an «acoustical signature.» The traces of your network activity will be «mapped» on a 12-channel audio system, resulting in an acoustical map of the electronic space which stems from your interactivity.[14]

The ability for listeners of the radio broadcast to participate at such an interactive level with the two performances and the simultaneous broadcast upends a more infantile idea of multimedia interactivity which often associates the term interactive with something as simple as the clicking of hypertext links in any given website to choose a pathway in and through the material on the site. Instead, Stocker's description clearly points to the active engagement of the at-home listener in the performance itself, to the extent that she becomes an active performer in the piece herself. Yet, beyond the triggering of a corresponding track of the CD as the website is navigated, which itself forms an intriguing facet of this project, the tracing of the network pathway between a visitor's computer and the server hosting the project website allows each individual surfing the site to be present in the performance regardless of physical limitation or level of spatiotemporal distance. Since neither of the performance spaces in Graz or Rotterdam serves as the focus of the project, and none of the five participants among the two groups of artists adopts a central role, the listeners navigating the website or those calling the voicebox in Vienna are easily mapped into the range of inputs that comprise the orchestration of the piece. In addition, this complex integration of the broadcast listener into the performance of the piece works to engage the listener at a deeper level with the range of source material on the website and with the active creation of the forty-two minute, forty-seven second broadcast.

The variety of telematic connections assembled to link the cities of Graz and Rotterdam, the collection of intermedial components of the performance, and the range of sources for the sound riffs that arise in the broadcast—when coupled with the complex level of interactive possibilities provided to each specific audience for the piece—prompt a type of dissolution of the borders set up spatially between the two cities and medially between the three versions of the performance:

> When the physical oneness of cause and effect is telematically sundered, the stability of places—based, as it is, on demarcation—also comes undone. Their parallel realities become transparent. Places flow into each other [06:08–06:25].

This dissolution of national boundary and spatial distance allows each artist group to establish a virtual presence in the space of the city where they are not located physically and triggers the dissipation of the feeling of security and stability that comes with a bounded sense of place. This stands in stark contradiction to the types of immigration policies being enforced to physically keep certain people out. That these artists accomplish this using the very same telematic networks that form the backbone for the new globalization economy reveals the

15 *Kunstradio*, «HORIZONTAL RADIO,» http:// www.kunstradio.at/HORRAD/horrad.html (accessed February 27, 2007). A second website providing conceptual and network infrastructure information in the lead up to the event existed on a server housed at the University of Graz and is no longer available: Gerfried Stocker, «*horizontal radio*,» http:// gewi.kfunigraz.ac.at/x-space/horrad/ (site now discontinued).

very intricate sleight of hand machinations that drive this economy, uncovering the duplicitousness that allows the easy transfer of information and marketable goods and services but forbids the physical movement and travel of human beings. *State of Transition* appropriates and splices into the data spaces of the global infrastructures of telecommunication and uses them tactically to amplify these social, political, and cultural discrepancies via broadcast and to highlight the possibilities of triggering actions remotely, when physical presence is not possible, or desirable.

Horizontal Radio
Transcultural Broadcast and Networks of Performance

Although the 1995 project *Horizontal Radio* consists of over one hundred DAT cassettes of material sent from over two hundred artists, composers, musicians, and authors from the twenty-five cities worldwide participating in the twenty-four-hour live event via fourteen public and ten independent radio stations on a range of frequencies and wavelengths along the electromagnetic spectrum, it is a difficult piece to capture in a textual medium without feeling something important has been overlooked.[15] With that said, however, *Horizontal Radio* is a rich and provocative event that incorporates a multidimensional and decentralized approach to the process of radio broadcast and transmission, avoiding the top-down hierarchical programming structures of many public, independent, and commercial stations through its transformation of the traditional role of radio as a transmission/reception medium. Instead, the horizontal approach to the radio medium focuses on flows of communication existing within a network of actively interconnected radio stations, which allows content to be produced, accessed, and broadcast by each of the stations participating in the event, such that broadcast content deviates from the typical one-to-many model of distribution and instead permits a more equitable playing field in the process of transmission. The end result is an opening up of an electronic, radiocentric space where all aspects of artistic production (conceptualization, collaboration, creation, and dissemination) could take place. The project combines the immaterial aspects of ethereality cited by Joe Milutis, the collaborative artistic potential lauded by Robert Adrian, the appropriation and re-tooling of telecommunications infrastructures supported by Dunne/Raby and Heidi Grundmann, and the itinerancy and free-flow nature of migratory communication theorized by Vilém Flusser to rethink, reconceptualize, and revive the radio medium as an active, thinking, and engaged medium of artistic performance. While the sheer magnitude of material associated with and produced by the rhizomatic structure of these live broadcasts is an indication of the project's success, the true nature of that success precedes and extends beyond its twenty-four-hour durational time frame.

The actual live broadcast took place from noon on June 22 until noon on June 23, 1995, yet the concept and planning process began one year prior to the event debuting at the Ars Electronica Festival, while reports, cassette tapes, and anecdotal stories continued to trickle in to the organizers from the twenty-five cities and four continents represented well past the broadcast's endpoint. These stages of the live broadcast are both important factors to consider for the combined levels of technical ingenuity and conceptual imagination that went into the planning of the broadcast, and for the experimental and cultural reverberations the project brought to bear on the continuing trajectory of movement in the sphere of radio art. Co-produced by twenty-nine public and independent radio stations in eighteen countries, *Horizontal Radio* was conceived by Gerfried Stocker and x-space, an interdisciplinary group of media artists and technicians, and co-organized with Heidi Grundmann in Vienna. Building on his participation and knowledge gained from the telematic broadcast and performance *State of Transition* from the previous year, Stocker also looked to a pioneering project spearheaded by telecommunications artist Robert Adrian in 1982 known as *The World in 24 Hours* for inspiration and guidance. This earlier work connected artists in fifteen cities to the central location hub in the Austrian city of Linz from noon on September 27 to noon on September 28 via telephone-based media (slow-scan TV, telefacsimile, computer network, and telephone sound) as part of the 1982 Ars Electronica Festival.[16] While the range of technologies integrated into this earlier work may appear pedestrian from our perspective in 2007, Robert Adrian's concept of combining the full potential of each individual tech-

16 For additional material, see Robert Adrian, «The World in 24 Hours,» http://alien.mur.at/rax/24_HOURS/main.html (accessed February 27, 2007).

17 Very detailed information regarding the network design vision was available as Gerfried Stocker, «network design,» http://gewi .kfunigraz.ac.at/x-space/horrad/network1 .html (site now discontinued); see note 15

18 Gerfried Stocker, «horizontal radio» (concept paper, *Kunstradio* Archives, ORF, Vienna, 1994), p. 2.

nology into a network of communicative tools for artists to use collaboratively from remote locations was an astounding achievement for 1982, both technically and artistically. It is this creative-technical ingenuity that Stocker sought to replicate with the new palette of technologies available to him in 1995, particularly extending the earlier telephonic networks to benefit from the growing omnipresence of computer- and digital-based networks. The network design that Stocker envisioned for the project allowed for different levels of connectivity through the participating radio stations, Internet nodes, regional subnetworks, the formation of a routing station located at the project's home base in Linz, remote-controlled MIDI (Musical Instrument Digital Interface) lines, the existing terrestrial radio network of the European Broadcasting Union and the *Ars Acustica* group, as well as standard and ISDN (Integrated Services Digital Network) telephone lines.[17] This layered, multifaceted approach to establishing network connectivity to the twenty-four hours of live broadcast was conceived to ensure that each radio station or performance group «does not have to establish direct contact to every other station in order to be connected to all of them.»[18] The technique of routing information, in this case sound objects comprised from noise, voice, text, music, interactive sound sculptures, installations, and so forth, through this distrib-

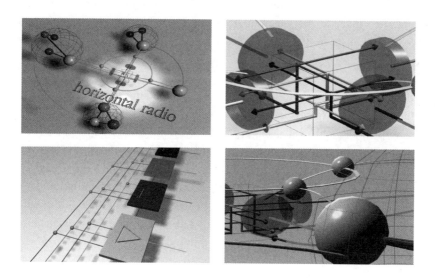

Horizontal Radio, graphics from the original concept paper, 1995.

uted network of radio channels, phone lines, and Internet servers also permits each participating station to «temporarily become the centre of the network» in their role as hosts. The range of possible access points to this horizontal communications network likewise assures that any participating station would be able to access the twenty-four-hour space of performance without a high level of technical skill and without a large financial buy-in, thus diminishing those issues of access related to socioeconomic factors. One facet of the network design conceptualized by Stocker, which merits more focused attention, centers on the varying levels of interactivity interspersed throughout the project. In addition to the range of varying network access paths organized and developed for the participating radio stations in each of the twenty-five worldwide cities represented in the event, Stocker envisioned a layer of interactive capacity that employs similar techniques interfacing a web-based hyper-environment and remote triggering of audio tracks such as those used in the *State of Transition* performance. In this instance, the notion behind his «Survey of Human Language: An Acoustical Maze» enables those surfing the project website to read and engage with a collection of poetry and short prose texts composed by writers from countries participating in the *Horizontal Radio* network. The navigation through this web-based collection would then activate voice recordings of these texts to be projected into the performance space at Ars Electronica in Linz and to be broadcast into the radio space of *Horizontal Radio*. Stocker describes this interactive aspect as initiating a type of maze:

> If only a few persons are in the network reading and navigating through the texts, we only will have a few voices (different languages, different sounds of speech). But if more people are doing this we will get a very dense multilingual maze or labyrinth. (As experience shows, the amount of activity in such a network varies very much, so we'll get very dynamic sound pieces.) In Linz we will put these voices into an installation with twelve loudspeakers spread out all over the room so that the voices will come from all directions. And we will put this «survey of human languages» periodically on air.[19]

19 Gerfried Stocker, «An acoustical maze,» http://gewi.kfunigraz.ac.at/x-space/horrad/ gerfrtxt.html (site now discontinued); see note 15.

This collection of texts would not be translated into a lingua franca or language of economic transaction but rather would be presented in the original language of their respective authors. This cacophony of world languages within the network and broadcast space of *Horizontal Radio*, and within the physical performance space in Linz, calls into question the premise behind a monolingual global economy and instead presents the vibrant, culturally rich, and enriching heritage of a world marketplace. Whether or not this aspect of interactive play was actually folded in to the live twenty-four-hour broadcast is unclear from the materials available describing the event, however it remains an integral notional point for understanding the scope of the project and for initiating and staging the itinerant processes of thought and dialogue in a multilingual, multicultural—and yet economically dependent and informationally narrow—world. Stocker relates this communicative routing of information to the metaphor of migration, in the sense of a *permigration* or nomadic movement where residency is not established:

The information fed into the network (and with it the listener) proceeds through:

Tyrolean Ensemble of New Music, *Horizontal Radio*, live performance, ORF Broadcasting House, Innsbruck, Austria, a TRANSIT project, 1995.

- Various levels of its technical reproduction
- Various levels of interactive and creative editing (manipulation)
- The geographic space delineated by the transmitting frequencies of the participating radio stations[20]

The unsettledness and lack of fixity which Stocker associates with the notion of information as it is conceived in a networked environment assists in demarcating the boundaries of broadcast space, revealing both the organic growth that occurs through iteration, versioning, or reproduction and the artistic and interactive manipulation that propels notions of artistic creation away from origin and toward collaboration. As the sound objects being fed into the network that make up this radio space are routed in and through the varying data feeds, Stocker claims the listening subject is also transported across the geographic space comprised from the frequencies of the participating stations. The nature of this networked radio space, its porosity, its non-hierarchical structure, its oscillatory flow of reception and transmission, provides a new frame for artistic production that transcends the limitations of spatial and temporal distance and allows for a collaborative space of performance. The extension of performance beyond the precise temporal measurement of broadcast time frames, even in this instance of live broadcast with its accompanying possibility of unscheduled, unintended, or uncharted occurrences, points to the incredible idea and power of an art form that undermines a strict sense of public time and bypasses a strict legislation of geopolitical boundaries in order to gain momentum and force along radio channels, electromagnetic frequencies, broadcast wavelengths, network nodal points, and Internet

20 Stocker 1994 (see note 18), p. 4.
21 Rupert Huber, *horizontal radio*, compact disc, ORF *Kunstradio*/Transit/Ars Electronica, © 1996 (2 compact discs).
22 Jamie Shea, «NATO Speech: Morning Briefing on Kosovo – 30. Apr. 1999,» NATO: NATO's role in Kosovo: Background Briefings, http://www.nato.int/kosovo/press/b990430b.htm (accessed February 13, 2004).
23 Additional information about the history of Radio B92 and a biography of Veran Matić can beaccessed at *Kunstradio*, «Veran Matic,» http://www.kunstradio.at/BIOS/maticbio.html (accessed February 27, 2007).

24 Both the live broadcast and CD remix are available on the *Kunstradio* website as streaming audio files: a) Gordan Paunović, *Other Voices–Echoes From A War Zone*, live broadcast streaming audio, *Kunstradio*, http://www.kunstradio.at/1999A/RA/99_04 _29.ram (accessed February 14, 2004); b) Gordan Paunović, *Other Voices: Echoes from a Warzone*, compact disc streaming audio, *Kunstradio*, http://www.kunstradio.at/2000A/RA/00_04_02.ram (accessed February 14, 2004). The compact disc is also available: Gordan Paunović, *Other Voices–echoes from a warzone. Vienna/Belgrade April 29 1999*, compact disc, ORF *Kunstradio*, © 1999.

pathways, offsetting the cultural homogeneity of traditional commercial radio and advancing an idea of broadcast that draws on a multiple array of sound objects that exist, thrive, and grow in the electronic space of radio. To a certain extent, an exact accounting of such an event is near to impossible, since its dispersed, decentered nature resists archivization, which makes the existence of a double CD sampler of the event all the more important for the types of audio tracks it does capture and provide of a world involved in live and virtual performance, of the world in sonic artistic motion.[21]

Sounds of Displacement
Other Voices–echoes from a warzone. Vienna/Belgrade. April 29, 1999

On the evening of April 29, 1999, NATO operation «Allied Force» began its thirty-seventh day of air operations with «the single most intense period of attacks over Belgrade.»[22] That same evening in Vienna from 10:15 to 11:55 p.m., *Kunstradio* broadcast a live mix by Serbian radio artist, and Radio B92 founding member, Gordan Paunović, described as one hundred minutes in support of the free voice of Radio B92.[23] This live radio broadcast and subsequent CD remix *Other Voices–echoes from a warzone. Vienna/Belgrade. April 29, 1999* perform on several levels.[24] They mix audible threads from within the ten-year media landscape that emerged in Serbia between 1989 and 1999. They trace the development of community-based radio and artistic practice within the Milošević era and tease out connections between the creation of alternative media spaces in support of democratic change in Serbia and the neglect of these media spaces by the global media event which arose around operation «Allied Force,» the NATO response to the conflict in Kosovo in the spring of 1999. They document those other voices that get lost or silenced in this folding together of repressive media policy, on the one hand, and the loss of local identity and local response created by an influx of global media conglomerates, on the other. And, finally, they demonstrate the collaborative interplay between the two cities of Vienna and Belgrade, inextricably linked through their common geographical, cultural, economic, and historic ties to the Danube, and now also linked through the intermeshing of their respective soundscapes. In the performances marked by Paunović's live broadcast and CD remix, the flows of information between Belgrade and Vienna along Internet channels, diary excerpts, e-mail correspondence, and radio waves stand in for the people of Belgrade, as they are caught between a minimized degree of mobility and the impossibility of movement. In the context of Gordan Paunović's radio performance, how are tactical appropriations of these telecommunications infrastructures providing new modes of interchange within the cross-border region between Vienna and Belgrade? To this end, how is the historical riparian network between Vienna and Belgrade via the Danube being recast in terms of electronic signal flow?

Gordan Paunović's radio art piece and the *Kunstradio* program's role in its broadcast provide an exceptional example of how artistic experimentation with the radio medium manages to break in to the globalized space of radio transmission and to help reposition and amplify the voices and ideas lost or ignored within these globalized information networks. Heidi Grundmann clarifies these types of experiments in the context of the *Kunstradio* program and its institutional support by the ORF in her essay, «But is it Radio?»:

> The position of *Kunstradio*—however marginalized—inside a public radio institution has made it possible for artists to exploit not only the institution's technical resources but also its mainstream program formats. There have been projects where artists were able to infiltrate other programs and/or channels of the ORF beyond the late-night ghetto, inserting radio-art into Ö3, the pop music channel, or into one or the other of several regional channels. Such interventions outside of the gallery-like space of the weekly national radio-art program are most successful, when they are not announced/perceived as art but are left to be incidents in the public space of everyday radio, anticipating an audience of passers-by who may or may not stop or hesitate for just a brief moment of irritation or even reflection.[25]

25   Heidi Grundmann, «But is it Radio?,» in *Anarchitexts: Voices from the Global Digital Resistance. A Subsol Anthology*, ed. Joanne Richardson (New York: Autonomedia, 2003), pp. 157–64, here p. 158.

26   For additional information regarding each of the individual sources employed in the live broadcast, see the accompanying website,

«Surface of the Project OTHER VOICES– ECHOES FROM A WARZONE, 29th of April 1999,» *Kunstradio*, http://www.kunstradio .at/1999A/ANEM_B92/index.html (accessed May 31, 2005).

27   Geert Lovink, «An Insider's Guide to Tactical Media (2001),» in *Dark Fiber: Tracking Critical Internet Culture* (Cambridge, MA: MIT Press, 2002), pp. 254–74.

Grundmann points to the playfulness involved in the broadcast of radio art. With terms such as «infiltrate» and «intervention» describing the methods used by *Kunstradio*-supported artists to broaden their audience base beyond the late Sunday evening time slot provided to the program by ORF, Grundmann's essay highlights what happens when the roles of technician and artist come together in the realm of radio production.

The live broadcast of *Other Voices* engages these modes of experimentation with the radio device through its performative routing of unique threads of information, each with their own specific spatiotemporal set of source histories and cultural reverberations or echo effects. The intertextual and intermedial play between these individual components of the overall broadcast prompt both the listener and the creator of the broadcast to think more critically about the relationships between each source of information, while also requiring them to delve more deeply into the respective trace histories of each source. In this sense, Gordan Paunović never claims ownership to the work, seeing himself instead as a thinking agent, as a stopover within the routing of information, where his own take, his own interpretation of the materials, is added to the mix before sending it back out into the network, or in this case over the radio waves. In total, twenty distinct verbal and artistic sound elements were utilized in the live broadcast.[26] This combination of ambient sound and personal documentary details the quick physical change of Belgrade's skyline and the slow process of coping with the impending loss of one's home, one's city, one's identity. Paunović's mixture of tracks from archived music productions, voice overlays, essay commentaries, and live Internet and audio feeds helps to trace these moments of changing experience and displacement of identity.

The live broadcast itself serves as a moment of self-referential tactical media practice, an idea of media that seeks in some way to appropriate the more traditional channels of media as relays of power and use them as relays for dissent and disruption.[27] The live piece begins with a reading of a short essay by Radio B92 founding editor Veran Matić entitled «Schaffung des Informationsraums: ‹Commando Solo.›» As the lead-in component for Paunović's live broadcast mix, Matić's essay introduces themes related to postmodern military practice and telecommunications into the broadcast space of the radio piece. Written during the NATO intervention in April 1999 and sent to the *Kunstradio* studios just two days prior to the live broadcast, the essay takes NATO's use of hybridized weapons combining high-powered bombs and imaging technologies to task and problematizes the use of captured images and recordings from these hybrid devices by mainstream journalists to provide popular backing for NATO's involvement. Among these are discussions about the Commando Solo aircraft to establish an alternative information space through military jamming of civilian radio and television airwaves, as well as the melding together of smart-bomb missiles and cameras to provide logistical and video analysis of targets being bombed:

> ... the only proof offered to us as the sole truth [is] the camera in the head of the rocket hitting its target. The daily repetition of the same or similar pictures recorded by these cameras is turning journalism into a superfluous profession, for the sole truth comes from the head of the rocket. In this way, brutal murders and destruction become palatable little video games.[28]

For Matić, the idea that the «truth» behind the success of the NATO intervention resided in a quick media consumption of images captured by smart bombs as they headed toward their targets demonstrates the failure of mainstream journalism to critically engage with the reality of the situation in Serbia and the war in Kosovo and turns the thirty-plus days of NATO bombing into a video game reminiscent of the first Gulf War. To put it more plainly, the global media event prompted by the NATO response to the Kosovo conflict in spring 1999 overlooks and diminishes the local experience of that event. These ideas about the hybridization of warfare technologies and telecommunications networks, and about the disappearance of any human experience of the NATO bombing in mainstream media coverage, serve to emphasize the artistic possibilities inherent in radio as foregrounded by Paunović's radio art piece and by the *Kunstradio* program's role in its broadcast. In June 1999, during production of the CD remix, Paunović writes:

> The mainstream media followed the directions of the political establishment on both sides and thus transformed reality into a giant stage for a

28 Veran Matić, «Schaffung des Informations-
    raums: ‹Commando Solo,›» *Kunstradio*,
    http://www.kunstradio.at/WAR/VOICES/matic
    -commsolo.html (accessed June 1, 2005).
    Translation provided by Richard Watts.

29 ORF *Kunstradio*, Other Voices CD Release
    Website, http://www.kunstradio.at/TAKE/CD/
    paunovic_cd.html (accessed June 1, 2005).
    Translation provided by Richard Watts.

propaganda spectacle. Beyond the Potemkin villages of the big television companies, however, a different life was taking place, the life of people who had spent years and decades battling against totalitarianism and nationalist hatred with their expressive power and creativity.[29]

Paunović's motivation for producing this radio performance piece centers on the artists, writers, and media producers who were denied access to the technologies of media production by both the Milošević media state and its broadcasts of the Serbian war as well as the large television corporations and their broadcasts of the NATO intervention. The function of Matić's essay as epigraph serves as a justification for Paunović's own creation of an alternative information space via live radio and Internet streaming broadcasts. In this regard, Paunović accomplishes the same type of takeover of radio space that the Commando Solo aircraft has been developed to do militarily. Yet, what Paunović's tactical use of the radio medium adds to the mix are the varying threads from spoken text and sonic elements that evoke the emotive atmosphere of Belgrade in April 1999 as well as traces of the historical, cultural, and political engagement with the post-1989 dissolution of Yugoslavia.

Gordan Paunović, *Other Voices—echoes from a warzone,* screenshot, *Kunstradio On Line,* 1999.

What is missing from the publicly proliferated media landscape surrounding the Serbian war in Kosovo and NATO's intervention are the haunting sounds of air raid sirens, the explosions generated by the aerial bombings, and the rationalized stories from those entrenched in Belgrade's cityscape, all of which arise as elements in Paunović's work. As the website associated with the live version of Paunović's piece points out, the broadcast is structured around three recurrent sound elements: a live audio stream of sounds of the NATO bombing picked up by a microphone hanging outside a window in Belgrade on the evening of April 29, original recordings of a one-minute air raid alarm from Belgrade sent to the studios in Vienna via an Internet feed, and excerpts from an orchestration by Arsenije Jovanović titled *Concerto grosso balcanico*.[30] Although the broadcast is bound by the spatiotemporal limitations set up by commercial radio programming time slots, Paunović's use of these live sound captures and integration of excerpts from topical texts allows the broadcast to transcend its one-hundred-minute time limit and also transforms the radio from a conduit of transmission and reception to a device that transports its listeners to the streets of Belgrade through a live, point-to-point flow of information. The noise of the bombings captured from the microphone and the air raid alarm taken from the Internet feed evoke the immediacy of Paunović's piece, while the use of Jovanović's earlier sound project invokes a sonic archaeology of the earlier Bosnian war. This 1993 soundscape is a disturbing triptych which blends the sounds of war with the anxious stirrings of animals (sheep, dogs, and wolves) confronted by these very human sounds.[31]

---

30   See note 26.

31   Arsenije Jovanović, *Concerto gross balcanico*, Real Audio file, *Kunstradio*, http://www.kunstradio.at/1993A/RA/concerto.ram (accessed February 14, 2004).

32   Excerpts from both Jasmina Tesanović's and Slobodan Marković's diaries are reproduced on the *Kunstradio* project's website: *Kunstradio*, «WAR DIARIES OF JASMINA TESANOVIC & SLOBODAN MARKOVIC,» http://www.kunstradio.at/WAR/DIARY/ (accessed February 7, 2004). Tesanović's diary and other personal diaries from Belgrade are gathered on the «Help B92» website where they can be read in English and their original Serbo-Croatian: Jasmina Tesanović, «Personal diaries,» <Help> B92, http://helpb92.xs4all.nl/diaries/jasmina/jasmina.htm (accessed February 27, 2007).

When quoting from the diary entries employed in the live broadcast and CD remix, I utilize direct transcriptions from the recorded audio, CD version. The first set of time settings in square brackets in the text refers to the location of the sound clip in the CD version of the radio art piece, and the second set refers to the location in the live broadcast. Wherever possible I also provide page numbers for these excerpts from the 2000 Midnight Editions version of Tesanović's diary, published as Jasmina Tesanović, *The Diary of a Political Idiot: Normal Life in Belgrade* (San Francisco: Midnight Editions, 2000).

33   Geert Lovink, «Kosovo: War in the Age of Internet (1999),» *Dark Fiber: Tracking Critical Internet Culture* (Cambridge, MA: MIT Press, 2002), pp. 318–28, here pp. 322–23.

The creation of a CD remix, released in March 2000 to coincide with the anniversary of the beginning of the NATO intervention, emphasizes this function
of the live broadcast as archaeological cache or archive and provides Paunović
the creative and reflective time necessary to engage with a particular facet of
the longer one-hundred-minute live broadcast. The relationship between the live
broadcast and CD remix as one of archive and iteration is one that could continue ad infinitum, and it is one which positions the live broadcast as having the
quality of rawness, as a never before heard, never complete, and never deceased
sonic snapshot of events occurring in Belgrade in spring 1999. At the center of
the CD are voiced excerpts dated from March and April 1999 from two electronic
diaries. One is by Jasmina Tesanović, a forty-five-year-old writer, filmmaker, and
feminist activist, and the other was written by Slobodan Marković, a twenty-one-
year-old computer science student at the University of Belgrade, independent
media activist, and founder of the online Serbian *Internodium* mailing list, which
addresses issues of open access to Yugoslav (.yu) cyberspace.[32] The electronic
format of both diaries illustrates two important details. First, it points to the
importance of the Internet for the sharing of information from two of Belgrade's
citizens during a time of war, which Geert Lovink contextualizes in his essay
«Kosovo: War in the Age of the Internet» in terms of the extensive media vacuum
that had arisen around the NATO intervention:

> It was hard to grasp that an entire region inside (Southeast) Europe is
> being turned into an information black hole … What the Internet was left
> with were Serbian witnesses, diaries, personal accounts, mainly from edu-
> cated urban citizens. Immediately, while the first bomb load was dropped,
> the Internet diaries started to pop up. Their psychogeography is limited,
> by nature, by the very definition of the genre. They did not produce theory
> or a critical analysis of politics and the war situation. Add to this situation
> the semi-personal touch of e-mail, and presto, you get an odd, once in a
> lifetime mixture of paranoia, reflection, pathetic pity, waves of despair,
> worrisome productions of subjectivity, with here and there valuable pic-
> tures of the everyday life under extraordinary circumstances.[33]

Although Lovink's commentary argues that the personal nature of these Internet
diaries makes them in some way less valuable theoretically and critically, I want

to suggest that it is exactly their personal overtones, their documentary character, that makes them accessible to the Internet medium, and transferable to the medium of radio broadcast. In this context of war and atmosphere of despair, the realm of the personal necessarily becomes the locus of knowledge production, and the foundation from which more critical and theoretical analyses can take shape. And the second important aspect of these diaries' respective electronic formats lies with their ability to illustrate once again the radio's transformation from a device for reception-only into a medium that interactively engages its listeners and its source feeds in an intellectual, cultural, and sociopolitical network of idea exchange. In a certain sense, both Tesanović's and Markovic's diaries can be viewed as early blogs, or weblogs, which themselves are types of textual broadcasts of information. The entries used from Slobodan Marković's e-mail postings originated from his own personal submissions to an Internet-based mailing list known as *The Syndicate Mailing List*, which was formed in January 1996 as a «loose affiliation of artists, curators, networkers, writers and festival organisers, most of them from Eastern Europe, who are working in the field of electronic- and media-art.»[34] In contrast, Jasmina Tesanović's diary began its unique life on the web almost by accident. As the publisher's note to the 2000 American publication of the diary explains, Tesanović did not personally post her diary entries to the web, rather a friend in Sweden took the step of sharing her personal writing with the world Internet community:

> Hours after NATO started bombing Yugoslavia, Jasmina Tesanović received an e-mail from a friend in Sweden, who wanted to know how she was doing. Jasmina didn't have time to write back, so she sent entries from her diary. Her friend, the writer Ana Valdes, posted Jasmina's diary entries on the website of a magazine she wrote for. Within a week, the diaries had been posted anonymously on fifty websites, translated into several languages and sent in e-mails throughout the world ... The diary of an anonymous woman from Belgrade had become everybody's diary.[35]

---

34 «About the Syndicate Network,» http://colossus.v2.nl/syndicate/about.html (site now discontinued).

35 Frédérique Delacoste, note from the publisher of Tesanović 2000 (see note 32), p. 10.

36 For more information regarding Jasmina Tesanović's work in the «Women in Black» movement in Serbia, see her online essay «Women and War: A Serbian Perspective,» http://www.geocities.com/Wellesley/3321/win23a.html (accessed June 5, 2005).

Unlike Marković, who knowingly posted his observations on the NATO bombing to the web, Tesanović's diary experienced its anonymous online celebrity through a more grassroots approach to media activism. Both diarists were able to garner a wide audience outside the boundaries of Belgrade and Serbia through utilizing the inherent networks associated with the Internet infrastructure, which facilitated the level of resonance that both achieved in a very short amount of time. With Marković's computer science background and active interest in supporting open artistic and media access to networks in Yugoslav cyberspace, as well as his involvement with media arts groups in Eastern Europe, it is not surprising to understand the reach that his e-mail postings found, nor the types of discussions they informed on several electronic lists in Europe and beyond. In Tesanović's case, the language of her diary entries propelled their movement along Internet streams, and this language, as we will see shortly, is informed by her involvement with feminist activist groups like «Women in Black» and their focus on the situation of women in the various wars in the former Yugoslavia.[36] In much the same way that the live feeds of sounds from Belgrade during the bombing add to the immediacy of the live radio art piece, the echoes of discussion and transmission generated by both of these diaries during the height of NATO activity add a sense of timeliness and urgency to Paunović's piece as well.

Paunović's implementation of the two electronic diaries for his versions of *Other Voices*—his adaptation of them through translation (into German in the case of Marković's entries, into English in the case of Tesanović's), his staging of them as individual channels for mixing into the live radio broadcast, his enlivening of their written thoughts through dramatic vocal readings, his placing of them into the electronic soundscape representing the city of Belgrade on this one particular evening in April 1999—reveals the importance of electronic signal flow as a substitution for the physical body, whose movements are restricted or disrupted by both the technologies of war and the technologies of global telecommunications. Both textual documentaries offer eyewitness testimony to the war in Belgrade—commentaries on the absurdity of NATO's missile targets and the civilian-based casualties that resulted from them, and rationalized observations of the developing chaos percolating around them. While Marković's e-mail transmissions recount in emotional detail the nightly destruction of NATO bombs in sarcastic and ironic tones, Tesanović's diary captures the human experience of the war in interstitial terms—of Belgrade's citizens caught between moments of sanity and nervous breakdown, caught between local compulsive patriotism and global compulsive guilt, and caught between the isolation of staying put and the anonymity of being displaced.

In the first voiced excerpt from her diary, listeners to the radio broadcast experience the reasoned paradoxes of this war—the human players set against the backdrop of the world that causes it. Dated March 26, 1999 at 5 p.m., the entry responds to NATO's first sortie of air strikes against Yugoslavia just two days earlier:

> I hope we all survive this war and the bombs: the Serbs, the Albanians, the bad and the good guys, those who took up the arms, those who deserted, the Kosovo refugees traveling through the woods and the Belgrade refugees traveling through the streets with their children in their arms looking for non-existing shelters when the alarms go off. I hope that NATO pilots don't leave behind the wives and children whom I saw crying on CNN as their husbands were taking off for military targets in Serbia. I hope we all survive, but that the world as it is does not [10:28–11:00; 54:59–55:37].[37]

Tesanović's remarkable ability to name and empathize with each group of people involved in the Kosovo war, regardless of their ethnic background, refugee status, or NATO involvement, points out that the degree of separation between perpetrator and victim, so important in past instances of war, is no longer a distinction that can be made in the age of a telecommunications-based war. Seeing images of their future attackers on CNN, watching the movements of Serb and Albanian troops on state-run television, hearing about the migration of Kosovo refugees from independent broadcasts, and seeing the nervous wandering of want-to-be refugees in Belgrade with their own eyes provides a continuum between the insanity of imagined war and the calm concreteness of the real war. Tesanović clarifies this balance in the same entry from March 26:

---

37 Tesanović 2000 (see note 32), p. 72.

Today is the second aftermath day. The city is silent and paralyzed, but still working, rubbish is taken away, we have water, we have electricity. But where are the people? In houses, in beds, in shelters. I hear several personal stories of nervous breakdowns among my friends, male and female. Those who were in a nervous breakdown for the past year, since the war in Kosovo started, who were very few, now feel better. Real danger is less frightening than fantasies of danger. I couldn't cope with the invisible war as I can cope with concrete needs: bread, water, medicine. And also, very important: I can see an end. Finally we in Belgrade got what all rest of Yugoslavia has had: war on our territory [11:00–11:48; 55:37–56:26].

Fear of the unknown, of how the war would be played out, is now replaced with a knowledge of how the war would affect their lives. There is a certain spatiality involved in knowing more about how one's life might end. This is a sense of space that becomes progressively smaller, that limits physical movement, and reduces the possibilities of expression. That Paunović places Tesanović's dramatized voice within a surrounding audio stream of air raid alarms, exploding bombs, and chill-

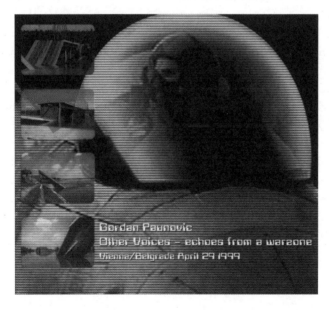

Gordan Paunović, *Other Voices—echoes from a warzone*, CD cover, graphic design by Matt Smith, *Kunstradio* CD edition, 1999.

ing cries in the night expands this sense of spatiality by positioning Tesanović's words as the unspoken thoughts of every citizen of Belgrade in the surrealist buffer of a city experiencing the loss of its most basic infrastructure. Not included in the radio broadcast, but available on the *Kunstradio* website, is her diary entry from March 31:

> Fear has entered in my mind: I don't know if I dare think what I do, I cannot cope with reality: is it possible that we are all sacrificed for somebody's lack of political judgment, or worse, madness. I am censoring my thoughts afraid to think in personal tones, afraid to be heard, judged and executed. The conflict is escalating, the atrocities are daily happenings ... My head and language are getting stiff, they have to incorporate all these controversial meanings; I despise getting along in war, no space for feminine language, no free space.[38]

One week into the NATO intervention, the nightly bombing and the daily Serbian war are taking their toll on her sense of self, and her sense of place within the world. Language is becoming other, transforming as her reality is transformed and not allowing her to write and think as she desires. Tesanović links the ever-decreasing sense of space, freedom of movement, and freedom of thought with equally decreasing possibilities for language. Here, her comment that there is «no space for feminine language, no free space» reminds us of her engagement with feminist-based NGOs, and with the founding of the first women's publishing house in Serbia called «94.» However, this comment does not mean she is somehow giving up her feminist perspective, on the contrary, as the importance of this feminist work for her sense of self, and her sense of well-being, is still a factor in her continued existence in the bombed city of Belgrade. This statement underscores, as well, the absurdity of being in a city which is being watched by the whole world, but whose citizens are not being listened to. The situational specificity of living in a city which is being attacked by NATO airplanes and barraged by Milošević propaganda has made her painfully aware of the lack of a space where such a feminist perspective is viable, or operational as a valid alternative viewpoint to bombs or half-truths. In the entry from April 12, Tesanović

---

38 See note 32.
39 Tesanović 2000 (see note 32), p. 89.

40 Zygmunt Bauman, *Globalization: The Human Consequences* (New York: Columbia University Press, 1998), p. 86.

reflects on the prospect of leaving Belgrade, her friends, her streets, her habits, her language; and becoming Other:

> I couldn't go to sleep last night, finally I took a tranquilizer, there it goes, I started to. I postponed all these weeks the use of drugs to stay normal, but I see that no normal person can stay normal without drugs, if you want to stay here. I do not want to go, I do not want to leave my city, my friends, my streets, my habits, my language. I do not believe in Other. I understand those who left, out of fear, out of needs, I could have been one of them too, but I want to stay. Friends from all over the world offer me flats, money, help. But the only thing I need from them and from others all over the world is to try to stop our war [16:42–17:33; 61:26–62:16].[39]

We hear the resolve in her voice, and again the steadiness of her words places a balance between the two wars that she and her fellow citizens have to locate themselves in, the Serbian war and «compulsive patriotism» during the day and NATO intervention and «compulsive sense of guilt» at night. In the final three spoken excerpts dated April 20, April 23, and April 26, we come face-to-face with this interstitial existence, with the impossibility of what Zygmunt Bauman terms «degree of mobility—the freedom to choose where to be:»[40]

> April 20, 1999. Now, what is my cross: NATO bombs, Serbian patriotic death. OK, between compulsive patriotism and compulsive sense of guilt, I guess there is no way out. It would take another life to do so [22:25–22:41; 67:09–67:24].

> April 23, 1999. Just yesterday I thought, now everybody is fighting for our souls, of us Serbs led astray, all these televisions, local and international. We even receive American leaflets from the planes telling us about us. Not even the Colorado teenaged killers could draw attention from our educational program [23:24–23:47; 68:08–68:30].

> April 26, 1999. I do not feel safe with the NATO or any other bombs, NATO being the only ones I know. I do not feel safe without bridges, in a boat, on a horse, on a bicycle, against NATO airplane; I do not feel

safe without schools, universities, libraries, against highly technological NATO countries. I am not afraid, not anymore, we are beyond good or evil by now, but my legs simply tremble, when I hear the NATO or any other planes with bombs above my head [25:39–26:12; 70:23–70:56].

Tesanović's personal diary documents her slow move into war, into isolation, into silence and then steady return back to identity, to community, and to expression. These last three clips evidence this narrative arc and also demonstrate Tesanović's realization that her mobility is restricted, in both a physical sense of movement and in an intellectual sense of sharing ideas and reflections. The strength of this work of radio art lies in Gordan Paunović's ability to amplify the steady, deliberate, and balanced words of Jasmina Tesanović, to turn the creative impulses of these journalists, musicians, and writers, who have been labeled «collateral damage,» back into the expressive forms of engagement they were originally intended to be. Her Internet-based diary and its place within Paunović's radio mix allows her to extend her body beyond the limitations of its physical nature, allows her to circulate her thoughts and knowledge outside the imposed boundaries of war-torn Belgrade, and allows her to take a position as an engaged global citizen. The collaboration between Paunović and the Austrian *Kunstradio* project—to draw attention to these «other voices» not captured by the global media network—highlights as well an engaged use of tactical media. Where a culture of fear is readily compounded by the global media event surrounding the conflict in Kosovo, the type of tactical media practice evidenced in Paunović's live broadcast allows for a different type of globalized network communication to occur, one that is not founded on easily digestible sound bites and the marketability of information, but rather one that mixes together a multiplicity of knowledge inputs and serves a wide range of outputs. The sounds of displacement—the fear of a disembodied identity that forms the heart of the broadcast's two diaries, the constant air raid sirens that creep into the background of the listener's minds—make the realities of this war audible, recordable, and traceable and transpose local experience, local identification with the war, onto the European and global imagination.

41 Ibid., p. 77.

While the notions of travel, exile, homelessness, and displacement each presume a relocation or dislocation of a physical body, charting this type of movement in the late twentieth century requires an additional investigation into the ways in which information, documentation, and surveillance stand in for the physical body. As Zygmunt Bauman puts it:

> In the world we inhabit, distance does not seem to matter much. Sometimes it seems that it exists solely in order to be cancelled; as if space was but a constant invitation to slight it, refute and deny. Space stopped being an obstacle—one needs just a split second to conquer it.[41]

In an epoch of globalized economies, media states, and convergent telecommunications networks, mobility and movement assume characteristics of instantaneity, where the distances of time and space become imaginary, as equally traversable by immobility or staying put as they are by physical movement. Gordan Paunović's implementation of these diaries into the ethereal flow of radio broadcast and Internet transmission opens a viable network space in which the power of Tesanović's words addresses the hegemonic forces that are keeping her physical body restricted: the nightly NATO bombing, the omnipresent weight of the Milošević regime, and the quelling silence parsed by the constant din of commercial Western media.

The trajectory of artistic and technical experimentation represented by the three projects discussed in the parameters of this essay demonstrates the power of a networked radio space in opening up lines of communication and collaboration between artists to circumvent traditional modes of radio broadcasting and bypass regulations seeking to limit access to networks within the global telecommunications infrastructure. The freedom to move information within these networks, but not to move or create knowledge, maintains them solely for the economic structures of globalization. The experimental modes of communication and thought behind the *State of Transition*, *Horizontal Radio*, and *Other Voices* broadcasts and performances appropriates the channels and relays of these same telematic networks and opens them up as a temporary autonomous zone of performance and dialogue that taps into the immaterial realm of artistic consciousness, provides possibilities for artistic collaboration, and transmits engaging, thought-provoking broadcasts back out into radio space for access and continued dialogue by the listening public.

LADA — L'Arte dell'Ascolto
(The Art of Listening)

A Festival in Rimini, Italy, 1991–98

Roberto Paci Dalò

LADA – L'Arte dell'Ascolto (The Art of Listening)[1] was an independent international festival dedicated to radio and art held in Rimini, Italy from 1991 to 1998, curated by Roberto Paci Dalò with the collaboration of Isabella Bordoni, produced by the artist group Giardini Pensili with varying collaborators and coproducers. LADA was a project in continuous evolution to reaffirm a creative approach to radio, conceived of as a place and a medium aggregating to other languages. An explorative relationship with municipal and public spaces emerged as a second characteristic of the festival.

LADA included radio works, concerts, live radio drama, performances, films and videos, installations, debates, and radio broadcasts (on the Italian and Austrian National Radios, Rai and ORF respectively, and other stations) and, in 1995, saw the launching of RADIO LADA as one of the first online radios. Every annual version of the festival was achieved with minimal economic resources, and it was all possible thanks to the collaboration of artists, scholars, and technicians participating with sincere enthusiasm and collaborative spirit.

Considering radio's situation in Italy today, having a strong audience but being dramatically diminished in terms of planning and production, I view our small L'Arte dell'Ascolto festival in Rimini and other experiences—such as the continuous production, distribution, and reflection of radio art on and by the *AudioBox* program on Rai (Italian National Radio) and its large international festivals of the same name—as somewhat the swan song of an age.

Today, *AudioBox* is no more, and the Rai regional radio headquarters are almost all sadly underutilized, with many of the extraordinary engineers and technicians that collaborated on the L'Arte dell'Ascolto festival now finding themselves «recycled» in the area of television, not having enough radio space in which to operate.

What follows is a short description of the respective annual L'Arte dell'Ascolto (LADA) festivals.

1991: Radio e audio art
(Radio and Audio Art)

The first time the festival L'Arte dell'Ascolto was held, it took place entirely in the Cineteca in Rimini, an evocative place with Roman mosaics on the walls, located inside the Gambalunga Library building, one of the most important humanities libraries in Italy. Among the many authors represented in the library with original works is Athanasius Kircher (a protagonist of acoustic imagination).

The following is excerpted from the text presenting the first annual LADA festival:

Contemporary radio work brings together and synthesizes different styles and trends including: present-day musical research, implementation of technology, a growing attention to everyday sounds, that is, sounds considered to lack «musical» value, and acoustic ecology or the relationship between human beings and the sound landscapes in which they live. Radio art, or hoerspiel, comprise all of these facets, facilitating a form of acoustic art, achieved specifically for radio, in which texts of any type—literary or poetic—are transported to an acoustic context, thus acquiring new meanings and relationships: sound that emphasizes silence and the awareness of our acoustic environment. Radio art can

1   A complete report about LADA – L'Arte dell'Ascolto is downloadable from http://giardini.sm/lada.

be considered to be a developmental process, starting from the few illustrative environmental noises in early radio drama and culminating in
complex works of sound that, not coincidentally, have brought composers and sound artists closer to radio, resulting in the realization of an
increasing number of compositions conceived for this medium. Their exploration of radio's intimacy and sense of community tends, even while
maintaining a special position for music, to dissolve into and integrate with
other media such as the visual arts, video, theater, performance, and film.

A section of the first L'Arte dell'Ascolto festival was dedicated to the multi-coded
AudioBox space—then a daily program on Rai Uno—emphasizing the production, presentation, and reflection of radio-specific work by artists and embedding
it into in-depth information on cultural events and developments in Italy and
abroad.

LADA 91 also saw the launch of the series *Audioritratto* (Audio Self-Portrait).
The first of these tributes was dedicated to the Australian composer/performer
Jon Rose in whose work radio to this day plays an important role. In the following
years, Audio Self-Portraits of Luc Ferrari, Mauricio Kagel, and Heiner Goebbels
were produced with an emphasis on their radio work.

All variants of the yearly LADA festivals were accompanied by presentations
of international radio art productions, networked projects, and CD productions.

1992: Guerre
(Wars)

The 1992 festival was witness to the Yugoslavian paradox. In this period—and
during the first left-centre government in the history of the Italian Republic—air
raids departed from the Cervia airport (twenty minutes from Rimini) to perform
their missions over Belgrade. Now war, thought to be exorcised from Europe,
was right in our own home. That this war was the responsibility of the European
governments, with active involvement of the Italian government, made it even
more tangible.

The festival of 1992—along with many other events—featured radio works by
Arsenije Jovanović of Belgrade, already established as an important protagonist
in the development of radio-specific aesthetics of «composition» (in a radio art

rather than a musical sense) using sounds from his very own, ever-growing archives. Implementing the first site-specific work at LADA, Spanish composer and musician Llorenç Barber realized *Dal sole al sole*, a concerto for one hundred bells (and a single performer, Barber himself). His concerto took place non-stop from sunset to dawn, inland from Rimini on the almost dry riverbed of the Marecchia River. What seemed to be an event for the few was transformed into an event of unexpected proportions, with an audience of several hundred people who spent the night in this place among bushes, shrubs, stones, and bonfires.

Canadian artist Robert Adrian and Austrian Gerfried Stocker presented their three-year project *ZERO–The Art of Being Everywhere*, which they had been curating at the time in Graz, Austria. *ZERO* included *The Big Net Jam–an interactive online opera* by Seppo Gründler, a musician-composer, radio artist, and innovative programmer from Graz. *The Big Net Jam* took place on FidoNet, used MIDI language, and was usable by whomever had access to a computer and modem. The MIDI data could be uploaded by telephone, played on a synthesizer, manipulated, altered, and retransmitted on the online database for further manipulation by other participants. Over the course of two days, the L'Arte dell'Ascolto audience could participate in *The Big Net Jam* through interactive hookups with an interactive installation located in front of the Austrian pavilion at the World Expo in Seville, Spain.

1993: L'infanzia del linguaggio
(The Infancy of Language)

1993 proved to be a crucial year for L'Arte dell'Ascolto. The need was felt for a different and more radial use of space, and thus we began to work in and for the city. In the 1993 festival, projects were created that allowed for a sense of distance and/or nearness. A psychogeography was triggered that sought to challenge the routine of canonic spaces.

The inauguration of LADA 93 took place outdoors at the Piazza Cavour in the historical centre of the city, with Italian sound ecologist and composer Albert Mayr performing *Time Events*.

For the first time, the festival had access to the *Publiphono*. The loudspeakers of this special «radio» were stationed over a length of fifteen kilometers of coastline, at a distance of approximately fifty meters apart. *Publiphono* was created by Renato de Donato in 1946. *Publiphono* president Ugo de Donato explained in 1993: «During the golden years of mass tourism with its unprecedented growth, in August we would sometimes broadcast an average of 150 messages a day, what with lost children and children found. We were the classic beach for families.» *Publiphono* remains part of the acoustic memory of at least four generations of beachgoers on the Adriatic Riviera.

Twelve artists received commissions to create original works for the festival's *Publiphono* broadcasts, transmitted first on Rimini's beach and subsequently by European radio networks. The *Publiphono* broadcasts took place on two days in August at 4:00 p.m. and lasted thirty minutes each. The very first broadcast even set off a small measure of panic, with *Publiphono*'s switchboard having been invaded by telephone calls from people alarmed by the «strange sounds» emitted. That same year, *La lunga notte* (The Long Night) was created, an internationally networked concert between Rimini, Innsbruck, Cologne, and Jerusalem, with participation in Rimini by Takumi Fukushima (violin), Gordon Monahan (piano), Horst Hörtner (interactive computer system), Giancarlo Cardini (piano), Quartetto Arianna (string quartet), Claudio Jacomucci (accordion), Roberto Paci Dalò (clarinet, voice, live electronics), Gerfried Stocker (data gloves, interactive

LADA festival,
Publiphono, documentary video,
Rimini, Italy, 1997.

computer system), and, live from Innsbruck's regional radio station, Sainkho Namtchylak (voice), from Jerusalem's KOL Israel studios the Israeli poet Yehuda Amichai and the Palestinian poet Samih Al-Qasim, as well as from Cologne Axel Otto at the Electronic Café International. The live radio line from Jerusalem did not work and was replaced by a telephone connection.

«Of course the signal was not pure but whatever the loss from a technical point of view, it makes this piece particularly touching. We can ‹feel› the distance. We can feel the desert.»[2]

1994: La casa
(The House)

The fourth annual L'Arte dell'Ascolto was a reflection on the house as a private place, with its ephemeral, vulnerable separations between inside and outside: a reflection on the sounds of the home, but also on the acoustic imagination of a private space; on the various daytime and nighttime moods of the house; on the occupied home, the bombed home, the desired home; as well as on houses, their invisible walls and acoustic crossings from floor to floor.

Among the radio stations participating were the Russian, Slovenian, and Polish radios, a further broadening of the scope that reflected the event's philosophy.

Live concerts and performances strictly linked to the radio medium were presented, among them Stefano Giannotti's *Canzoni Naturali* (Natural Songs) and Sergio Messina's *RadioGladio*.[3]

The section *Radio pour les yeux* (Radio for the eyes) opened to the image in movement with videos by Konstanze Binder and the German intermedia artist Wolf Kahlen, who founded the twenty-four-hour artists' radio *Ruine der Künste* in Berlin (Ruins of the Arts, 1988–1994).

Again, works by international artists were commissioned for *Publiphono*, which also broadcast some of the *Messages to Belgrade*, an Austrian project in which international artists created messages to the independent radio station B92 in Belgrade.

2   Isabella Bordoni and Roberto Paci Dalò in a presentation of their work in the symposium/ exhibition ZEITGLEICH (1994). See also exh. cat. *Zeitgleich* (Vienna: Triton, 1994), p. 111. Or see http://www.kunstradio.at/TAKE/ zgcatalog.html.

3   See Sergio Messina's essay, «Airtime,» in this volume.

4   Arthur and Marilouise Kroker, *Lecture* (Rimini and San Marino, 1995).

1995: Radio Lada, Horizontal Radio, Arte a parte
(Radio Lada, Horizontal Radio, Art Aside)

«Consequently, what is necessary is not the recovery of the ear as a privileged orifice for the nostalgic return of oral culture, but the growth of new ears—digital ears—as a sign of nostalgia for the future.»[4]

Five years before the end of the millennium—five years during which, due to digital technologies, radical changes in daily life, in education, in art would occur—LADA became border-crossing: its program was distributed across the border from Italy to the small Republic of San Marino.

The festival aimed to constitute an instance for reflection and discussion premised on the project *Horizontal Radio*, which had been realized on June 22 and 23 of the same year, with the participation of artists, technicians, and many others around the world. Within its Mediterranean sub-network (Italy, Spain, Israel, Palestine, Greece, San Marino), three Italian National Radio (Rai) channels along with several independent radios had contributed eight hours of live broadcasting and several on-site events at various locations in different cities, among them Bologna. LADA 95 was intended to pursue a debate on art and artistic work faced with new technologies and the changes in perception they provoked.

Concise introductions were dedicated to how CD-ROMs, digital radio, Internet, hypertexts—among other things—function and how they might be utilized at the same time in artistic and scientific contexts.

During the festival, *Radio LADA*, a web radio, was launched. This ensured that festival events created between Rimini and San Marino could potentially be listened to throughout the world and be picked up by radio stations.

A main conference was held between Rimini and San Marino with the participation of international artists and theoreticians.

The future headquarters for Rimini's museums became the evocative space for *Arte a parte* (Art Aside): a modernist building that had been closed for many years, it was used in its entirety in order to give each artist ample space for his or her installation. Some of the installations were site-specific, but all of them were based on the relationship between sound and space. Light played a fundamental role in the exhibition.

In San Marino, exhibits were created in a private home and at the Pinacoteca Museo di San Francesco. All festival events were faciliated in collaboration with San Marino RTV (San Marino National Radio).

Some of the works were spread out over the open-air market that is held twice weekly, filling various piazzas in the historical centre of Rimini. There, among clothes, food, and objects, the sounds of the audio and radio works of the festival moved in an almost subliminal way, superimposing themselves on the sound-scape of the market's sites.

Also, a live radio broadcast was transmitted on Rai's Radiotre *AudioBox* and on the Internet.

1996: Circuiti del desiderio (Circuits of Desire)

Bodies? Partial machines. The 1996 festival revolved around the body and the senses. At the centre of the project was the conference *Partial Body*, implying the body understood as partial machine. This comprised an investigation of the possible forms of relationships between the body and technology, of the conventions and codes sanctioning the territory of standards and normality. Underscoring the necessity of practical theory and a laboratory, the conference *Partial Body: Conference vs. Laboratory* was held in three different moments at Smoke, a coffee bar in Rimini close to the beach, and at the SUMS Citizens' Club in San Marino.

The festival became increasingly aware of the spaces used for its projects and events. Places as «found objects» turned into extraordinary spaces the moment in which they were experienced in other contexts.

Again, works by international artists were broadcast through *Publiphono*, over the sandy beaches of the Riviera. Video and interactive installations were located at a Palazzo in Rimini and a church in San Marino, while the coffee bar Smoke in Rimini featured photographic work. Live performances took place in different locations, among them a theater and a club, broadcast on channels of several national radios and on commercial regional stations: Rai (*AudioBox*), San Marino RTV, ORF (*Kunstradio*), Radio Mediterraneo, and Radio Melody.

1997: Misure
(Measures)

The 1997 festival was dedicated to noises and silences in networks, the measuring of time and space; to a phantasmagoric encounter between archaic and contemporary things; and to reflections on the relationship between pop culture and «high» culture, between Internet and radio, between political and aesthetic reflection, between the North and the South in the world.

The festival was centred at the Palace for Tourism, a small, late-nineteenth-century building located in front of the legendary Grand Hotel, an icon of the films of Federico Fellini. This unusual partnership network brought together radio stations, independent associations, discotheques, and government agencies. The German playwright Heiner Müller was the guiding figure of the entire festival and the subject of an international symposium entitled Heiner Müller, Radio, Digital Technologies.

The section *HeinerMüllerMaterial* comprised two events: the first was *Dance Floor: HeinerMüllerMaterial (Uno)* with Sam Auinger, Rupert Huber, Roberto Paci Dalò, Norbert Math, Davide Riondino, Isabella Bordoni, and Rachel de Boer

LADA festival,
documentary video,
Rimini, Italy, 1997.

(VJ), with live performances broadcast on the radio on *Suoni e Ultrasuoni* Rai Radiodue; the second was *HeinerMüllerMaterial (Due)* with Rita Maffei, Fabiano Fantini, Antonio Catania, and E Zezi live on Rai Radiotre *AudioBox*.

In collaboration with the Communications Science course «Media Dramaturgy: Radio & Internet» at the University of Siena, the main project for the network involved a laboratory for the creation of the online radio *Itaca* (which actually never started).

The first collaboration of LADA with the oldest Italian labor union, the CGIL (*Confederazione Generale Italiana del Lavoro* [General Italian Labor Confederation], created in 1906), and with the association of solidarity, Hammada, resulted in an explicitly political project. The Gruppo Operaio di Pomigliano d'Arco E Zezi presented a concert of solidarity with the Saharawi people in the Western Sahara.

In an autumn version, *Publiphono* became a live event on a Sunday morning with the beach populated not by tourists, as during the high season, but by the natives out taking a walk, as is typical during Sunday off-season mornings. Austrian sound and radio artist Sam Auinger executed a two-hour live concert using the fifteen kilometers of amplification.

As part of the festival, the third section of the *Kunstradio* project *Recycling the Future I–IV* was achieved with live broadcasts on Österreich 1 and the *Kunstradio* website. The LADA festival thus became part of *Kunstradio*'s preparations for the celebration of its tenth anniversary with the «on line – on air – on site» *Recycling the Future IV* festival in Vienna in December 1997.[5]

LADA also saw the first experiment of an «instant documentary» at the festival by Salvo Cuccia. Filmed and edited in real time, it was shown at the festival's conclusion and embodied an example of artistic practice strongly linked to the development of digital work.

5   Episodes 1 and 2 of *Recycling the Future* took place in the *Hybrid WorkSpace* at documenta X in Kassel and at the Ars Electronica Festival in Linz. See http://kunstradio.at/FUTURE/index.html.

1998: Ascoltare il mediterraneo
(Listening to the Mediterranean)

The last time the festival was held, the need for a dialectic encounter between the cultures of the Internet and a special tradition became evident—a tradition conceived of in an innovative manner that finds an explicit place of action in a well-defined geographic area: the Mediterranean.

The leading figure and inspiration of the festival was the writer and linguist Predrag Matvejević, who was born in Mostar (Bosnia-Herzegovina, ex-Yugoslavia) and emigrated to become an Italian citizen. Matvejević's writings and complex notions on the «Mediterranean» and «World Ex,» his memento to the «wound» of Sarajevo, and the destruction of the famous old bridge in Mostar were the focus of LADA 98.

The central event of the festival was the performance of *Mondo Ex* in which Predrag Matvejević read from his texts to a flux of live streams from different ex-Yugoslavian cities. The preparatory work took several months since it involved putting back into contact people and places who had been dispersed by the war. The reestablishment of these contacts resulted in the forming of a strange, para-doxical (and moving) *Yugoslav Electronics Federation* that was created in the space and for the duration of one night. Along with Matvejević, the musicians Luigi Lai (one of the great heirs of the Sardinian tradition and maestro of *is launeddas*), Lullo Mosso, and Massimo Semprini performed on-site in Rimini.

The entire festival was transmitted through live streams on the Internet, and a workshop and mix of presentations was achieved under the guidance of *Itaca & Aria Network*, a Euro-Mediterranean radio and telematics project involving Barcelona, Lisbon, Marseille, Rimini, and Vienna.

Diaries occupied an important place within this festival thanks to the presence of Elena Tosi Brandi (written diary) and Stefano Ricci (drawn diary), to which were added the animation films of Gianluigi Toccafondo.

In addition to *Mondo Ex*, other performances, almost all linked to the writings of Matvejević, were presented: *Reading from a Mediterranean Breviary* with Nicoletta Fabbri and Pierpaolo Paolizzi; *Maqam* live sounds from the Mediterranean, dance floor between electronic and traditional; *Mediterraneo* with Predrag Matvejević, and webcasting from various cities; *AudioBox on-line*, webcasting with the participation of Pinotto Fava, Pino Saulo, the artists in Rimini, and hookups to artists in many other places via the Internet.

A Conclusion, A Departure

Aside from conveying my personal reflections on this adventure, it has been my aim in this essay to furnish information on participants, places, and works, so as to create a kind of Polaroid of a project such as this, with its fragile, volatile, and broad nature. I have attempted to give an overall vision of something that by its very nature was inevitably multiple, collective, rhizomatic.

LADA also witnessed the birth of the fertile relationship between radio and the Internet. The festival was the direct eyewitness of a special period during which Internet became accessible. Everything that is «obvious» today (streaming, uploading, or downloading something) was at the time—just a few years ago, really!—a genuine adventure.

Projects like *Horizontal Radio* can no longer exist, not so much due to technology issues—since now everything is available practically right in your own home—but rather to the changes in people, in the institutions, and in the public radio organizations. The personal and institutional conditions no longer exist, in short, in which to create projects on this scale. Whether this will prove beneficial or detrimental is not up to us to decide. All we can do is take note of the present state of affairs and never stop erecting active «coming communities.»

Increasingly, I believe that, for the development of these processes, it is crucial to set up activities on a daily basis, also in relation to specific physical locations. For this reason, we initiated the *Velvet Factory* project in 2006:[6] an unusual contemporary arts centre created within the Velvet Club, a venue well-known across Europe for its electronic, rock, and quality pop music programming. Located in the hills near Rimini, it is a three-story building—approximately 2,500 square meters—facing a lake, averaging more than 180,000 visitors annually. The *Factory* has post-production facilities, several different spatial typologies, and artist-in-residence programs, where people can gather to establish further collaborative strategies both on local and international scales. An open laboratory for sensorial adventures focuses on digital cultures, urban explorations, sound, image, and radio—a project devoted to the development of the Cultural District and the Creative City, where we try to continue the experiences of LADA daily, locally, and internationally. This is the future for me and, as always, there is so much to do!

6   See *Velvet Factory* at http://velvet.it.

The Medium as Midas

On the Precarious Relationship of
Music and Radio Art

Christian Scheib

The very first show in December 1987 in the *Kunstradio–Radiokunst* series initiated by Heidi Grundmann for the cultural program of ORF (Austrian Broadcasting) featured an interview with Klaus Schöning, the renowned radio colleague
from WDR (West German Radio). Covered topics included Schöning's *Ars Acustica*
section curated for documenta 8[1] and, as the first artistic contribution to the new
radio art series—as strange as it may sound at first—a version of an opera created for this medium. The work was based on a performance from the Frankfurt
opera house, *Europera 1 & 2* by John Cage, a work that had been commissioned
by the Frankfurt opera. From the beginning, then, there has been a close and,
at the same time—when a matter of working out aesthetic differences between
forms of experimental music, on the one hand, and radio art, on the other—not
only a close but also a precarious relationship between music and radio art. What
a theory of radio art and its precarious relationship to music—radio art makes
sound even when it does not involve language—and to radio—its medium—
must achieve, based upon the existing theoretical approaches to both realities
of art, one oriented more to sound, the other more to media, is to develop a new,
stand-alone, constructivistically open aesthetic. Radio art is incongruent with
radio and music in their respective traditional self-perceptions. It has been and

remains necessary to, again and again, force the radio medium to see itself not only as a medium, but as art. And as far as the acoustic arts are concerned, it was and still is necessary to fight for assertion that the traditional belief in a certain sought-after work in its intended form does not always or necessarily want to be applied, for one because a materiality of sound is replaced or supplemented by a materiality of communication. This essay sets out to outline a theoretical approach to resolving this situation.

The focus on the art projects considered in the following lies in the thought concepts of large-scale, globally networked *Kunstradio* projects, not so much in the works carried out by the various artists operating mainly with sound, field recordings, electroacoustic procedures, languages, et cetera. Attempting to create a new aesthetic for these works closer still to an intersection of experimental radio play and experimental music or electroacoustics may not prove as essential as for those networking projects in which numerous aspects that are taken for granted, even by «traditional» experimental art, are thrown overboard, for example beginning and end, comprehensible form, predictable mode of appearance, and so forth, as was developed, for example, in the undertakings *Horizontal Radio*, *Sound Drifting*, or some contributions to *Art's Birthday* and the like. The Achilles heel of a radio art that has long since left behind all simple temporal, media-based, phenomenological restrictions is still of course the—very—simplicity of the loudspeakers of the radio medium. But *Kunstradio* began attacking and abandoning precisely this restriction at a very early stage, with its motto of «on air – on line – on site,» and any attempt to set up a theory that draws on theoretical roots of music as well as on those of media theory must take this situation into account.

Although this essay reflects on aesthetic attitudes of the major networked projects, the numerous «everyday,» or rather now «every-Sunday,» works are of course equally of tremendous importance for the subject of this essay, for the precarious relationship between music and radio art. *Kunstradio* began with John Cage and continued with many musicians, internationally from Max Eastley

1 See Klaus Schöning, «Auf den Spuren der ‹akustischen Kunst› im Radio,» vol. 1, and «Audiothek,» vol. 2, in *Documenta 8: Kassel 1987, 12. Juni–20. Sept.*, ed. Monika Goedl, exh. cat. documenta 8 (Kassel: Walther & Weidemeyer, 1987), ISBN 3-925272-13.5.

2 Brandon LaBelle, *Background Noise: Perspectives on Sound Art* (New York: Continuum International, 2006), pp. 280–81.

3 See also Robert Adrian, Telecommunication Projects, http://alien.mur.at/rax/BIO/.

4 Robert Adrian, quoted in LaBelle 2006 (see note 2).

5 Robert Adrian, «Electronic Space,» in «Im Netz der Systeme,» *Kunstforum International* 103 (1989).

to Bill Fontana to Alvin Curran or Roberto Paci Dalò and regionally from Gary Danner, Josef Klammer, and Seppo Gründler to Mia Zabelka, Andrea Sodomka, Patrizia Jünger, and many, many others. And in the phase of self-discovery and constitution of *Kunstradio–Radiokunst*, really in the years before the final formation of the new show, it would seem to have been above all the realm of telematics, the development and use of an «electronic space» and a network idea, that helped this new self-image of art find its identity. As early as 1979—the media location not yet *Kunstradio* by a long chalk, but an ORF/Österreich 1 show produced by Heidi Grundmann[2]—Robert Adrian and Richard Kriesche, at the I.P. Sharp Office in Vienna, along with Gottfried Bach and Heidi Grundmann, live from the *Kunst heute* show studio, collaborated on the global telecommunications art project *Interplay*.[3] Demonstrating the possibilities of the new electronic networks not only precipitated a search for new forms of art; moreover, the demonstration of the possibilities inherent in the new electronic networks, along with other objectives—and this embodies the truly radical approach to a new, telematically oriented art—was regarded as worthy of being art itself, as Robert Adrian has stressed in retrospect: «… the basic theoretical concept was: … To demonstrate the global nature of electronic networks … To challenge the hegemony of the one-to-many broadcast media by using the telephone system for one-to-one multi-media interaction … To make a statement about a new role for the artist in the age of electronic media as a creator of the space for art rather than as a mere producer of objects.»[4] Just how hard telematic art, even in its early days, had striven to break up a traditional concept of space—and telematically oriented art was concerned in these years with exploring and/or conquering a new, namely an electronic space—is also emphasized by Robert Adrian: «[While] Performance Art had shown how artworks could be related to duration (time-based) and Conceptual Art had shown how they could be located in conceptual space (dematerialized), it was Mail-Art with its concept of postal space—a blizzard of images circling the globe through the integrated postal services—that made it possible to conceive of artworks in the electronic space of the new networks.»[5] This course, with its various stages, shows that during these years—indicating, in the context of this essay, the years prior to and around the founding of *Kunstradio*—what was involved was a slow artistic development and exploration of the network concept: abandoning the concept of «one-to-many broadcasting» in favor of an electronic space, discovering and developing networks as a new spatial conception.

John Cage; the numerous musicians involved from the outset; the tele-matic—this outline sets out from this initial situation with the aim of forging the desired link between thoughts from the world of music and from the world of (tele)media. The first attempt: John Cage—and, for all the seriousness involved, we cannot avoid a slightly ironic smile in Cage's spirit—was, as we know, a kind of manic liberator, a magician in releasing this and that and everything into a lib-erty devised by the magician himself. In this sense, everything was released and relieved of its serving function, everything was entrusted to self-determinedness. Once tone pitch had been released from its serving function within a harmony, rhythm from its serving function within a meter, timbre from its serving function within an overall sound, the note from its serving function within a structure, structure from its serving function within a context of tension, the context of ten-sion from any function within a dramaturgy, and so on, and in any case, funda-mentally, hearing from its serving function within a circumscribed and restricted or restricting social reality—space, and thus the media space, could naturally not remain unliberated either, and that alone makes Cage's strategies equally rel-evant to radio and media art. In Cage's work, however, this was a goal achieved in stages; to begin with, space in Cage's conception served to liberate other things, such as time, or rather a linear conception of time—after all, Cage hailed from the time-based art of music. «Don't think of the work outside of time. Instead of controlling possibilities, instead of letting them emerge only in succession, break their linearity and run them simultaneously, immediately and all at once.»[6] Big simultaneous projects such as *HPSCHD* or *Musicircus* were then carried out, in which space was used to achieve overlaps of time, nonlinearities. The aim was to achieve the «liberation of time» by means of an «invasion of space.» But soon it was also a matter of breaking up space, or rather a traditional conception of space. «My concern was to avoid having to deal with some sort of ‹spatial ob-ject,› and thus, likewise, a ‹finite temporal object› with a beginning, a middle, and an end.»[7] Such proclamations come very close to the reality of a project such as *Sound Drifting*,[8] and another step that would follow ended up resolving the definable space of the listeners completely into the innumerable, superim-

6   John Cage, *For The Birds* (Salem, 1981), pp. 198–99.

7   Ibid.

8   See http://kunstradio.at/SD/index.html. Also see *Sound Drifting: I Silenzi Parlano Tra Loro: Documentation with essays, images and two audio CDs*, ed. Heidi Grundmann (Vienna: Triton Verlag, 2000), ISBN 3-85486-082-X.

Tyrolean Ensemble of New Music, *Granite Head*, an eight-hour radio and Internet event with a live audience on a stone-sculpture site in the alpine valley Pitztal, Austria. A contribution to the international networked project *Rivers & Bridges*, a TRANSIT project, 1996.

posed, independent media spaces of radio listeners and Internet users—if we read Cage's thoughts from the nineteen-seventies from this perspective: «Space arises out of the fact that the works are superimposed and accumulate ‹their own› spaces. There is no single space, finally—there are several spaces and these spaces tend to multiply among themselves.»[9] We will come back to Cage in this regard later in this essay.

The second attempt: the fact that, as mentioned above, many artists involved in early *Kunstradio* hailed from the sphere of music made a program with roots, recognizable from John Cage, appear plausible throughout, but this also led to very different patterns of action and interaction that occasionally (with an ironic wink) gave the *Kunstradio* ideology something akin to the bliss of a musician's jam session, for example when an extremely heterogeneous group of artists—stylistic and aesthetic in origin—performs as «*Kunstradio* All Stars» for its tenth anniversary. Musicians such as Andrea Sodomka, Sam Auinger, Rupert Huber, Bernhard Loibner, Norbert Math, all from Austria, jammed with Bob Ostertag, Andres Bosshard, GX Jupitter-Larsen, Jon Rose, Scanner, and Roberto Paci Dalò, among others, as All Stars; musicians and artists such as Winfried Ritsch, Elisabeth Schimana, Josef Klammer and Seppo Gründler, Mia Zabelka, Karlheinz Essl, Günther Zechberger, Igor Lintz-Maues, Tamasz Ungvary, Gerfried Stocker, Horst Hörtner, Matthias Fuchs, Rick Rue, Jim Denley, Warren Burt, Amanda Stuart, Martin Daske, Gordan Paunović, José Iges, Concha Jerez, and many more performed in projects such as *Recycling The Future*,[10] *Rivers & Bridges*,[11] and many others. Of course, the boundaries between «*Kunstradio* ideology» and «music-making attitude» were continuously blurring. In the later years of *Kunstradio*, series were developed that—like a belated analogy to the «session» genre—were explicitly dedicated to certain genres: sitcom, road movie, thriller. And in all of these cases, a secret of the aesthetic strategy seems to lie in operating experimentally on a meta-level, meaning to see the «material» of the artistic work as being not so much the sound or the word itself but rather the genre as whole, or rather certain characteristic traits. Which is why the All Star sessions never found themselves in the normalcy of a musical session, and why Familie Auer[12] was never caught up by the banality of a sitcom, at least not unintentionally. Because radio art does not believe in the phenomenological aspect of the acoustic

9   Ibid.
10 See http://kunstradio.at/FUTURE/index.html.
11 See http://kunstradio.at/RIV_BRI/index.html.
12 See http://kunstradio.at/AUER/index.html.

material but rather works on the materiality of the media, telemedia, or a particular genre, all of this is transformed Midas-like under its hand into something different, materializing in an every-Sunday metamorphosis into radio art. We will come back to this metamorphic aspect again later on in this essay; but let us begin with some comments on the «*Kunstradio* ideology» asserted above, as a third attempt at outlining a theory.

The fact that art has something to do with ideology, and not only with aesthetics, has been clearly and frequently illustrated by *Kunstradio*. And this is intended not as criticism but rather as the beginning of an attempt to suggest wherein lies the special feature, because then the «artistic» aspect of something that is so far removed from a socially accepted notion of «artistic,» as was sometimes the case in some *Kunstradio* projects, cannot be grasped with the conceptual tools already accepted by society as an aesthetic stock-in-trade. Instead, you have to look elsewhere, to the realm of ideology, and to begin with you end up outside the sphere of art, subsequently working your way back. Although this metaphor is in fact wrong: you do not «work your way back» into art, rather you work to ensure that art catches up with you again, that it grows across, as it were, to the place where you are now.

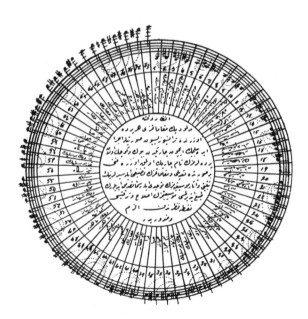

Rupert Huber, *Darb – I Fetih*, installation, performances, radio and Internet project, 1996–97.

And that may be real places, or «place» as a metaphor. The real place of radio art, according to the old *Kunstradio* radio art manifesto,[13] is the place where people hear under precisely those conditions in which people hear. Radio art thus does not have one place but an indeterminate number of places. And, logically, it has no final, no unequivocally definable, determinable manifestation. Pure constructivism of the aesthetic: every radio art listener hears a different piece, unchangeably, and everyone creates their own final version from a framework of possibility. Such was already the way of things when radio art consisted simply in producing pieces for radio. The further development of radio art toward using multiple technical media is usually described such that the changing communication technologies were so «enticing» that, as soon as they appeared, they were also used to make art, in this case radio art. As clear as it is that insight into the realm of technology, its history, utopias, possibilities, and above all its restrictions has always shaped this kind of art more than could the restrictions of the five staves from the musical notation storage medium ever define composition—to the extent, then, that artists, knowing this, have indeed oriented themselves to what is technologically possible—so should we perhaps view the expanding of the concept of radio art not from a technological vantage point but as a consequence of this constructivist conception of art that was applied from the outset. If someone seriously believes that art is not the broadcast piece itself, but rather the act of hearing the broadcast piece—«Radio art is composed of sound objects experienced in radio space ... Radio happens in the place it is heard,» the manifesto avers—then the expanding of the concept of radio art beyond actual, real «radio» is already inherent in the first approach, and use of the Internet and any other media-based and likewise non-acoustic dimension always goes as much without saying as the concept of the no longer controllable—or rather no-longer-willing-to-be-controlled—network and, of course, also the decentralized multiperspectivist aesthetic. Hence, all of this, I would suggest, is not only conceivable by means of «technologies» but rather had been so thoroughly conceived from the outset that the expanding of the concept was always inherent in the concept that was applied.

Of course, there are aesthetic exemplars outside of radio art, too. If we add to «multiperspectivist» such concepts as indeterminacy and experiment, what we

13   See http://kunstradio.at/THEORIE/index.html.

14   See Desmond Mark, ed., *Paul Lazarsfeld: Die Wiener RAVAG. Study 1932. Der Beginn der modernen Rundfunkforschung* (Vienna and Mülheim an der Ruhr: Guthmann–Peterson, 1996), ISBN 3-900782-29-6.

have are some of the key terms from the music aesthetic of John Cage and David Tudor. And yet, when radio art conquered all of this terrain through *Kunstradio*, it sounded like and was indeed more ideology than aesthetic. And the reason is that radio art does not take place at a certain place dedicated to art—unlike Cage and Tudor when they experimented in galleries, museums, and also concert halls—but rather on the radio, a mass medium. This is why something like the pursuit of multiperspectivist indeterminacy was, in this context, not a shocking aesthetic program to begin with but rather a media ideology.

And this medium—radio—does not have much to do with art, and, if it does, then with the broadcasting of art, and here again, from the outset, listener surveys have demonstrated that the strict chamber of chamber music was pretty near the bottom of popularity rankings in Lazarfeld's study even when radio as a spreading medium was still young.[14] The fact that this medium claims to be not only a transporter of art but, in its intrinsic characteristics, «capable of being art» itself had been left to the dreams of Futurists, just as progressive artists had been needed at Bauhaus and elsewhere to reconceive the record medium from being a player for art to a medium capable of being art. So from this angle, while radio art happens on and through radio, it happens as art in spite of radio.

How does art get into radio and how does it get out again? Through artistic work, we might conclude, media-related ideology has caused precisely this work to become an aesthetic of radio art. From the viewpoint of music, the above-mentioned tension is of particular interest: to what extent do we find that aesthetic of experimentation here that also has a musical component or tradition and, at the same time, to what extent does it nevertheless differ from it. By way of trial, after applying Cage's key concepts of experimentation and multicenteredness, we will apply a key concept from European, Adorno-trained thought, asking quite simply what this «material» of radio art is. Sound, the answer would be, if we still went by the radio art manifesto, for example. But the history of the fought-for expanded concept of radio, the aforementioned «on air – on line – on site,» having long since been concerned with much more than sound waves emanating from radio loudspeakers, renders this view obsolete. To reflect a moment on the famous «historical status of the material» with regard to radio art, however, it would make sense to at least postulate a material in this context. Among other things, in order to contemplate an expanded concept of radio art, that, according to the usual genre designations, lies somewhere in a simultaneous intersection of performance, installation, radio play, music, literature, network art, media art—just name it—thus to likewise contemplate its manifestations and form, a concept of «material» or an Adorno postulate such as «that the form given to content is itself a sedimented content» may be a useful tool.

But what, then, is the material of radio art? Sound waves, as the radio art manifesto itself still maintains? No, that is the whole point—it is a different materiality and has been for a long time, one that is not conceived acoustically but rather also simultaneously in terms of media, and therein lies the difference. Precisely because the above-outlined crusade of ideology toward achieving an aesthetic was successful. The material of radio art, as pursued by *Kunstradio*, is more communicative than acoustic. What is involved is a materiality of communication, as is the title of one fine old book from the nineteen-eighties.[15] The material of this art is interaction, the simultaneity in the same media space, or rather, to be more correct and paradoxical: in the same media spaces. And that means that—although it is an art that is ultimately received through some loudspeaker somewhere, vide the radio art manifesto—the acoustic result per se often appears surprisingly unimportant in its details, to the artists, technicians, and producers alike. Prototypically, it does not so much involve building final acoustic results—and I emphasize this despite knowledge of how many artists have worked on this and in this way for *Kunstradio*, but now I am deliberately thinking more of the big networked projects than of small-scale studio works—for often the work focused to a lesser degree on acoustic details as on creating networks and connections. And even whether or not they work is sometimes surprisingly irrelevant. What does seem relevant is the intention of having conceived and organized the network, all errors occurring along this path being accepted as part and parcel of the artwork, just as Duchamp simply declared the fragments of his *Large Glass* to be an artwork instead of mourning the loss of an artwork.

But perhaps this is actually wrong, and artists and producers alike have simply learned a kind of professional equanimity in handling all these error-prone systems from which, inversely, we should not draw any aesthetic conclusions. But it is appealing as an intellectual game, for one thing because there is something Duchampesque, if you will, about this act of a prototypical *Kunstradio* satellite/Internet/radio project in another way, too: if the material is not just sound

---

15   Hans Ulrich Gumbrecht and K. Ludwig Pfeiffer,
      eds., *Materialität der Kommunikation*
      (Frankfurt am Main: Suhrkamp, 1988).

Bob Ostertag with Mark Dressler (bass),
Gerry Hemingway (percussion), and
Phil Minton (vocals), *Say No More In Person*,
Vienna, Austria, a TRANSIT project, 1994.

waves but rather, at the same time, telecommunications in whatever form—so if, in a way, the network itself becomes a material capable of being art—then this strategy does of course have something of this Midas-like Duchampian effect in that something that served quite profane purposes is transformed into art and subjected to a metamorphosis without any change on the phenomenological side. Arthur C. Danto[16] summed up this strategy as *The Transfiguration of the Commonplace*, a book title that he himself had borrowed. And seen this way, it is indeed a fine intellectual game to reflect on these open forms and movements—«Form & Flow» is the title that Heidi Grundmann once gave to an article on this topic[17]—to briefly rethink these «open systems» in the sense of the Adorno quotation: the fact that form in such projects as *Sound Drifting* and their world-spanning, constantly moving, and, in their details, undefinable forms—the fact, then, that this «form» itself is supposed to be sedimented content—would indeed seem to have something to it, aptly describing the intention, even if we must productively misunderstand Adorno's words to make it so, because what he originally said was that form is given to content and is not content itself.

In view of changing attitudes in all systems of thought and society—in contrast to old definitions of form as demarcation, centering, and animation—a concept of form that is conceived more in terms of system theory deploys an extensive range of calculation instruments, autopoetic systems, difference-form, self- and foreign reference, to create a world or realm of imagination for itself in which border definition and forming loses all stasis. The «system» is now such a flexible instrument that form becomes obsolete once and for all as something that we could get a grip on or capture in a definition for a moment. The prerequisite for the «old» definition of form to work is an unquestioned subject-object relationship between the artists and the artwork; no solely or ultimately responsible artist, no distinguishable artwork is required in a flexible system of rules. For *Kunstradio*'s 1999 network project *Sound Drifting*,[18] dozens of artists working simultaneously at sixteen nodes on three continents transmitted (mostly gener-

16 Arthur C. Danto, *Art After the End of Art* (Princeton: Princeton University Press, 1997), p. XV.

17 Heidi Grundmann, «FORM & FLOW,» in *Form – Luxus, Kalkül und Abstinenz* (Saarbrücken: Pfau, 1999).

18 *Sound Drifting: I Silenzi Parlano Tra Loro*, September 1 (0:00)–September 9 (24:00), 1999, Ars Electronica, *Kunstradio*, 1999 (see note 8).

19 Winfried Ritsch on *Kunstradio*, September 5, 1999.

ated acoustic) data sets. These were, for example, clustered into a stream in Linz, Austria, that could then via the Internet be relayed and broadcast to all other nodes in their own respective streams and on-site/on-air versions. In *Sound Drifting*, there is no ultimately responsible artist sitting behind the studio mixing desk any longer, deciding what may be acoustically represented how and when. Instead, generative programs at the various locations take charge of this task. In Linz, this was the «Sound Drifter,» a program developed by Winfried Ritsch. The key agents of such computer programs are reactive sound files and micro-compositions allowing previously unrelated elements to interface with each other. «The sound objects,» as Winfried Ritsch explains his Linz Sound Drifter, «are treated like little micro-machines. They move around between computers, also communicating control data, meaning they group up, communicate their rhythm, in order to control the composition.»[19] On the basis of these programs, sound files, and micro-compositions, called SoundLives by Ritsch—which, as moving systems, are constantly drawing and changing borders—as well as the generative programs and interactive systems used at the other locations, the entire *Sound Drifting* installation—spanning continents with the aid of computers, with its local manifestations as installation, occasional performative elements, and radio

Will Sergeant, *Frozen Tear Drop in Space*, installation, *Sound Drifting*, Lancashire, U.K., 1999.

programs[20]—becomes a mechanism or organism that is constantly changing its structure, both its inner composition and its appearance. Its form can only be described by thinking in terms similar to those of system theory, as a distinction machine that, controlled by programs, draws a temporary, intangible borderline between art and environment instead of adding further sound objects to the world.

Here is the dividing line, if you will, at which it becomes clear why radio art—although in principle acoustic, like music, and based upon media, like radio—is incongruent with radio and music in their respective traditional self-perceptions. As mentioned above, it has been and remains necessary to, again and again, force the radio medium to see itself not only as a medium, but also as art. And with regard to the acoustic arts, it was and still is necessary to fight for assertion that the traditional belief in a certain sought-after work in its intended form does not want to be applied, for one reason, among others, because a materiality of sound is replaced or supplemented by a materiality of communication. And from this it follows that it is not only the traditional European conception of a single author and his or her intact power of expression that fails to work here. But ultimately, the aforementioned aesthetic postulates, stemming from American experimental tradition, may have anticipated many things and also have much in common—for instance, the above-noted multiperspective approach and more—but when it comes to the question of material, they (in continued reference to the postulates from American experimental tradition) have nevertheless remained in the phenomenological physical sphere—be it music, multimedia, intermedia—not replacing or (without meaning to sound ambiguous) transcending the materiality of the social-media reality.

Ultimately, any thematic, critical discourse on quality, success, and failure must be conducted from this (media-related) viewpoint. One of the critical points of current radio art could perhaps best be reconceived from a dual viewpoint, from that of a phenomenology of sound and from that of the media, meaning the translation of a giant network structure into perceptible reality. Of course, this has often been discussed in the past, because the Achilles heel of transmitting a

20   From its base in Linz, the Sound Drifter also generated an eight-hour *Long Night of Radio Art* on Österreich 1, ORF's culture program. In Weimar, Germany, three streams of the fifteen other nodes and local on-site versions of the I/Osonic system were processed at all times and broadcast for one as a non-stop stereo radio sculpture on the frequencies of two independent radios (and made available worldwide via audio stream): more than 108 hours long total (September 1–6, 1999).

universe of art reality, operating in many cases synchronously through multiple satellites and dozens of streams, is found in the very realm where it should in fact do justice to its name—in radio, with its two or even five loudspeakers. Perhaps this thinking—in terms of the possibility of translating into direct, possibly also storable and documentable, physical, sensorially comprehensible phenomena— is already wrong in principle since it is bound to the «old,» purely artistic conception and not primarily to social media realities and their presence. Perhaps we should change the perspective, not seeking to conquer additional possibilities of representation, stereo or 5.1, but rather to operate circumstantially in the sense of a refusal to represent or of a voluntary iconomachy.

Simultaneity, multiperspectivity, dissolution: these processes—from the perspective of «iconomachy,» or rather, in this context, let us simply call it ignorance or negligence toward «representation,» the pressure of media representation— are evidently all employed intentionally or unintentionally as artistic strategies against the definiteness of acoustic and optical images. These strategies also work beyond mere technical irritation, because the pictorial or symbolic nature of (electronic) communication assumes the status of the material to be processed. The interaction between (acoustic and optical) image symbols becomes the ob-

Seppo Gründler
and Elisabeth
Schimana,
Die Große Partitur,
performance,
Ars Electronica,
2004.

ject of processing and questioning, the level on which reflection must take effect. While acoustic work on and with, for example, cracked sound software, equipment used contrary to the intended purpose, and so forth, thus—contrary to its prefabricated sound production—comes close to classical compositional work as regards the condition of the material, networked projects, with numerous, sometimes uncontrollable contributions, shift the focus to the materiality of the interaction patterns and communication channels. In contrast to the existing elements to be cracked and attacked in the iconoclast's view, streamed sounds and images in networked constellations rather play the cool role of referencing the key contexts beyond the image itself. With iconodulic imperturbability, the aim is to work on dissolving concrete, acoustic, and optical «images,» in the sense of units of sense, on shifting meaning from the seeable/hearable phenomenon to communication and context, that is: to a materiality of communication. If artistic interest shifts more and more to the «whether» and «how» of data exchange instead of the «what» of that which is exchanged, it seems that a paradoxical form of self-imposed iconomachy, in the above sense, takes effect: what is depicted in each case is clearly taken from the real world but lacks any function that could make its pictoriality a threat or a delight. An attempt to conceptualize these images would prove impossible. The controversy of the image and the concept that codifies it has shifted: the worshipped image is communication itself. In order to avoid the potentially ensuing paralysis, however, artists develop mechanisms of objectifying detachment that—using the channels of communication—are intended to bring their self-referentiality to light, thus concurrently questioning the idol of communication. This significance, which in another context is accorded the materiality of a violin tone or oil paint, emerges in an advanced radio art aesthetic of communications materiality.

The Imaginary Network

Peter Courtemanche

The act of sharing images and sound is one
of our basic human needs: the need to communicate. We also need to travel, physically and
especially psychologically. Without our day-
dreams, we would go crazy. We need to project
ourselves into the landscape of our imagination
in order to feel the spiritual strength that keeps
us alive. We also need the real sensual pleasure
of sitting down and having a good meal with
friends...Conversation is an art and communications art is the art of conversation. E-mails zip
back and forth, people complain about the
glitches in the technology that get in the way
of sending images and sound. Everyone is trying
to be seen and heard, just as they would at a
dinner party.[1]
—Lori Weidenhammer

Noise to Eternal Network

In 1988, I was doing radio; a weekly program of live noise art; feedback, intense
collage, crashing and banging, tape loops, field recordings (found sound), ethereal phone-in manifestations; no distinct voices. GX Jupitter-Larsen, a regular visitor to the radio show, introduced me to mail art networks by handing me a list of
addresses and encouraging me to send out audio cassettes to other artists, radio
show hosts, and zine publishers. Within the radio art network, exchanged audio
included everything from rough recordings (to be used as components of a larger
mix) to finished works and cassette releases. Ron Lessard of RRR records used
to have an open call for cassette tapes. People from around the world would send
him material, and he would use it live on-air and send out copies of the resulting
collages. In response to mail outs, artists sent back a variety of materials: audio
tapes, CDs (which were very new back then), poems, books, zines, et cetera. In
1989, I worked with Hank Bull of the Western Front on *Hyperspace Radio* (*Art's
Birthday*, January 17, 1989)—a project that joined together four radio stations

in Western Canada through a conference call. The hosts then participated in an elaborate journey into the future, based on a loose script that ultimately was effected by technical glitches, telephone system echoes, feedback, and the nefarious natures of the individual radio programs. Ironically, my awareness as an audio artist started in December 1987 with the first broadcast of *Absolute Value of Noise* radio. This was the same month that French Fluxus artist Robert Filliou died, and since that time his ideas about art, communication, and network have had a growing influence on my own work and philosophies in relation to the network paradigm.

Filliou traveled across Canada in the nineteen-seventies. He had a significant impact on the Artist Run Centre[2] movement, particularly in Vancouver (Western Front), Calgary (Clive Robertson and Arton's), Toronto (Art Metropole), Montréal (Véhicule), and Québec City (Le Lieu). In Canada, Filliou was introduced to *video* and the possibility of translating many of his ideas (that had been realized through objects and text) into this new (at the time) electronic medium. Filliou's work in the sixties was intent on separating the creation of art from art institutions (galleries, dealers, museums). He worked with the idea of Permanent Creation, of incorporating the creative sense into aspects of everyday life. He also worked with the absurd—putting forth proposals that were tongue-in-cheek but at the same time conveyed serious and profound ideas about life, art, economy, social responsibility, and the importance of individual creativity. Along with his collaborator, George Brecht, he developed the concept of the Eternal Network[3] and used this in his writings and mail art practice. In the seventies, many young

1   *The Grim Nymph*, diary from ..*devolve into II*.. (March 20, 2002). See http://absolutevalueof noise.ca/2002_devolve/online/diary.html.

2   The Artist Run Centre movement in Canada started in the late nineteen-sixties. Influenced by Fluxus and ideas of the «artist-determined culture» that could (and should) exist outside of the control of institutions, many groups created their own gallery, studio, and performance spaces. In 1973, the Canada Council for the Arts decided to provide funding for several centres across Canada. This movement has continued to this day and includes both gallery spaces and media arts production centres.

3   Eternal Network is both a real network (put in place through mail art, correspondence, and later telecommunications art) and a philosophical proposal about the nature of network and knowledge. A brief text of the proposal is published in an exhibition catalogue compiled by Sharla Sava and Scott Watson: *Robert Filliou: From Political to Poetical Economy* (Vancouver: Morris and Helen Belkin Gallery, 1995), p. 8.

4   Keith Wallace, introduction to *Whispered Art History: Twenty Years at the Western Front*, ed. Keith Wallace (Vancouver: Arsenal Pulp Press, 1993), p. 2.

artists in Canada were struggling with similar ideas, and the inclusion of Filliou (both as collaborator and mentor) within this crowd was a natural fit. These artists brought Filliou into their world of youthful performative happenings, dinners, tennis matches, video art, and excursions up the coast. Through this exchange and the correspondence art that ran through it all, the concept of the Eternal Network became firmly incorporated in the work of groups like the Western Front. Keith Wallace, writing about the Western Front, paraphrases the Eternal Network:

> This term was coined by French artist Robert Filliou, who optimistically expressed a belief that artists should be in communication at all times in all places without dependency upon art establishment. Within the Network, artists most often used correspondence through the postal system as a means of exchanging ideas and images. In this context, making art was a shared activity and not dependent upon the individual artist creating objects within the isolation of the studio. The Network also challenged the idea that certain cities constituted geographical art centres; through the medium of correspondence each artist could be connected internationally without having to live in a major urban centre.[4]

Robert Filliou, *And So On, End So Soon*, Western Front Video, Vancouver, Canada, 1977.

Filliou's writings indicate that the Network exists whether we acknowledge it or not. It is inherent in the space where people come together to share knowledge, ideas, skills, criticism, food, et cetera. From this point of view, Filliou's Eternal Network is a way of looking at the world. As an economist, philosopher, and artist, Filliou's ideas went beyond the realm of art by artists (and activism by artists) and were put forth in the context of a larger society. Eternal Network de-emphasizes the «director» and emphasizes the collaboration that we engage in our daily lives. It strengthens the role of the individual within a «collaboration of life (and art)» that promotes social responsibility. Eternal Network also puts forward the idea that the complexity of knowledge and ideas makes the concept of objective experience passé. Experience becomes increasingly subjective and notions of assessing art («what is good and what is bad»), as well as notions of the «avantgarde,» become obsolete. Within this Network, art is a never ending exchange of objects, ideas, and social contexts.

One of Filliou's projects within this realm was *Art's Birthday*—an extension of his ideas about the creative enactment of leisure time, *La Fête*, and the importance of playfulness in life and art. *Art's Birthday* was first realized in 1973, on January 17, in Aachen, Germany, where a municipal holiday was declared. Filliou proposed that «1,000,010 years ago, art was life, 1,000,010 years from now it will again be.» *Art's Birthday* was embraced by mail artists in Canada and the U.S., who celebrated it in tandem with a mail art awards ceremony, the *Decca Dance*, in Hollywood in 1974. Since Filliou's death in late 1987, many artists from around the world working with telecommunications, mail art, and artist-run spaces have collaborated to keep *Art's Birthday* and its underlying philosophy of exchange and the Eternal Network alive.

Starting in 1989, the Western Front has hosted annual *Art's Birthday* celebrations. Over time, these events have evolved to include four to five days of activities, both local and networked, tied in with events at other points around the world. In recent years (2004–2006), each celebration has taken on a theme which the global participants interpret in their own way, adding or subtracting

5 Robert Filliou, «Whispered Art History,» published in several places including *FRONT Magazine* (Western Front Society, Vancouver) (January 1990), p. 9, within an article by Alain Gibertie, translated by Phillip Corner. This is the origin of *Art's Birthday* as related (paraphrased) above. *FRONT Magazine* is published in Vancouver by the Western Front Society: http://front.bc.ca/frontmagazine.

6 Transcribed from «Porta Filliou,» a video tape made with Clive Robertson in 1977. Transcript published in Sava and Watson 1995 (see note 3), pp. 75–87.

local interests and ideas. The work is focused around performance and social activities in local spaces, with connections through the Internet, and satellite radio
broadcasts in Europe. The Western Front acts as one hub of this global network,
situated on the Pacific Rim, connecting the participants together through the
«artsbirthday.net» website. Since 1999, *Kunstradio* has acted as another important hub, situated in Europe, connecting the artist network into the EBU (European Broadcasting Union) radioscape. Tetsuo Kogawa, with *Radio Kinesonus*, forms
yet another hub, bringing more artists from different parts of the world into the
annual celebrations. The contemporary *Art's Birthday* network takes as its starting point Filliou's promotion of a culture of collaboration, exchange, creative enactment of social space, and his original text entitled «Whispered Art History»[5]
(the story of *Art's Birthday*). Filliou's idea of *Art's Birthday* doesn't necessitate
the long-distance connection of social-art environments through telecommunications technology or the Internet, but it is interesting to note that artists inspired
by the idea chose to realize *Art's Birthday* through an electronic network.

> So the way I see the *Network*, as a member of the *Network*, is the way it ex-
> ists artistically through the collective efforts of all these artists in Europe,
> in North America, in Asia, in Australia, in New Zealand—everywhere.
> In Africa also (I have received communication from Yemen for instance)
> each one of us artistically functions, in the *Network*, which has replaced
> the concept of the avant-garde and which functions in such a way that
> there is no more art centre in the world.
> Concentrating silently. Sending waves of greetings. Weatherluck. Man-
> luck. Womanluck. To any or all of the members of the *Eternal Network*
> the world around.[6]
> —*Robert Filliou*

Telecommunications Art
Telematics
Radio within a Network

Starting in the nineteen-seventies, with the advent of intercontinental cables and
satellites, telecommunications networks became possible. Artists used the new
global long distance infrastructure to explore the potential of a shared communi-

cations space. The network was created by opening up many connections at the same time through an elaborate system of relaying messages from one point to another. The relay network was enabled by audio and video recording technology. At any particular node the artists would: make the phone call, record the exchange, hang up the phone, make the next call, play back the recording from the previous call, record a new exchange, and so on. During these events, the network invariably became a vast, ephemeral collage, where the playback of recordings would be interrupted and altered with each new transmission. Faxes could be altered with the pen, sound and video could be layered, the modem tone signals themselves (images encoded as audio) could be altered by singing into the telephone line during transmission. Some of these networks existed without the need for relaying. Telephone companies would occasionally sponsor a conference call between participants. Norman White, working in Toronto, helped artists gain access to an intercontinental time-sharing system owned by I.P. Sharp Associates. In 1980, Robert Adrian worked with this system to develop ARTEX (Artist's Electronic Exchange Network)—an «intercontinental, interactive, electronic art-exchange program designed for artists and anybody else interested in alternative possibilities of using new technologies.»[7] This electronic mailbox network for artists existed until 1991, during a time when international electronic networks were confined primarily to academia and large corporations. It became a focal point for organizing and realizing a number of pivotal projects including *The World in 24 Hours* (1982),[8] *Wiencouver IV* (1983),[9] and *La Plissure du Texte* (1983)[10]—this last work used ARTEX as a medium for passing text around the world, with artists at each location adding to a collaborative online narrative.

7   Robert Adrian, ARTEX, and the I.P.Sharp network. See http://www.medienkunstnetz.de/ themes/overview_of_media_art/ communication/15/.

8   *The World in 24 Hours* (1982). For a good chronology of telecommunications projects involving Robert Adrian and his various collaborators, see http://alien.mur.at/rax/ BIO/telecom.html.

9   *Wiencouver IV* (1983) is described in Heidi Grundmann, ed., *Art + Telecommunications* (Vancouver: The Western Front Society and Vienna: Blix, 1984). This book also describes other *Wiencouver* events from 1979 to 1983.

10 *Plissure du Texte* (1983) is described by Roy Ascott in his essay «Distance Makes the Art Grow Further: Distributed Authorship and

Telematic Textuality in *La Plissure du Texte*,» in *Precursors to Art and Activism on the Internet*, ed. Annemarie Chandler and Norie Neumark (Cambridge, MA: MIT Press, 2005), pp.282– 96. It contains many interesting essays on telecommunications and artist-activist networks. The Western Front component of *Plissure du Texte* is described in Keith Wallace 1993 (see note 4), pp.82–84.

11 Video documentation of *Pacific Rim Slow Scan* is available in the collection of the Western Front Society, Vancouver.

12 Slow Scan Television (SSTV) was a method for transmitting video images over radio or telephone lines. In black-and-white, it took eight seconds to send an image, and in color, it took from twelve seconds (low resolution) to forty-eight seconds (high resolution).

One of the earliest telecommunications networks of which I was aware was documented on video in 1979. Bill Bartlett, working at Open Space (an artist-run centre in Victoria) and the Vancouver Art Gallery, organized *Pacific Rim Slow Scan*—a network of scientists and artists exchanging black-and-white video images at eight seconds per frame via satellite and telephone.[11] Within this project, it is interesting to note the instant collaboration among people from very different backgrounds—artists, scientists, Western academics, communities in the South Pacific, and so forth. Each participating node sent live images over Slow Scan TV[12] to the Vancouver Art Gallery and other locations, who recorded them and sent them on to other participants. This work didn't differ very much from the nature of several artist-only telecommunications exchanges that followed it in the eighties and nineties. It is the exchange of stories that gives life to the network, whether real events (the butchering and cooking of a giant sea turtle as transmitted from a beach in the South Pacific) or imagined narratives (performance art activities, poetry, and animations).

Telecommunications art focused on the telephone as a means to provoke exchange, build networks of artists, and engage in discourse around the role of global networks in culture (it was informed by utopian ideas of electronic net-

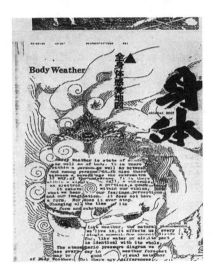

The World in 24 Hours, with the Tokyo contribution coordinated by Kazue Kobata, participants including Min Tanaka, Yoshi Nobu, Kazue Kobata, fax scroll, Body Weather Laboratory, Tokyo, Japan, September 1982.

works and the history of artists communicating and collaborating across distance through travel, mail art, and other forms of dissemination). The traditional European model of the artist is an individual who produces work that is then sent out into the world for many people (as many as possible) to see. This is mirrored in the broadcast model of media (institutionalized and commercial radio and TV) where a show is transmitted from elite creators to a mass audience. Telecommunications art broke down notions of the author and the audience. Projects were aimed at connecting people (artists in particular, but not exclusively artists) over distance to create what was effectively (perhaps ideologically) a long distance community. In this sense, the art form is about «communication.» We can think of telecommunications art as a foreshadowing or as a «crude precursor to» the Internet, but early artist networks imagined something quite different—an empowerment of individuals in their own network, under the radar (or beyond the control) of the commercial networks. The Internet both enables and contains this imagined network, but this type of network is not the entirety of the Internet.

In the mid-nineteen-nineties, artists working with telecommunications shifted from using the telephone lines and video phones to using the Internet as a conduit for webcams and various audio streaming technologies. Many of these artists realized at once that the Internet is not so much being used as a medium of exchange and communication as it is exploited as a medium of distribution.[13] This is evident in the proliferation of websites, download content, broadcast model streaming, et cetera. (It is important to note that websites, at their fundamental and conceptual level, are built on a technology that is intended purely for downloading and reading text.) This is the one-to-many model of delivering product (even if the product is free or open source). Within this realm, the network communities exist and proliferate, but they are blurred into the background by the incessant noise of capitalist media culture. Passive viewing, the main entertainment of the last century, has conditioned people to experience media largely as audience instead of creator. The utopian idea of using the Internet as a dynamic continuous social environment hasn't been realized.

13 Anna Couey. This idea was put forth in a loose web-text communications art project from 1996. I have read two versions of it. See «A Conversation with Hank Bull,» Interactive Art Conference on Arts Wire, November 1996, http://www.well.com/~couey/interactive/bull.html. Related conversations on Arts Wire can be found at http://www.well.com/~couey/interactive/guests.html. This is a strange text to read if you don't have any personal knowledge of the participants. It is a conversation between friends that takes place over an extended period of time on the Internet.

Art's Birthday, fax, Banff Centre for the
Arts, Banff, Canada, 1991.

Peter Courtemanche
The Imaginary Network

This duality of the Internet provides an interesting context for developing projects that attempt to alter the information interface and question the mass-media approach to the World Wide Web. In her writing about networked radio art, Heidi Grundmann talks about the «sonority» of the Internet:[14] the many sounds constantly streaming and living in the network that can become both a source and destination of material for a broadcast (national radio) station. This approach allows for new ideas of long distance collaboration within the realm of a local broadcast medium. It enables radio to connect into many different spaces as sources for sound, in the same way (conceptually) as it connects to many different listeners as the destinations for sound. It also makes radio, in a sense, a multidisciplinary medium, taking it away from the purely aural into the realm of new media, network content (text, image, online communities), and real world social spaces. One example of this is *Radiotopia*,[15] realized for the Ars Electronica Festival in 2002. *Kunstradio*'s component of *Radiotopia* involved gathering sound from artists by snail mail, e-mail, uploads, live streams, and so on. The project combined a vast array of networked audio sources that were channeled both through a website and into a six-hour radio broadcast on the FM, shortwave, and AM radio bands. *Radiotopia* called for «artists of all fields and from all over the world»[16] to submit sound works and written texts (poetry, manifestos, historical documents, etc.) that would be read live on-air. In this way, it encouraged an «open source» or democratized approach to the networked-radio form.

The Integration of Old and New Technologies

There's a growing recognition that the culture industry is doing for our culture what the forest industry is doing to our forests. The Big Media want to sell us 500 more channels where «interactive TV» means you get a «buy» button on your remote. On the net there are an infinite number of channels; every viewer is also a transmitter, and this has seen the blossoming of an incredible on-line culture. We hear that in the future

14 Heidi Grundmann, «But is it Radio?,» published online at http://subsol.c3.hu/subsol_2/contributors0/grundmanntext.html.

15 *Radiotopia* (2002), http://www.kunstradio.at/RADIOTOPIA/.

16 *Radiotopia* (2002), quote from the «call for participation,» posted online at ibid.

17 Quoted from an article about *TV Freenet*: «Jeff Mann, Artist in Residence,» *FRONT Magazine* (Western Front Society, Vancouver) 5, no. 4 (March/April 1994).

18 http://projects.front.bc.ca/2003/scrambled/; catalogue: Peter Courtemanche, ed., *Scrambled_Bites: Art's Birthday 2004* (Vancouver: Western Front, 2004).

we'll be able to send video over the phone. I want to prepare for this using desktop video technology, low-power transmitters, VHS cassettes, the Internet, and whatever means necessary.[17]
—*Jeff Mann*

Contemporary telematic art (art using computer networks)—from the Western Front, *Kunstradio*, and other progenitors of this form—ultimately refer to (and sometimes include) other mediums of exchange: old communications technologies that are «semi-simulated» on the web, radio networks, pirate broadcasting, telephones, satellite transmission, and so forth. Each medium or method of sending sound and image over long distances has its own peculiarities and its own history in terms of its use by artists. Early works used text, single-line telephone connections, and modem tones to transmit video images and MIDI information (musical notes encoded as digital information). *Telephone Music I* and *II*, in the early eighties, encouraged artists to compose music that fit within the frequency limitations of the phone line. In 1991, *Text Bombs and Video Tape*—a reaction to the Gulf War—had one of its most interesting manifestations as fax art: collages and hand-drawn protests, scattered around the world by fax, often altered and sent onwards.

On the Internet, software and software development become key features of this type of work. In my own practice, I use software to create collaborative frameworks, to incorporate different (often older) technologies into these frameworks, and to enable autonomous-seeming software organisms. One example is *Scrambled_Bites*,[18] produced at the Western Front in 2003. *Scrambled_Bites* played with the idea of a «data stream» connecting robotic devices, sensors, and noisemakers in different locations around the world. Here the idea was not to become transfixed with the web as the focus of network activity, but instead to use the Internet as a means of shipping data from one location to another, to be activated in a space with a live audience. One of the inspirations behind this project was an interest in subverting the concept of Internet streaming at a fundamental level. This was done by introducing a new self-defined form of streaming and reducing the entire system to something very minimal. The *Scrambler* (our homemade server software) did not stream audio or images. Instead it transmitted a slow collection of numbers that were largely abstract and removed from their origins. The Internet and communications technologies in general can rapidly become vast, complex systems. The intent of the *Scrambler* was to strip back this complexity to reveal the basic underpinnings of data flow and exchange.

A certain amount of early critical writing (circa mid-nineties) about the Internet was fascinated with bandwidth, virtual communities, and networked virtual reality. One predominant view predicted that the world would become an amazing and wonderful place when we could finally push full frame multi-dimensional video through an Internet connection, enabling people to live in each other's imaginations (or imaginary living rooms). Some people view the emergence of cable modems as an important leap forward in the history of the Internet. Others take a different approach and view «access» as the most impor-tant historical change in the nineties. Ultimately a network is made up of indi-viduals, and for the network to have a significant impact on society, a significant proportion of the world's population must be connected to the network and be able to participate in its cultural structures. This idea of accessibility is key to networked radio art, both in terms of audience and in terms of enabling re-mote participants to collaborate from disparate cities and cultural milieus.

Designed in the era before the ubiquitous cable modem, the ..*devolve into*..[19] pieces (commissioned by *Kunstradio* in 2000 and 2002) were aching-ly conscious of bandwidth. In any work of this nature, it is important to en-able both the artists and the larger public to access a high degree of depth and complexity on a connection that may be slow and prone to interruption. Within this context, some ingenious work has been done. In the seventies and eighties when artists were working with Slow Scan TV—where it takes up to forty-eight seconds to send a single frame of color video over a telephone line—live animation (and interference) was a common form. On the Internet in the nineties, using the browser's cache effectively enabled you to send little pieces of sound and image over a 14400 baud modem and have the receiving computer use those tiny segments to create something that had the sound and look of a denser, more complicated broadcast. ..*devolve into II*.. played specifi-cally with these ideas and techniques by managing live and recycled content and running simple generative algorithms to create a landscape that felt much big-ger than the original pieces that were fed into the system. The first version of the piece from 2000 played with questions of predetermined navigation by forcing

19   For ..*devolve into*.. (*I* and *II*) (2000 and 2002),
     see http://absolutevalueofnoise.ca/2000
     _devolve/ and http://absolutevalueofnoise
     .ca/2002_devolve/online/.

20   http://projects.front.bc.ca/2005/reverie/;
     catalogue and audio CD: Peter Courtemanche,
     ed., *Reverie: Noise City* (Vancouver: Western
     Front, 2005).

21   *Walled City* was described in William Gibson,
     Idoru (New York: G.P. Putnam's Sons, 1996).

22   See http://alien.mur.at.

the browser to travel through an ever-changing matrix of works in order to find all of the different streams. .. *devolve into II*.. (2002), produced in collaboration with Roberto Paci Dalò, focused additionally on ideas of the ephemeral (live streams) versus the document (recordings of those streams), and on the notion that all digital material will eventually mutate (as it is copied and moved from archive to archive) and go through a process of decay over time.

Reverie (2005)[20] was a virtual city of sound art on the web. It referred to William Gibson's *Walled City*[21] and other non-fictional, online virtual communities (MUDs, chat groups, networked gaming groups, etc.). *Walled City* exists as a distributed network game that requires continuous human interaction to keep it alive and functioning. The players adopt a persona and take responsibility for maintaining different parts of the city. These parts are then passed from player to player as the participants log in and out of the game. In a similar fashion, *Reverie* imagines a city that is activated purely through the ongoing activities and exchanges of sound artists. This project was initially inspired by an early version of antarcti.ca (a map of Antarctica that acted as an interface to organizations and information on the web) and by *Alien City*,[22] an artwork by Alien Productions created by Austrian artists Martin Breindl, Norbert Math, and Andrea Sodomka,

..*devolve into II*..,
installation,
intermedium II, ZKM,
Karlsruhe, Germany,
March 2002.

exploring the concept of the city as a dynamic, evolving place for exchanges and cultural practice. An early proponent of the virtual city, within the context of communications technology, was Hank Bull, who invented *Wiencouver*. *Wiencouver* is a virtual city in space that was developed in the late nineteen-seventies and early eighties. It became the basis for one of the first consistent series of telecommunications events that linked artists around the world and created a community through long distance exchange.

> *Wiencouver* is an imaginary city hanging invisible in the space between its two poles: Vienna and Vancouver...In 1979 I flew from Vancouver to Vienna to attend *Audio Scene '79*, where I talked about radio by artists. I said that radio, like other intermedia arts, removes the art world that normally mediates between the artist and the public. Radio, I said, was sculpture. I talked about an aesthetics of social action and international communication between artists, that we comprise an important network.[23]
> —*Hank Bull*

The Fast Future

By creating network projects that refer to earlier (pre-Internet) experiments and models, we can explore the larger history and context of this shifting realm. One of the reasons that I like to embed seemingly archaic technologies in with the new is to imply that perhaps the world isn't evolving as fast as we think it is. There are more and more new products every day—but the idea of «product» is far from new. There are more and more software tools—but the concepts of software and hardware, biology and consciousness, are also very old. What we are seeing as technological leaps forward are most often improvements on existing ideas—make the hardware faster, smaller, cheaper, more disposable; make the software bigger, flashier, more complex, more essential to work flow.

I stopped programming computers for about six years from 1988 to 1994. When I returned to it, mostly out of interest in the Internet and the potential of networking, I was surprised to see how little had changed in that time. The structure

[23] Quoted from the original proposal for *Wiencouver* (1979) in Grundmann 1984 (see note 9).

of the Internet (its raw underpinnings) was almost identical to earlier network protocols. Operating systems were much as I remembered them. This had a great effect on my view of technological development. Obviously the notion of rapid development of software and hardware is evident in usage and access, but is not necessarily reflected through or into changes in the basic paradigm or structure of the system. Transcendent development (changes to the fundamental building blocks of a system) isn't necessarily about speed or bandwidth, but is instead about ideas and experimentation.

One of the most fascinating aspects of change within contemporary cultures is our relationship to software. Software has its origins in a very particular scientific-military-industrial ideology. It mutates, expands, works its way around the world and into many aspects of life. It affects the way we work, the way we play. It creates a peculiar symbiosis between the machine and the «user,» a symbiosis that alters our consciousness and cognitive processes. We change our languages so that software can encode them more easily. We change our methods of remembering and relating stories—from mnemonics, to the printing press, to the word processor. To what degree is this a process of enlightenment or, ultimately, cultural reprogramming?

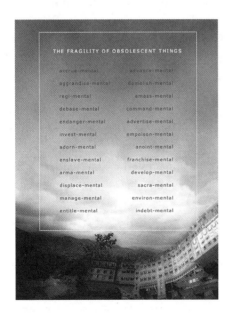

Reverie: noise city,
Internet project, *Art's Birthday*, 2005.

One of *Kunstradio*'s most interesting (and ambitious) Internet (on air – on line – on site) projects was *Sound Drifting, I Silenzi Parlano Tra Loro* (1999). «[It] was formulated as an experimental non-biological organism: a network or community of generative algorithms constituting a virtual autonomous organism living, interacting, breeding and ultimately dying in the matrix of the Internet.»[24] *Sound Drifting* referred to the idea that all complex systems have an inherent intelligence and consciousness, even if the human mind and body is unable to measure it or relate to it. *Sound Drifting* also referred to the ephemerality of net-worked communities and saw this as a natural phenomenon. If the network exists as communication and exchange (real-time occurrences), then the network does not exist when the communication ceases or fades away—in the same way that a dinner party is over when the guests go home. The existence of ephemerality in the network can be a point of difficulty in many network art projects. In most of the projects I've done on the Internet, the artists want the work to live on without them after the project has finished. What is this fascination with storing and retrieving data rather than viewing connectivity and connections as the essence of the network? By emphasizing the information or documentation of a work, we de-emphasize the human component of the process. Perhaps within this realm of networked communications art, we can view the human interaction (and thus human memories) as more important than the computer memory.

In his book *Silence Descends* (1997),[25] George Case describes the end of the Information Age from a vantage point five hundred years in the future. He describes a world that has suffered through a series of natural disasters. People have left the virtual behind in order to survive. The virtual does not only exist in the electronic domain of information systems and global networks, but it is also evident in the capitalist, consumer-driven society where economy is linked to purchases and market shares instead of to the well-being and health of a com-munity. George Case's future is not a world without network(s), but it is a world without the virtual trappings that are used as rationale for oppression. Will the

---

24 Heidi Grundmann, introduction to *Sound Drifting*, ed. Heidi Grundmann (Vienna: Triton, 2000), p. 3.

25 George Case, *Silence Descends* (Vancouver: Arsenal Pulp Press, 1997).

26 «Poetical Economy» was an idea put forth by Robert Filliou, initially as part of a manifesto: «A problem, the one and only, but massive: money, which creating does not necessarily create. A *Principles of Poetical Economy* must be written. Write it.» See Sava and Watson 1995 (see note 3), p. 21.

27 *The Grim Nymph*, diary from ..*devolve into II*.. (March 18, 2002). See notes 1 and 19.

Information Age burn out like so many social and political movements that have come before it? As more and more information is added to the system, it becomes impossible to maintain. Links are broken, older software fails to run. The integrity of the data is lost. This broken information becomes less important than the references contained within—the articles and people who, like ghosts, are implied by the vanishing content. In 2005, I worked with several artists to produce *Reverie: noise city*. In the space of a few months, this virtual city went from inception, through rapid growth, and into the realm of historical architecture—a process that takes a real city many decades, often centuries, to complete. As time passes and technology evolves, the city will slowly decompose. The sounds will become incompatible with new software and the design will shift with browser obsolescence. This is a metaphor that the artists discussed in the early phases of the project—the idea that at some point the city would crumble into digital dust. Like many experimental contemporary practices, *Reverie* is ephemeral. Projects of this nature are interventions into a public (yet virtual) space that are intended to make passersby stop, look, and experience something out of the ordinary before continuing on with their daily activities. These projects are also intended as social networks between collaborators. This particular network space is transcendent; it is the Imaginary Network that is yet to be fully realized; an economy that is poetical;[26] perhaps it will be found five hundred years in the future.

> I think in the digital realm, we must acknowledge the pixel. Rather than being ensconced within the stone museum and protected by archivists and restorers, we must know our work is more akin to writing in grains of sand.[27]
> —*Lori Weidenhammer*

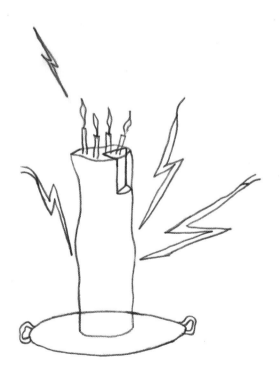

Peter Courtemanche,
cake fabriacted
by sonic currents,
Art's Birthday,
pencil on paper,
Vancouver, Canada,
2008.

Sonic Postcards

Excerpts from an Online Diary Inspired by
Art's Birthday 2007

Lori Weidenhammer

I'm a Radio
Jan. 14, 2007

These days everything gives off signals. Cell phones, Wi-Fi, satellite dishes, and radio towers all pump out signals connecting privileged people around the world. The world is a global village, but only to a select few. We are the lucky ones. Communication is taped to our fingertips, wrapped around our ears, and tied to our tongues. Communication artists are fascinated by sending and receiving signals and noise. We are seduced by high-frequency chatter and low-frequency hum. Sometimes our bodies travel alongside the radio waves, but even when our bodies are still, we continue to vibrate with internal messages zooming along neurons and dendrites. Communication keeps us alive.

Peter Courtemanche,
performance with
bicycle-wheel and
low-frequency antenna,
Art's Birthday,
The Western Front,
Vancouver, Canada,
2007.

Everything gives off signals. Scientists have discovered that the queen bee gives off at least nine pheromones that help direct behavior in the hive. Evolution in technology means that new frequencies of complex whale song can be recorded and recognized. Life constantly whirs and hums in surges and ebbs. To live is to transmit. Death is the absence of communication.

Yesterday we met for dinner: Anna, Roberto, Glenn, Peter, and I. After months of separation and communication via telephone and e-mail, we have the luxury and the pleasure of talking face-to-face, unmediated by technology. This itself is an occasion to celebrate. Roberto cuddles with our son on the couch, reading about Scooby-Doo. Anna knits her camouflage leggings, and Glenn snaps off a piece of a Zotter chocolate bar.

Time-Sensitive Sound
Jan. 15, 2007

The vessels that contain, send, and receive sound are constantly decaying and evolving. In the collaborative webcast called *Wiencouver—1906–2006*, the artists mixed the sounds of the present with those of the past. Volkmar Klien recorded sounds made by navigational devices and instruments that are housed in museums in Vienna. Anna Friz vocalized the *dits* and *dahs* of Morse Code and played an antique recording of a hymn («Lead, Kindly Light») written by John Henry Newman in 1833 while he was at sea. *Absolute Value of Noise* (Peter Courtemanche) transformed silent waves of radiation into audible drones. Glenn Gear sifted through photographs of sailors and dour Victorian women long since passed away.

The images we saw were projected onto a screen within the constant frame of a round porthole. Glenn uses footage that he has sourced from archives, images he has filmed in Newfoundland, and his own sequences of animation. All of his images were tied together with a seafaring theme: sailboats, lighthouses, sailors, sunlight on water. We see a cartoon of two little characters rowing a boat who are swallowed up by a black sea monster. An octopus's eye emerges from the murky depths, visual representations of sound waves (wave forms) are layered over the snowflake patterns of a kaleidoscope.

The images and sounds integrate seamlessly in this session. The images appear to emerge and dissolve through visual static in the same way the sounds emerge from a sea of textural noise. It's as if Captain Nemo is taking me on a trip through his subconscious mind. Growing up on the prairie, I always thought of the basement in our house as the main metaphor for my submerged memories and fears. Maybe it's different for someone like Glenn, who grew up near the ocean.

The result of this «sonic séance» was a layered experience evocative of the past. We can intimate how much imagination and courage it must have taken to believe in the possibility of transatlantic communication. The drive to communicate must have been very strong. Sometimes I forget that sense of longing that comes out of isolation—the deep need to seek a call and response from one soul to another. It was this strong desire to communicate and connect with the living (and even the dead) that inspired the inventors of radio and the early broadcasters such as Reginald Fessenden.

Wiencouver: this ethereal city exists somewhere between Vienna and Vancouver, between the past and the present. This city is amorphous, created by that same deep need to collect sounds, create sounds, and send them across the ocean.

Lori Weidenhammer, *I'm a crow*, improvisation, Grand Lux performance space, The Western Front, Vancouver, Canada, 2007.

Calling Vienna
Jan. 16, 2007

(with apologies to Joni Mitchell)

Can you hear the distance between us?
Can you count the candied violets laid in a row across the country?
How many sacher tortes would it take to reach your shores?
I'm a cell phone baby. Every cell in my body is calling to you.
I'm a little bit crazy to share all my sushi,
a little bit happier than yesterday.

It's winter now, but the blizzard is over. We lost a lot of trees.
Lost some big old trees. Pulled right out by the roots. Lost that big old
tree in front of the building. Did you see?

Can you hear the ocean from your house, or is it just the traffic,
the white noise that whistles down your day?
How many glasses of wine does it take to reach you baby?
How many dark winter days has it been?
I know this big old house lets in a lot of ghosts, but I like it that way.
I'm a cell phone, baby. I'm sending you blue butterflies
when I close my eyes to see you,
I'm sending you little icebergs on a video screen.
I'm a cell phone baby,
wishing you a happy birthday by the light of the laptop screen.

The Crow
Jan. 18, 2007

Peter asked me to come down to the Front on Wednesday and jam with Guy van
Belle in Prague. When you go deeply into improvisation, you can create a channel right into your imagination. I've been watching the behavior of crows in the
snow, and the image of embodying a crow came right to the front of my mind.
Singers are trained to make beautiful sounds, but it is a real pleasure to explore

the throaty croaks of the crow. Crows are expressive, opinionated birds. They are good subjects for performers to study.

I experimented with mixing melodic sounds and crowspeak. Anna Friz joined in with her xylophone. I was grateful to have a companion in my madness. The sounds coming from Prague were haunting—some of them sounded theremin-inspired. Mimicking, mocking, imitating, laughing, I tried to draw out the sounds trapped down in me for many years. It's been six years since I cleaned out those sounds. I ended with some elongated and elided words about avoiding storms and fleeing blizzards. Anna and I tapped out a rhythmic ending.

Hello Guy in Prague and thanks for the dance!

Wish You Were in Wiencouver
Feb. 28, 2007

I recently read an article in the *Globe and Mail* about a writer who had decided to create sound souvenirs from his global travels. Instead of just taking photos, he wanted to record some of the essential sounds that captured the essence of the far-flung places he visited. He collected sounds that would trigger the memories of a particular time and place. I had to chuckle at this, because it's something sound and communications artists have been doing for years. They regularly pack their suitcases with the sounds of home and leave with luggage full of the sounds of foreign countries.

From mail art exchanges with cassettes and CDs to interactive Internet broadcasts, sound artists have used their desire to communicate to create a body of collaborative sonic correspondence. Some of the raw material for these projects is «found» in the live environment, other sounds are created by the artists. A group of artists in Vancouver (and beyond) are fortunate to have developed this kind of correspondence with a group of artists from Vienna (and beyond). When the *Wiencouver* group meets and shares sounds and images, wonderful things happen. Rich associations in nonlinear patterns are sifted, layered, and sculpted into a variety of limitless forms. The artists agree on concepts that inspire the content and shape each collaboration. There is jazz, noise, radio art, Filliou, and Freud. There are dreams, markets, myths, and radiation. Above all, there is history, community, food, friendship, and a spirit of celebration. This makes the work a perfect fit for the occasion of *Art's Birthday*.[1]

1   For further diary entries, see http://projects.front.bc.ca/2007/artsbirthday/blogs/lw_front_bc_ca/.

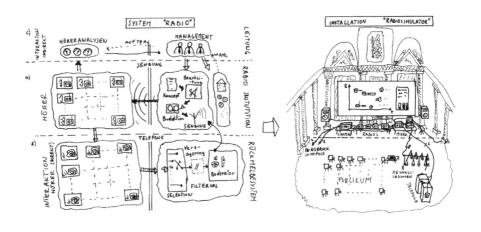

Winfried Ritsch,
Automated Radio, diagrams.

Automated Radio

A Project by Winfried Ritsch

The radio whispers into the listener's ear: «...I want to tell you something,... but don't ask who I am...»

Radio brings the world to the listener, who has seen a lot and who wants more than the world as it is.

Automated Radio is an experiment with the radio system. It involved developing a radio simulator, a piece of machinery that simulates the functions of radio and that can be used to create radio programs.

The radio simulator is a network of electronic devices that are controlled by a central computer and constitute a reaction system. A reaction system in that the sequence and content of the program can be determined by parameters influenced by the listener. The listener determines the radio program. The audience can thus explore this system.

The key components of the radio simulator include a control computer, announcement generator, remote replay machines (radios), and audience contributions in the form of phone statements, audience microphones, and opinion sensors.

The content of the radio program is produced «live.» The ingredients are a database of announcements, recordings from other radio programs, and audience statements. The audience is instructed to react to the installation, that is, to the radio program in the making, on the basis of associations, with the presenter raising different questions.

The individual parts appear as microworlds that, once joined together, create a new world determined by the structure (macroworld) of the sequence of events. The components are joined together by means of a specially developed computer program, a finite-state machine with access to a database of microworlds and a time pattern generator.

The audience becomes part of the installation and performs a function in the radio machine just like the other parts.

Are they actually in electronic space or in their own reality?

This project description is reprinted from *Interferenzen: Die Geometrie des Schweigens*, concept and organization by Heidi Grundmann and Robert Reitbauer, exh. cat. Museum Moderner Kunst Wien (Vienna, 1991), out of print.

August Black
and Markus Seidl,
Vienna Augarten,
Austria, 2002.

Blind Sight is 20/20

August Black

From 1998 until 2003, I developed a practice of radio making with two separate collaborators on two separate free radio stations in two separate cities in Austria; but with many overlapping themes and ideas. The first of my collaborative radio developments was a one-hour weekly show with Markus Seidl on Radio FRO in Linz (1998–2003). We called it *Fundamental Radio*. The second was a monthly radio hour in collaboration with Rupert Huber on Radio Orange in Vienna (2000–2003). That one was called *Standup Radio*. Each of these collaborations carried themes of (mis)communication, translation, and disinformation through conceptual play and through an experimental use of networking and radio infrastructures.

Fundamental Radio began as a weekly live radio show of raw sound and experimental chitchat but quickly evolved into a concept band, producing works for television, gallery installations, workshops, and public intervention. Our very first show premiered somewhat by chance during the *Recycling the Future* project of *Kunstradio* in 1997. We called that one *All that space and nowhere to go* with focus on a central question: what to do with a space you cannot inhabit. It was live and unprepared, as were most of our shows. I wore a Captain America helmet (as the show was also webcam'ed) and Markus asked questions. The show was fluid and talkative. We both had a particular liking to a live, no-holds-barred kind of attitude. After all, most of what you hear on the radio is so homogeneous that almost any kind of ridiculous behavior would be of interest. Or, so we thought.

We took that energy and those ideas to Radio FRO in Linz, being one of the very first regular shows to air on the newly licensed free radio station, meeting every Wednesday evening at 8 p.m. The idea was to practice radio as a form of live media theater. In some ways, this was done in total disregard for an audience. What is an audience anyway nowadays? Are they still just consumers? To our saving grace, there was a jazz show before us and a nice electronic music show called *e-verteiler* after us. We made these guys look good.

Our show was sometimes noisy, scratching LPs, shouting poetry, shouting in general. Sometimes we even played pop music. We often had guests. One month we spent talking about two chairs in an empty room. Another month we spent exploring the two no-no's of radio: silence and feedback. We'd have silence as a guest to our show, invite him to speak, and then wait for a long, long time, silently, until someone called in about the «dead» air. No, it was not dead, it was just silent. We'd take the Real Audio stream (they hadn't yet switched to the more politically correct MP3 format until later) and fold it in on itself. We'd get the loop started with our voices and then let it ripple, so that you could hear the latency and effects of compression. The output was of course broadcast on FM. We recorded washing machines, refrigerators, train rides, and walks through the town, and so on. Anything that was about an hour's duration. Then we'd play them back, one-to-one. (The washing machine show was called *propaganda* for obvious reasons. A few listeners called in to guess what kind of a machine it was that was being played. GE? Eudora? It was a Zanussi.) We mixed languages. German. English. We even created our own language, Ö, with other artists on a residency in Tasmania.

While all of this was happening, broadband and wireless Internet technologies were just hitting the scene. With cable modem and packet radio, we were able to take the show outside of the studio, almost at whim. Whenever we didn't have an idea (if you practice radio religiously as we did, you WILL run out of ideas), then we would just take the show to someone's dinner and mic the cooking and/or eating.

This act of extending the production studio became second nature. How could we make content about the act of being somewhere else? This was becoming a central question for us. The end results were often bizarre and evocative, as the location at hand became our «content.» Here are some examples: our first real excursion was to Lapland, Finland where we stayed up late at night to produce five shows over the course of a week, from 1 a.m. till 5 a.m. under the midnight sun. The last show was made with a bottle of whiskey and many guests on the roof of the University of Lapland.

In Amsterdam, we took our show to the streets on the Leidseplein. Drawing power and network cables through the window of the DeBalie, we set up two mics and a direct MP3 stream to the Radio FRO transmitter. There, we exchanged beer for thirty seconds of content from the people passing by. It was BYOC:

bring your own content. All kinds of craziness unfolded. In Hobart, Tasmania, we developed our own Dada-esque language with twelve other media artists from around the globe for a live spoken-word radio event at the Tasmanian Museum of Art.

One of the most interesting endeavors, however, was the very first live underwater radio show, where we took our show to a kiddy pool on the top terrace of an apartment building in Linz. Obviously, we were directly inspired by visual and conceptual artists like Tom Marioni, Hank Bull and Patrick Ready, and Bill Fontana. Not to mention benefiting from the rich tradition of radio art in Austria through the *Kunstradio*.

Standup Radio started in 2000 on Radio Orange in Vienna. The approach was somewhat similar to *Fundamental Radio*, but much more deliberate. With a month of time in between shows, we had enough foresight to make some preparations, timing the shows to overlap with our respective schedules. And, since it was a morning show at 11 a.m., the tone was also much softer and more listenable. We developed shows based on the theme of travel. We recorded train stations and airports and other places around the same time as our radio slot to pick up on the time announcement for arrivals and departures. We'd record our-

Fundamental Radio, singing the gospel of free software with Erich Berger, Linz, Austria, 2001.

Fundamental Radio, *Live underwater radio à la HP Radio Show*, condom cover mic in a small pool of water with Rupert Huber, video still, Linz, Austria, 2000.

selves taking a trip together the day or week before. We'd go to places like the local public pool or run some other errand together, all the time recording.

It was a kind of radio concrete. But, on-the-fly. The next day, this would become the base of our show on top of which we'd layer other nuances. Often, one of us was away and would have to phone or stream audio live to the station. Once, I was calling in from my cell phone while stopping off to shop at Hofer on the way to the radio station. We had shows that were at least partly made from Rome, Berlin, Hamburg, Karlsruhe, Linz as well as various locations in Vienna. Radio is everywhere and should thus come from everywhere and/or anywhere at once. Why limit it to the studio? So what if we don't have a budget? The costs were becoming cheaper and cheaper.

Anomalies were also inevitable, as good ideas and running jokes would develop. For instance, for the underwater show of *Fundamental Radio*, Rupert selected Dave Dudley's «Six Days on the Road» to be the acoustic backdrop, played on loop. Where else would a road song be more appropriate than underwater? We discovered that there were almost a hundred different recorded versions of this one song; some in foreign languages. Inevitably, this needed to become a source for content. And, indeed, we made a typical call-in request show, but where everyone requested different versions of the same song. Needless to say, country music isn't very popular in Vienna. Needless to say, radio is sometimes the subject of radio: it would be almost impossible to spend that much time with any given medium and not develop some sort of modernist critique of form.

While it is impossible to give a full impression of such a diverse body of activity from over five years and hundreds of hours of audio, this hopefully sheds some light on the ABC's of radio making from a particular perspective and from a moment in time where previously separated media ecologies are becoming more and more ensconced in one another. I'm sure similar ideas and activities have been seen elsewhere, and some ideas here were directly borrowed and reappropriated. That's just how it goes when you are dealing with a moving target. From this somewhat visual approach to radio, sight itself is blind. The best images end up on the radio frequencies. From this perspective, radio is the blind spot between the ears and behind the eyes.

Net Literature and Radio

A Work-in-Progress Report

Johannes Auer

«Speech and dialogue-based radio art concepts are nearly completely missing within artistic attempts to create interactive web-based audio works,» Sabine Breitsameter wrote in 2001.[1]

In the meantime, however, there have been a few promising attempts to close this gap from the field of European net literature. Between 2003 and 2005 there were productions for the *Kunstradio/Art Radio*, in 2005 for the German-Polish artists' radio *Radio_Copernicus*, and in 2006 for the Festival *RadioRevolten* in Halle.

This essay reports on radio-broadcasted net literature projects which have taken up the challenge of working with the traditional medium of radio.

On the level of protocols, Internet and radio are quite close, or at least both use a lot of so-called «broadcasting» processes. For example, routing tables are «broadcast» in the net, and radio networks «broadcast» their SSIDs, their network names on the air, like radio.

And the Internet is likewise bi-directional on the protocol level. It has the feedback or communication channel that radio lost through the state monopoly on broadcasting, and which Bertolt Brecht demanded back vehemently in his 1932 theory on radio: «Radio must be transformed from a dissemination apparatus into a communication apparatus.»[2] The link between net literature and radio can, in line with Brecht's intention, open up the possibility for listener participation.

A Digression
Apple Games

Hence, it is fair enough to claim that net literature is only an apple's throw away from radio, and this claim can be backed up with a short digression, which at the same time pays brief hommage to Reinhard Döhl, the Stuttgart author, artist, radio play and media sciences expert, and net literature contributor. From 1996 until his death in 2004, I cooperated with him on numerous literature projects for the Internet.

The best-known work by Reinhard Döhl is the «*apfel*» (apple, 1965), an incunabulum of concrete-visual poetry. In this poem, the form of the fruit is produced by the repetition of the word «*apfel*.» And in the middle of this apple picture is a word worm.

In 1997, I created a computer animation of Döhl's concrete poem as «worm applepie for doehl,»[3] in which the word worm eats up the apple picture, and thus sated, slowly digests itself back to its original size, only to start eating again.

Admittedly, the «worm applepie» can perhaps still be seen as kinetic art or film, but the next step in the evolution of the «*apfel*» as a «codework» clearly has a close affinity to the computer and net.

Concrete poetry is based on the elements of language. And «codeworks,» whose program code provides the material of the artistic work, are based on the elements of digitalism, that is, the program code, the zeros and ones, which are always text:

1   Sabine Breitsameter, «Audiohyperspace – From Hoerspiel to Interactive Radio Art in the Digital Network,» 2001, http://netzspannung.org/ database/37545/de (accessed June 10, 2007).

2   Bertolt Brecht, *Gesammelte Werke*, vol. 18 (Frankfurt am Main, 1967), p. 129.

3   Johannes Auer, «worm applepie for doehl,» http://auer.netzliteratur.net/worm/applepie .htm (accessed February 11, 2007).

4   Florian Cramer, «Wenn Schrift sich selbst ausführt: Über Codes und ihre Reflexion in Literatur und digitalen Künsten,» http://www .netzliteratur.net/cramer/schrift_selbst _ausfuehrt.html (accessed February 11, 2007).

5   This code line is the book title of: *$wurm = ($apfel>0) ? 1 : 0; experimentelle literatur und internet: memoscript für reinhard döhl*, ed. Johannes Auer, edition cyberfiction (Zurich and Stuttgart, 2004).

For there is one thing ... that the work of digital artists ... has in common with concrete poetry and the experimental use of language for poetry: it is art as a form of aesthetic hacking, of dissecting structures and making them visible ...

Apart from Morse, the Internet is the first modern medium—or rather the first modern information technology—which is based on a code. If one defines «text» in general terms as a succession of single (discrete) signs drawn from a finite repertoire (an alphabet), then 01 codes are also texts and all digital technologies are textual technologies ... [This is] text which is written in computer languages and then transported, transformed, and executed as digital writing code.[4]

Thus, the apple poem from 1965 can be translated in program code as:

$wurm = ($apfel>0) ? 1 : 0;

This code,[5] written in the computer script language PHP, can be roughly translated into words as: *Ist der Apfel größer Null, is(s)t der Wurm. Ansonsten is(s)t er*

Johannes Auer, *worm applepie for doehl*, screenshot of the online work, 1996.

nicht. If the apple is larger than zero, then the worm exists (eats). Otherwise it doesn't exist (eat).[6]

In addition to program code (in codeworks) and the computer screen (in «worm applepie for doehl» as film or kinetic art), net literature also works with databases and Internet search engines.

In *appleinspace*[7] by René Bauer and Beat Suter, the stream of search terms being entered in the search engine «Fireball.de» hits a database which stores all of Reinhard Döhl's online texts. If one of the words entered in the search engine is contained in a Döhl text, then the relevant section of the text appears in the form of an apple on the screen. This is instant net communication, interacting here with the text corpus of Döhl's work on the Internet.

The net installation *appleinspace* was adapted for radio and expanded into a «multilayered auditive human-search-engine-cooperation.»[8] The «noise» of the search engine terms as they hit Döhl's text corpus over and over again was made audible, acoustically commented by city sounds and collaged with further auditive material from the net.

appleinspace – search the world was broadcast on November 7, 2004 by *Kunstradio*, as the first item in the *curated by*[9] series *.ran.*

The five-part series *.ran [real audio netliterature]*,[10] broadcast between November 2004 and February 2005, was an attempt to bring together various approaches of net literature with the medium of radio.

.ran deliberately did not focus on the issue of listener participation but looked instead at the other possibilities and themes relevant for net literature in radio, such as code, montage/collage, questions of authorship, text-visuals-acoustics indifference, human-machine cooperation. I will take up these questions later.

6   Translator's note: here there is a German play on *ist* = is and *isst* = eats.

7   Beat Suter and René Bauer, *appleinspace*, http://appleinspace.cyberfiction.ch (accessed February 12, 2007).

8   See http://www.kunstradio.at/2004B/07_11 _04.html (accessed February 12, 2007).

9   *Kunstradio, curated by*, http://www .kunstradio.at/PROJECTS/CURATED_BY/index .html (accessed February 12, 2007).

10   *Kunstradio, .ran [real audio netliterature]*, curated by Johannes Auer, http://www .kunstradio.at/PROJECTS/CURATED_BY/ran/ (accessed February 12, 2007).

11   Benjamin Whooley, *New Media-Worlds* (London, 1992), p.165.

12   Uwe Wirth, «Literatur im Internet. Oder. Wen kümmert's wer liest?» http://www .netzliteratur.net/wirth/litim.htm (accessed February 12, 2007).

13   Johannes Auer, «Text im Bild // Marcel Duchamp,» in Reinhard Döhl and Johannes Auer, «Text – Bild – Screen // Netztext-Netzkunst,» *Literatur in Westfalen*, vol. 8, *Beiträge zur Forschung*, ed. Walter Gödden (Bielefeld, 2006), pp. 295ff.

14   Ben Fry, «genome valence,» http://acg.media .mit.edu/people/fry/genomevalence/ (accessed February 12, 2007).

Death of the Author and Compulsive Control

One question these apple games have not anwered is as to who is writing—the author or the reader or the computer? Ever since the appearance of hyperfiction in 1996, this major question has been repeatedly raised. The postmodern argument ran as follows: in the Internet every reader is also an author, since he or she can determine the form of the text through the links clicked. The reader collages the text while reading and in fact produces the text in the process of reading. According to Benjamin Whooley, «everyone is an author, which means no one is an author: the distinction from the reader disappears. Exit author ...»[11]

Does the phenomenon of the Wreader (meaning of the reader who is also an author or writer) really mean the click of death for the author? This question has quite rightly been anwered with a «no» by Uwe Wirth, among others:

When hypertexts forgo structure or internal coherence so that they are completely open to whatever the reader decides to do with them, then the line between interpretation and use is no longer evident. A completely open text is thus completely uninterpretable.»[12]

Or, to phrase it differently: an open hypertext is meaningless. A hypertext which is meaningful to read still requires the author, at least as a director who sets limits for the different readings and is thus to a certain extent in control.

However the question is not merely as to whether the author has control of the text. There is also the question of whether the author has control over the computer with his or her concept—or whether the computer has control of the author with its structures, its programming logic, with the potentials and limitations of its interfaces, with the power of the screen.

Given in particular the seductive, overwhelming power of the display, it seems fitting to apply Duchamp's rejection of «retinal art» to the computer screen. «Retinal» was the term Duchamp used for art which drew its aesthetic appeal from the surface, from the pictoral composition, from optics, and not from an underlying idea or artistic concept.[13]

Ben Fry's data visualization, in which data like the gene code in «genome valence»[14] are translated into an arbitrary optical show, seems to me a good illustration of the problematics of «retinal» computer art.

Without going into the matter any further at this point, one could nevertheless ask whether in blogging, for example, the author has not in fact lost control of the text to the logic of programming.

In *The Famous Sound of Absolute Wreaders*, I posed questions about the control of text, work, and machine the artistic subject. *The Famous Sound of Absolute Wreaders* is comprised of two parts—firstly, a radio production for *Kunstradio*,[15] broadcast on September 7, 2003, and secondly, a net project.[16] Since this was the first work attempting to link net literature and radio productively, as far as I know, I will thus present it in more detail.

The material used as the basis for the radio program and the Internet consisted of the texts of six net authors (Reinhard Döhl, Sylvia Egger, Martina Kieninger, Oliver Gassner, Beat Suter, Johannes Auer), who were asked to write about certain selected net projects carried out by the others. The only requirement was that the texts had to be printable on paper and recitable.

The text for broadcasting was collaged out of these texts and performed by the two speakers, Christiane Maschajechi and Peter Gorges, in the studio of *Kunstradio*. The program broadcast consisted of four ten-minute-long sections.

The first part called *Collage* was based on a text selection carried out by me, in other words it was under «human control.» In the second part, *Remix*, the speaker's text was randomly put together by the computer and was thus «computer-controlled.» The text basis for the third part, *Dialog*, was created in the same way, but this time the speakers had the task of commenting on the text spontaneously and thus regained some of the human control over the text. In the fourth part, *Rauschen*,[17] the same happened as in part three, but this time the speakers were drunk. People can decide for themselves who was in control of what in this last part.

15 See http://www.kunstradio.at/2003B/07_09_03.html (accessed February 13, 2007).

16 See http://kunstradio.cyberfiction.ch (accessed February 13, 2007).

17 Translator's note: *Rauschen* refers to the noise of static and contains the word *Rausch*, meaning intoxication.

18 *Kunstradio, Literatur als Radiokunst*, http://www.kunstradio.at/PROJECTS/LITERATURE (accessed February 17, 2007).

19 *Kunstradio, Familie Auer*, http://kunstradio.at/AUER (accessed February 17, 2007).

20 See http://kunstradio.at/AUER/auer_info.html (accessed February 17, 2000).

In advance of the broadcast, there was an upload area in which anyone who wanted could upload whatever digital material they chose. This material was deleted successively during the broadcast.

The net project utilized the text basis of the radio broadcast. Each of the authors involved used the text written by one of the others about the project of another as the source text for a new work.

This hybrid form—radio broadcast and extension through a website—is a form already introduced and practiced in the literary productions of *Kunstradio*. From 1999 onwards, for example, the exceptional series *Literatur als Radiokunst (Literatur as Radio Art)* has existed, which has been concerned with «finding forms of presenting literature on the radio beyond the traditional genre of ‹readings› [*Lesung*] and ‹plays› [*Hörspiel*].» Authors are given a net extension within the homepage of *Kunstradio*.[18]

Similarly, in *Familie Auer*[19] (broadcast from January 1996 to January 1997) the accompanying web platform was a fundamental and complementary element of the project. Thus a connection could be made between the old form of «the SitCom and the new cultural technologies.»[20]

The Famous Sound of Absolute Wreaders
Upload von Dateien

Durchsuchen...

Upload

Bitte beteiligen Sie sich und laden Sie vor der Sendung Dateien (Text, Bilder...) auf unseren Server [max. Dateigrösse 70 kb].

Johannes Auer,
*The Famous Sound
of Absolute Wreaders*,
upload tool, screen-
shot, 2003.

Love Talk

«Hypertexts are in fact just as unsuitable for reading out as source code is,» said Heiko Idensen in his project description of *.ran4 – Idensen live!*.[21] If he is right, then his radio program, testing precisely the possibilities of an audio hypertext, was just as pointless as the next section of my essay might be.

As already mentioned, what codeworks and concrete poetry along with Dada have in common is a reduction to the elements of language (or program language, respectively). Isn't it likely, then, that it should be possible to hear features common to Dadaistic sound poetry and to audible renderings of program source codes?

On May 4, 2000, a computer worm spread itself extremely rapidly per e-mail. «I love you» was the subject heading, leading to the virus being named «Loveletter.» Franco Berardi Bifo performed the source codes of this Loveletter virus at the d.i.n.a. Festival in Bologna on May 24, 2001.[22] Audio material from his performance was collaged into the radio broadcast *.ran5 – Codeworks*[23] by Florian Cramer (et al.). Anyone listening to Bifo's performance will feel strongly reminded of Dadaistic sound poetry.[24]

However, there is a serious difference to concrete poetry and Dada. This «code» doesn't just become a sound event.[25] It can cause damage when read by a computer: it is also a program code which executes itself!

21 See http://www.kunstradio.at/2005A/30_01 _05.html (accessed February 13, 2007).

22 An MP3 and a video of this performance can be found at http://www.epidemic.ws/dina_en .html (accessed February 13, 2007).

23 Broadcast by *Kunstradio* on February 20, 2005, http://www.kunstradio.at/2005A/20 _02_05.html (accessed February 13, 2007).

24 This may be largely because Franco Berardi Bifo spent a lot of time on Schwitters's sound poetry in preparation for his own performance, as Florian Cramer mentioned in a conversation we had. This supports rather than disproves my claim that program code is well-suited for interesting experiments in the tradition of sound poetry.

25 The partiture of Schwitters's *Die Ursonate* (*The Primal Sonata*) is, in a non-technical sense, also a «code to be executed» in a performance.

26 Sabine Breitsameter, «Die Apparatur hinterfragen: Telekommunikationskunst im Radio,» http://netzspannung.org/cat/servlet/ CatServlet/$files/272719/breitsameter.pdf (accessed February 17, 2007).

27 I was not aware in 2003 of the parallels to Hans Flesch's *Zauberei*.

28 See here Reinhard Döhl, «Zu Richard Hughes' ‹Danger,›» http://www.uni-stuttgart.de/ndl1/ hspl_hughes.htm (accessed February 17, 2007).

29 Sylvia Egger, for example, followed «*DADAspuren im Netz*» («DADAtracks on the Net») before the broadcast (*.ran3 – DADA TO GO. a walkthrough (levels)*), and the noise of the search engine terms in *.ran1* was recorded before the broadcast and collaged with other material. Heiko Idensens *Hoerhypertext* in *.ran4* was an auditive collage and thus a simulation of a hypertext reading.

Retrospective and Interim Résumé

The examples outlined above as early attempts to link net literature with radio reveal surprising parallels to the development of the radio play.

Hans Flesch's *Zauberei auf dem Sender* (*Magic on the Radio Channel*) was the first German radio play to be broadcast, on October 24, 1924. Briefly, in this «radio broadcast grotesque,» instead of the symphony concert on the program, listeners heard a chaotic mixture of numbers, dance music, the barking of dogs, and some announcers claiming «the radio channel has gone mad!» A magician had taken over the radio station and caused the sound chaos. The program director asked, horrified: «But what will happen if everyone just does as he likes?» He believed that the «centralized, hub-and-spoke system of radio was in danger.»[26]

Hans Flesch addressed the question of control in his play: who is in charge of the medium, and thus who decides how and what is broadcast?

The Famous Sound of Absolute Wreaders also deals with these issues of control (who is in charge of the text—the author, the reader, the computer?) and loss of control (drunk speakers in the fourth part ignore large sections of the text presented by the author and reworked by the computer and, instead, «do as they like»).[27]

It is natural for a young medium to concentrate on itself in the early stages. However, drawing on what is familiar is a tried and tested way of approaching new territory.

The first radio play ever is considered to be *A Comedy of Danger* by Richard Hughes, broadcast by the BBC on January 15, 1924. Hughes used a trick to make his play suitable for the radio: during a mine inspection the lights fail, and in this way the dialogue and the radio play can commence. The radio play becomes «Theater für Blinde,»[28] (drama for the blind) and thus creates a setting for the new form of radio play (lights out), which allows the adaptation of the familiar form of a stage play for the radio.

It seems justified here to claim that there are parallels between the «drama for the blind» and «radio art for non-users of the net» with the series *.ran* and *The Famous Sound of Absolute Wreaders*. In all these productions, reference to the net was made in advance of the broadcast or was a simulation[29] but at any rate had a decisive influence on the concept and material of the radio play. One can say that the Internet here was (reflexively) the occasion for the radiophone language game.

At this point it is worth remembering Georges Perec's excellent radio play, *The Machine* from 1968. Four speakers—«three memories» and a «controller»— simulate the work of a computer which is intended to systematically analyze Johann Wolfgang von Goethe's poem «Wanderers Nachtlied» (Wanderer's Night Song):

> It becomes clear to the attentive listener that this play on language does not merely describe the way a machine works, but also reveals the internal mechanism of poetry itself, though on a far more subtle level.[30]

As a provisional conclusion, one can say that there appear to be three possibilities for adapting net literature for the radio (and all three are hybrid forms):

1. The performed reading, either as a radio text or radio play (example: *The Famous Sound of Absolute Wreaders*) or as sound poetry (example: Loveletter).
2. The collage of differently generated sound material (example: *.ran1 – appleinspace* or *.ran3 – DADA TO GO*).
3. The algorythmic generation (example: *.ran5 – Codeworks* and *.ran2 – authorship and its automatic generation*). The supposition here is that the more the text/tone is generated throughout the course of the program, the more it is heard as a «musical» experience.

This provisional conclusion excludes, however, a very significant aspect of the potential of net literature—radio: interactivity or listener participation.

So far I have deliberately omitted this, as a reflection of my own emphasis in working with net literature and radio. For a long time the hyperfiction euphoria, which started in Germany in 1996, overshadowed other interesting aspects of net literature (see «A Digression: Apple Games» above). Interactivity was triumphantly declared to be the death of the author and trivialized into mere «clickability» as a form of «user participation.» In the series *.ran – real audio*

---

30 Georges Perec, *Die Maschine*, first broadcast by SR (Saarland Radio) and WDR (West German Radio), November 13, 1968.

31 «Copy and paste,» a basic operation in handling computer data.

netliterature I thus expressly aimed at placing emphasis on the other aspects of net literature (such as program codes as a base, use of databases, collage and montage).[31]

In *The Famous Sound of Absolute Wreaders*, the future listener could participate by uploading digital material in advance, but the «insolent» way the user data was erased without being used in the course of the broadcast was, if anything, a demonstration of the power of the author and not of listener participation.

The above résumé illustrates that this form of adapting net literature for the radio leads to interesting artistic experiments with language, which reflect the medium they were conceived for. Nonetheless, I have to admit that for the listener the form remains largely «traditional.»

Authentic Interactivity
Speculation

Is interactivity the decisive element which can turn net literature on the radio into a new acoustic form and experience?

Familie Auer was an innovative «sitcom» for radio, Internet, and other media. Over seventy authors (visual artists, musicians, writers, sound and performance artists, and sound engineers) collaborated over a year to develop new methods, strategies, and forms for working in the era of the convergence of mass media and computer-based communications technology, 1996–97.

Sabine Breitsameter regards the bi-directional communication possibilities as having great potential for radio art:

> Since the digital networks came up recently, the electroacoustic media space which radio art is based on has altered. Its new architecture makes available a shared environment, a distributed space, with—finally—bi-directional communication possibilities.

She then gives precise instances of how radio art can become interactive:

1. Dramaturgies based on navigation.
2. Productions based on the flexibility of the sender/receiver relation.
3. Concepts based on network-architectural principles («distributed space» and «shared environment.»)[32]

Of course, there were attempts to involve the listener in radio plays in pre-Internet times,[33] and also early forms of «dramaturgies based on navigation.» A good example is Richard Hey's *Rosie: Ein Radiospektakel zum Mitmachen für Stimmen, Musik und telefonierende Hörer,* Südwestfunk, 1969 (*Rosie: A radio spectacle involving voices, music and phone-in listeners*), in which listeners could determine the course of the broadcast by phoning in to the radio studio. This tradition was picked up electronically in 1996 on *Kunstradio* in two parts of *Familie Auer,*[34] whose conclusion listeners could decide per e-mail.

At the same time, interaction requires that the public is prepared to become involved, as Dieter Daniels commented:

> I think that interaction will always be confronted with the problem that it runs counter to the human desire to be offered something, to be entertained passively. Of course we all like to be told a story. And all of this

32 Sabine Breitsameter (see note 1).
33 Sabine Breitsameter (see note 26).
34 *Kunstradio, Familie Auer. Familienausflug I* (broadcast on March 21, 1996) and *Familien-ausflug II* (broadcast on March 28, 1996), by Renate Pliem and Reinhard Köberl.

35 Quoted after Sabine Breitsameter, «unter-haltungen im internet. hörspiel als interaktion. ein radiophoner essay,» in Auer 2004 (see note 5), p. 34.
36 Ibid., pp. 33–34.

potentially resists any movement in the direction of interaction. These are poles which cannot easily be reconciled.[35]

This is well illustrated by a dialogue with a listener who phoned in during Richard Hey's *Rosie*:

Moderator: «Studio *Rosie*,» Good evening.

Listener 4: Well, hallo. I'm calling from Durmersheim. I reckon the young man ought to give someone a good thumping. And the person he ought to thump is Mr. Hey. I've often listened to radio plays from him in the past but I don't like this one at all.

Moderator: Why not? Don't you want to give your opinion and influence the plot?

Listener 4: No, I want to be entertained.

Moderator: Well aren't you being entertained right now?

Listener 4: Maybe, but not the way I want to be.[36]

```
EIN DORF IST LEISE ODER EIN BLICK IST NAH
JEDES HAUS IST SPAET. EIN BILD IST STILL
EIN FREMDER IST OFFEN. NICHT JEDER GRAF IST OFFEN
NICHT JEDES AUGE IST SPAET. KEIN TURM IST STILL
EIN KNECHT IST LEISE UND NICHT JEDER TURM IST FREI
NICHT JEDES SCHLOSS IST LEISE. NICHT JEDES BILD IST DUNKEL
KEIN KNECHT IST WÜTEND UND KEINE Bühnenbeleuchtung IST LEISE
KEIN GAST IST GROSS. KEIN HAUS IST GROSS
EIN RADIO IST FREI, SO GILT NICHT JEDES BILD IST LEISE
JEDES HAUS IST GROSS. NICHT JEDER sex mit tieren IST HÖRBAR
NICHT JEDER GAST IST TIEF. NICHT JEDES AUGE IST FERN
NICHT JEDER BAUER IST STARK, SO GILT JEDER BAUER IST WÜTEND
JEDE Bühnenbeleuchtung IST GUT. KEIN GAST IST TIEF
NICHT JEDER Diskussion IST GROSS. KEIN WEG IST OFFEN
NICHT JEDER BAUER IST WÜTEND. EIN Drachenfahnen IST TIEF
JEDER KNECHT IST GROSS: KEIN HAUS IST STILL
```

stochastische texte 1959   ///////   search lutz 2006

Johannes Auer, *search lutz!*, web interface, screenshot, 2006.

The public's reluctance to participate seems to me a particular problem of «dramaturgies based on navigation,» since the interaction is generally restricted to selecting from a limited number of predetermined options. This means that the listener is not really a genuine player, but, maintaining the metaphor, at best a referee.

As I see it, the greatest challenge in an interactive radio play is achieving authentic participation. I have made a few attempts myself in this direction with *free lutz* and *search lutz!*, live broadcasts for *Radio_Copernicus*[37] and *RadioRevolten*.[38]

In 1959, a calculator generated a literary text for the first time ever. Theo Lutz wrote a program for Zuse Z22 to create stochastic texts. On the advice of Max Bense, he took sixteen nouns and adjectives out of Kafka's *Schloss*, which the calculator then formed into sentences, following certain patterns. Thus every sentence began with «*ein*» or «*jeder*» («one» or «each») or the corresponding negative form «*kein*» or «*nicht jeder*» («none» or «not every»). Then the noun, selected arbitrarily from the pool of sixteen, was linked through the verb «*ist*» («is») with the likewise arbitrarily chosen adjective. Then the whole assembly was linked up through «*und,*» «*oder,*» «*so gilt*» («and,» «either,» «thus») or given a full stop. Following these calculation instructions, by means of this algorithm, the machine was able to construct such sentences as:

EIN TAG IST TIEF UND JEDES HAUS IST FERN
(A day is deep and every house is distant)
JEDES DORF IST DUNKEL, SO GILT KEIN GAST IST GROSS
(Every village is dark, thus no guest is large)[39]

---

37 *free lutz*, broadcast by *Radio_Copernicus*, Wrocław, December 8, 2005, http://radio-c .zkm.de/radio-copernicus.org (accessed February 19, 2007) and http://copernicus .netzliteratur.net (accessed February 19, 2007).

38 *search lutz!*, broadcast by *Radio Corax* as part of the festival *RadioRevolten*, Halle, September 30, 2006, http://www.radiorevolten .radiocorax.de/cms/index.php (accessed February 19, 2007) and http://halle.netzlit eratur.net (accessed February 19, 2007).

39 Theo Lutz, «Stochastische Texte,» *augenblick* 4, no.1 (1959), pp. 3–9, http://www .stuttgarter-schule.de/lutz_schule.htm (accessed February 19, 2007).

40 The live search by Fireball and other search engines displays the stream of terms as they are entered by users in the search engines. See http://www.fireball.de/livesuche (accessed February 19, 2007).

41 «It is possible to ignore the fact that a person is behind the texts on the screen, whereas one is automatically aware that one is talking to a person in FTF communication. In this respect, the threshold for insulting someone seriously is lower. It is no wonder that in Netiquette users are admonished not to forget that there is a person on the other side of the screen with whom they are interacting.» From Gloria Dabiri and Dörte Helten, «Psychologie & Internet,» http://userpage.fu-berlin.de/~ chlor/werk.pdf (accessed February 19, 2007).

For the live broadcast *free lutz* and *search lutz!*, I used a web conversion of Theo Lutz's program which I wrote in PHP. The web interface generated stochastic texts on the basis of Lutz's algorithm but permitted additional word input. The nouns and adjectives of the original vocabulary could be replaced by listeners through the Internet or the audience at the performance through a terminal. Furthermore, in *search lutz!* words from the live search of the search engine Fireball[40] could infiltrate the text generation process.

In 1959, computer texts were connotated as literary texts twice over, firstly through the «Kafka» vocabulary, and secondly through corrections carried out by Theo Lutz. In an edited print out of a selection of stochastic texts, Theo Lutz corrected minor grammar errors and punctuation omissions by hand, and thus, out of keeping with the programming, he acted as a «traditional» author. In the live broadcast, reference was made to these literary features (or one could almost say «human touches») of the first computer-generated texts in several ways. The first was through the co-authorship of the listeners, the second was the inclusion of terms which at that instant were being entered in a search engine, and the third was the literary production of the computer texts by a professional speaker reading off the screen and performing them as they were generated.

A real-time performance with a speaker seems to me crucial in the pursuit of authentic interactivity. To illustrate this, I would like to make one closing, brief digression.

Almost everyone has at some point experienced a significant difference between the way Usenet and mailing list subscribers behave online and the way they would behave if they were in similar exchanges with people in «real life.»[41]

I would claim that the (linked) computer is not so much a machine that serves to establish dialogue with others as an apparatus that facilitates autistic monologues. In front of the screen, people communicate with themselves or products of their own imagination. The space in front of the computer is not net space but a space filled with one's own projections and images. The fact that e-mail writing has less to do with letter writing than with holding imaginary dialogues explains, in my opinion, the strong tendency for Usenet and mailing list subscribers to flame others. This includes even those who in «normal» life remain calm in discussions but who turn here very quickly to sharp, insulting responses. When I imagine angrily how I would give someone «a piece of my mind,» and when

I compare this with what I would probably say in a real conversation, then it is the uninhibited, aggressive internal monologue which corresponds to the e-mail.

If my supposition is correct, then how can the autistic attitude (and posture) of the computer user in front of the screen be transformed into one of participation?

I believe this can only happen by «humanizing» the interface. Authentic interaction can, in my opinion, only work if users experience an authentic presence on the other side.[42]

In *free lutz* and *search lutz!* I attempted to create this situation with a speaker. The speaker does not merely read off the text, but he performs it, interprets it, and thus gives it meaning.

When the listener in this live play interacts through the computer and enters words, then the answer out of the radio does not come from an algorithm but from a human being.

---

42 And definitely not through the ELIZA principle, whereby a program within the limits of its algorithm is able to react so skillfully that its answers fulfill the projected expectation of the «dialogue partner.»

An Anatomy of Radio

August Black

Imagine for a minute that we live in a metaphysical world of telepathy where any kind of message can be sent at instantaneous speeds to any individual or group at any distance, near or far. It is a world of pure radiological communication. Any transmission of any size can be delivered without considerations of bandwidth or physical linkage. If you send a message—let's say it's a 3D animated sequence of a detail that is so vast that it appears to be infinite—the message is not only received by all at the moment of broadcast but can be decoded and «viewed» without error or excessive effort. It can be changed and modified by the recipients on-the-fly and then re-broadcasted and received simultaneously with the original broadcast to everyone else. There are no issues of compatibility, and the reception itself is guaranteed to be deliverable and processable.

This, of course, is an imaginary scenario. Despite the fact that our present world of radio is also a virtual nonphysical world, as we experience it through mediated environments such as terrestrial broadcast or Internet, it is still one heavily tied to the physical realities of tension, vibration, and friction of matter in ambient space. This imagined scenario is also a rather boring one. While a transmissive world such as the one described above would certainly create an interesting fluidity in the style, genre, and form of message making (content?), the art of radio can probably be best attributed to the threshold of its own physical limitations. The parts of radio—it's tools, instruments, and structure—are a significant portion of what provides the formal characteristics, style, and language of radio.

Radio is, of course, much more than a portion of the electromagnetic spectrum, much more than the electronic devices used to tune in to a frequency channel, and much more than the stations and the organizational efforts to slice time into schedules of music, talk, and advertisement. Radio is many things simultaneously, a plurality. It is the broadcaster (radio transmitter), it is the message (the radio signal) and organizer of that message (the radio station or radio show), as well as the device you use to listen to what is «on» the radio: a radio. Nowadays, it is your walkie-talkie, your cell phone, the web and Internet, both streaming and on-demand. All together, it is the stuff of connectedness. It is an evolving definition, ever-changing, that adapts to our understanding as we create new and more evocative systems and devices for producing interconnectedness among men and machines.

As such, radio is a system to been seen as consisting of multiple parts that are mutually dependant. Without the transmitter, a receiver is useless, and vice versa. Without bandwidth limitations over cabled networks, compression formats, which seriously add to the complexity of online audio production, would be unnecessary. Without software capable of the decoding of compression format X, streaming in such format would be a practice in futility. Additionally, while software may be readily available to receive and decode audio format X, there is no guarantee that any amount of users will download, install, and use that decoding software. Users are rightfully lazy. On whole, as a system of connectedness, radio is an ever-flowing dynamic of relationships between «hard» things such as devices, wiring, and accessibility as well as «soft» things such as usage, expectation, organization, and scheduling.

But, what are these systems and devices? What are the tools that connect? And, how are these connections shaped by the various instruments, structures, and protocols that have recently come about? Are new «stuff» of connectedness created? If so, how have they changed the face of radio in the past few years? In short, what is the current anatomy of radio?

For the sake of understanding, I will try to break these things down into two separate category pairs of data and data-flow, as well as between static and live transmission. While the signal and data, as well as the flow of those things, better represents the material of radio (as a mixture of solidity and fluidity), the timing and scheduling is characteristic of its personality.

The Data
Compression Codecs and Audio Formats

I think it is fair to say that practically all current digital communications channels that have been established for some form of public use and consumption—including everything from cell phones to satellite radio to online streaming—use a compression codec of some form or another. Compression is simply a way of taking a digital signal, live or statically recorded, and making it smaller in size for easier storage or transmission. For transmission purposes, the size of the signal is referred to as bitrate and is a measure of how many bits must be sent to produce a second of audio. The unit of measurement is in bits per second. The effects of compression, especially to networked radio events, is difficult to judge and often hard to perceive. They are, however, integral to the process of making radio online. Without compression, audio streaming would be next to impossible

August Black,
Radio graffiti,
Copenhagen,
Denmark, 2001.

for a general audience on the given global networks. Without compression, it would also be MUCH easier to develop software and maintain standards for the exchange of audio online.

The point of all compression is to reinterpret the original signal (X) into another form, whereby, when you subtract unnecessary data, the resulting signal (Y) is of smaller bit size. The act of compressing a file is known as encoding. The act of getting the «original» signal back from the compressed data is known as decoding. The codec is the name of the encoding/decoding software and can usually control the amount of compression that is desired. Each codec has specific characteristics, but in general, more compression equals a lower bitrate equals a more degraded signal and a signal that is more easily accessed by online users, who may not have a high-speed Internet connection. And, vice versa.

The important thing to get out of this is that compression is a necessary characteristic of digital transmission due to limitations, both imagined and real, in bandwidth on both wired and wireless networks. Nowadays, instead of hearing the statics, pops, and hiss of AM or FM transmission, you hear the warble, garble, and stutter of digital compression and its artifacts as it is stalled and delayed by the network. The sound is very different and can be tuned to sound even more different depending on need and intent. It is part of the sound of transmission and is essential to the psychology of distance inherent in a radiophonic world.

Data-Flow
Unicast, Multicast, and Broadcast

It is unusual to me that the telephone, as was initially conceived by Alexander Graham Bell, was thought to be more like a cable subscription network. Families with a telephone were to subscribe to a telecast, and at a certain time of day the receiver would ring and then would be taken off the hook, set down, and all would listen to what was being said over the line. However, due to whatever reason, the telephone really took off when it was used to connect individuals in direct conversation. What was initially thought of as a broadcast cable network quickly changed to private, isolated point-to-point connectivity. Oddly enough, the new methodology of telephony—cell phones—are built upon wireless technologies. As the world becomes increasingly engrossed in the speed and efficiency of communications media, it is becoming difficult to differentiate between wired and wireless modes of communication. From the point of view of making radio, it is almost irrelevant whether or not you are connected with a physical link, so long as the connection is there and is reliable. The important difference for radio makers is not the linkage per se, but whether the system of transmission is configured for broadcasting, single connection, or some sort of mix thereof. The issues involved stem from latency, buffering, and bandwidth and evolve into higher-level issues of style and procedure of transmission. The space that is delineated and evinced by a certain network configuration will determine the type and amount of usage. For some, the amount of audience is not as important as the kind of audience that is to be met through a connected environment.

Radio is typically thought of in terms of broadcasting and is structurally characterized by a single transmitter and multiple receivers. Whether by state consolidation or by public or commercial interest, the classic understanding of broadcasting necessitates a larger organizational structure to plan round-the-clock scheduling, to accrue funding to pay staff and licensing fees, house equipment, and so forth. Broadcasting is monolithic in stature and local in scope. It is a space of news, ritual, and homogeneity. Broadcasting produces listeners, and in cases of commercial broadcasting, it produces consumers.

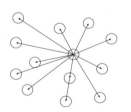 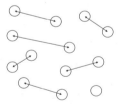 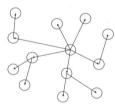

Broadcast   Unicast   Multicast

By contrast, the telephone is a typical example of unicasting. It is private, personal, and intimate. It is the space of gossip, chat, and emergencies. The telephone connects two people at any given time for any given amount of time, requiring little more than a cheaply bought telephone and service. Of course, in some parts of the world, telephone service is more of an issue than in others. However, cell phones have come into popularity, and telephone networks based on wireless technology have become easier to build and maintain than old-fashioned cabled telephone networks. They are also less reliable as they can often cut out when the radio signal is weak.

Multicasting is a technical term for a type of network routing. In cabled networks, the typical way of streaming audio would be to have a single server streaming some encoded audio at a fixed or variable bitrate. Each person who wants to listen to the stream, also known as a client in technical terms, would connect to the server and receive the streamed data. Now, for each client that connects, the bandwidth used at the point of the server is increased by the bitrate of the stream. To elevate this bottleneck, multicasting routes the data amongst nearby clients as well as between the clients and the server. In short, it is a way of distributing bandwidth amongst clients, reflecting the data stream ad hoc from one client to the next, allowing for larger bitstreams to be sent over the line. Multicasting builds a space of flows. It is meant for live, real-time data and is most used in video-chat software architectures such as VideoLAN.[1]

There are, of course, many other ways to configure a communications structure, but I feel these demonstrate the most basic differences. And to all of this, I would argue that while old-fashioned radio was broadcast-, signal-, and audience-centric, the current mode of radio (as much of everything else) is network-, data-, and user-driven, centering around the arbitrariness of connectivity and focusing on content only when usage is collectively adhered to certain expectations and abilities for understanding and managing the network. The characteristics of communication are shaped less by the difference between wired and wireless structures than by the network topology itself, as many modes of networking can be implemented and/or simulated over various links.

1   http://videolan.org
2   http://www.orang.org
3   http://cba.fro.at

Static Transmission
Scheduled, On-Demand, and Automated

Classical radio is an interesting interface between people, linking them through scheduling over time and through an ongoing dialogue. What is being played and listened to now is almost as important as what is remembered to have been played at this specific time last week. This is often called the «programming» although has more to do with the manipulation and guidance of interest throughout the days, weeks, and months of the year than with the manipulation of computational processes. This kind of radio is more often driven by regularity and repetition. Like the beating of a drum, it delineates time so that it is more easily and more enjoyably passed, syncing groups of listeners to a common habitual rhythm.

However, with the onslaught of computer technologies, available bandwidth and storage, and overall «cheapness» of digital content, listening is increasingly becoming more fragmented and dispersed among audiophiles, and scheduling less appetizing. From the perspective of a listener, one might argue that radio is little more than a sanctioned playlist—a linear list of audio content selected by a disk jockey. The demand for individual control in the selection of audio is on the rise, and with the current popularity of portable MP3 players, capable of easily loading audio from the net (in a few set formats), new species of radio-on-demand are already solidifying for entertainment purposes.

This speciation of distribution methods can be traced back to early experiments such as the now-defunct Open Radio Archive Group (ORANG)[2] by Thomax Kaulmann. ORANG was a simple and effective database system that allowed anyone to upload audio content, tag it with descriptors, and then create and store individual playlists. It was a simple and effective system used by many radio makers to store and categorize audio material for later reuse and redistribution. It was, however, a centralized database with all audio material residing in (mostly) one format (Real Audio) and on one computer. Another centralized example is the Cultural Broadcasting Archive (CBA),[3] initiated by the Free Radios of Austria. Again, a centralized database is used to store audio content, however the content itself is comprised by the archives and raw material from radio programs of the various Free Radios of Austria (in mostly MP3 format)—the purpose being to allow for easy exchange of material between the free radio stations. Many programs here are archived with automation software.

The Frequency Clock,[4] by r a d i o q u a l i a, was a similar experiment at creating a new species of online radio, however more decentralized. *Frequency Clock* allows users to not only create playlists, but to create playlist schedules of both live and static audio that is stored on dispersed machines in many formats using various compression codecs. It builds an interesting mix between individually selective playlists and communal scheduling of traditional radio and has two main components: a media player and a scheduler. The scheduler is a server and database application that allows users to develop playlists and time them throughout the day. The player regularly calls on the scheduling server for playlist updates and queues them for playback as requested. Because the playlists are only a list of URLs for online media, and the audio is then streamed to the player as it is being played, it can schedule and play any media from the Internet, be it a statically stored file or a live audio stream.

Audio blogging and what is (unfortunately) known as podcasting are two of the latest and simplest forms of on-demand radio. Audio blogging is practically the same thing as podcasting, only with audio blogs a user browses a website periodically (or is informed via RSS feeds when updates are available) and then manually clicks on links to download and/or play the audio. It is browser-based and is generally accompanied by a written description by the blog author. Podcasting gets its name from Apple's iPod portable audio player and is a style of on-demand radio broadcasting, whereby an audio playing application (such as the Apple iTunes or Rhythmbox on Linux) can be programmed to retrieve audio content as it becomes available. It is not unusual for websites to offer both possibilities as does *Democracy Now!* with Amy Goodman.[5]

As the distribution of media becomes more and more software-based and more varied, features, standards, and compatibility amongst software become more of an issue. While it is easy to add new features to any given software, it is difficult to have those features accepted and understood among a user base. The social aspect of software is here demonstrably perceivable. It is also questionable whether more diverse forms of audio as well as more diverse audiences are thus created by this development, but it looks as if that is the case.

4   http://radioqualia.va.com.au/freqclock
5   http://www.democracynow.org

Live Transmission
Wiggling and Inter-Re-Active

Arguably, the most exciting form of radio is when it is live on-air, where the act of listening is simultaneously tied to events in real time. More interesting, however, is when the act of listening is not only tied to an event, but also when the listeners are connected to each other and can partake in the dynamics of the event structure.

There are species of radio that have come about through mixed networking that provide interactive and/or reactive exchanges. The most simple and effective of these is the telephone call-in, which mixes the intimate personal conversation of the telephone with the public stage of broadcasting, linking person-to-person to many people at the same time. Other forms include peer-to-peer networks and live text-to-speech on the radio. The more complicated and experimental forms involve home-brewed software, which require and evoke an attitude of collective democratic participation in the production of publicly audible content. A few examples include ninjam, streaps, and the author's own userradio.

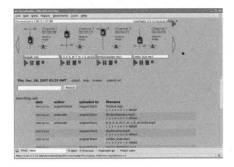

r a d i o q u a l i a, *The Frequency Clock*, net.radio installation, timetable and player, screenshot, 1998– 2001.

August Black, UserRadio, web inter- face, screenshot, 2004.

Peer-to-peer networking is a software-based system of exchanging data between individuals whereby each client also acts as a server. Popular implementations include Napster,[6] Bittorrent,[7] and Gnutella.[8] When you join the network as a client, and search and download illegal MP3s, bootleg movies, and pornography (for what else would you use these things?), you open up a portion of your hard drive to other clients looking for the material you are now downloading or have already stored on your drive. It is notable, I find, because its topology is reflective of both live and on-demand communication, as well as mixing methods of broad-, multi-, and unicasting. It is only «on» when users are connected, as they provide the content as well as the network.

There have also been numerous attempts at text-to-speech radio events, whereby text from IRC channels or some other online chat forum as well as from cell phone text messaging allows users to voice thoughts and opinions live on-air. At Radio FRO in Linz, Austria, where I held a weekly show for five years, this was possible on many occasions. I've also witnessed similar events elsewhere such as at *Kunstradio*[9] and *ääniradio*.[10] Text is probably the easiest interactive protocol to understand (next to speech) and provides effective low-tech interactive possibilities.

Ninjam[11] is a kind of live peer-to-peer network software that allows users to «jam» music online. In order to deal with synchronization over the network, it quantifies latency as musical measures so that users are synced to a beat rather than a specific point in time. Streaps[12] is an interesting software configuration that mixes a fixed number of audio streams in Ogg Vorbis format at the central server. Users can select multiple streams to mix from a matrix-like user interface that can be controlled through a web browser. UserRadio[13] is a similar server-client application with a web interface that allows an unlimited number of individuals to mix multiple channels of audio simultaneously and together from anywhere online using a standard flash-capable browser. Users can select audio on separate channels of the mixer from a database of stored content or from live streams online. With all of these, there is a possibility of linking the online streamed output with an FM transmitter for classical broadcast capabilities as well as of mixing the output from one software to the input of another for more intricate (as well as complicated) software architectures.

6   http://www.napster.com
7   http://www.bittorrent.net
8   http://www.gnutella.com
9   http://kunstradio.at
10 http://www.aaniradio.org
11 http://www.ninjam.com
12 http://streaps.org
13 http://aug.ment.org/userradio

There are other such applications that, by mixing broadcast and unicast technologies, provide interactive possibilities to an otherwise one-dimensional and scripted media platform. While these software applications and general connectivity allow for a new (and sometimes exciting) interaction, often with a form of democratic control structures, popular implementations of these kinds of interactivity are slow to come about—with the exception of peer-to-peer networks and text interaction on television, where the focus is on the consumption of entertainment.

Whether it is wired or wireless, micro or macro in scale, digital or analog, or whether it is standardized and popular, or nonstandard and/or fragmented, radio is at least partially defined by its physical and organizational makeup. As the computer—in desktop, laptop, and other alternative forms—becomes more and more integral to the functioning of our daily lives, this makeup converges in the fluid morphology of software and network topologies.

The possible anatomy of radio is virtually endless. The initial explosion of digital and network technologies highlighted the visibility of changes in communication, while the current development is distinguished by the subtle co-evolution of software communication systems and the manufacture of collective intent. Despite the fact that most of this text emphasizes the «soft,» high-tech components of radio, the powers and possibilities of «hard,» low-tech components should not be underestimated: two cans and a long string tied in between can be an effective form of radio. Or, how about a large megaphone? Or, just some simple graffiti? Or, a cassette player set in a palm tree and running on solar power?

Radio as Art

Classification and Archivization of Radio Art

Anne Thurmann-Jajes

Examining radio art as a cultural asset to be preserved in its mediality and ephemeral structure and to be made accessible to a general audience interested in art is the aim of the ensuing discussion. The focus rests on those radio art-works broadcasted by broadcasting corporations, independent radio stations, and web radios, and only marginally on that sphere of radio art that is also classified as telecommunications art. This essay picks up the thread of a research project aimed to collect, archive, and develop radio art and to make it accessible.[1] The difficulties, premises, and objectives involved in this context are presented in the following.[2]

Radio Art in a Field of Conflicting Systems

The core problem of radio art is its restricted accessibility, making any comprehensive investigation, treatment and research, mediation and presentation nearly impossible. Only with some effort is it possible to listen to radio art programs stored in the nonpublic archives of public service broadcasting corporations. Things can get even more difficult for those wanting to listen to programs produced autonomously by artists, for which the artists worked in local stations such as campus or community radios, or in town stations or other forms of limited-range independent radio stations.

One result of this lack of accessibility has been that art science research, for example, has largely disregarded radiophonic artworks. This also applies to some extent to literary studies and other disciplines. Often even the artists do not have access to their works held by public service broadcasters, particularly if they are early productions stored only on tape. As a result, these artistic productions have only come into the public eye to a very limited extent, the more so as they were usually only broadcasted late at night. Radiophonic artworks practically do not exist in the traditional understanding of art, featuring neither in art education and mediation nor in museum education. Hence, one subset of cultural assets is largely «nonexistent» in society, to put it somewhat drastically.

While artists at independent stations have worked with the simplest of means, improvising and often neglecting to record their works, being, as they were, totally occupied with production, the situation differs completely with public service broadcasters. They have been in a position to offer artists technical equipment without which many radio artworks would not have been possible. Particularly in the German-speaking world, since the nineteen-sixties, seminal developments have taken place that have founded and established radio art in Europe. But precisely these works are not accessible to the public.

The general task of nonpublic broadcaster archives, for example in Germany, is generally seen as collecting (studio) recordings of their own programs and archiving them for the purpose of using them again for later productions, repeating them, or making them available to other broadcasters. Widespread publication would run counter to the basis of their own work. Over the years, however, all broadcasters have come to see their audio material equally as assets, founding subsidiaries to market them and publishing the individual works as audio CDs, formerly as cassettes, and allowing fee-based recording for private use.

1   This is a research project of the Research Centre for Artists' Publications (*Studienzentrum für Künstlerpublikationen*) and the Research Association Artists' Publications (*Forschungsverbund Künstlerpublikationen*).

2   My thanks extend to Heidi Grundmann for numerous supplementary references.

3   The Research Association Artists' Publications is a scientific association with the task of initiating basic research in the field of artists' publications and establishing it as a new field of scientific work. The Research Association is funded by the University of Bremen, the Jacobs University, the University of the Arts, Research Centre for East European Studies, and the Weserburg–Museum for Modern Art via the Research Centre for Artists' Publications.

Rationalization and restructuring measures within the public service broadcasting corporations, a shortage of space, and diminishing interest due to a change of generations have led and still lead to a situation in which, in particular, old recordings/tapes decay, disappear, or even get thrown away. The broadcasters' interest is in infinitely reusable, rather popular program material, which unconventional artist programs precisely are not. At best, such programs get replayed on the artist's eightieth birthday. This reveals the profound misunderstanding on the part of the broadcasting corporations. For radio art is both program and artwork, a form of art that, as a program, exists only in its audio form. Hence, of relevance here is the non-accessibility of art, of artistic production.

Public service broadcasters are in a quandary. On the one hand, they are blocking the public's rightful access to their cultural assets. Indirectly, they are hindering science and research, a fact that making programs available for a recording and licensing fee does nothing to change, as researchers, university facilities, and museums cannot raise the necessary funds. On the other hand, the broadcasters are forced to create income, to reuse existing programs, and to take the various copyrights and licenses into account.

Because broadcasters cannot afford to make these programs available, the Research Centre for Artists' Publications at the Weserburg–Museum for Modern Art along with the Research Association Artists' Publications[3] have taken the initiative and founded a radio art research project. In this context, an archive of radio art is being built, to be housed at the Research Centre. The aim is to depict and document radio art in its overall context, its history and development—presenting it, making it accessible to the public, as well as available for research by means of an audiovisual overview.

The archive is being created in cooperation with artists and various broadcasting corporations. The programs are made available to the museum for the archive in the form of permanent loans from the broadcasters and artists. The museum cannot derive any rights from this. The only rights retained are to store the programs on a server, to index them, and to allow visitors, artists, scientists, and students to listen to them. All other rights remain with the radio stations and copyright holders. With its radio art archive, the Research Centre assumes the role of scientific mediator by providing research material for teachers, researchers, and educators. The result is the first facility in which radio art is available for in-depth research and public access for interested parties, students, and scientists.

On Radio Art

The archive holds all kinds of relevant forms of radio programs in the broadest sphere of what artists have done with, on, and for radio. But to what, generally speaking, does «radio» refer here? And to what conceptions of radio do the artists refer? Taking technical developments into account—from terrestrial broadcasting to telecommunications media and media fusion—what we are dealing with is a changing concept of radio that spans a spectrum from wireless technology to tube technology to Internet radio.[4] As a concept, «radio» denotes both the radio set and radio or sound broadcasting, as well as telephony, telegraphy, radar, wireless communication, facsimile transmission, the transmitter, et cetera. Or, in other words: «Radio is the remote transmission of acoustic and optical messages by means of electric waves ... to a spatially unlimited, indeterminate number of people. Radio is ... characterized by the fact that—like the press—it is an indispensable means of mass communication and a crucial factor in shaping public opinion.»[5] The idea of radio as a technological and symbolic medium also derives from the meaning of the word «radio» in social communication, that is, in what is heard and reflected upon in the form of radio. Hence, the radio concept is also informed by the social manifestation of its technical possibilities. In this sense, artists focus on «radio» in its full range, referring very differently to its technical, media-based, and symbolic diversity—be it by incorporating the transistor radio as an object, creating telecommunications projects based on different radio technologies, or dealing with radio as a mass medium.

Artists have examined the radio medium on both institutional and autonomous levels. The artists who have been producing radio art programs in their studios or on local radio stations since the nineteen-sixties have seen radio as a space of information and communication, working, for the most part, with the simplest of means. On this basis, they have improvised with everyday objects and often with the most basic technology, but with such a conceptual approach as to create works of special artistic succinctness in the sense of an «economy of means.»[6] This is also based on an independence from the rules and norms of big institutions and producers' aesthetic ideas. In contrast, since the sixties, public service broadcasting stations, particularly in Germany, have been able to offer artists

---

4   See Wolfgang Ernst's essay in this volume.
5   Kurt Koszyk and Karl Hugo Pruys, eds., *Handbuch der Massenkommunikation* (Munich: dtv, 1980), pp. 279–80. Translation of quotation provided by Richard Watts.

6   Here I am referring to an expression coined by Michael Glasmeier.

production and broadcasting opportunities not obtainable elsewhere. They have procured access to the infrastructure and to cutting-edge production studios, including the special radio play studios, without which certain works would not have been possible. In their projects, they have been supported by well-trained sound engineers, although, it must be said, some sound engineers have lacked an appreciation of the artists' ideas and wishes, thus precluding collaboration. Their acoustic works on records—those not referring to the medium of radio or not considered radio art—have also likewise been broadcasted. By means of appropriate fees for commissioned works, broadcasters such as WDR (West German Radio) have been able to support and promote artists. But in Germany and internationally, only few artists have received commissions from public service broadcasters. A few open-minded, farsighted producers have played a key role in the development of radio art.

Individual radio artworks, but also series, are associated with a number of publications. On the one hand, these comprise works conceived and designed by artists themselves, for instance audio CDs, photographs, films/videos, graphics and conception drawings, cassettes, artists' books, artists' magazines, objects/multiples, scores, and records. The «visual» artworks that make reference to or

WDR radio play program, Cologne, Germany, 1979.

are based on radio art are, for example, concepts or scores by Gerhard Rühm or Franz Mon, objects or multiples created, for example, in the context of the «on air – on line» sitcom *Familie Auer (Kunstradio)*, or artists' records and audio CDs, for example the signed and numbered audio CD *Radiosonate* by Dieter Roth or the *Radiotaxi* record project. In this sense, the radio art archive is based on the Research Centre's existing inventory of radio artworks published on cassettes, records, or CDs.

On the other hand, documentary materials such as invitations, audio CDs, photographs, correspondence, posters, publications, program booklets, and newspaper or magazine articles are collected at the Research Centre in the context of fonds. These materials are an important addition to radio art as such and make a major contribution to its appreciation.

In this context, then, radio art can be assigned to the sphere of artists' publications to the extent that artists' publications are taken to mean all forms of published and multiplied art. Hence, the paradigms of artists' publications are also of relevance for radio art.[7] For radio artworks are artworks published by radio stations or Internet radio that are based on the transmission of «acoustic signals.» Similar to newspaper, book, or record, radio is a mass medium that artists use to create artistic products, meaning artworks. The production of radio art programs is much influenced by a democratization of art, which should be accessible and affordable for everyone. Potentially everyone who could hear radio in a station's broadcast radius would be able to listen to a radio artwork broadcast by this station. The artists' intention in this regard has been to reach not only a small «elitist» group of people but as many as possible. By abandoning the idea of the original in art, this new conception of art has manifested itself in a special way in artists' publications and in the particular independence from the art context that radio has offered. The artists' programs have become fora for their own individual, artistic public. At the same time, the artists have conquered the public space. With their actions, happenings, performances, concerts, cabarets—having taken place on the street, in universities, and in all manner of places—they have not only blasted traditional conceptions of art, integrating the viewer and leaving the spaces traditionally allocated to artists. Moreover, this has led to the creation

<hr />

7   The following comments are based strongly on the following essay: Anne Thurmann-Jajes, «Ein künstlerisch-kommunikativer Zwischenbereich: Zur Bedeutung des künstlerischen Beziehungsgeflechts im Kontext der Künstlerpublikationen der 1960er bis 1980er Jahre,» in *Künstlerpublikationen: Ein Genre und seine Erschließung in Bibliotheken, Museen und Sammlungen*, vol. 2, ed. Sigrid Schade and Anne Thurmann-Jajes (Cologne: Salon Verlag, 2008).

of numerous radio art programs. The artists who have been working with radio (and/or at local stations) have also been involved in the international exchange of artists' publications that, starting from correspondence art, was based on the achievements of mail art, having led in the nineteen-sixties through eighties to an international network of artists transcending all political borders. They sent each other their works on cassette and later on CD, often for publication without any copyright. The focus of their intention was on art as information. Some cassettes even got through to radio art producers at public service broadcasting corporations but were only rarely broadcasted, owing to the inadequate sound quality compared with radio standards. Hence, artists have used radio to present their artistic concepts, building a public that they had themselves initiated and that may also be regarded in the sense of a counter-public. By way of studio productions, the work of a few pirate radios or independent stations, dedicated airtime on local stations or *Bürgerrundfunk* (community broadcasting), as it is known in Germany, artists have attained institutional independence but have almost always worked without a budget or fee, paying any costs or charges for airtime themselves. The programs have taken place in a state of artistic independence, with the autonomy of the artist as the declared aim.

Radiotaxi, Edizioni Lotta Poetica & Studio Morras, Verona and Napoli, Italy, 1982–84.

Radio art began, starting in the nineteen-sixties, evolving very slowly in Germany, France, Italy, the Netherlands, Austria, Sweden, Spain, and so on—earlier in some countries, later in others. The artists created and broadcasted radio art within the framework of the disparate national media-political situations and according to the possibilities available in public service or independent broadcasting stations. The situation was quite different in the countries of Eastern Europe, where in many countries such as Hungary, Poland, the Czech Republic, or Slovakia an official radio art had been emerging since the seventies within the framework of the state-censored media, but where an independent radio art scene was in some cases also forming in the underground. In South America, alternative conceptual artists had only limited access to the radio medium in many countries during the military dictatorship era, for example in Brazil, where Paolo Bruscky's weekly *Rádio Clube* series was broadcast in the seventies. As a result of media developments that were due in part to the geographical size of these countries, the United States, Canada, and Australia saw the arrival of specific broadcasting systems that led, among other things, to the aforementioned local radio stations and that were set up almost everywhere in Canada. Special radio art projects were thus likewise developed in these countries as early as the sixties.

Problems in Defining Radio Art

The term «radio art» is problematic due to its complexity, as there is no radio art «as such.» Rather, a creative, conceptual breadth of artistic analysis of radio technology, radio as a mass medium, and the perception or effect of radio must be discussed. The question of what exactly is—or should be—classified as radio art and what not cannot always be answered definitively. The vast sphere of broadcasted radio art is concentrated in two premises:

- The restriction to broadcasted material, material intended for broadcast, and broadcasting material.
- The focus on works by visual artists, including works by inter-disciplinary writers and musicians.[8]

8 Works by sound artists or musicians who work exclusively with digital music, for example, are not classified as radio art.

Consequently, radio art dwells in an artistically interdisciplinary sphere in the context of visual art, experimental literature, and new music. This breadth is also reflected in the art movements in which the various works of radio art may be set: conceptual art, conceptualism, electroacoustic art, electronic music, digital music, Fluxus, land art, sound poetry, mail art, minimal art, musique concrète, new music, performance, pop art, telematic art, video art, visual and concrete poetry, et cetera.

In view of the complexity of individual forms, a definition of radio art must describe the dependencies and conditions of these forms. In this respect, that means finding a structure in which the various interdisciplinary and intermedia forms of artistic analysis of radio may be positioned and classified. Indirectly, this allows an overview of radio art and creates a basis for attempting to define and differentiate radio art. However, it must also be taken into account that radio artworks have been created and broadcasted in the context of a wide range of radio broadcasts and programs, literary, musical, and artistic trends and developments. Without these extended contexts—also leading to a kind of «fraying» of possible definitions—it is not possible to understand radio art in its diversity. For the artists have not aimed to conform to definitions or categories of radio art—instead some of them have themselves explained their conception of radio art.

With regard to broadcasted radio art, four values can be distinguished that help define radio art or classify radiophonic works. They may also be described as subgenres of radio art.

1. Original radio art comprises works by visual artists that were specially conceived for broadcasting on the radio and that usually reflect on the medium. These programs, often live and unpredictable, represent radio by artists in the most original sense. The basis of radio artworks is a concept often recorded in a score or written/drawn form, in which the focus is on language or sound as material as opposed to a narration or story. The individual genres or varieties in which radio art can occur are based on sound and, at the same time, demonstrate the diversity of conceptions and possible artistic implementations: collage, discussion, documentation, feature, radio play (*Hörspiel*), audio piece (*Hörstück*), composition, concert, live mix, mixed media, noise, performance, remix, road movie, radio essay/radiophonic text, soundscape, sound sculpture, et cetera.

Radio art is manifested in individual series, projects, or programs. Series are identical to individual programs, such as *Kunstradio*, being explicitly dedicated in their entirety to radio art in its various forms. Series may last for a year or even span over several years or decades. In the context of broadcasted radio art, radio art projects are radio programs combined under a title, with individual works linked in a topic or by different artists. They constitute certain more or less fixed episodes in a set period of time and may last for a few days, weeks, or months. Individual programs are radio artworks created by artists independently of series or projects or individually in all types of broadcasting contexts. They are produced by one or several artists.

Almost every series also features productions that cannot be referred to as radio art. Often they are by writers or musicians, for example Karlheinz Stockhausen, Luigi Nono, Phil Glas, or Terry Riley, whose work was not explicitly cross-discipline but who did have a great influence on visual artists. Their works cannot be classified as radio art but rather as literature or music, specifically new music or electronic music, but they are part of the Research Centre radio art archive as they have proven extremely important in the context of the development of radio art—for one, because of the principle of origin and, furthermore, because of their significance and influence. These programs are appropriately flagged in the archive.

2. Networked projects are extensive cross-media and, often, international radio art projects that take place synchronously or asynchronously under one title, frequently in conjunction with events such as performances, festivals, or exhibitions. Via phone, Internet, radio, and/or satellite transmission, artists work simultaneously at multiple locations—at broadcasting stations, art centers, that is, museums or galleries, concert halls, studios, semipublic spaces such as university buildings, or in the «public space»—in different countries and sometimes in a global network to create a joint, temporary artwork. The focus is on the networked production by the artists and not necessarily on what the individual artists produce and release into the network.

Three different levels of networked projects can be distinguished, each of which takes place in a different way depending on the particular concept. Pure broadcasting projects involve several broadcasting stations, creating productions on the basis of an exact score. They are either broadcasted simultaneously straight away or first compiled into a mix according to the score and then broadcasted simultaneously. The stations are, so to speak, distributed voices in a distributed «radio orchestra» with a «conductor.» On a second level, artists in different places are networked with each other and participate in the joint production, although one artist usually acts as director on the basis of his or her score. Most complex are networked projects in which all participating nodes, be they broadcasting stations or an individual artist in his or her flat or studio, are equal partners who simultaneously transmit and receive and then process and resend what they receive. The various streams may be incorporated on-site into radio programs, performances, or installations, thus reaching a local audience as different part versions of the overall project. Such versions being created at individual nodes of the network can then be input into the network again. This is a constant exchange in the course of which nothing persists and everything changes, a continually changing give-and-take in which the whole cannot be perceived. Everything that the individual radio stations broadcast during their more or less limited airtime, for example, can never be more than an excerpt, a local selection from the whole, a small version of a far larger overall work. The individual artistic contributions may be anything, from readings to concerts, installations or performances, without being a radio artwork themselves in the strict sense.

3. Objects, net artworks, environments, interventions, or installations conceived on the basis of radio or transmission technologies constitute one area of radio art as such that exists outside the realm of broadcasting and which is often referred to as «expanded radio.» In the wealth of technical transmission and communications media that were developed on the basis of the invention of radio technology, it is practically irrelevant which transmission technologies (Slow Scan, GPS, etc.) the artists have used for their works, the crucial factor being the artistic intention or conception geared to radio and its media manifestations. Quite a few artists

have criticized the paradigm and forms of radio as a mass medium with their installations, developing alternative models of communication. The works are capable of transferring information, outputting received signals, or transmitting autonomously. On the one hand, they are increasingly being classified as media art or telecommunications art and, on the other hand, as broadcasted radio art since their sound versions can be broadcasted on radio. Such broadcasted radio versions are usually one or several excerpts from the whole sound material that are representative of the work. The authorized selection by the various artists makes them an autonomous work in the context of broadcasting. As acoustic artworks, the broadcasted work references are an integral part of the radio art archive.

4. Like radio art, sound art is situated on the borderline between art, music, and literature. Every work of sound art is potentially suitable for broadcasting on air. Radio has played a key role in its dissemination, as it has allowed the artists to reach a larger audience, to disseminate the works and make them known. For sound poetry and acoustic poetry, radio has become the culminating medium. But at this juncture, radio is just a medium that serves the sole purpose of technical transmission of readings, sound poetry, spoken texts, and much more. Sound art is not primarily geared to broadcasting on the radio, but rather its distribution is by means of sound recording media such as the record, cassette, and audio CD or by means of live presentations such as readings or text recitals. Sound art and its nineteen-twenties beginnings formed one of the preconditions for radio art, having played a key role in the emergence and development of artists' treatment of radio. Sound art and radio art have a «reciprocal relationship.» For one, broadcasted sound art constitutes an expanded sphere of radio art, and secondly, radio art published on sound recording media may be seen as a subset of sound art, as a generic label for auditory and acoustic artistic works.

In addition, the radio art archive will feature a secondary sphere of radio art. This will comprise programs about radio art in the narrower sense. As of the nineteen-seventies, radio art was appraised directly via radio, specifically by the protagonists of the radio art scene, who hailed from literature (e.g. Klaus Schöning,

AKROSTICHON FÜR JOHN CAGE (1986)

```
                                        jodeln
                            jodeln      orchester
                jodeln      orchester   hafen
    jodeln      orchester   hafen       niesen

jetzt   offen       hier        nennen
        jetzt       offen       hier
                    jetzt       offen
                        jetzt

                                                    jodeln
                                        jodeln      orchester
                            jodeln      orchester   hafen
            jodeln          orchester   hafen       niesen
            orchester       hafen       niesen      celesta
            hafen           niesen      celesta     atmen
            niesen          celesta     atmen       gong
            celesta         atmen       gong        explosion

chor            all             gang            ewig
nennen          chor            all             gang
hier            nennen          chor            all
offen           hier            nennen          chor
    jetzt       offen           hier            nennen
                    jetzt       offen           hier
                                    jetzt       offen
                                                    jetzt
```

```
die wörter unter der trennlinie werden gesprochen, die wörter über der
linie bezeichnen geräusche. die obige notation ist eine vereinfachende
(platzsparende) darstellung, denn die gesprochenen wörter beziehungs-
weise die geräusche überlappen sich nicht, sondern sind unmittelbar
aneinandergeschnitten (es handelt sich um ein tonbandstück), wobei
sich beide gruppen in ihrem simultanen ablauf vom jeweiligen gemein=
samen ansatzpunkt an gegeneinander (ihren einzelnen dauern entspre-
chend) verschieben. jede wort- beziehungsweise geräuschwiederholung
erscheint um eine lautstärkenstufe leiser ("jodeln" und "jetzt" haben
demnach von normal abnehmend acht kontinuierlich differenzierte laut-
stärkegrade); zugleich verändern sich mit den wiederholungen die ton-
höhen - diese allerdings gegenläufig: die geräusche nach oben, die ge=
sprochenen wörter nach unten.
```

the words below the dividing line are spoken, the words above the dividing line indicate noises. the above notation is a simplified (space-saving) representation as the spoken words and the noises do not overlap but are rather cut together (this is one tape recording), with both groups shifting against each other in their simultaneous sequence from their respective common starting point (according to their respective durations); every repetition of a word or noise appears one volume level quieter (thus, «jodeln/yodel» and «jetzt/now» have eight continuously differentiated volume levels decreasing from normal level); at the same time, the pitches change with each repetition, albeit in the opposite direction: the noises go up, while the spoken words go down.

Gerhard Rühm, *Akrostichon für John Cage*, radio play partitura (*Hörspielpartitur*), 1986.

Klaus Ramm, and Helmut Heißenbüttel), or music (e.g. Hans Otte), or visual art (e.g. Heidi Grundmann). Like radio art as such, this stock of radio programs was absolutely not previously available to the public and, being time-bound features, are usually not repeated by radio stations. These secondary sources are, however, an important basis for the scientific research of radio art. Programs about radio art and sound art from this period are particularly apt reflections of the atmosphere and authenticity of the works from the sixties to eighties.

Compilation and Indexing in the Radio Art Archive

The Research Centre's radio art archive is conceived as a «work in progress» and is intended to contain as many important international programs and projects as possible both from public service broadcasters and autonomous independent stations. In addition, it will feature projects and programs by individual artists who have worked completely independently. Initially, the archive will feature Europe in the form of programs by *Kunstradio* at ORF in Vienna, having become one of the most important exponents of radio art since 1987, the *Studio Akustische Kunst* at WDR, *Ars Sonora* at RNE, and also *pro musica nova* at Radio Bremen, which, apart from a few concerts, has not explicitly represented radio art but was the first interdisciplinary series as of 1961, having since exerted a great influence on visual arts. Other series or projects originate in Canada, France, Great Britain, the United States, and so forth. In addition, the archive will integrate the radiophonic works of the precursors of radio art, such as Hans Flesch or Orson Welles, from the nineteen-twenties and thirties, along with the aforementioned secondary programs about radio art as a separate section.

The breadth of radio art archivization takes place at three levels. Firstly, it involves digital archivization of the radio artworks proper (audio files), secondly compilation of the radio artwork metadata, the associated «visual» artworks, and documentary material. Thirdly, archivization also involves physical safekeeping of the artworks and documentary material, meaning proper storage and correct conservational packaging, physical retrievability, and permanent preservation with on-site measures regarding personnel, technology, and space without time limitations. The first step of archivization is compilation, which involves ascertaining

9 See Angelika Menne-Haritz, *Schlüsselbegriffe der Archivterminologie*, 3rd ed. (Marburg: Archivschule Marburg, 2000), pp. 63–64.

10 Ibid., p. 67.

and identifying the archive material. Indexing is comprised of two tasks: itemization and ordering. The result is the inventory represented in the finding aid.[9]

The radio art archive inventory has been structured in order to make radio art readily accessible and available to interested parties on-site. For this purpose, the archive was roughly structured or divided to provide a general overview by country, with the individual series and radio art projects, and by international networked projects and individual broadcasts. The list of contents contains a structured list of all recording units for each item. The finding aid is drawn up on this basis and contains all of the indexed individual works according to this division.[10]

Itemization of the radio artwork metadata is of particular importance since, to begin with, it has never before been compiled in its full breadth, and because, furthermore, it is necessary to research all data for indexing, and this data usually cannot be ascertained from the work. Without this data, no basis exists for classification by content and structure, which is, however, necessary for scientific indexing. But the first step was to work out the necessary facts for compilation in the context of the radio art archive and to generalize and verify these in the context of criteria, so as to define data fields for indexing. Along with basic data, for example artist name and title, it is also necessary to compile broadcasting data and additional information on the work's creation and reception history. Compilation of this information or data is based on facts that are sometimes easier, sometimes more difficult to research.

The situation is quite different when it comes to the details of the work itself and its classification. For example, it may be difficult to ascertain the material and technology involved, as it is not, or only rarely, possible to identify the technological processes just by listening. What technological process did the artist use, what material was employed to create the sound? Without any immediate information, it is not always possible to say whether the acoustic material is found or recorded. Was the artist able to work autonomously in the studio or did the institutional context have to be taken into account? How can networked projects be indexed, the different links reflected? How can a program based on an action or installation be correctly archived? Can the installation references be reflected in their entirety? How can radio artworks or projects be archived in terms of content? How can thematic links of the works and the intentions of the artists be taken into account and recorded? Is it possible to archive the meaning of a work?

At this point it becomes clear that radio art—like artists' publications in general—cannot be archived by recording art-related and discographical data alone. Compilation, as it is performed in a collection of art, for example, must be supplemented by archival indexing. This means that, in the context of a finding aid index, it is necessary to integrate additional information in the form of various texts on a particular work and special aspects of the works. These additional texts consist of descriptions and explanatory information, in-depth background information, and texts from secondary literature.

In view of its diversity and interdisciplinarity, compiling and indexing radio art can only be performed in conjunction with and on the basis of references to art studies, literary studies and musicology, technology, media, archivization and discography, as well as in terms of content and context. As a result of the complexity involved, a complete appraisal and representation of radio artworks can probably only be successfully accomplished in close cooperation with the specific artists and radio station producers. In this respect, indexing radio art is impossible without research.

Documentation versus Authenticity

The radio art archive consists of digitized acoustic material that is stored and made available on a server on the basis of the finding aid. The archive of individual radio artwork audio data is thus a digital archive that raises several questions regarding the artistic value of the archived radio art. Is radio art only art in the context of broadcasting? What does the archivization of radio art imply for radio art? How is the space of radio to be understood? What does documentation mean in this context?

Documentation signifies proving, preparing, and transmitting information and knowledge. A document is a record, a piece of evidence detached from the context of its creation and having lost the context of its formation.[11]

In this sense, the digitized and archived radio artwork would be a document, as it is not broadcasted, or is not in the process of being broadcasted. It would correspond to documentation in the presentation and verification of a broadcasted work, or in terms of the notion of broadcasting a specific work as such. Listening

11 Ibid., p. 59.

to radio thus implies the experience of listening at a specified time, at a particular locality, on the basis of a specific transmission technology, in an irretrievable mood and atmosphere, and with the knowledge that thousands of other people are having the same experience at the same time, thus giving rise to a radiophonic metaspace. The listener has a very special perception of a unique moment. The radio artwork is geared to this perception. The archived radio artwork, however, is diametrically opposed to these contexts, all of which are no longer true. Archivization turns the radio artwork into a contextless document. Although, in all honesty, only a live program—be it a terrestrial or digital broadcast—really conforms to this perception. Thus, when considering the perception of radio programs, it is necessary to distinguish between live programs, analog programs, repeats, digitized and digital programs. Programs for which special contracts were concluded with the artists or that are public domain—which, again, radio art programs from the sixties to eighties were not—can be placed online.

But how is the perception of Internet radio different, where programs remain permanently available? The digital radio artwork can be perceived at any time, in any place, with a delay, in unlimited repetitions, in a wide variety of situations. The situation with digital radio art is thus the same as with archived radio art.

RADIO ART: The End
of the Graven Image,
brochure with texts by
Willem de Ridder and
William Levy, ed. Gallery
A, Amsterdam (1981).

The various states of existence of radio art must therefore be assessed differently for analog and for digital radio art. While for analog-broadcasted radio art, publication of records, cassettes, audio CDs, and archivization constitute a documentation, the situation with digitally broadcasted radio art is different. Internet stream, podcast, audio CDs, and archivization correspond to an identical perception, the possibility of individual reception that can be retrieved for listening at any time. The development of digital media has also altered perception of radio, of radio art—signifying that Internet radio is no longer radio in the original sense of analog radio, that podcast already implies archivization, and that radio has ceased to exist as an experience of a broadcast, as an irretrievably lost moment. The podcast manifests the sign of the end of radio, the end of a unique radiophonic perception. But is it also the end of the authenticity of a radio artwork?

Technological development has turned radio into a digital medium that no longer has de jure anything in common with the perception of analog radio, while de facto nothing has changed in terms of the individual broadcast. The recipient does not distinguish between terrestrial and digital radio, although the reception options of digital radio and online representation are convenient for the listener and also the artist. Yet radio as a symbolic medium can also be expected to disintegrate in years to come, to be assimilated in social communication in the context of a «multifunctional medium.» Although perception changes, among other things due to the changed behavior of recipients, authenticity remains. The authenticity of the recording and of the moment of reception becomes the authenticity of the broadcast, regardless of the form of transmission or reproduction.

> In the twentieth century, authenticity is not a state that results from the one, true, good, right, beautiful determinant, but rather is the result of a certification process taking place in a locality and at a certain time, which may occur again and again without guarantee ... Such a nonnormative aesthetic concept of authenticity would thus be a concept bound to space and time that structurally reflects mediality.[12]

12 Susanne Knaller, «Genealogie des ästhetischen Authentizitätsbegriffs,» in *Authentizität: Diskussion eines ästhetischen Begriffs*, ed. Susanne Knaller and Harro Müller (Munich: Wilhelm Fink, 2006), pp. 32–33. Translation of quotation provided by Richard Watts

Accordingly, authenticity would be the same in terrestrial and digital radio and geared solely to the broadcast as such. And indeed, radio as a phenomenon per se is still regarded as a supposedly «transitory» moment regardless of the form of broadcasting. This understanding impacts authenticity, leading to a wish among many listeners to record individual programs or to order recordings, so as to be able to listen to them at any time and, indirectly, to counteract this transient aspect. For the digital is equally volatile and irrecoverably deleted at the push of a button. For scientific access to radio art in the form of an open-access radio art archive, in contrast, the individual radio artwork becomes the documentation of its media-based function. As such, the archive as a non-authentic place or authentic non-place is the only place where authenticity still exists.

Radio in the Chiasme[1]

Tetsuo Kogawa

Radio has been analyzed by the set of two concepts: sender and receiver, or sending and receiving. This is a convenient metaphor, but it prevents an understanding of what is really happening in radio. In my view, the sending-receiving metaphor is wrong. As Maturana and Varela have already argued, «there is no ‹transmitted information› in communication» but «communication takes place each time there is behavioral coordination in a realm of structural coupling.»[2] It is necessary to understand radio as a «structural coupling» and as a holistic event.

Radio has been seeking to further the range of the service area. This corresponds to the basic trend of the machine technology underlying the invention of the steam engine, the functionally required spatial environment, and the modern lifestyle. Now that the machine technology is finally ending and has been integrated into the electrodigital technology, radio is gradually less interested in expanding its service area. In fact, it becomes technically easier to cover the entire world with sounds and images by using satellites and the Internet. No longer too much energy for expanding. That's why digital radio and high-definition television is up-to-date. However, exploration and exploitation of the quality of sound and image will not fulfill the most radical potential of radio. What do we see behind the horizon of the end of modernist use or radio? What is the new potential of radio in the age of post-electrodigital technology?

Increase of channels and stations is only a development of content. The structural relationship between transmission and reception has not been significantly different, even in community radio, micro radio, and digital radio. They are not free from conveying messages and cannot overcome the sender-receiver metaphor. If transmission and reception are considered different in structure, concepts such as «content» and «form» must be reconsidered. If the point is re-invention of radio, it should be done both in the transmitting and receiving form and in the content. But the more important point would be a structural re-coupling of radio in transmission and reception.

Consciously or unconsciously, radio art has been providing many experiments of such re-coupling. As an art form, radio art need not be concerned with conveying messages. The Futurists critically pushed the message to the wall of anti-message, but John Cage overcame the modernist antagonism and dichotomy. Mini FM, the postmodern radio, turned out to constitute a unique challenge for changing the structure of radio transmission and reception. Given the limited and much smaller service area as compared to community radio, the listener had to come closer to the station for catching the airwaves; then the station became a party place and «radio party» started. Intentionally and accidentally, Mini FM neglected to broad-cast and even narrow-cast: it deconstructed «cast» (a throwing out) itself. Phenomenologically bracketing the range of transmitting airwaves, radio party of Mini FM found a micro model of the structural coupling of transmission and reception.[3]

Radio is not only a media form but also a phenomenon of radiation. This argument lets us re-think radio from a different perspective and reminds us that radio is, first and foremost, an emitting action/process rather than receiving, as receiving would be the counterpart of transmitting. In any physical process, there is no receiving process that is simply passive as is, in the beginning, radio emission.

1 Maurice Merleau-Ponty, *Le visible et l'invisible* (Paris: Gallimard, 1964), p. 172. English translation: Maurice Merleau-Ponty, *The Visible and the Invisible*, trans. Alphonso Lingis (Evanston: Northwestern University, 1968), p. 130.

2 Humberto R. Maturana and Francisco J. Varela, *The Tree of Knowledge* (Boston: Shambhala, 1992), p. 196.

3 More in Tetsuo Kogawa, «Toward Polymorphous Radio,» in *Radio Rethink* (Banff: Walter Phillips Gallery, 1994), p. 287. See also http://anarchy.translocal.jp/non-japanese/radiorethink.html.

4 Denis de Rougemont, *Penser avec les mains* (Paris: Gallimard, 1972), p. 151: «de penser avec ses mains [est] la vraie condition de l'homme.» At the Radiophonic 2003 festival, I presented my radio art performance under the theme of «hands.»

5 Merleau-Ponty 1964 (see note 1), p. 176: «Par ce recroisement en elle [mon main] du touchant et du tangible, ses mouvements propres s'incorporent à l'univers qu'ils interrogent, sont reportés sur la même carte que lui.» Translation quoted from Merleau-Ponty 1968 (see note 1), p. 133.

Even receiving by a radio set emits something. An action of radio transmission and reception would be a kind of self-oscillation, and the relationship between this action and the audience would be a resonance that induces our various emotions that literally move our body.

My performance series using tiny transmitters comprises an aspect of experimenting with such a re-coupling by minimizing the range of transmission and reception. In my radio performance *Penser avec les mains*, the audience is present at the process of transmission-reception initiation, with my hands functioning both as a transmitter and as a receiver, the borders between electronics and human body intertwining.

The point of contact between technology and nature is our body. While Denis de Rougemont wrote that «thinking with the hands» is «the true condition of man,»[4] Merleau-Ponty noted that «through this crisscrossing within it [my hand] of the touching and the tangible, its own movements incorporate themselves into the universe they interrogate, are recorded on the same map as it.»[5] If our hands are the minimal unit of our body, to transmit and receive with my hands might temporarily provide a visual and audible process where technology, art, and our existence resonate together.

Tetsuo Kogawa, *de-Radia transversal*,
performance live «on air – on line – on site,»
musikprotokoll, Graz, Austria, 2007.

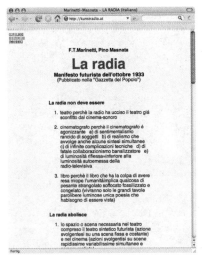

Robert Adrian and Nobert Math, *Radiation*, screenshots, 2002.

Radiation

An Installation for Shortwave Radio
by Robert Adrian and Norbert Math

In the second year of the twentieth century, the signals from Guglielmo Marconi's first transatlantic radio transmission[1] began their journey across the solar system. Since then, radio waves have become as common as air, and our planet has become a new source of radio waves in the galaxy. All the radio signals ever produced since Marconi's experiment are still radiating outwards through space. The history of our century exists at the speed of light in the dark spaces between the worlds.

Marconi's radio used long wavelengths requiring very large antennas for transmission and reception. This remained the case for about twenty years — until the technicians trained for the First World War returned home and began to experiment with shortwave technology. It was discovered that shortwave signals could be transmitted thousands of miles by being bounced off the ionosphere.

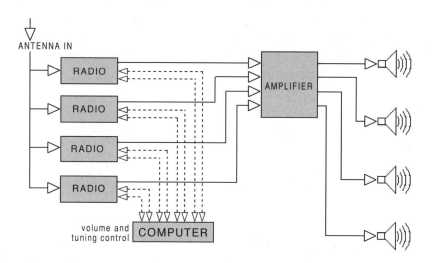

Robert Adrian and Nobert Math, *Radiation*,
concept diagram, 2002.

By the mid-thirties, all the major countries were employing shortwave radio for military and diplomatic communication. During the Second World War, radio technology became more sophisticated in response to the need for communication with armies and navies spread out across the world, for the rapid deployment and control of air forces, as well as for subversive information warfare involving encryption, deception, and propaganda.

The *RADIATION* project concentrates on shortwave radio—the wavelengths used mostly by security and espionage agencies, national propaganda and information stations, and by amateur radio operators. Many shortwave transmissions are received as bursts of coded or scrambled signal—Morse, fax, or image transmissions and secret commercial or political data. The shortwave spectrum contains every human language and every kind of music. Shortwave signals are often distorted by atmospheric conditions, bursts of electromagnetic activity on the Sun, interference from other transmitters, or local static—with shortwave radio, it is «radio» itself that is in the foreground.

Project Description

The sounds from four shortwave radio receivers, each tuned to a different source, are fed into an amplifier and distributed to four loudspeakers installed about 400 cm apart and 3 meters high A computer program controls the receivers so that they are always tuned to active and interesting sources.

There were four versions of *RADIATION*:

1998:   installed at Ars Electronica '98.
2002:   installed at the *Broadcasting – dedicated to Nikola Tesla* exhibition, Technical Museum, Zagreb.
2004:   installed at *Re-Inventing Radio*, Radiokulturhaus, Vienna[2]
2006:   installed at the *Waves* exhibition, Latvian National Museum of Art, Riga.

1   See http://www.ucs.mun.ca/~jcraig/marconi .html.
2   The big public concert hall and its radio studio at the ORF Broadcasting House, Vienna, was one of the sites of the *Re-Inventing Radio LongNight of Radio Art*, an internationally networked «on air – on site – on line» event with eight hours of live broadcasts from Vienna and Linz on the national cultural radio channel Österreich 1. Other parts of *Re-Inventing Radio*, September 2004, were a conference and three on-site projects at the Ars Electronica Festival (r a d i o q u a l i a: *Radio Astronomy*, Smith/Wintner: *Audiomobile*, and *The Time Machine*, an installation by Aleksandar Vasiljević). See also: http://kunstradio.at/PROJECTS/REINVENTING/index .php?c=3.

Robert Adrian and Nobert Math, *Radiation*,
installation, *Broadcasting*, Technical Museum,
Zagreb, Croatia, 2002.

Robert Adrian and Norbert Math, *Radiation*,
installation, *Waves*, Latvian National Museum of Art,
Riga, Latvia, 2006.

RADIATION RADIO VERSION, Technical Museum Zagreb and Vienna. *Kunstradio* Studio, Broadcasting House, Vienna, 2002.

For the *Kunstradio* broadcast,[3] the Zagreb installation had been expanded to include four microphones, a mixing desk, a computer for MP3 encoding, and an Internet connection:

- The four microphones were placed on stands in front of the loudspeakers.
- The signals from the microphones were fed into the mixing desk for Norbert Math to mix and encode them as an MP3 stream for the Internet.
- In Vienna, the MP3 stream from Zagreb was fed into the mixing desk in ORF studio RP4 for sound engineer Gerhard Wieser to make the broadcast version, mixing the Zagreb stream with the original material («*La Radia*» by Marinetti and Masnata converted to Morse Code).
- The Vienna mix was broadcast in stereo over VHF on ORF Österreich 1, in mono over shortwave on Radio Austria International, and re-encoded as Real Audio for *Kunstradio On Line* where it can be accessed from the *Kunstradio* home page.
- The shortwave signal from Radio Austria International was received in Zagreb by at least one of the radios in the installation and played over the loudspeakers where it was picked up by the microphones and recycled through the system.[4]

3 See http://kunstradio.at/2002A/27_01_02.html.
4 For more information, see http://alien.mur.at/ rax/BIO/ and http://kunstradio.at/2002A/27 _01_02/index.html.

Distory

100 Years of Electron Tubes, Media-Archaeologically Interpreted vis-à-vis 100 Years of Radio

Wolfgang Ernst

Reginald Fessenden's «radio broadcast» on Christmas Eve, December 24, 1906 may still echo in our ears—but regular entertainment radio, meaning radio in the mass-media sense, did not start even in the U.S. until November 1920. Not until then does radio in the classic sense begin, ending the media-archaeological epoch of radio, in which the primary message of the medium was not the structured, macrotemporal programming flow (the «flow» defined in Cultural Studies),[1] but rather the electromagnetic frequencies themselves, oscillating in the time-critical range literally as «sparks.»

It's not the inherent time of electronic media but instead the old-fashioned historical discourse that engenders the logic of calendrical cycles of memory according to the law of symbolic figures in our decimalized culture («100 years,» while the ancient Babylonians, for example, already would have celebrated after «60 years» based on the sexadecimal system—and we promptly impinge upon sixty years of the tube-based electron computer, the ENIAC [Electronic Numerical Integrator And Computer], as we will take up later). What meaning do these advent-of-radio dates have, besides the fact that they—to the delight of today's broadcasting institutions like the ORF—produce a whole series of «anniversaries» (1906 into the nineteen-twenties), thus up to the year 2020 and beyond; in

Vienna, the state-owned RAVAG has been broadcasting official news and music for detector receivers since 1924. According to my thesis, all of these dates fail to mark the beginning but rather signify the end of radio as a producer of media knowledge; the beginning of radio as mass medium refers to yet a different radio.

100 Years of Radio?

Still remembered well by me is how in Germany «75 years of radio» were celebrated (approximately) in October 1998 on the part of the *Deutsches Runkfunkarchiv* (German Radio Archive) with special radio shows and multimedia websites featuring the first public radio broadcast from the Vox House building in Berlin. My meager arithmetic skills tell me that in the time between 1998 and today, that is, in a good eight years, the time span between 75 years of radio and 100 years of radio cannot already have passed—unless media time itself generates, in terms of Minkowski and Einstein, a spatial and temporal dilation. The media-archeological view virtually lurks, waiting for such moments of uncertainty in order to formulate them as opportunities for venturing other means of perception, for blazing other memory trails—as an alternative to the media historical viewpoint.

At first glance, we seem to be experiencing an anniversary in media history: one century of radio. But is radio, when playing, ever in a historical state? Isn't it in fact always in a present one? The medium only appears to conform to the logic of historical epochal concepts; in actuality, it undermines this logic and sets a different temporal economy. For example, an original recording resonating today from an old tube radio, provided it can still run on 220 volts, hardly makes history audible. A tube radio thus practices *compressed* time as respects our sensory perception, as long as this is not overlaid with «historical meaning,» which cognitively does not correspond to the actual media workings of radio but rather to the logic of inscribed historiography.

Let's now examine the question of the temporality of electronic media. What about the being and time of radio? Seemingly historical media objects are purely

1 See Raymond Williams, *Television: Technology and Cultural Form*, 2nd ed. (1975; repr., London: Routledge, 1990).

2 Martin Heidegger, *Being and Time*, trans. John Macquarrie and Edward Robinson (New York: Harper Collins, 1962), pp. 431-32. For the original German publication, see Martin Heidegger, *Sein und Zeit*, 16th ed. (Tübingen: Niemeyer Verlag, 1986), p. 380.

of the present time as soon as they function. Martin Heidegger already asked in 1927: «How far is such equipment historical, when it is *not yet* past? ... Or do these ‹Things› have ‹in themselves› ‹something past,› even though they are still present-at-hand today?» What's past—even after 100 years of radio—is «nothing else than that *world* within which they belonged to a context of equipment and were encountered as ready-to-hand and used by a concernful Dasein who was-in-the-world ... But what was formerly *within-the-world* with respect to that world is still present-at-hand.»[2] The within-the-world existence of radio 100 years ago—in keeping with this timing—pinpoints a media-epistemological artifact at the heart of radio, namely the (at that time new) electron tube, an electrotechnical artifact in the interspace of radio, its soul.

In 1906, the year Lee de Forest patented his triode tube, radio was above all still an epistemological entity for generating knowledge on the essence of electromagnetic waves themselves. During the same year, the Viennese telephone factory owner Robert von Lieben registered a patent for an amplifier tube in the form of a cathode-ray relay. His invention is referenced by Albert Einstein in a Berlin speech held on August 22, 1930 at the opening of the 7th Great German Radio and Audio Show, aptly addressed to «Honored Listeners, Present and Absent» (to

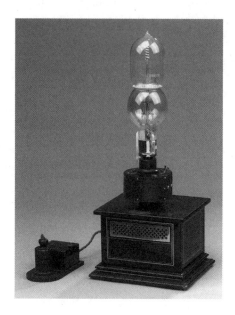

Robert von Lieben tube.

which we can still listen today as a message from the depths of the relativistically enmeshed space-time): «Think especially of Lieben, who invented an unprecedented measuring instrument for electric pulses, the electric valve tube. It was also an ideal and simple instrument to generate electric waves.»[3]

The two inventions by von Lieben and de Forest proceeded to copy each other back and forth, helping to spur each other on. In 1907, de Forest applied for a further patent, for he had discovered that the radio tube could not only be employed as an amplifier but could also perform the same work as a crystal detector. Here, the semantic message, the modulated speech (that is, the audible, low-frequency portion), is separated from the high frequency as the actual transmission medium. The essence of the tube-based «Audion circuit» of the receiver is no longer purely electrical but rather cybernetic: feedback. The radio waves, having passed through the Audion, are once again fed back into the input circuit in order to influence it in a way that is favorable for reception. In 1913, Meißner improved on the perfected feedback circuit: the electrical current oscillating in the anode circuit exerts an effect back on the grid circuit, and the feedback builds up until the entire anode current pulsates in the rhythm of the incoming waves. The Audion's anode and grid circuits thus end up resonating—«music» even *before* any acoustic application for human ears. Ever since then, the radio tube has been able not only to improve reception but also to send its own waves out into the ether (*sit venia verbo*).

Von Lieben's patent first applied functionally only to telephony; in actuality, broadcasting before radio was in fact not wireless—radio as a current of electrical sparks—but rather telephone, for example the Telefon Hírmondó wire radio system in Budapest invented in 1893 by Theodor Puskas as a «talking newspaper.»[4] De Forest's tube circuit—with its threefold function of attenuation equalization of the oscillating circuit, demodulation of the HF signal, and amplification of the resulting LF signal—served the purpose of making speech

3 Translation of Einstein's speech, quoted twice within this essay, is excerpted from the following sources: David E. Rowe and Robert Schulmann, eds., *Einstein on Politics: His Private Thoughts and Public Stands on Nationalism, Zionism, War, Peace, and the Bomb* (Princeton: Princeton University Press, 2007), p. 237; http://www.einstein-website.de/z_biography/speechfunkausstellung.html (accessed October 20, 2007).

4 Oskar Blumtritt, *Nachrichtentechnik: Sender, Empfänger, Übertragung, Vermittlung*, 2nd ed. (Munich: Deutsches Museum, 1997), p. 79.

5 On this type of «remote telephone system,» see Franz Pichler, «Telegrafie- und Telefonsysteme des 19. Jahrhunderts,» in *Vom Verschwinden der Ferne: Telekommunikation und Kunst*, ed. Edith Decker and Peter Weibel (Cologne: DuMont, 1990), pp. 253–86, here p. 281.

more understandable, thereby favoring radio in the sense of a mass medium. The name chosen by de Forest for his patent, Audion, itself indicates that his triode vacuum tube was genuinely meant for the broadcast of sonic articulation. In 1910, the system was used to broadcast a performance by the singer Caruso from the Metropolitan Opera in New York; in 1912, de Forest used the electron tube as an oscillator for oscillation generation, thus perfecting wireless telephony.[5] The von Lieben tube, by contrast, served primarily to minimize the distortions in telephone lines, so it literally had a different techno-logical connection; it acted as a relay fortifying the rapidly weakening, electrically converted signals in telephone lines. This made it possible to communicate over distances up to 1,000 kilometers; the electron stream was controlled from outside using a magnetic field (the improved von Lieben tube was the first to be equipped with a control grid). Previously, Valdemar Poulsen had already developed a process to electromagnetically record telephone conversations through induction onto an uncoiling wire. In the Telegraphone, electric voice transmission has found its congenial storage medium, forming, so to speak, a continuum of both processes in the electromagnetic field. Hence, the miracle is explained, that we in principle can still today with electricity hear the language entrusted to this field (whether telephone or radio), articulated 100 years ago, in its own medium (namely, electromagnetism).

Let's listen once again to Einstein's Berlin speech, where he admonishes us: «And everybody should be ashamed who uses the wonders of science and engineering without thinking and having mentally realized not more of it than a cow realizes of the botany of the plants which it eats with pleasure.» Therefore, let us not only consider the role played by the tube in radio but also look into the tube itself, embracing 100 years of radio as 100 years of electron tubes. Although when we treat radio not as mass medium and broadcast format but instead examine the perspective of its concrete epistemological entity, the electron tube, connections emerge to a media temporality at odds with «radio history.» A media theory of the electron tube attempts to contribute to pluralism—the tube as a basis medium, which transversally unites various media complexes (radio, oscilloscope, television, computer). Media-epistemological entities are at odds with those histories that further differentiate media only as the process of such technologies developing into mass media.

Not (merely) the Prehistory,
but the Alternative to the Mass Medium of Radio

The media-archeological early phase of radio represents not merely the prehistory but also the alternative to the mass medium of radio. When Heinrich Hertz discovered that electromagnetic waves propagate by means of high-frequency excitation of an open oscillating circuit, it was the result of a research query. Radio meant at first specifically not language and music but rather radio waves for wireless telegraphy, particularly radio telegraphy in marine radio after 1900. The word «radio» was accordingly meant literally, in order to emphasize the specific properties of electromagnetic fields, namely the radial effect of the waves, broadcasting on the physical plane. It is therefore not enough to characterize radio simply as a device for receiving radio broadcasts, referring primarily to their content. Based on radius, that is, ray, the message is above all the medium: electromagnetic waves and high-frequency electrical signals, transmission, and sound.[6] This is the message that radio underhandedly, thus latently, enunciates to our senses over and over again, notwithstanding all manifest programming significance. The radio of the twentieth century was an ongoing massage[7] for the perception of sound prevailing in occidental culture. The electrotechnical transformation of speech into signals, of signals into waves, into recording and radiation has impressed the collective consciousness with the fact that linguistic meaning in the media always turns into sound, sound into signal, signal into noise; even the voices of leaders and dictators were thus «nothing more than a wave in the air.»[8]

However, wherever academic endowments and grants failed to provide funding for these types of purely inquisitive experiments (for example, the Prussian professorial system), great minds like Thomas Alva Edison were forced to finance their research themselves through marketing. This was likewise the strategy pursued by Guglielmo Marconi, who took up Popov's St. Petersburg experiments with

---

6   This is the explanation given in the German entry under «Radio» in the online encyclopedia Wikipedia, http://de.wikipedia.org/wiki/Radio (accessed December 2006).

7   In the sense of Marshall McLuhan and Quentin Fiore, *Das Medium ist Massage* (Frankfurt am Main et al.: Ullstein, 1984).

8   Paul DeMarinis, text accompanying his installation *Firebirds und Tongues of Fire* at the Singuhr-Hörgalerie of the Parochial Church of Berlin-Mitte, June to August 2004.

9   Hagen Pfau in *Mitteldeutscher Rundfunk: Radio-Geschichten*, ed. Steffen Lieberwirth (Altenburg: Kamprad, 2000), p. 10.

10   This is emphasized by Pfau in ibid., p. 13.

the coherer as thunderstorm detector and combined it with the idea of a transmitting antenna, with man himself replacing the natural lightning as transmitter.
Like Edison, Marconi was also impelled to finance his invention as a business;
he practiced wireless telegraphy. In 1901, communication bridged the Atlantic «using electromagnetic waves for the transport of informative signals.»[9] But
«wireless» has not always been synonymous with radio. The patent registered in
1904 by Marconi's engineer, John Ambrose Fleming, further developed an effect
detected by Edison in light bulbs, by which electricity can flow from filaments to
an additional enclosed electrode, even if no direct contact exists. In his patent
manuscript of 1884, *A Manifestation of the Edison Lamp*, Edison explicitly describes electricity flowing through the vacuum «without wires»—literally «wireless,» radio inside the evacuated, etherless tube itself.

The media-epistemological break is even starker when we speculate on the
birth date of radio: «In order to return to the beginnings of wireless transmission of speech and music, we must separate ourselves from the spark gap transmitters of the first broadcasters. They generated only attenuated, pulse-shaped
waves»[10]—meaning signals, not signs, hardly in a position to transport sounds
and tones to the recipient—which also solves the riddle of why Heinrich Hertz
didn't already consider radio content in his experiments.

Early radio was closer to Morse Code than to what we know as radio today,
or, to put it differently: it was literally digital before it became, through speech
and music modulation, an analog medium. The digital only managed its reentry
through pulse code modulation—with which radio in fact finds its way back to its
original potential as broadcast medium. This being the case, we may reflect on
the year 1906, when the International Wireless Conference in Berlin regulated
the handling of wireless communication, though it was only with the introduction of tube technology that the human voice or music lastingly replaced Morse
Code. Radio is the function of a technological escalation: the tube. The opposite
of such electronics based on low-voltage current was the Telefunken high-frequency machine transmitter of 1912 with a frequency of 10 kHz, which could be
transformed up to 170 kHz, making telephony attempts from Königs Wusterhau-
sen to Vienna possible in 1913. The mechanical limits of this wave generation
virtually forced the paradigm change to the field of nearly inertialess electronics,
the realm of the modulatable electron stream in a vacuum—thus to the electron
tube transmitter. As we know, speech takes place in a frequency range that lies

far beneath those higher frequencies radiated by electric transmitters in free space. Speech must therefore be inscribed as signal flow onto the high-frequency ranges by causing a low frequency generated by speech to *modulate* an emittable high-frequency oscillation. The modulation of electrons is actually the definition of «electronics» as opposed to sheer electricity. The triode invented by de Forest, followed forthwith by von Lieben's further development of the *modulatable* thermionic tube, allowed for just such generation of high-frequency oscillations and the amplification of modulated currents enabling amplitude modulation. Henceforth, *«funken ohne Funken»* was possible, meaning to telegraph wirelessly without sparks, as Ferdinand Braun noted in his Nobel Prize acceptance speech in 1909. Allow me here a moment of frequency ontology: the waves emitted by a tube in combination with an antenna are of an entirely different nature to those of the spark gap transmitter, as only the tube—as an Audion circuit—can emit truly evenly and continuously, thus making it a medium (and not only a machine). Electromagnetic sparks are no longer transmitted *as* encoded information (Morse Code), but they themselves instead constitute a high-frequency medium through which low-frequency signals (speech, music) can then be sent—an escalation of epistemological dimensions.

In the United States, the tube rapidly gave rise to the mass medium of radio, while in more radio(/spark)-oriented Old Europe it long remained primarily an entity of knowledge—an entity *of* and *for* research. When Hertz proved with his experimental setup that electromagnetic waves produced by sparks moving through a gap behave in principle like light waves, this was not the beginning of radio as mass medium but rather the end point of a question of applied media theory—of Aristotelian media theory as the question of what happens in between (*to metaxy*). In a narrower sense, Hertz's experiment was designed as a media-technological verification, namely as the empirical proof of, on its part, an idea couched in theory: Clerke Maxwell's mathematical calculation of the electromagnetic field discovered by Michael Faraday. This was prompted by an incident when, on the experimentation table during Oested's lecture, the surrealistic proximity of a magnetic needle, while an electron stream was being

11 Freely formulated after a contribution by Hartmut Petzold to the workshop «Archäologie, Theorie und Künste der Elektronenröhre,» Kunsthochschule für Medien, Cologne, June 4–5, 1997.

12 Ferdinand Braun, «Ueber ein Verfahren zur Demonstration und zum Studium des zeitlichen Verlaufes variabler Ströme,» in *Annalen der Physik und Chemie* (February 15, 1897).

conducted through a wire, accidentally, as well as necessarily, caused the needle to deflect—the laboratory as media theater. In fact, Faraday with his neologism of an electromagnetic «field» (with which he came to grips, at least semantically, with the induction effect he had discovered experimentally) in effect placed the concept of medium on an epistemologically exciting new basis. From this perspective, the electron tube of 1906 is much more of an end point to 100 years of electromagnetic phenomena analysis. Only then does it switch tracks to herald the birth of further, different 100 years of radio-as-broadcast, which today, in the age of Internet radio, is gradually drawing to a close, while the radio as actual wireless medium in the media-archeological sense is surreptitiously back at work in the form of Radio Frequency Identification (RFID) of goods in our supermarkets, without either speech or music.

100 Years of Radio (Tubes)

A media archeology of 100 years of radio (tubes) makes our uncertainty as to the question of where radio history begins productive as knowledge. It proves impossible to write an organized or even chronological history of development of the tube, because the tube has no linear discursive history but instead, especially in the beginning, followed more of a zigzag course of experimental groping in the dark.[11] For technological archeology, the defect is the true index of the real. The tube is thus a dispositive, compared to which its concrete realizations and differentiations (radio, television, computer) are more representative of deviations.

The von Lieben tube as monument to amplification technology is not necessarily coupled with the radio idea. In the media-archeological phase, medium means primarily measurement. Already before 1906, namely in 1898, Ferdinand Braun discovered the cathode-ray tube as a measuring instrument for time-dependent electrical quantities by way of depicting electrical signals on a fluorescent screen, the media-archeological archetype of the television picture tube.[12] The history of Braun's tube anticipates the history of the tube we know so well from radio. As deployed by Braun, the new medium is at first itself the message: about making visible the oscillations of the new alternating current generator at the Strasbourg electricity works in February 1897. While the radio tube has largely disappeared, replaced by transistors, the picture tube prevails today as television picture tube and as computer monitor, as Franz Pichler wrote just several years ago.[13] It should not be taken for granted in information technology for a device to stay around, retaining its principal, physical mode of functioning over a period of 100 years. But this epoch is now rapidly, even abruptly, coming to an end, as cathode-ray tubes are replaced by flat screens for computer and television—with consequences for their graphic ontology (raster display). On the level of the display, this last stronghold of the «analog,» the culture of electronics, is now also being replaced by the (digital) aesthetic of information. This was already suggested by the alternative use of the cathode-ray tube: while in television the picture tube generates pictures as representations of analog values, its application as computer monitor enables digital display; every pixel here is the function of a binary code word. One and the same (basically analog) electron tube is now an analogizing, now a digitizing entity.

For a Culture of Noise

This is the point at which I lapse into a nostalgic, melancholy tone, as a token of bidding farewell. The trend, discernable at the IFA Consumer Electronics Trade Show 2006 in Berlin, toward digitization of shortwave radio (Digital Radio Mondial)—and the latest rumors indicating a potential shutdown of analog shortwave reception in the U.S.—give us occasion to speculate about the media-epistemological sacrifice associated with this digitization. When broadcasts are transmitted over a digitized mediumwave frequency, we may not hear anything with an analog receiver, but neither do we hear much more than noise—digitally encoded signals cannot be calculated for our ears by the analog receiver.

Digital reception is touted as advantageous due to its elimination of noise; compared to the existing analog AM radio, this means, according to a trade publication: «With DRM ... strong noise and fading in reception are of the past.»[14] But it is not classical radio that is finding its way back to its original potential here,

13 Franz Pichler, «100 Jahre Braunsche Röhre. Ein Jubiläum für einen Interfacebaustein,» *PLUS LUCIS* 2 (1997), pp. 14–16, here p. 14.

14 Thomas Riegler, *DRM. Digital Radio Mondiale: Theorie und Empfangspraxis* (Baden-Baden: Siebel, 2006), p. 13.

15 P.R. Masani, *Norbert Wiener 1894–1964* (Basel et al.: Birkhäuser, 1990), p. 85, citing Norbert Wiener, «The harmonic analysis of irregular motion (Second Paper),» *J. Math. and Phys.* 5 (1926), pp. 99–121, § 6.

16 Norbert Wiener, *I Am a Mathematician: The Later Life of a Prodigy* (New York: Doubleday, 1956), p. 40.

but rather radio transformed into information. Though it may still be electromagnetic waves wafting through the ether, atop them now ride digitized signals, in their capacity as information. Decoding them is an act of mathematics, or mathematics machines, meaning computers, an act that can no longer be mastered by the classical tube radio by means of classic demodulation of high-frequency waves to low-frequency speech and music. Instead, without a decoder, all that can be heard is digital noise, a strange return of noise to the otherwise noise-free space of digital transmission.

Exactly this noise and flickering of electrons in the vacuum tube were what inspired Albert Einstein and Norbert Wiener to equate it with the familiar phenomenon of Braun's molecular movement (for example, of pollen) and with thermodynamics (gas particles) in order to no longer deal with this disorderliness and randomness only electromagnetically and cybernetically, but above all mathematically. At this point, we may commemorate a different «hundred years»: Ludwig Boltzmann, founder of statistical physics, voluntarily took his own life in September 1906. Boltzmann's entropy formula ($S = k * \log W$), which built the first stable bridge between classic physics and nuclear and quantum physics, is chiseled into his gravestone at Vienna's Central Cemetery—time's arrow is relentless. If you throw a tumblerful of water into the sea, you cannot get the same tumblerful out again, noted James Clerk Maxwell, anticipating the concept of the irreversibility of molecular or atomic movements. The same applies to the emission and stream of electrons in the vacuum tube. In the mid-nineteen-twenties, Wiener's attention was drawn to the aptly named «shot effect» in electronic amplification. Einstein had theorized that thermal agitation of electrons in a conductor would generate random fluctuations, and in 1918 Walter Schottky developed the model of this effect further. The so-called «tube noise» was too slight, however, for then-available measuring instruments to pick up; the theoretically proposed shot effect could not be demonstrated experimentally until 1927.[15] When Wiener, like Einstein, discovered the analogy between this shot effect and Braun's molecular movement of organic substances, he interpreted this by applying a basically similar mathematical analysis as the «result of the discreteness of the universe.»[16] The electron tube therewith virtually became a macro monad. Although Leibniz in his monadology believed neither in vacuums nor remote effects, he nonetheless asserted the perceptual capability of remote monads; with a measure of imagination, Wiener therefore sees an «analogy between this mirroring acticity of the monad … and the modern view in which the chief activity of the electrons consists in radiating to one another.»[17] Xenakis's stochastic music conveys the same to our ears in the form of sound clouds.

Computing Radio
Radio as Calculation

It's true that the amplitude modulation of analog radio is already sheer encoding, and speech and music can only be heard when they are demodulated—that is, decoded. Digital transmission works the same way, but this encoding is of a different epistemological and practical nature. What is today entering into the medium of radio is this kind of operational mathematics: computing. Now that the 100-year-old tube has vanished from radio, we can celebrate it anew in connection with computing, depending on one's point of view, as a centennial, as a semicentennial, or as «Babylonian» 60 years.

The decisive escalation of the amplifier tube was—as mentioned—attributable to the fact that it was capable of feedback. This not only made radio possible for the masses; feedback also entails a special case that would divergently yield unforeseeable consequences: electron tubes were negentropically taught to no longer merely amplify their incoming signals in an analog manner but also to output them digitally, hence making them calculable. The tube itself cannot count or detect whether it is transmitting analog or digital signals, but by heterodyning analog oscillations, digital signals can be generated (as Fourier's analysis already demonstrated).

Formerly a transit medium for electron and radio streams, the tube can suddenly, when switched as a twin in an Eccles-Jordan circuit, itself serve as a storage medium for a binary position.[18] The combination of two electronic tubes as relays is in effect a flip-flop, an electronic trigger switch. The electron tube is a media-epistemological entity insofar as it is simultaneously concrete (in its materiality and electrotechnics) and paradigmatic. What was still concrete in the days of Edison (the light bulb), appears by de Forest's time no longer as an iconic object but as a technical drawing, as a switch—crossing over to the symbolic

---

17 Norbert Wiener, «Back to Leibniz! (Physics reoccupies an abandoned position),» in *Tech. Rev.* 34 (1932), p. 202.

18 Johannes Arnold, *Abenteuer mit Flipflop* (Halle: Mitteldeutscher Verlag, 1970), p. 16; also in this sense, see Bernhard Siegert, *Passagen des Digitalen* (Berlin: Brinkmann & Bose, 2003), p. 405.

realm. The electron tube is thus able to survive its own demise, for the transistor remains a semiconductor with a «tube-like relay effect,» albeit thermally less susceptible—medium cool. The process familiar from radio was thus echoed in the computer, but with a phase shift: first the electromechanical relays in Konrad Zuse's «Z1,» then the tube-driven computer (ENIAC), and finally, in 1958 Heinz Zemanek builds in Austria the «Mailüfterl» («May Breeze»), a transistor computer.

100 years? More like 90: Schottky's tetrode of 1916 already implemented a form of the integrated circuit; this likewise applies to the Loewe threefold tube «3NF» of 1926, co-developed by Manfred von Ardenne, the central component of the legendary Loewe local receiver (OE 333), which helped leverage private radio due to its low price—so it's actually 80 years of radio. The 3NF encases the assembly of three tube systems in *one* glass (vacuum) space, with four resistors and two capacitors fused-in, and is declared in terms of radio history to be «the world's first integrated circuit»; the media-epistemological cross-reference for this tube is in actuality more to the computer. As integrated resistor-coupling circuit, the tube transcends itself here, except that in the form of the 3NF it is not a logical («digital») but rather analog electron-stream control element. The

Radio receiver OE 333 with the Loewe threefold tube 3NF.

actual integrated circuit of the computer (a 1959 concept) is characterized by the fact that the wiring is flattened from three-dimensional space in favor of the two-dimensional lithographic procedure.

The tube is thus—depending on use—an analog/digital hybrid. Tube and psyche: von Lieben's electron tube not only has a link with *Wien* (Vienna), but also with Norbert Wiener, the founder of the discourse on *cybernetics* as a mathematical discipline. Vacuum tubes appeared to Wiener to be the ideal means of depicting instrumental equivalents to nerve circuits and nervous systems. For the electron tube (unlike electromagnetic relays) is the only example of where, like neuronal synapses, the voltage increases until, upon reaching a specific voltage level, it flips, functioning as a digital switch. None other than the great heir to Sigmund Freud, Jacques Lacan, once correlated the unconscious as function with a series of discrete states, explicitly taking recourse to electronics: «All those who have dealt with a radio know it—a triode tube.»[19] In Lacan's psychoanalysis, the modulatable electron tube stands paradigmatically for the imaginary function of the Ego. In this way, what Freud still called a «psychic apparatus» becomes a tube-based electron calculator. It is thus the electron tube of all things—that media-epistemological entity, serving both as analog amplifier and as digital switch without becoming something else—which enables the return to *Wien*, to the Vienna of Freud and von Lieben, and to Wiener's techno-mathematics.

As soon as the tube is no longer used for radio purposes alone, but instead as a digital switching element in computers, it changes its status of being, without however modifying one bit of its technical nature as inertialess modulation of a current. Tube-as-radio *versus* tube-as-digital switch: the electron tube thus divides two epochs and media systems *a*historically, in its pure media-archeological activation. The tube functioned as medium for electro-mathematical calculations at exactly the half(-life) period of that epoch of «100 years of radio,» which (apparently) is only drawing to a close with today's digitized, wireless communications media. The analog electron tube of radio technology comprises both a beginning and an end as pertains to the realm of the digital: to the discrete medium of telegraphy and to the beginning of the digital computer. Here, history turns back on itself like a Möbius strip, and that means: the present is shadowed by the inverse omens of its past.

19   Jacques Lacan, *Das Ich in der Theorie Freuds und in der Technik der Psychoanalyse, Das Seminar Buch 2*, 2nd ed. (1954–55; repr., Weinheim et al.: Quadriga, 1991), p.156.

For when we approach the question of 100 years of radio not only from the standpoint of mass media history but also mathematically, it all of a sudden looks completely different. Digital radio does not denote the end of the analog. Jean Baptiste Fourier demonstrated in the early nineteenth century in his *Analytical Theory of Heat* that even discontinuous signals, which include digital impulses, can be interpreted approximately as the sum of individual analog oscillations; consequently, the so-called digital can be described within the bounds of the analog. And the sampling theorem enables the digital reproduction of analog signals in such a way that they not only appear original (in high fidelity) to our human senses with the limited speed of their nerve stimuli, but their complete information content is also effectively maintained (including quantization noise). Digital radio has long since been able to simulate the aesthetic feel of analog radio—*Kunstradio* (art radio).

The veritably radio-active half-life period of 100 years of radio tubes is inevitably evocative of 50 years of tube-based computer music as well, being that Lejaren Hiller at the University of Illinois first programmed a computer to compose a piece of music, resulting in the *Illiac Suite* for string quartet. Likewise 50 years ago, Max Mathews realized at Bell Labs the first synthetic sounds using

Heinz Zemanek's transistor computer «Mailüfterl,» 1958.

digital technology.[20] The electron tube in this computer application is in fact a moment in which the interplay of materiality and encoding recalls the occidental connection between music and mathematics. Electron tubes, once brought into oscillation, not only bring sound to radio as transmitter or receiver; they were also employable for the mathematical synchronization of data cycles, as technological form of musical *harmonía*. As soon as we artificially/artistically sonify the cycling units of early tube computers of the ENIAC type, that is, acoustically reveal them through deceleration (with the program SuperCollider), the units audibly accelerate to create a rhythmic tone—ENIAC as Techno.[21]

Lecture presented at the conference 100 Years of Radio – The Return of Wireless Imagination, ORF Broadcasting House, Vienna, a collaboration between *Kunstradio* and the Ludwig Boltzmann Institute Media.Art.Research. The conference was part of Vienna *Art's Birthday* Celebrations, January 17–19, 2007.

Acknowledgements
With thanks to Dr. habil. Renate Tobies (Technical University of Braunschweig) for casting a critical glance over my remarks.

20 See http://www.computing-music.de (accessed October 2006).
21 The demiurge of this program is Martin Carlé, media scientist at Humboldt University in Berlin. See Martin Carlé, *ENIAC NOMOI: Eine seynsge-schichtliche Durchführung der poetischen Weisen des ersten Computers nach Klang, Tanz und Skulptur*, http://www.medienwissenschaft.hu-berlin.de/~mc/KVV_SS05_M4.php.

Interview with Robert Barry
October 12, 1969

Ursula Meyer

Let us go back to your pieces made of extended wire.

Yes. The wires were so thin and were in certain pieces stretched so high above the ground that it was virtually impossible to see them—or to photograph them. And from that I went to things that could be neither seen nor perceived in any way. My father, who is an electrical engineer and always worked with carrier waves and radio transmitters, ever since I was a kid, helped me out and that was the thing I knew about. I guess it was the first invisible art. It could not be perceived directly. And in the «January 5–31, 1969 Show» (Seth Siegelaub) I included several carrier wave pieces. One was called *88 mc Carrier Wave* (FM) and another *1600 kc Carrier Wave* (AM). Since you cannot photograph a carrier wave, we had to photograph the place where the carrier wave existed. The carrier waves have several very beautiful qualities. For example, they travel into space with the speed of light. They can be enclosed in a room. The nature of carrier waves in a room—especially the FM—is affected by people. The body itself, as you know, is an electrical device. Like a radio or an electric shaver, it affects carrier waves. The carrier waves are part of the electromagnetic spectrum of which light waves are also a part. A carrier wave is a form of energy. Light waves are made of the same material as carrier waves, only they are of a different length. A person is also a source of some kind of a carrier wave. Let me call that telepathy. The form of a piece is affected because of the nature of the material that it is made of. The form is changed by the people near it although the people may not be aware of the fact that they are affecting the actual form of the piece, because they cannot feel it.

Can it be measured?

For any transmitter, a receiver can be built that picks up what the transmitter sends out. It is interesting that these carrier waves, which go over the radio spectrum, can be picked up on the radio. When I left the carrier waves clean and turned on the radio, the stations went silent where the carrier waves were.

This interview is reprinted from: *Interview (October 12, 1969): Robert Barry*, interview by Ursula Meyer, UbuWeb Papers, http://www.ubu.com/papers/barry_interview.html.

Another piece was the *New York to Luxemburg CB Carrier Wave*. On January 5, I sent the CB carrier wave on a ham radio to Luxemburg. Seth wanted the dimensions of the piece. I gave him the megacycles and watts. And then there was this piece in Seth's show: *40 KHz ultrasonic soundwave installation* (January 4, 1969). We call it sound wave, I do not know why, because we cannot hear it. Ultrasonic sound waves have different qualities from ordinary sound waves. They can be directed like a beam, and they bounce back from a wall. Actually, you can make invisible patterns and designs with them. They can be diagramed and measured. I will do a piece for Jack Burnham for his show. I believe in the Jewish Museum.[1] I have to go to the place and work with the walls right then and there. My piece *0.5 Microcurie Radiation Installation* (January 5, 1969), Barium 133 (1969) consists of small radioactive isotopes—buried in Central Park—that emit radiation. Once again we photographed the place. Radiation waves are way up in the upper echelon of the electromagnetic wave spectrum; they are much shorter than light waves. Light will stop at the wall. Radiation will go right through it. A radioactive isotope is an artificial material. It has what they call «Zero time»—beautiful expression! That is the time when it is created. On the label of the small plastic vial in which it is contained, its «Zero time» is printed. From that moment on, it starts losing its energy. Now the «half-life» in this particular case was ten years, which means that every ten years its energy is decreased by half; but it goes on to infinity, it never goes to nothing. Some isotopes have a half-life of a millionth of a second, some have a half-life of four billion years, and some of fifteen minutes, meaning every fifteen minutes the energy is halved. But it never goes out of existence. They are perfectly harmless. A world of things can be done with this incredible material. And it is just letting them do what they are supposed to do. You cannot change a carrier or radiation wave; you can only know what it is supposed to do and let it do it. That's enough.

This is very important. Vibrations having substituted for thinghood.
Could it be said that you made an art form of vibrations?
Of energy.

An art form of energy?

Yes, everything is energy. There is not anything that is not energy. You may say of a Minimal sculpture that the object itself is the art even though it may emit these energies. I would say it's the energy that's my art. Then it seemed to me that the object that was producing the energy was getting in the way. Isotopes, transmitters, et cetera. I chose to work with inert gas because there was not the constant presence of a small object or device that produced the art...I got involved with energy without an object-source of energy. I did that using mental energy. I did a «telepathic piece» for Seth Siegelaub's exhibition, 1969, at Simon Fraser University in Vancouver. In the catalogue it states, «During the exhibition I shall try to communicate telepathically a work of art, the nature of which is a series of thoughts; they are not applicable to language or image.» I guess this was the first work I did that really did not have a place to be photographed. There was nothing visual that could be tied to it.

How do you feel about the missing aesthetic aspect? How does it affect you having either transcended or pushed aside the visual experience? Did you feel a sense of loss, as though you gave something up?

Robert Barry, *Inert Gas Series: Neon*, from a measured volume to indefinite expansion. On a hill near a valley in Los Angeles, overlooking the Pacific Ocean, one liter of neon was «returned to the atmosphere,» Los Angeles, CA, U.S., March 4, 1969.

No, not at all. I like the word «transcend.» I think you have to see it in those terms. Making art is not really important. Living is. In my mind, art and living are so closely interlocked. Trying to be involved in living and in the world around me makes this satisfactory. It seems to me that you have to give up something for an advance you are making. For any new truth that you discover for yourself, you have to discard some favored old belief. I would like to get away from calling things art. Robbe-Grillet has a beautiful line: «If art is going to be anything, then it has got to be everything.» Fortunately—in recent years—the term «art» has lost any solid meaning. I guess if I call something art, I am saying: «Look at this thing, consider it carefully and that is all it means.»...I am using art to draw attention to something.

ı   *Software, Information Technology: Its New Meaning for Art*, curated by Jack Burnham, Jewish Museum, New York, 1970.

Joyce Hinterding and Parasitic Possibility

Douglas Kahn

Joyce Hinterding wants to cook her meals on Channel 7, to direct the energy of the broadcast signal toward something useful. Of all the signals radiating metropolitan areas, those of broadcast television carry the most energy. Concentrating this power provides a spark that illuminates Tesla's dream of transmitted electricity, if not the reality. The prosaic reality is that the magnitude of power marshaled to flood these signals across large populations is nothing more than testament to an intrinsic political desperation at the center of control. It is from this location and through these channels that electromagnetic wave propagation becomes the carrier wave for propaganda. Using it diminishes the signal, but the amount of energy that reaches an individual antenna is miniscule compared to that being transmitted, so it would take a huge swarm of antennas to sap the tiniest loss from signal strength; a suspension bridge in the path of transmission would be a better bet. For one exhibition in New Zealand in the early nineteen-nineties, Hinterding wanted to start with a gallery space cluttered with antennas, following a story she had heard about a house in England intent on scavenging their energy from the air, but it proved to be too expensive. Yet, even if Hinterding could gather enough antennas for domestic use for her home in New South Wales, it would still be distasteful knowing that Prime Minister Homunculus Howard melted cheese while sending troops to Iraq.

For Hinterding, antennas in themselves have important sculptural implications because they demonstrate via electromagnetic induction—«the most extraordinary concept»—that «everything is active; all materials are active.» She had earlier become interested in incorporating sound into her work because resonance and sympathetic vibrations in sound exemplified «what exists between things rather than things.»[1] Rather than being driven by drives and exercising mastery over inert objects, electromagnetic induction served Hinterding as an analog that enabled, in effect, an affective wave function of attunement with the physical world.

Her interest in using antennas was first excited by an article by Tom Fox, «Build the ‹Whistler› VLF Receiver,» in the 1990 *Popular Electronics Hobbyist Handbook*. Whistlers are naturally occurring electromagnetic waves generated primarily by a full spectrum of electromagnetic bursts from lightning interacting with the ionosphere and magnetosphere. These are signals reflected and refracted lens-like through the upper atmosphere and, at times, travel great distances, while spiraling around magnetic flux lines of the magnetosphere, across the equator, and far out into space, from one hemisphere to the other, sometimes bouncing repeatedly between hemispheres. Being electromagnetic waves, they are traveling at the speed of light. Because they are exceedingly long waves that, moreover, travel thousands and hundreds of thousands of kilometers, they end up falling into the human audible range of frequencies once they are translated, transduced into vibrations in the air.

This patch of the electromagnetic spectrum is properly called the «audio frequency range,» or VLF (Very Low Frequency) for short, since it is dominated though not exhausted by the VLF range. It represents one of only two places on the spectrum that intersect experientially with human vision and audition. The other place is well known: visible light. Humans can perceive light unaided whereas it takes simple technology to transduce electromagnetism into sound. Such technology may include hair, fur, pine needles, and grasses when polar aurorae are heard. Whistlers and other ionospheric VLF phenomena can be heard through simple transducers alone—a long wire with a simple telephone receiver

1   Joyce Hinterding, interview with Josephine Bosma, August 24, 1998, http://www.nettime .org/Lists-Archives/nettime-l-9808/msg00074 .html.

2   S. W. Robinson, «Ringing Fences,» *Science* 2, no. 75 (December 3, 1881), p. 573.

3   Gene Fowler and Bill Crawford, *Border Radio: Quacks, Yodelers, Pitchmen, Psychics and Other Amazing Broadcasters of the American Airwaves* (Austin: Texas Monthly Press, 1987), p. 34.

4   Charles K. Wolfe, *Classic Country: Legends of Country Music* (London: Routledge, 2001), p. 10.

as the transducer will work—whereas radio signals outside the audio frequency range must be transposed up or down, or rendered from data, in order to fall within the range of hearing.

The sounds of ionospheric VLF are fascinating and beautiful, ranging from short bursts of noise that have been described as metallic bacon frying, to bird-like chirping, to the ethereal glissandi of whistlers themselves, and the echo trains of whistlers piled up from bouncing back and forth between the polar hemispheres of the earth. Tom Fox recounts how the first sounds he heard after he built his solid-state VLF receiver were not the mysterious sounds of whistlers, but the sound of Omega Navigation system operating between 10–14 kHz (Omega beacons ceased transmission once GPS became more widely available). The real fun, he said, «starts when you pick up a whistler. That strange sound starts as a high-pitched whine, at about 20 kHz, and sweeps down in frequency to a pitch like that of a high-soprano singer; it lasts about a second.»

Fox decided to test a little low-tech hearsay. He «strung 125 feet of #22 wire along the top horizontal support of the wood fence [encircling his] children's play yard,» and listened with his headphone set. He heard weak Omega Navigation signals and thus knew that he could conceivably hear whistlers. There is a history of fences containing sound, ringing property with wires and lines, containing properties and property rights. Henry David Thoreau reveled in the Aeolian properties of telegraph lines, even as he feared the lines would improve the South's slave trade. «Ringing fences,» the sounds produced by walking past picket fences—«a curious musical tone of initial high but rapidly lowering pitch ... with a duration of perhaps a quarter second»—were the topic of one scientific paper in the late nineteenth century.[2] Tales of radiophonic fences grew in the nineteen-thirties with the advent of border radio. In 1935, radio station XERA started broadcasting a directional signal of one-million watts, blasting into the United States from across the Mexican border. The signal was so strong that unsuspecting birds were barbequed in mid-flight. «Ranchers were startled to find their fences electrified by the high-powered broadcasts of hillbilly performers.»[3] Country music singer June Carter agreed; hang a tin can off any barbed-wire fence, she said, and you could hear the Carter Family.[4] For Tom Fox, the border was the equator. With his backyard in Michigan, he was hoping to hear sounds produced by lightning occurring at conjugate points located on the same geomagnetic line of force in the southern hemisphere. Just find the opposite latitude, add ten degrees to the longitude, and listen deep into the night.

Joyce Hinterding remembered reading the Tom Fox article and thinking it was about listening to lightning. The high-pitched sounds of VLF can be thought of as the upper register of lightning, with thunder filling out the bottom. Thunder plods away at the speed of sound and dissipates quickly on short horizons whereas VLF is a globe-trotter. Having studied electronics at technical school (TAFE), she soon became well-informed about the generation, propagation, and reception of VLF, gaining the technical skills that necessarily accrue to those sculptors and installation artists where the idea comes first. Still, she says, it is important not to get too specific since, like many artists, like many people, «All my things are determined from a slight misunderstanding.»[5]

In 1991, Hinterding was in-residence at the Greene Street Studio in New York through an Australia Council Fellowship. When she first turned on her VLF receiver and antenna inspired by Tom Fox, she hoped to hear the Omega Navigation signal that would in turn let her know that she was at least in the right neighborhood for whistlers, but all she heard was the 60 Hz hum of the U.S. electrical grid and, strangely, a Christian fire-and-brimstone preacher instructing everyone through the hum to «Stand in front of the mirror. Repent! Repent!» She didn't understand why there could be a broadcast that low, apart from reaching sinners wherever they might be. The saving grace was that it made her wonder whether «Repent! Repent!» was pulsating just outside the window, resonating sympathetically in the conductive mass of the fire escape, and it made her wonder where else was the call to repent in that big rat's nest of vibrating metal called a city.

She finally heard natural radio for the first time during the same year at Walter De Maria's *Lightning Field* in New Mexico, where she camped out and made recordings deep into the night. She was not there to watch lightning—it's not good to be too close to lightning while recording VLF—instead she was there on an artistic pilgrimage and because of the isolation the site provided from electrical grid that interferes with VLF reception. Following instructions, she found the Omega tracking signal and knew her antenna and receiver were working.

She had been in New York to work on a commission for the Sydney Biennale called *Electrical Storms* (1991), which used two large electrostatic speakers connected to a VLF antenna. To my knowledge, this is the first exhibited artwork that used VLF. Alvin Lucier had attempted unsuccessfully to use VLF in a live per-

5   Joyce Hinterding, interview with the author,
    Riga, Latvia, August 24–26, 2006.

formance for a composition called *Whistlers* in 1968, and was subsequently successful in *Sferics* from 1981. He composed a related piece called *Navigations for Strings* (1991), which was an attempt to exorcise the earworm tones of the Omega Navigation beacon that got stuck in his head like a bad advertising jingle, while making the recording for *Sferics*. Lucier lists *Sferics* as an installation as well as a composition, thus, more precisely, Hinterding's *Electrical Storms* may be the first VLF artwork to have been completed and exhibited. It included two custom-built electrostatic speakers that used high voltage, had very low distortion, and elicited a palpable sense of 3-D spatiality. One system had the existing ambient electromagnetism, while the other had the recordings made at De Maria's *Lightning Field*. The presence of high voltage in the electrostatic speakers lent immediacy to the experience of the energies involved in the terrestrial and exoterrestrial production of these sounds; the low distortion ironically meant greater definition to the noise; and the spatiality worked to give a sense of the *fields* of electromagnetic activity, rather than utterances and messages that animate putative communications.

While in New York, Hinterding met someone who had been going around the city to listen to stairwells and fire escapes in order to hear whether or not they

Joyce Hinterding,
Electrical Storms,
VLF antenna, *Sydney Biennale*, Australia,
1991.

were receiving radio. If the fire escape could induce «Stand in front of the mirror. Repent! Repent!» and if simple wire wrapped about Tom Fox's backyard fence could draw down sounds from across the equator and from outer space, then the conductive expanses of any given city were obviously not the only unwitting antennas. Since the nineteenth century, telegraph lines, railroad tracks, cables, plumbing, wire and barbed wire fences, and a multitude of other inductive lines and surfaces had crisscrossed the earth in a web of unwitting antennas receiving natural radio, VLF, long before the earth had been theorized into a noosphere or cyberspace.

Writing in 1873, the cartographic mind's eye of one American author reveled in an image of the railroad system cast across the continent: a swarm of life organized around and through the dense, intricate network of the black lines of its tracks. In comparison, however,

> if we could rise above the surface of the earth, and take in the whole country at a bird's-eye view, with visual power to discern all the details, the net-work of the telegraph would be still more curious to look upon. We should see a web spun of two hundred thousand miles of wire spread over the face of the country like a cobweb on the grass, its threads connecting every important center of population, festooning every great post-road, and marking as with a silver lining the black track of every railroad.[6]

Further, to place the telegraph system itself into perspective, the mind's eye grows an additional sensory capacity:

> The observer, whom we have supposed capable of seeing electricity, would find that the whole surface of the earth, the atmosphere, and probably the fathomless spaces beyond, were teeming with manifestations of the electric force ... Our observer would see that these great earth currents infinitely transcend the little artificial currents which men produce in their insulated wires, and that they constantly interfere with the latter, attracting or driving them from their work, and making them play truant, greatly to the vexation of the operators, and sometimes to the entire con-

6 «The Telegraph,» *Harper's New Monthly Magazine* 47, no. 279 (June–November 1873), p. 332.

7 Ibid., p. 334.

fusion of business. If a thunder-storm passed across the country, he would see all the wires sparkling with unusual excitement.[7]

In 1876, Thomas Watson, working as Alexander Graham Bell's assistant, put a telephone «in series,» also called «in circuit,» with a half-mile long experimental iron line running over housetops in Boston. He could hear the faint signals of Morse Code from the surrounding telegraph lines, but at night he heard what he called «stray electric currents,» a sound no one had ever heard.

I used to spend hours at night in the laboratory listening to the many strange noises in the telephone and speculating as to their cause. One of the most common sounds was a snap, followed by a grating sound that lasted two or three seconds before it faded into silence, and another was like the chirping of a bird. My theory at the time was that the currents causing these sounds came from explosions on the sun or that they were signals from another planet. They were mystic enough to suggest the latter explanation but I never detected any regularity in them that might indicate they were intelligible signals.

Joyce Hinterding,
Electrical Storms,
installation, *Sydney Biennale*, Australia,
1991.

He was confident that «... I, perhaps, may claim to be the first person who ever listened to static currents.»[8] The sounds he heard were the slurred overtones of an unheard thunder, and, in this way, he listened to «wires sparkling with unusual excitement» that had unwittingly become antennas. The man who had lived a very good life, but was destined to be the historical sidekick of Bell, had discovered radio before it was invented. What Bell was to the social conduct of communication, Watson was to a commune with the inductive nature of the electromagnetic, of «the whole surface of the earth, the atmosphere, and probably the fathomless spaces beyond ... teeming with manifestations of the electric force.»

A newspaper reporter from the *Lawrence American* (Lawrence, Massachusetts) wrote of a telephone demonstration conducted by Watson who, failing in his attempt to communicate using speech or music, nevertheless heard, as he thought, the *loose electricity* of the «Northern Lights and found his wires alive with lightning.»[9] Thunderstorms, atmospheric electricity, magnetic storms, and auroral activity were known to produce sparks and explosive sounds as they interrupted and debilitated telegraphic technology, a small sacrifice when compared with the noisy effects of lightning on exploding armories and screaming church bell ringers, who tried to acoustically fend off thunderstorms by pulling on their wet ropes. Once the telephone was placed in the circuit of existing telegraphic technology, more discrete sounds could be heard.[10] Even when lightning was far off on the horizon, it sounded «something like the quenching of a drop of molten metal in water, or the sound of a distant rocket,» in the words of William Channing,

8   Thomas A. Watson, *Exploring Life: The Autobiography of Thomas A. Watson* (New York: D. Appleton and Company, 1926), pp. 80–82.

9   Ibid., p. 21.

10   «Towards the afternoon of Sunday the 4th Earth currents became very strong on the 1865 cable. They increased so much as to produce sparks on turning switch, accompanied with a sharp crack like the explosion of a percussion cap. Specially attracted by this rare phenomenon.» See G. E. Preece, «Earth Currents, and the Aurora Borealis of 4th February,» *Journal of the Society of Telegraph Engineers* 1, no. 1 (1872), pp. 102–114, here p. 103.

11   William Channing, cited by W. H. Preece in Alfred Ritter von Urbanitzky, *Electricity in the Service of Man: A Popular and Practical Treatise on the Applications of Electricity in Modern Life* (London: Cassell and Company, 1886), p. 713; see also John Joseph Fahie, *A History of Wireless Telegraphy: 1838–1899* (Edinburgh: William Blackwood and Sons, 1899), p. 80.

12   Alexander Graham Bell, «Researches in Electric Telephony,» *Journal of the Society of Telegraph Engineers* 6 (October 31, 1877). On the Brown group, see Robert V. Buce, *Bell: Alexander Graham Bell and the Conquest of Solitude* (Ithaca: Cornell University Press, 1973), p. 225.

13   C. E. McCluer, «Telephonic Reminiscences,» *Telephony* (January 1908), pp. 42–45, and http://earlyradiohistory.us/1908rem.htm.

a member of the group of physicists at Brown University in Providence, Rhode Island, who assisted Bell in the early development of the telephone.[11] Similar but fainter sounds were heard when lightning was hours away. Physicist and Professor Emeritus John Peirce, also at Brown University, «observed the most curious sounds produced from a telephone in connection with a telegraph-wire during the aurora borealis.»[12]

In 1876, C. E. McCluer, the Western Union Telegraph Company office manager in Lynchburg, Virginia, built his own telephones using Bell's description, placing them on a short private line between his office and boarding house.

From the night the telephones were installed my attention had been attracted to the mysterious whisperings and strange frying noises which were heard almost constantly through the telephones, particularly during the quiet hours of the night. It became my custom when I went home at night, no matter how late it was, to spend a few minutes listening to the strange and at times almost uncanny noises that the telephone gave forth, and speculating as to their origin. My telegraph instruments had never offered any indications of earth currents, except during the prevalence of an auroral display, and while I had learned that the atmosphere was continually traversed by electric currents in greater or lesser profusion, it had never occurred to me that the bosom of old mother earth was permeated and torn by similar electrical manifestations. Hence the weird noises and faint peculiar cracklings which my telephones for the first time revealed to me were fascinating to me, and I spent much of my leisure time in a study of the interesting phenomena, with the hope of arriving at a satisfactory solution of their origin. The subject of electrical leakage and induction had not then been brought to my attention, and I listened to the faint and mysterious utterances of the telephones as though they were spirit whisperings from another world.[13]

Alfred Ritter von Urbanitzky writing in 1886 described how «earth-currents» ever-present in the wires will normally produce a crackling noise, «not unlike the rushing of broken water,» and will increase their power with aurorae. He also described what were no doubt the sounds of natural radio: «Sometimes a peculiar wailing sound is heard, which an imaginative correspondent of mine likened to ‹the hungry cry of newly-hatched birds in a nest.›»[14] In contrast to the regular static of earth currents, these sounds were considered to be *musical*, and may be produced by «the swinging of the wires across the magnetic lines of force of the earth,» a combination of wire and magnets of the type that had been put together more purposefully by Faraday and used in the musical telegraphy that immediately preceded telephony. In this notion, music was produced in an Aeolian fashion with the wind swinging the wires, or the geomagnetic perturbations oscillating across the wires, such «that these vibrations may succeed each other in the necessary rhythmic order to produce musical tones.»[15]

Clearly, the telephone was not just a communication device. From the very beginning, and for decades to come, it was considered to be a scientific instrument of great sensitivity and versatility. It was doing for the ear what the microscope had done for the eye: it revealed hitherto unheard-of phenomena. Electrical interferences in telegraph lines and cables had been known through the sound of their consequences, when equipment malfunctioned or sparks flew, fly, but their subtler forms had not been detected. On April 2, 1877, Alexander Graham Bell attached his telephone to the telegraph line leading from Boston to New York and noted two categories of electrical phenomena attracted to the lines: induction currents and earth currents.

> When a telephone is placed in circuit with a telegraph line, the telephone is found seemingly to emit sounds on its own account. The most extraordinary noises are often produced, the causes of which are at present very obscure. One class of sounds is produced by the inductive influence of neighboring wires and by leakage from them, the signals of Morse alphabet passing over neighboring wires being audible in the telephone, and another class can be traced to earth currents upon the wire, a curious modification of this sound revealing the presences of defective joints in the wire.[16]

14 See von Urbanitzky 1886 (see note 11), p. 713.
15 Ibid.
16 Bell 1877 (see note 12).
17 Ibid.
18 Fahie 1899 (see note 11), pp. 80–85.

19 McCluer 1908 (see note 13).
20 Charles Süsskind, «Observations of Electro-magnetic-Wave Radiation Before Hertz,» *Isis* 55, no. 179 (March 1964), pp. 32–43, here p. 33.

William Channing heard music in a telegraph line when none was being transmitted. It was, simply, music heard over wireless or, rather, over an expanse of air between wires that were not connected with each other. He heard five of Edison's musical telephone concerts from New York to Saratoga, Troy, and Albany, New York, received on a mile-long wire strung over the rooftops of Providence.[17] Corroboration came from Charles Rathbone in Albany, New York, who heard six of the concerts between August 28 and September 11, 1877, after he attached a telephone to a private telegraph line.[18] McCluer also heard cross-talk in Virginia or rather cross-singing from two separate concerts that produced a «weird music.»[19]

Finally, Eli W. Blake reported that Morse «leakage» could be heard when a telephone receiver was attached to railroad tracks. This meant that the systems of railroad tracks and telegraph wires that had been separated by our mind's-eye observer in 1873 above had in fact been joined all along as antennas, and that the natural radio age began to spread markedly as networks of tracks were laid. As for human-made radio, as Charles Süsskind has stated, «Observations of electromagnetic-wave propagation from man-made electrical disturbances have been made probably for as long as there have been means for producing moderately large sparks.» One example he gives is of vivisectionist techno: «In 1780, Luigi Galvani observed that sparking from an electro static generator could cause convulsions in a dead frog at some distance from the machine.»[20] From the perspective of induction and antennas, at least since 1876, that is, once the telephone was put in-circuit with telegraph and telephone wires, radio was discovered before it was invented: Morse Code was heard on a regular basis without wires when Marconi was two years old; and music and voice was heard without wires and Fessenden was ten years old.

This is the induction that Hinterding calls «the most extraordinary concept.» It tempers the conceit that humans are the authors of radio, and it opens the technology to the environment. This is basis of an ecological complement to Bertolt Brecht's desire for communications technologies to be used for radically democratic communication, actual communication, by proposing that communications technologies need not be used for communication between humans at all, but can be used to appreciate phenomena outside the immediate exigencies of sociality. Calling things such as telephones and telegraph lines communications technologies in the first place is, therefore, not entirely accurate.

Certainly Hinterding's best known work involving induction and antennas is *Aeriology* (1995). Much like Tom Fox wrapping his kids' playground fence with wire in a big loop antenna, Hinterding wrapped 20 to 30 km of wire—at V2, 26 km of .6 mm magnet wire—around columns in the warehouse exhibition spaces. It is a stunning sculptural presence, cordoning off a space like a fence with an oddly diaphanous, huge expanse of metal and palpable concentration of labor. It is suspended in tension but seems to be moving in the way it shimmers as you move. You soon realize that it is a large VLF loop antenna, reaching far out from the containment of the exhibition space as it resonates with its electromagnetic environment. You can hear it in the speakers, fifty or sixty cycles with the static grit and grime of the urban electromagnetic ambience. The speakers are not connected to any obvious power source.

She did connect an oscilloscope in order to reveal that «there's some kind of vibration inside of things in the world,» which is confirmed because «it's just a big humming thing.» The fields of the wire resonate with ambient electromagnetic energy, but the slight gaps in the wrapping, what lends *Aeriology* its diaphanous quality, and the minute space given by the wire insulation itself, accumulates and stores the energy. Also, the way the sections are cut—it's not one continuous line—reinforce one another, like sections in a voltaic pile, an early incarnation of the battery. It collects enough energy to be self-sufficient and independently power the speakers. So it's not merely an antenna, it's an energy scavenger and big, inefficient battery. As Hinterding has said, «It explores technology in a very different way to mainstream thought: not looking so much for efficiency but simply possibility.»[21]

If she were to install *Aeriology* in as isolated a locale as De Maria's *Lightning Field*, the ionospheric radio signals would not be overwhelmed by the radiation that vibrates the city. Yet, although Hinterding has a politics of the signal, it is not coincident with a discourse on pollution, one that began with Thomas Watson and others as the electrical grid and tramlines edged in on their reception of VLF. As insult to injury, VLF and other induced signals—they were called disturbances, interference, noise, and, as if Michel Serres were an engineer, parasites or parasitics—were considered pollution and systematically eliminated

---

21   Hinterding interview (see note 1).

Joyce Hinterding, *Aeriology*, installation, Artspace, Auckland, New Zealand, 1995.

Joyce Hinterding, *Aeriology*, installation, Artspace, Sydney, Australia, 1997.

from communications systems. But Hinterding is neither mainstream nor mountain stream. *Aeriology* is pinned at the crossroads of brute industrial force and a lighter touch on the earth. It is only possible through a systemic excess of materials and labor, of mining and smelting, and grimy manufacturing that shines in the wire, configured in one of the carcasses of abandoned industrial spaces where you often find grassroots arts spaces. At this location, a self-exploited cohort of fully caffeinated Bohemian volunteers wind wire for hours and hours into what appears to be a working simile for the frailest of failed dynamo coils, but what is instead, in 1995, an early form of energy scavenging, that itself has gained industrial attention lately in RFID, mobile media, and remote sensing. As a prescient energy scavenger, Hinterding had her antennas tuned to the noises generated by the parasite of possibility.

On Resonance

Nina Czegledy

The marvel of the invisible and often inaudible electromagnetic realm keeps me mesmerized. This fascination guided me to explore the magnificent and enigmatic polar lights, a magnificent geo-specific phenomenon. The aurora (known as borealis in the north and australis in the south) are created as a consequence of high-energy particles refracted from the sun soaring into the earth's atmosphere, colliding with gas molecules and captured by the earth's magnetic field. The resulting dazzling phenomena are not merely brilliant natural revelations; the aurora also make dramatically visible the invisible world of electromagnetic activities, thus the enigmatic phenomena retained over centuries a near-mythical status in most cultures. Historically, Nordic people envisaged the fluttering lights as many different things, from supernatural creatures fighting fierce battles in the sky, to old women dancing or hovering in the air. Most of the interpretations have been forgotten, but a surprising amount of folklore is still vibrant, as it has been carefully passed down from generation to generation to this day and age.

The extensive knowledge and familiarity with nature in ancient tribes contained venerable wisdom. It is the contemplation of these myths vis-à-vis contemporary science, which often provides a source of inspiration for present-day interpretations. To create a dialogue between a naturally occurring electromagnetic disturbance and our constructed technological environment, we had initiated with Stephen Kovats the first *Aurora Universalis* project a decade ago. While research and collaborative practice have remained an essential element, over the last decade the project has been expressed in a variety of forms and attracted various participants. Today, a plethora of online real-time auroral data is available for professionals as well as the general public, yet many riddles exist unresolved, and essential questions remain unanswered. Curiously, in the process of the extensive knowledge transfer, the physical sky and the symbolic sky became somehow separated.

Over centuries auroras provided a constant source of mystery, awe, and inspiration for artistic exploration, for representing the phenomena through photography, film and video, dance, performance, and audio-based projects. Regrettably, the most fascinating feature, the sublime experience to behold the aurora, remains often missing. I became acutely aware of this a few years ago during our winter residency with Luke Jerram in Lapland at the Sodankyla Geophysical Observatory. More than a hundred kilometers north of the Arctic Circle, each evening—lasting late into the night—we watched, from the warm comfort of the guesthouse, the online magnetic conditions on the Internet, including the all-sky camera images. As soon as we suspected increased magnetic activity, we would don our arctic clothing and rush out, waiting for the amazing aurora displays. Each and every time the sights provided an unforgettable, sublime experience. These and previous encounters motivated my ongoing electromagnetic research and the production of subsequent aurora exhibitions, conferences, texts, and lately public art projects.

My continued investigations lead to the topic of biomagnetism in the form of the production of a magnetic field by a living object such as the human body. The ancient concepts of the magnetic and electric properties of the human body date back thousands of years. The earliest accounts of magnetic therapy have been traced to Africa, where ground bloodstone (natural magnetite) has been used for approximately 100,000 years in food and potions. Most ancient civilizations, including the Hebrew, Arab, Indian, Egyptian, and Chinese, used magnets for healing as chronicled in the Chinese chi, the Hindu chakras, and other ancient texts. Nevertheless, recorded accounts of biomagnetism, bioelectricity, and magnetic therapy show an often-controversial and highly debated history. Contemporary understanding of biomagnetism, based on the interaction of living organisms with electromagnetic fields, led to the new discipline of bioelectromagnetism: the study of electromagnetic phenomena within and between biological systems.

In the course of studying the electromagnetic spectrum, I became deeply interested in the pioneering concepts and eccentric life of Nikola Tesla. He believed—ahead of his time—that everything that exists, organic or inorganic, animated or inert, is responsive to electromagnetic stimulus, and he asserted that each human body has an electric potential, which fluctuates incessantly.

Over the last fifty years with renewed interest in bioelectricity, it has been shown that the human body functions like an electromagnetic machine, each body cell containing electrical currents, unique to the individual. It has been confirmed that physical and mental body functions are controlled by electromagnetic impulses from the brain, the pineal gland, and the central nervous system. The findings of biogenic magnetite in human tissues had been validated when high-resolution transmission electron microscopy and electron diffraction technologies became available in the nineteen-nineties. As a result of the research and clinical studies, it became clear that the balance between negative and positive magnetic forces greatly impact our existence.

Luke Jerram, *Waiting for Aurora*, Sodankyla Geophysical Observatory, Lapland, 2003.

Tesla postulated that there is no breach in this process, the same law governs all matter, and the whole universe is alive with electrical vibrations. He alleged that thought, memory, and motion are feedback processes and that he was a kind of «automaton of cosmic forces» endowed with abilities to think and move. He considered the invention of teleautomatic control as a result of this process. While many of his concepts and dreams remain utopian, including a world of limitless cheap light for (community) public use, control of weather, and extraplanetary communication, he nevertheless eerily predicted, more than a century ago, future technological advances. His original research and the hundreds of his patents cover nearly every aspect of science and technology. Tesla began working on remotely controlled devices in 1893, continuing to automatic mechanisms beyond the line of vision and predicting that teleautomata will eventually be capable of acting as if possessed of their own intelligence. The patent granted to him in 1898 on the radio control of guided vehicles remains a cornerstone for the development of space exploration. Thus, remotely controlled exploration of the cosmos began a century ago when Tesla demonstrated in New York his first working model of a robot guided by radio waves. Tesla was ridiculed and his credibility questioned among professional scientists for his claim to receive signals of extraplanetary origin. I was reminded of this ridicule at the well-attended scientific sessions on searching for extraterrestrial intelligence at the recent 57th International Astronautical Congress in Valencia, Spain, where the realization of extraterrestrial communication was treated with great respect.

Tesla lived in a world of magnetic waves, light, and vibration. His visionary concepts combined with his extraordinary personality captured the imagination of hundreds of people, including myself and my friend and colleague Louise Provencher. The *Resonance Electromagnetic Bodies* project began with our reflections on Nikola Tesla. In the following, I provide a personal and subjective narrative of this project. Clearly such independent projects require a significant amount of venue negotiation, administration, fundraising, and so forth, however this text remains focused on the project concept, history, the participating artists and their work, with nominal reference to pragmatics.

Before our conversations with Louise and Charles Halary (who in 2003, and again in 2004, organized significant *«electromagnetique»* conferences in Montreal), I had already twice visited the Tesla Museum in Belgrade, had lengthy discussions with Velimir Abramović, a remarkable Tesla scholar, and Maria Sesic, who later became director of the Tesla Museum. Velimir offered a wealth of relevant information, as well as philosophical and biographical interpretations of Tesla's life and concepts. In the—always vibrant—cafés of Belgrade, we talked at length about Tesla's exceptional ability for visualization, his notions of the cosmos, as well as the contemporary heritage of invention in Serbia. (I have been told that in the back alleys of Belgrade budding inventors are fabricating devices to this day in the hope of future fame.) In the Tesla Museum, in addition to his working models, numerous documents, hundreds of letters, many personal items such as umbrellas, hats, walking sticks, and white gloves are also stored. I had hoped that one day I would be able to integrate these fascinating objects in a future exhibition among scientific instruments and artworks. Alas, this never came true, but while in Belgrade, I collected many books and diaries and other items for the future project.

How can the art and science aspects best be reflected in such a project? The deliberation of the scientific, technological origins leading to symbolic elucidation required extensive consideration. Louise and I spent a long time taking into account relevant artworks as well as finding a fitting project title. Working with the basic principles of resonance and vibration, finally we settled on *Resonance Electromagnetic Bodies*, which reveals an awareness of vibration and alerts us to pulses subtly traversing and informing the human body. We assumed that the primary aim of the project is to consider the scale of the human body (as well as other living organisms) simultaneously as a source, an echo, and a transmitter, and as a point of resistance to electromagnetic waves. Within the framework of the project we intended to find works that examine the nature of invisible yet discernible material forces and explore how these dynamic energies impact on our sensory perception.

At the outset, Canadian artists were approached, who either produced work in this field or were interested in developing an appropriate work for the project. The investigation of the historical background of artists working with electromagnetisms provided rewarding results—from Warhol's Electric Chair screen prints, to Takis's early telesculpture, to Jasper Johns's brass light bulb installation, to Catherine Richards's embodied sculptures, a long list of artists explored the relationships between transcendental forces and human existence. From our previous collaboration, I have been familiar with the work of Catherine Richards, who is one of the best-known Canadian artists exploring the electromagnetic realm. Richards repeatedly examines the blurred boundaries between our bodies and the wired world. In the closed circuit of her *Curiosity Cabinet at the End of the Millennium* (1995), the participant/visitor is supposedly shielded from magnetic interference and becomes «unplugged» from the «plugged-in» state of our contemporary surroundings. The cabinet becomes a secure space, an impervious skin from electronic and magnetic currents. In contrast, *Charged Hearts* (1997) invites visitors to become part of the electromagnetically charged atmosphere. Thus the installations compliment each other—one by plugging the visitor into the electromagnetic atmosphere, and the other by unplugging the visitor. In 2000, Richards took this metaphor further by creating *Shroud/Chrysalis*. This work became a fundamental component of the *Resonance* project. Here the visitors are wrapped in a protective sheet of copper taffeta and once again are safely shielded from the electromagnetic surroundings. Richards conveys the notion that we all are permeable to the invisible, human-generated electrical magnetic spectrum as well as its technological displays, and it seems that to separate ourselves from our mediated environment we have to enter a shielded cabinet or «wrap» ourselves into the safety of copper taffeta.

A «historical» signifier not only grounds a contemporary art project (as I firmly believe) but also serves as a benchmark of critical importance. Norman White—best known for his pioneering robotics artwork—created *Abacus* in 1974. It is an elegant, seemingly simple-looking piece, but by White's admission it represents a turning point in his production of electronic sculptures in the mid-seventies. To quote White's description of his artwork:

> *Abacus* employs random and structured principles working in harmony to produce a stochastic effect … partially predictable, partially not. However, whereas my preceding electronic works manifest their internal logic by producing light patterns on grids of small bulbs, *Abacus* does so mechanically, causing aluminum tubes to shuttle back and forth erratically over arched steel rods. Two years after completing *Abacus*, I abandoned light sculptures altogether, and focused my attention entirely on robotic work.

Abacus served as a touchstone among the current works throughout the *Resonance* tour.

Reflections on the electromagnetic environment provide broad readings and diverse symbolic interpretations by the artists. These were often expressed in *Resonance* through indirect references to the electromagnetic spectrum. Nevertheless, the wide range of topics investigated by the artists included data and audio flow, gravity, nanotechnology, levitation, X-ray radiation, and electromagnetic photography. Throughout the project, in addition to the ten Canadians, more than thirty international artists participated in the five European exhibitions. The detailed description of all of these projects is outside the scope of this text; consequently, I will focus on selected themes and works.

An important question raised by the *Resonance* project is exposed by Jocelyn Robert's title *Saint-Georges et le dragon*. What prompts us to search for «heroes» such as Saint George or Nikola Tesla? Is this question raised here because Tesla might have himself chosen to play the role of a hero? Or is it because heroic characters function as a kind of magnet on the collective and individual imagination for our eternal quest of individual identity? In one of Abramović's texts on Tesla, I have discovered some relevant questions: «Why theorists and empiricists

Paulette Phillips, *Homewrecker*, installation, *Resonance Electromagnetic Bodies*, The Centro Cultural Conde Duque, Madrid, Spain, 2006.

of modern physics of time are so interested in reconstruction of Tesla's missing theory of physical reality and his view on electromagnetic phenomena? Shall we consider Tesla to be a spiritual precursor of a new scientific and technological civilization named as Tesliana?»

Sparks, an experimental video by AElab, contextualizes the backdrop behind Tesla's inventions and explores various aspects of an inventor's life, through contemporary interviews. Tesla often presented in a spectacular way electric phenomena in his laboratory. During these theatrical presentations, he made use of the seductive power of his own persona, a conscious strategy that is apparent in surviving photo documentation, where he looks with great intensity at the viewer. Paulette Phillips displays this «gaze» metaphorically in her *Homewrecker* installation. By her own admission, the concept of this work grew out of Phillips's interest in electromagnetism as a metaphor for desire. The visitor is confronted by the seductive stare of a female figure. The surrounding space around her expands and shrinks in turn, implying the electrically charged environment. A ghostlike levitation, presented in the form of small electromagnetic sculpture, compliments this film loop. The installation is a reminder of Phillips's deep interest in invisible or imagined phenomena such as telepathy, hypnosis, and electromagnetism.

Simone Jones in *Camera Exercises*, a ten-minute film loop, also explores levitation and gravity as a fantastical phenomenon. The grainy, black-and-white film evokes the physical challenges of real-time body performances of the seventies. Jones's interest in the relationship between the real and the imaginary is presented here by a figure that seems to be suspended by an invisible power defying the tendency of falling toward the center of the earth. The interplay between fact and fiction is further suggested by David Tomas's *Matrix for Yellow Light*, introducing contemporaries of Tesla's time: Pierre and Marie Curie. The audio and power point installation is focused on radioactivity simultaneously evoking the (yellow) color of radium in a fictive laboratory.

Jean-Pierre Aube has perceptibly confirmed the strength of invisible electromagnetic waves surrounding us in our everyday environment. *Spying the Electromagnetic Work Force* utilized mini VLF (Very Low Frequency) receivers to survey, analyze, modify, and re-represent the electrical flow of the buildings where *Resonance* was shown. Simultaneously, the work revealed the invisible and frequently inaudible dangers of electromagnetic pollution.

The power of evocative electromagnetic or Kirlian photography is based on placing an object or body part directly onto a piece of photographic paper and then passing a high voltage across the object. Marie-Jeanne Musiol, while investigating metaphors conveyed by photography, began to use this method to capture the invisible energies surrounding objects, a fundamental although unseen component of life. Through a series of photos on the same subject, the artist reveals various phases of the aura encircling objects such as plants or a human finger. She claims that via her art, she has conveyed meaningful information on the physical and psychic state of objects and their interaction with the environment. In the installation *Bodies of Light*, the visitor's presence triggers the illumination of light boxes in the dark to create the perception of a radiant universe: a small cosmos lit from inside and intensified by the highlights of a video.

From the very beginning, we intended to create a flexible modular structure for touring *Resonance* across Europe. This process-based structure allowed a diversity of participants in each venue. Reflections on history of science and technology are often missing from the so-called art and science projects. We have tried to rectify this by including historical working models (by Hertz and Tesla), whenever there was a possibility. From the start, we intended to collaborate with

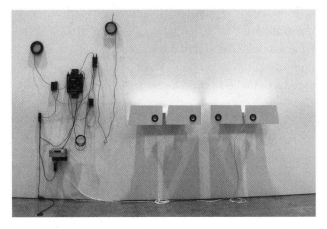

Jean-Pierre Aube, *Spying the Electromagnetic Work Force*, installation, *Resonance Electromagnetic Bodies*, ZKM, Karlsruhe, Germany, 2005.

local co-curators, thus extending the range of the interpretation of the thematic concept as well as the scope of the events. On one hand, this revealed fresh interpretations on the Canadian artworks, simultaneously creating a new reading of the whole project by the changing cultural context. From the audience's point of view, the Canadian works were experienced in a different way at each phase of the tour. Based on previous experience, the significance of a dedicated project website was recognized and followed up with step-by-step production, adding a separate page for each venue. Starting from Canada, *Resonance* toured five European countries including Germany, Spain, the Netherlands, Hungary, and France and had over 50,000 visitors. In addition to the exhibitions, the adjunct events included conferences, performances, and concerts.

«The future is mine!» declared Nikola Tesla at the turn of the twentieth century. In 2006, the International Belgrade Airport was renamed Belgrade Nikola Tesla Airport. One of the craters on the moon as well as an asteroid orbiting between Mars and Jupiter bear the name of Nikola Tesla. Celebrating the 150th anniversary of his birth, 2006 was proclaimed Nikola Tesla year by UNESCO and the governments of Serbia and Croatia. While these accolades recognize Tesla's enormous contribution, notwithstanding his enduring efforts, the effects of electromagnetism still present an enigma to scientists and artists alike.

The *Resonance Electromagnetic Bodies* project, an interdisciplinary collaboration, provided an opportunity for reflection on the legacy of Nikola Tesla's vision. The participating artists utilized simultaneous readings of scientific information with an aim to question or to better understand our natural and man-made electromagnetic habitat as a living medium. The art projects seemed to recapture the often-lost connection between science, art, technology, and the natural world. On examination, a remarkable intersection is revealed between aesthetics and indiscernible magnetic energies. Hence, these artworks often restore the magic of our electromagnetic environment.

Radio: An Agent of Audification?

Honor Harger

In r a d i o q u a l i a's artistic practice, we have encountered radio in multiple guises. Radio is, for us, a many-headed beast which can take any of the following forms, depending on the context:

1. A carrier wave: radio waves propagate through space carrying information or energy
2. A mechanism of reception: receivers take delivery of signals in the radio part of the electromagnetic spectrum
3. A system of distribution: transmitters distribute content to an audience of listeners
4. An apparatus of communication: a means by which people communicate
5. An agent of audification: radio instruments allow the electromagnetic spectrum to be heard

Observing that radio is a carrier wave, a receiver, or a system of distribution is fairly tautological. It could also be convincingly argued that Bertolt Brecht (1932),[1] the amateur radio movement Tetsuo Kogawa,[2] and activists involved with free radio have made an excellent case for radio as «an apparatus of communication.» But it is perhaps not quite as obvious how radio could be considered «an agent of audification.» In our artistic practice, r a d i o q u a l i a surmise that radio «audifies» the spectrum, making the otherwise aphonic realm of electromagnetism audible. In order to unlock this idea, it is helpful to refer to the theoretical work of auditory display researchers, such as Gregory Kramer. This text will briefly introduce this field, along with r a d i o q u a l i a ' s artistic practice in relation to radio. It will continue by demonstrating ways that radio has been used to reveal the hidden aural attributes of the electromagnetic spectrum, not only noting artistic experimentation in this area, but also appraising the experiences of scientists who engage with radio as a tool to monitor and classify natural and man-made radio phenomena.

Exploring Hertzian Space

r a d i o q u a l i a ' s artistic work stems from an interest in the convergence of old and new technologies. We began practicing in Australia in 1998 shortly after arriving there from New Zealand. Our early works were networked radio systems which used the Internet, streaming audio, and FM radio. Some of our projects have tactically engaged with the social contexts we have operated in and have involved listeners in the practice of radio making—through projects such as *The Frequency Clock* (1998–2004)[3] and *self.e x t r a c t i n g.radio* (1998).[4] We also allude to the history of free radio and how it relates to contemporary technology with *Free Radio Linux* (2002–2004).[5] Whilst many of our projects reposition the listener as producer, holding to the notion that «people are radios,»[6] our recent

1   Bertolt Brecht, «Der Rundfunk als Kommunikationsapparat,» *Blätter des Hessischen Landestheaters* (Darmstadt) 16 (July 1932), quoted in *Video Culture: A Critical Investigation*, ed. John G. Hanhardt (Rochester: Visual Studies Workshop, 1986), p. 53. See also Bertolt Brecht, «The Radio as an Apparatus of Communication,» in *Brecht on Theatre*, trans. and ed. John Willett (New York: Hill and Wang, 1964).

2   Tetsuo Kogawa, «If you had the same number of transmitters as receivers, your radio sets could have completely different functions» (1990), quoted from «Toward Polymorphous Radio,» in *Radio Rethink: Art, Sound and Transmission*, ed. Daina Augaitis and Dan Lander (Banff: Banff Centre Press, 1994).

3   http://radioqualia.va.com.au/freqclock/

4   http://www.radioqualia.net/ser

5   Micz Flor, «Hear me out: *Free Radio Linux* broadcasts the Linux sources on air and online,» Walker Art Center, Minneapolis, published online in 2002, http://netartcommons.walkerart.org/article.pl?sid=02/05/12/038213&mode=thread (accessed March 26, 2006).

6   Honor Harger and Adam Hyde, «Frequency Shifting Paradigms in Broadcast Audio,» *Revolutions Per Minute*, broadcast on Radio New Zealand, April 18, 2004.

pso.Net and other projects of the networked
project *Sound Drifting*, installation, OK Center
for Contemporary Art, Ars Electronica Festival,
Linz, Austria, 1999.

work is also concerned with radio as a part of the natural environment. As John Cage memorably commented to fellow musician Morton Feldman in a radio conversation in 1966:

> But all that radio is, Morty, is making available to your ears what was already in the air and available to your ears, but you couldn't hear it. In other words, all it is, is making audible something which you're already in. You are bathed in radio waves.[7]

r a d i o q u a l i a build transmitters and receivers in the locations we visit and use these tools as musical instruments and artistic objects to explore and «audify» the radio waves which surround us. *pso.Net* (1999),[8] and the installation version of *The Frequency Clock*, treated radio waves as sculptable materials. *Free Radio Linux* kindled our interest in presenting abstract information in sound, a process sometimes called «sonification.» Making the imperceptible audible became one of the key aspirations of projects such as *Van Eck TV* (2002)[9] and, later, *Radio Astronomy* (2004–present).[10]

Revealing the Inaudible

Whilst the term «sonification» has become something of a «catch-all» phrase to describe the representation of information in sound, auditory display researchers such as Gregory Kramer[11] and Scaletti (1994) tend to use it to specifically describe the mapping of numeric data onto acoustic outputs. Many musicians and artists employ data sonification in their work, inputting data sets into sound software such as MaxMSP and using the data to generate compositions. New York based artist, Andrea Polli, uses sonification techniques to great effect, as evidenced by the project, *Heat and the Heartbeat of the City* (2004),[12] which sonically models the impact of global warming on New York City.

7   John Cage, excerpt from *Radio Happenings I–V*, performed with fellow musician Morton Feldman in 1966–67 at WBAI in New York City.

8   http://www.radioqualia.net/psonet

9   http://www.radioqualia.net/makrolab/vaneck.html

10 http://www.radio-astronomy.net

11 Gregory Kramer, «An Introduction to Auditory Display,» in *Auditory Display: Sonification, Audification, and Auditory Interfaces (Santa Fe Institute Studies in the Sciences of*

Complexity, Proc. Vol. XVIII), ed. Gregory Kramer (Reading, MA: Addison Wesley, 1994).

12 Andrea Polli, *Heat and the Heartbeat of the City*, commissioned by Turbulence, launched December 1, 2004, http://turbulence.org/ Works/heat/ (accessed March 26, 2006).

13 Kramer 1994 (see note 11).

14 Hayward, «Listening to the earth sing,» in Kramer 1994 (see note 11), pp. 369–404.

Kramer[13] uses the term «audification» to refer to direct signal-to-sound conversion. This differs from sonification, in that data is treated directly as a sound waveform and is not mathematically or digitally altered. Audification can be thought of as the most simple way of representing information in sound. An example of a familiar audification device is a Geiger counter, which indicates the presence of radioactivity in minerals or other materials through a series of clicking sounds. Writers such as Chris Hayward[14] have also suggested that seismic data audifies well, because sound transmitted through the air has similar physics to seismic vibrations transmitted through the earth.

r a d i o q u a l i a ' s interest in the use of sound as means to represent inaudible information began with the work *Free Radio Linux*, which broadcast the entire source code of the open source operating system Linux. Each of the 4.1 million lines of computer code was read aloud by computer voice and sent as sound live on the Internet, resulting in a 593-day-long broadcast. In essence, the code from the Linux software was «sonified» using text-to-speech synthesis. The intention was to use audio to demystify something which most people consider to be impenetrable—computer code. By relaying the code as audio, rather than as written text, the project invited its audience to consider code in a different way.

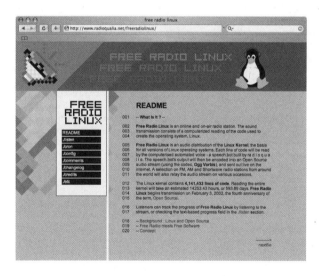

r a d i o q u a l i a,
Free Radio Linux,
broadcasting the
code of the Linux
kernel, screenshot,
2002–2004.

The sonic reading revealed both the functional and opaque qualities of the code. It could be contended that listening allowed audiences to gain a deeper understanding of the processes described by the code. The format of the broadcast alluded to free radio stations, software radio stations from the nineteen-eighties,[15] and the enigmatic number stations which broadcast sporadically on shortwave radio.[16] *Free Radio Linux* twinned sonification techniques with various methods of radio broadcasting and piqued our interest in sonifying inaudible phenomena.

r a d i o q u a l i a ' s next experiment in this area came about whilst we were in residence at the *makrolab*[17] in the remote Scottish Highlands in 2002. We became acquainted with research by a Dutch engineer named Wim van Eck, who published a paper in 1985 outlining a form of surveillance which used computer monitors' electromagnetic fields.[18] At *makrolab* we began the research project, *Van Eck TV* (2002), using transistor radio receivers to detect radiation from monitors. The presence of electromagnetic fields emitted by computer monitors could

15 Flor writes in 2002 (see note 5), «In the late 70s and early 80s, pirate broadcasters would exploit the fact that in the early days many computers would store and retrieve code by using audio tapes. The ZX Spectrum is probably the most popular home computer using this technology. Broadcasting such an audio signal allowed listeners to tape the software and load it into their computers. Systems employing different ways of storing data would require special software to modulate it into audio signals which would then be demodulated by the users at the receiving end. One of the first stations to broadcast computer code was the Dutch station NOS in 1979/80. In their programme ‹Hobbyscoop› they would deliver software for specific computers whose storage methods were acoustic. In the UK, Radio West in Bristol and Radio Victory in Portsmouth were doing the same for their regional communities. The idea was so successful that even the BBC decided to go along with the idea and launched the ‹Chip Shop› in the mid-80s.»

16 Harry Helms, «Shortwave Mysteries,» *Popular Communications* (August 1990), pp. 12–14.

17 *Makrolab* is an itinerant art-science research laboratory developed by Slovenian artist Marko Peljhan.

18 Wim van Eck, «Electromagnetic Radiation from Video Display Units: An Eavesdropping Risk?» *Computers & Security* 4, no. 4 (1985), pp. 269–86; http://www.sciencedirect.com/science/journal/01674048 (accessed March 26, 2006).

19 Stephen P. McGreevy, *Auroral Chorus II: The Music of the Magnetosphere. A Collection of Earth's Mysterious VLF Radio Phenomena*, S.P. McGreevy Productions, U.S., (1996).

20 It is worth noting that historically some people have controversially spoken of sounds associated with auroral displays, often describing them as crackling, hissing, buzzing, or whistling. The Wikipedia entry on aurora borealis notes: «Danish explorer Knud Rasmussen mentioned them indirectly in 1932...the same sounds in the same context are mentioned in an account written by Canadian anthropologist Ernest Hawkes in 1916... But despite these anecdotal reports there are scientific problems with the idea of the sounds being true sound waves originating in the auroras. The energy of the auroras and other factors make it extremely improbable that any sounds directly produced by auroral discharges would reach the ground.» See http://en.wikipedia.org/wiki/Aurora_borealis (accessed May 26, 2006).

21 Douglas Kahn, «Radio was discovered before it was invented (bringing amber to Riga),» at *Art + Communication: Waves*, Riga, Latvia, August 2006.

clearly be heard as interference on radio receivers. Aside from the fact that we made some progress in demonstrating van Eck's theories, we were particularly excited by the way that radio created a sonic «impression» of these otherwise imperceptible fields. A non-audible presence—the fields—was made audible by the utilization of the radio. To our ears, radio was beginning to sound like an agent of audification.

Nature's Radio

Using radio technology to represent inaudible phenomena is not purely an artistic pursuit. Amateur radio hobbyist Stephen P. McGreevy has created a vast archive of unaltered field-recordings of very low frequency (VLF) emissions of the Earth's magnetosphere and its interaction with the Sun and solar wind[19]—often known as «natural radio.» Natural radio phenomena, such as the aurora borealis (or northern lights), cannot be heard by the human ear.[20] But when a radio receiver is used to monitor the aurora, it deciphers the electromagnetic energy as sound, enabling listeners to clearly hear these atmospheric phenomena. Douglas Kahn noted in 2006 that natural radio «can be thought of as a ... place where acoustics and electromagnetics meet, at least from the purview of human audibility.»[21]

As we have intensified our own experimentation with radio, r a d i o q u a l i a have come to understand that many scientists and engineers use the audifying characteristics of radio to identify, monitor, and analyze natural and man-made electromagnetic phenomena. After years of practice, a radio engineer can tell the difference between the sound of a lightening strike, the sound of overhanging power lines, and the sound of an aurora in his or her radio headset. A rapid rise in volume, or a change in the character of a signal, clearly denotes a noteworthy occurrence.

Rob Stammes, an electrical engineer from the Netherlands, is an excellent case in point. Stammes spends most of his spare time assembling, maintaining, and managing a vast array of electrical equipment which he uses to count meteors and detect the occurrence of the aurora borealis. Using his highly honed VLF receiving system, he can get a very accurate reading of the occurrence of an aurora from his base in the Netherlands and then inform tourism agencies in Norway that it is there for tourists to watch. Detecting an intermittent occurrence such as the aurora takes diligent, persistent observation. Whilst magnetospheric signals are recorded graphically on paper strip-charts, using these charts to identify an aurora in real time would take constant, concentrated attention. Stammes instead uses his radio receivers to audify the signals. His VLF receivers are plugged into loudspeakers, which he listens to continuously from his home. As he noted in an interview in September 2006,

> It's nice to have a lot of channels with information on paper, but you must look to the paper. When you can listen to your detecting signals, you can read a book, you can look to the television. Your ear is the best instrument. When there is a little change in the noise or in the sound you can hear it, and that is a good signal [that] something is happening … on the Sun or in the Earth's magnetosphere.[22]

Celestial Radio

The work of McGreevy, Stammes, and other radio hobbyists who work with natural radio resonates with an eminent branch of physics, which also utilizes radio to monitor natural phenomena. Radio astronomy, the study of celestial phenomena at radio wavelengths, was invented after the accidental discovery of cosmic radiation by radio engineer Karl Jansky in 1933.[23] Radio astronomers use radio receivers and antennas to survey the spectrum from 30 kHz to 105 GHz.[24] Some astronomical objects can be detected within the part of the spectrum which is also used for broadcast and amateur radio. The Sun, for instance, can be detected between 17–30 Mhz. The planet Jupiter can be monitored between 17–23 MHz. These frequencies fall within the range of shortwave (and sometimes FM) radio receivers. As with the emissions collected by McGreevy and Stammes, the elec-

22 Rob Stammes, interview with the author, Heidelberg, Germany, September 10, 2006, 16:57.

23 Karl Jansky, «Electrical disturbances apparently of extraterrestrial origin,» *Proc. IRE* 21 (1933), p. 1387.

24 W. D. Brundage and B. Lilie, «Frequency Allocations and Footnotes for Radio Astronomy and Passive Radio Services,» International Telecommunications Union (ITU), in the U.S. by the National Telecommunications and Information Administration (NTIA), the Federal Communications Commission (FCC), 1996.

25 On April 6, 1955, Bernard Burke and Kenneth Franklin announced that they had discovered radio emissions from Jupiter. Documented in Kenneth L. Franklin, «The Discovery of Jupiter Bursts,» in *Serendipitous Discoveries in Radio Astronomy*, ed. Kellermann and Sheets, proceedings of the NRAO Workshop held at the National Radio Astronomy Observatory (Green Bank, West Virginia, May 4–6, 1983), pp. 252–57.

26 Richard Flagg, *Listening to Jupiter*, 2nd ed. (Hawaii: Radio-Sky Publishing, 2003), p. xii.

27 Ibid.

28 Ibid., p. 1.

tromagnetic energy of the Sun and Jupiter are not audible. Sound waves cannot propagate in the vacuum of space. However, as with the phenomena McGreevy and Stammes scrutinize, it is also possible to listen to radiation emitted from Jupiter and the Sun by using common radio receivers as an intermediary between the radio waves and our ears. By acting as agents of audification, our radios can give us an aural awareness of the principal planet in our solar system, and of the Sun itself.

The experience of Hawaii-based engineer Richard Flagg, one of our collaborators on the *Radio Astronomy* project, illustrates how radio can build sonic knowledge of astronomy. Flagg has been involved in designing and building radio receivers and antennas to detect and study Jupiter almost since the birth of the field in 1955.[25] Like Stammes today, Flagg and his colleagues in the nineteen-fifties and sixties monitored their equipment by ear, rather than exclusively by visual readouts. Flagg recalls:

You could spend all night listening to static at the radio observatory.[26]

Flagg and his colleagues would use loudspeakers attached to their receiving units to listen for the L-Bursts (long bursts of radiation) and S-Bursts (short bursts of radiation) of an approaching Jupiter noise storm.

The observer would sit for hours waiting for a radio noise storm ... then it would begin, perhaps with a couple of weak L-Bursts in one channel. And then more bursts. The storm spreads to other frequencies. L-Bursts and S-Bursts blasting from the loudspeakers. An experience not soon forgotten. Finally all the activity subsides and all that remains is the quiet rush of radio static from the galaxy.[27]

Over the years, Flagg developed a systematic understanding of the auditory quality of emissions from Jupiter. He has written about the way in which the different Jovian emissions can be correctly categorized by their differing aural attributes.

L-Bursts sound like ocean waves breaking up on a beach. S-Bursts sound like a handful of pebbles thrown onto a tin roof. If you don't have a tin roof, think of the sound of popcorn popping.[28]

Broadcasting the Music of the Spheres

Douglas Kahn has noted that «the development of radio astronomy since Karl Jansky can be credited with finally taking astronomy out of its silent film period,»[29] and Flagg's recollections certainly provide some substantiation of this. Yet radio astronomy is today a largely visual science, with data being represented in computerized graphs and digital diagrams. Similarly, in popular culture, we have no sense of what space sounds like. Though the weight of images associated with space is overwhelming, hardly any of us could describe the sound of a single planet or star.

r a d i o q u a l i a ' s project *Radio Astronomy* attempts to stimulate an auditory understanding of astronomy. We became fascinated by the idea that radio enabled us to hear something which was physically present, but imperceptible to our senses. So we created *Radio Astronomy* to allow listeners to tune into different celestial frequencies, hearing planets, stars, nebulae, and the constant hiss of cosmic noise. The intention was to unearth the sonic character of objects in our universe, and in the process perhaps making these phenomena more tangible and comprehensible. As Joe Milutis cogently observes,

> What the work of much radio art reveals is the struggle to reveal what is already there.[30]

We collaborated with several astronomical institutions—including the American Space Agency, NASA; Flagg's Windward Community College Radio Observatory, Hawaii, U.S.; and the Ventspils International Radio Astronomy Center, Latvia—to make the project. It launched at ISEA in August 2004 in Finland.[31] Celestial radiation was received by our international network of radio telescopes, common radio receivers were used to make the radiation audible, and the resulting sound was then broadcast online, on FM, as well as being relayed live inside an astro-

29 Kahn 2006 (see note 21).

30 Joe Milutis, «Radiophonic Ontologies,» in *Experimental Sound and Radio*, ed. Allen S. Weiss (Cambridge: MIT Press, 1996), p. 58.

31 The International Symposium for Electronic Art (ISEA) was held in Helsinki and Tallin in August 2004.

32 Nicholas Zurbrugg, «Sound Art, Radio Art and Post-Radio Performance in Australia,» ed. Brian Shoesmith and Alec McHoul, *Continuum: The Australian Journal of Media & Culture* 2, no. 2 (1989), pp. 26–49; http://wwwmcc .murdoch.edu.au/ReadingRoom/2.2/2.2.html (accessed March 26, 2006).

nomical observatory called URSA, in the form of a site-specific installation. On any given occasion, a listener may have encountered the roaring waves and spitting fire of Jupiter's stormy interactions with its moon Io, the Sun's fizzling solar flares, pulsars' metronomic beats, or the eerie melodic shimmer of a whistler in the magnetosphere. Many listeners observed that audified by radio, the textured glistening soundscapes of the universe bore some aesthetic correspondence to experimental electronic music or avant-garde sound art. Since it's first outing in 2004, *Radio Astronomy* has been shown as an installation in several forms and continues to broadcast online and occasionally on-air. It is radio astronomy in a literal way—a radio station devoted to broadcasting sounds from space.

Nicholas Zurbrugg writes that

> ... radio art might be identified as that creativity predominantly dependent upon radio technology for its conception, for its realization, and for its distribution. In its most pure form, radio art might be thought of as exclusively radiophonic materials orchestrated and disseminated by radiophonic technology.[32]

RT-32 and RT-16 antenna at Ventspils International Radio Astronomy Center, Irbene, Latvia.

For *Radio Astronomy*, we attempted to use radio in every stage of the project. For us, the nature of celestial radiation, which propagates as radio waves, invited inherent comparisons to the medium of radio. We reasoned that the phenomena called for the media. To refer back to the taxonomy used in the introduction, we not only used radio as «a mechanism of reception» (radiation was received by radio telescopes) and «an agent of audification» (receivers made it audible), but also as «a system of distribution» (the audified sounds were resent by radio transmitters, back into space). *Radio Astronomy* completes a cycle of transmission begun billions of years ago by the emission of radiation from stars in our Universe.

An Interface between Radio Waves and Our Ears

Thus radio shifts its function with its context. In r a d i o q u a l i a' s practice, radio is sometimes a receiver, frequently a transmitter, and often an ebullient enactment of Brecht's wish for an apparatus of communication, but radio can also be an interface between radio waves and our ears. It can make the intangible materiality of the electromagnetic spectrum audible, thus opening up the Hertzian space around us, and above us, to our aural sense.

The Realization of
Radio's Unrealized Potential

Media-Archaeological Focuses
in Current Artistic Projects

Inke Arns

> I'll throw the damned rearview mirror out of the
> damned window because I don't want to know
> where I've come from, but where I'm going.[1]
> — *Frank Lloyd Wright*

The American architect is said to have been driving when he made the above remark in the nineteen-thirties, and to have snapped off and tossed out of the window the vehicle's rearview mirror as he spoke. This declarative break with the past amounts to a near-perfect self-stylization of the historical avant-garde. That his dramatic avowal of being fixated exclusively on the new was not wholly accurate (since even the avant-garde movement adopted and adapted elements from the past) is made clear by a 1929 photograph of Alexander Rodchenko. It captured, in the rearview mirror of a car driving through Moscow, the reflection of the Russian artist, sitting next to a pipe-smoking man, presenting an almost uncanny answer to the statement later made Frank Lloyd Wright.

Contemporary artistic projects are increasingly using a similar rearview mirror in order to focus on their own movement into the future by recording what lies behind. In Eastern Europe especially, the (media) art projects of the last decade have displayed growing interest in the technology-related utopian dreams and fantasies of the past. The work of artists such as the «retro-utopians»[2] (Marko Peljhan, Vadim Fishkin, Cosmokinetic Cabinet Noordung, and others) does not automatically, as was still the case in the nineteen-eighties, equate the utopias of the avant-garde with totalitarian leanings but scrutinizes such visions for the projections and blueprints they contain in regard to media technologies. In the early twentieth century, visions of this kind came not only from artists and theorists associated with the avant-garde, but equally from scientists and engineers. Velimir Khlebnikov, Bertolt Brecht, Nikola Tesla, Nikolai Fedorov, and Hermann Potočnik Noordung are among the names that recur in that connection. The last name is that of a Slovenian engineer who lent his name to the Cosmokinetic Cabinet Noordung and inspired the design of the space station that rotates round its own axis in Stanley Kubrick's film *2001: A Space Odyssey* (1968). Potočnik, who was a pioneer of space medicine, described the station with precise drawings and technical details in *The Problem of Space Travel: The Rocket Motor*, a book first published in German (as *Probleme der Befahrung des Weltraums – Der Raketenmotor*) in Berlin in 1929. Kubrick's legendary film creates a monument to the space station, the revolutionary idea that in the post-1945 era via the agency of Wernher von Braun had captured the collective imagination of the United States of America.

The growing media-archaeological interest of art projects in these early utopian technological fantasies of the avant-garde was symptomatic of a significantly altered relationship to the notion of the utopia(n) in the nineteen-nineties. The clearly negative associations of utopianism with political totalitarianism was giving way to increasingly positive political connotations with emancipating or even visionary-spectral potential («utopicity»).

The mass usage of the Internet and other new digital media that began in the nineteen-nineties, and which in Eastern Europe coincided with processes of

1 The 2004 Ars Electronica used the quotation to illustrate the theme «Timeshift – The World in Twenty-Five Years.»

2 See Inke Arns, *Objects in the Mirror May Be Closer Than They Appear! Avantgarda v vzvratnem ogledalu* (Ljubljana, 2006) and Inke Arns, *Objects in the Mirror May Be Closer Than They Appear! Die Avantgarde im Rückspiegel* (Brussels, forthcoming).

3 See Dieter Daniels, *Kunst als Sendung: Von der Telegrafie zum Internet* (Munich, 2002), pp. 254–57.

4 Siegfried Zielinski, *Archäologie der Medien* (Munich, 2002), back cover; see also Timothy Druckrey, «Imaginary Futures,» *Media Archaeology* (dossier), http://www.debalie.nl/dossierpagina.jsp?dossierid=10123 (accessed May 29, 2007).

5 In reaction to the 1918 revolution, the jurisdiction of the German Reich was applied to the creation and operation of transmitting and receiving equipment. Moreover, a decree from 1922 (repealed in 1923) prohibited private individuals from receiving radio transmissions. From 1923 onward, the technical possibilities of receiving devices were restricted, and a ban on feedback was introduced along with the requirement for licensing and fees.

6 Wolfgang Ernst, during the 100 Years of Radio conference, Vienna, January 2007.

7 See Inke Arns, «Interaction, Participation, Network: Art and Telecommunication,» in *Media Art Net*, ed. Dieter Daniels and Rudolf Frieling (Vienna, 2004), http://www.medienkunstnetz .de/themen/medienkunst_im_ueberblick/ kommunikation/ and Reinhard Braun's essay in this volume. See also Edith Decker and Peter Weibel, *Vom Verschwinden der Ferne: Telekommunikation und Kunst* (Cologne, 1990).

political and social transformation, was certainly crucial for the growing interest in the historical roots of new media technologies. However, artistic interest in the history of technical systems aims to do more than merely provide teleological confirmation that the present situation has a history of coming into being. Rather, the media-archaeological interest of contemporary artists applies to—and here I use a phrase coined by Dieter Daniels—the *unredeemed (technical) utopias* of, for example, the historical avant-garde, which are simultaneously the reverse side of the *realized anticipations* of the historical avant-garde.[3] This recollection of potential—since never realized—futures of mediums, of the forgotten minor branches of technological history, of the ideas, concepts, and visions that remained in the realms of the technological-imaginary, is at the same time *not nostalgic*. In fact, such a retrospective media-archaeological survey of utopias, which Siegfried Zielinski terms «movement in the deep time of media-technological thought and operation,»[4] reactivates past potentials and thus becomes a *corrective for current and future developments*.

This reactivation also, and primarily, applies to notions of radio. With the emergence in the mid-nineteen-nineties of the Internet as a potential (mass) medium with a feedback channel—and at present above all with wireless communication networks (cell phone networks, W-LANs, etc.)—the former potential of radio as a global wireless radio and communications technology is being reinstated in unexpected contexts and to a hitherto unforeseen degree.

This amounts to the rediscovery of a historical aspect of the medium of which few people, aside from amateur radio enthusiasts, remained aware after radio became subject to state regulation (in Germany, as of 1918),[5] namely the fact that before the regulation and centralization of radio—*as a simultaneous receiving and transmitting device*—it had already once signified unhindered access to a realm of global communication. In Germany, the vertical and centralized broadcasting principle of the radio mass medium («for everyone») replaced the horizontal, cross-connected communication medium radio. Wolfgang Ernst succinctly summarized how this development truncated that of the radio medium: «The beginning of broadcasting was the end of radio.»[6]

A return to, or the recollection of, an alternative history of radio first came about with the Internet of the nineteen-nineties and its expansion into the «realm» beyond fixed ethernet cables. From the sixties onward, artistic telecommunications projects,[7] and radio art projects in particular, possessed some awareness that an alternative history existed. However, it is not just the *technical feasibility of a feedback channel* that is currently leading to a genuine «re-invention» of radio (keyword: *Horizontal Radio*).[8] Equally important, if indeed not more so, is a growing awareness of the perception of space that surrounds us as a *realm shot through with electromagnetic waves*, as an *augmented space*. This electromagnetic spectrum resembles an unknown continent that must be explored and mapped. In this process, it soon becomes clear that the waves by which we are surrounded are not exclusively of natural origin but that the electromagnetic spectrum, as a zone of combat over frequencies and licenses, is dominated by political and commercial interests. This situation was most recently made clear by the exhibition *Waves* mounted in Riga in 2006 under the curatorship of Armin Medosch, Rasa Šmite, and Raitis Šmits. There were clear references to Nikola Tesla in *Broadcasting Project, dedicated to Nikola Tesla*, curated by What, How & for Whom (WHW) in the Zagreb Museum of Technology (2002),[9] as well as in Nina Czegledy's exhibition *Resonance: The Electromagnetic Bodies Project* (2005–2006),[10] Marko Lulic's video *Tesla 21* (2002),[11] and Craig Baldwin's *Spectres of the Spectrum* (1999), a film examining Tesla's influence on popular culture.

In the following, I intend to illustrate the media-archaeological interest of a young generation of artists on the basis of several projects specifically addressing the «disintegration of radio in the form of apparatus and the renaissance of wireless.»[12] The examples are provided by the group convex tv., the International Necronautical Society (INS), Suzanne Treister, r a d i o q u a l i a / RIXC, and Marko Peljhan and/or Projekt Atol. These artists and projects are linked not only by their shared interest in contemporary developments in the electromagnetic spectrum, but also by the interest shown in the history of that which came

8 As early as 1995, Gerfried Stocker, Heidi Grundmann, and x-space carried out at the Ars Electronica Festival their *Horizontal Radio* project, the basic concept of which was to superimpose over the classical transmission medium radio the mechanisms and structures created (as a network metaphor) by the Internet. Some twenty-five radio stations in Australia, Canada, Europe (including Russia), and the U.S. participated for twenty-four hours on all frequencies over the two-day period June 22–23, 1995.

9 See http://projectbroadcasting.mi2.hr/index.htm.

10 See http://www.resonance-electromagnetic bodies.net/.

11 In *Tesla 21*, Marko Lulic combines his personal research with the various mythologies that surround Nikola Tesla and sets out in search of the latter's topographical and historical traces, a journey that takes him from the house where Tesla was born in Smiljan, through the small Croatian town of Gospic, to New York. Lulic posits that while the modern movements failed, this is not true of the utopias by which they were fuelled.

12 Armin Medosch, during the 100 Years of Radio conference, Vienna, January 2007.

International Necronautical Society, *Second First Committee Hearings: Transmission, Death, Technology*, Witness Heath Bunting (on screen), INS Chief of Propaganda Anthony Auerbach and INS General Secretary Tom McCarthy (*left to right*) and Witnesses Mukul Patel and Manu Luksch (on screen), INS First Committee Delegation Anthony Auerbach, Tom McCarthy, Zinovy Zinik (*left to right*), Cubitt Gallery, London, U.K., 2002.

to be and has thus been actualized (the technological structure by which we are confronted today) as well as of that which was prevented from developing and therefore did not come to be—in other words, the still-existing reservoir of techno-utopian potential. All these examples make it clear that these media-archaeological projects are not concerned merely with illustrating or citing history but with genuinely picking up the loose threads of the techno-imaginary that they view as conceptual inspiration for current developments.

In the suggestively titled 1997 manifesto «there's a bandwidth playing on the radio,»[13] the *net.radio* collective convex tv., founded in Berlin in 1996, briefly outlines the third space opening up behind the «old, almost pitiable» radio medium: «Ever since the format dictatorship was imposed on radio—although consumers had long since been zapping through dozens of TV channels—the medium has seemed like an obsolete, almost pitiable, technology. convex tv. answers the routine public-station statements from the few *to all* and their dismissal as a permanently reconstituting collective form: precisely because radio, in the form of format radio, is utterly in ruins—its public-station antipode still mourning the golden age of highbrow culture transmitted top-down—a third space is opening up in the ether.» Wholly in the spirit of the early amateur radio pioneers and of the original concept of radio, convex tv. founded the *German Schwarzsender*. During a term of residence in the *Hybrid WorkSpace* set up at the documenta X in Kassel (August 8 to September 1, 1997), the collective established a distributed, self-organizing network of some two hundred radio transmitters and receivers within which anybody would be able, as the motto ran, to transmit whenever they wanted («*jeder jederzeit senden kann*»). The objective of the *German Schwarzsender* was to integrate the medium radio into the debate emerging about distributed networks as the Internet evolved.[14]

The declared aim of the International Necronautical society (INS), a pseudo-bureaucratic organization founded in London in 1999, is to examine radio in all its (necro-)poetical and simultaneously political dimensions. The society's self-confident founding manifesto declares death to be «a type of space.»[15] Modeled on Soviet and corporate organizations as well as on the structures of early-twen-

---

13 convex tv., «there's a bandwidth playing on the radio,» 1997, http://www.art-bag.org/convextv/pro/object.htm (accessed May 29, 2007).

14 In 1998, convex tv., together with mikro e.V., organized the Net.Radio Days in Berlin, one of the first events dedicated to the subject of net radio. See http://www.art-bag.org/trimmdich/anno.htm.

15 See http://www.necronauts.org.

16 See http://www.hexen2039.net.

tieth century avant-garde movements, the INS operates in the «mediasphere,» according to its General Secretary Tom McCarthy. Its interventions to date include the reenactment of a Mafia shooting in a wind tunnel in the Netherlands (2001), public *Committee Hearings into Transmission, Death and Technology* (2002), the infiltration of the official BBC website (2004), and the establishment of a transmitter unit in London's ICA (*Calling All Agents*, 2004). The last of these projects, which involved more than fifty participants in elaborate text- and data-processing processes, fused together scenes from Jean Cocteau's film *Orphée* (1950) with William Burroughs's world of control centers, in this way having produced a steady stream of cut-ups—lyrical, frenzied propaganda—broadcast over a VHF transmitter to the London area, and over the Internet to participating stations in Europe and the U.S.

By contrast, the Institute of Militronics and Advanced Time Interventionality (IMATI), founded by Australian artist Suzanne Treister in 1995, is interested in the history of the subversive manipulation techniques described by William Burroughs in *The Electronic Revolution* (1971) and, more specifically, in the combination of occult and military technologies in the twentieth and twenty-first centuries. For Treister's *HEXEN 2039: New military-occult technologies of psychological warfare* (2006),[16] she invented a time-traveling explorer, Rosalind Brodsky, who in 2039 reveals the most improbable connections in the course of her research on the twentieth and twenty-first centuries: for instance, connections between the Remote Viewing program, operated by the Stanford Research Institute from 1972–1995, and the film *Stargate*, produced by the Metro Goldwyn Mayer (MGM) Studios in 1994; between the British occultist Aleister Crowley and the researcher Jack Parsons, who developed rocket fuel in the Pasadena Rocket Research Labs; or between the *Silent Subliminal Presentation System*, patented by Oliver Lowery in 1992, and the psychological and subliminal techniques of warfare deployed in Iraq, in Abu Ghraib, and in Guantanamo. Rosalind Brodsky also links these research projects—which serve primarily military goals—with a number of poetic elements, including the film *The Wizard of Oz*, Modest Mussorgsky's *A Night on the Bare Mountain* (1867), the walpurgis night (*Walpurgisnacht*), the Brocken peak in the Harz mountains, a typology of transmitter towers for television and other purposes, the 1936 Olympic Games in Berlin, Walt Disney's film *Fantasia* of 1940 and the development of the *Fantasound* sound system, as well as (unlikely though it sounds) lists of articles sold in Dortmund at the Moondaughter Wicca Shop, a retail outlet for «witchcraft accessories and ritualistic supplies.» Treister subjects this list, and likewise one of all the places in which M15 and M16 were based from 1924 up to the present day, to a gematriacal[17] analysis, attempting to discover concealed meanings in the numerical values thus obtained.

In the manner of the classical conspiracy theory, the Brodsky–Treister duo weave disparate elements and fragmentary observations into gigantic associative networks which are then recorded in delicate ink-and-pencil drawings. Suzanne Treister's *HEXEN 2039* is a (media-)archaeology of our present-day, written from a future-based perspective, obsessive and fascinating yet highly realistic. Her deliberate blending of fact and fiction succeeds in destabilizing that which we purport to know for sure, thus opening a retrospective—or forecasting—view of possible futures.

For some years now, the group r a d i o q u a l i a of New Zealand has been preoccupied with the equally interesting phenomenon of audification. The two members, Honor Harger and Adam Hyde, have been working in the net radio context for over a decade.[18] Launched in 2003, their *Radio Astronomy*[19] project translates into sound the data collected globally by various radio telescopes and distributes this stellar sound over the Internet or via FM radio. Developed in collaboration with astronomers, engineers, and radio astronomy stations,[20] the project facilitates public listening of various «heavenly» frequencies—planets, stars, and cosmic noise: in other words, the sound of the universe.

The *solar listening_station* (2003/2006), based on *Radio Astronomy*, formed a part of the *Solar Radio Station* project (2006),[21] a collaborative project involving artists from r a d i o q u a l i a along with RIXC, Riga, the musicians of Clausthome, Riga, and the scientists working at the Ventspils International Radio Astronomy Center VIRAC in Irbene, Latvia. *solar listening_station* was devoted to

17 Gematria is the attempt to interpret letters mystically by converting them into corresponding numerical values in order to obtain new meanings. Gematria is an old method of using the numerical values of letters in order to detect the assumed hidden meaning of a word. See http://en.wikipedia.org/wiki/Gematria (accessed May 29, 2007).

18 r a d i o q u a l i a, http://www.radioqualia.net.

19 *Radio Astronomy*, http://www.radio-astronomy.net.

20 With, among others, the VIRAC radio telescope in Irbene, Latvia; the Windward Community College Radio Observatory, Hawaii, U.S.; the Radio Jove Network operated by NASA; and the Interplanetary Scintillation Radio Telescope Array in Mexico.

21 *Solar Radio Station* took place from May 16 to July 23, 2006 in the framework of the show *mit allem rechnen. Medienkunst aus Estland, Lettland, Litauen* (English title: *Face the unexpected: Media art from Estonia, Latvia, and Lithuania*), Hartware MedienKunstVerein, Museum am Ostwall and PHOENIX Halle, Dortmund. See http://www.hmkv.de/dyn/e_program_exhibitions/detail.php?nr=1225.

RIXC, Clausthome, r a d i o q u a l i a, and VIRAC, *Solar Radio Station*, installation, Dortmund, Germany, 2006.

RIXC, Clausthome, r a d i o q u a l i a, and VIRAC, *Solar Radio Station*, performance, Dortmund, Germany, 2006.

the audification of the radiation emitted by the sun. This electromagnetic energy is the cause of white noise on the radio but, if discharged in sufficient quantities during so-called sun storms, can also cause considerable disruption to the earth's radio spectrum and to electronic devices, as well as damage to satellites orbiting the earth. r a d i o q u a l i a is interested in the space surrounding us that is filled with data streams of terrestrial and extraterrestrial origin. The audification of these streams serves to make perceptible a highly differentiated radiophone urban soundscape.

The work of r a d i o q u a l i a was crucially influenced by the *Acoustic Space Lab*, an international symposium on the subject of radio and satellite communication that was organized by RIXC and held at VIRAC in Irbene, Latvia in August of 2001.[22] The VIRAC commands a satellite telescope of thirty-two-meter diameter (v-32), abandoned by the Red Army in 1992 and partially dismantled. During the Soviet era, the KGB had used the telescope to monitor satellite communications between Europe and the U.S. Today, it counts among the world's five most precise radio telescopes accessible to civilian research. The twenty-five media artists, activists, musicians, and theorists participating in the *Acoustic Space Lab* jointly attended workshops with the VIRAC radio technicians in order to examine the possibilities of creatively deploying the former military technology to which artists rarely have access. The parabolic antenna was used to generate sound and also to monitor satellites of the INMARSAT network. The monitoring results were made freely available on the Internet as acoustic «raw material.»

Marko Peljhan numbered among the artists who took part in the *Acoustic Space Lab* in Irbene. The Slovenian artist co-developed with Projekt Atol the *makrolab*,[23] which was first set up at the documenta X in Kassel in 1997 and later operated on the west coast of Australia in early 2000, in Scotland[24] in the spring of 2002, and on the island of Campalto by Venice from June to December 2003. The *makrolab* is an autonomous research, working, and residential unit that, with the aid of all manner of technical equipment and varying research crews, maps the «topography of signals»[25] throughout the electromagnetic spectrum—as a kind of private ECHELON system. The laboratory is equipped with vast transmit-

22 *Acoustic Space Lab*, Irbene, Latvia, August 4–12, 2001. Documented in detail at http://acoustic.space.re-lab.net/lab/.

23 *Makrolab*, http://makrolab.ljudmila.org (accessed May 29, 2007).

24 See Rob La Frenais, Gillean Dickie, and Paul Khera, eds., *makrolab*, exh. cat. The Arts Catalyst and Zavod Projekt Atol (London, 2003).

25 Dieter Daniels in *cITy: Internationaler Medienkunstpreis 2000* (Karlsruhe: SWF Baden Baden, 2000), pp. 94–97, here p. 95.

Marko Peljhan/Projekt Atol, *makrolab*,
Rottnest Island, Australia, 2000.

ting and receiving antennas covering various signal ranges, in which they are able to record circulating data streams (private telephone calls, satellite-controlled navigation systems, and military and commercial communications). The *makrolab*, which was conceived as a ten-year research project, has been set up at preferably non-urban locations remote from the exhibition circuit; preparations are in progress for its permanent installation in the Antarctic as of 2007.

Peljhan terms the strategy pursued in this project one of «insulation/isolation.»[26] He is referring to a combination of total physical isolation with a state of being totally connected via media with the outer world. The objective is to better enable the observation—from outside—of signal streams, and to intensify the communication among crew members inside the *makrolab*. Peljhan's thesis is that under conditions of such intense isolation, a small number of individuals will be able to produce more «evolutionary code» than large political movements. Due to the suggestion that this model might function for society as a whole, the idea of an isolated small elite of researchers remains strangely ambiguous. At the same time, however, the «insulation/isolation» engenders on the microlevel of the *makrolab* a specific subjectivity, an «affective sociality,»[27] that, according to Kodwo Eshun, distinguishes the *makrolab* from the sterility of most projects linking science and art.

26 Marko Peljhan, «makrolab | lecture 310897; the makrolab lecture in the 100 days program,» lecture, documenta X, Kassel, 1997, http://makrolab.ljudmila.org/reports/published/peljhan/.

27 Kodwo Eshun, «Makrolab's Twin Imperatives and Their Children Too,» in La Frenais 2003 (see note 24), pp. 6–14, here p. 7.

28 Marko Peljhan in ostranenie 95: 2. Internationales Video-Forum an der Stiftung Bauhaus Dessau, exh. cat. Stiftung Bauhaus Dessau (Dessau, 1995), p. 324.

29 The Russian (Cubo-)Futurists did not share their Italian counterparts' enthusiasm for technology and modernity. The Russian «futurians» were interested above all in the development of new linguistic concepts. See Hans Günther, «Befreite Worte und Sternensprache: Der italienische und der russische Futurismus,» in Literarische Moderne: Europäische Literatur im 19. und 20. Jahrhundert, ed. R. Grimminger, J. Murasov, and J. Stückrath (Reinbek, 1995), pp. 284–313.

30 Combination of «lad» (Old Russian for harmony, living creature) and «mir» (peace, world, universe)—«both these parts are conjoined by the vowel O, for which Khlebnikov has devised the meaning of THE LETTER THAT INCREASES SIZE»; see Peljhan's makrolab lecture 1997 (see note 26).

31 Aage Hansen-Löve, «Faktur/Gemachtheit,» in Glossarium der russischen Avantgarde, ed. Aleksandar Flaker (Vienna and Graz, 1989), pp. 212–19, here p. 212.

Peljhan understands evolutionary code to mean the experimental exploration and development of strategies and modes of behavior in present-day and future societies, initially tested under laboratory conditions in the *makrolab* so that they may later be deployed in everyday life. And herein lies the utopian potential of the *makrolab*: it is first a question of making us conscious of the immaterial data space that has imposed itself over the material world like a new dimension. The second step consists in making clear the antagonistic power interests existing in this data sphere, together with their strategies of data collecting, surveillance, and control. In a third step, the *makrolab* has developed a «counter-surveillance» method to counter these strategies. These tactics involve the inverting, or opening and making accessible, of techniques and technologies that can normally be pursued only by institutional, governmental, or commercial entities.

The *makrolab* is part of the *LADOMIR-FAKTURA* project series conducted by Marko Peljhan together with various collaborators since 1994. According to Peljhan, the title of the series refers to the «findings derived from the works of Velimir Khlebnikov, his mathematical works on time and history, his linguistic research … as well as his poems and literary works.»[28] Velimir Khlebnikov (1885–1922) was one of the foremost exponents of Russian Futurism.[29] The project title *LADOMIR-FAKTURA* contains both a direct allusion to Khlebnikov's poem «Ladomir» of 1920, which according to its author describes the universal realm of the future,[30] as well as a reference to the *faktura* («facture»), one of the core artistic methods formulated by the Russian Formalists. The notion of *faktura* or «surface quality» describes the «totality of all those material and plastic characteristics of the picture surface which in Cubo-Futurism no longer mimetically simulates the space but has been reified to an independent three-dimensional object (‹relief›) of haptic perception (tactile sense).»[31] Prerevolutionary Russian Futurism aimed to eliminate illusionism in painting (and literature), to abolish the referential—and thus likewise the symbolic—character of the image and the word. In the eyes of the Futurists, the non-illustrative and radically desemiotized painting or word artifact, thus reduced to its pure materiality, gained in reality as a «word as such.» This radical desemiotization led to heightened sensitivity to materiality and increased attentiveness to the «surface quality» of the «material artifact.» Thus, *faktura* firstly produces an intensified sensory perception in general, but secondly an estrangement effect consisting in the «disclosure» or «baring» of the procedure that makes the overall structure of the artwork the object of reflection.[32] Marko Peljhan himself uses the Formalist term *faktura* as a «technical designation of the method of work, which is struggling to give a sensorial and tactile quality to abstract elements in art and science.»[33] Accordingly, the term describes a method by means of which Peljhan creates tactile, sensorially perceptible surfaces for invisible communications spaces shot through with invisible data streams.[34]

In his poem «Ladomir» (1920), Velimir Khlebnikov describes a future scenario resulting from wars, the destruction of the old order and the creation of a new. Khlebnikov's «science of the individual,» by which he means a kind of synaesthesis of abstract-scientific and tactile-sensory processes, is a training and testing phase for establishing contact with this novel environment. According to Khlebnikov, wireless radio and communication play an important part in the exploration of new spatiotemporal concepts. The individual must gather experience with this new space-time and reflect scientifically upon the changing constellations of harmony (Old Russian: *lad*) and peace/world (Russian: *mir*).[35] Centrally important to the latter is, as Marko Peljhan noted in 1994,[36] the strategy

32   Ibid., p. 213.

33   Marko Peljhan, «Information on Pact, Collaborators and Projekt Atol,» in *LADOMIR-FAKTURA: Cetrta povrsina – povrsina stika! Ritmicno-scenska podobe. Materiali* (*LADOMIR-FAKTURA: Fourth surface – the surface of contact! Rhythmical-scenic structure. Writings*), ed. Projekt Atol (Ljubljana, 1996), p. 16.

34   For an analysis of the highly interesting connection between the Formalist concepts of *faktura* and *poverchnost'* (surface) and that of the interface, see Inke Arns, «Faktur und Interface: Khlebnikov, Tesla und der himmlische Datenverkehr in Marko Peljhans makrolab (1997–2007),» in *«Ohne Schnur: Art and Wireless Communication*, ed. Katja Kwastek, exh. cat. Cuxhavener Kunstverein (Frankfurt am Main, 2004), pp. 62–79.

35   See Johannes Birringer, «MAKROLAB – A Heterotopia,» *Performing Arts Journal* (Autumn 1998), http://makrolab.ljudmila.org/birringer.html.

36   Marko Peljhan, «Science of the Individual – Mapping of Ladomir» (1994), reprinted in

Marko Peljhan, «makrolab,» in *Politics-Poetics: das Buch zur documenta X* (Ostfildern, 1997), pp. 784–85.

37   Velimir Khlebnikov, «The Radio of the Future,» in *The King of Time: Selected Writings of the Russian Futurian*, ed. Charlotte Douglas, trans. Paul Schmidt (1921; repr., Cambridge, MA, 1985), pp. 155–59.

38   See Dubravka Oraic-Tolic, «Die Sternensprache,» in Flaker 1989 (see note 31), pp. 448–55.

39   Khlebnikov worked in Piatigorsk for the «Tergubrosta.» See note in Velimir Khlebnikov, *Tvorenija* (1986). Accessed at the Russkaja Virtual'naja Biblioteka (Russian Virtual Library), version 1.4, on September 23, 2000, http://www.rvb.ru.

40   Khlebnikov in Douglas 1985 (see note 37), p. 186.

41   Ibid.

42   See, for example, the two photomontages showing Nikola Tesla sitting in his laboratory under static discharge in Margaret Cheney, *Tesla – Man out of Time* (Englewood Cliffs, 1981).

of «insulation/isolation.» It is a matter of equipping the individual in a situation of «intensive isolation» with contemporary interfaces enabling him to find his bearings in spaces that are increasingly influenced by immaterial information-based structures.

Marko Peljhan's preoccupation with Khlebnikov is concerned with emphasizing central concepts and ideas of the Russian Futurist. These include the emphasis Khlebnikov placed on the positive effects exercised on a global consciousness by the deployment of new technical media such as the radio[37] (in «The Radio of the Future,» 1921, and elsewhere), on the significance of the dimension of time, or the «temporal axis,» for a future spatiotemporal global order, as well as his notion of a «universal language,» the «stellar language» to whose construction the Futurist poet devoted himself from 1915 up to his premature death in 1921.[38]

In his short poetic text «The Radio of the Future,» Khlebnikov develops his vision of the future rule of the mass media radio and television. He describes the Russian Telegraph Agency (ROSTA), for which he worked in Piatigorsk in 1921,[39] as the «consciousness of man,» as his «brain,» as the «uniform point of the people's will,» and as the «spiritual sun of the country.» Equated with the «consciousness of the people» within Khlebnikov's visionary framework, the central transmitting station or the media network—«the whole country will be covered with radio stations»[40]—becomes immeasurably important: «The main Radio station, that stronghold of steel, where clouds of wires cluster like strands of hair, will surely be protected by a sign with a skull and crossbones and the familiar word ‹Danger,› since the least disruption of Radio operations would produce a mental blackout over the entire country, a temporary loss of consciousness.»[41] In his description of the immaterial connection routes emanating from the main radio station, Khlebnikov on the one hand tries to find material-haptic images for immaterial radio connections (streams, swarms, ropes, nets), while on the other hand he operates with metaphors based on lightning and electricity («annihilating» and «flaring» bolts of lightning, «bright blue ball of spherical lightning,» «stream of lightning birds») reminiscent of the mystical-technical aura of many experimental procedures investigated by Nikola Tesla:[42] «Let us try to imagine Radio's main station: in the air a spider's web of lines, a storm cloud of lightning bolts, some subsiding, some flaring up anew, crisscrossing the building from one end to the other. A bright blue ball of spherical lightning hanging in midair like a timid bird, guy wires stretched out at a slant. / From this point on Planet Earth, every day, like the flight of birds in springtime, a flock of news departs, news from the life of the spirit. / In this stream of lightning birds the spirit will prevail over force, good counsel over threats.»[43]

Thus, the radio of the future solves the «problem of celebrating the communion of humanity's one soul, one daily spiritual wave» by, among other means, almost instantaneous message transmission: «Earthquakes, fires, disasters, the events of each twenty-four-hour period will be printed out on the Radio books.»[44] The radio, this «newspaper without paper and without distance,»[45] would in this way «forge continuous links in the universal soul and mold mankind into a single entity.»[46]

The ubiquity enabled by radio, that is to say, the capability conveyed by media of being omnipresent, meaning of being everywhere and seeing everything immediately,[47] of hearing things evidently taking place thousands of kilometers away—until then an attribute of the divine—was still able to evoke euphoria in 1921: «But now what follows? Where has this great stream of sound come from, this inundation of the whole country in supernatural singing, in the sound of beating wings, this broad silver stream full of whistlings and clangor and marvelous mad bells surging from somewhere we are not … ? … Are these perhaps the voices of heaven, spirits flying low over the farmhouse roof? No … The Mussorgsky of the future is giving a coast-to-coast concert of his work, using the Radio apparatus to create a vast concert hall stretching from Vladivostok to the Baltic, beneath the blue dome of the heavens.»[48] Khlebnikov further writes: «Now the reading-walls grow dark; suddenly the sound of a distant voice is heard singing, the metallic throat of Radio beams the rays of the song to its many metallic

43 Khlebnikov in Douglas 1985 (see note 37), p. 155.
44 Ibid., p. 156.
45 Lenin, quoted in Winfried B. Lerg, «Ein Pionier des Sowjetrussischen Rundfunks: Vor 40 Jahren starb M. A. Bontsch-Brujewitsch,» Studienkreis Rundfunk und Geschichte, Mitteilungen 6, no. 3 (July 1980), pp. 136–38, here p. 136.
46 Khlebnikov in Douglas 1985 (see note 37), p. 159. In a speech given at the opening of the 7th Great German Radio and Audio Show on August 22, 1930, Albert Einstein used similar phrasing; see Albert Einstein, «Die wahre Aufgabe des Rundfunks: Einzigartige Möglichkeiten zur Völkerverständigung,» Beiträge zur Geschichte des Rundfunks 12, no. 3 (1978), pp. 89–90.

47 See Paul Virilio, Revolutionen der Geschwindigkeit (Berlin, 1993), p. 15.
48 Khlebnikov in Douglas 1985 (see note 37), p. 157.
49 Ibid., p. 158.
50 Virilio 1993 (see note 47), p. 52.
51 Ibid. A very precise description of a modem, that is, of a modulator-demodulator necessary for remote data transmission, can be found in Khlebnikov: «Surges of lightning are picked up and transmitted to the metal mouth of an autospeaker, which converts them into amplified sound, into singing and human speech.» Khlebnikov in Douglas 1985 (see note 37), p. 156.
52 Khlebnikov in Douglas 1985 (see note 37), pp. 157–58. Khlebikov's text is genuinely

singers: metal sings! And its words, brought forth in silence and solitude, and their welling springs, become a communion shared by the entire country.»[49] This fascination in face of the instantaneous approachment of remote places, the telescoping of near and far, and the abrupt shrinking of the «wide world»—Virilio would later call it the «infra-mince»[50] of the world—seems to anticipate the technological euphoria evoked by the Internet in the nineteen-nineties.

This «infra-mince» is already preformulated in Khlebnikov's notion of the radio of the future, for the «flickering of those apparitions being instantaneously transmitted»[51] evidently encompasses not only texts (messages, scientific information, and educational programs) but also visual information: «Today Radio is using its apparatus to transmit images in color, to allow every little town in the entire country to take part in an exhibit of paintings being held in the capital city. This exhibit is transmitted by means of light impulses repeated in thousands of mirrors at every Radio station. If Radio previously acted as the universal ear, now it has become a pair of eyes that annihilate distance. The main Radio signal tower emits its rays, and from Moscow an exhibit of the best painters bursts into flower on the reading walls of every small town in this enormous country, on loan to every inhabited spot on the map.»[52]

Tesla III Millenium,
in homage to Nikola
Tesla's 140th Birthday,
invitation flyer, Belgrade,
Yugoslavia, 1996.

Khlebnikov thus intended radio to become, wholly along the lines of «tele-audiovision,» a carrier for text, audio, and visual information. Beyond this, he also imagined the transmission of smell and taste sensations, that is to say, olfactory sense stimuli that would enable consciousness to be influenced remotely: «Every simple, plain but healthful meal can be transformed by means of taste-dreams carried by Radio rays, creating the illusion of a totally different taste sensation.»[53] The biblical image of water being transformed into wine here alludes above all to the deceptive potential of media and its conceivable deployment for the purposes of propaganda: «People will drink water, and imagine it to be wine. A simple, ample meal will wear the guise of a luxurious feast. And thus will Radio acquire an even greater power over the minds of the nation.»[54] Accordingly, radio in the future will be able to «act also as a doctor, healing patients without medicine.» Further, Khlebnikov adds, it was known that «certain notes like ‹la› or ‹ti› are able to increase muscular capacity, sometimes as much as sixty times»—and he goes on to imply that nothing could be more logical than

utopian not only in regard to television but also to radio, since he foreshadowed the technical implementation by at least one year. The famous radio transmitter built by Shukov—which Khlebnikov termed the «main Radio signal tower»—was first completed in the summer of 1922. Using the code word «Moskva Komintern,» the station was on-air from September 17, 1922 onward with some degree of regularity; see Lerg 1980 (see note 45), p.138.

53 Khlebnikov in Douglas 1985 (see note 37), p.158.

54 Ibid.

55 Bertolt Brecht attacks, in his «Radio Theory» (1927–32), which appeared some ten years after Khlebnikov's «Radio of the Future,» precisely this ultimately manipulative deployment of the new medium. Brecht presumably had no knowledge of Khlebnikov's text. See Bertolt Brecht, «Radiotheorie,» in *Schriften zur Literatur und Kunst*, vol.1, 1920–1939 (Berlin and Weimar, 1966), pp.127–47.

56 Khlebnikov in Douglas 1985 (see note 37), p.158.

57 Brecht 1966 (see note 55), p.146. Hans Magnus Enzensberger's text, «Baukasten zu einer Theorie der Medien» (1970), reformulates Brecht's radio theory in regard to the new (electronic or digital) media, «egalitarian in structure.» Enzensberger contrasts the repressive and emancipating usage of media. Emancipating usage turns every receiver (a means of consumption) into a potential transmitter (meaning, a means of production). See Hans Magnus Enzensberger, «Baukasten zu einer Theorie der Medien,» in *Kursbuch Medienkultur: Die maßgeblichen Theorien von Brecht bis Baudrillard*, ed. Claus von Pias et al. (Stuttgart, 1999), pp.264–78. Referring to Brecht's «great conversations,» John Perry Barlow in 1996 described the availability of the Internet as a two-way communication channel for growing numbers of users since the early nineteen-nineties as «The End of Broadcast Media and the Beginning of the Great Conversation.» See John Perry Barlow, «The Best of All Possible Worlds,» in *Communications of the ACM, 50th Anniversary Issue* (1997), http://www.nettime.org/nettime.w3archive/199612/msg00011.html.

58 Velimir Khlebnikov, «Swanland in the Future» (1915/1928), in *Collected Works of Velimir Khlebnikov: Letters and Theoretical Writings*, vol. 1, ed. Charlotte Douglas, trans. Paul Schmidt (Cambridge, MA, 1987), pp.392–96.

to use this wonder means in «periods of intense hard work like summer harvest time.»[55]

An aspect mentioned by Khlebnikov only fleetingly, namely the technical implementation of the possibility of a «game of chess between two people located at opposite ends of Planet Earth, an animated conversation between someone in America and someone in Europe,»[56] that is to say, of dialogical two-way communication instead of monological one-way communication, would become a central Brechtian demand.[57]

Whereas Brecht was clearly concerned with a tangible political utopia to be realized by means of radio as a «communication apparatus in public life,» Khlebnikov's «Radio of the Future» was a matter of poetically approximating the medium itself. Written almost ten years before Brecht's «Radio Theory,» Khlebnikov's text is palpably closer to the early fascination with the radio medium. In that phase, there was still great interest in the deterritorializing attributes of radio («international understanding»), which harbored the potential to unify humankind. The fascination with the immaterial utopia of radio still predominated, which Khlebnikov attempted to capture with material metaphors. For Peljhan, Khlebnikov's visionary achievement above all lay in the stress he placed upon the temporal dimension of space (whereby he often transcended the boundary to the irrational). It must be said that in the twentieth century this temporal dimension was primarily seized upon by economic interests in a way that deprived this space of significance. However, if we follow Peljhan, then Khlebnikov has placed in our hands means by which it will be possible to win back the dimension of time (for example, by means of Peljhan's above-described «counter-surveillance» tactics).

In «Swanland in the Future» (1915/1928), Khlebnikov refers to so-called «skybooks,» which he describes as high white walls or clouds onto which the latest news can be projected, thus reminiscent of «large books opened against the dark sky.» His list of projected matter reads: «News flashes about Planet Earth, the activities of that great union of worker's communes known as the United Encampments of Asia, poetry and the instantaneous inspirations of members, breakthroughs in science, notifications for relatives and next of kin, directives from the soviets.»[58] Marko Peljhan uses Khlebnikov's poetic concept of the «skybooks» as a metaphor for the immaterial world of signals being created in Khlebnikov's time, for the invisible radio connections traversing the heavens today via military and civilian communication satellites, whose open pages should, as demands Peljhan, be legible not only to the secret services.

The creation of an all-embracing holistic system is what makes Khlebnikov's work so interesting to Peljhan. For the latter, the development of such a complex, interdisciplinary system is today the only possible form in which to cultivate «sensual organs,» or metabolical/machinic interfaces, appropriate to the new (im)material communications spaces. However, Peljhan is not concerned with a simple «application» or implementation or even an «illustration» of Khlebnikov's ideas, but rather with the interdisciplinary mode of thought that today, in an era of renewed large-scale «tectonic activity,» makes the Russian seem so current.

Next to Khlebnikov, Nikola Tesla likewise plays a major role in Peljhan's work. A series of performances delivered jointly by Marko Peljhan and Carsten Nicolai starting in 1997 were devoted to the ideas of the Serbian engineer and inventor who emigrated to the United States in 1884 and there became, in the words of Erik Davis, the «ultimate visionary crank.»[59] The recent «rediscovery» of Tesla in the context of media art projects is due not least to the fact that he was the first to propagate the notion of global wireless transmission/communication.

All the projects described thus far are concerned less with imaging the visible world than with making accessible to human perception the world surrounding us that is increasingly based on invisible and immaterial (but yet no less powerful) structures. Margaret Morse formulates the ambition of such projects as follows: «The vocation of an art of the kind that reflects on electronic crowds and networks is not the representation of the visible world but the visualization of what is otherwise inaccessible to perception and is difficult to imagine because of its cosmic or microscopic scale, its discontinuity in space and time, or its impenetrability—from the insides of the body, the atom, or the black box to the outside of our galaxy and our universe.»[60]

59 Erik Davis, *Techgnosis: Myth, Magic and Mysticism in the Age of Information* (New York, 1998), pp. 68–75, here p. 69.

60 Margaret Morse, *Virtualities: Television, Media Art and Cyberculture* (Indiana, 1998), p. 192.

61 Knut Ebeling, «Die Mumie kehrt zurück II: Zur Aktualität des Archäologischen in Wissenschaft, Kunst und Medien,» in *Die Aktualität des Archäologischen in Wissenschaft, Medien und Künsten*, ed. Knut Ebeling and Stefan Altekamp (Frankfurt am Main, 2004), p. 20.

62 Ibid., p. 16.

63 Gilles Deleuze and Félix Guattari, *A Thousand Plateaus* (Minneapolis, 1997).

64 Ebeling 2004 (see note 61), p. 22.

65 Siegried Zielinski, quoted in Wolfgang Ernst, «Medienarchäologie: Provokation der Mediengeschichte,» in *Schnittstelle: Medien und Kulturwissenschaften*, ed. Georg Stanitzek and Wilhelm Vosskamp (Cologne, 2001), pp. 250–67, here p. 258.

66 Zielinski 2002, back cover text (see note 4).

That artistic projects point out the increasing importance of the electromagnetic spectrum by returning to the origins of radio is remarkable. However, the truly exciting aspect lies in these projects not focusing on the media *history* where only that which came into being or was actualized counts. In fact, it is precisely those *non*-realized, «unbecome,» and hidden futures of media that occupy the foreground—those blueprints and prospects whose status never exceeded that of potential, which were unable to be realized and were ultimately excluded by technological progress (and thus discarded by media history). Whereas the history of media and technology describes that which came into being, media archaeology, in its capacity as a «central cultural tech unearthing what was previously concealed,»[61] is interested in the unbecome, the unconfirmed, in other words in that which did *not* contribute to the emergence of the «completed materiality,»[62] namely of the technological systems that now surround us.

In *A Thousand Plateaus*, Gilles Deleuze and Félix Guattari describe becoming as an «antimemory.»[63] Just as becoming is contrary to derivation (and history), so archaeology too is preoccupied with «discontinuities, transpositions, and codings, and less with continuous transmissions from authentic pasts.»[64] According to Siegfried Zielinski, media archaeology lays claim to «working out in the largely linear and chronological construction of history the resistant local discourses and expressive practices of knowledge and the conceptualization of technologically based world-views and visual worlds.»[65] In his *Archäologie der Medien* (2002), Zielinski more radically formulates his approach by dedicating his media archaeology—along the lines of opening up the present to the future—decidedly not to the exploration of completed materialities, that is, to what came into being, but instead to the *research into concealed potentialities*: «Under the dictates of feasibility, the possibilities of the future are at present viewed as being identical with technological media. Traditional histories fit into this scheme. They are committed to the concept of a linear progression from the simple to the complex. This archaeology takes a different route. It bends the arrow of time out of the here-and-now and directs it into a possible future via past events and persons. In a generous searching movement, it retraces ideas, designs, and practices that deal with forgotten, suppressed, or hitherto unknown adventures of an impossible present of the mediated.»[66]

The searching movement of this media archaeology is distinguished by a paradoxical belatedness, for in orientation it is not simply retrospective (or nostalgic) but *retrospectively prospective*, in other words geared toward extrapolating the futuristic potential,[67] toward opening up the past to the future.

This searching movement, likewise constituting a distinguishing attribute of the artistic projects described in this contribution, stresses the importance for the future of that which did not come into being.[68] Media art, then, explores «not just the existing mass-media dispositives but envisions what did not become.»[69] As noted in my introduction, the media-archaeological interest of contemporary artists extends to the *unredeemed (technical) utopias* of, for instance, the historical avant-garde movements, which are at once the reverse side of the *realized anticipations* (Daniels) of the historical avant-garde. With its many truncated developments, the prehistory of radio offers potential alternatives to the broadcasting principle of the radio mass medium. A glance in the rearview mirror attempts to discover, in searching the medium's past, bygone potential futures of the medium and to extrapolate this potential that was not actuated. The reactivation of these past potential futures, the turning to the «unconfirmed technologies»[70] of the hobbyists and amateurs, to the wild assumptions regarding electromagnetic waves in space and a Fourth Dimension, to the fantasies of Russian Futurists and engineers—in short, to the paths of media and technological history not embarked upon—is *not nostalgic*. It is rather the case that such a retrospective, media-archaeological survey of the utopias reactivates bygone potentials and in this way becomes a *corrective to current and future developments*. Thus, only today can radio possibly realize the state it was prevented from attaining in the course of the past ninety years. Hence, radio's unrealized potential is more significant than its historical consequence—including for reflection upon what the future may hold.

67 See Eckhard Lobsien, *Wörtlichkeit und Wiederholung: Phänomenologie poetischer Sprache* (Munich, 1995), p. 189.

68 On the notion of «potential» in Giorgio Agamben, see Adam Thurschwell, «Specters of Nietzsche: Potential Futures for the Concept of the Political in Agamben and Derrida» (September 1, 2004), http://ssrn.com/abstract=969055 (accessed May 29, 2007).

69 Reinhard Braun, during the 100 Years of Radio conference, Vienna, 2007.

70 Armin Medosch, during the 100 Years of Radio conference, Vienna, 2007.

Acoustic Space Laboratory

Rasa Šmite and Raitis Šmits

> By creating mobile ad-hoc networks or by
> pointing antennas towards outer space or the
> depth of oceans, artists literally open up the
> horizons towards the possibilities of a new way
> of seeing and interacting with the world.
> —*Armin Medosch*

The *Acoustic Space Lab* is a series of co-projects that explores acoustic dimensions of networked media space. Initiated by RIXC and E-LAB from Riga, Latvia, the *Acoustic Space Lab* projects involve various sound artists, *net.audio* content contributors, radio community activists, as well as radio amateurs and radio scientists from all over the world. By building a network-based platform for collaborative experimentation on a translocal/global scale, the *Acoustic Space Lab* fosters creation of new forms in creative self-expression, social communication, and art and science collaboration.

Acoustic Cyberspace

Back in 1996, together with Jaanis Garancs, we first founded the E-LAB (electronic arts laboratory) in Riga[1] in order to start working with the Internet and electronic media. Since then, our primary fields of interest have included two interconnected elements: sound and networked communication. Perhaps a reason for raising this particular interest was our education—having a visual arts background, the world of sound seemed for us a new and unexplored territory. Other possible reasons were the consequences of the political regime—

a lack of information and communication during the Soviet period in Latvia, which fostered a need for establishing connections and cooperation networks on an international scale.

Our first *net.audio* projects—*Riga net.radio OZONE*[2] and *Xchange net.audio network*[3] were launched in 1997. The intent was to create a network for collaborative experimentation with real-time sound and emerging streaming technology on the Internet.

The theoretical context for these early *net.radio* activities, as well as for many other projects later implemented by the E-LAB and RIXC, was framed by a San Francisco-based writer and culture critic, Erik Davis, who gave a talk on «Acoustic Cyberspace» during the second Art+Communication Festival *Xchange on-air session* in Riga (November 1997).[4]

In his lecture, Erik Davis talked about «some abstract ideas, some images, some open-ended notions about acoustic space.» His intent was «to get at some of the deeper issues about sound and the ways it constructs surrounding environment (and subjectivities) and can act as a kind of map.» Having introduced this notion, he proposed to start

> with a distinction that Marshall McLuhan draws between visual space and acoustic space. McLuhan used the notion of visual space as a way to describe how Western subjectivity has been organized on a technical basis since the Renaissance ... McLuhan contrasts this construction of visual space, and the kind of subjectivity associated with it, with what he calls «acoustic space.» Acoustic space is the space we hear rather than the space we see, and he argued that electronic media were submerging us in this acoustic environment, with its own language of affect and subjectivity.[5]

1   E-LAB was founded in 1996. Based on the E-LAB concept, RIXC (The Centre for New Media Culture) was founded in 2000. See http://rixc.lv.

2   For more on *Ozone, Riga net.radio*, see http://ozone.re-lab.net/.

3   For more on *Xchange net.audio network*, see http://xchange.re-lab.net.

4   Erik Davis, «Acoustic Cyberspace: Acoustic Space #1,» presentation at the *Xchange* conference, Riga, Latvia, November 1997. See http://www.techgnosis.com/acoustic.html.

5   Ibid.

6   Ibid.

7   Raitis Šmits, «Xchange Open Channel: Co-broadcast Experiments in the Net,» in *Readme!*, ed. Josephine Bosma et al. (Brooklyn: Autonomedia, 1999), pp. 349–50.

What we didn't know before (considering that the art history lessons we had had in the eighties and nineties missed twentieth-century art entirely), we tried to do intuitively. None of us had any prior radio experience, nor did we initially realize that we wanted to gain some. However, the notion of «Internet radio,» and what it could be, inspired us to try. By doing *OZONE live net.radio* sessions, we simply tried to express our own and our friends' (musicians, journalists, poets, and other young Latvian artists) creative ideas audibly over the Internet, whereas in building the *Xchange* mailing list, we wanted to be connected with other net.broadcasters in remote places, thus developing a context for collaborative experiments on the Internet.

In the *Xchange* experiments with streaming sound on the Internet, the main intent was neither the creation of specific content—such as radio programs, electronic music, or sound art transmissions—nor the facilitation of live streams from clubs and other events, nor even collaborative streaming performance from remote locations. Rather, the collaborative *Xchange* live online sessions were a mixture of all above-mentioned elements, following Erik Davis's notion of an «acoustic space that isn't limited to a world of music or sound; the environment of electronic media itself engenders this way of organizing and perceiving the other spaces we intersect.»[6] In addition to focusing on creating specific content, *Xchange* aimed to «provide the context for communication and information exchange among the creative net broadcasters.» The content—what to contribute to the co-sessions—was created independently by the participants themselves.

The most interesting of the *Xchange* co-broadcasting experiments and events took place in 1998. Most of the live online co-sessions took place without any pre-planning—immediate expression of ideas over the Net was the main feature of the so-called «*Xchange* Open Channel» sessions.[7] The *Xchange* mailing list was used to announce open calls, where everybody was invited to join in with their live Real Audio stream for a co-broadcast session. What we first and foremost tried to do was to simply establish connections with each others' live streams. Meeting and coordination happened online in the IRC chat channel, where we agreed upon who would send out their stream how and when, as well as upon how these outgoing streams would be picked up one after another by different participating locations. Thus, we managed to create a constant loop, comprised of a number of remote broadcasters streaming from different places around the world, including *Backspace* in London, *MZX* in Ljubljana, *XLR project* in Berlin, *OZONE* in Riga, *Radio 90* in Banff, Canada, *L'Audible* in Sydney, and many others.[8]

There also were some interesting experiments with collaborative content taking place—Rachel Baker from *Backspace* in London proposed to prepare PPP news (a personal news service) as a contribution to *OZONE live* Tuesday sessions; Borut Savski and Martin Schitter from Ljubljana, in their discussion on radio and its future on the Internet, tried to involve other remote participants. «Discussion in loop» was also organized by the *OZONE* team from the workshop at Polar Circuit II in Tornio (Finnish Lapland),[9] where Monika Glahn in Berlin, Peteris Kimelis in Riga, and those of us in Tornio were operating the loop (consisting of three parallel live streams) by switching off and on the feedback in order either to hear remote participants asking questions or for us to answer them at the right time—with as little overlap or delay as possible.

The looping sound via the Internet—often created by more then three remote netcasters (once we succeeded in connecting seven remote locations)—made an unimaginable noise. Since a Real Audio stream needs several seconds for rebuffering (that is, it downloads some data to your hard disk in order to be able to start playing back the stream), these loops created a feedback effect because delay often was four to ten seconds, and sometimes longer. Audio inputs coming from different physical locations joined together in a common (cyber)space were in fact creating not one simultaneous stream but rather multiple layers of looping sounds. The noise of sound in the feedback was reminiscent of chaos. Listening to this noise, we first experienced the existence and spatiality of this nonphysical, counter-geographical (cyber)space. We became aware of what Erik Davis had meant with the specificity of nonlinear spatial organization in the networked media environment: «Acoustic space is capable of simultaneity, superimposition, and nonlinearity … Where visual space emphasizes linearity, acoustic space em-

8   For more on *Xchange Open Channel*, see
    http://re-lab.net/netradio/workshop01/05/
    index.html#b.

9   *net.radio workshop* at Polar Circuit II, held in
    Tornio, Lapland, Finland, July 1998. See
    http://re-lab.net/polar/. More information
    about *net.radio* is available on the *net.radio
    workshop* (1999–2000) website at http://re
    -lab.net/netradio/workshop01/index.html.

10 Net.Radio Days '98: Trimm Dich, the first
    international meeting of experimental Internet-
    Radio-Projects, Berlin, June 1998. See http://
    www.art-bag.org/convextv/pro/trimmdich/
    anno.htm.

11 *Xchange net.audio network*, netcasting project
    at the Ars Electronica Festival, Linz, 1998. See
    http://xchange.re-lab.net/56h/info.html.

12 net.congestion, international festival of
    streaming media, Amsterdam, October 2000.
    The festival was devoted to new forms of
    broadcasting and live programming that have
    emerged on the Internet (the so-called
    «streaming media»), such as net.radio, net.tv,
    net.film, and the hybrid media. See http://
    straddle3.net/context/art/a_001006.en.html.

phasizes simultaneity—the possibility that many events occur in the same zone of space-time.»

The first larger international *net.radio* meeting in real space took place in Berlin in June 1998. It was organized by the Berlin-based Mikro initiative. The *Xchange* mailing list was used to inform and coordinate participants, events, and locations. The main focus of the Berlin Net.Radio Days was about connecting Internet, radio, and physical space. Every day, a new event was taking place in another location in Berlin-Mitte. Highly important features of this event—as of many other *net.radio* events—were not only the presentations and workshops, but also the parties and socializing. Only in such an informal and open atmosphere—where the sound and screened images are created for the environment—can one better experience the meaning of the acoustic space.[10]

In September 1998, the *Xchange* project received an Award of Distinction in the net category of PRIX Ars Electronica, and *Xchange* was invited to be present at the Ars Electronica '98 Festival in Linz, Austria.[11] The *Xchange* proposal was to create a live audio environment during the entire Ars Electronica Festival, using real-time Internet audio technologies (Real Audio). This included an open broadcasting studio in the «real» space as well as the creation of a virtual sound environment in cyberspace, involving both on-site and remote participants. The event was entitled *Acoustic Space: 56h LIVE* and it was the first international *Xchange* meeting in «real space,» where many of the participants met face-to-face for the first time. It brought together twenty-five net.broadcasters from all over the world (Zina K./Sydney, b2men/Pararadio/Budapest, Borut Savski/MZX/Ljubljana, Honor Harger/r a d i o q u a l i a/Adelaide, and many others from Riga, Berlin, Ljubljana, London, Amsterdam, and Budapest) and connected more than ten remote locations.

Since then, a number *net.radio* events, meetings, and *net.radio* nights by *Xchange* participants have taken place in the framework of various international media art festivals, workshops, temporary labs, and other new media events. These include the *net.radio* night at Art Servers Unlimited, London, July 1998, the *net.radio workshop* at Polar Circuit II in Tornio (July 1998), *net.radio live* at Comm_X_Change '98 in Basel (October 1998), Art+Communication in Riga (1997 and 1998), the *Streaming Media Workshop* at the Next Five Minutes conference in Amsterdam (March 1999), and the net.congestion festival for streaming media in Amsterdam (2000).[12]

Very soon «the summer of *net.radio* '98» was over—and real-time Internet broadcasting gathered huge attention from commercial Internet Service Providers (ISPs) and industries. Due to commercialization of Real Media, more and more artists became interested in MP3 and other open source streaming formats. To get beyond the confusion of streaming media standards and commercialization, RIXC initiated the project entitled *Acoustic Space Research Lab*. It intended to reapproach the notion of «*net.radio*» and to set up a new context for research on «data ecology,» development of new audio communication tools, as well as co-experiments in the field of networked media, radio, and satellite technologies.[13]

In collaboration with several international artists' groups and individuals from the *Xchange* network—RIXC/E-LAB (Riga, Latvia), Derek Holzer (Amsterdam, Netherlands and U.S.), r a d i o q u a l i a (London, U.K. and Adelaide, Australia), *Projekt Atol* (Ljubljana, Slovenia), *L'audible* (Sydney, Australia), *Radio90* (Banff, Canada) and others—an international symposium for sound art, radio, and satellite technologies took place in August 2001 in the forests of western Latvia, in Irbene at the site of a Soviet-era, thirty-two-meter diameter dish antenna. Formerly used to spy on satellite transmissions between Europe and North America by the KGB, the antenna was abandoned and nearly destroyed when the Russian Army withdrew in 1994. The dish was successfully repaired by the VIRAC (Ventspils International Radio Astronomy Center) radio astronomers.[14]

During the symposium, an international team of approximately thirty sound artists, Internet and community radio activists, and radio amateurs, in cooperation with VIRAC scientists, explored the possibilities of the antenna. The participants used the dish in three main ways:

1. The dish was explored in an acoustic fashion. Its groans, buzzes,
   and sirens were recorded, and the dish itself was used as a massive
   parabolic microphone to scan the surrounding environment.

13 *Acoustic Space Lab*, international symposium for sound art, radio, and satellite technology, held in Irbene, Latvia, August 2001. See http://acoustic.space.re-lab.net.

14 VIRAC, Ventspils International Radio Astronomy Center, Riga, Latvia. See http://www.virac.lv.

2. The dish was used in its «original» fashion. Satellites from the INMARSAT network were located and snooped on. Analog mobile phones, ship-to-shore communications, air traffic control signals, and data packet transmissions were monitored and recorded.
3. The dish was used in its «retrofitted» fashion. Jupiter, Venus, and (most successfully) the Sun were located and scanned using precise radio astronomy equipment operating in the 12 GHz range.

The recorded data was immediately processed by participating artists in a temporary lab space and uploaded to the server for later processing and to be made available to other artists via the Internet.

It was a great chance for artists to access and work with this big antenna. But most important was that this «old and heavy» technology—the big dish, with its secret past, it specific location in such a remote place, and its previously unexploited potential for civilian use—succeeded in facilitating the common ground for collaboration among artists, scientists, and radio activists.

RT-32,
Acoustic Space Lab,
Irbene, Latvia, 2001.

Rasa Šmite and Raitis Šmits
Acoustic Space Laboratory

As an outcome of this symposium and follow-up research, the DVD *RT-32 – ACOUSTIC SPACE LAB* was published by RIXC and first presented at the World-Information.org exhibition in Amsterdam in 2002.[15]

The DVD constitutes multimedia research of the VIRAC radio telescope RT-32. It covers the history of this top-secret, Soviet-era military object, including precise technical data and its conversion to scientific and civilian use. It also presents the international *Acoustic Space Lab* symposium results.

The *Open Source Sampling* project, initiated by Derek Holzer, invited sound and video artists to reinterpret the symposium material available on the Internet and «to add their own thematically related material to the mix.» The *Open Source Sampling* project was released on CD and distributed together with the *Acoustic Space Lab* DVD.[16]

The second edition of the DVD featured another follow-up project—the CD *Radio Astronomy* that was initiated and compiled by Adam Hyde. This CD is a collection of sound pieces by various artists, featuring recordings of the Sun, Jupiter, and Venus made by r a d i o q u a l i a as part of their *Radio Astronomy* project at the VIRAC radio telescope in Irbene, Latvia. *Radio Astronomy*[17] is a project that enables listeners to tune into different celestial frequencies, hearing planets, stars, nebulae, and the constant hiss of cosmic noise.

At the close of the *Acoustic Space Lab* symposium, the former director of VI-RAC, Edgars Bervalds, expressed his delight that the Irbene antenna had been explored by *Acoustic Space Lab* participants in so many ways, adding that, though such an object (as the antenna) ought to be used primarily for science, «artists can use [it] to fill the vast spaces in our Universe that science cannot reach.»[18]

15 World-Information Exhibition in Oude Kerk, Amsterdam, November 15 to December 16, 2002. The exhibition outlined the evolution of communication technologies and their consequences in relation to society, exhibited historic and state-of-the-art control and surveillance technology, and displayed digital artworks and installations. See http://world -information.org/wio/program/amsterdam.

16 *Open Source Sampling* was initiated by Derek Holzer as a follow-up project of the *Acoustic Space Lab* symposium, Latvia, August 2001. Derek Holzer was also international coordinator of the symposium, writing related texts and creating a symposium website: http://acoustic.space.re-lab.net/lab/.

17 *Radio Astronomy*, project by r a d i o q u a l i a. See http://www.radio-astronomy.net.

18 Mukul, *Acoustic Space Lab*, WIRE, September 2001, London.

19 *Solar Radio Station*, collaborative project by RIXC, Clausthome musicians, r a d i o q u a l i a, and VIRAC scientists. See http://rixc.lv/solar.

20 *Solar Radio Station* in PHOENIX Hall, organized by Hartware MedienKunstVerein in Dortmund, May–July 2006. See http://www.hmkv.de/dyn/ e_program_exhibitions/detail.php?nr=1221&ru bric=exhibitions&.

21 Clausthome is a group of noize musicians based in Riga, Latvia. See http://www .claustrum.org/clausthome/.

Solar Radio Station

One of the recent RIXC projects is *Solar Radio Station*, which is a continuation of creative explorations with the Irbene antenna. *Solar Radio* Station has specifically focused on co-production, in which different parties—artists and scientists—are involved. The project is an ongoing collaboration between the artists of RIXC (Latvia), r a d i o q u a l i a (New Zealand), Clausthome musicians (Latvia), and the VIRAC – Ventspils International Radio Astronomy Center scientists (Latvia).[19]

The first exhibition of the Solar Radio project took place in the PHOENIX Hall at the Hartware MedienKunstVerein (HMKV) in Dortmund, Germany during the spring and summer of 2006.[20] It encompassed two parts: a «live installation» exhibition and performance took place in Dortmund, while a temporary «real-time scanning» laboratory was set up at the site of the RT-32 dish in Irbene.

Real-time scanning of solar systems and other objects of the universe, performed in Irbene using the VIRAC radio telescope, was provided by a team including VIRAC scientist Dmitry Bezrukov (who operated the dish) and the RIXC crew involving Signe Pucena, Agnese Rucina, and Davis Bojars, who were coordinating and providing the live stream for the Internet.

There was a specific observation arranged for this project at the Irbene radio telescope. Two evenings, for two hours each, four objects in the universe—two planets: the Sun and Venus, and two constellations: Taurus and Cygnus—were scanned with the Irbene 32 m dish. The real-time signal was down-sampled to an audible frequency and transmitted live via the Internet. Thus the signal was made available for the Clausthome musicians[21] in Dortmund, where they turned the noise from space into a real-time sound modeling performance. The sound interpretation was complemented by a live video mix created by Mārtiņš Ratniks.

There were two particular qualities to this event. The first was the «access» it provided. Lauris Vorslavs from Clausthome expressed his enthusiasm for this unique possibility for interpreting a completely «fresh» signal, received in real time from various locations of the universe, since he as well as other sound artists and noise musicians are accustomed to searching NASA and other Internet sources for material to be used in their music. The second quality of this work was «connectivity»—how the signal was received, down-sampled to the audible frequency, encoded again into live stream and sent via the Internet, subsequently received in Dortmund, and transformed into a noisy, cosmic radio soundscape.

In fact, the show in Dortmund was a live, networked installation, in which remote transmissions from the radio telescope and live interpretations by the artists in the exhibition space were an integral part of this live set-up.

Waves

The most recent project and the largest representation of networked media art dealing with deeper issues of electro(magnetic) acoustic space organized thus far by RIXC is the *Waves* project. *Waves* was based on an original idea and concept developed by Armin Medosch. His proposal was to set up a large-scale, international exhibition that looks at the phenomenon of electromagnetic waves as the principle material and the medium of media art, and waves as a universal principle. In a joint collaborative effort between Armin Medosch and RIXC, lasting nearly two years, we co-curated *Waves*, an international exhibition in conjunction with the Art+Communication 2006 Festival, having taken place in August and September 2006 in Riga.[22] In the *Waves* concept introduction, Armin Medosch wrote:

> The artists of the *Waves* exhibition are challenging conventional knowledge about and perception of waves. Electronic media such as radio, TV and the Internet are of defining influence on today's societies. Subsequently the information sphere is tightly controlled and subject to various artificially imposed political limitations. Yet artists with their electronic and digital DIY kits are exploring numerous ways of thinking outside the box, making their own waves, creating alternative networks and engaging with strange scientific phenomena—which points at actually existing utopian potential.[23]

The *Waves* festival program consisted of an exhibition, a conference, open presentations, workshops, performances, and film screenings. The two-day Spectrum conference facilitated a theoretical background for the artworks displayed at the

22 Art+Communication 2006: *Waves*, 8th international festival for new media culture, held in Riga, Latvia, August 24 to September 17, 2006. See http://rixc.lv/waves and http://osdir.com/ml/culture.internet.spectre/2006-05/msg00096.html (press release).

23 Armin Medosch, *Waves* concept, 2005–2006.

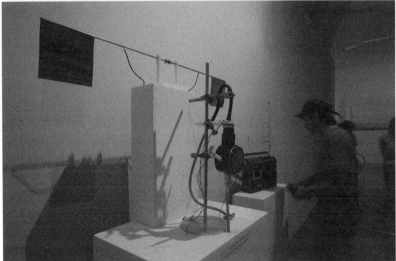

Marko Peljhan and Sašo Podgoršek, *Ladomir
Qikiqtaq*, installation, *Waves*, Riga, Latvia, 2006.

Paul de Marinis, *Rome to Tripoli*, installation,
Waves, Riga, Latvia, 2006.

exhibition hall, while a specific program of classic and contemporary experimental movies, curated by Erwin van't Hart, a film curator from the Netherlands, introduced the visual space of the electromagnetic spectrum, and the performance program in the RIXC Media Space endeavored to mix the two acoustic and visual spectrums.

The *Waves* exhibition took a look at electromagnetic waves not just as carriers of information but also as the material and/or theme of the artwork. It featured about forty international works of (media) art by seventy artists from eighteen different countries.[24] The exhibition took place at the Exhibition Hall ARSENALS of the Latvian National Museum of Art from August 24 to September 17, 2006.

The artworks on display at the *Waves* exhibition covered a wide range of topics. To give an overview on the variety of waves interpretations, Armin Medosch wrote:

> Some of the works engaged with interesting scientific phenomena to provide unusual aesthetic experiences such as listening to the background noise of the universe (Franz Xaver/AT) or engaging with the visual and aural qualities of light bulbs (Artificiel/CA). As the human sensory perception system gives us only limited access to electromagnetic waves, sonification and visualisation of scientific data were a major component of the exhibition. Other works explored social and political implications of wave regulation (Bureau d'Etudes/FR) and offered viable alternative com-

24 The *Waves* international exhibition took place in the Exhibition Hall ARSENALS of the Latvian National Museum of Art (see note 22). Participating artists included: Robert Adrian and Norbert Math (Austria), Artificiel (Canada), Jean-Pierre Aubé (Canada), Erich Berger (Austria and Finland), Bureau d'Études (France), Paul DeMarinis (U.S.), Disinformation (U.K.), Antanas Dombrovskij (Lithuania), Farmersmanuel (Austria), Judith Fegerl (Austria), Mark Fischer (U.S.), Gints Gabrāns (Latvia), Bulat Galeyev (Romenia), Dmitry Gelfand and Evelina Domnitch (U.S.), David Haines and Joyce Hinterding (Australia), Usman Haque (U.K.), Bengt Sjölén (Sweden), Adam Somlai-Fischer (Hungary), Steve Heimbecker (Canada), Adam Hyde (New Zealand), Aleksandar Erkalović (Croatia), Lotte Meijer (Netherlands), Luke Jerram (U.K.), Voldemārs Johansons (Latvia), Aaron Kaplan (Austria), Doron Goldfarb (Italy and Austria), Yunchul Kim (Germany and Korea), Jacob Kirkegaard (Denmark and Germany), Anthony McCall (U.S.), Jay Needham (U.S.), Marko Peljhan (Slovenia), Sašo Podgoršek (Slovenia), Oskars Poikāns (Latvia), Julian Priest (U.K. and Denmark), r a d i o q u a l i a (New Zealand), Mārtiņš Ratniks (Latvia), Clausthome (Lativa), RIXC (Latvia), Scanner (U.K.), Sine Wave Orchestra (Japan), Nina Sobell (U.S.), TAKE 2030 (U.K.), Bas van Koolwijk (Netherlands), Derek Holzer (U.S. and Netherlands), Martins Vizbulis (Latvia), Franz Xaver (Austria). The *Waves* exhibition materials, audio and video archive, as well as publication are available online at the *Waves* website: http://rixc.lv/waves.

25 Armin Medosch, «Waves – an introduction,» *Acoustic Space #6: WAVES* (Riga: RIXC, 2006).

Re-Inventing Radio

504

munication systems (Marko Peljhan/SI). Whereas some works were based on screens and audio-visualisations of waves (Aaron Kaplan/AT), many works relied on physical objects (Joyce Hinterding & David Haines/AU), obscure or forgotten communication technologies (Paul DeMarinis/U.S.) and the antenna as an art object.

Those are just a few examples out of a large scale exhibition which interrogated the conventions of media art exhibitions. Bringing together experienced and well known artists with young experimentators between art and science, *Waves* succeeded to make a statement by being the first large scale international exhibition to focus uniquely on waves as the material and medium of art.[25]

The Spaces of Openness

The main idea behind all of the *Acoustic Space Lab* projects is to push the boundaries of electronic networked media environments—not just to discover and explore, but rather to independently build new autonomous spaces for creative self-expression and communication.

Bas van Koolwijk and Derek Holzer, *Ozone*,
installation, *Waves*, Riga, Latvia, 2006.

Rasa Šmite and Raitis Šmits
Acoustic Space Laboratory

Waves, as the most representative project of the *Acoustic Space Lab* series, aimed to expand the context of electronic networked media arts. On the one hand, it was a return to the «fine arts» context (in terms of the creation of «imagery»), where the key element is the imagination as opposed to a concept or a visualization. By utilizing communication technologies in the arts, and attempting to fuse the fields of art and science, imagery is the key which opens up a new vision. Imagery also is a way of communicating science and making it, if not completely comprehensible, at least (audially or visually) conceivable. In this way, imagination is also enhanced in the consciousness of a human being.

On the other hand, *Waves* created a context within which to bring together artists from all over the world, artists who don't hesitate «to ask the big questions about fundamentals such as time, space, energy and substances.» Thus for us, *Waves* was more than just an exhibition or festival theme—it was a fundamental concept within which we wished to contextualize those creative experiments, social dynamics, and artistic processes in the acoustic space of networked media, which have been expressing themselves in our work for the past ten years.

But in addition to looking at the past, we hope that *Waves* is also a turning point that will become a new stage for further «acoustic space» explorations. Bringing this essay to a close, we would like to concur with Erik Davis, who remarks that «it's incredibly important to maintain electronic communications media as a space of openness, of indetermination, of the affects of the unknown.»

Radio Tower Xchange (RTX)

A Networked Project

Radio Tower Xchange (RTX)[1]—a networked sound performance event—took place online on April 27, 2007. Sound artists from various countries and the *Xchange* network were contributing live streams and audio artworks in relation to the «radio towers,» «antennas,» and «waves» themes.

The main live stream was provided by RIXC from Riga, featuring artists' contributions by Martin John Callanan (UK), Jan-Peter E.R. Sonntag (DE), Horia Cosmin Samoïla/Spectral Investigations Collective (FR), Nils Edvardsson (SE), Superfactory (TM) (DE/LT), Mārtiņš Ratniks and Clausthome (LV), rx-tx (SI), and others. Other contributions included live streams from Bratislava and Brussels, both coordinated by OKNO, a live stream from Orléans, provided by Ellipse, as well as a recorded session from the RTX event in Ljubljana organized by Projekt Atol.

It was artist Adam Hyde (r a d i o q u a l i a) who developed the concept for the *Radio Tower Xchange* event as a continuation and further step in the artistic exploration of *Waves*. In his concept, Adam Hyde explains: «The idea behind this event is both paying homage and a critique of the broadcasting philosophies and histories the radio towers represent, and an investigation into the evolving practice of unregulated online broadcasting.»

In connection with the notion of unregulated online broadcasting, Hyde also refers to the early *Xchange* collaborative broadcasting experiments on the Internet:

In these unregulated spaces *Xchange* has been provoking cultural, artistic and theoretical practice and discourse since the advent of streaming media in the mid 90's. *Xchange* reflected the new approach to collaborative, autonomous ad-hoc broadcasting. Network broadcasts were commonplace for the first years of *Xchange*, with each node in the network contributing to an online cacophony where no single node could be distinguished in the mix from another. Ownership was impossible to maintain and hence forgotten.

Radio Tower Xchange (RTX) was co-organized by RIXC (Latvia), Okno (Belgium), Tesla (Germany), Ellipse (France), Projekt Atol (Slovenia), Performing Pictures (Sweden), and others.

Participation became the goal. The sharing of transmissions was more exciting than the simultaneous reception of the same transmission.

The doors to the broadcast towers were not forced open by these pioneers but ignored, and the landmark symbols of one-to-many broadcasting was replaced by rambling a network of many-to-many net.casters.

The following are a few examples of the variety of artistic concerns in the different contributions to the *Radio Tower Xchange* in April 2007: the RTX session started with the Riga live stream, featuring RIXC resident artist Martin John Callanan (UK) who set up his *Sonification of You* equipment. He was scanning the various radio spectrum frequencies used by mobile phone devices, Bluetooth, WiFi networks, and others within an area around the Riga TV and Radio Tower. The data information was represented by assigned audio sounds indicating activity, distance, and strength of signals. Thus he created an interactivity that became ambient, as the artist himself puts it, adding that «[t]he invisible becomes audible and therefore visible. Allowing individuals to become aware of their constant connectivity.»[3]

The sound contribution *VLF* in Paris, France was exploring the surroundings of the Eiffel Tower. Horia Cosmin Samoila from the Spectral Investigations Collective contributed recordings that were revealing both VLF and electrosmog activity at the site of the Eiffel Tower in Paris: «Urban sites like country landscapes are immersed in a new kind of electromagnetic flux and pulsations with the rise of the last generation communication technologies. The old analogic radio modulation waves are supplanted by digital discontinuous signals. This constitutes a new environment in which ecological, biological and cognitive aspects of our society are in constant mutation and evolution.»[4]

German artist Jan-Peter E.R. Sonntag from Berlin contributed his work *Campa-Sacrow*. For producing his work, Sonntag used the facilities of the Saviour's Church at Sacrow, Germany (close to Potsdam and Berlin)—as its campanile was the first antenna tower or «radio tower» and transmission station in Germany as early as 1897. The inner architecture of this church was used by the artist «to re-play a part of [his] *RAWextension f5*...into a Raw-Morse-video (which can be downloaded on your mobile).»[5]

The RTX event also introduced hydro-towers, which, in spite of never having been meant for transmissions, are still generating sounds...The sound art project *Power Lines in Sweden* was the contribution by Nils Edvarsson, who considers «the sound of the power lines to be the sound of the modern society, a big string instrument that responds to our daily chores.» He introduces us to the changing sounds of electricity. «When current flows through the power lines, different sounds are generated.»[6]

Another «radio tower» represented in the RTX session was, of course, the RT-32—former Soviet military antenna in Irbene, Latvia. Sound recordings from *Solar Radio Station* transmissions were contributed and remixed by Clausthome musicians from Riga.

Solar Radio Station is an ongoing collaboration among artists of RIXC (LV) and r a d i o q u a l i a (NZ), Clausthome (LV) musicians, and VIRAC – Ventspils International Radio Astronomy Center (LV) scientists. The *Solar Radio Station* performance for RTX used pre-recorded files from Irbene live scans and turned this noise from the space into a real-time sound modelling performance.[7]

Horia Cosmin Samoila /
Spectral Investigations
Collective, *VLF*, Paris,
France, 2007.

Martin John Callanan,
Sonification of You,
2007.

In his introductory text to RTX, Adam Hyde writes:

As well as being architecturally significant, Radio Towers have played a re-markable role in history and a valuable role in the evolution of radio science since the beginning of last century.

However with the recent developments in wireless internet technologies, these towers that were sites exclusively used for government and commer-cial broadcasts are now largely symbols of frequency commodification. The stately towers and masts now are encircled by a multitude of self-organising public WiFi networks. Thousands of wireless routers form chaotic meshes of public radio space around these huge broadcast icons similar to how ram-bling city markets surround the towering commercial buildings in many cities of the world. In these places public broadcasting takes on a new meaning, it is the public that broadcasts, not a broadcast provided FOR the public. Reg-ulated broadcasts are monolithic, like the towers built to support them which require huge amounts of resources to sustain and generations to change. Unregulated space, the new public broadcast space, is infectuous, it finds new ways to communicate new things, and broadcasting is becoming a behaviour which is daily and inevitable. Transmitting is becoming part of the fabric of urban existence, it is perhaps now a more common practice to

1 http://rixc.lv/waves/rtx/en.html. This text
   was compiled by Rasa Šmite, RIXC.
2 http://rixc.lv/waves
3 http://sonification.eu/rtx
4 http://www.ghostlab.org/article.php3?id
   _article=203
5 http://www.sonarc-ion.de
6 http://www.nilsjc.com/kraft/kraftledningar
   _EN.html
7 http://rixc.lv/solar

Paradigms Shifted

Matt Smith

Personally, I believe that it is no longer relevant to distinguish media by its transmission format—that is, broadcast by terrestrial radio, or satellite, or downloaded from the Internet—for media is simply a form of encoded data, and its transmission is completely removed from its content. At the same time, my own experience and background has been shaped by the era of monopolized mass-one-way-media and by an accompanying frustration. Radio is a perfect departure point for discussing the future of independent media. This is due to the unique way in which it serves as the prime technology for the transmission of content (digital and analog) over a geographic distance, while still remaining the most prevalent mass-media format. In 2004, I presented a paper in Mexico City at the Radio Biennale dealing with the history of radio as a technology and media format. I had also made some dire predictions as to where I thought we were headed if commercial interests were to prevail without interference. Not quite three years later, these aspects of my presentation sound overly pessimistic and naïve, and I now understand what I could not grasp then: digitization is now practically complete, with all new media being created digitally and with analog transmission systems increasingly being shut down. Hence, it seems to make less and less sense to distinguish between different transmission formats, such as radio, television, or downloaded interactive content. But before I elaborate on such points, I would like to present a section of my paper from 2004, introducing my version of how we ended up with the mediascape of the twenty-first century:

In the last 100 years, radio has come full circle: from serving as a utilitarian communication tool for ship-to-shore communication to developing into the most powerful and controlled propaganda tool ever used by governments and their favored businesses. Radio enabled the development of television, arguably the most influential mass medium, which in turn transformed radio into a mainly commercial product (especially in North America) that is still a very viable business proposition (FM frequencies are still a hot commodity, basically a license to print money in terms of advertising revenue). Most recently, by virtue of its technological concept, radio transmission has quickly emerged as the main tool for person-to-person communication (through cellular telephones, etc.) as well as machine-to-machine communication, being the fastest growing carrier for data transmission (satellites and Wireless Local Area Networks).

Respecting content, digital satellite and terrestrial broadcasts will only further diminish the relevance of distinguishing between moderated, linear radio and individual producers of audio. Pay-Per-View and On-Demand concepts in the commercial television world are probably a good, if clumsy, example of what digital radio will eventually look like. Considering the increasing integration of financial micro-transactions in the distribution of digital media, there is no reason not to replace the current subscription model of satellite and cable radio (and television) with something similar to the 99¢-per-download model of current online audio services. The newer digital players incorporate FM radio receivers and in the future will certainly feature digital radio receivers, permitting the instant download of an album, song, or live soccer broadcast, maybe even with an image when necessary. The political danger here is obvious: as independent artists and producers, we face being locked out of these emerging distribution delivery systems, because we cannot demonstrate any immediate commercial value for the network providers. Cell phone networks are probably the best currently existing example of how the providers keep complete control over what information can be sent on their equipment. All services available to cell phones are accessed through the provider, who charges an arbitrary amount for providing this access or service. So effectively, there is no way to access free, uncensored content with a cell phone—the technology has specifically been designed to give complete control to the operating entity, as opposed to the user.

This scenario can easily be applied to emerging digital broadcast formats, especially when one considers the pressure the recording industry is currently under. The broadcasters who are introducing digital transmissions are strongly connected to the big media companies, so the face of digital radio is going to be shaped very much by the corporate interests of the media and telecommunications conglomerates involved in its promotion. Unless independent artists and producers act now, by actively subverting and reappropriating the corporate rules and boundaries of media creation and distribution, we will end up with a sanitized, controlled, and hermetic media system completely dominated by corporate interest, with the willing collusion of government in return for free airtime—on a globalized scale.

Well, I was wrong: thus far, no cataclysmic Orwellian clampdown has occurred, probably because the focus of information management is directed toward the military and propaganda aspects of The War on Terrorism as opposed to the home front of complaining media corporations and their nemesis, the software and content pirates besieging the shores of the traditional distribution channels. Or perhaps nobody really cares about the plight of the struggling entertainment giants. However, these developments have forced the hand of all big media corporations, who currently are reacting by releasing a vast amount of content into the digital realm, in the hopes of attracting and holding an audience on the network and its mobile extensions. This represents the conclusion of a major paradigm shift for the large corporations, the shift from being a business based on owning delivery channels and production facilities—transmitters, cable networks, studios, and editing suites—to being a model where the main asset is content, and delivery is done any way possible and desirable to the audience. The revenue stream is similar as far as the big content owners are concerned: try to reach as large a number of people as possible while providing advertising opportunities to other large corporations that can be sold in bulk for large sums of money. Whereas this may or may not work, it is nevertheless the current fashion in developing new distribution models by the large content owners in the face of peer-to-peer networks.

Coming back to our chosen perspective—the media arts community—this basically means that some really big fish have just entered the pond in which we have all been splashing for the past twenty years. One of the obvious ramifications is that there will be much more competition for memory on personal media players, with the world of podcasting and live streams having just received a huge boost in advertising and general levels of inanity. This increase in significance cuts both ways: from one perspective, it acknowledges what artists, activists, and scholars dealing with the digitization and networking of our culture have long been predicting and reflecting, and from another, it also ends an era of experimentation, where formats and styles were yet fluid.

One obvious effect of the complete digitization of the media world, and to a certain extent the physical world, is the change of the role of technologies and their providers in our lives. The average person in the «developed» world is surrounded by such a vast number of devices that this same average person has no real grasp of their complete—or sometimes even basic—functionality. All the «user» has to know is its basic purpose and how to apply it appropriately, a simple example being a car: most people who know how to operate one have no idea how it actually functions. With digital technologies, there is no way the average user of a given gadget can guess what the device does just by looking at its insides, much less its exterior, which may be multicolored, adorned with flashing lights, buttons, and little color screens, but is essentially an arbitrary variation of the little black box. What makes this interesting is the fact that, for the first time since the advent of serious mass production, the producer can maintain absolute control over the product and, by extension, its use. A perfect example for this would be the average DVD player: the little circuit board—which handles the decoding of the data being fed to it by the DVD drive and then sends it to the screen—could potentially play any kind of digital format, but manufacturers will implement restrictions on some models and not on others, in order to create model and feature variations on store shelves. The irony here is that the identical device without restrictions is often more expensive than the one with restrictions. As a buyer, what you are paying for here is obviously not a physically different product; instead, you are paying for all the features of which the technology is capable or, more pointedly, for access to a wider variety of content. Naturally, a whole subculture for subverting these locks and barriers in various electronic items exists, but generally one can assert that the industry has learned to protect and market their «intellectual property.»

This subculture, however, is probably the most interesting aspect arising from this situation, as it represents the so-called bleeding edge of the counterculture and, as such, also has a partial crossover with the media arts community: it often pushes the limits or, these days, runs up against the limitations of «consumer» technologies. Circumventing, appropriating, and subverting these limits and limitations has traditionally played a strong role in many telecommunications and network-based artworks, and still does.

Until recently, most artists involved with art and telecommunications have had a background in a different media form and have come to telecommunications and broadcasting through a desire to collaborate with others and/or distribute their work independently to a wide, mediated audience. Initially, existing broadcast media were used, then the early computer networks were incorporated, and finally the Internet became public and allowed for a convergence of direct delivery to an interested audience, thus facilitating collaboration on a truly global scale: the integration of affordable media production (PC/digital audio/video) with an immediate distribution system. Throughout this development, the desire to build an alternative mediascape to the dominating one-way outlets of television, print, and radio was an overarching motivator for all kinds of art and activism. Now that this has been achieved, alternative media can hardly be distinguished from the «mainstream.» The current and coming generations of artists and producers dealing with media and communications are bound to use a completely different set of paradigms than the previous generations.

The newest generation of media artists, however, has a completely different vantage point on media, its production, and distribution. They have grown up with the Internet and have, to a large extent, shaped its current paradigms. A good example of the influence of this development is that the formats dominating all kinds of subcultures for the last thirty years, namely handmade photocopied magazines and leaflets as well as pirate radio, have all but disappeared in the Western world. Now anyone can have their own podcast or live stream or can rant away to their hearts' content on a blog that literally thousands of people can—and do—access. Combined with the concept of immediate mobile data transmission (smartphones, etc.), we have a previously unseen amount of broadcasting and telecommunications power literally at the tips of our fingers. What unifies the old-school electronic arts crowd with the fresh kids is an interest in using the networking and related technologies for exploration of the potential and capacity for cultural expression, and, ironically, this is what the media corporations are also forced to do if they want to be part of this flat and vast many-to-many media network.

The ongoing fragmentation of what was called «mainstream culture» is a conundrum for the corporation and the artist alike. Phenomena such as Elvis Presley and Michael Jackson are becoming increasingly unlikely to occur, precisely because no single marketing machine exists today with the clout to dominate all available channels of media. Respectively, it is also more difficult for an independent artist to make a splash or just plainly get noticed outside of their peer group. Another effect of this fragmentation is the erosion of support for more traditional forms of expression, for example radio plays. Radio plays are on the cusp of being a historic art form which may soon cease to exist as a generally known format. Radio plays have their roots in theater and writing, and the medium radio has allowed the magic of combining sound effects, distinct voices, and the listeners' imagination to unfold. In order for this particular magic to work, the listener needs to engage with the medium in a specific way, essentially closing out the surroundings to participate in the mediated world: just like in those faded, black-and-white photos where the whole family is seen huddled around the huge transistor radio, rapt in awe at what is transpiring from the single, fuzzy speaker. Generally, people can no longer be found engaging with radio in this manner. The way radio is perceived these days is in three- to five-minute sections of music, interspersed with ten- to thirty-second advertising messages: ClearChannel is actually experimenting with one- to five-second ads, and a few jokes from the host. This does not mean that radio plays are not worth doing or cannot be relevant or exciting, but certainly it will be increasingly hard to get support from radio stations for their production, and a reaction like the one *War of the Worlds* provoked is unimaginable. But, at the same time, it is quite possible for a person in their basement to produce a weekly podcast that has a following of thousands around the world and to actually distribute it without ever asking a single person for permission or support. Of course, this podcast could be a radio play ... This kind of evolutionary tale could be told for many mass-media content formats, as the lines between traditional distinctions such as «TV,» «radio,» «telephone,» and «Internet» slowly blur completely.

The other radical change is how digitization and consecutive transmission have affected the sheer amount of content that is made available on a daily basis. Twenty years ago, it was a privilege of major news corporations to be able to have a live video or audio feed from the front lines of a war zone or from the heart of a riot. Now, anybody with a decent cell phone can do this, and nothing short of shutting down the network or a bullet to the phone can stop it from happening. This is quite exciting, however another important effect of the proliferation of digital consumer technology is the acceptance of a wide spectrum of quality levels in all kinds of media. Again, twenty years ago it would have been completely unacceptable for a television station to be broadcasting footage shot with consumer-grade video cameras (admittedly, this was around the birth of the first Sony Handycam, and quality has improved since), but now CNN regularly has full segments with talking heads being piped in via a satellite link, sporting a level of digital artifacts and distortion that makes a person wish for the still photographs and crackling telephone lines of yesteryear. The combination of these two factors alone has allowed for an enormous increase in available material, and much of it is available immediately—often even initially—live. However, all this content is easily stored, again due to its digital nature, for future reference, so is it still important to create live content when access to a file is about as immediate as it can get: what difference does listening to a live newscast on FM radio make when your latest voice mail is right beside BBC's world news podcast in the playlist on your smartphone?

Obviously, the answer is that it completely depends on the application, which again illustrates my point that in future the technology used to create and distribute art in the digital realm will be less relevant to the actual work that is being made. One excellent example of how seamlessly old and new concepts of media can coexist without any apparent conflict—uniting traditional practices in radio with the new realities of instant connection via the latest incarnation of mass radio, the cell phone—is *Radio Tag*, a project conceived and produced by Rob Gauvin, an artist and host at Co-op Radio, a legendary community radio station in Vancouver. It involves a flexible number of people who actually travel through the city, following a personalized instruction sheet informing the participants when and from which location to make a phone call to the radio station. The call is then placed directly on-air, together with ambient sounds prepared by Rob specifically for the show. During each phone call, the participant does something specific, for example describes the people in the immediate surroundings or just reads all the numbers that can be seen at the location from which the call is being made. Normally there are between eight to twelve participants, each on their own trajectory, sometimes intersecting with each other. Rob is meanwhile in the studio, creating a live mix with the prepared sounds, phone call schedule, and up to two callers at the same time. The first versions concentrated on phone booth locations around the city, but quickly cell phones were used, and it has become even more dynamic with participants being able to call in from nearly anywhere while directly involving random people they encounter.

As people continue to shift their attention away from mass media in its current forms, focusing more and more on the content of their combined digital memories and playback devices, it is clear that the prophecies of the nineties, proclaiming the end of distinction between audience and performer, media consumer and producer, are coming true in the form of websites like youtube.com, flickr.com, or blogs in general. At the same time, with the incorporation of cameras into cell phones, that, just for the record, operate completely in the digital realm and communicate by radio, Brian Eno's (I think ...) ancient prediction that «the telephone book will be the same thing as the TV guide» is also being fulfilled.

Not only is this going to affect the artists making and distributing digital work in all the aforementioned ways, it will also be very interesting to see how the established cultural and commercial institutions involved with traditional media react to the changing paradigms. Virtually every organization based on a traditional understanding of culture and media is being forced to adjust to the new reality to some degree. Newspapers are struggling to justify an actual printed version of themselves; television stations are cooking up deals with cell phone providers to make huge catalogues of old shows available to mobile devices; radio stations are sifting through their archives to find content to podcast; and fine art galleries are finding themselves hiring computer technicians instead of conservators to install the latest and greatest in contemporary art.

In practice, as it becomes easier and cheaper to obtain and maintain hardware and software, «traditional» artists are also becoming more present in the digital realm. Musicians having previously used the net hardly more than as an electronic flyer for their next gig are now developing generative audio engines using online data; painters who snubbed their noses at on-screen reproduction are now creating digital catalogues of their work for curators, exhibitors, and potential buyers; and video artists are suddenly shooting nonlinear video based on viewer input via webforums. As digital media become more ubiquitous, so-called traditional art forms are embracing them, again leading to a feedback loop in which more digital content is being created and added to the universally referable bitstream. On the other hand, there are hordes of kids coming out of art, film, animation, and IT school, armed to the teeth with technical expertise, ready to make some crazy digital stuff, not knowing much about analog media and its genealogy, only really perceiving it as historical content, ready to be re-cycled and referenced in new work that uses Control-C and Control-V as its main tools ... Could all this mean that there is now a second wave of cultural change and evolution rising just beyond our horizon? Or are we just about to enter an era of technological bliss, where everybody just slowly melts into the digital bitstream, permanently jacked in via their personal-digital-life-enhancer? Personally, as an old-school media jammer, I would of course prefer the former, but probably it is going to be a bit of both. Either way, the number of channels of in- and output to

Matt Smith, *eastside wireless (made with my cell phone)*, Vancouver, Canada, 2006.

the mediated world is continuously increasing with the digitization of content. I cannot deny that I am finding it overwhelming, ironically, since I dedicated a lot of time to promoting the use of the Internet and all other available channels of digital distribution among arts and activist crowds: but hey, I grew up with two channels of state-run television! So I find myself standing back and watching the show for a bit, pondering how to create content for all these available combinations of digital technologies and networks that reflects this new-to-me reality now that the battle for creating alternative, non-profit channels for distribution and access is over.

What I am expanding on is the conclusion that the production and transmission of digital data is now a solved problem, reduced to technicalities. This is resulting in a situation in which—instead of worrying about how to distribute content freely among as many interested parties as possible, against the odds of strictly controlled regulations imposed by government agencies—we find ourselves confronted with a noise level in the mediascape that seems impenetrable, not by design but by its nature. The world has changed radically: the politics in the media landscape are not about getting the word out, but about making it heard. In a sea of outrageous home video clips, personal playlists of easy listening, amateur porn, and endless slideshows of digicam snapshots—intermingled with blogvertising, blinking banner ads, and TV-On-Demand offerings, ideally all piped straight to your latest sexy slice of silicon miniaturization in the pocket of your sweat-shop-free designer jeans—its a challenge to even penetrate your friends' spam filters with an invite to your band's webcast. Consequently, this implies that a focal point for electronic art practices still needs to lie in the art of communication, especially in the continuing expansion of available channels for its expression.

Herd Listening

Andrew Garton

> The radio is on. There is static. It hisses
> and sputters like only a drifting radio can.
> It's unclear if the radio is drifting or the
> signal is drifting. Out of the static and hiss
> some Russian is heard... Tonight's concert
> continues for hours, drifting from Chinese
> to static and hiss, Russian, Indian and noise
> and noise again. The performance is excellent,
> not unlike a rendition of John Cage's aleatoric
> works for radios. The sounds drift from one
> context to another based on some underlying
> aleatoric force. The direction of the wind. The
> heating of the radio's analogue components,
> weary and drifting...
> *— Stephen Holtzman*

Drifting

USB flash disks with built-in radio receivers, proprietary messaging protocols embedded in domestic appliances, micro wireless devices are increasingly being worn, and I've dreamt of jewellery that talk to each other.

And whilst analog is being abandoned for the digital spectrum, it is becoming easier and cheaper to build transmitters supporting analog frequencies.

Amidst the fury of networks, the gaggle of formats and standards, staggeringly complex legislations and international governance bodies, artists have now more mediums and hybrids of them at their disposal, more liberal copyright options, and populations that become more curious as their governments become less transparent, where despots are more easily recognized but, try as one may, become less marginalized.

In London, I saw the future of radio, and it was free, playful, discrete, and yellow.[1] In Brazil, Creative Commons[2] was revolutionizing the way the government conducts its business, and at the iSummit[3] held there in June 2006, we were invited to «Share the past, create the future,» and we did, seeking collaborators and guidance on pressing licensing issues, but many were to leave with more business cards than substance.

In Dhaka, I would walk behind a column of stone-throwing strikers, leaving them to the ravages of the Bangladeshi police who had earlier beaten and hospitalized sixteen journalists at Chittagong Stadium. As I, a participant in the Asia ICT Policy Consultation,[4] entered the BRAC Center Inn, protesters were hidden in a plume of tear gas, and riot police appeared as if grown instantly from the pavement. Later that day, the police would indiscriminately beat women and men alike, their actions recorded on the front pages of the next morning's papers.

On this day I would present «A Vision for the Community Use of Digital Television Spectrum,»[5] prepared by Open Spectrum Australia, and I would meet several Bangladeshi community radio station operators, yet none broadcast in that country. I would also be informed that community stations in Sri Lanka are deprived of any community consultation and engagement in programming and management, despite the self-congratulatory reports published by UNESCO and their consultants.[6]

In Sarawak, I would watch lovingly shot footage of Sarawak tribes in the mid-nineteen-fifties, footage that would be used in Malaysian courts to prove indigenous ownership of lands rapidly gutted—non-renewable wealth—flora, fauna, and human cultures facing extinction, if not many already, at a cost that will no doubt be shouldered by future generations.

1 I'm in London looking at a bright yellow mobile network wearable. Porta-pak is the public interface to the PORTA2030 performance described as an «urgency network exercise» for ten participants. Porta-pak «…recalls a reel to reel porta-pack which was launched by Sony Japan in the 60s and fostered a generation of video art and community video. The updated porta-pack for PORTA2030 takes up…portable network technology to envision a portable, sustainable and responsive social network.» See http://www.porta2030.net. PORTA2030 is a Hive Network project which is deserving of an entire paper in itself: http://hivenetworks.net/tiki-index.php.

2 Creative Commons: http://creativecommons.org.

3 The second iCommons Summit, dubbed iSummit 2006, was designed to «collaborate with organizations and communities from around the world to demonstrate and share best practice, and discuss strategies for continuing the positive impact that ‹sharing› practices are having on participation in the cultural and knowledge domains.» See http://icommons.org/isummit/ and http://rights.apc.org.au/culture/2006/09/me_myself_and_i_the _summit.php.

4 Organized by the Association for Progressive Communications and hosted by the Bangladesh Friendship Education Society, the APC Asia ICT Policy Consultation sought to identify ICT policy priorities and advocacy strategies. For many, it was the first face-to-face meeting with colleagues with whom we had worked for a good many years. One such meeting was with South Asian journalist Frederick Noronha. Based in Goa, India, Frederick had been known to me since the early nineteen-nineties as editor of Pegasus Netnews and Satellite Dispatch, two of the earliest Internet and community communications journals distributed via e-mail. From jamming community radio to lowering telephony costs, an article on the APC Asia ICT Consultation by Frederick Noronha: http://www.apc.org/english/news/index.shtml?x=5038217.

Andrew Garton listening
to the Ithala bush, South
Africa, 2006.

Alexei Blinov (Raylab),
PortaPak, London, U.K.,
2006.

Andrew Garton
Herd Listening

Ithala,[7] a reserve hosting the world's oldest rock formations, located in northern KwaZulu-Natal, South Africa, would have me barely two meters from baboons that propelled themselves effortlessly through the dense mountain scrub. Barely making a sound, human-like forms agile amidst ancient flora and insects of exquisite proportions. It was chilling. I had never felt so far removed from my own environment as I was at that moment, my instincts buried, my eyes blind to the genius complexity I was immersed in. But I could feel them watching, listening, and smelling, and they knew I was vulnerable, standing there with my headphones on, a microphone outstretched, the African bush amplified in my head louder than would be considered hospitable!

What Has Any of This to Do with Radio?

When all is said and done, whether you or I harvest our information via broadband, dial-up, AM, FM, 3G, 802.11b or g, satellite, microwave, two-way, through computer games or the cinema, from interactive media or what many believe to be the new platform for narrative and cinematic expression—machinima[8]—there

5   A «Vision for the Community Use of Television» was prepared in response to the concerns of third sector broadcasters, producers, researchers, and associations for the need for community broadcasting license allocation within the digital spectrum in Australia, in particular community television. The paper was written by Ellie Rennie and builds on the premise that community broadcasters boost Australia's creative workforce and encourages content innovators from which free-to-air frequently draw fresh talent. See http://www.apcasiaictpolicy.net/a-vision-for-the-community-use-of-digital-television-spectrum-0/.

6   I met Nalaka Gunawardene in Dhaka at the APC Asia ICT Rights Consultation. He's head of Television Eduction Asia Pacific, an education-based production house based in Sri Lanka. He's also Arthur C. Clarke's scribe or something of an assistance. Our conversations were never dull. Nalaka shared with me his concerns regarding the state of community broadcasting in his home country. I knew of several people in my own country, some who were foreigners studying there, who

had created quite a decent academic career for themselves out of these few UNESCA-backed projects in Sri Lanka. In short, the notion of what is and what isn't community is rather vague. That the so-called communities these stations are to serve have no input into daily programming—that everything that goes to air must be vetoed by some government authority does not sound like community broadcasting to me. Nalaka writes openly, as one must, on the myth of Sri Lankan community radio: http://rights.apc.org.au/resources/2006/05/busting_the_sri_lankan_community_radio_myth.php.

7   Ithala is an eco-reserve in KwaZulu-Natal, South Africa. I was told that neighboring Zulus did not understand why so many animals could graze freely in the reserve when they could be hunted. Despite political improvements in South Africa, economic development was still in the hands of the former leadership of the country, the white Afrikaans.

Dhaka post-midnight,
Bangladesh, 2006.

will be dwindling reserves of energy and water, warming of the polar ice caps, and governments less and less capable of solving these problems, and societies in the developed world less able to critique and improve themselves.

Whether we re-invent radio or no, whether the artist is summoned as a child from crayon to a student of Processing,[9] whether we hurl ourselves to the Moon and back, televising this daring route, whether we tune our theremins[10] to a vowel-based harmony or stream generative[11] sound simultaneously from remote locations, does it ever cross your mind to ask, «Is anyone listening?»

For whom are we re-inventing radio? Neil Armstrong and Buzz Aldrin first walked on the Moon as a result of sheer creative indulgence from which we are left with the miracle of Teflon, freeze-dried food, and scratch-resistant lenses. An estimated 600 million people, one-fifth of the world's population in 1969, tuned into the first global simulcast, and Australians witnessed those auspicious moments 6.3 seconds before the rest of the world.[12]

At the time of writing, 1,043,104,886[13] people are net connected, well over 1,752,183,600[14] rely on mobile telephony, and more than 2.5 billion tune in around the world on 1.5 billion shortwave radio receivers.

8 Machinima is a production technique based on real-time and interactive environments created entirely within computer game development engines. A popular development platform is Unreal Tournament, which I was introduced to by artist John Power. John creates vast, architecturally impossible environments with the Unreal Engine in which he improvises live visual performances.

9 «Processing is an open source programming language and environment for people who want to program images, animation, and interactions.» See http://www.processing.org/.

10 *Touchless* was a vowel-based improvisation conceived by Elisabeth Schimana for the International Theremin Orchestra. Two versions of the composition resulted in the performances *Touchless I* and *Touchless II*, which were recorded and released by *Kunstradio*. See http://kunstradio.at/PROJECTS/TOUCHLESS/TL01/ and http://kunstradio.at/PROJECTS/TOUCHLESS/.

11 I began the creation of generative works in 1996 after the release of SSEYO Koan Pro. I found this a terribly liberating form of composition. For one, it could not be commodified easily. And secondly, it provided me with endless complexity from which to harness fresh ideas.

12 Australia's Parkes Observatory was critical to the success of the television broadcasts NASA was reliant on during the international simulcast of the Apollo 11 landing on the Moon. See http://www.parkes.atnf.csiro.au/apollo11/introduction.html and http://www.honeysucklecreek.net/Apollo_11/Australian_TV.html.

13 On July 30, 2006, 16 % of the world's population was connected to the Internet; http://www.internetworldstats.com/stats.htm.

14 The number of mobile phone users is likely to have significantly increased since the most recent figures, compiled in 2004, were released in January 2006 via the CIA Factbook: https://www.cia.gov/cia/publications/factbook/. This graph—http://en.wikipedia.org/wiki/Image:Mobile_phone_use_world.PNG—provides an overview of mobile phone penetration on a global scale.

Whilst we consider re-inventions, reconfigured, multichanneled, and interactive radio, let us not forget the 2.5 billion people who still rely on conventional radio.

What are we to say and to whom?

What will be heard and what will be understood?

The broadcaster and listener are, in my immediate world, less and less different from each other ... The more we are aware of similarities, and the more we are capable of accepting our differences—perfection is an aberration—the future of radio seems more and more like unhindered diversity. The artist ensures and protects this ... across all mediums and platforms, whether it be a stencil to a wall or a hive of wireless.

Postscript

Amidst the homogeneity, diversity grows still, and the means to communicate and nurture diversity becomes more and more necessary. Radio, the most resilient of all electronic communication mediums, persists. How will it endure the digital migration? If a story can be told in only so many ways, radio will adapt to deliver those stories whether it be a multi-platform mobile media device in Vienna or a hand-cranked, solar-powered radio receiver in Kashmir.

Contributors

Robert Adrian is an artist who began working with telecommunications technology in 1979 and, during the nineteen-eighties, organized a number of projects involving fax, slow-scan TV, amateur radio, BBSs, et cetera. In April 1995, he initiated *Kunstradio On Line*, the website of the ORF radio art program *Kunstradio*, continuing as webmaster of *Kunstradio On Line* until April 2000. He has also continued to work with different media including installation, model-making, photography, painting, sculpture, radio, and computer. His work has been included in many international exhibitions. He writes and publishes about the postindustrial revolution and its effects on art and culture. Robert Adrian was born 1935 in Toronto and has resided in Vienna since 1972.

Inke Arns is artistic director of the Hartware MedienKunstVerein, Dortmund, starting in 2005. From 1988–96, she studied Slavistics, Eastern European Studies, Political Science, and Art History in Berlin and Amsterdam, with her 2004 PhD (Dr. phil.) from the Humboldt University Berlin with a thesis researching a paradigmatic shift in the way artists reflect the historical avant-garde and the notion of utopia in visual and media art projects of the nineteen-eighties and nineties in (ex-)Yugoslavia and Russia (published in Slovenian translation by Maska, Ljubljana, in 2006). Since 1993 she has been an independent curator and author focusing on media art, net cultures, and Eastern Europe. Her curatorial work includes international exhibitions, festivals, and conferences, most recently History Will Repeat Itself (HMKV Dortmund/KW Berlin, 2007–2008) and irational.org (CCA Glasgow, 2007). Books include *Netzkulturen* (2002), *Neue Slowenische Kunst* (2002), and *Avantgarda v vzvratnem ogledalu* (*The Avant-garde in the Rear-View Mirror*, Ljubljana, 2006). She has published numerous articles on media art and net culture and edited various exhibition catalogues. Inke Arns was born 1968 in Duisdorf/Bonn. http://www.inkearns.de

Johannes Auer is an artist residing in Stuttgart. He has collaborated on various award-winning net literature and net art projects and worked closely with Reinhard Döhl. He has contributed to numerous exhibitions and art projects in different countries. His productions in the scope of net literature and radio have involved *Kunstradio*, *Radio‑Copernicus*, and *RadioRevolten*. He has published theoretical essays on net literature and net art and edits both netzliteratur.net and stuttgarter-schule.de. In 2005 and 2008, he curated the Net Literature Festival Literatur und Strom at the Literaturhaus Stuttgart. He teaches at the Merz Akademie Stuttgart. http://auer.netzliteratur.net

Robert Barry is known as one of the fathers of conceptual art and has exhibited paintings, drawings, sculpture, slide projection, video, and other media since the nineteen-sixties on an international level. He took part in the epoch-making exhibitions When Attitudes Become Form (1969) and Documenta V (1972). His works are included in the most important public and private collections worldwide. Early in his career Barry created minimally composed drawings and paintings, which lead into his work with intangibles: artworks consisting of inert gases, radiation, and radio or electromagnetic waves. Barry found language as a means to describe the intangible and adopted it as an artistic tool. Language has since become an essential element in his oeuvre for decades of artistic innovations. Barry's use of language creates an entirely unique linguistic system, one neither prose nor poetry, but instead a system where groups of words floating across the surfaces of canvases, video screens, paper, walls, or even windows and grass fields have lead to open-ended contemplations, which are guided and shaped in ways that are specific to each individual's thought pattern. Robert Barry was born 1936 in New York City.

Gottfried Bechtold is an artist living and working in Hörbranz (Vorarlberg), Austria. Starting out as a sculptor, he became influenced by post-minimal art, land art, and concept art. His apprenticeship as a stonemason in Hallein was followed by stays in Great Britain, the United States, and Canada. He has been a visiting professor both in Austria and abroad. During the late nineteen-sixties, he began working in a great variety of different media including photography, film, and video, focusing his analytic interest on their specific qualities as systems of communication. While his film work was still largely dominated by a process of translating the sign elements of language into cinematic terms, his videos, created from 1970–73, indicated a much greater involvement with the examination of the specific reality defined by the medium of video, which was new at the time. The speculative and experimental character of his works has often borne similarity to the way laboratory test series are set up. In addition to such largely conceptual approaches, he has repeatedly engaged in efforts to expand the classic concept of sculpture. In his public realm installations developed after intense immersion in the specific realities of a given site, he also integrates the elements of time and space and the immaterial medium of light. Gottfried Bechtold was born 1947 in Bregenz, Austria.

August Black is an artist, researcher, and developer of new tools and instruments. His research and praxis is based in the general overlap of culture, craft, and code. He was once a resident artist at the University of California, Santa Barbara (UCSB) BioImage Informatics Lab, researching in the areas of volume rendering, multimedia database applications, and high resolution tiled display systems. He is currently pursuing a PhD in Media Art and Technology at UCSB. His radio work is mostly defined by its characteristic misuse of dialogue, sound, and communication infrastructure within a live broadcast environment. He was first introduced to the artistic use of radio as an intern at *Kunstradio* in 1996. From 1998–2003, he produced a weekly radio experiment with Markus Seidl under the name of *Fundamental Radio* (http://funda.ment.org) on Radio FRO in Linz, Austria. From 2000–2003, he produced a monthly hour of radiophonic content with Rupert Huber (http://aug.ment.org/standup/) on Radio Orange in Vienna.

Reinhard Braun is an author and curator and has been publishing, lecturing, and conducting research on the history and theory of photography and media since 1990. He has conducted project-oriented work with artists in the field of media and telecommunica-

tions. In 1992, he was a founding member of the HILUS group; in 1999, he founded MiDiHy Productions/Media.Theory.Art.Culture; from 2003–2006, he was a curator and editor for *Camera Austria*; and since 2007, he has been serving as fine arts curator at the Styrian Autumn Festival. Reinhard Braun was born 1964 in Linz and now lives and works in Graz. http://braun.mur.at and http://midihy.org

Peter Courtemanche is a contemporary sound and installation artist from Vancouver. He is the former Director and Curator of the Western Front's Media Arts Program. He creates radio, installations, network projects, performances, curatorial projects, and handmade CD editions. His artworks often have a literary basis—inspired by narrative texts and the history of specific installation sites. Works include: *Divining for Lost Sound* (1996–99), *.. devolve into II..* (commissioned by *Kunstradio*, 2002), *Spark-Writing* (2004), and *Preying Insect Robots* (2006).

Nina Czegledy is a media artist, curator, and writer and has collaborated on international projects, produced time-based and digital works, and participated in workshops, forums, and festivals worldwide. *What will you do* and the *Aurora Feast* collaborative public art projects were exhibited in 2006–2007. She has shown with the ICOLS group and with the Girls&Guns collective. *Resonance*, the *Electromagnetic Bodies Project*, *Digitized Bodies Virtual Spectacles*, and the *Aurora Projects* reflect her art-science-technology interest. She has curated numerous media art exhibitions and exchange programs. Her academic lectures and conference presentations have lead to numerous publications worldwide. Czegledy holds positions as: Senior Fellow at KMDI, University of Toronto; Adjunct Associate Professor at Concordia University, Montreal; Honorary Fellow at Moholy Nagy University, Budapest; co-chair of the Leonardo Education Forum.

Dieter Daniels is professor for Art History and Media Theory at the Academy of Visual Arts (HGB) in Leipzig, starting in 1993. In 1984, he co-founded the Videonale Bonn and has contributed to numerous projects, exhibitions, and symposia in the field of media art. From 1991–93, he headed the Mediatheque at the Center for Art and Media (ZKM),

Karlsruhe. He has extensively published on twentieth-century art, a.o. on Marcel Duchamp, Fluxus, media art. He is coeditor of *Media Art Action* and *Media Art Interaction* (with Rudolf Frieling), and recent book publications include *Kunst als Sendung* (2002) and *Vom Ready-Made zum Cyberspace* (2003). From 2001–2005, he conceived and coedited Media Art Net (www.mediaartnet.org). Since 2005, he has served as director of the Ludwig Boltzmann Institute Media.Art.Research. in Linz. Dieter Daniels was born 1957 in Bonn.

Wolfgang Ernst is chair of Media Theory at the Humboldt University, Berlin, having studied history, the classics, and archaeology with a 1989 PhD thesis on historicism and museology. His teaching experience and guest professorships in cultural history and media studies have extended among various universities (Leipzig, Cologne, Weimar, Bochum, Paderborn, Berlin). His recent publications include *M.edium F.oucault* (Weimar, 2000), *Das Rumoren der Archive* (Berlin, 2002), *Im Namen von Geschichte* (Munich, 2003), and *Das Gesetz des Gedächtnisses* (Berlin, 2007).

Bill Fontana is a sound artist who studied philosophy and music at the New School for Social Research in New York, with Phillip Corner and others. Following a prolonged stay in Australia, he was a guest artist in Germany and Japan. The composition of sound sculptures began in 1976, and he has since produced a large number of works in this genre. The compositions and live sound sculptures realized for the Studio Akustische Kunst of the German radio station WDR have been of central importance for his artistic development; they include *Distant Trains*, *Metropolis Cologne*, *Satellite Ear Bridge Cologne – San Francisco*, *Journey Through My Sound Sculptures*, *The Sound of an Unblown Flute*, and *Soundbridge Cologne – Kyoto*. Bill Fontana was born 1947 in Cleveland, Ohio.

Anna Friz is a sound and radio artist, and a critical media studies scholar. She has performed and exhibited installation works at festivals and venues across North America, Europe, and in Mexico. Her radio art/works have been commissioned by national public radio in Canada, Austria, Germany, Denmark, and Mexico and heard on independent airwaves in more than fifteen countries. Anna Friz is a free103 point9.org transmission artist, and a doctoral candidate in the Joint Graduate Programme in Communication & Culture at York University and Ryerson University in Toronto.

Andrew Garton is an artist and producer who began producing and performing music in the late seventies as a synthesist, saxophonist, and spoken word performer. He has composed numerous documentary soundtracks, has conceived and produced interactive installations, both on- and offline, has published articles on independent media, generative music, and radio art, and has worked with the pioneer community Internet provider, Pegasus networks. He produced perhaps the first generative sound piece for Australian radio and Internet in 1997, a collaboration with Stelarc, for *The Listening Room* (now off-air) and co-produced a series of live audio-video collaborations commencing in Melbourne in 1998 and culminating in a series of works for the opening of the Taipei International Arts Festival in 2001. From 1997–99, he co-founded, wrote, produced, and performed with the Austrian-based Electro-Pathological Consort, and in 2005 he curated the innovative generative sound series, *Frequency Post*, for the Vienna-based *Kunstradio*. He has presented numerous papers on networking and new media initiatives at a wide range of international conferences. His most recent works have been published in At a Distance (MIT Press) and the online journal Sleepy Brain and Filter (Australian Network for Art and Technology). He is an MA graduate of RMIT University, Melbourne, Australia and member of the Association for Progressive Communications. Andrew Garton was born 1962 in Guildford, New South Wales, Australia. http://apc.org.au/ and http://toysatellite.org/

Daniel Gethmann is currently teaching Media and Design Studies at the Institute of Art History and Cultural Studies at the Graz University of Technology, Austria. He is the author of *Die Uebertragung der Stimme: Vor- und Frühgeschichte des Sprechens im Radio* (diaphanes Verlag, 2006) as well as the coeditor of *Apparaturen bewegter Bilder* (LIT Verlag, 2006), *Politiken der Medien* (diaphanes Verlag, 2005), and *Daumenkino – The Flipbook Show* exhibition catalogue of the Kunsthalle Düsseldorf (snoeck Verlag, 2005).

Daniel Gilfillan is Assistant Professor of German Studies and Information Literacy in the School of International Letters and Cultures at Arizona State University. He earned his PhD in German Studies from the University of Oregon in 2000. Research emphases include history of media technology in the German context, and studies of textuality across various media. His first book, *Pieces of Sound: Experimental Radio in Germany*, will appear in 2008 with the University of Minnesota Press. Daniel Gilfillan was born in 1965.

Heidi Grundmann is a lecturer, curator, and consultant in the field of new media with a special focus on radio and communications art. In 1987, she created the radio program *Kunstradio* (original artworks for radio) on ORF, the Austrian National Radio. She has curated international conferences, events, and exhibitions and has been involved in many innovative radio art projects. She has edited several publications, including *Art + Telecommunication* (1984), *The Geometry of Silence* (1991), *On the Air* (1993), *ZEITGLEICH* (1994), and *Sound Drifting* (2000).

Wolfgang Hagen is college lecturer at the Humboldt University, Berlin and head of the cultural departments of a German radio station, *Deutschlandradio Kultur*. He is author of numerous works on the history of media, with emphasis on photography, radio, and the computer. His most recent publication is *Busonis Invention: Phantasmagorien und Irrungen in Zeiten des Medienübergangs*.

Honor Harger is an artist and curator with a particular interest in artistic uses of new technologies. She was educated in New Zealand and has lived in Europe since 1999. From 2004, she has been director of the AV Festival in Newcastle, Gateshead, Sunderland, and Middlesbrough in the U.K. (http://www.avfestival.co.uk). Her artistic practice is produced under the name r a d i o q u a l i a, together with collaborator Adam Hyde. Their work has been exhibited at the ICC in Tokyo, New Museum of Contemporary Art in New York, Gallery 9, Walker Art Center in Minneapolis, Sonar in Barcelona, Ars Electronica in Austria, Artspace in New Zealand, among other places. In August 2004, r a d i o - q u a l i a were awarded a UNESCO Digital Art Prize

for the project *Radio Astronomy* (http://www.radio-astronomy.net). Honor Harger was born 1975 in New Zealand.

Andreas Hirsch is an expert in conceiving and engineering cultural systems. For more than two decades his work for leading cultural organizations in the arts, theater, music, film, literature, and the media has included conceptualizing and curating as well as developing and managing projects and institutions. He is especially interested in the cultural implications of technology and globalization and their effects on cultural memory and diversity, as well as in the creation of common public goods and the development of sustainable solutions for a more just and peaceful world. He is based in Vienna, Austria. http://electrolyte.net/

Candice Hopkins is the Director/Curator of Exhibitions at The Western Front where she has recently curated exhibitions on the themes of networks and art, architecture and disaster, and time and obsolescence. She has an MA from The Center for Curatorial Studies, Bard College where she received the Ramapo Curatorial Prize for the exhibition *Every Stone Tells a Story: The Performance Work of David Hammons and Jimmie Durham*. Her writing is published by MIT Press, NYU, Walter Phillips Gallery, and Museum London among others, and she has given talks internationally, including at the Dakar Biennale and the Tate Modern.

José Iges is an intermedia artist, musical composer, and radio art producer with a PhD in Sciences of Communication. With the coauthorship of the artist Concha Jerez, since 1989 he has been making sound and sight installations, intermedia concerts, radio artworks and performances in Austria, France, Finland, Italy, Germany, and Spain. Since 1985 he has been a producer of *Ars Sonora* at RNE Radio Clásica. He also served as coordinator of the Ars Acustica/EBU group from 1999 until 2005 and authored the doctoral thesis «Radio Art, a Sound Art for the Electronic Space of Communication» (Madrid, 1997).

GX Jupitter-Larsen is an artist, based in Hollywood, California, who has been active in a number of underground art scenes since the late nineteen-seventies. Underlying all of his work is a mix of aesthetic and conceptual obsessions, particularly entropy and decay, professional wrestling, and a self-created lexicon consisting mainly of personalized units of measurement such as polywave, the totimorphous, and the xylowave. In 2006, he designed and manufactured his own ruler based on his own ideas of measurement. http://www.jupitter-larsen.com, http://www.noisyvideo.com, http://www.polywave.us, and http://ebooks.jupitter-larsen.com

Douglas Kahn is Professor of Technocultural Studies at the University of California, Davis. He is the author of *Noise, Water, Meat: A History of Sound in the Arts* (MIT Press), coeditor of *Wireless Imagination: Sound, Radio and the Avant-garde* (MIT), and is writing a book on electromagnetism and the arts for the University of California Press. He also serves as editor of the Leonardo Music Journal (MIT), the journal Senses and Society (Berg), and the Technoculture and the Arts book series from the University of California Press. He received a 2006 Guggenheim Fellowship for work on the historical discovery of natural radio. He currently lives in San Francisco.

Friedrich Kittler is chair of Aesthetics and Media History at the Humboldt University Berlin, starting in 1993. He studied German and French Literatures and Philosophy at the University of Freiburg/Breisgau. From 1987 to 1993, he served as chair of German Literature at the Ruhr-University Bochum. He is a member of the Hermann von Helmholtz-Zentrum für Kulturtechnik in Berlin and the research group «Bild Schrift Zahl» (DFG). His publications include: *Aufschreibesysteme 1800/1900* (München, 1985; 4th edition, 2003), translated under the title *Discourse Networks 1800/1900* (Stanford University Press, 1990); *Grammophon, Film, Typewriter* (Berlin, 1986), English translation *Gramophone, Film, Typewriter* (Stanford University Press, 1999); *Dichter, Mutter, Kind* (München, 1991); *Draculas Vermächtnis: Technische Schriften* (Leipzig, 1993); *Essays: Literature, media, information systems* (Amsterdam: G+B Arts International, 1997); *Eine Kulturgeschichte der Kulturwissenschaften* (München, 2000); *Optische Medien* (Berlin, 2002), *Musik und Mathematik I, Hellas 1: Aphrodite* (Paderborn, 2006). Friedrich Kittler was born in 1943.

Tetsuo Kogawa is a performance artist who—aside from being a university professor in the Department of Communication Studies at Tokyo Keizai University, the director of the Goethe Archive Tokyo, and a prolific writer on media philosophy, information technology, film works, Kafka, and various contemporary themes—has been teaching workshops for many years, showing people how to build their own FM transmitters from simple electronic components. These workshops also provoke those involved to consider the technical, political, and social ramifications of electromagnetic broadcasts. By building transmitters the workshop participants inevitably deconstruct broadcasting, challenging their own notions of what broadcasting is now and what it could be. He has been likewise challenging radical experiments of radio art using and exhibiting his invented devices in various cities of Europe and North America. Since the mid-nineties, he has also been involved in creating and organizing his own webpages. http://anarchy.translocal.jp

Richard Kriesche is a media artist and director of «kulturdata» (culture data), since 2004 at the Landesmuseum Joanneum, Graz. In 1963, he received his teaching credentials for Artistic Pedagogy at the Akademie der Bildenden Künste (Academy of Visual Arts) and the University in Vienna. In 1964, he earned a Master's in Graphic Arts and Painting at the Akademie der Bildenden Künste, Vienna. He has held professorships in Austria, Germany, and France in the field of electronic and digital media. Main exhibitions include: documenta 6 and documenta 8 in Kassel; the 34th, 42nd, and 46th Venice Biennales; Ars Electronica in Linz in 1989, 1994, and 2003; ARTSAT–Space Station MIR in 1991 (the first art project in the history of the Russian spaceflight on the space station MIR). He has an artistic interest in media, initially analog, but since the early seventies, digital. He ranks among those pioneers in media art who, in a most rigorous way, have applied strategies to analyze the inherent qualities and limits of the medium. Richard Kriesche was born 1940 in Vienna and lives and works in Graz. http://iis.joanneum.at/kulturdata

Katja Kwastek is an art historian and researcher at the Ludwig Boltzmann Institute Media.Art.Research. in Linz, Austria, where she directs the research projects on Interactive Art. Previously, she worked as assistant professor in the Art History Department of the University of Munich and was a Visiting Scholar at the Rhode Island School of Design in Spring 2006. Her research focuses on digital media art, for example on changing spatial conceptions due to the rise of communication technologies, and on the aesthetics of media. She has curated exhibition projects, lectured widely, and published many books and essays, including *Ohne Schnur: Art and Wireless Communication* (2004).

Brandon LaBelle is an artist and writer working with sounds, places, bodies, and cultural frictions. He is the author of *Background Noise: Perspectives on Sound Art* (Continuum, 2006) and coeditor of the *Surface Tension* (Errant Bodies) series. His recent work *prototypes for the mobilization and broadcast of fugitive sound* was exhibited at the Enrico Fornello Gallery, Prato. He teaches at the University of Copenhagen and is currently developing projects on auditory design, emotional geographies, and street cultures.

Caoimhín Mac Giolla Léith is a critic, curator, and Senior Lecturer at University College Dublin. He is a contributor to various journals including Artforum, Frieze, and Parkett. Recent publications include essays on Miroslaw Balka, Thomas Demand, Keith Edmier, Ellen Gallagher, Candida Höfer, Karen Kilimnik, and Thomas Scheibitz. He has curated exhibitions at the Irish Museum of Modern Art, the Douglas Hyde Gallery, and Kerlin Gallery (Dublin), the Drawing Room (London), Tanya Bonakdar Gallery (New York), and de Ateliers (Amsterdam).

Norbert Math is an artist active in the fields of radio art, electronic music, installation, and Internet. He is co-founder (with Andrea Sodomka, August Black, and Martin Breindl) and network designer of alien productions, an artist's network for theory and aesthetics of new technology and media. His radio works include *State of Transition* (with Sodomka and Breindl and x-space, 1994), *Tempest* (with Ludwig Zeininger, 2001), *Radiation* (with Robert Adrian, 1998–2006), and *XT* (alien productions and

Machfeld, 2007). Norbert Math was born 1962 in Bolzano, Italy and now lives and works in Vienna. http://alien.mur.at

Doreen Mende is a curator and author based in Berlin. She earned her Diploma in Music from the University of Music and Theatre in Leipzig and completed studies in Electroacoustic Music at the Sibelius Academy in Helsinki. She has curated *What If … #2* (JET, Berlin, 2005), *Ear Appeal* (Kunsthalle Exnergasse, Vienna, 2006), *Not Right But Wrong* (JET, Berlin, 2007), and *LOGE* (performance/installation series at General Public) and has been writing texts and editing publications in connection with the projects above. Since 2006, she has been assistant professor in the Exhibition Design and Curatorial Practice program at the University of Media Art and Design in Karlsruhe (HfG). She is editor in chief of the publication series *DISPLAYER*, published by HfG, and is co-founder of the collective/project space General Public in Berlin. Currently she is doing a PhD in Curatorial/Knowledge at Goldsmiths College, University of London. http://www.artnews.info/doreenmende

Sergio Messina is a musician, journalist, sound designer, and performer. He's a regular columnist for the Italian edition of *Rolling Stone* magazine and teaches Sound Design at the Istituto Europeo di Design (IED) in Milano. His latest project is a stand-up sociology show on digital pornography called *Realcore*. http://www.radiogladio.it

Ursula Meyer was an artist and professor born in Hanover, Germany in 1915. She studied in secret under Bauhaus Masters from 1934 to 1937 and later continued her studies in Italy at the Reggia Scuola in Faenza, finally completing her education in the U.S., with a BA from the New School and a Master's Degree from Columbia in 1962. Meyer became a professor of sculpture in the CUNY system, in 1963. She participated in numerous solo and group shows, including shows at the MOMA, Brooklyn Museum, Aldrich Museum, Newark Museum, Hudson River Museum, the Finch College Museum, the Amel Gallery, and the A. M. Sachs Gallery. Meyer was frequently reviewed, including by *The Village Voice*, the *New York Post*, *Art News*, *Arts Magazine*, *Arts International*, and *The Washing-*

ton Post. She wrote *Conceptual Art* (New York: Dutton, 1972) and more than ten magazine articles about art. Throughout a vigorous career, intellectual passion, conceptual mastery, and a breathtaking range of inventiveness marked Ursula Meyer's work. After retirement from CUNY in 1980, Meyer continued to create hundreds of new pieces of artwork, which have never been shown, including several very large sculptures. She was wildly experimental and prolific until the end of her life in 2003.

Roberto Paci Dalò is an Italian artist, theatre director, filmmaker, composer/musician. Since 1985, he has served as director of the performing arts group Giardini Pensili, and since 2006, artistic director of the contemporary arts centre Velvet Factory (Rimini). His works are presented in Europe, Russia, the Middle East, and the Americas in major festivals, theatres, museums, and as site-specific art in the public space. He curates international art projects based on telecommunications systems and was director of the radio festival LADA – L'Arte dell'Ascolto (1991–98). He is a member of the Internationale Heiner Müller Gesellschaft Berlin. His latest book, coedited with Emanuele Quinz, is titled *Millesuoni: Deleuze, Guattari e la musica elettronica* (2006). He has taught Media Dramaturgy and New Media at the University of Siena and collaborates with Italian and Canadian universities. He lived for several years in Berlin, where in 1993–94 he was a guest of the Artists-in-Berlin Programme of the DAAD. He currently lives in Rimini, Italy, and feels at home in Vancouver. http://giardini.sm

Sarah Pierce is an artist based in Dublin. She regularly publishes *The Metropolitan Complex* papers and organizes a project of the same name that taps into locality, the personal and incidental, using a variety of platforms. She has contributed to such publications as *Curating Subjects*, *Make Everything New*, and *Put About: an anthology of independent publishing*. Ongoing projects include *The Meaning of Greatness*, *Affinity Archive*, and *Paraeducation Department*. In 2006, she co-curated *Enthusiasm!*, a four-part radio program on communism for London's Resonance FM. She is currently doing a PhD at Goldsmiths, London.

Winfried Ritsch is professor at the University of Music and Dramatic Arts Graz (KUG) in the Institute of Electronic Music and Acoustics (IEM), starting in 1989. He studied Sound Engineering at the Technical University Graz and at the University of Music and Dramatic Arts Graz. In 1998, he founded the Graz-based NetzKunst (Net Art) network and has also founded the artists' group fond and atelier algorythmics. He has done artworks and performances in the field of radio art along with compositions (especially with computer music), sound installations, telematic artworks, and net art. http://mur.at

Christian Scheib is a musicologist, radio editor, and music producer. Currently, he is editor of new music programs at the Austrian cultural radio station Österreich 1 and program director of the new music festival «musikprotokoll im steirischen herbst» (http://oe1.orf.at/musikprotokoll). He has edited and written several books, has been lecturer at the California Institute of the Arts (1998), and continues to lecture on aesthetics at the University of Music Vienna. Together with Sabine Sanio he has edited books such as *das rauschen* («static's music,» 1995), *Form – Luxus, Kalkül und Abstinenz* («form,» 2000), *Bilder – Verbot und Verlangen in Kunst und Musik* («(no) graven image,» 2001), *Übertragung – Transfer – Metapher* (Kerber, 2004). He and Susanna Niedermayr have jointly written and published two books as well as two CD packages about music in the eastern half of Europe under the title *European Meridians: New Music Territories* (Pfau, 2003). Christian Scheib was born 1961 and currently lives in Vienna.

Tom Sherman is an artist and writer. He works in video, performance, radio, and text. His interdisciplinary work has been exhibited internationally, including shows at the National Gallery of Canada, the Museum of Modern Art, and the Venice Biennale. He performs and records with Bernhard Loibner in a group called Nerve Theory. His latest book is *Before and After the I-Bomb: An Artist in the Information Environment* (Banff Centre Press, 2002). He is a professor in the Department of Transmedia at Syracuse University in New York but considers the South Shore of Nova Scotia, Canada his home.

Rasa Šmite and Raitis Šmits are Latvian artists and new media activists, founders of the E-LAB (1996), RIXC (2000), and the Art+Communication Festival in Riga, Latvia (1996). Since 1997, they have been interested in «acoustic space» research and are initiators and founding members of the *net. radio OZONE* (1996) and *Xchange* network (receiving PRIX Ars Electronica in 1998) as well as editors of the *Acoustic Space* publication series (since 1998) and organizers of the Acoustic Space Lab symposium at the Irbene Radio Telescope (2001). In collaboration with r a d i o q u a l i a, Clausthome, and VIRAC, they have developed the live installation and streaming project *Solar Radio Station* (2006) and, together with Armin Medosch, are curating the international exhibition *Waves*. They are the initiators, founders, and participants of various other co-projects, networks, and mailing lists (NICE, Locative Network, Trans-European Cultural Mapping [TCM], etc.). Since 1996, they have organized and participated in numerous conferences, exhibitions, symposiums, and festivals, have lectured at the Latvian Arts Academy, Riga Stradina, and other universities, and have served as experts and members of various boards on new media culture. Rasa Šmite is presently director of the RIXC center for new media culture and is working toward a PhD in social sciences, culture, and communications at the Riga Stradina University. Raitis Šmits teaches in the Visual Communication Department of the Art Academy of Latvia and also works as program leader of *net.radio OZONE*, director of E-LAB, and coordinator of the RIXC Media Lab.

Matt Smith is an artist who started out as a media designer at the Ars Electronica Center in Linz, Austria in 1995. He left in 1997 to set out on an online diary project on the West Coast of North America. In 1998, he settled in Vancouver, where he has since been working on projects of his own as well as collaboratively with various local and international artists and groups. He also continues to do select contract work for artists and institutions when he is not at the Audio Visual Department of the Vancouver Art Gallery. Highlights have included founding the Artist Run Limousine Collective and the resulting project *Audiomobile*, which has been performed seven times in five cities since 2003. Before that he was actively involved with all kinds

of Internet broad- and narrowcasting adventures, mostly in form of the *FirstFlooRadioShow*. It was started originally at the Ars Electronica Center as a broadcast on pirate radio relayed to the transmitter via the Internet, eventually becoming a late-night fixture on CITR 101.9 FM in Vancouver for five years between 1999 and 2004, while also being involved in network projects around the world. Currently Matt has been investigating robotics and photography, with varying success. He is part of the Second Site Collective and has recently exhibited a pond-roaming robot called *The Ponderer* at VanDusen Gardens in Vancouver.

Anne Thurmann-Jajes is head of the Research Centre for Artists' Publications at the Weserburg– Museum for Modern Art and teaches at the Institute of Science of Art and Art Education at the University of Bremen. She has curated numerous exhibitions as well as authored and edited many catalogues and books, including *Painters' Books – Artists' Books: The versatility of a medium in the art of the 20th century* (2001), *Book – Media – Photography* (2004, with Sigrid Schade), and *Sound Art: Between Avant-Garde and Pop Culture* (2006, with Sabine Breitsameter and Winfried Pauleit).

Lori Weidenhammer is a performance-based artist, originally from Cactus Lake, Saskatchewan, who now makes her home in Vancouver. In her piece called *The Weidenhammer Wunderkammer* she traveled to disappearing prairie towns in the Artist Run Limousine. In *The Madame Beespeaker Project* she channeled Madame Dolittle, a time-traveler who uses her scientific knowledge and extrasensory perception to communicate with honeybees. For the past two years, she has been studying and working on issues related to food security, organic farming, and creating a sustainable food culture.

Sandra Wintner is a Technical Director at the Western Front Artist Run Centre in Vancouver. Since 1997, Sandra has worked on numerous web-based productions (organization, web design, streaming audio, video documentation) for *Kunstradio*, Vienna, including *Recycling the Future* at the Ars Electronica Festival 1997, *..devolve into II..* in spring 2002, and the global streaming network *Radiotopia* in autumn 2002. Sandra assisted *Kunstradio* in realizing events in Vancouver within the framework of the telecommunications project *Wiencouver 2000*, including *I AM THE ONE WHO SAYS: HERE I AM* by Bruno Pisek and Anna Friz. She was involved with Matt Smith's Artist Run Limousine and co-created *AUDIOMOBILE* with Matt Smith and Winnipeg artist Ken Gregory.

Elisabeth Zimmermann is a cultural manager living in Vienna. She studied at the International Centre for Culture and Management (ICCM) in Salzburg and has been involved in organizing, coordinating, and curating radio art projects, symposia, CDs, publications, and international telematic art projects. She has held various presentations and lectures on radio art projects at national and international festivals. Since 1998, she has been the producer of the weekly radio art program *Kunstradio–Radiokunst* (http://kunstradio.at) on the cultural channel of ORF (Austrian National Radio). In 1999, she founded «werks»—an art association dedicated to the realization of artistic projects in telecommunications media.

Links

(accessed January 30, 2008)

Preface, The Editors
classes.design.ucla.edu/Fall06/10/
    CybernationToInteraction.pdf
www.mediafiles.at
scan.net.au/scan/journal/display.php?journal
    _id=92
www.werks.at

Inventing and Re-Inventing Radio,
Dieter Daniels
alien.mur.at/rax/KUNSTFUNK/index.html
www.usatoday.com/tech/news/2005-02-09
    -podcasting-usat-money-cover_x.htm

Blanking: A Text by Tom Sherman
www.kunstradio.at

Becoming Radio, Anna Friz
s171907168.onlinehome.us/civicspace/
    ?q=en/taxonomy/term/15
anarchy.translocal.jp/radio/micro/howtotx.html
www.free103point9.org
www.somewhere.org/NAR/writings/apple.htm
www.simultaneita.net/promiscuoustechn.html

Landscape Soundings: A Project by Bill Fontana
kunstradio.at/TAKE/CD/fontana1.html
kunstradio.at/FONTANA/LS/index.html

Art without Time and Space? Radio in the
Visual Arts of the Twentieth and Twenty-First
Centuries, Katja Kwastek
www.ok-centrum.at/ausstellungen/open
    _house/ligna.html
ace.uci.edu/penny/works/loyoyo.html
www.artmuseum.net/w2vr/archives/Kluver/
    04_Oracle.html

Audiomobile: A Project by Matt Smith and
Sandra Wintner
www.firstfloor.org/ARL/Audiomobile/
www.firstfloor.org/ARL/

Radio as Exhibition Space, Doreen Mende
kunstradio.at/BREGENZ/KIDS/index.html
www.ridderradio.com
www.tate.org.uk/britain/exhibitions/audioarts/

Media Space: Networked Structures in Early Radio
Communication, Daniel Gethmann
foucault.info/documents/heteroTopia/foucault
    .heteroTopia.en.html

Networked Radio Space and Broadcast Simultaneity:
An Interview with Robert Adrian, Daniel Gilfillan
alien.mur.at/rax/TEXTS/ra-eraum-e.html
alien.mur.at/rax/TEXTS/elecism.html
alien.mur.at/rax/24_HOURS/24-catalog-e.html
www.kunstradio.at/TEXTS/manifesto.html

Hank Bull: From the Centre to the Periphery,
Candice Hopkins
www.artpool.hu/Fluxus/Higgins/
    intermedia2.html
www.aec.at
kunstradio.at/REPLAY/
alien.mur.at/rax/BIO/
telematic.walkerart.org/overview/overview
    _adrian.html
en.wikipedia.org/wiki/The_Pleasure_of_the
    _Text
openspace.ca/web/outerspace/
    NormanWhiteInterview2

Radio Amidst Technological Ideologies,
Reinhard Braun
wps.com/FidoNet/
www.kunstradio.at/2007A/14_01_07.html
www2.tu-berlin.de/~soziologie/Crew/schulz
    -schaeffer/pdf/AkteurNetzwerkTheorie.pdf
www.voorthuis.net/texts/Manuel_DeLanda
    _The_Machinic_Phylum.doc

RadioZeit: A Project by Richard Kriesche
www.kunstradio.at/1989A/19_1_89.html

Past and Present of Radio Art: A 1995 Perspective,
Heidi Grundmann
www.aec.at
alien.mur.at/rax/KUNSTFUNK/index.html

Kunstradio On Line
www.kunstradio.at
orf.at

Broadcast Space as Artistic Space: Transcultural
Radio, Itinerant Thought, and the Global Sphere,
Daniel Gilfillan
    www.kunstradio.at
    www.kunstradio.at/TEXTS/manifesto.html
    www.kunstradio.at/1994B/stateof_t.html
    www.kunstradio.at/HORRAD/horrad.html
    alien.mur.at/rax/24_HOURS/main.html
    www.nato.int/kosovo/press/b990430b.htm
    www.kunstradio.at/BIOS/maticbio.html
    www.kunstradio.at/1999A/RA/99_04_29.ram
    www.kunstradio.at/2000A/RA/00_04_02.ram
    www.kunstradio.at/1999A/ANEM_B92/index
        .html
    www.kunstradio.at/WAR/VOICES/matic
        -commsolo.html
    www.kunstradio.at/TAKE/CD/paunovic_cd.html
    www.kunstradio.at/1993A/RA/concerto.ram
    www.kunstradio.at/WAR/DIARY/
    helpb92.xs4all.nl/diaries/jasmina/jasmina.htm
    www.geocities.com/Wellesley/3321/win23a
        .html
    alien.mur.at/state_of/

LADA – L'Arte dell'Ascolto (The Art of Listening): A
Festival in Rimini, Italy, 1991–98, Roberto Paci Dalò
    giardini.sm/lada/
    www.kunstradio.at/TAKE/zgcatalog.html
    kunstradio.at/FUTURE/index.html
    velvet.it

The Medium as Midas: On the Precarious
Relationship of Music and Radio Art,
Christian Scheib
    alien.mur.at/rax/BIO/
    www.kunstradio.at/SD/index.html
    www.kunstradio.at/FUTURE/index.html
    www.kunstradio.at/RIV_BRI/index.html
    www.kunstradio.at/AUER/index.html
    www.kunstradio.at/THEORIE/index.html

The Imaginary Network, Peter Courtemanche
    absolutevalueofnoise.ca/2002_devolve/online/
        diary.html
    front.bc.ca/frontmagazine
    www.medienkunstnetz.de/themes/overview
        _of_media_art/communication/15/
    alien.mur.at/rax/BIO/telecom.html
    www.well.com/~couey/interactive/bull.html

www.well.com/~couey/interactive/guests.html
subsol.c3.hu/subsol_2/contributors0/
    grundmanntext.html
www.kunstradio.at/RADIOTOPIA/
projects.front.bc.ca/2003/scrambled/
absolutevalueofnoise.ca/2000_devolve/
absolutevalueofnoise.ca/2002_devolve/online/
projects.front.bc.ca/2005/reverie/
alien.mur.at
antarcti.ca

Sonic Postcards: Excerpts from an Online Diary
Inspired by Art's Birthday 2007, Lori Weidenhammer
    projects.front.bc.ca/2007/artsbirthday/blogs/
        lw_front_bc_ca/

Net Literature and Radio: A Work-in-Progress Report,
Johannes Auer
    netzspannung.org/database/37545/de
    auer.netzliteratur.net/worm/applepie.htm
    www.netzliteratur.net/cramer/schrift_selbst
        _ausfuehrt.html
    appleinspace.cyberfiction.ch
    www.kunstradio.at/2004B/07_11_04.html
    www.kunstradio.at/PROJECTS/CURATED
        _BY/index.html
    www.kunstradio.at/PROJECTS/CURATED
        _BY/ran/
    www.netzliteratur.net/wirth/litim.htm
    acg.media.mit.edu/people/fry/genomevalence/
    www.kunstradio.at/2003B/07_09_03.html
    kunstradio.cyberfiction.ch
    www.kunstradio.at/PROJECTS/LITERATURE/
    www.kunstradio.at/AUER/
    www.kunstradio.at/AUER/auer_info.html
    www.kunstradio.at/2005A/30_01_05.html
    www.epidemic.ws/dina_en.html
    www.kunstradio.at/2005A/20_02_05.html
    netzspannung.org/cat/servlet/CatServlet/
        $files/272719/breitsameter.pdf
    www.uni-stuttgart.de/ndl1/hspl_hughes.htm
    radio-c.zkm.de/radio-copernicus.org
    copernicus.netzliteratur.net
    www.radiorevolten.radiocorax.de/cms/
        index.php
    halle.netzliteratur.net
    www.stuttgarter-schule.de/lutz_schule.htm
    www.fireball.de/livesuche/
    userpage.fu-berlin.de/~chlor/werk.pdf

An Anatomy of Radio, August Black
www.videolan.org
www.orang.org
cba.fro.at
radioqualia.va.com.au/freqclock/
www.democracynow.org
www.napster.com
www.bittorrent.net
www.gnutella.com
www.kunstradio.at
www.aaniradio.org
www.ninjam.com
www.streaps.org
aug.ment.org/userradio/

*Radio as Art: Classification and Archivization
of Radio Art, Anne Thurmann-Jajes*
www.weserburg.de
www.kuenstlerpublikationen.de
www.nmwb.de/nmwb_deu/1tp_aspc.php

Radio in the Chiasme, Tetsuo Kogawa
anarchy.translocal.jp/non-japanese/
radiorethink.html

*Radiation: An Installation for Shortwave Radio
by Robert Adrian and Norbert Math*
alien.mur.at/rax/BIO/
www.kunstradio.at/2002A/27_01_02/index
.html
www.kunstradio.at/PROJECTS/
REINVENTING/index.php?c=3

*Distory: 100 Years of Electron Tubes, Media-
Archaeologically Interpreted vis-à-vis 100 Years
of Radio, Wolfgang Ernst*
www.einstein-website.de/z_biography/
speechfunkausstellung.html
de.wikipedia.org/wiki/Radio
www.computing-music.de
www.medienwissenschaft.hu-berlin.de/~mc/
ENIAC_NOMOI_eng.php
www.medienwissenschaft.hu-berlin.de/~mc/
KVV_SS05_M4.php

…ith Robert Barry (October 12, 1969),

…m/papers/barry_interview.html

*Joyce Hinterding and Parasitic Possibility,
Douglas Kahn*
www.nettime.org/Lists-Archives/nettime
-l-9808/msg00074.html
www.earlyradiohistory.us/1908rem.htm

*Radio: An Agent of Audification?,
Honor Harger*
radioqualia.va.com.au/freqclock/
www.radioqualia.net/ser/
netartcommons.walkerart.org/article
.pl?sid=02/05/12/038213&mode=thread
www.radioqualia.net/psonet/
www.radioqualia.net/makrolab/vaneck.html
www.radio-astronomy.net
www.turbulence.org/Works/heat/
www.sciencedirect.com/science/
journal/01674048
en.wikipedia.org/wiki/Aurora_borealis
wwwmcc.murdoch.edu.au/ReadingRoom/
2.2/2.2.html

*The Realization of Radio's Unrealized Potential:
Media-Archaeological Focuses in Current Artistic
Projects, Inke Arns*
www.debalie.nl/dossierpagina
.jsp?dossierid=10123
www.medienkunstnetz.de/themen/medien-
kunst_im_ueberblick/kommunikation/
projectbroadcasting.mi2.hr/index.htm
www.resonance-electromagneticbodies.net
www.art-bag.org/convextv/pro/object.htm
www.art-bag.org/trimmdich/anno.htm
www.necronauts.org
www.hexen2039.net
en.wikipedia.org/wiki/Gematria
www.radioqualia.net
www.radio-astronomy.net
www.hmkv.de/dyn/e_program_exhibitions/
detail.php?nr=1225
acoustic.space.re-lab.net/lab/
makrolab.ljudmila.org
makrolab.ljudmila.org/reports/published/
peljhan/
makrolab.ljudmila.org/reports/published/
birringer/
www.nettime.org
www.rvb.ru
ssrn.com/abstract=969055

Acoustic Space Laboratory, Rasa Šmite and
Raitis Šmits
    www.rixc.lv
    ozone.re-lab.net
    xchange.re-lab.net
    www.techgnosis.com/acoustic.html
    re-lab.net/netradio/workshop01/05/index
        .html#b
    www.re-lab.net/polar/
    www.re-lab.net/netradio/workshop01/
        index.html
    www.art-bag.org/convextv/pro/trimmdich/
        anno.htm
    xchange.re-lab.net/56h/info.html
    www.straddle3.net/context/art/a_001006
        .en.html
    acoustic.space.re-lab.net
    www.virac.lv
    www.world-information.org/wio/program/
        amsterdam
    acoustic.space.re-lab.net/lab/
    www.radio-astronomy.net
    www.rixc.lv/solar/
    www.hmkv.de/dyn/e_program_exhibitions/
        detail.php?nr=1221&rubric=exhibitions&
    www.claustrum.org/clausthome/
    osdir.com/ml/culture.internet.spectre/2006-05/
        msg00096.html
    www.rixc.lv/waves/

Radio Tower Xchange (RTX): A Networked Project
    www.rixc.lv/waves/rtx/en.html
    www.rixc.lv/waves/
    www.sonification.eu/rtx/
    www.ghostlab.org/article.php3?id_article=203
    www.sonarc-ion.de
    www.nilsjc.com/kraft/kraftledningar_EN.html
    www.rixc.lv/solar/

Herd Listening, Andrew Garton
    www.porta2030.net
    www.hivenetworks.net/tiki indcx.php
    www.creativecommons.org
    www.icommons.org/isummit/
    rights.apc.org.au/culture/2006/09/me_myself
        _and_i_the_summit.php
    www.apc.org/english/news/index
        .shtml?x=5038217
    www.apcasiaictpolicy.net/a-vision-for-the-com
        munity-use-of-digital-television-spectrum-0
    rights.apc.org.au/resources/2006/05/busting
        _the_sri_lankan_community_radio_myth.php
    www.processing.org
    www.kunstradio.at/PROJECTS/TOUCHLESS/
        TL01/
    www.kunstradio.at/PROJECTS/TOUCHLESS/
    www.parkes.atnf.csiro.au/apollo11/introduction
        .html
    www.honeysucklecreek.net/Apollo_11/
        Australian_TV.html
    www.internetworldstats.com/stats.htm
    www.cia.gov/cia/publications/factbook/
    en.wikipedia.org/wiki/Image:Mobile_phone
        _use_world.PNG

Re-Inventing Radio
Aspects of Radio as Art

Edited by
Heidi Grundmann, Elisabeth Zimmermann
Reinhard Braun, Dieter Daniels,
Andreas Hirsch, Anne Thurmann-Jajes

Editorial Office: Dawn Michelle d'Atri

Translations:
Pablo Abril
Suzanne Branciforte
Angeles Ezquerra
Nicolas Grindell
Thomas Morrison
Jennifer Taylor-Gaida
Richard Watts
Teresa Woods-Czisch

Graphic Design: Martha Stutteregger
Assistance: Tom Albrecht

Cover Illustration: Phelan/McLoughlin/
Bourke, studio still from *Yellow: minimum
analysis, maximum action*, video installation
for supermarkets, 2 min. 40 sec. loop, 2004.
Photograph by Brendan Bourke.

Printing: Typo Druck Sares GmbH

Lithography: pixelstorm litho & digital imaging

Published by

Revolver
Archiv für aktuelle Kunst
Bethmannstrasse 13
D-60311 Frankfurt am Main
Tel.: +49 (0)69 44 63 62
Fax: +49 (0)69 94 41 24 51
info@revolver-books.de
www.revolver-books.de

ISBN 978-3-86588-453-4

Printed in the European Union.

A publication by Verein werks in cooperation with
the Ludwig Boltzmann Institute Media.Art.Research.
(Linz), MiDiHy Productions (Graz), and the
Research Centre for Artists' Publications at the
Weserburg–Museum of Modern Art (Bremen).

Illustration Credits

Supported by